MW00795761

William Colby
and the CIA

Other Books by John Prados:

Vietnam: The History of an Unwinnable War, 1945–1975

Safe for Democracy: The Secret Wars of the CIA

Hoodwinked: The Documents That Reveal How Bush Sold Us a War

Inside the Pentagon Papers (written and edited with
Margaret Pratt Porter)

The White House Tapes: Eavesdropping on the President
(written and edited)

Lost Crusader: The Secret Wars of CIA Director William Colby

Operation Vulture

America Confronts Terrorism (written and edited)

The Blood Road: The Ho Chi Minh Trail and the Vietnam War

*President's Secret Wars: CIA and Pentagon Covert Operations
from World War II Through the Persian Gulf*

*Combined Fleet Decoded: The Secret History of American
Intelligence and the Japanese Navy in World War II*

The Hidden History of the Vietnam War

Valley of Decision: The Siege of Khe Sanh (with Ray W. Stubbe)

*Keepers of the Keys: A History of the National Security Council
from Truman to Bush*

Pentagon Games

The Soviet Estimate: U.S. Intelligence and Soviet Strategic Forces

*The Sky Would Fall: Operation Vulture: The U.S. Bombing
Mission in Indochina, 1954*

William Colby
and the CIA

The Secret Wars of
a Controversial Spymaster

John Prados

UNIVERSITY PRESS OF KANSAS

© 2003, 2009 John Prados

All rights reserved

This book was originally published by the Oxford University Press in 2003 under the title
Lost Crusader: The Secret Wars of CIA Director William Colby.

Published by the University Press of Kansas (Lawrence, Kansas 66045), which was organized
by the Kansas Board of Regents and is operated and funded by Emporia State University, Fort
Hays State University, Kansas State University, Pittsburg State University, the University of
Kansas, and Wichita State University

Library of Congress Cataloging-in-Publication Data

Prados, John.
William Colby and the CIA : the secret wars of a controversial spymaster / John Prados.
p. cm.
Includes bibliographical references and index.
ISBN 978-0-7006-1690-9 (pbk. : alk. paper)
1. Colby, William Egan, 1920– 2. United States. Central Intelligence Agency—Biography.
3. Intelligence officers—United States—Biography. I. Title.
JK468.I6P724 2009
327.12730092—dc22
[B]
2009024895

British Library Cataloguing-in-Publication Data is available.

Printed in the United States of America

2 4 6 8 10 9 7 5 3 1

The paper used in this publication is recycled and contains 30 percent postconsumer waste. It is
acid free and meets the minimum requirements of the American National Standard for Perma-
nence of Paper for Printed Library Materials Z39.48-1992.

To

Danielle and Natasha

with Love

. . . For the world, which seems
To lie before us like a land of dreams,
So various, so beautiful, so new,
Hath really neither joy nor love, nor light,
Nor certitude, nor peace, nor help for pain;
And we are here as on a darkling plain
Swept with confused alarms of struggle and flight,
Where ignorant armies clash by night.

Matthew Arnold, *Dover Beach*, Stanza 4

CONTENTS

Preface to the Paperback Edition

IN THE ORIGINAL EDITION OF THIS BOOK, published early in the war on terror and before its excesses had become known to the public, I wrote that the Central Intelligence Agency (CIA) would one day wish it still had a William E. Colby. A certain spectrum of the agency's officers chose to pillory Bill Colby, their former director and this book's subject, because they saw him as giving away the CIA's secrets in the face of congressional inquiries into United States intelligence activities during the "Year of Intelligence," 1975, when revelations of CIA domestic activities ignited inquiries into all facets of CIA operations. A number of those activities skirted, parsed, or transgressed U.S. law or widely held moral standards. Agency officers' rejection of Colby was rooted in a preference for secrecy rather than law as a means of protecting the agency and its operations. Colby understood that standing fast on secrecy would fan flames of opinion that could potentially sweep away the agency. He instead sought protection through a modicum of cooperation with the investigations plus the elaboration of a new set of legal provisions for CIA activities, in effect a charter for the agency that would reflect the national consensus. Agency stalwarts and the Ford administration—spearheaded, believe it or not, by Dick Cheney—thought they had succeeded in establishing secrecy as the polar guide for U.S. intelligence. The disgrace of Bill Colby followed. Now America has come full circle. Excesses during the presidency of George W. Bush again raise the question of a troubling season of inquiry. Now is indeed the time, and today the day, for CIA officers to wish anew for a leadership capable of navigating the dangerous waters of public outrage over CIA operations conducted in secret.

I had no specific knowledge, when I wrote this book in 2002, of the CIA rendition programs, its "black" prisons, or its torture of prisoners. But it was perfectly evident—and perfectly predictable—that a muscular prosecution of the war on terror, putting force in the place of subtlety, would lead to actions damaging to United States purposes, and to public confidence in the CIA. As I write today, the U.S. Senate has just agreed on modalities for a year-long investigation of CIA activities, the White House is conducting an internal review, the Justice Department is completing a preliminary inquiry into possible obstruction of justice at the CIA, and there is substantial political pressure for a public truth commission on a wider-ranging inquiry into the Bush (II) administration's conduct of the war on terror. The horrors of the Bush administration's arrogation of prerogatives threatening even to the United States Constitution, beginning with subversion of the First and Fourth Amendments in the name of counterterrorism, are only starting to come into view.

It has been established that the CIA's deputy director for operations, Jose A. Rodriguez, ordered the destruction of ninety-two videotapes taken of prisoners under interrogation in the agency's black prisons, against the advice of CIA counsel, and that the agency, even while it possessed these records, certified to a federal court that they did not exist, said to amount to hundreds of hours of video. The United States has also issued an official affirmation that it utilized sovereign British territory, the Indian Ocean island of Diego Garcia (where basing rights had been extended to the United States by international agreement but for no such purpose) for the CIA activities. Kidnappings of individuals carried out by the CIA by patently illegal means on the territories of friendly nations, including Italy, Germany, Sweden, and Albania, are known, as are the infamous "rendition flights" that touched on many lands, but remain to be explored in any depth. All this is without even considering the excesses at Guantánamo Bay, Cuba; or Bagram, Afghanistan. I note these things not to make charges that may or may not prove to be accurate but simply to illustrate that the "flap potential"—a wondrous CIA term of art from the bad old days—inherent in the current controversy is enormous, perhaps even off the scale.

To believe that such an array of controversial activities can be dealt with secretly despite their political sensitivity, in a free democracy so damaged by these actions, is wishful thinking. Congressional leaders and Obama administration officials have begun this new season of inquiry professing to look forward, not back, and hoping that the Bush excesses can be disposed of quietly. But the tinder is already in the firebox, and it is in the nature of secrecy that the sordid details of excess will scandalize in such a fashion that they will inevitably see the light of day. Under those circumstances—and to avoid charges of sweeping this mess under the rug—some of the laundry will have to be aired in public. The odds are better than even that private investigation will lead to public inquiry.

All of which brings us back to Bill Colby and the CIA. The investigations on his watch are the only precedent for today, and thus they are the major point of historical reference for such an inquiry into secret activities. That example compels our attention. Colby is the paradigm case of a CIA director attempting to act with grace under fire, and the course he charted is instructive. Director Colby attempted—as this narrative will show—to tread carefully among his bosses in the Ford administration, the congressional inquisitors, his own people at CIA, and the American public. It was, as the game theorists would say, a *satisficing* strategy—not optimal with respect to any one of those audiences, but the best that could be managed among all of them given the realities that stood to be discovered behind the smoke and mirrors of CIA secrecy. Hardly understanding the delicacy of the real problem, both the Ford White House and a slice of the CIA's spooks chose to make the director a scapegoat.

Bill Colby's example is instructive in another way as well: it demonstrates the inevitability of a public accounting for borderline or illegal intelligence activities. In the Vietnam war, in which Colby was a major protagonist, he supervised a neutralization campaign known as the Phoenix program against covert Vietnamese operatives. The effort has clear similarities to the methods the CIA used in the war on terror. The controversy that Phoenix engendered dogged Colby for the rest of his life. That experience today shows why a public accounting is in fact necessary: participants in this latest round of excesses will not actually be able to put this behind them unless the society comes to an understanding of what happened and why.

The CIA officers who struggled in Afghanistan, Iraq, Somalia, Italy, Germany, and elsewhere steeped themselves in a belief that Americans would support anything done in the name of counterterrorism. That responded to a national consensus after the September 11 attacks that did prevail, up to a point, but at a moment yet to be established the operatives stepped across a line. Absent a legislative charter for the CIA, there was no real polar star for guidance—the day-to-day opinions of lawyers are no substitute, and indeed have become a major cause of complaints about what intelligence people now speak of as "risk aversion." Bill Colby supported a charter that could be drawn in a fashion such as to provide statutory authorization for appropriate CIA operations. The Ford administration actively worked to prevent that. Today, agency officers are again hoisted on the petard of the failure to secure a charter at that time.

The world was different then—but the same—again in ways that are instructive. In Bill Colby's day, the height of the Cold War, the CIA's cult of secrecy seemed appropriate because the agency was ranged against an ultimate enemy. In the contest between the West and the Union of Soviet Socialist Republics, the entire social and political systems of the sides appeared to be at risk. Even then, however, certain methods and techniques of the spy agencies were not acceptable to a democratic society. In its zeal for prosecuting the Cold War, the CIA had used many of these, especially in the third world. Presidents had demanded operations; the CIA, officers would say, merely carried out their orders. That same profligacy applied in the days after September 11, when President George W. Bush referred to terrorist leader Osama bin Laden in the same terms from the American Wild West once used in Vietnam in the Phoenix program's "Wanted" posters that security operatives put out. Bush administration rhetoric evoked the same imagery of ultimate struggle as in the Cold War. In a way it is not surprising that excesses occurred.

But the world *has* changed. And so has the CIA. The sense of purpose that prevailed during the Cold War disappeared for a decade until September 11, which was followed, at the agency, like Wall Street, with something akin to irrational exuberance. There was a sense the gloves were coming off. Then came the Iraq war, followed first by the huge imbroglio over intelligence failure at 9/11, the Bush manipulation of intelligence to bring the Iraq war on, then the frustration of discovering the conflict did not seem affected by the CIA's operations, and finally the Pentagon intrusion into traditional CIA preserves led by Secretary of Defense Donald Rumsfeld. The establishment of a new director of national intelligence as the supreme commander of the community took away more rice bowls. The agency never quite regained the stature it had had as America's premier Cold War agency. Afghanistan and counterterror were the areas the spooks reserved, and they appear to have concluded that Americans' anger after September 11 made unnecessary any effort at building a national consensus. That is clearly no longer the case, if it ever was.

In his statement responding to the latest round of investigations, the current CIA director, Leon E. Panetta, said, "The CIA is a highly professional, mission-driven organization. Our engagement with the Senate intelligence committee is important. Our work on counter-terrorism is decisive. We will keep our focus right where it belongs—on protecting the American people. The work you do is far too critical to accept anything less. I believe Congress, and the country at large, would agree." But the underlying political situation remains that a public with little confidence in, or understanding of, the CIA has been confronted first with a succession of apparently boneheaded agency mishaps, and then with real transgressions. The challenge to CIA methods is implicit. In this climate, any new evidence of past misdeeds, and certainly any new spy fiasco, can sweep away the agency. This is a Colby moment.

During the intelligence controversies of the 1970s, the Central Intelligence Agency proved fortunate to have as its director a man who understood the true dangers inherent in the politics of that day. Colby realized that unless the CIA gave way on some forms of openness and accountability, it would have no future. Despite his roots in the CIA's heroic era and his work on classic CIA operations—breeding grounds for the agency's felt need for secrecy—that director did what he felt necessary. The process itself was painful, and for his pains, Colby would be ostracized by those incapable of appreciating that a new era had dawned.

President Gerald R. Ford, who was careful to stay in the background and say only generally supportive things, stood with the opponents of change. Ford resorted to cosmetic reforms in an executive order to forestall any statutory charter for U.S. intelligence. This passage from the briefing book prepared for President Ford's decision gives the flavor of the exercise: "Some changes could and should be made administratively, but they need not alter the present system and we should oppose attempts on the part of Congress to repeal the flexibility given under the National Security Act of 1947." Ford's lead operative in this back-alley fight was the then-deputy White House chief of staff, Richard Cheney. In fact, Cheney's files are the main repository of presidential records on the intelligence investigations of 1975. This book outlines Cheney's role, but I wish I had been able to highlight it in greater detail. Unfortunately, a number of key records on the White House role were secret at the time, and requests for declassification, even those filed well before the writing of *William Colby and the CIA,* were answered only long after the book had not only been published but had disappeared from shelves across the country. The more recent declassification of those and other records, however, further underlines the importance of the White House fight to avoid accountability. There is a direct line from the Ford administration's success then to America's troubles today.

William Colby and the CIA illuminates a heroic age—from World War II to the Cold War—and how good men and women who thought themselves engaged in an ultimate struggle marched into a practical and moral abyss that undercut the very values for which they fought. Above all, it is the story of one man, William Egan Colby, his own path through that era, and how he tried to cope with the dilemmas and contradictions that had emerged by that age. Colby was among the anointed, a CIA officer who had participated in the most classic actions, from commando operations in World War II, to the Soviet penetration missions, to political action in Italy, to long association with the CIA effort in Vietnam. That he could be destroyed by his stand is itself an astonishing element of the story. *William Colby and the CIA* is a parable for today, when U.S. intelligence again stands in need of visionary leadership. One man's swim against the tide, despite its personal and professional costs, offers hope for those who see the need for change now.

Within the narrative, specific questions about Colby and his times are examined for what they reveal about the Cold War–era CIA, as well as agency activities that remain dimly understood even today. The same is true of the Vietnam war. For fifteen years between 1960 and 1975, Colby worked at the heart of Central Intelligence Agency operations in Vietnam and in the Far East more generally. Some of Colby's relationships in Saigon came back to bite him later, such as his cultivation of Pierre Hautier, a French doctor connected by marriage to a senior Vietnamese general, an associate of Nguyen Van Thieu. As a result of this book, the CIA, which in the 1970s learned from French counterintelligence that the doctor was a Russian spy, declassified that case. Other programs conceived in Vietnam have been subjects of continuing controversy. Phoenix, to mention one, has even been invoked in Iraq and the war on terror as a model for how the United States should combat its foes. This is a good moment to recall the actual experience of that project. As the head of the CIA—and the entire U.S. intelligence community, as the director's job was structured at that time—Colby also presided over changes in the way intelligence analysis is performed that created the system still used today. In all his roles, Colby exemplified those Americans dedicated to the Cold War crusade, but as director, he encountered the cauldron of political turmoil where the old ways no longer sufficed.

This biography is primarily a study of Bill Colby's life and times. The key substantive interests are tracing CIA activities in the Cold War, in Vietnam, and in the Year of Intelligence. The details of Colby's private life are covered to provide the context for the larger story but they are not the principal focus. Overarching issues are how the CIA set up its operations against Russia; how U.S. efforts to influence Italy were affected by CIA efforts; and how Colby, given his early concentration on European and anti-Soviet operations, ended up as perhaps the CIA's key player on Vietnam. Within the Vietnamese context, the assassination of Ngo Dinh Diem is a crucial event, and this narrative offers what I believe still stands as one of the closest analyses of CIA participation in those events that is available. Colby's role in opposing the Diem plots is more nuanced than previously understood, as the evidence will show, but the conclusions he drew from this experience would color much of his subsequent work on the war. For pacification in South Vietnam—Phoenix in particular—the evidence suggests that neither critics nor apologists have gotten the story quite right, in part because of the passions aroused by Vietnam policy, but also as a result of a desire to discredit Colby.

As already suggested, Colby's service as director of central intelligence remains the least understood of all the passages in his life. Critics of a very different bent than those who opposed the Vietnam war, and perhaps egged on by the Ford White House, would accuse Colby of destroying the Central Intelligence Agency. The evidence from formerly secret CIA and White House records shows quite a different picture. It was presented in this book for the first time and remains the only detailed account available of Ford administration efforts to head off the intelligence investigations. The lessons in direct manipulation that Dick Cheney learned in 1975 undoubtedly became the foundation for the methods that Vice President Cheney used during the second Bush administration. The imperfections in the system of intelligence oversight that resulted from Ford White House machinations made possible the excesses in the Reagan secret wars of the 1980s, as well as certain facets of CIA activity that supported the Iran–Contra affair. The Ford administration did not quite have its way, and oversight did accomplish something—without it, Iran–Contra really would have swept away the CIA—but not enough. For those who believe in centralized national intelligence, the most important lesson in Bill Colby's life lies here. In the post–Cold War world, even in an age of terror, responsible action positively requires a fresh national consensus on the role of the Central Intelligence Agency.

This is in no way an authorized biography. I knew Bill Colby slightly, having encountered him once during his CIA days and a number of times through his postgovernment career. On several occasions, we shared podiums or lectured the same audiences. We also shared many views on nuclear arms reduction and debated the CIA and Vietnam, but we were not close enough to be friends. I have also met members of the Colby family to discuss cooperation short of an authorized project, but the family expressed a desire to maintain their privacy. I have respected that wish. Most recently I advised Carl Colby, Bill Colby's son, on historical aspects of a documentary film Carl is now completing.

Many different sources have contributed to the material used to create this book. Most important have been government records, in particular those of the Central Intelligence Agency, the National Security Council staff, and the files of various White House political advisers. Interviews and oral histories supplemented the documentary material, and a wide array of memoirs, news accounts, and secondary sources added to the research ensemble. Congressional hearings, reports, and investigative papers contributed as well. In many instances, individuals brought important material to my attention.

Materials have been accessed in various ways. Secret documents were declassified directly, by application through the Freedom of Information Act or by Mandatory Declassification Review, an alternate procedure; through the government's general declassification schedules; or as a result of similar efforts by other scholars. The declassification process continues to be frustrating and cumbersome. Some documents that would have been relevant and were requested long before writing began remain outstanding. Some declassified documents have been so heavily excised they are virtually worthless. Some sources became available literally days or weeks before the manuscript had to be finished, and others long after it went to press. To take only the latest example, days before writing this new preface to a six-year-old book, I received a set of CIA official histories of activities in Vietnam and Laos that would have been useful (and no doubt will inform fresh scholarship), but it was in response to a Freedom of Information Act request that I filed in 1992. Even more disturbing, the CIA chose to supply these histories—actually written after the request was filed—in preference to supplying monographs the existence of which it refuses to confirm or deny. Present declassification procedures provide for a research process that is in some respects a random walk.

Having said that documentary research proved frustrating, let me hasten to add that casting a wide net has nevertheless resulted in a plenitude of source material. I believe the text and notes amply demonstrate its richness.

I used many collections of U.S. records during the course of this research, and I wish to acknowledge the help I received with all of them. The staff at the National Archives and Records Administration offered great assistance. The Nixon Library Project of the National Archives was a repository of important records, and since the first publication of this book, it has become a truly ample source. Helpful at the John F. Kennedy Library were Maura Porter, Michele DeMartino, and Paul Lydon. At the Lyndon B. Johnson Library I am indebted to Regina Greenwell, Linda Seelke, Ted Gittinger, and formerly, Nancy Smith. At the Gerald R. Ford Library, I had the help of Karen Holzhausen and Donna Lehman. The Gerald R. Ford Foundation, in addition, funded a portion of my research at the Ford Library, for which I remain grateful. Historians William Hammond and Graham Cosmas at the U.S. Army's Center of Military History fielded relevant questions at key moments.

The most useful set of William E. Colby papers are at the Vietnam Center of Texas Tech University. I used them there with the help of Bruce Cammack, Michael D. Lerner, James Ginther, and Danette Owens, several of whom have since moved on to greater things—good luck! There are some Colby papers at Princeton University also. In Washington, D.C., important sets of records of the CIA, the U.S. military, Joint Chiefs of Staff chairman General Earle Wheeler, and intelligence operative Edward G. Lansdale are held by the National Security Archive housed at George Washington University. I made use of these and other of its Vietnam records collections. Many persons at the archive were of great help, including Thomas Blanton and Malcolm Byrne.

In addition, many people offered assistance that was vital to this work in various ways. Among those who answered important questions or confirmed information were Gerald K. Haines, J. Kenneth McDonald, Oleg Kalugin, Paul Redmond, and Michael Warner. I was furnished leads to material or provided documents by Kai Bird, Guenter Bischoff, William Burr, Anne Cahn, Mario del Pero, Daniel Ellsberg, Kay Reist, Jeffrey Richelson, Jeff Stein, Mark Stoller, Bruce Vandervoort, and Howard Zinn. Special thanks go to Douglas Valentine, who happily provided access to his extensive collection of Vietnam war pacification research materials. For reading portions or all of the manuscript, I wish to thank Mario del Pero and Ellen Pinzur. For hand-holding and other assistance, let me thank Russell Galen, Bill and Abbot Kominers, Roothee Gabay, and Danielle and Natasha Prados. All these persons contributed things of value to this book. I am solely responsible for its errors and omissions.

John Prados
Washington, D.C.
March 2009

Acronyms

AFL–CIO	American Federation of Labor–Congress of Industrial Organizations
BBC	British Broadcasting Corporation
BNE	Board of National Estimates
BPP	Border Patrol Police
CAT	Civil Air Transport
CBS	Columbia Broadcasting System
CDNI	Committee for the Defense of National Interests
CIA	Central Intelligence Agency
CIDG	Civilian Irregular Defense Group
CIO	Central Intelligence Organization
CORDS	Civil Operations and Revolutionary Development Support
COSVN	Central Office for South Vietnam
CTT	Counter-Terror Team
CVT	[Vietnamese Confederation of Labor]
DCI	Director of Central Intelligence
DDCI	Deputy Director of Central Intelligence
DDO	Deputy Director of Operations
DDP	Deputy Director for Plans
DI	Directorate of Intelligence
DIA	Defense Intelligence Agency
DO	Directorate of Operations
DST	Direction du Surveillance de Territoire
FBI	Federal Bureau of Investigation
FE	Far East
GAO	General Accounting Office
HES	Hamlet Evaluation Survey
IB	Military Intelligence Bureau of Sweden
ICC	International Control Commission
ICEX	Intelligence Coordination and Exploitation
IOB	Intelligence Oversight Board
ITT	International Telephone and Telegraph
IVS	International Voluntary Services

JGS	Joint General Staff
KIQ	Key Intelligence Question
LBJ	Lyndon Baines Johnson
MACV	Military Assistance Command Vietnam
NID	*National Intelligence Daily*
NIE	National Intelligence Estimate
NIO	National Intelligence Officers
NLF	National Liberation Front
NLRB	National Labor Relations Board
NORSO	Norwegian Special Operations Group
NRO	National Reconnaissance Office
NSA	National Security Agency
NSAM	National Security Action Memorandum
NSC	National Security Council
OCI	Office of Current Intelligence
OCO	Office of Civil Operations
OG	Operation Groups
ONE	Office of National Estimates
OPC	Office of Policy Coordination
OSO	Office of Special Operations
OSS	Office of Strategic Services
PARU	Police Aerial Recovery Unit
PAT	People's Action Team
PCI	Partito communista Italiana
PFIAB	President's Foreign Intelligence Advisory Board
PIC	Provincial Interrogation Center
PKI	[Indonesian Communist Party]
PMKRI	[Indonesian Catholic student group]
PRU	Provincial Reconnaissance Unit
PSDF	People's Self-Defense Forces
RAF	Royal Air Force
RDC	Revolutionary Development Cadre
ROTC	Reserve Officers Training Corps
SAPO	[Swedish intelligence]
SAS	Special Air Service
SAVA	Special Assistant for Vietnam Affairs
SEAL	Sea Air Land soldier
SEPES	[Diem's personal intelligence service]
SFHQ	Special Forces Headquarters
SGU	[Hmong special guerrilla unit]
SHAEF	Supreme Headquarters Allied Expeditionary Forces
SIS	Secret Intelligence Service
SNIE	Special National Intelligence Estimate
SOE	Special Operations Executive
USAID	U.S. Agency for International Development

USIB	U.S. Intelligence Board
USIS	U.S. Information Service
VCI	Viet Cong Infrastructure [hidden in Vietnamese villages]
VIAT	Vietnam Air Transport
WSAG	Washington Special Action Group

1

THE MYSTERY OF BILL COLBY

No ONE PAID ATTENTION until Sunday night. That was when weekenders left the Maryland shore, returning to jobs in Washington. But next to this weekender's house the sport-utility vehicle stood idle, unused. The Cobb Neck home, a yellow wood frame structure with a pleasant deck just back from the shore of Neale Sound, belonged to William E. Colby, former director of the Central Intelligence Agency. The retired spy practiced law, wrote a column that analyzed risks for an investment newsletter, gave interviews and policy advice on request, and spoke at public meetings and scholarly conferences on subjects ranging from disarmament to the Vietnam war. There was plenty to keep him busy in Washington.

Yet there stood the car. Colby had been seen around the Cobb Neck house the previous evening, and soon after sunset that Sunday neighbors stopped by to see if they could help. There was no sign of Bill Colby, though sound came from inside. The door was unlocked. The noise had been coming from the radio, and a computer was on, but there was no Colby. In the sink were unwashed dishes and mussel shells, remains of a recent meal. A glass of wine stood on the table. Colby's canoe was gone from its usual spot near the house.

What turned out to be Colby's canoe had already been recovered by Cobb Island resident Kevin Akers. An unemployed carpenter, Akers had been boating with his family that morning. As Akers, his wife, and their young daughter came up to Rock Point, a promontory in the Wicomico River just around from Neale Sound, they found a green canoe tipped on its side. The craft was so swamped it took them an hour to empty the water from it. Akers then attached a line and towed the canoe to the Cobb Island docks. The mystery of the canoe—why it was partially submerged and where was its owner—led to the knock on Colby's door.

Charles County authorities were told of Bill Colby's disappearance at 7:45 P.M. on April 28, 1996. Sheriff Fred Davis treated the report as a typical missing person case. With the canoe a clear indication of a boating accident, Charles County dive rescue teams were summoned to help the search.

William Porter, chief of the Dive Rescue Team, organized an intense manhunt, with more than forty divers; on April 29, a Coast Guard vessel and a couple of helicopters also took part in the search. Maryland and Virginia rescue personnel, plus U.S. Navy divers from Little Creek, Virginia, cooperated. Rescue teams reached the scene quickly, scouring the area around the dock behind Colby's house until almost midnight, resuming their search the next morning. As it was late spring, water temperatures were in the upper fifties and divers could spend no more than thirty-five to forty minutes under the water. Once the search moved to the river, the muddy silt on the bottom and the opaque water became a problem. The teams felt with their hands, while small boats dragged the bottom with a hundred-foot weighted line.

There was nothing. No body. No detritus. A dog worked by handlers near the Cobb Neck house sensed something, and another trained dog, brought to confirm that indication, also caught the human scent, but searchers came up empty-handed. There was only the canoe at Rock Point, just a few hundred yards from the Colby house. It might as well have been on the moon for all the clues it yielded.

BILL COLBY'S DISAPPEARANCE and the lack of a body allowed free rein to amazing claims for what had happened to him. Few American spies vanish, and quite certainly no director of the Central Intelligence Agency (CIA) had ever faded into thin air. The incident brought out resentments some CIA officers had harbored for Colby since the 1970s when, as director, he had faced the most serious political crisis in United States intelligence history. Some agency people appreciated Colby's problem. Others saw him as giving away the company store. Indeed, there was corridor gossip at CIA headquarters in Langley, Virginia, that the director himself might secretly be an enemy agent, the long-suspected and sought Russian penetration agent, or "mole," allegedly planted within the CIA during its early years.

Of course there was no one at the time who would walk up to the director of central intelligence and accuse him of being a Russian spy, but the corridor gossip inevitably reached Bill Colby's ear. One spring day in 1978 at lunch with a reporter, the by-then-retired Colby actually mentioned the charge himself: "The latest story about me," Bill Colby revealed, "is that I'm the mole. You know, on the side of the Russians . . . I've had lots of bum raps. I shake them off."[1] But the bum rap lived on among CIA adherents of the cult of secrecy.

Oddly enough, another incident that had occurred in 1978 contributed to resuscitation of the allegations about Colby when he disappeared years later. That was the very similar death of retired CIA officer John Arthur Paisley. Less than forty miles from where Colby vanished, Paisley, also in a boat, also on the Chesapeake Bay, had disappeared one September day. Like Colby's canoe, Paisley's sail boat *Brillig* had been found abandoned and partly submerged. A twenty-five-year veteran of the Central Intelligence Agency, Paisley had had a varied career that ranged from shipping out as a sailor in the merchant marine in World War II, to working a radio for the United Nations plenipotentiary in Palestine at the time of the first Arab-Israeli war. John Paisley had been both an experienced intelligence officer and skilled sailor. So was Bill Colby, who a year before his own death had expertly brought his own thirty-seven-foot sailboat *Eagle Wing II* back to harbor despite a gale that ripped her sails apart. As for Paisley, the thirty-four-foot, sloop-rigged *Brillig* was his second sailboat, one he had navigated as far as Florida and the Caribbean from a homeport in the Chesapeake.

When Paisley disappeared, his boat drifted inshore along the coast of Maryland's Point Lookout State Park where it was recovered by a park ranger. That triggered a hunt that ended days later with the discovery of a body in the bay. The body identified as Paisley's had been shot in the head with a 9mm bullet and went into the water weighted with two skin divers' belts. Although the death appeared to be a suicide, Maryann Paisley, who had lived separately from her husband for several years, expressed reservations regarding the identity of the body. Paisley's girlfriend of the time, Beth Myers, further reported him as being upbeat, not depressed.

Among the less charitable speculations in the Paisley case was the notion that the man had been a Russian spy, and the Chesapeake Bay incident had been contrived to disguise Paisley's defection to the Soviet side. Though it was true that the Russian embassy maintained a farm for recreation purposes on Maryland's nearby eastern shore, *Brillig* was nowhere near there when Paisley disappeared. Other allegations, such as one claiming that Paisley had stepped onto a Russian submarine, were really farfetched; a transfer to another boat was conceivable, but why bother with supplying a decoy body? One excessively conspiratorial speculation charged that Paisley, the CIA officer, was actually a Russian national who had been switched for the real John Paisley at some earlier time of life (such as when Paisley, the merchant seaman, visited Murmansk during World War II, or when Paisley, the CIA agent, went to any number of places in Europe. John Paisley had been deputy director of the CIA's Office of Strategic Research and had played an important behind-the-scenes role in the Team B report of 1976, an outside critique of the perceived inadequacies in CIA estimates of Russian military power; but although he may have been a desirable target for Russian intelligence schemes, there is no sign that Paisley himself worked for Russia as a mole. Indeed the Senate Select Committee on Intelligence looked into the Paisley case and reported no evidence that his death was anything other than a suicide, or his life anything other than that of a patriotic American intelligence officer.

As with John Paisley in 1978, so with Bill Colby in 1996. Some from the CIA recalled Colby as having liked Paisley when Bill was still director of central intelligence. And there were, of course, already allegations of a Russian espionage role for Colby himself. Comparison of the two disappearances tended to bring back the old fears, the old charges. So while divers were out dragging the bottom at Rock Point, magpies busily speculated again. The old fears became a subtext in many of the stories on this new search in the Chesapeake.

No one need believe any of these allegations, especially those regarding William Egan Colby. What is significant is that such suspicions were entertained at all. They were based not on notions of how an enemy had gained advantage from a spy, but rather some sense that the Central Intelligence Agency, U.S. intelligence, or the United States as a whole had been "damaged" by Bill Colby's actions as director of central intelligence. The source of the damage, in this view, was Colby's conduct at the time of the U.S. congressional investigations of intelligence in the mid-1970s. But those investigations were not brought on by Colby; rather, they had been the response of the United States Congress to a widespread public perception that the CIA, and U.S. intelligence more broadly, was out of control, a "rogue elephant" in the idiom of that day.[2]

In 1975 the CIA was about to be reined in. The case officers, analysts, technical specialists, and spies could accommodate to that, they could get out of the way, or they could fight. If they had fought, in all likelihood the Central Intelligence Agency would have been shattered—broken into a thousand pieces, as John F. Kennedy had once talked of destroying it in the wake of the CIA's utter failure at the Bay of Pigs in Cuba. Bill Colby's recourse would be that of an expert sailor—to keep close to the wind, tacking smartly, giving enough to satisfy investigators without compromising the core values of U.S. intelligence. But to the hardliners, adherents of the dedication to secrecy, Colby was little better than a traitor.

The idea that the director of central intelligence could be a traitor is unique in the annals of CIA history. For Bill Colby personally, the image, aside from how preposterous it must have seemed, would be highly ironic. In fact, Colby stood among the annointed, one of the original secret warriors in the Office of Strategic Services in World War II, an early recruit to the CIA and a participant in the agency's classic programs against the Russians. A devout Catholic, Colby would have appreciated the metaphor that he had received all the intelligence sacraments. On the front line of the secret wars from the beginning, the only thing that really separated Colby from the cultists would be his belief that the Central Intelligence Agency needed a political compact with the American people. That made Colby suspect to the secrecy cultists, opening a fissure among the denizens of the wilderness of mirrors. How that cleavage rent the CIA's world, and what happened to American intelligence in consequence, is both the real mystery and the real tragedy in the story of the Central Intelligence Agency.

PEOPLE SAW BILL COLBY on Cobb Island the day before he vanished. At the Lighthouse Marina directly across Neale Sound from his vacation house, Colby had worked on his sloop *Eagle Wing II*. That afternoon, presumably on the way home, Colby appeared at Jack's Crab House, where proprieter Jack Yates sold him a dozen mussels. Later would be a telephone conversation between Bill and his wife Sally Shelton who had traveled to Texas to visit family that weekend. And Colby was seen around the house in the evening. There the trail went cold. A last sighting of or communication with the victim in a setting related to the disappearance, a key element in organizing a search, was just not there.

Returning from Texas, Sally Shelton came to Cobb Neck and described for investigators a favorite canoe route the couple often used, sailing to Rock Point for wine and quiet moments in the evening. Paul Colby, a son from Bill's first marriage, also came down and participated with divers in the search operations. Sally persisted in hopes that Bill had simply been stricken somewhere and awaited rescue. Hopes rose when the dog teams caught a scent but fell as nothing significant was found. The number of divers working the bottom settled at about two dozen, but with fishermen helping on the water, plus neighbors and police combing the land, the number involved in the hunt for Bill Colby grew to a hundred or more.

Days passed with no sign of the missing spy chieftain. It developed that Colby had not been the only man to disappear on the Chesapeake that day; on the Severn River near Annapolis a sixty-one-year-old man had fallen off a sailboat and was also missing. Wolfgang Siebeck, an Eastern Shore resident, a waterman for most of his life had been as unlikely as William Colby to have had an accident on the water. Meanwhile, four official agencies and dozens of hunters found nothing. Sally Shelton awaited news with trepidation.

"It's much more frustrating than you could believe," explained Maryland Natural Resources police lieutenant Mark Sanders, "until you do it yourself. When I first started it was, 'Okay, we know where he went, let's go to work and get him.' "[3] But no witness had seen Colby on the water, so notions of where he had gone were no more than inference.

The weather continued windy, as it had been when Colby vanished, and rainy, which made things worse for everyone. Spring runoff from the mountains agitated the bottom, cutting visibility under water to just inches at a time. This search remained grim, tedious work.

Sally Shelton stayed on at Cobb's Neck, friends sustaining her. She and Bill had had the house for four years, and it was full of happy vacation memories. Their canoe outings to Rock Point had featured white wine and dreams of custom-building a new home at that very place. Colby's canoe indeed turned up at Rock Point but Bill himself was not there. Every day, no news seemed less like good news.

The mystery of Colby's whereabouts ended the morning of May 6. Two hours after starting his shift, Corporal Leonard Sciukas of the Maryland Natural Resources Police cruised near Rock Point on his regular patrol. Roughly a hundred feet from the shore, Sciukas motored near the opposite side of the point from where the canoe had been found. Suddenly he noticed something red drifting near the shore. The patrolman nosed his boat inshore and grounded it. He quickly realized the object had to be a body. Coming from the beach side, Sciukas saw Bill Colby's head and shoulders near marsh weeds and in foot-deep water. Colby had been wearing a red windbreaker, along with khaki pants and a blue-and-white-striped polo shirt. There were no shoes, leading to speculation he might have fought the water, kicking off his shoes to swim better. Corporal Sciukas recalled, "He was in the water, right up on the edge."[4]

Medical examiners from the Maryland Department of Health and Mental Hygiene concluded that Bill Colby died from exposure—the water on April 27 had been cold enough for hypothermia to set in within fifteen to twenty minutes—and drowning. He may have suffered a stroke or heart attack before falling in the water in the first place, but in any case he died soon after eating. His blood alcohol content was gauged at 0.07 percent, a significant but not intoxicating level under Maryland law.

As for those who glimpsed dark conspiracies in the disappearance of Bill Colby, it is worth noting that the waterman who had fallen into the Severn River the same day Colby drowned in the Wicomico surfaced the same day. Wolfgang Siebeck's body, like Colby's would be recovered on May 6.

Sally Shelton held a brief press conference to thank all the people who had helped in the rescue operation and to try for a higher perspective: "Bill had a magnificent life. There was not much that was left undone for him. He fought the fascists and he fought the communists, and he lived to see democracy taking hold around the world. He was just thrilled. . . . He left the world a lot safer place than when he entered it."[5]

President William J. Clinton also issued a statement on this day: "Throughout a quarter of a century at the CIA, William Colby played a pivotal role in shaping our nation's intelligence community. . . . He made tough decisions when necessary, and he was always guided by the core values of the country he loved."[6]

A week later there was a quiet, private service, and William Egan Colby was laid to rest in Arlington National Cemetery, right behind his father. On Tuesday, May 14, more than a thousand people attended a public remembrance at Washington's National Cathedral. Among the guests were colleagues from the Office of Strategic Services in World War II, from the Central Intelligence Agency's secret wars, from Vietnam, and from his years in the Nixon and Ford administrations. The group included Vietnam war commander General William C. Westmoreland, Laotian secret army chief General Vang Pao, secretary of state Henry A. Kissinger, and many more. It seemed a wide assortment of luminaries had come to honor a man who had lately been disparaged in life, sometimes by these same individuals. One wonders how this could all happen. So, with perhaps the hint of a smile on his face, Bill Colby went to the grave leaving behind one final mystery.

2

BAPTISM OF FIRE

GEORGE SHARP THOUGHT he had a problem. Heading the Western Europe section in the Special Operations branch of the Office of Strategic Services (OSS), Sharp was struggling to put together a program to help win World War II. William J. ("Wild Bill") Donovan, the legendary swashbuckler who had infused the OSS with his own brand of derring-do, made a distinction between special intelligence, or spying, and special operations. Donovan saw the latter as activities designed to harass, confuse, disrupt, deceive, intimidate, frighten, injure, and at best, destroy the enemy. Special operations could be either offensive or defensive; Wild Bill perceived them as a component of psychological warfare, but later they developed into a wholly separate endeavor.

George Sharp's problem in 1943 was to get something going. In the various countries in Europe for which Sharp held responsibility, there were active Resistance movements against the German occupation. British intelligence, through liaisons with the spy services of the exiled governments and through an entity of its own called the Special Operations Executive (SOE), was already actively assisting the Resistance. Sharp's OSS unit, hampered by the infancy of the OSS and its only very recent establishment of a base in Great Britain, had not accomplished much of anything. In the summer and fall of 1942 there had been a plan for OSS to field men who would form joint teams with the British as well as a third country's services, such as the French, to be inserted within Resistance cells. American Army intelligence, always intensely suspicious of OSS, attacked the plan as a security risk and contrived to have it rejected in October 1942.

George Sharp was a lawyer—in fact, a partner—in the New York firm Sullivan and Cromwell, whose lobbying would have much to do with the creation of independent intelligence agencies in the United States. Sharp knew the kinds of bureaucratic maneuvers used to undermine the Resistance

7

support plan. Sharp was also son of the man who had been America's ambassador in Paris at the time the Versailles Peace Treaty had been negotiated to end World War I, and he understood that the European Resistance needed help. By the summer of 1943 plans for an invasion of Western Europe had become the most important issue in Anglo-American alliance strategy, and the invasion was going to need help from the Resistance. The project to form teams and parachute them to the Resistance had to be revived. The OSS convinced Army Chief of Staff General George C. Marshall to go along. Special Operations would be responsible within OSS for this initiative, which would be called the Jedburgh project.

Inception of the Jedburgh program left Sharp a new headache—actually recruiting Americans willing to undertake these dangerous missions behind enemy lines. Sharp worked on the recruiting with Franklin O. Canfield, another Sullivan and Cromwell lawyer, who had represented the firm in Paris. Canfield would become the OSS liaison officer with the Allied invasion planners in England and later with the forward echelon of the main military command, Supreme Headquarters Allied Expeditionary Forces (SHAEF), under General Dwight D. Eisenhower. Sharp and Canfield, with their subordinates, had little to tell prospects other than that they represented a secret organization looking for qualified parachutists who were proficient in foreign languages. Recruits would be given special training but then would have to participate in perilous missions. Sharp and Canfield worried about finding as many as fifty recruits. By November 1943 they had a hundred.

Bill Colby believed, and wrote years later,[1] that the act of true heroism occurs not in the middle of a mission—amid the frantic action, under the eyes of friends, and with the thought of the objective at the back of the mind—but in the initial act of volunteering, when information is scanty and the pressures of the moment absent. Colby ought to know. Bill Colby was among the volunteers for the Jedburgh program.

IN THE SUMMER of 1943 William Egan Colby was cooling his heels at Fort Benning, Georgia, just another number, an anonymous young paratrooper in the replacement pool. Colby had been a staff officer in a parachute artillery battalion of the 82nd Airborne Division before it shipped out to Europe, but his inefficient commander got the boot, and the new boss swept clean, bringing in a fresh set of trusted minions to run the unit. Colby had a little less time assigned than some because he had broken an ankle during jump training, and he ended up in the officer replacement pool. As an Army brat it was a fate Bill could well understand; but he was a dedicated young man, one who had joined the Reserve Officers Training Corps (ROTC) in college and had picked up his commission as soon as he reached the required age (ROTC at that time would not commission any person not yet twenty-one years old) and the academic year had ended, so for him, the events at Benning had to be an intense disappointment.

This was the Good War, where the issues were drawn in white and black and few questioned the evils of fascism or the enmity of adversaries like Adolf Hitler. Now Hitler controlled Western Europe and his propagandists touted it as a veritable fortress. To be part of fighting that enemy was the right thing, and Bill showed his mettle by joining the Army even before America entered the war. Two years later, after so much preparation, Colby seemed to have been left behind. He would not languish at Benning for long however, for it was there that the OSS found Bill Colby. Those bombers, battleships, and divisions that were going to crack Fortress Europe needed the help the Office of Strategic Services could give them, as did the French Resistance and the other opponents of Hitler. Thin, wiry Bill Colby quickly volunteered. So did most of his companions in the pool that day. Fluent in French, Colby would become a Jedburgh; he would be at the heart of the intelligence covert operations supporting the Allied campaign in northwest Europe.

Over the next few months the Office of Strategic Services winnowed its assorted volunteers, paring the hundred men George Sharp had found to half that number. In November 1943 the newly formed SHAEF headquarters officially became responsible for OSS activities in the European theater, and the British government approved the use of English bases to mount OSS operations. Bill Colby and his fellow recruits crossed the Atlantic aboard the *Queen Elizabeth* just before Christmas. They landed at Glasgow and were sent to a commando training camp in the western part of Scotland.

This place gave the Jedburgh program its name. Along the Jed River in the Scots borderland of Roxburghshire was Jedburgh, known for an abbey and for Judge Roy Bean-style "Jeddart Justice," in which the accused is hanged first and tried later. The Scotland sojourn lasted just a few days, however. Within the fortnight the OSS trainees moved to a facility about fifty miles north of London, an estate called Milton Hall in the county of Peterborough. Here the Jedburghs' training began in earnest.

Men learned lockpicking from a paroled British burglar. Weapons experts taught them about guns, demolition specialists instructed them in explosives. They had classes on how to run a radio secretly, use forged documents, encode messages—all the clandestine skills. Major Fairbairn, formerly of the Shanghai police, taught the Jedburghs to kill silently with a knife in the side and a hand over the victim's mouth. Fairbairn was said to have learned this skill from the Chinese *tongs*, the gangsters of that land. Bill Colby later recalled with relief that he had never seen the sharp commando knives used for anything except opening ration cans.

Jedburghs also had to know how to behave like a typical citizen of the place they were sent. They needed military planning and had to be able to call on Allied sources to funnel support to the *maquisards*, as the French Resistance fighters called themselves. Learning to be a Jedburgh was a big job, and after a long day of training, a nighttime favorite of the officers at

Milton Hall was to call out the Jeds for a field exercise. By the time the Normandy invasion actually happened in June 1944, Jeds had been through all the practice routines dozens of times.

All the work did not prevent a lot of hard play. Fortunes were won and lost in endless poker games during the weeks before D-Day. Indeed, Bill Colby met his future Jedburgh team boss over poker, or at least grew to know him that way. Using the cover name "Jacques Favel" to protect his family living in France, Camille Lelong was quick, able to take care of himself in a pinch, tough when the cards did not go his way, and altogether a deadly player. Colby saw Lelong amaze English girls, pull out incredible hands at cards, and tell hair-raising stories of the Free French and Algeria. Lelong also seemed much more accessible than other Frenchmen because his father, who had owned a cotton plantation in Louisiana, had sent Camille to high school there. Jedburgh teams were self-selecting; not made up of assigned recruits. The rules were that a prospective team had to have one British or American officer (an earlier stricture that teams have one of each had been abandoned); one who was French, Belgian, or Dutch; and an enlisted radio-man. Colby and Lelong began to work together and soon constituted them-selves as a Jedburgh team. French Sergeant Roger Villebois (with the cover name "Louis Giry") completed the group. Though Major Colby outranked Lieutenant Lelong, it would be the Frenchman who led the team.

So elaborate were the plans for D-Day that they provided for a variety of help for the *maquis*—the French Resistance fighters. Bill Colby and his friends learned how to carry out their roles knowing little of the overall picture. Invasion plans called for over eighty Jedburgh teams to parachute into France.

Behind them were four units the OSS called Operational Groups (OGs), commando teams of thirty-four men each who could be sent to accomplish specific military missions. The British allies held two full regiments of their Special Air Services (SAS) parachutists for insertion alongside the *maquis*, while the French prepared two battalions of light infantry paratroops (*chas-seurs parachutistes*). With Royal Marines in the invasion and other com-mando units, there were as many as 5,000 special warfare troops acting in support of the Normandy invasion. Jedburgh in many respects formed only the tip of the spear. Preventing individual line crossers, teams, and the larger units from stumbling over each other was a major task; therefore on May 14, 1944, still several weeks ahead of D-Day, the British Special Operations Executive and the Special Operations Branch of OSS began jointly running an operations room at SHAEF headquarters.

Fifty more Americans—enlisted radio operators to complement the Jed-burgh officers—were added, doubling the U.S. contingent. Milton Hall re-ceived an equal number of British Jeds, and there were a hundred assorted French, Belgian, and Dutch officers and men. All the Jeds were divided into teams and kept in a revolving training cycle, from which the most appropriate teams would be chosen whenever one was needed in the field.

Among the wild bunch of the Jeds, Bill Colby seemed rather ordinary. His OSS colleagues included an Argentinian who had made a name as a stunt man in Hollywood; a sailor who had gone around the world in a small boat, and fought with the French in 1940 and then as a Marine on Guadalcanal; and a Greek scholar from Cambridge who had been in the Spanish Civil War. Lucien E. Conein, a Kansas City boy born in Paris of a mixed nationality couple, also had been a veteran of the French defeat in 1940. There were Jedburghs who would go on to fame as journalists, lawyers, judges, scholars, and, like Colby himself, spies. This was a society of accomplishment.

As D-Day neared, the secret warriors put finishing touches on their training. British women instructors, telegraphy experts, labored to bring the Jeds to the point that they could send and receive Morse code on the radio at a rate of twelve words per minute—quite a pace for neophytes.

The Jedburghs practiced commando functions again and again, but Colby wondered why they received so little instruction on political matters. One day he walked into a London bookstore and bought a copy of *Seven Pillars of Wisdom*, T. E. Lawrence's classic account of the guerrilla campaign in World War I that earned him the sobriquet "Lawrence of Arabia." The book became Colby's political advice manual. He recounts, "I suppose I fantasized myself becoming, if not exactly a Lawrence of Arabia, then at least . . . Colby of a French Department [i.e., county]."[2]

William Egan Colby may not have been flamboyant and his experience may have been limited, but he impressed enough superiors in the Office of Strategic Services to be promoted repeatedly. A couple of weeks after the Normandy invasion, SHAEF established its forward headquarters on French soil for the first time, and Frank Canfield took an OSS liaison detachment to France to coordinate with the high command. Canfield's unit included representatives of all the OSS branches. David K. E. Bruce, who had come to OSS from the American Red Cross and became the OSS chief in London, soon visited. William Colby went with the unit as Jedburgh adviser. While most OSS personnel pitched their tents in clearings among the hedgerows, Colby and two others shared a room with Bruce in the farmhouse near Carentan occupied by top officers.

During June and July 1944 the Germans managed to contain Allied forces within Normandy and the military campaign focused on attrition. However, at the end of July both British and American armies made breakthroughs. Fast Allied mobile forces began to spill through France. From the special operations standpoint, the OSS/SOE problem changed from delaying German reinforcements bound for Normandy to protecting the flanks of the Allied forces. A particular problem was General George S. Patton's Third U.S. Army. This force moved so quickly that in less than a month men who had started by fighting a positional battle in Normandy were nearing the German border, and a French division had captured Paris. Third Army intelligence officers asked OSS for more line crossers, agents who could provide important tactical information, because the American troops were in danger of outrunning their intelligence. On another inspection trip to France, David Bruce wired OSS/London on the subject. But the Third Army by then had thrust deep into France and had far outdistanced any flank protection. George Patton believed in letting the enemy worry about flanks, but his superiors were not so sanguine. As part of their effort to assist Patton's fast-driving tank units, SHAEF's special forces headquarters decided to commit Jedburgh Team "Bruce." This became Bill Colby's moment.

AT MILTON HALL the Jeds now had a mission list and team Bruce had reached the top of it. Bruce was Colby's Jedburgh team, led by the Frenchman Camille Lelong. They went through briefings for central France, to join *maquis* forces in the Yonne district (*department*) southeast of Paris. Located beyond Patton's army, they could expect to encounter German garrisons plus any combat units moving up from the south to oppose Patton. Unknown to Team Bruce, Allied forces were to invade the Mediterranean coast of France within days, and German forces could also be expected to recoil up the valley of the Rhone River.

Jedburghs and other special operations in Europe were backed by regular air missions called "Carpetbagger" flights. The arrangement had been completed in September 1943 and the first two squadrons activated that November. The units used modified B-24 bombers, four-engine aircraft flying with equipment containers instead of bombs and with armament reduced to accommodate passengers. The B-24 had a mid-fuselage gun turret underneath the plane, and the entire assemblies for these were removed from Carpetbagger aircraft, creating a large hole in the belly of the bomber. In OSS parlance these were called "Joe holes" because OSS agents were collectively termed "Joes." A flight would take the Jedburgh team to its destination, the men would drop through the Joe hole, and the containers of equipment would follow them—all by parachute.

That was the ideal, at least, and the way Carpetbagger missions were planned by the 801st Bombardment Group (Provisional), located at Harrington field in England and led by Lieutenant Colonel Clifford J. Heflin. The group had 64 B-24 bombers assigned by the time of D-Day and carried out an average of 650 flights per month that June and July. David Bruce and one of his deputies, Gerald Miller, visited Harrington on August 2 for lunch with Colonel Heflin and a briefing on the latest techniques and operations. Heflin's Carpetbaggers were flying with losses averaging just 1 per cent, somewhat less than typical bomber losses in the strategic air campaign against Germany.

Though the loss rate boded well for Team Bruce, there were no guarantees everything would go as planned when their turn came, and indeed it did not. Lieutenant Lelong moved his Jedburghs to Harrington and they took off with favorable weather on the evening of August 14, 1944, aboard a B-24 whose nose sported fanciful art plus the name "Slick Chick." It was half past midnight as they neared the target area, and 12:45 when the pilot decided he had found the proper drop zone. The airmen were not certain the *maquis* reception committee supposed to be on the ground below were sending them the correct recognition signal for that day, so they made another circuit of the area to check. But the pilot decided to proceed with the drop. Colby and his mates dived through the Joe Hole in good order, parachuting from about 1,500 feet. Dangling from his static lines Colby got an inkling things might not be as advertised—the lights on the ground were a single large fire, not the separate bonfires made by *maquisards*. Lieutenant Lelong saw this too and quickly decided they were seeing a village set aflame by the Germans.

Mistakes on the drop were not unusual for Carpetbagger missions, or in most airborne operations for that matter. Team "Giles," which parachuted into France's Brittany peninsula under the Jedburgh Greek scholar, Bernard B. M. W. Knox, also learned the hard way that OSS/SOE intelligence on drop zones was out of date and strictly limited. When he went to supply officers to draw the team's equipment, Knox discovered there was so little expectation the Jeds would survive that the authorities did not want to bother getting his signature on receipt forms. Team Giles was supposed to drop where it could link up with the Resistance and then hit the Germans; instead, it came down right in the middle of the tough Luftwaffe 2nd Parachute Division. Barely evading capture, Team Giles did manage its linkup and neatly turned the tables on the enemy, as *maquisards* working with Knox ambushed a full battalion of the Luftwaffe troops, inflicting heavy losses on them.

Bill Colby's Jedburghs did not have such good luck, at least not at first. Lieutenant Lelong proved quite right—the three Jeds had landed in gardens among the houses of Montargis, a town on the road between Paris and Clermont-Ferrand. Townspeople wakened by the noise of the equipment containers crashing down on their homes quickly set the Jeds straight on where they were—at least twenty miles from the planned landing zone. The townspeople also told Colby and his mates that Montargis held a German garrison; it was a good idea for the Jeds to get out. With their equipment containers scattered all around, it was clear the Jedburghs could not even find their radio without a lengthy search. Lieutenant Lelong made the only choice he could: he ordered Team Bruce out of town through fields toward the southeast. At dawn the three men hid in a ditch by some woods where they remained hunkered down all day. German soldiers in Montargis naturally discovered the abandoned Jedburgh equipment containers and combed the town for any sign of the infiltrators.

The second night Team Bruce tried to follow a compass bearing toward a prearranged safe house, but a storm blew up with such ferocity that the team members had to tie themselves to each other to avoid becoming lost. Careful maneuvers became impossible under the circumstances. Then the Jeds heard voices. Afraid of German patrols, Team Bruce had to find a hiding place fast. Lightning revealed a farmhouse in the distance. The men made for it, and Lelong knocked on the door while Colby and Roger Villebois covered him with pistols. Amazingly, the cottage turned out to be a Resistance radio post manned by an operator who himself had arrived from London just a week earlier. Team Bruce could now inform headquarters of their arrival, loss of equipment, and status. The *maquis* arranged a new rendezvous with the Resistance units Team Bruce intended to join. They had had plain dumb luck!

The following day a car appeared, a French Citroen converted to burn charcoal, and took the Jedburghs to the safe house that had been their original destination. This house had been arranged for at the last minute on the insistence of Team Bruce, and it turned out to be the root of their success in the Yonne department. From it, the Jeds contacted *maquis* leader Roger Bardet, whom they met at a café in the tiny farm village of Sommecaise. This act plunged Bill Colby into the complexities of Resistance politics, where loyalty and betrayal often hung by the merest threads.

Roger Bardet led a *maquis* group of some five hundred fighters. Colby sat down, pulled out a map, explained the Jedburghs were there to help the Resistance fight Germans, and asked Bardet to brief him on the situation. The Frenchman stared back at Colby and said nothing.

Gradually the Jedburghs learned that Bardet was in competition with others to be the top *maquis* leader in the Yonne. This the men of Bruce only discovered once they had met Adrien Sadoul ("Colonel Chevrier"), a Metz lawyer and former reserve officer who was constantly on the move and in touch with the Resistance networks. Sadoul claimed he had orders from a headquarters in Paris to command all *maquis* forces in the Yonne; Bardet insisted he had identical orders from a headquarters in Switzerland. While the Jedburghs tried to figure out who was really supposed to be in command they held back on air drops of arms and ammunition that would have greatly increased *maquis* firepower.

Below the top command level there were rivalries among *maquis* bands. Four hundred French fought under "Georges" in one sector, six hundred under "Vernouil" in another. The French communists had their own *maquis* of 300 under "Yvon." Bardet could not seem to accomplish much on his own, but he encouraged the other Resistance leaders to refuse the "command" of Colonel Chevrier. Bill Colby, who had heard of most of these forces only through Chevrier, and Team Bruce, which was soon working directly for Chevrier, to create liaisons with the different bands, had difficulty understanding why there was any problem. Chevrier, unlike Bardet, quickly provided the Jedburghs with potential drop zones for air supply, and the beginning of arms deliveries a week or two later stood as clear affirmation of Chevrier's standing. An order eventually came from London confirming Chevrier as Resistance commander for the Yonne. This led to an incipient revolt at the end of August, when *maquis* leaders, fed up with Chevrier's imperious manner, became restive. But Chevrier, in a demonstration of effective leadership, convinced and cajoled the others to stay in the game, then renounced the post of "commander" in favor of being "chairman" of a committee that brought together senior *maquis* leaders. At this point, coordination among the Resistance actually improved.

Meanwhile, Roger Bardet proved an unusually weak reed. Not only had he been quite uninformative when Colby sought information about the *maquis* in the Yonne, but he had behaved more like a petty bureaucrat than the dynamic leader of a band of freedom fighters. Bardet almost never suggested actions and often came up with reasons why those proposed by others should not be carried out. Bardet had been deputy to Henri Frager, a brave and dynamic Resistance leader, and it may have been in deference to Frager's memory that subordinates continued to follow Bardet. Frager would be seized by the German Gestapo in Paris in early July, leaving Bardet with that strong *maquis* in the Yonne.

Bill Colby was not impressed by Roger Bardet, but during the Team Bruce mission he never suspected the Frenchman. This was not true for "Nicole," the twenty-one-year-old Englishwoman who had parachuted into France during April, months before Colby's team arrived, to serve as a courier. Nicole was Peggy Knight, a typist from Walthamstow of mixed French-British parentage. She had so impressed SOE executives who overheard her speaking French in a restaurant that they had recruited the woman and sent her where her almost-native French could help the Resistance. Knight went to France with less than two weeks' training and only a single practice parachute drop— from a static balloon. She proved efficient, modest, self-effacing, expert at shorthand, and able to be quite inconspicuous—all qualities that impressed Bill Colby. Some thought Knight naive, but she was shrewd enough to be wildly successful moving about in German-occupied France.

Within days of her arrival Peggy Knight had arranged her first receptions of arms, and Frager had sent her to Paris with messages for his associates. Knight made the Yonne-Paris trip many times; even after the Allied breakout from Normandy she was still moving around relatively freely. As American troops from the Third Army neared and there were actual battle lines, Knight crossed them repeatedly. Twice stopped by Germans, she talked her way out of her situation. Nicole [Peggy] told one German officer she just *had* to cross the lines because she had a terrible toothache and her dentist was in the next town; the Germans gave her coffee and aspirin. Peggy Knight left with a positive identification of the German unit in this area to be passed along to the Third Army.

In true *maquis* style, Peggy Knight also used her gun, a British Sten submachine gun. Many of these weapons were delivered to the Resistance, and Nicole helped teach *maquisards* how to use them. Her own Sten gun got its baptism of fire in the ambush of a German truck convoy. The most terrifying night, however, came sometime after D-Day, a night Peggy spent at Frager's network headquarters, the Château de Petite-Hermite. German soldiers came up and surrounded the place, then mounted an attack. Knight fought her way out among thirty or so *maquis* survivors. Nicole found it highly suspicious that Roger Bardet had been absent from the château that night. She continued to work with Bardet, but once the Jedburghs turned up, the pretty English girl began to take her marching orders from Team Bruce.

(Nicole proved right in the end: after the war Roger Bardet was arrested and tried for collaboration with the Germans. At his trial it came out that Bardet had not only betrayed various *maquis* missions, but had helped arrange the rendezvous at which his chief, Frager, was taken. The French court condemned Bardet to death but that sentence was never carried out; instead, it was commuted to twenty years, and Bardet was released in 1955. The Germans executed Frager by hanging at the Buchenwald concentration camp on October 4, 1944.)

One of the most important Jedburgh functions remained strengthening the Resistance through air drops of arms and supplies. In the Yonne, especially after *maquis* leadership rivalries had been worked out, strength increased markedly. The 2,000 Resistance fighters in the Yonne doubled, then tripled, before the end of the campaign. These accretions in strength only occurred at the point of German exhaustion, however, with the occupiers but a week or two away from completely abandoning this part of France. Team Bruce concluded that although its mission had been a success, it could have been much more successful if the Jedburghs had gone into France two to four weeks sooner.

Beyond the time factor, *maquis* development also lagged because arrangements with London were so cumbersome. Carpetbagger flights were most successful in areas where planes could actually land somewhere. Not only were equipment containers not lost that way, but loading went more rapidly, parachutes and containers could be saved for places they were needed most, and the aircraft could take people or things with them back to England. Team Bruce's attempts to initiate flights into the Yonne show how this ideal could fail in practice because of red tape, timidity, and inefficiency among the decision makers.

One of the larger towns in the Yonne was Auxerre, possibly best known because Napoleon Bonaparte had studied there as an officer candidate for the French army in the eighteenth century. Auxerre was liberated on August 26, 1944. The next day Jedburghs inspected its airfield and determined that it was able to handle C-47-type aircraft. Major Colby had taken a training course on the requirements for landing these planes and was the resident expert on the subject. Resistance people helped check the airfield for mines and clear those that were found. The news went immediately to London; authorities there waited a week to reply, and then said, there was a rumor that the Auxerre field was mined. Colby got in a car and drove all over the airfield without detonating anything, then, again, told London immediately. On September 5 London finally sent a long message detailing a system for lighting the field different from what Colby had learned, then insisted they would go ahead only if a trained expert was on hand to manage the air effort. The "expert" London sent, Lieutenant MacCready of the 1st Special Air Service Regiment, had exactly the same knowledge that Colby did as they had attended the same class on C-47 landings. After that, London separately supplied Team Bruce and Lieutenant MacCready with a stream of messages containing conflicting instructions for recognition letters. On September 7

London sent what it called a "final" order, then changed that system twice more. After Team Bruce radioed London insisting that Bill Colby had the relevant training, headquarters acquiesced in Colby's handling the activity but later asked if the Auxerre area was truly safe for daylight C-47 flights. Assurance that it was had already figured in one of Team Bruce's first messages. On September 14 the unit cancelled its request for arms shipments by air; by then local *maquis* fighters were being reorganized into infantry battalions for the French army. The OSS and SOE weapons would have been wasted. As the frustrated Jedburghs noted, "The handling of this operation by the London Headquarters was such as to destroy what faith we had in it."[3]

As for Resistance activities and targets, London appears to have been inadequate there too. Rather than sending specific directives and objectives, London radioed messages filled with amorphous generalities and exhortations. As George Patton's Third Army neared, this became a serious problem, for the Jedburghs needed explicit instructions if *maquis* actions were to dovetail with the activities of American troops. At first the Resistance could simply lay traps and ambushes as they had always done, but without a coordinated strategy, these activities became less and less satisfactory.

Late in August, William J. Casey, chief of the OSS Secret Intelligence Branch in London, went to Paris to begin establishing a new main headquarters closer to the front. Casey immediately started visiting the command posts of the American armies. At the Third Army, in a pair of meetings, Lieutenant Colonel Robert I. Powell, the OSS detachment boss under Patton, laid out the army's plans, and Resistance leaders agreed to a set of coordinated operations to protect Patton's flanks. Casey attended both briefings and carried the news up the line within OSS.

Team Bruce consequently received orders in General Patton's name to organize a defense of the region, seizing towns, blowing bridges on the Loire and Yonne rivers, and generally channeling the retreating Germans into sectors that could not threaten the Third Army. At the Jedburghs' request, "Rip" Powell radioed OSS London to ask that Team Bruce be given priority for weapons deliveries to accomplish this mission.

Maquis bands began capturing towns one after another, with German troops, actually quite anxious to escape the area, not putting up much of a fight. The Resistance could get cocky, however, as when a German liaison plane, apparently out of gas, landed on a road amid the farms. Bill Colby participated in the subsequent attack as the *maquis* tried to capture the aircraft and German troops defended it. The French were soundly defeated. Colby took away the lesson that lightly armed irregular troops should never attempt frontal attacks. Outcomes could go the other way too, however—a *maquis* force of 150 found a German gasoline dump when they took over the town of Moneteau. Later that day 200–300 German auxiliaries with superior weapons tried to regain the position but were defeated.

At another command session in Sens on August 31, Rip Powell issued orders to blow up river bridges. Major Colby began a survey with Colonel

Chevrier, visiting each of the bridges in their area to check which had been destroyed and arrange the demolition of those still standing. There were problems here as well. At Briare, where Colby found the bridge standing, he made his arrangements to destroy it and moved on, only to discover later that Colonel Powell had issued a new order to save that bridge. At Sancerre, disputes with the local *maquis* band delayed action. La Charité held a German garrison so strong that *maquis* attack seemed impossible, so the Resistance began moving a 120mm artillery gun it had captured, with the idea of shelling the bridge. Team Bruce also asked the Allied air force to bomb the bridge at La Charité and the latter claimed to have destroyed it. When Colby checked, the bridge stood untouched. The Germans evacuated La Charité on September 8 and blew up the bridge themselves.

By now the war, long a faraway thing, had arrived and almost passed the Yonne. In mid-August, French and American armies landed in the south of France. Rapidly ascending the Rhone valley, those armies soon linked with Patton's Third Army. From there too came a new Resistance leader, a man with orders to assume control of *maquis* forces not only in the Yonne but in several adjoining departments. Team Bruce helped link Patton's troops and those coming up the Rhone by taking location and route information directly from small units of one army and passing it to formations of the other. The linkup actually came in Bill Colby's sector.

As the Allied armies formed a unified line against the German frontier, the Jedburgh mission became superfluous. Former Resistance fighters were being integrated into the French regular army. The Yonne had been liberated. Speeches, champagne, and parties replaced clandestine plotting. When they had had their fill of celebration, Team Bruce headed for Paris, where the Jedburghs were regrouping. Lieutenant Lelong took the others on a detour to let him reconnect with a former girlfriend, but the Paris reunion came soon enough. Bill Colby found that his friend Bob Anstett, a fellow law student at Columbia, had also survived his Jedburgh mission. In fact, Anstett's team managed to waylay fleeing French collaborationists with the Vichy regime, and he ended up with the black Cadillac formerly used by Vichy prime minister Pierre Laval. When Anstett was ordered back to England, he bequeathed the auto to Bill Colby. Colby thereafter rode around in style, though he missed a second Jedburgh mission into the French province of Alsace— which was canceled when the Germans pulled out of the targeted area. Major Colby's French companions moved on from the Jedburghs to their own national army. Lieutenant Lelong fought through the war and later returned to Louisiana. Sergeant Villebois stayed in the French Army to be sent with the Expeditionary Corps which Paris dispatched to Vietnam. Roger Villebois died in combat in Indochina in late 1945. Bill Colby had not the faintest inkling that one day he would follow Villebois to that fateful place. For the moment, Major Colby would be a man in search of a mission.

3

TIANJIN TO TRONDHEIM

REST AND RECUPERATION in Paris, as Bill Colby awaited his next OSS assignment, could not be described as hard duty, even though the City of Light scarcely lived up to that name after four years of German occupation. Having a car also gave Colby great mobility. It permitted Bill to have a reunion with his father Elbridge Colby, an event at least as important as his recent one with the Jedburghs. The elder Colby served on the staff of General Courtney H. Hodges' First Army, then located not too far from the French capital. Like Bill, whose work with the OSS fulfilled his dream of doing something important in the big war, Elbridge was also thrilled to be on the Continent with the field armies. This assignment held special meaning for Elbridge Colby because during World War I, he had been with the Army's garrison in Panama, guarding the Panama Canal.

Bill Colby's behind-the-lines exploits resonated with his father in another way as well. Elbridge's World War I experience, *before* he joined the Army, had also been behind the lines, though in a much different function. The elder Colby had worked in the Balkans, in what is now Bosnia, on war relief. He was awarded the Gold Medal of the Serbian Red Cross and, after Versailles, when this area became Yugoslavia, that nation's Order of Mercy. In much the same way, his son William, for different behind-the-lines service, would one day receive the French croix de guerre.

This was heady stuff for a New York City boy, the son of a Columbia University chemist, who had passed away when Elbridge was very young. He and two sisters had been brought up by their mother. She worked incredibly hard for all the children, and got Elbridge through Columbia College, from which he graduated summa cum laude in 1912. His college years gave the boy time to think of meaning and life—he converted to Roman Catholicism during this period—as well as to collect a Phi Beta Kappa key. He seemed to be on the way toward a comfortable academic life, instructing at

Columbia University while working toward a Ph.D. in English. Once he got his master's degree, Elbridge Colby had accepted a teaching position at the University of Minnesota. He moved to St. Paul and began a doctoral dissertation. It would be St. Paul that Elbridge Colby left to meet the challenge of the human suffering caused by the world war.

What brought Colby back to Minnesota after Armistice Day was his bride. In St. Paul Elbridge had met a wonderful and religious girl named Margaret Egan. She came from an Irish Catholic family; her father was active in Democratic politics and was the former agent of an Indian trading post. Margaret proved irresistible and the two married before Elbridge left for the war. Their St. Paul reunion in 1919 proved memorable, for William would be the result, born in St. Paul on January 4, 1920. Margaret's maiden name became Bill's middle one, a family touch that turned out to be appropriate, for Margaret and Elbridge would never have another child. Margaret's health and the couple's lack of money were the reasons. Elbridge resumed teaching and writing his dissertation, but he worried about supporting a family—a reflection of his own difficult childhood.

The United States Army offered him a solution. Although he had been an enlisted man in his World War I Army service, Elbridge Colby parlayed advanced academic standing into an officer's commission. There was something about the Army, not just the money, though the Army helped Elbridge complete his doctorate in 1921. And it was not the heat and humidity of the Panama Canal Zone, where Elbridge had been an enlisted man, or the Army's lack of appreciation for Colby's Serbian relief work—only many years later would the military begin to see such efforts as forming part of what it now calls "civil affairs." Elbridge Colby became a twenty-nine-year-old lieutenant in the small interwar Army, moving from post to post as the personnel office dealt him assignments.

At Fort Benning in 1925 Colby experienced an early crisis of sorts. Three years before, the Army had brought one of its regiments of African-American soldiers, the 24th Infantry, to Benning. The men of the 24th, officered by whites, were trained in their military duties but relied on for a variety of chores. These were high days of segregation in the South, and the men of the 24th did roadwork, hauled concrete for a stadium that was under construction, delivered coal to officers' quarters, cleaned up, and cut trees. Maintaining the post stables was considered a prestige job. Elbridge Colby could not help but see all this, and he did not like it one bit. In 1925 an incident occurred in which a soldier of the 24th was shot down in cold blood because he would not get off the sidewalk for a white to pass him. An all-white jury acquitted the murderer. Colby, who handled press relations and the post newspaper at Fort Benning, wrote an angry article on the affair, published in the liberal magazine *The Nation*.

Rather than helping correct the problem, Elbridge Colby's protest became a scandal that blighted his career. Georgia newspapers and even congressmen attacked him for speaking out. The African-American press came to Colby's defense, but it had little power. The Army demonstrated its displeasure by assigning Colby to the 24th Infantry Regiment. There followed hard years of soldiering, and even his next duty assignment in a post in the North did not free Elbridge from the stigma.

Young Bill Colby remained blissfully unaware of the tribulations that beset his father. Instead, he came to personal awareness in a most exotic setting. When Bill was nine years old, Captain Elbridge Colby went to China for a tour with the 15th Infantry Regiment at Tianjin. These were the days of European colonialism and extraterritorial rights in China. Tianjin, a port up-river from the Bohai Bay and considered the gateway to Beijing, had had Western garrisons since the Boxer Rebellion of 1900–1901. One of the bat-talions of the 15th Infantry had been in place since that time; the other arrived in 1912. Since the start of World War I, when Tianjin's German garrison had been interned, the Americans had occupied the Germans' portion of the in-ternational quarter. Kaiser Wilhelmstrasse became Woodrow Wilson Street, and the former German concession became the American one, containing a barracks, a hospital, a service club and recreation hall, a post headquarters, and diplomatic facilities. Tianjin at the time was a city of about 900,000, with perhaps 4,400 foreigners in the International Concession. Among them were some 700 Americans, outnumbered by their protectors in the 15th In-fantry, which fluctuated in strength from 700 to 1,200 troops. For a brief time the year before Elbridge Colby's arrival, during heightened tensions in the Chinese Civil War, the U.S. Command had been reinforced by a 4,500-man Marine brigade under Brigadier General Smedley Butler. Political ten-sions had eased considerably by the summer of 1929; Butler's Marines were gone, part to Shanghai, part back to the states.

A bachelor officer could rent a room above the officer's club, but there was no housing in Tianjin for the 15th Infantry's families. Officers like Colby had to rent outside the compound, though still in the International Conces-sion, where all foreigners lived. A house of five to ten rooms rented for fifty to 250 Chinese dollars; that currency, colloquially called "Mex" by Ameri-cans, traded for the U.S. dollar at a ratio of 1.8 to 1 in 1925. Almost all tasks were performed by Chinese—even infantry companies in the field had laborers who set up officers' tents, worked under the cook, and so on. At home there would be a head boy to supervise the help, one or more maids and gardeners, a cook, an *amah* for the children. Wages for a typical lineup of five household servants, as recommended by a 15th Regiment guidebook printed in 1926, would be eighty-five Chinese dollars. Nor did this change very much over time—General Earle G. Wheeler, who served with the 15th in China in 1937–38, long after Elbridge Colby had left, paid his single servant $5 to $8 per month.

Chinese language training had been mandatory for officers of the 15th from the mid-20s, but not so for their families, who could pretty much get by in the International Concession with nothing but English. There were recent Hollywood movies several times each week at the regimental club plus a limited library. Ten-year-old Bill Colby went to the American School, run by an association of the Americans residing in Tianjin, and Chinese was not required there either. Young Bill no doubt picked up a smattering anyway but he must have lost it later—none of Colby's Far East work for the Central Intelligence Agency indicates he retained any boyhood Chinese.

These were breathtaking years in China, with the land dominated by warlords but with a social revolution under way. The traditional Chinese imperial system had been swept away. In its wake there was a conflict of modernization between the nationalists of Chiang Kai-shek and the communists of Mao Zedong. Japanese encroachment from the north also began in the year of Colby's arrival, with the deliberate destabilization, and subsequent Japanese takeover, of Manchuria. There were direct repercussions at Tianjin where the Japanese, worried after violent outbreaks in Shanghai the year before, increased their garrison from 600 troops to more than 6,000.

The political nuances of all these matters were beyond a boy of ten, but Colby did respond to hero figures like Chiang Kai-shek. In particular there had been an American missionary movement in China and Chiang's nationalists were favorites of the evangelists. Margaret Colby remained a strong Irish Catholic and had friends among the mission families; Elbridge wrote articles for Catholic publications stateside; Bill's Catholicism flourished in this environment and, with it, his appreciation for the Chinese nationalists.

Beyond observation of the historical forces at work in China there were the simple concerns of a boy. North China is arid, with summer temperatures of more than a hundred degrees Fahrenheit common, and summering at the seashore was almost *de rigeur*. Qinhuangdao and Weihai were the popular resorts. The plains surrounding Tianjin also lent themselves to riding. There was an endless kaleidoscope of characters residing, or passing through, the International Concession—some of the missionaries, expatriate Russians more or less stateless after the Russian revolution, traders, Chinese business agents, not to mention eccentric American soldiers, who were numerous in the 15th Regiment. This unit had many of the longest-serving men in the U.S. Army, as well as one of the highest rates of alcoholism and *the* highest rate of venereal disease. There were also outings, ceremonies to watch, and parties, all very dear in expatriate life. Despite the conflicts raging all over China, the International Concession remained safe enough for the children to walk to school. As a third grader, Bill walked over to the academy with his *amah*, but in fourth and fifth grades he went independently.

Personal safety did not mean lack of danger, however. For Americans especially, disease became a powerful enemy. Bill had to endure inoculations for a long list of maladies beginning with cholera and hepatitis. He could not use the local water to brush his teeth, nor could he eat any fresh food. Household staff became indispensable to life and health. That, in turn, became a lesson for Bill about the East: Americans should learn to see Asia as the Asians do. They should allow Asians to interpret and moderate their local reality for them, the Americans. Years later Bill Colby would write, "My boyhood experiences of China . . . prepared me for the exoticism of Asia."[1]

As Elbridge Colby's tour of duty in China wound toward its end, and Bill grew older and wiser, upheavals continued in the land around them. Japan completed its takeover of Manchuria in late 1931 and 1932. In Washington, Secretary of State Henry L. Stimson declared the United States would not recognize territorial gains made by force. Chinese and Japanese forces in Shanghai clashed once more, leading to a major military encounter. Though tranquillity would be restored—the conflict between China and Japan did not escalate to full-scale war until 1937—even a twelve-year-old could see the clouds on the horizon. As his family returned to the United States, William Egan Colby had much to ponder.

FOR MOST KIDS GROWING UP, high school and college are the most memorable passages. To judge Bill Colby by his own writings, in spite of the places the Army sent his family, including China and Panama, he too held most fondly the teenage years and the young adulthood of college. Bill felt this without regard to his father's duty post, which, during high school, was as instructor in the Reserve Officers' Training Corps (ROTC) detachment at the University of Vermont. As a consequence, Bill Colby spent three years in Burlington, Vermont.

Burlington, the shire town of Chittenden County, Vermont, proved a very pleasant place. Though the town had fewer than 40,000 people within its boundaries, locals called Burlington the "Queen City of Vermont," and perhaps it did rise to the level of a cosmopolitan place because of its university. When Vermont first became a state, its constitution provided for a university, and the school was chartered in 1791, the same year the state entered the Union. The town stood on the wooded shore of Lake Champlain, with the university set back a bit, so that approaching by boat, a visitor would see the college buildings rise like the classic castle atop a hill.

Founded in 1763, the town is named for the largest landholders of that age, the Burling family. Burlington would be the source of a number of the Green Mountain Boys, the Revolutionary War militia that played a key role early in the conflict by capturing the British Fort Ticonderoga. Indeed the leader of the Green Mountain Boys, Ethan Allen, became one of Burlington's prominent citizens after the Revolution when he retired to a farm north of town. Allen died in February 1789, and his family, caught in state tax law, lost all their property after Vermont became a state, but his example of fighting for principle was a perfect model for a young man coming to adulthood during the 1930s.

The value of innovation would be another lesson Burlington's history could teach. Throughout the first part of the nineteenth century Burlington acted as a communications hub for the entire Lake Champlain region because Gideon King had seen the lake as a thoroughfare. King became a magnate, a friend of John Jacob Astor who was then building a fortune in the fur trade; Burlington became a center of lumber milling and textile manufacturing. In 1808 the steamer *Vermont*, only the second in the United States to be operated commercially with success, was built in Burlington. By mid-century a Burlington company dominated the lake but the area would have a valuable lesson in how quickly new technology can change fortunes when the railroad came and the shipping firm quickly expired.

Bill Colby might have missed the lesson about technology, but he is unlikely to have neglected the example of Ethan Allen. Not only had Bill himself witnessed revolution under way in China, but both Bill and his father had a sense of history. Elbridge, teaching at the University of Vermont, was working for an institution founded in part by Ethan Allen's brother Ira. At Bill's school, the only high school in Burlington, there were plenty of social events, including many commemorating Ethan Allen. Bill may also have been especially drawn to tradition as he had the feeling, common among children in military families who move often, of always being the new boy in town. Also, as a Catholic in Protestant New England, Bill needed any element of commonality he could develop.

Bill Colby spent three years in Burlington. It would be the longest period of his childhood spent in one place, but it ended all too soon. Some of the schools Bill attended in his peripatetic wanderings had taught him well, moving him ahead quickly, so that in Burlington he came to the end of high school at age sixteen. Bill had had notions of applying to West Point, following his father into the service, but now he was too young, so instead Colby applied to Princeton College. Accepted there, William E. Colby left in the fall of 1936 for Princeton, where he remained very much the odd man out—a public school kid from the middle class among the privileged scions of America's best families.

The town of Princeton, with a population of less than 7,000, could truly be said to live for its university. Its train station was built to the same pattern of collegiate Gothic as the more recent university buildings. As a visitor came from the train station onto University Place there were dormitories nearby, as well as tennis courts and the gymnasium. These were the days of Princeton's snobbish "eating clubs," which substituted for fraternities, and they fronted on Prospect Avenue, within the campus. Only upperclassmen were permitted to join, and in any case Bill Colby lacked the money or social standing for such things. He ate in the cafeteria—in fact, he had to have a student job waiting tables at Madison Hall. Princeton remained a very closed community: in 1936 no African American had ever attended the college, and the admission of women was still four decades away.

Then as now, Princeton prided itself on the broad liberal arts education offered students, of whom there were 2,388 during Colby's sophomore year. The first couple of years were filled with arts and sciences survey courses that formed the core curriculum. Freshmen got to take only a couple of electives; Colby, reflecting his exposure to foreign cultures in China, chose anthropology. He found it very exciting; perhaps, in later Vietnam years, those lessons became relevant to his work on pacification.

During Christmas break of his freshman year, Bill Colby turned seventeen and could apply to the United States Military Academy at West Point. He submitted all the materials necessary, but West Point functions on the basis of appointments mostly given by legislators, and applicants are selected by congressional members after meeting West Point's basic performance criteria. One of those, health, required all applicants to have a full physical examination. Already nearsighted, Colby failed the eye exam. With any chance of entering West Point closed to him, he stayed at Princeton throughout his undergraduate days.

Life at Princeton proved simultaneously profoundly stimulating and socially constricting. Religious Catholic that he was, Bill had a problem with the Princeton rule that first- and second-year students had to attend at least half of Sunday chapel services, as the school was strongly Presbyterian. Colby fulfilled this requirement by becoming an altar boy at the Catholic Chapel. Students were forbidden to have a car in Princeton or drive anyone else's. Liquor was prohibited in dorms, as were unescorted women at any time, or escorted women after six in the evening. A Princeton man could not marry without permission of the dean. In academics, an honor system required each student following any test to sign an affirmation that he had not cheated.

On the other hand, the place had been and remained an intellectual hothouse. From their sophomore year Princeton men joined small reading groups guided by a preceptor who expanded their course work through extra readings. The overall program consisted of thirty-six semester courses through the undergraduate years plus, in the student's major field, a comprehensive examination and a senior thesis. Then there were the informal exchanges with other students, with graduate students, and with faculty members. Many, if not most, of the 365 faculty of that day had international reputations in their fields, and they were the preceptors for the reading groups.

There were other sources of excitement as well. At the foot of Nassau Street stood the five-story red brick building that then housed the offices of the Institute for Advanced Study, created in 1930 to facilitate independent research beyond the doctoral level. The institute began with mathematics, but added economics and politics in 1934 and humanities the following year. The best known of the institute's denizens was the physicist Albert Einstein, who lived in a small frame house with his daughter and secretary and was sometimes seen at the movies or occasionally at Princeton's McCarthy Theater. Bill Colby later recalled his own pleasure at sharing the campus with mental giants, specifically Einstein.

The departments of history, politics, sociology, and economics at Princeton were located within a hybrid called the School of Public and International Affairs. Colby majored in politics and excelled in the military education program of the ROTC, in which he became cadet captain. He took seminars with Edward S. Corwin, a luminary on American political systems, and constitutional law expert Alpheus T. Mason. Enthusiastic and excited by President Franklin D. Roosevelt's New Deal, Colby studied contemporary political and social problems. At one point he researched abridgments of civil liberties in the Jersey City politics of that day. Jersey City was nearby and could be studied relatively easily. Another time his inquiries focused on the Cuban sugar trade, quotas for which were a constant political issue in the era before 1960. Colby also looked into issues of education for African Americans.

In the classical vision of American liberalism, activist social proclivities are coupled with international interventionism. William E. Colby fit that profile well. This was the time of the rise of dictators—in Germany, Italy, and Japan. Colby had witnessed Japanese expansionism firsthand; then the late 1930s had brought the Spanish Civil War, in which Germany and Italy took sides with Francisco Franco's nationalists. Princeton had been a politically active place despite the university rule that participation in a riot, which protest marches sometimes became, was grounds for expulsion. Just a few years before, student feeling against foreign interventionism had been expressed in the creation of an activist group calling itself the Veterans of Future Wars. American feeling in favor of Franco's opponents, the Spanish republicans, can be gauged in Princeton by the demise of that student group. Whereas the Veterans of Future Wars had stood against the absurdity of war, Bill Colby was typical of the antifascist interventionist sentiment of his age.

Elbridge Colby arranged for his son to spend the summer of 1939 with a French family living in the Loire valley. This became an idyllic time spent among farm villages, and bicycling in the valley, not far from where Colby would later be sent for his first OSS mission; visiting châteaus, and relaxing in local cafés. Bill learned French, saw something of French politics, and loved the people. When World War II began with the German invasion of Poland, Colby saw the beginning of the conflict from a front row seat. The trip home would be aboard a British ocean liner that had been given an armed detachment to ward off submarines and merchant raiders.

At Princeton in his senior year, Colby split with mainstream political feeling, which now favored U.S. neutrality in World War II. There were demonstrations by masses of angry protesters. For his senior thesis Colby examined French policy toward the Spanish Civil War. It enabled him to pursue interests in things French as well as take a position on military intervention. Now France had had a very mixed policy in that civil war, compounded from the succession of short-lived governments holding office during that period, and also from the political position of the French communist party which, though strong, remained a minority. France gave diplomatic support to the republicans, and sold them some weapons late in the civil war, but an earlier and more forthright stance could have made a real difference, a point that could also be made about British foreign policy in this conflict. In any case, Bill Colby emerged from studying for his thesis convinced both that interventionism had been the correct course and that communism had been a blight in French, and all, politics. This stance of activism and anticommunism made Colby a true believer when the Cold War crusade began against Russia.

France would be in crisis as Colby and his Princeton classmates sang their "Cannon Song," a graduation ritual that led to ceremonial breaking of clay pipes on the breech of a Revolutionary War cannon sunk into the ground behind the administration building, Nassau Hall. German armies overran France in the short space of six weeks. Convinced of the folly of failure to intervene in the Spanish Civil War, which later predisposed Colby to friendship with OSS Jedburgh mate and Spanish Civil War veteran Bernard Knox, Bill wanted to get ready for the war he knew to be coming. But though he had graduated with an ROTC certificate, Colby, as he had been for West Point, remained a year young. He could not be commissioned in the United States Army.

By this time Elbridge Colby had a headquarters assignment in Washington, D.C. Bill went home for the summer. He had decided to go to law school and had been accepted by Columbia in New York City, which pleased Elbridge very much. Bill spent his time working as a pump jockey at a gas station, where he discovered employees were not unionized. Colby had ambitions of becoming a labor lawyer as a way of participating in New Deal social change, so he became an agitator for unionization among gas station workers until time to go to law school. That fall Bill left for New York. He had nothing to say about the drudgery of being a first-year law student, but he did later tell an Italian journalist, with respect to his union organizing, that as a youth he had been a "radical."[2] The high point of his year would be a blind date set up by a friend on which he met Barbara Heinzen, then a Barnard College junior. Bill and Barbara took to each other instantly. They went all around the city, argued politics, partied. Bill would be incensed by a communist demonstration at Columbia where coffins were carried to stigmatize President Franklin D. Roosevelt's policy of aid to Britain.

Though Colby already felt he wanted to marry Barbara, in that year of 1940–41 he was only waiting out the months until he could assume an Army commission and he did not propose to her. In the summer of 1941, Colby applied for his commission and that August left for basic training at Fort Bragg. When the Japanese attacked Pearl Harbor young Second Lieutenant William E. Colby remained at Bragg. Shortly thereafter he went to Fort Sill, Oklahoma, for advanced training as an artillery officer. Colby did so well on the field artillery course he was kept over as an instructor for new classes of officer candidates as the Army began its rapid expansion to fight World War II. Desperate to get to the war, Colby hated the Fort Sill assignment and volunteered instantly the day he saw a notice soliciting men to sign up to be paratroopers.

As did West Point, the parachute branch wanted to be elite and insisted on physicals for its recruits. Bill Colby, wiser than when he applied to West Point, contrived to undress near the eye chart and memorize the line that would show he had acceptable, but plausible (for a man who wore glasses),

20/40 vision. Unfortunately, when the time came the prospective paratrooper recited the letters from the eye chart backward. Colby's subterfuge was exposed. The doctor asked him to read the next line and he could not do so. But the Army was desperate too; the doctor merely asked Bill if he *really* wanted to be a paratrooper. Assured this was the case, the doctor approved the medical papers with the comment that Colby's vision was at least good enough to see the ground underneath him.

And so it happened that William E. Colby's station would be Fort Benning when the Office of Strategic Services came calling. The OSS *needed* paratroopers. Colby became a Jedburgh. Then came his mission to France. Soon enough Bill Colby went after another OSS assignment. Once again it would be different from what he wanted, but the new mission marked the highlight of Colby's service with OSS.

BY AUGUST 1944, Gerry Miller could be heard talking to European OSS chief David Bruce about what he should do after the war ended. This euphoric mood, widespread at the time, came from the impression that Hitler's Germany had been defeated, pressed back against the ropes. One more push—and Allied armies were thrusting across France and into Belgium and the Netherlands at that very moment—and the Germans would cave in. German withdrawal from all but isolated enclaves in Alsace seemed to confirm the trend. That withdrawal scotched the second Jedburgh mission planned for Major William Colby, but Germany's apparent disintegration proved illusory. As the German armies recoiled on their own frontier, their resistance stiffened. Soon the Germans were fighting hard along a stabilized front line and even, unknown to Allied commanders, preparing the counteroffensive that became the Battle of the Bulge.

The headquarters for the Office of Strategic Services in Paris concerned itself primarily with intelligence information in support of the armies. The various *maquis* functions, being quasi-military, or "paramilitary" as the term would soon become, continued under the control of Special Forces Headquarters (SFHQ) in London. Bill Colby cooled his heels in Paris for a time, awaiting the message from London that might set his future, but Paris soon lost its luster. More effective would be returning to London, where he could stalk the halls of SFHQ until an assignment came open. At least in London Colby would be in the faces of his superiors, a constant reminder that he was available. He returned there in October 1944.

Major Colby, of course, would be only small fry for SFHQ. London had much bigger things on its plate. Of these, the *maquis* effort in Norway continued to be a headache. The Germans had a large garrison in Norway, over 350,000 through the end of 1944, and the Resistance forces were nowhere near that large. There were an estimated 40,000 *maquisards* in the Resistance organization known as the *Milorg*, and renamed the Home Forces in the fall of 1944, and at that time only a quarter of them were armed. The Allied strategy was to permit the Germans to pull as many men out of Norway as they wished, simplifying the military situation in Norway. The Norwegians themselves, on the other hand, demanded to be let loose against the hated Nazis. A careful exfiltration operation in August brought to London Jens Christian Hauge, the Norwegian lawyer who had built the Home Forces into a true national resistance movement. Hauge proved willing to go along with Allied policy, but the Norwegians worried that a Germany *in extremis* might destroy Norway to scorch the earth it was losing.

In October the Allied strategy would be reaffirmed, but just days later SFHQ approved limited railway attacks in Norway so as to keep the Home Forces from losing their edge. When the British Royal Air Force succeeded in sinking the German battleship *Tirpitz* at her moorings in northern Norway during November, opening the door to intensified attacks on German shipping along the Norwegian coast, avoidance of strikes against land transportation routes made less strategic sense. London still resisted any large-scale commitment of the Home Forces, instead using sabotage parties from the British Special Operations Executive (SOE) that had previously been landed in Norway. But the available SOE commandos were few in number and only isolated acts of sabotage were possible. In January 1945, SFHQ mandated much more extensive attacks against four major rail lines. These strikes were carried out on March 14 by more than 1,000 *maquisards* of the Home Forces. A major strike against Norwegian railway offices also occurred directly in Oslo.

As the war neared its end, Home Forces focused on preventing any German scorched earth program. But the need for transportation strikes remained, and there were Americans agitating for an OSS role in Norway alongside that of SOE. In France, Italy, and Yugoslavia, among other places, the OSS had achieved some success with its own brand of commando teams called "Operational Groups" (OGs). In the D-Day invasion, for example, OGs were credited with cutting eleven power lines or communications trunks, mining seventeen roads, and destroying thirty-two bridges. All this in addition to killing 461 Germans, wounding 467, and taking the surrender of 10,000 more. The idea of sending one or more OSS Operational Groups to Norway seemed a good proposition.

One day Major William Colby found himself in the office of OSS Jedburgh chief Gerry Miller. Offered command of the Norwegian Special Operations Group (NORSO), Colby accepted. Only then did Miller ask if Colby knew how to ski. Thanks to his years at Burlington High School, he did: he had been one of the first members of its ski club, and because the nearby White Mountains had no chair lifts, Bill had gone up the hard way. His ski experience was not really sufficient for the NORSO assignment, but Colby got the job anyway for he had the rank to lead and happened to be there at the critical moment.

The operational group had been resting after a mission in France at a manor north of London. Norwegian-American members of OSS plus Norwegian volunteers were integrated into the unit to constitute NORSO. Major Colby moved the oversized group—about a hundred men, almost three times the size of a typical OG—to Dalnaglar Castle in the Grampian mountains of Scotland, otherwise known as OSS Area P. Colby put NORSO through a regimen of physical hardening, miles of route marches and jogging plus shooting. When snow came in the winter of 1944–45 they practiced skiing as well. Many of the Americans had been through the ski training program at Fort Hale, Colorado, that had produced the 99th Mountain Battalion; others were skiers in civilian life. And parachute training became another issue: apart from the OSS men, many NORSO commandos had none. The eventual plan would be to deploy only an advance party by parachute and have the rest follow in a seaborne landing.

The Royal Air Force (RAF) supported the Norwegian Home Forces and other Resistance efforts in Norway. Between January 1, 1945, and May 2, when air activity ceased, the RAF flew 469 successful flights into Norway, delivering 6,850 containers and 1,854 packages, more than three-quarters recovered by the Resistance. But the RAF refused to carry NORSO, possibly due to British fears of U.S. encroachment in Scandinavia. Major Colby then had to rely on the 801st Bombardment Group (Provisional) at Harrington Field. With weather always critical in Norway flights, no American crew had ever made one, and many of Heflin's pilots were reaching the ends of their combat tours. Long service B-24 crews were replaced by fresh ones who had neither mission experience nor flight records. The Norway route required staging through Kindloss in Scotland, long over-water navigation, then landfall very close to intended drop zones. The missions would have been tough under the best of circumstances.

Operation "Rype," code name for Bill Colby's assignment, had the objective of disrupting the Nordland rail line in the North Trondelaag region of Norway; this rail line had been used by the Germans to move an estimated 150,000 troops retreating from Finland after Russia knocked that country out of the war. The line moved a thousand soldiers a day from Narvik through Sweden to Trondheim, where they were shipped to Germany. Disrupting this traffic seemed worth a commando mission. Colby separated his group into two units, NORSO I of thirty-three men led by Colby, plus another twenty in NORSO II under Lieutenant Roger Hall. Colby would parachute first and summon NORSO II as a reinforcement to break the Nordland line in several places. The plan dispensed with any seaborne landing.

Parachute drops had to be carried out in total darkness, which meant during "new moon" days of the month, further complicating aerial navigation for Heflin's B-24 crews. Only by February 1945 were the NORSOs judged ready, and Major Colby started with an advance party under his deputy, Lieutenant Tom Sather, including his Norwegian liaison man, his best radio operator, and a couple of others. The B-24 lost its way on the long flight and only returned by jettisoning everything on board to lighten the plane and extend its range. At the next new moon the Norwegian exile press reported the Germans adding to their defenses in the exact sector Colby wanted to strike. The plan had to be changed. NORSO tried again on March 24. Gerry

Miller came out to Harrington to wish Colby's men well as they boarded eight B-24s. The planes were to fly to Lake Jaevsjo, north of Trondheim, for the drop. There a reception party of Home Forces were to meet the NORSOs and guide them. Colby divided his officers, men, and supplies in such a way that the load carried by any plane would sustain the men for forty days of independent action.

That had been the plan. Reality proved both messier and tragic. Three of the 801st Group B-24s turned back without ever reaching the drop zone. Another aircraft navigated poorly and parachuted its OSS commandos into Sweden. Roger Hall, one of a later NORSO contingent, wondered at the frequency with which pilots mistook one country for another. Colby's own plane blundered into Sweden also, but the pilot discovered his mistake and found the lake in Norway where fires lit by the Resistance marked the goal. The OSS men parachuted in from 500 feet. Then Major Colby with sixteen commandos were on the ground, though scattered over a thirty-six-square-mile area. The NORSO men themselves had not rigged the parachutes on their supply containers, nor had they had responsibility for attaching them to the static lines on the planes, so there was no way to tell if they had been rigged properly. Some containers had no parachutes at all; other parachutes did not work; these containers simply buried themselves in the snow. Other containers were found only after a long search. A mere portion of the supplies was recovered.

Colby's group had dropped correctly in spite of its navigational error, and the major soon saw men standing around one of the fires by the lake. Bill gave the password, which was to ask if the fishing was good—sort of silly since the lake froze solid in the winter—and got back only a laugh. The Norwegians were supposed to reply that fishing was especially good in the winter. Doubts were resolved because the Resistance men instantly recognized Lieutenant Herbert Helgesen, Colby's liaison, a Home Forces hero for earlier exploits. Team NORSO spent several days looking for its supplies and hiding out.

A week later the 801st tried to bring in the remainder of NORSO I, but this time all the aircraft aborted the mission when the weather over the lake, perfect a few moments earlier, closed with mist. On the return flight one of the B-24s crashed in the Orkney Islands killing six OSS men and seven of the eight aircrew. On April 7, a further attempt was to be made with the same result. This time one of the Harrington B-24s crashed into a cliff within earshot of Colby's group. Aside from the crew, Lieutenant Blain Jones and three OSS commandos perished. NORSO listened for the British Broadcasting Corporation (BBC) broadcast that would alert them to the next attempt, but instead London SFHQ canceled the endeavor, ordering Major Colby to proceed with the men he had.

The primary objective for NORSO had been to destroy the railroad bridge at Grana, but that would have required Colby's full operational group. Destroying railroad tunnels seemed the next best thing to do and NORSO spent a good deal of time figuring out how to place explosives on tunnel ceilings. Years later Bill Colby learned that this technique, often used to *construct* tunnels, would only have scattered rubble on the tunnel floors that trains could steam right past. Colby abandoned the concept, not because experts warned him but because the scheme seemed too dicey—in a reprise of the "Great Locomotive Chase" from the American Civil War the idea had been to seize a train and ride it until the explosives ran out, blowing every tunnel and bridge along the way before derailing the train itself.

A simple bridge blowing, as Colby had done in France, became the fallback solution. Colby selected a stretch of line and the team left its hideout soon after the final air drop failure. Each man carried fifty pounds of equipment and many pulled sleds with sixty pounds of explosives. In about a week they covered a hundred grueling miles in zero degree temperatures, up and down mountains and through snowstorms, until reaching the heights above the bridge at Tangen, where the Nordland line skirted a lake at the foot of cliffs. Colby skiied ahead with two men to scout Tangen but found it too heavily defended. Then he found a smaller bridge, just eighteen feet long, at the head of the lake. Helgesen, an expert skiier, thought that descending the mountain above the bridge was impossible; Colby, a neophyte, ordered the men to sit down on their skis when the going got too rough. Colby proved right, the sole mishap would be Helgesen's—the Norwegian broke a ski on the descent. He was given a replacement and sent to check NORSO's escape route. Major Colby dispatched Lieutenant Sather and four men with a radio to warn of approaching trains; he hoped to catch a German troop train or alternately refrain from blowing the bridge if the train were loaded with Norwegians. No train appeared, however, and once the demolition expert, Lieutenant Glen Farnsworth, finished rigging the explosives the OSS team simply blew the Tangen bridge.

Alerted, the Germans sent truck patrols to catch the commandos. A fifty-six hour running battle ensued as NORSO retreated. Gradually Colby's men pulled away. One craggy mountain, "Sugartop" on the map, Colby called "Benzedrine Hill" for the pills Bill credited with getting the sixteen Americans and seven Norwegians of his party over it. Guide Hans Liermo broke trails enabling the others to follow quicker. Major Colby turned north along the Swedish border and the team made it to their base at Lake Jaevsjo, where they rested and ate elk provided by the Norwegians.

At this point NORSO added a few more OSS men. The group that had landed in Sweden, four corporals led by Staff Sergeant Lief Oistad, joined up after adventures of their own. Oistad had ended up fifty miles inside Sweden where his party faced off against Swedish police. Narrowly averting a shoot-out Oistad had let himself be interned. The Swedes, after letting the NORSO men rest, permitted them to escape to rejoin their comrades.

On April 18 Major Colby radioed London of the success at Tangen bridge and NORSO's arrival at its hideout. The tension of their situation had been broken by Helgesen, who had wished for a dish of pineapple. Colby put that request in the message, and on April 22 a supply flight, along with food, soap, and cigarettes, delivered a case of canned Hawaiian pineapple.

The next day the operational group moved off again to sabotage railroad tracks as the Germans had restored service on the Nordland line. Another three-day trek brought them to the railroad at Snasa. Colby scouted the line with guide Lierma and a radioman whom he had given a battlefield promotion to second lieutenant. Colby picked spots and late that night NORSO divided into eight teams, each to wire thirty points for demolition. Soon after midnight a one-and-a-half-mile section of Nordland blew up all at once. German guards emerged everywhere, shooting at anything they thought could be a commando. The firefight brought Colby as close to death as he ever came—a bullet richocheted off a pebble to hit Bill's forehead—but the wound was slight. Colby's men made it back to base in less than a day. Unlike the affair at the Tangen bridge, this time the damage to the Nordland line slowed German traffic to a virtual halt; during the last month of the war the Germans were estimated to be able to move only 1,000 men on the railroad.

At Lake Jaevsjo soon after, a Lapp reindeer herder told Colby where to find the wreckage of the B-24 that had carried the Jones group. The OSS men recovered the bodies and buried them with military honors. A day or two later a patrol of five Germans chanced on NORSO when they ran into one of the Norwegian fighters and shot him. Commandos heavily outnumbered the Germans and Colby convinced them to surrender, only to have one of them begin shouting as the Americans lowered their weapons. A quick exchange of gunfire wiped out the Germans.

Meanwhile London SFHQ halted Carpetbagger flights to Norway. Food ran low and could not be replenished. Snow had begun to melt and Colby was convinced the Germans would come after them soon. Major Colby knew he had to move and his Home Forces people pressed for a maneuver in the open, the seizure of a town. At length Colby decided that was a pretty good idea and chose the town of Lierne, where there would be food and the NOR-SOs could fan out to hit German columns moving through the region. It would have been a repeat of Colby's French Jedburgh exploits. Special Forces Headquarters denied permission. Colby stood his ground, radioing back, "I am here, I know what I am doing. I know I can do it; the Resistance wants me to do it, and I intend to do it."[3]

London repeated its rejection: "ANY UNAUTHORIZED CONTACT BY YOU WITH ENEMY WILL SUBJECT YOU TO IMMEDIATE DISCIPLINARY ACTION."[4] But the German capitulation came shortly thereafter and Bill Colby found himself contacting the German area commander to take the surrender of his troops. Worried the Germans might yet fight, Colby took just two men with him and had NORSO take up covering positions. But if anything, the Germans were even more nervous; they gave up on May 11 without difficulty. Major William E. Colby corralled 10,000 German soldiers.

That was incredibly good for NORSO, which, even after the arrival of Lieutenant Hall's contingent (following the surrender), was made up of just thirty men. The group marched toward Trondheim in what quickly became a triumphal procession as the populace, freed from the German yoke, went wild. Norwegian Crown Prince Olaf came to Trondheim for a heartfelt national day parade on May 17; Colby's NORSO formed his honor guard and marched in the parade. NORSO's last mission in Norway would be to move up the coast and secure the town of Namsos, around which were indeed 10,000 Germans. There would be problems with some German naval patrol boats, but Major Colby announced a surprise inspection the next morning and after that the Germans yielded. Then came a few days in Oslo, a leisurely flight to London, and a visit to OSS-Paris, where Bill would be reunited with Elbridge Colby, by then working at SHAEF headquarters in Versailles. Suddenly Bill Colby's war looked quite different.

4

THE CRUSADE BEGINS

COLBY DID NOT LEAVE the European Theater without one more attempt to stay on, and his effort proved indicative of the direction this true believer would take after the war. The OSS heard from Colby during his Paris visit, when the major suggested he wanted to be part of any mission to Spain designed to rout Spanish fascism. Forty-five-year-old Russ Forgan— in civilian life the Chicago banker (and Allen Dulles intimate) James Russell Forgan, who succeeded David Bruce as European chief—knew the United States had not gone to war with Spain. Forgan had not the slightest intention of mounting a Spanish operation. Colby's proposal, which followed from Bill's own preoccupation with the Spanish Civil War, was met with amusement if not derision. By then most Jedburghs had been reassigned to the Pacific Theater for the climax of the War against Japan, primarily on missions into China or, shortly, Indochina. Bill Colby now got similar orders and found himself on a troopship bound for New York en route to the Far East.

In his memoirs Bill Colby wrote of his failed Spanish proposal, "I learned that America's mission in Europe was not purely ideological."[1] But the episode is equally, if not more, revealing of the man himself. It shows Colby willing to reach into the prewar (distant) past to settle an account. Colby seemed ready to punish Spain regardless of that country's neutral, though pro-German, stance in World War II, and ready to consider Spain's ideological stance and politics a *casus belli*. Moreover, nonbelligerence did not matter, nor did the absence of a state of war between the United States and Spain. This kind of exuberant activism, interventionist to a fault, would be precisely what characterized America's secret warriors during the Cold War. This episode from his OSS days shows William Egan Colby to have been a cold warrior in the classic mold.

The rest of Bill Colby's war passed as an anticlimax. Retooling for the Pacific, the Office of Strategic Services ordered Colby there but had to give him home leave along the way. Bill's troop ship landed at New York. There was a joyful reunion with Barbara Heinzen, now graduated from Barnard, and a whirlwind courtship. Heinzen had become an advertising copywriter for the New York department store Abraham & Strauss. Living in Brooklyn, she was a little removed from the center of city life, but Colby was happy to cross the East River in search of her. Then came the end of the Pacific war, after the early August atomic bombings of Hiroshima and Nagasaki. Bill Colby's resolve to avoid marriage evaporated with the atomic bombs. Within two weeks Bill and Barbara were engaged, and the marriage took place at St. Patrick's Cathedral on September 15.

Faith continued to be bound up in Colby's life equation. Not only did he see a necessity to break with his wartime routines—he paused at a Catholic church "to confess the lively bachelor life I had lived as a paratrooper."[2] Colby felt his Catholic discipline reinvigorated. He would be amused when his mother Margaret thanked the Irish saints, as opposed to any others, that her prospective daughter-in-law was a good Catholic as well. Elbridge Colby, yet to return from SHAEF headquarters in Versailles, could not attend the New York wedding.

Margaret Colby accompanied Bill to Washington, where she provided her contacts as he canvassed Army personnel authorities looking for further assignments. The Office of Strategic Services, never popular with the Army hierarchy, quickly disbanded with the end of the war. Major Colby would have been sent to Fort Leavenworth, to the Command and General Staff College, a key passage for career officers and one Elbridge could have been proud of, but Bill was more interested in finishing law school. Columbia was ready to take him back if he returned immediately, and living in New York meant Barbara could continue her life with minimum disruption.

These days were dizzying for Bill. In the space of two weeks the young officer married, secured a good postwar assignment by the grace of his mother's contacts in the Army family network, and arranged for a return to Columbia Law School in New York.

The Columbia maneuver proved possible only because Colby could get himself discharged from the service instantly. The Army had adopted rules for separation that were a compromise between its need to carry out postwar missions and the popular desire to bring the boys back home. This resulted in a system that assigned points to servicemen and women based on their time in the military, participation in combat zones, medals and awards for bravery, and so on. Bill Colby had a long time in service, having joined up before Pearl Harbor, and an array of medals ultimately to include ones from three countries, including the French croix de guerre and the Norwegian St. Olaf's Medal, as well as the U.S. Bronze Star. An award of the Silver Star to Colby, for his campaign in Norway, was in process. Points entitled Colby to immediate demobilization, and he took it.

But Major Colby wore his uniform one more time, for a mass gathering of Office of Strategic Services personnel that climaxed his frantic fortnight.

It was the final stand down of the agency and a most poignant moment, the evening of a mild and sunny day, September 28. That Friday, many from the OSS left the temporary buildings that housed their headquarters and walked down a hill to enter Rock Creek Park. Near where the park met the Potomac River the Riverside Skating Rink then stood, and the OSS took it over for the night. Deputy Director Ned Buxton spoke to pay tribute to General William J. Donovan, then presented him with a plaque as an Army honor guard looked on.

"Wild Bill" himself addressed the audience, many of whom already sported civilian clothes, some of them just realizing that other people they had known during the war, also present, were actually members of the OSS. "We have come to the end of an unusual experiment," General Donovan remarked. "Within a few days each one of us will be going on to new tasks, whether in civilian life or in government service. You can go with the assurance that you have made a beginning in showing the people of America that only by decisions of national policy based upon accurate information can we have the chance of a peace that will endure."[3]

The chief of the Office of Strategic Services then presided over a ceremony at which OSS members were honored for medals most recently awarded. William Egan Colby stood among that group, next to John Wester, an officer who had distinguished himself in Thailand during the last days of the war. Colby had already received his Bronze Star, one of 773 earned by OSS personnel, but his Silver Star (one of 148) had only just come through. General Donovan went down the line pinning medals on each of the honorees. When he came to Colby, Wild Bill, who had won the Medal of Honor in World War I and had once been considered America's most decorated soldier, lamented never having gotten the Silver Star himself. Bill Colby replied affably that the medal indeed might have completed Donovan's trove. The brief exchange would be recalled later when Young Bill and Wild Bill met once more.

COLBY DOES NOT WRITE MUCH about his last years at Columbia Law School. He did well enough to make law review and spent long hours in the library, but Princeton remained his true love. To one school buddy, surprised at his disappearance for several days, Bill admitted he'd gone back to Princeton to inhale its atmosphere and regenerate. Still, Colby built ties at Columbia too. This author encountered him first at Columbia during Colby's tenure as CIA director. Again after his retirement, I ran into Colby in the halls of Columbia. Law seemed interesting and important to Bill and the program at Columbia worthwhile. Barbara Colby worked for their spending money and Bill's veterans' benefits just about covered the cost of their Upper West Side apartment. War experience remained an emotional high point; it was the daring of the OSS that had carried Colby to manhood.

This Minnesotan's great good fortune would be to be able to play on the fringes of both the law and the spy game when he graduated. Wild Bill

Donovan provided this remarkable opportunity. Like young Bill, Wild Bill lived in Manhattan, on fashionable Sutton Place. He attended OSS reunions that Colby also frequented. After a couple of those meetings came a dinner invitation. Once Colby left law school in February 1947, William J. Donovan asked Bill to join his firm. As a freshly minted lawyer—granted, one with the prestige of having worked on the *Columbia Law Review*—Bill Colby instantly became an associate at Donovan, Leisure, Newton, Lumbard, and Irvine, of 2 Wall Street.

But the Donovan firm proved much more than it appeared, which may have been why Wild Bill decided a job offer to Young Bill would be suitable. In just the month surrounding Colby's graduation, the United States gave up efforts it had been making to mediate between Chinese communists and nationalists in that country; the United States and its allies signed a treaty ending the state of war that existed with Italy and the minor Axis nations; and the United Kingdom decided to submit the issue of Israeli statehood to the United Nations. Within a couple of weeks more, the British told Washington they could no longer support Greece, as they had been doing since 1944–45, leading to what became the Truman Doctrine and the Marshall Plan. William E. Colby's career finally would have something to do with every one of those international issues, and some of that work came to him while he was at the Donovan firm.

Wild Bill Donovan kept his fingers in many pies beyond his law firm, principally following his interest in intelligence. The World Commerce Corporation, an import-export firm that seems to have functioned as a cover for a commercial information gathering network, formed under the leadership of Donovan's wartime British and Canadian colleagues led by Sir William Stephenson, with the Donovan, Leisure firm as their legal advisers. Wild Bill personally kept in touch with many former OSS people, not just the ones he hired, and used his influence to advocate the creation of a peacetime U.S. organization along the lines of the Office of Strategic Services. In 1947 such an entity came into being and became known as the Central Intelligence Agency (CIA). When the CIA, in turn, formed its own covert action apparatus, which it called the Office of Policy Coordination (OPC), the head of that unit would be yet another Donovan friend, Frank Wisner, a lawyer and former OSS operative who worked upstairs at 2 Wall Street for the firm Carter, Ledyard, and Milburn. Wisner eventually got so many phone calls in which Wild Bill told him he ought to be doing one thing or another that the OPC chief stopped taking Donovan's calls. Wild Bill simply switched to calling another wartime associate, CIA's general counsel Lawrence Houston.

On the China front, William Donovan spent weeks consulting with Claire Chennault, the famous wartime leader of the "Flying Tigers," on the legal foundations of the Civil Air Transport (CAT), a form that in fact became a front company, or "proprietary" of the CIA. The Donovan firm filed papers for CAT, and Wild Bill served as intermediary of sorts when the Central Intelligence Agency began its relationship with the company, advancing money toward the end of the Chinese Civil War. During the first year of the Korean War the degree of CIA involvement in CAT expanded to the extent that Chennault's aviation company became a wholly owned appendage of the agency.

Donovan's firm continued to work a wide variety of cases, many like the CAT affair, international matters with vague links to the nether world of intelligence. There were conventional cases as well, and Wild Bill argued at least one before the United States Supreme Court. But it would not be until 1950, when the Donovan firm had twenty-one partners and thirty-four associates, that it posted its first million-dollar profit.

This came after Bill Colby's time, but the fact is that the work of an associate was not all pedantic. Drafting and polishing legal briefs no doubt did not seem all that exciting, and it could not be trial work. Corporate law is about tax liabilities, legal filings, establishment and merger of companies, board and shareholder meetings, stock issues, and the like. Colby took notes when partners met with clients, and advised when corporate minutes showed a company to be skating at the edge of the antitrust laws. The firm made an effort to season Bill, committing him to public defender work with the New York Legal Aid Society, and to cater to Colby's interests by giving him labor law cases when they came in.

Still, the most interesting things were those that recalled OSS days. In a firm with partners who included not only Wild Bill, but former senior OSS officials Otto C. Doering, Richard Heppner, and Walter Mansfield, plenty of interesting matters came up. Donovan was just one of several principals pressing for the formation of a peacetime intelligence agency. There were also inquiries from former OSS members, promotional activities for OSS memoirs, veterans benefit cases, and assistance for the principals on their correspondence with former colleagues. Sometimes things got more personal, such as Colby's participation with the American Veterans Committee, which began during his last year at Columbia as part of an effort to prevent takeover of the Manhattan chapter of that organization by some of its communist members. Here came a chance to engage directly with the totalitarian enemy and Bill Colby relished it. This issue would be fought out over a resolution that the group condemn the right-wing government of Greece in its fight against Greek communists. The resolution went down to defeat, but the more extreme members subsequently continued obstructing attempts by liberal veterans to give the group a voice in the issues of the day.

Greece became the key issue of Colby's time with the Donovan firm. On May 8, 1948, the Middle East radio correspondent for the Columbia Broadcasting System (CBS), George Washington Polk, Jr., disappeared in Salonika, Greece. Some days later his body surfaced in Salonika bay. About a week after that a number of distinguished journalists, organized by the well-known columnist Walter Lippmann, joined in the Overseas Writers Special Committee to Inquire into the Murder of George Polk. This group hired Wild Bill Donovan to conduct its investigation into the affair.

This resulted in several trips to Greece by Donovan, where his primary investigator was James G. L. Kellis, a man who had been with OSS during 1944–45. Kellis, an Army major like Colby, had led an OSS operational group in Greece code named Chicago, and by war's end he knew most of the key personalities on the Greek scene. In New York, Bill Colby himself would be Wild Bill's main man in this matter.

Within weeks Jim Kellis established that the Greek communists, who were being accused of the Polk murder, lacked the ability to manipulate the local authorities in Salonika, the freedom of movement, and the knowledge of Polk's activities necessary to have perpetrated the action. Kellis finished a report to that effect on July 22 and gave it to Donovan. The alternative explanation was that Polk's murderers were either the Greek government or certain elements of the government, and subsequent evidence also suggests participation by British operatives and possibly American ones. In any case, the United States government, and especially the CIA, showed special interest in this case and were in touch with William Donovan when he visited Athens. Soon after the Kellis report, Donovan took his investigator off the case.

Meanwhile George Polk's bride of seven months, Rea Coccins-Polk, a Greek national and former airline stewardess whom Polk had met while flying from Salonika to Athens on a previous trip, found herself harassed by Greek authorities and bruited about as a suspect in the murder. She fled to America and arrived in New York late in June, to be met by William E. Colby. The Donovan firm associate quizzed Rea hard about her suspicions of right-wing Greek involvement in the murder. Bill and Barbara Colby became friends of Rea Polk, who followed Barbara to the Upper West Side to enroll at Barnard College. They had pleasant evenings together, but also official dealings, as early in 1949 Donovan had convinced Polk to give him a power of attorney. Most disturbing was an incident, which Rea reported to Colby, in which she was threatened by several Greeks, including relatives of top government officials. Donovan himself returned to Athens for the trial in Greece where, a former Greek communist was accused and convicted based on contrived evidence.

Walter Lippman's committee of journalists would never be apprised of either the Kellis report or the opinions of Rea Polk recorded by Colby, even though it had employed the Donovan firm. James Kellis went on to a job at the CIA, and there can be little doubt that Wild Bill Donovan had played the CIA's game. At a minimum the CIA had conspired to manipulate justice in Greece and had used the Donovan law firm to intimidate Rea Polk, the one person with clear standing to blow the lid off this affair.

Not long after the Polk case, Bill Colby left the Donovan firm. Colby presented this move in his memoir as based simply on family and personal considerations, but he saw himself as a liberal Democrat with a desk at a Wall Street law firm whose partners were conservative or Republican. Then there was Donovan's handling of the Polk business. One did not have to oppose United States interests or, for that matter, those of the CIA, to be distressed by the methods used here.

Moreover, in conversations with Rea Polk, Bill Colby discovered the commonalities that existed between him and George. Polk had been in China while Colby attended Princeton, and had been educated at the Virginia Military Institute following his father, much as Bill had wanted to go West Point. To the degree his professed friendship with Rea had been a real one, the issues raised by the Polk affair must have bothered Colby.

Indeed, "disturbed" would be a common response to the Polk case. James Kellis, who served long and honorably with the CIA, including tours in Korea and Japan, and who would be considered for station chief in Athens in the mid-1950s, was disturbed also. "While I was in Greece," Kellis wrote after retirement in 1977, "I often heard the statement that national interests had to be given a higher priority than discovering the real murderers of George Polk. I could not accept then, and I do not accept today, that we could support national interests by disregarding moral principles."[4]

For a few months Colby could still immerse himself in American politics. Manhattan was effervescent in the 1948 election. Bill joined his local Democratic club in what was then the 7th Assembly District. He pushed doorbells and canvassed residents for the party. On the day Harry S. Truman defeated Thomas E. Dewey in that surprise upset, Bill Colby worked as a poll watcher in a New York precinct. But for the long run, Manhattan seemed increasingly unattractive to Colby. Raising a family in the city looked like a poor idea, and Bill and Barbara already had a son, Jonathan, born in 1947, and were about to be blessed with daughter Catherine. The suburbs, a mortgage, another level in the Donovan firm, those things began to look to Colby like a treadmill.

Early in 1949 Young Bill and Wild Bill took a trip together to Norway, where the Norwegians were about to dedicate a memorial to the OSS mission that had helped liberate their country. The world beyond Wall Street beckoned more strongly than ever, while Bill Donovan's legerdemain in the Polk case continued to rankle. Bill came back with a Norwegian medal and the determination to make a new start.

Returning to his interest in labor and law and unions, Bill Colby submitted an application for a position with the National Labor Relations Board (NLRB). The job required moving to Washington, but that got the family out of Manhattan, and with Elbridge now retiring from the Army to teach journalism at George Washington University, it brought them close to the grandparents. Bill got the job and the Colbys moved that autumn. Bill's first NLRB case benefited garment workers in Philadelphia who were trying to form a union. He also worked on briefs opposing big farmers in California who were breaking strikes by their migrant grape pickers. But already the Central Intelligence Agency beckoned, and in June 1950 came the outbreak of the Korean War. Bill Colby rallied to the flag.

THE SIRENS' CALL that attracted Bill Colby came, not anonymously, but from an OSS buddy. Like Colby, Gerald E. Miller, his former London supervisor in special operations, was a lawyer. After the war Gerry Miller returned to Detroit and resumed his practice there, mostly banking, some law. But when another lawyer, Frank Wisner, went to the Central Intelligence Agency to create its Office of Policy Coordination (OPC), Gerry moved to Washington also. Miller had known Wisner in OSS, for which Frank had led an agent team into Rumania. Now in the CIA's Office of Policy Coordination, Gerry Miller effectively got back his old job, being made chief of the Western European Division. If anything, it was a promotion, as now he supervised all covert activities. Miller quickly learned that Bill Colby was in the nation's capital, and not long after, Gerry invited Bill to lunch.

At the beginning of 1950 Colby had just begun his stint at the National Labor Relations Board, and though the CIA post that Gerry Miller offered seemed tempting, Bill did not permit himself to be drawn in. Colby readily concurred about the sharpness of the threat from Stalin's Russia, which Miller portrayed as so dire it had induced him to give up a lucrative banking career, but Bill could not walk away from the Labor Relations Board just a few weeks after taking the job. Such a move would neither look good on his record nor be fair to NLRB. At the same time, however, Colby did not wish to miss out on having a relationship of some kind with the intelligence agency, so he agreed to consult on matters that seemed appropriate. Bill consented to the background check the CIA carries out on prospective employees and provided the information to start such an investigation. He went on to his Philadelphia union case.

In both the departure from the Donovan law firm and the first, truncated, job in Washington, there are clues to the later William Colby. Here was evidence of a particular attitude toward fairness as well as a stand on principles. On the other hand, the testimony of Rea Polk to students of her husband's case,[5] which amounted to an affirmation that Colby never told her the truth about the position Wild Bill Donovan had assumed in the matter of the murder, shows Colby solidly in the camp of those driven by Cold War ideology. His end-of-the-war willingness in OSS to participate in an operation in Spain betrays the same kind of ideological motivation.

Of course the Korean War furnished the perfect occasion for the careful and cautious Colby to switch ships, leaving the NLRB behind forever. It is difficult today to evoke the atmosphere of 1950. With the Cold War ended there is no global tension with which to compare; the closest available analogue would be the Russian intervention in Afghanistan of 1979, an event that many Americans (mistakenly) saw as the start of a conventional military offensive that could reach as far as the Persian Gulf. There followed a spate of volunteers for the U.S. military and the CIA. In 1979 the specter of global conflict soon passed, but in 1950 it did not. Just five years after the end of World War II, less than two since the Berlin blockade, with a pall of constant tension and fear over Europe that that continent would be the scene for a further Russian power play, the Korean conflict possibly betokened World War III. To join seemed an act of patriotism, and the CIA of that era, if known to outsiders at all, appeared vaguely alluring, with the mystique of the old Office of Strategic Services combined with the cadre of dynamic, well-educated Americans who descended on Washington in the summer of 1950. Suddenly, for Bill Colby to quit the Labor Relations Board to join the CIA became not only acceptable but perfectly logical.

Within the CIA, Colby went to Frank Wisner's Office of Policy Coordination. He came to OPC as a known quantity. Not only had he been acquainted with Gerald Miller, but Frank G. Wisner himself had been opposing counsel in an ownership suit, over land in Rumania, that had been fought out between the Donovan law firm and Carter, Ledyard and Milburn. Although the CIA's training activities would not become regularized until 1952, when the agency opened its facility at Camp Peary near Williamsburg, Virginia, as a former OSS man, the newly minted CIA GS-12 rank civil servant could be considered mostly trained and was inserted directly into OPC projects. In addition, Colby would be excused from taking a polygraph test by virtue of his status as a former OSS member, which also expedited issuance of his security clearance.

The Office of Policy Coordination had been the product of initiatives taken after the creation of the Central Intelligence Agency. The National Security Act of 1947, which formed the charter for the CIA and also merged the military services into a new Department of Defense, did not provide for covert operations as a CIA function. But a catch-all provision existed that required the CIA to perform such "other" missions as the National Security Council (NSC)—also an entity of the 1947 act—might from time to time direct. At the State Department, America's architect of containment, George M. Kennan, pushed for and secured the agreement of the Defense Department, and subsequently the NSC and the rest of the government, to an organization to carry out psychological warfare against Russian communism. This effort, sanctioned in a policy paper called NSC-4/A in late 1947, would be expanded in the summer of 1948 to include a range of "covert," or unattributable, actions. The Office of Policy Coordination, administratively housed within the CIA but actually loosely suspended among that agency, State, and the Pentagon, carried out the covert program. Frank Wisner proved acceptable to the CIA and the Pentagon as director because of his wartime work with the OSS. State seemed amenable to the appointment as well—for a brief time after the war ended Wisner had been assistant secretary of state for Eastern European lands the Russian military had overrun in their rush to defeat Germany.

Director Wisner recruited a number of people whom journalist and former OSS colleague Stewart Alsop characterized as "Bold Easterners," often liberal internationalists from Ivy League schools. Many were lawyers like Gerry Miller and Bill Colby. The CIA had no parking lot in those days, but the curbs closest to OPC offices were clogged with sports cars or late model fancy machines, whereas the rest of the area would be filled in with the usual hodgepodge of older, sometimes battered, vehicles. This was consistent with the well-heeled Ivy League crowd who then predominated at the agency. The CIA could offer only regular civil service wages, by law, but it was not coincidental that Frank Wisner frequently did not bother even depositing his salary checks (his secretary once discovered almost a year's worth of checks squirreled away in Wisner's desk). The OPC chief would be typical in this regard, with people like William E. Colby as the exceptions. Colby came to CIA without means of external support and, in this respect, became more dependent on the agency than some of his peers.

Agency employment did not lead to Colby's changing the routines that had evolved during his time at the NLRB. He continued to carpool with friends who worked for the District of Columbia government, but then caught a crosstown bus to CIA headquarters. The children were in a cooperative preschool and stayed there. Barbara Colby participated in the major decisions—whether to join the CIA, to take an overseas tour, and so on. Yet Barbara accepted being told nothing of the details of his CIA work or knowing his relationship to the other agency officers she encountered at official functions. Civilian friends winked with private knowledge, as CIA officers' obfuscations in describing their government work instantly revealed their real status, but they cooperated in preserving Bill's rather shallow cover story. His life changed forever that day in November 1950 when Colby first went to work at OPC.

William E. Colby became one of many fresh officers in the rapidly expanding Office of Policy Coordination. This CIA unit had been slated for major growth since decisions made in 1948 and 1949, and State and the Pentagon simply demanded even more actions they saw as desirable, necessitating further OPC expansion. Thus neither the Korean War per se, nor President Harry Truman's approval of the policy paper NSC-68 earlier in 1950, which mandated an American military buildup, caused the increases in the Office of Policy Coordination. At most, Korea accelerated a trend already set. In 1949 the OPC had had about 300 officers with a budget of $4.7 million. By the time of Korea there were 500, and when fiscal year 1951 ended on June 30, 1951, some 1,531 CIA officers labored for what Frank Wisner liked to call his "Wurlitzer," the brand name for a type of large pipe organ produced for movie theaters in the early decades of the twentieth century. A year after that Wisner had 2,812 personnel and a budget of $82 million, with a substantial headquarters staff and no fewer than forty-seven stations in foreign countries.

Colby expected to work on Korean War–related activities, as would have been most consonant with his China past. But such an assignment was almost impossible in Gerry Miller's Western Europe Division. Instead Miller took advantage of Colby's OSS Norway experience and sent him to the Scandinavia Branch of the division. The Office of Policy Coordination wanted to provide for a resistance network that would fight on, like the *maquis*, in the event the Russians succeeded in taking over Europe. Unlike World War II, the CIA notion started from the assumption that a *maquis* movement would work much better if it were set up in advance and were not dependent on air supplies and infiltration. Bill Colby had been in Norway and obviously had some knowledge of what resistance forces might need in terms of supplies, and how those materials might be stored. Division chief Miller promptly put Colby in charge of planning what the CIA began to call "stay-behind networks" for Scandinavia, with minimal revelation of this fact, even within the CIA. Branch chief Lou Scherer gave Colby the available intelligence data, limited in some cases to old OSS reports. Bill forged ahead.

There were many difficulties for the CIA planners. Some were political, others operational or practical. In Norway and Denmark, allied with the United States by the North Atlantic Treaty, there had to be a certain coordination. Sweden professed to be neutral in the East-West conflict so there could be no overt association there, but the Swedes strongly maintained their prerogatives and the CIA could hardly carry out significant activities in the country without the Swedes' knowledge and acquiescence. Colby writes about Finland as well, but there is no evidence the CIA got anywhere with stay-behind networks in that land. Meanwhile the simple need to identify suitable storage places or prospective agents became a major headache, and demands on supply officers to furnish material for the nets were disturbingly large, especially in view of the CIA's need to focus on the Korean War.

Identifying local recruits who were possibly open to working with the CIA meant getting a hand on the most current information, and that meant data from the Office of Special Operations (OSO). The OSO members were the CIA's spy managers, an agency component that actually did the legwork of finding valuable intelligence in foreign countries. Under an Army general, Robert A. Schow, the Office of Special Operations labored hard in the spy business, considered itself the inheritor of the mantle of the OSS, and thought of the OPC as upstarts. Schow had been an associate of the director of central intelligence who appointed him, Rear-Admiral Roscoe H. Hillenkoetter. Both of these men spent the first part of World War II as attachés in the rump United States embassy in Vichy France. Frank Wisner's appointment had been the common denominator of choices by several agencies. Their organizations, the OSO and the OPC, remained uneasy allies at best. In fact, the hostility had been so great that a new director of central intelligence, General Walter Bedell Smith, who came aboard just a month before Colby began work, made achieving an accommodation between the OSO and the OPC one of his major goals. Director Smith's efforts led in 1952 to a merger of the two CIA units.

Thus in Sweden (and elsewhere) when Bill Colby took the field, OSO reporting could not be used very easily by an OPC officer for a recruiting list. This was especially so in that the OSO wanted its own stay-behind nets to maintain open channels in the event they would be needed. Colby had to work from scratch, developing methods he would profit from later in South Vietnam.

Meanwhile, Sweden was vital to operations even more important than those of the OSO Scandinavia Division. The Soviet Bloc Division, headed by Harry Rositzke, strained every muscle to put agents on the ground inside Russia, which then included the Baltic states (since reemerged) of Latvia, Lithuania, and Estonia. All those countries had active anti-Soviet resistance groups—not nebulous stay-behind networks but flesh-and-blood partisans begging for help. Sweden and its islands in the Baltic were key operating bases for Russian activity. The CIA, hungry for intelligence that the Baltic partisans could furnish, made Rositzke point man for this project, with his OSO Baltic chief Gerhardt Meyer consequently sensitive regarding Bill Colby's OPC initiatives in Stockholm.

Then there were the British. In truth the CIA were new to all this, but the Baltic resistance had been active from the end of World War II, and the British Secret Intelligence Service (SIS or MI-6) had long since forged links with it. In the SIS organization the "northern area" included both Russia and Scandinavia, and the "Controller Northern Area," Harry Lambton Carr, already had his own favorites, both individuals and espionage rings. American intelligence, bound to cooperate with the British in consequence of a wartime secret agreement between the two governments, had to make some accommodation with SIS.

In April 1951 the CIA's Harry Rositzke led a delegation of six agency men to London for talks with the SIS. They were to do a comprehensive review of all operations against the Russians and some of the Soviet Bloc countries. Bill Colby was among the Americans. Consonant with his poor cover, Colby used his regular passport, in his own name, and told border control officials he would be in England on legal business. The drill would be the same in Denmark and Norway. Colby had known since early in the year, when Gerry Miller called him into his office, that he would be heading for Stockholm to start an OPC franchise there. That required suitable arrangements with all the allies for such details as supplies, security protocols, and training of local nationals who would go on to train the recruits in their own countries.

England's Harry Carr, meanwhile, had been disputing with the Americans for over a year over *whose* Baltic allies were penetrated by the Russians—the SIS and the CIA both agreed the Russians were getting inside information on Allied intelligence operations. The earlier stages of this argument had been observed by a real Russian double agent, the SIS liaison in Washington, Harold A. R. ("Kim") Philby, but he had come under suspicion from CIA counterespionage expert James J. Angleton and his colleagues at the Federal Bureau of Investigation (FBI). Only a month later the defection to Russia of British diplomats associated with Kim Philby left the SIS officer all but exposed as a Soviet agent. The London talks with the Americans were conducted without Philby. British and American spies never did agree upon exactly which of their local collaborators might be Russian spies, but they did set up modalities for further activities. A party of four housed in Sweden and staged through the CIA base at Munich had been scheduled for parachuting into Lithuania late in April. The men landed on the 19th but were swept up by Russian secret police. It was an OPC agent team; Bill Colby later learned about the fiasco.

At that point Colby, the newly minted CIA officer in the final stages of preparation for his overseas assignment, began classes in espionage tradecraft. Not required to train in basic close combat, weapons, or parachute drops because of his OSS service, Colby learned to spot and evade watchers; use so-called safe houses, places unknown to the adversary where meetings could be staged or an agent go to ground; make contact with an agent; use secret writing, miniature cameras, other espionage equipment, and similar measures. Lessons in the psychology of recognizing prospective agents and recruiting them were interesting, but Colby preferred the more straightforward technique of simply building a friendship with someone. The CIA officers also got a primer on communist theory and tactics, which Bill found quite second-rate compared to what he had learned as an undergraduate at Princeton.

Bill and Barbara found the orders to Stockholm somewhat surprising—this time he had expected to be assigned to Norway. But clearly Sweden stood in the front line of the secret war whereas Oslo, if not becalmed, at least constituted a rear position. Stockholm also beckoned as someplace new, and Colby's plan for a stay-behind network had to be carried out in person, at a high level. His initial effort, to get an itinerant OPC officer to inspect a potential storage site with a Swedish official, failed because the Swede did not want to be seen in company with an American agent. The CIA needed someone who could be in place long enough to build confidence, and at a high enough level to override local prejudices. Bill completed his advanced espionage training, he and Barbara added another son, Carl Colby, and in April 1951 the enlarged family left for Sweden. William E. Colby now had cover as an ostensible member of the diplomatic service, a Foreign Service Reserve Officer at the United States embassy.

The American embassy in Stockholm, quite off the beaten track in ordinary times, would be quiet enough in this Cold War age so as not to be watched much, unlike installations in places like Berlin, Vienna, and Hong Kong. Bill Colby nevertheless used his tradecraft and took precautions, and he would be careful to keep fences mended inside the embassy as well as without. At the embassy the CIA's Office of Special Operations (OSO) chief had been at work longer than he, and though Colby had theoretical independence through his OPC chain of command, the OSO man would in practice be regarded as station chief. The Swedes, not to mention the various Balt emigré groups, did not make distinctions among different strands of the CIA. Neither would Ambassador W. Walton Butterworth, actually an Asian specialist who had been in Washington before the explosive growth in the Office of Policy Coordination, so for him, the OSO man *was* the CIA chief. Bill Colby carefully kept the OSO apprised of all his moves, doubly necessary because the OSO remained involved in running its own operations into Russia using the same emigré groups with which Colby would deal.

In fact, it would be the espionage man, the OSO chief, who arranged Colby's first meeting with a potential recruit for the stay-behind network, then introduced them at a CIA safe house in Stockholm. The Office of Special Operations continued to keep a weather eye on OPC activities in Scandinavia. Bill Colby went about his work, avidly at first but more as a routine as months stretched into years and the stay-behind project remained oriented toward an eventuality that every day seemed more remote. Colby found and recruited lead agents, inserted them into a CIA training cycle; brought them home to spot, recruit, and themselves train subagents; and arranged for the necessary provision of equipment for training and for stockpiles. He located places for arms and radio caches, and secured permissions from the owners for that use of their land. In some instances he benefited from expatriate Americans who owned farms or other land. In Norway, Colby could work officially in liaison with that nation's secret service, which set up the networks itself and merely called on the CIA for equipment and technical assistance. In Denmark, official cooperation was lukewarm, with a handful of Danish functionaries assigned to work with Colby at a high level and for specific purposes.

Swedish activity remained complicated both by the neutral status of the country and by the rivalries of local security services. The national intelligence service (SAPO by its Swedish acronym) and Sweden's Military Intelligence Bureau (IB) never cooperated openly, but the chief of its technical office, Thede Palm, apparently joined the network. Through one of these sources Colby learned that there was an anti-communist underground in Sweden predating his own organizing efforts, one with World War II and early postwar fascist roots. The CIA man had to be doubly careful in Swedish recruitments to avoid persons from the other network. The Swedes were also very sensitive in their concern that people in their underground might be revealed by being known to the CIA, and Colby had to insist on special precautions for documents regarding the stay-behind network. Nevertheless, enough agents joined up and recruited enough subagents that estimates have put the size of Sweden's stay-behind network at between 1,000 and 2,000 persons.

According to the account of Daniele Ganser, an expert on the European stay-behind programs, the Swedes were also officially creating their own network under a colonel named Anders Grafström. This too could cut across the purposes of the CIA effort. Though the Swedish security services took a largely benevolent view of Colby's effort to recruit an underground, Ganser reports that problems developed between the CIA and Swedish officials over whether Americans could control the prospective underground. Colby apparently had to expel Swedish intelligence officer Thede Palm from the network, though cordially enough that they remained friends afterward.

Toward the end of Colby's tour in Stockholm the Swedes opened an investigation of the competing proto-fascist underground, known as the Sveaborg organization. Shortly after Bill moved on to his next post, the Swedes arrested and put on trial Otto Halberg, the chief of that group, leading to fears that prosecution might reveal overlaps between the Sveaborg organization and the CIA stay-behind network. The investigation could have been a warning to the CIA to respect the Swedish government's primacy in these matters.

Meanwhile the Swedes remained active in other ways that freed Colby to operate within their country. On numerous occasions, for example, they imposed restrictions on Russian diplomats and suspected spies, whereas there is no evidence of similar measures against the CIA. As late as 1976 Swedish journalists reported there had never been a case in which CIA personnel or agents were brought to trial in their country.[6]

Under Frank Wisner's Wurlitzer concept, molding opinions would be among the OPC's functions. One man who served the CIA in this role in Sweden, Austin Goodrich, worked for the Columbia Broadcasting System (CBS) in Stockholm as a part-time reporter, or "stringer," from 1951 on. Goodrich had a perfect cover through journalism for his intelligence work. As case officer, Colby claims, he made it clear to headquarters he would not instruct agents of influence like Goodrich on what to write or broadcast, and that their standing with cover companies like CBS would depend entirely on their product for those employers. Though Colby's conviction was the right one, there is little doubt officers under deep cover in situations like this thought hard about what the CIA would want them to say on issues of the day regardless of whether they had orders. As for CBS, its cozy relationship with the CIA would be a curious role reversal from the adversarial one in the 1948 murder of correspondent George Polk. A year after Colby left Stockholm, a CBS manager who took a familiarization trip to Europe and did *not* stop by Stockholm to see Goodrich would be criticized by two CIA officers for failing to do something that contributed to the cover of their man. The meeting to air the CIA's complaint took place in the offices of CBS executive William S. Paley, who denied knowledge of these events when they came to light two decades later.

Directing local agents, not an especially onerous task in Scandinavia, lacked excitement after the first few iterations. Much more exciting, though also not all that dangerous in this particular espionage environment, were deliveries of equipment Colby sometimes made personally. Once he used a family road trip to disguise a series of radio deliveries to cache sites in Denmark. The radios weighed so much the back of his car drooped noticeably. Colby worried he would be stopped by authorities, but his diplomatic passport saw him through. At carefully arranged stops the family would go for walks in the woods while local agents unloaded the radios.

As an embassy political officer Bill tried to live his cover, doing diplomatic work that a real foreign service person might engage in. Barbara Colby added depth to that cover by involving herself in women's issues and consumers' rights in a way that brought the couple into contact with people at all levels in Swedish society, from the royal family on down. Bill saw Barbara's activism as useful both in terms of his status as a diplomat and in bringing him into contact with people he might find useful in other ways. Barbara Colby, meanwhile, in going beyond her earlier forays into American party politics, acted in ways that would one day lead to some interesting places.

The most important intelligence business going on had nothing to do with any of the projects Bill Colby ran; rather, it reflected his care in dealing with his OSO colleague. Getting the OSO and the OPC to cease being rivals became very important to CIA director Walter Bedell Smith. One measure Smith took would be to bring in one of the Office of Strategic Services "greats," Allen W. Dulles, to be assistant director in control of both the rivals. To make this happen, Director Smith unilaterally moved to absorb the Office of Policy Coordination into the CIA, ending its convenient perch between agencies. When no one complained, Frank Wisner had no choice. But Bedell Smith muddied the water by trying simultaneously to perpetuate the budget arrangement under which State and the Pentagon *paid* for the OPC's political action and paramilitary projects. This permitted Wisner to make end runs to the other agencies, initiating projects by getting money for them. Allen Dulles and Bedell Smith then squabbled themselves, until in August 1951 Smith kicked Dulles upstairs to be deputy director of central intelligence. An Army colonel, Kilburn Johnson, became caretaker deputy director, but that arrangement proved unsatisfactory because lacking Allen Dulles's stature, Johnson found it difficult to knock OPC and OSO heads together.

Observers such as author John Ranelagh maintain that the merger of the OPC and the OSO into a new Directorate of Plans flowed very simply from General Smith's takeover of Wisner's Wurlitzer. In fact, the offices' rivalry persisted while Bedell Smith's temperature rose. The director called in OSO chief Lyman B. Kirkpatrick, Jr., and had him study a unified operations directorate. General Smith then used the result to justify direct orders for the reorganization. Kirkpatrick went on an international tour to promote the change during the summer of 1952, expecting to become the deputy director for plans (DDP), as the head of the operations unit would be known. Instead, Kirkpatrick contracted polio while in Bangkok and ended up in the hospital, later to become the CIA's inspector general. Frank Wisner became the DDP. Meanwhile, Kirkpatrick's tour never reached Stockholm, so the emissary there would be Lou Scherer, still the responsible OPC branch chief. Because Bill Colby had been coordinating his OPC activities with the OSO chief all along, he had no difficulty with the new arrangement.

As before, the most delicate coordinating, indeed an aspect of Colby's work that also directly concerned the State Department, involved the Baltic emigrés. Colby found this work exciting, although keeping track of the al-

phabet soup of exile groups and personalities, not to say their varied jeal-
ousies and agendas, could be a major headache. Not just the locus of innocent
conversation, or even simple intelligence-gathering, Sweden happened to be
a major source for exile recruits who would be given paramilitary or espionage training in Germany and, beginning late in 1952, the United States. That
spring several Latvians went to Germany escorted by Fred Launags, a Latvian
working with the CIA, who had been active in resistance movements since
volunteering at the British embassy in Stockholm back in 1945. As the
OPC's man in Sweden, Bill Colby had had the job of bringing the Latvians
into the fold.

The resistance activities were tragic. Heavily infiltrated by Russian secret
police, who had turned around many previous agents and made them work
against the CIA and its British allies, the resistance suffered divided loyalties.
The close Russian control of exiles' homelands also gave the adversary huge
advantages. When the Latvian recruits from Sweden parachuted into their
native country in August as part of a four-man team they were immediately
arrested. That fall the German Max Klose, who ran a Baltic boat service,
using former German naval craft (an E-boat) to support the CIA and the SIS,
made a trip to the Lithuanian coast to drop off another party of four and
bring one agent back. Unknown to Klose, one of the infiltrators, as well as
the man he brought out, were Russian police agents. Again the others would
promptly be arrested. In mid-May 1953, yet another Latvian was parachuted
into his country, sent with almost no knowledge of local conditions and with
instructions to make contact with a supposed resistance leader who was really
a Russian policeman. Paul Hartman, a Riga-born CIA officer who supervised
the final mission training of these spies and sent them off, insisted to Fred
Launags that there was nothing wrong with losing so many brave men: "It's
all part of our mission."[7]

But the losses did disturb Bill Colby, who thought also about the slim
chances of the stay-behind networks that were his main preoccupation. The
picture could not be a bright one. At the same time, the OSO/OPC merger
had become final; the head of the new Baltic Branch would be George N.
Belic, who had headed that unit of the former OSO. Belic had been with
Frank Wisner in Rumania at the end of World War II, and the Odessa-born
officer would become a star in the CIA's Russian operations. But the change
did not bode especially well for Colby, who had not been a Wisner protégé.
His man, Gerry Miller, had been bumped out of CIA headquarters to become
station chief in Rome. Colby responded with alacrity when Miller invited
him to visit Rome and then offered a posting in the CIA station there. As in
the late 1940s, Italy remained one of the most important fronts in the secret
war, with the Rome station at the center of the action. There were new fields
to master as well. Where Stockholm had been about paramilitary operations
in the grand OSS style, Italy would be about something that became a Central
Intelligence Agency hallmark, something called political action. Colby accepted gratefully.

5

POLITICAL ACTION

TWO GENERATIONS OF Central Intelligence Agency officers knew Allen Welch Dulles as the "Great White Case Officer." In agency parlance, a case officer recruited and ran agents or networks comprising a primary agent and one or more subagents. There could be all kinds of networks, as Scandinavia had shown Bill Colby. In Stockholm he had run paramilitary nets plus agents of influence while his OSO colleague had had the intelligence beat. Allen Dulles, who succeeded Bedell Smith as director of central intelligence in early 1953, after the inauguration of Dwight D. Eisenhower as president of the United States, often seemed to build relationships with his officers exactly like a case officer and agent. It would be that, as much as Dulles's legendary recruiting of Nazi spies, that gave him the sobriquet. Bill Colby personally experienced unusual treatment from Dulles when the new director passed through Stockholm on a worldwide inspection trip to see the CIA in action.

Bill Colby's encounter disappointed him. Colby's version has Allen Dulles taking a bath while, on the other side of the bathroom door, Colby talked about the format the CIA used to present its intelligence reports. Noncommittal, making liberal use of his "Ho, ho, ho" Santa Claus laugh, Dulles remained elusive. Gerry Miller, on the other hand, had an experience in the classic style of Dulles in action. The Shah of Iran, in an operation colluding with both the CIA and Britain's SIS, signed decrees removing from office his constitutionally selected prime minister, then fled to Italy to await the outcome of this CIA-sponsored coup d'état. Meanwhile, Allen Dulles and his wife, Clover, came to Rome, where they stayed at the same hotel as the Shah, permitting clandestine contacts. On the critical night in mid-August 1953 the CIA director kept vigil in the communications vault of the Rome station, where Miller accompanied him. It was an opportunity for the station chief to provide Dulles a detailed appraisal of political trends in Italy. What

Gerry Miller talked over that night with Allen Dulles kept Bill Colby busy for several years.

Having turned fifty, with experience giving him good background for the Italian challenge, Gerry Miller, as did Colby, fit the CIA's mold of Ivy League button-down activism. A Yalie, Miller had run OSS paramilitary activities with aplomb, while telling his wife Dorothy that his role had been very tiny: "I handed out arsenic tablets at the airfield in case they got caught."[1] At the OPC's Western Europe Division, Miller had presided over a series of political influence efforts in places like France and the western zone of Germany, plus giving subsidies to translational groups like the Congress on Cultural Freedom. These and other countries and groups were all influenced by Wisner's Wurlitzer, and CIA subsidies led to many outlets for pro-American propaganda.

Gerald Miller once impressed an audience by declaring that he had been on the dagger edge of the OSS's cloak-and-dagger business, and it seems that in Italy as chief of station for the CIA he wanted to get back to traditional activities like spying or even the paramilitary stuff. Miller was instrumental in setting up one of the CIA's biggest stay-behind networks, Project Gladio, after the Latin word for the short sword of a Roman soldier. Gerry Miller would be the American signatory to the 1956 agreement between the CIA and Italian intelligence arranging cooperation in this effort. The CIA promised a training base in Sardinia, money to pay participants (and their survivors in case of death), weapons, communications gear, and equipment for several kinds of action teams. Over 600 primary agents were recruited and trained for Gladio, and these Italians enlisted numerous subagents, up to 15,000 by some counts, though the most accepted figure hovers around 2,000. There were no fewer than 132 arms caches to support them, some located at Italian police barracks. Creating Gladio became a major endeavor, one that remained hidden until 1972, when the investigation of the deaths of three Italian *carabinieri* uncovered elements of the network.

In Rome, Miller no longer had to manage a political action program from afar. Rather, he had direct responsibility for implementing it. But instead of taking on the job, Gerry Miller brought Bill Colby down from Stockholm. He asked Colby, who *had* run a paramilitary project, to do the political action that Miller had managed on a large scale, while Gerry himself tossed daggers in the paramilitary scheme Gladio.

As for political action per se, at that time the Central Intelligence Agency Operatives were avid practitioners of an art unknown to the general public, but one that differed little if at all from the subversion Americans attributed to Russia. Quietly acquiring means of spreading propaganda could involve hiring "agents of influence," surreptitiously placing books and articles in the media, controlling means of dissemination such as newspapers, funding centers of information and advocacy like institutes or associations, or funding and supporting political parties. Neutralizing opposing means of propaganda began with gaining allies in friendly security services that could put pressure on the other side without the CIA's hand being visible. In Allen Dulles's book *The Craft of Intelligence*, published after his CIA years during which this very kind of political action effort had been carried out in Italy, the former CIA director wrote that Russian strategy relied on the "secret penetration" of other states, through communist political parties; front groups uniting people who believed in different causes, who could be mobilized at election time; penetration of the local military and security services; and the use of "all the instrumentalities of [Moscow's] propaganda machine." In his delineation of the CIA role in countering this Russian subversion, Dulles notes the need for intelligence to warn U.S. leaders as to the target nations; the necessity that agents infiltrate the enemy subversion machinery; and the need for the CIA to assist the local security services by making them aware of the nature of the threat, thus building up their defenses. "Among the tasks assigned to intelligence," Director Dulles concludes, "this is one that ranks in importance alongside those I have described: collecting information, counterintelligence, coordinating intelligence and producing the national estimates."[2]

The technique of political action, which Allen Dulles does not name in his inventory of CIA tactics against Russian subversion, is nevertheless a major CIA function he holds as important as the agency's critical intelligence missions. In Italy, Project Gladio certainly amounted to a penetration of the local security services; CIA subsidies to political parties were not different from Russian ones; the CIA's support to single-interest groups and front organizations proved identical to the Russian practice; and both sides were similarly on the lookout for media sources they could bend to influence opinion. In short, Italy would be a battleground for both sides in the Cold War political struggle. In that battle, William E. Colby would be America's leading secret warrior.

THE AUTHORITY UNDER WHICH CIA political operatives worked in Italy had not changed since early 1951, when President Harry S. Truman approved a National Security Council (NSC) policy paper called NSC 67/3. That paper resulted from an eight-month process of drafting, consideration by the NSC, and redrafting. The final product, not very different from the initial version, saw the U.S. objective as being "to prevent in that key country conditions unfavorable to our national security." The text of this NSC directive, declassified in 1981, orders political actions such as "combatting communist propaganda in Italy by an effective United States information program," and "giving increasingly more encouragement and support [deleted] to Italian personalities, groups and organizations which have proved their worth."[3]

The presidential decision enjoined Americans to pay special attention to "assisting and encouraging" noncommunist labor organizations. This already amounted to a major headache by 1951, for two years earlier Italy's general trade union had splintered into smaller units reflecting four major political tendencies: Catholic, communist, social democratic, and fascist. By Colby's time the tendencies were even more pronounced. In Italy the Roman Catholic Church was a player, and it was fortunate that the CIA's chief political operator happened to be Catholic himself and could build lines of communication into the Vatican, where Pius XII would remain Pope until his death in 1958. Pope Pius had underlined his conservative stance as early as 1949, when he simply excommunicated all Italian communists. Catholic Action, the religious political grouping (not a party) affiliated with the Church, counted three million members. There were also key regional differences in Italy, where the agrarian, generally poor south contrasted with the industrial north. Italy's major new economic resource, natural gas discovered in the valley of the Po River after World War II, further increased the disparity in favor of the north.

When Bill and Barbara Colby arrived in Rome, there was already a new sense of urgency. The need for political action in Italy had been part of the original raison d'être for the OPC, and an earlier round of CIA subsidies has been credited with making the difference in the Italian elections of April 1948. Those elections resulted in an overwhelming victory for the Christian Democrats, who thereafter held an absolute majority in the Italian parliament. Alcide de Gasperi led eight cabinet governments between 1945 and the summer of 1953. At that point political realignment followed a new election, in which the Christian Democrats, though still the leading party, became dependent upon coalition politics to retain power. Their majority shrank from 301 seats in the 590-seat lower house, to a less-than-commanding 261. The communist electorate picked up about a third of the parliamentary seats, with monarchists and fascists holding another 10 percent. Suddenly Italy had four prime ministers within seven months. Ambassador Clare Boothe Luce sent Washington the dire warning that worse lay in store if U.S. inaction continued. That would be the background for Bill Colby's mission.

Wife of the Time-Life corporate chairman Henry Luce, Clare had been appointed by President Dwight D. Eisenhower, not least for her and her husband's influence on American media. A formidable figure, Clare embodied the Cold War activism that favored "rolling back" the Iron Curtain by means short of war—in effect, CIA covert action. She would be an avid supporter of Gerry Miller's Rome CIA station. Within that station, however, Bill Colby remained isolated even though he and Luce favored the same kinds of action, because Luce responded to the Italian right wing while Colby believed it necessary to play to the center and liberal wings of Italian politics. Luce was regarded by Italian potentates as a prime figure for cultivation and she played the game back. Colby, of course, began as a mere subordinate CIA officer.

Rome would be a plum diplomatic post, its embassy a glittery whirl of activity, from receptions to private meetings to quiet lunches with figures of influence. Embassy resources could be used to build relations between America and Italy in the best diplomatic tradition. Still under State Department cover, Bill Colby loved every minute. Barbara liked Rome so much she began learning Italian, continuing to study the language long after they had moved on. Another child, Paul, was born to the Colbys in 1956. By then Bill's political actions showed promise and there came promotion in his notional State Department guise, from special assistant to embassy first secretary. In truth, Colby's stature grew within the rarified circles of the CIA's crusaders.

Political action in Italy remained as delicate as it had been in the days when the OPC worked on the 1948 election, studded with pitfalls and booby traps. Both American policy and Bill Colby personally were determined to pursue their course without offering additional aid to Italian fascist or monarchist elements, for example. But any number of these authoritarian types worked for the Italian police and security services or had enlisted in the Project Gladio secret army. To the extent that the CIA cooperated with those entities, they were helping the least desirable Italian political tendencies. Similarly, religious groups like Catholic "Civic Committees" harbored some of the same right-wing extremists, and the group, Catholic Action was a mixture of progressives and conservatives, yet no political action in Italy could be carried out without them. Colby did what he could to limit disbursements to the less-favored groups. He also emphasized practical help such as instruction in political organizing, which gave assistance without putting quantities of money in the wrong hands.

Other pitfalls existed within the Central Intelligence Agency itself. William E. Colby had been preceded in Italy by other CIA officers, including some with a continuing stake. Among these characters the most important was James J. Angleton. Like Colby, Angleton had served with the OSS, where he had specialized in counterintelligence. Starting in North Africa and continuing through the Allies' wartime invasion of Italy, Angleton had plied his trade on the peninsula, had kept up those ties after moving on to England, then renewed them on returning to northern Italy late in the war. Unlike Colby, when the OSS disbanded, Angleton stayed on with its successor organizations, first the Special Services Unit, then the Central Intelligence Group. Angleton's networks and single agents became the basis for the OPC's covert action in Italy. Jim Angleton saw communism as a monolithic conspiracy, without nuance, so it was enough that his agents were anticommunist. But in Italy the Partito Communista Italiana (PCI) never succumbed to Stalinism, though it remained close to Moscow, and significantly increased its apparent independence in the early 1950s. It was strongest in central and northeast Italy, richer regions with a strong socialist background and a record of resistance in World War II. In view of Italian realities, Bill Colby felt it necessary to be *for* something, not merely against communism, and he tried to recruit accordingly.

Besides their differences in overall approach, Colby and Angleton stumbled across each other over specific agents. Though Jim Angleton remained in Washington from 1954 on as chief of CIA counterintelligence, he maintained relationships with Italians recruited years before. As late as the 1960s several high-ranking Italian police or government officials would be identified in the local press as Angleton agents, and it is quite probable that these and other Italians were run unilaterally by Angleton in the 1950s. Indeed, Tom McCoy, an officer in the Rome station during this period, ultimately Colby's deputy, recalls, "Jim had a couple of people in Italy who did work for him and did not work for the station, including a source in the Vatican."[4]

One of the CIA's undercover officers in Rome also fell into this category. Code-named "Charlie," the man had been with Angleton in the OSS contingent in northern Italy toward the end of the war. There he made friends with many of the Italians only then beginning to restore the nation's political system. By the 1950s those people were at the apex of Italian politics and Charlie knew them all. From time to time he returned to visit, and Charlie reports reflected the very highest levels of Italy's political leadership. Gerry Miller was supposed to handle Charlie's accommodation in Rome; but as station chief, Miller had high visibility, and CIA headquarters decided to keep Charlie on the scene to provide a steady stream of reports. Miller introduced Charlie to Colby, who thereafter handled him. Astonished at the range of Charlie's contacts, Colby also discovered that his reports were being pouched direct to Washington, outside embassy and even CIA channels. That was a typical Angleton touch. Colby went ahead with the operation but managed to regularize it so that Charlie's intelligence would be available to the embassy, the station, CIA headquarters analysts, and others who needed it.

In 1956 a split developed between the PCI and the Italian social democrats of Pietro Nenni. This opening to the left, or *apertura alla sinistra*, seemed perfect for Colby's strategy of energizing the center in Italian politics. Tom McCoy became a go-between reaching out to socialist elements. Colby also had a half dozen officers outside the embassy under deep cover, and several of them, like Charlie, made the acquaintance of socialist figures. At CIA headquarters, Tom Braden of the International Organizations Division advocated this development, which Bill Colby favored. But within the embassy, Clare Boothe Luce resisted U.S. encouragement of the socialists. She remained suspicious of their sincerity and their aims, and found a kindred voice at the CIA, where James J. Angleton questioned the socialists' professions of independence from the PCI. Bill Colby deferred to the ambassador; the CIA never actively courted the Italian socialists.

There is no evidence that Colby and Angleton began to war against each other at this stage, but there would be other times that they crossed swords. A growing antipathy between Colby and Angleton would have repercussions in Southeast Asia and Washington. Moreover, the views on counterintelligence that Colby developed, which later had a strong impact on CIA practice, were conditioned by his dislike for Angleton. Those sores began to fester in Rome, where not everything was *la dolce vita*.

Meanwhile Frank Wisner was still the CIA's deputy director for plans, and his interest in the Wurlitzer remained intense. As Colby put it, "Washington expected action in the press field."[5] The political action chief in Rome would be faced with recurrent suggestions that CIA funds invested in Italian newspapers or magazines should prevent publication of stories inimical to American interests or, conversely, encourage favorable ones. Colby's position, that enemies would always be able to find some outlet for anti-American broadsides, seems reasonable. By stalling, Bill often succeeded in derailing these schemes, but he did not always manage to divert CIA media projects. It was on Colby's watch that the agency began putting money into the *Rome Daily American* newspaper, and before that process ended, the CIA actually owned 40 percent of the paper, a controlling interest. A fact that hints at some of the larger dimensions of CIA political action is that the printing press used by the *Daily American* also produced the newspaper of one of the Italian leftist groups.

Colby's CIA also worked in tandem with the United States Information Service (USIS), whose Italian operation grew to rival the agency's. In 1956 the USIS had almost fifty Americans in Italy and employed 250 Italians in offices throughout the country. This unit performed overt propaganda functions, at times supporting shows of American technological achievement; at others, illustrating democratic values; in some, promoting the "Spirit of Geneva," an early détente that followed the Geneva Summit of 1954. Articles and press releases flowed from USIS like water from a fountain; it also sponsored tours by prominent American figures.

In Rome, the intelligence specialists at the CIA station, people like John Leader, another of Gerry Miller's intimates, had the main responsibility for liaison with the Italian security services, who provided the CIA with some very good data. Many of the officers had served with the old OSO and before that the OSS, and they relied on long association with their Italian counterparts. In the quest for a media outlet it would be the Italians who furnished the lead to an editor happy to utilize CIA information in feature stories with an anti-Russian bent. Data on labor and political groups also piled into CIA in-boxes.

Sometimes the difficulty became separating the "positive intelligence" function of espionage from straight political action. Italian politicians and labor leaders who gave the CIA information often took money or asked for advice from supposedly sophisticated Americans. Results were tabulated in Washington, where Eisenhower's Operations Coordinating Board monitored conditions in Italy. The Board worried about a weakening of the Italian political coalition of the center but felt satisfied with labor activity, as illustrated in this November 1955 report: "The greatest success against the Left occurred in the trade union sphere where the . . . program, political screening for individual Italian plants benefiting from U.S. direct aid and procurement programs, U.S. encouragement of free unions, and the increased organizational efficiency of the free unions, were decisive factors." Programmatic instructions in National Security Council documents remain secret even today, but they undoubtedly featured the CIA in a key role.[6]

When James Angleton supervised the CIA's political action a decade earlier, Italians could get money out of their American case officers just by laying out plans for a poster or a leaflet campaign. Angleton's had been a short-term strategy aimed at a single election, but it continued to be the approach favored by Ambassador Luce. Bill Colby, in contrast, wanted to pursue a long-term strategy of giving the political parties of the Italian center and right-of-center the tools and organizational skills necessary for long-term political development. Most of Colby's activities, as had Angleton's, involved direct subsidies with CIA cash, but the aims were different. The cash amounts—$20 million to $30 million dollars per year over several years— made Colby's Italian program the largest political action effort ever carried out by the Central Intelligence Agency. The CIA's estimates were that the Russians were putting as much as $50 million per year into the PCI, but there are no hard data on the actual size of the Soviet effort, and no real way to compare it with the program of the CIA, which continued to invest large amounts of money over a narrower range of items.

Clare Boothe Luce would not remain in Rome long enough to see the fruits of her labor. Complaining of her health, she returned to the United States in 1955 for medical help, and arsenic poisoning was identified as the cause of her symptoms. Gerry Miller began an investigation of everyone at the embassy with the access and ability to poison Luce, and the CIA dispatched a team of technical experts to Rome to discover what technique had been used against the ambassador. Rather than discovering a plot, the technicians inadvertently uncovered environmental contamination—flakes of paint that contained arsenic were being dislodged from the ceiling and chandeliers in Luce's bedroom when people moved around or when a washing machine was used on the floor above. These things could be fixed; Ambassador Luce returned to her post but after little more than a year she resigned, arriving back in the United States on December 27, 1956.

At that point Bill Colby's political action still had eighteen months to run before the Italian elections. Colby went ahead with his long-term emphasis on cadre training and organizational resources. As the elections neared, the CIA nevertheless insisted on summoning political action specialists it had assigned to Greece, where the agency had had some success. As a result the Italian elections could not be a fair test of Colby's longer term methods versus the shorter span strategy of intervention in an election. Equally true, in Italy the basic decision to reject any Italian opening to the left prevented meaningful political realignment. When the elections took place in May 1958, the Christian Democrats picked up eight seats in the lower house of parliament and one in the senate, so they did not lose ground; but they remained a minority party in the government, beholden to coalition partners. Similarly, the PCI did not increase its percentage of the vote, but it remained a strong force and an implacable opposition party.

The CIA's budget assessors judged the Italian political action by the standards Clare Luce would have applied. The operation could not be judged a failure, as the Christian Democrats had increased their seats in parliament, but Italy could hardly be rated a success. The cash that had poured through the Rome station dwarfed what had been spent on the wild victory of 1948—amounting to more than five times as much—but the result was paltry, a handful of seats. Headquarters seemed reluctant to buy Colby's argument that the agency's efforts had strengthened the foundations of the Italian centrist parties.

Bill Colby had reached a crossroads of sorts; it was time for a change. Two years before, headquarters had offered him an assignment in South Asia. The Chinese communists had intervened in Tibet and a revolt had begun there. The Central Intelligence Agency would become heavily involved in Tibet, but not Colby, who stayed in Rome to finish the job on the Italian elections. By the summer of 1958, however, Colby felt he needed new turf and requested reassignment himself. He wanted to go to the Far East somewhere. That would be exactly what happened.

6

Journey to the East

WHEN BILL COLBY got selected to go to Vietnam, Frank Wisner no longer held the keys to the kingdom. In fact, Colby, Gerry Miller, and Clare Boothe Luce had seen Wisner fall apart. The occasion was 1956, when Hungary rose against its Russian occupiers. At the time Frank had been traveling, making a European inspection tour, and had read the early cables on the Hungarian revolt while in England and Germany. A proponent of rolling back the Iron Curtain, Wisner had labored long and hard within the CIA to get covert action going in Eastern Europe. When it did happen, the agency had no part in the Hungarian action, though many in Europe and elsewhere believed otherwise and lambasted the American spy agency. Wisner went to Vienna and to the Austrian side of the Hungarian border to see the refugees fleeing the Russian crackdown.

More than a sad moment, for Wisner the Hungarian uprising came as a psychological shock. The story has been related widely that the deputy director of the CIA went to Athens, where he ate bad clams and became infected with hepatitis. Less well known is his sojourn in Rome. Aside from his status as a CIA official, Frank Wisner was a friend of Clare Luce. During the Hungarian uprising, the ambassador more than once made the gesture of attending a Catholic Church with a Hungarian pastor and priest, and after one of these occasions, she returned to the embassy residence, the Villa Taverna, to find Frank drinking himself into a stupor. He seemed disoriented, upset. At the embassy Bill Colby could not avoid noticing too. Soon after Wisner returned to Washington he collapsed. In the months that followed, CIA colleagues worried about the Wurlitzer man. Back home after an ensuing trip—to the Far East, where the CIA conducted a paramilitary operation in Indonesia in 1958—Wisner succumbed to a mental collapse.

Thereafter, a new man came to head the directorate of plans in Washington; it was not Frank Wisner's deputy, who had been Richard Helms, but Richard

M. Bissell, Jr. A brilliant technocrat, responsible for the CIA's breakthrough in technical intelligence by use of the U-2 spy plane, Dick Bissell had become close to Allen Dulles. Articulate, quick to appreciate an argument, Bissell learned fast. Everything he knew about covert operations came from his work with the Marshall Plan in the late 1940s, when the CIA had used this aid program as a conduit for some of its political action payoffs. Now Bissell rapidly learned to feel comfortable running projects as complex as the Tibetan revolt, and later the Bay of Pigs invasion. But he wanted, and Dulles agreed, to continue with the aircraft (SR-71) and satellite (Discoverer, Corona) programs that followed U-2. Bissell simply did not have time to do everything in the DDP. Wisely, he left much of the action to his deputies for the various regional and functional divisions of the clandestine service.

Heading the Far East Division was Desmond A. FitzGerald, who took over more or less simultaneously with Bissell. FitzGerald had been deputy to two Far East division chiefs, more recently had headed a task force trying to spy on the People's Republic of China, and had served in the Philippines in charge of CIA activities there. Bill Colby's request to transfer to the Far East Division automatically went before FitzGerald. By now Colby clearly figured as a "comer," a rising star in the agency firmament, executor of the CIA's biggest political action program and chief of political operations at a major agency outpost. Were Colby to be reassigned to Asia there would have to be a post commensurate with that stature.

FitzGerald had worked in the Far East Division since coming to the CIA in 1950. Covert action in Korea, operations into China mounted from Burma and Japan, and the beginnings of the Tibet project were all his special interests. He had had some exposure to political action in the Philippines, where CIA election support had helped the party in power. In Japan, where his China mission had been based at the Yokosuka naval base, CIA political action supported the ruling Liberal Democratic party, but that had been a compartmented activity unknown to the China specialists. In any case, secret warfare against China became the primary mission of the Far East Division under FitzGerald. As a young U.S. Army officer, Desmond FitzGerald had served in Burma and China as a liaison officer to the Chinese nationalist 6th Army, and he had a romantic attachment to this mission. Bill Colby's boyhood in Tianjin leapt off the page when FitzGerald saw it. Colby's father's command of African-American troops in the Army also resonated with FitzGerald when he interviewed his CIA colleague, for his initial Army assignment had been commanding a platoon of African Americans. The two men also had parallel postwar experiences prior to the CIA, both having resided in New York City and worked for Wall Street law firms. FitzGerald, flashier, had lived more extravagantly, with a Park Avenue apartment followed by an East Side brownstone, and a divorce after his return from the war; but there had been enough in common for Bill Colby, with his CIA and OSS experience in both paramilitary and political action, to pass muster.

There were two places in the Far East Division that beckoned as emerging points of confrontation with China. One was in Malaya, now Malaysia, where British Commonwealth troops fought a communist insurgency rooted among an ethnic Chinese minority. Colby could have fit into Malaya without difficulty. The other possibility was South Vietnam. The pro-Western Vietnamese leader Ngo Dinh Diem continued struggling to make South Vietnam into more than the temporary regroupment zone provided by the 1954 Geneva agreement that had ended the Franco-Vietnamese war. China had helped the Vietnamese communists in that war, and Americans who feared Chinese encroachment saw Beijing as taking over Southeast Asia, starting with Vietnam. Diem and the Vietnamese spoke French as their land had been a French colony. Fluent in French, Bill Colby seemed a perfect fit for South Vietnam, where the post of CIA deputy chief of station was open. Malaya forgotten, Vietnam came to define William E. Colby's life in the Central Intelligence Agency.

When an officer was given a fresh assignment, the practice at the CIA always required reading into the new subject. Sometimes a case officer needed weeks simply to prepare to assume control over an agent in the field. For a deputy chief of station, who needed to be familiar with every aspect of CIA activity in his country, the effort could be quite extended. Colby also needed to brush up on his French. It would be February 1959, almost six months in all, before Bill Colby reached Saigon.

In reading into the situation in Indochina, Colby learned that the Central Intelligence Agency had been active there since 1951. The CIA adventure in Indochina began slowly but grew steadily. At first there were simple efforts to develop sources willing to provide better information than the material France supplied the United States at the official level. Under the pressure of military operations of the Franco-Vietnamese war, the agency's proprietary Civil Air Transport (CAT) began to fly into Vietnam and Laos in 1953, and it played a crucial role in supplying French forces at the battle of Dien Bien Phu in 1954. The American desire to have an "international volunteer air group" that could, in a way not attributable to the United States, fly warplanes the way CAT flew transport aircraft, led to techniques used by CIA air operators in covert actions in Guatemala, Indonesia, and Cuba.

The French were endlessly suspicious of American meddling but very desirous of U.S. help. For their part, CIA officers built on skills developed in the Korean war and encouraged the French in "unconventional warfare"—that is, paramilitary operations. Obvious candidates for such a role in southern Vietnam were several politico-religious sects. One day in a rubber plantation on the road to the headquarters of one of these sects, the owner found a jeep containing the bodies of two American embassy women. What they had been doing visiting the Cao Dai, the sect involved, would never be divulged, and the incident was hushed up, but French suspicions soared. Sure enough, later on, when defeat at Dien Bien Phu and the consequent Geneva agreement pushed the French out of the way, an alliance emerged between certain sects and the CIA that had a key impact on South Vietnamese political development.

Another paramilitary project would be started by the French themselves. That was development of a guerrilla force to fight the Vietnamese communists behind their own lines. By the fall of 1953 two Americans were permanently stationed with the French commando headquarters to fill requests for assistance. That December a top CIA manager visited Saigon to receive a full briefing on the guerrilla project. Washington documents of early 1954 talk of contributions the CIA had begun making to French unconventional warfare efforts. The French defeat led their commando leaders to propose to the Americans that CIA take over full responsibility for the guerrilla project. Though the French held another detailed briefing for a senior CIA man who followed up, in early 1954, the agency eventually rejected the French proposal.

Much as happened with the sects, however, the CIA *wanted* those programs, but it wanted them unilaterally, without the burden of cooperating with Frenchmen, who in fact competed for control of the sects, successfully at first. A special mission of a dozen CIA officers arrived in Vietnam in July and August 1954, and a detachment of that unit set up shop in Hanoi and Haiphong, at the time those cities were gradually being evacuated by the French. The paramilitary program was under Major Lucien Conein, veteran of the OSS Jedburgh program as well as an earlier assignment to Indochina at the end of World War II. Conein and his colleagues recruited Vietnamese, trained them at a secret CIA base on Saipan, then inserted them into the flow of refugees leaving South Vietnam for the north. Boats and CAT aircraft carried eight and a half tons of equipment north to support this stay-behind network, which for once in the CIA's experience would have to be an active rather than a hypothetical unit. Among the equipment brought in were 300 pounds of explosives, 350 pistols and carbines, fourteen radios, ammunition, and more. The network had minor successes at sabotage in Haiphong, and disseminated some scary leaflets, but in large part it proved to be a bust. By 1956 the Vietnamese had rolled it up. Bill Colby wondered about the staying power of the networks he had worked on in Scandinavia and had seen in Italy. Vietnam showed how fragile those nets would have been.

Conein's activity had been subsumed into a large Saigon Military Mission led by Colonel Edward G. Lansdale whose purpose was primarily psychological warfare and political action. Lansdale had made a name for himself in the Philippines and first showed up in Vietnam in 1953 as one of a group of U.S. military officers supposed to review French conduct of the war. In 1954 he came back in an active capacity. Aside from more or less sophomoric psychological ploys, the real importance of the CIA mission, which functioned under military cover, would be that Lansdale introduced himself to and forged a relationship with South Vietnamese prime minister Ngo Dinh Diem. Appointed to the government during the last stage of negotiations on the Geneva agreements that ended the French war, Diem tiptoed carefully between the Americans, French, and pro-French Vietnamese.

Diem's political dance came to a climax in the fall of 1954 when pro-

French Vietnamese army officers moved against him. Lansdale helped Diem overcome that threat by diverting the Army officers and making an alliance with the sects. In the spring of 1955 the sects, in their turn, rose against Diem, who suppressed them using Vietnamese army paratroops. In the middle of all that, the American embassy decided to withhold support from Diem but was outmaneuvered by Lansdale, whose actions amounted to de facto help, and who encouraged the Vietnamese leader to point to them as evidence of American aid. For a time relations between the CIA and the State Department in the Saigon embassy remained rather delicate.

A similar problem existed within the CIA itself because, for a time, there were effectively *two* CIA stations in South Vietnam. Lansdale's Saigon Military Mission focused on psychological warfare. Spying and traditional intelligence functions were the province of the real station, under Emmett McCarthy. Lansdale's communications ran through McCarthy, who considered the spy warrior an amateur. Lansdale did not like McCarthy either, and what is more, he could do something about it, because he knew the brother of the CIA director, John Foster Dulles, who happened to be secretary of state. Dulles made a visit to Vietnam in early 1955 and Lansdale, who had been honored with the presidential National Security Medal in a ceremony Dulles had attended, complained in a way sure to get to Allen Dulles. McCarthy would be replaced by John Anderton, a Japanese linguist during the war, instrumental in the decoding and translation of key messages revealing the Japanese Navy's plans for what became the battle of the Philippine Sea. Anderton and his deputy, Philip Potter, another former OSS man and old hand in Asia (he had been a member of the CIA's first base in Red China, at Shenyang), cooperated more amicably. In the 1955 sect crisis, in fact, CIA cash payoffs to Ngo Dinh Diem from Lansdale had been delivered through regular station channels by Potter, who was acting station chief at that moment.

John Anderton never overlapped with Bill Colby, but Colby had known him as far back as Princeton, where Anderton had been captain of the boxing team. There would also be a connection with Anderton's successor, who became Colby's boss. Nicolas A. Natsios had served in Italy with the OSS and had stayed on after the war in Milan until shortly before the Angleton election operation of 1948. Natsios had joined the CIA and, as a Greek American with fluency in the language of his first country, had been assigned to the agency's mission in Salonika soon after George Polk's murder. Ironically, Natsios and Colby never met until Saigon.

Bill Colby fell under the spell of the Far East Division, the CIA's face to the exotic East, which he saw has having its own heritage and special character. Des FitzGerald he perceived as an exemplar of enthusiasm and daring, Nick Natsios as an inspirational leader and fine manager who could get his officers to do anything, even what they disagreed with, while swearing by their boss. Saigon was still the "Paris of the Orient," many of its streets still bearing their French colonial names, and the Colby family's villa lay near the presidential palace. (Ngo Dinh Diem had assumed the title president after the crises of 1954–56, driving out Emperor Bao Dai and engineering a constitution proclaimed in July 1956. There had been legislative elections the summer before the Colbys arrived.)

Contained within the U.S. embassy, the CIA station then comprised slightly more than three dozen officers. Neither Colby nor anyone else suspected that the station would grow into the largest operational deployment of the Central Intelligence Agency, dwarfing the anti-Soviet installations in Europe and the anti-Chinese ones in Japan, Korea, and Taiwan. William Egan Colby would become a major player in that evolution.

UNKNOWN TO COLBY, his arrival in Vietnam coincided almost exactly with the decision of the Vietnamese communists, in Hanoi as well as South Vietnam, to take up arms anew, this time against the Diem government. Diem's crackdown against the political-religious sects had been only the beginning of repressive campaigns that expanded steadily through the late 1950s, soon focused on the Viet Minh who remained in the south after the 1954 Geneva agreements. The agreements provided for reunification of North and South Vietnam and a national election by 1956, universally expected to be won by Ho Chi Minh. Hanoi saw every reason to await this triumph peacefully. The United States encouraged Diem to renounce elections and reunification except on his terms, and Diem's presidency, constitution, and anticommunist laws were his alternative to the course stipulated by international agreement. Security actions against Viet Minh cadres were the inevitable corollary, and these eliminated many networks. Southern cadres appealed to Hanoi for arms and support, but the national front leadership, intent on economic development in the north and hoping for some compromise with Diem, long counseled patience. From the fall of 1957 some guerrilla bands, unable to accept Hanoi's advice, resumed fighting; and at the beginning of 1959 the Hanoi leadership officially declared its support for them by adopting a resolution changing its emphasis from political struggle to armed struggle. The supply unit that would smuggle arms to the south along what became known as the Ho Chi Minh Trail formed in May 1959.

For all that, Saigon seemed a somnolent place when Bill Colby arrived. One of the first things he did was take Barbara to the French military cemetery, where they sought out the grave of his former Jedburgh cohort, Roger Villebois. Barbara gave birth to daughter Christine in Saigon. Their first house gave way to a bigger second place, one with two floors and a kitchen in the back. Daughter Catherine attended a religious girls' school and the boys went to a French school until the intricacies of schoolyard politics brought their relocation to the American School. Colby and son Jonathan went on a train trip up the Vietnamese coast, then by car across Route 9, the road that crossed the breadth of Vietnam just below the Demilitarized Zone, to enter Laos and connect with the Mekong River. From the hills below the Zone Colby could look across into what was then North Vietnam, where flags waved atop villages he knew to be the enemy. Another time there was a family trip to Phu Quoc, the largest Vietnamese island, in the Gulf of Siam off the coast of Cambodia. And the Colbys joined the Cercle Sportif, the French-created social club that brought together Saigon's elite, the French expatriates, and the new American proconsuls.

At first Colby's life was not that different from what it had been in New Jersey or, for that matter, in Rome. The worst events that happened on the family outings were when son Carl spotted a big shark near the boat rented on Phu Quoc, or when the locomotive pulling Bill and Jon's train north to the Demilitarized Zone derailed, forcing them to stay overnight in the middle of nowhere. Vacations to Vietnamese cultural centers like Hue, or resorts such as Dalat, Vung Tau, and Nha Trang were popular among Saigon's American community. For outings, Colby drove the family up to Tay Ninh for a Sunday picnic. They saw the colorful pink cathedral of the Cao Dai religious sect.

But the CIA was still the CIA, and it was not in the business of employing Americans merely to furnish opportunities for tourism. Bill Colby's first emergency began only minutes after he arrived at Saigon's airport, Tan Son Nhut, on Tet, the lunar new year of 1959. The station officer who had met the Colbys and was driving them into town stopped the car when he saw a gesticulating American woman. She got in, turned out to be his wife, and warned that a cable had just reached the CIA station reporting trouble afoot in next door Cambodia.

Prince Norodom Sihanouk, the Cambodian leader, had extended diplomatic recognition to the People's Republic of China and made a state visit there in the summer of 1958. This flew in the face of American policy to ensure the isolation of "Red" China. At a meeting of the South East Asia Treaty Organization shortly afterward, Sihanouk became convinced the United States had persuaded its alliance partners to go along with the overthrow of the neutralist Cambodian government. It is suggestive that the U.S. ambassador to Thailand at the time, John Puerifoy, was the same man who was instrumental during the Eisenhower administration in mounting a CIA operation to overthrow the Guatemalan government in 1954. It is also true that a plot against Sihanouk *did* exist, which CIA authorities, including Colby, admit.

The question is, whose plot? According to Colby, this had been a Vietnamese-Thai covert action against Cambodia, which the CIA discouraged and expected to fail if the plotters went ahead. Ed Lansdale also rejects the charge that the CIA stood behind this *attentat*. On the other hand, Lansdale himself was among the Americans, including senior U.S. Pacific theater commanders, who visited Cambodian General Dap Chhuon just days before the plot emerged. Lansdale and the others were traveling on a survey of United States military assistance programs and stopped in Cambodia.

Another element in this is U.S. foreknowledge—of at least four months' duration. President Eisenhower was first briefed on the Dap Chhuon plot as early as November 5, 1958, when it was identified as a Saigon machination. By New Year's the CIA knew Dap Chhuon's name and knew of both Thai and South Vietnamese involvement. On January 7 Ike would be told that Dap

Chhuon's plots were continuing, and two weeks later that the Cambodian general planned to declare autonomy in February. The Cambodians slated to have the active military role in the plot, Khmer Serei and Khmer Krom irregulars, would later tie themselves openly to the CIA and the U.S. military.

Like the Puerifoy item, the Lansdale claims, Eisenhower briefings, and Khmer Serei connections have to be regarded as suggestive. What is beyond dispute is that when Sihanouk sent Cambodian army troops to arrest Dap Chhuon on February 21, along with him they captured a CIA radio and its agency operator, Victor M. Matsui. (U.S. weapons, South Vietnamese agents, money, and other communications gear were also taken in this action.) Dap Chhuon never made a full statement on the affair because he died, allegedly attempting escape, before Sihanouk could ever interrogate him.

The truth appears somewhat prosaic. Richard Bissell, still feeling his way as DDP, had major preoccupations absorbing his attention. Two of Bissell's technical collection programs—the spy satellites code-named Corona, and the Oxcart SR-71 supersonic aircraft—were entering crucial stages of development. During this same week, indeed, a rocket bearing Corona would be launched for the first time. Cambodia meant distraction. Bissell wanted to know about Cambodian events as the plot unfolded, perhaps to see how these things worked, so he ordered special assistant Charles S. Whitehurst to place a communicator with the plotters. That became Matsui. Whitehurst had been involved in Far East operations since the Korean War and knew the agency would be exposed by Matsui's presence, especially if the CIA had no other role. He cautioned against the move. Bissell insisted on it. Then the DDP went back to his other concerns. The capture of Victor Matsui was almost foreordained.

Bill Colby's morning arrival emergency in Saigon revolved around how to free Matsui. Colby believed the Whitehouse version of the communications man's role. Norodom Sihanouk reached different conclusions: "The CIA was in the forefront (except, when it suited their purposes, to remain concealed) of every plot directed against my life and my country's integrity. From 1954, until diplomatic relations were broken in 1965, my intelligence services listed twenty-seven known CIA agents . . . and the list was certainly incomplete."[1]

Sihanouk did let Matsui out of Cambodia, but he never trusted the Americans again. That distrust would cost dearly in a few years, when there was active insurgency in South Vietnam and Sihanouk gave the insurgents a free hand to use Cambodia for a supply base.

Meanwhile the CIA constantly pushed for better sources of information in Saigon. This meant recruiting South Vietnamese agents. Nick Natsios, whose experience in the Greek Civil War had been that the local ally always told the Americans what they thought Washington wanted to hear, put even more than the usual CIA emphasis on recruiting human sources. Everyone in the Saigon station was encouraged to develop Vietnamese contacts, Bill Colby no exception. At the Cercle Sportif, at the government ministries, Colby met Vietnamese he judged good sources and cultivated those contacts. The CIA, as did Russian intelligence, considered the key step in recruiting to be getting a prospective agent to sign something—in particular, a receipt for money. Signed documents could be used to prove a relationship and, if necessary, to blackmail. Colby went by the book the first couple of times but soon realized that if a spy was going to deny everything, having his signature would not matter a whit. More important was to have a solid friendship that could be prevailed on as a reason to give key information. Subsequently Colby relied on that technique.

Using his own methods shortly became easier, for William Colby reached that rarified plateau for CIA officers, the status of chief of station. This happened at first informally, in the summer of 1959, when Natsios went on home leave. The occasion also represented more familiar ground for Colby, as these were the months of the run up to the Saigon legislative elections, held on August 30. One of the CIA's most important functions was to maintain a liaison with parallel elements of the South Vietnamese government, so acting as station chief, Colby suddenly found himself in touch with some of the top Vietnamese leaders, including Ngo Dinh Diem and his brother, Ngo Dinh Nhu. The latter had no official job title other than counselor, but he actually ran the Vietnamese intelligence services and much of Diem's political machinery. Colby tried to convince his Vietnamese counterparts that they needed to post a fair election result, but he ran afoul of the cultural differences between Vietnamese and Americans. Vietnamese province leaders, who owed their jobs directly to Nhu, were more interested in demonstrating their loyalty. In the elections all but two of the 123 seats were won by candidates loyal to Diem.

That summer it also became apparent that the civil war had revived. In the early evening of July 8, American advisers at a town north of Saigon were watching a movie in their messhall when it was attacked by a squad of Vietnamese communist guerrillas. Major Dale R. Buis and Master Sergeant Chester M. Ovnand became the first Americans killed in the new Vietnamese war. "It came as a bolt out of the blue," Colby recalled. "It was hard to identify too clearly where [the attack] came from and who started it."[2]

Ngo Dinh Diem had already issued decrees to legalize a variety of measures against the Vietnamese communists who remained in the south after the 1954 Geneva agreements, and he sent the Vietnamese army on constant field operations against them as well as the politico-religious sects. The pejorative "Viet Cong," a contraction for the the words in the admonition to kill Vietnamese communists, became the universal name for the guerrillas. The Viet Cong, with some help from the sects and from Vietnamese north of the Demilitarized Zone, began to cut a swath of terror and destruction across the lands of Diem supporters.

Bill Colby liked to argue there was nothing much to the Viet Cong, that if you went out into the real countryside what you saw was a nation in the throes of modernization, a revolution from above in the style of Turkey's Ataturk. Both in his memoir and in interviews Colby uses the example of a school in Ca Mau province, the southernmost point of Vietnam. "It was one of those ceremonies that there are too many of," Colby told interviewer Ted Gittinger; "I've been through them forever."[3] Out along a canal, ten or fifteen miles down in fact, from the provincial capital, the nearby village had been abandoned during the French war and only reoccupied a year or two before. Now the authorities were dedicating a rebuilt school. Colby stopped by Ca Mau on his way back to Saigon, where he found a map showing the province had had just two or three schools in 1954—all in the provincial capital or district seats—but now had something on the order of thirty or forty. Bill saw that as evidence of social dynamism in South Vietnam. Yet in Washington, CIA headquarters reported in April 1959 that in Ca Mau province the communists had "achieved virtual control over whole villages and districts."[4] In fact, in Hanoi that summer the North Vietnamese general supervising delivery of weapons by sea to South Vietnam would be presented a coconut from Ca Mau as a token from the South's first liberated zone. Was something wrong with Colby's picture?

Colby became painfully aware of one element that he could do little about. His periodic encounters with President Diem and weekly sessions with Ngo Dinh Nhu keyed the CIA officer to the combination of technocratic precision, philosophical jumble, and political interest driving Saigon's top leaders. Diem could make dynamic arguments for doing nothing or order frantic activity when inaction would have been the right thing. The Ca Mau school example can be extended: to make use of newly implanted facilities strewn across the land, Diem and Nhu innovated a program they called "agrovilles." Gathering the villages into de facto towns, even small cities, provided reasons for such things as hospitals, high schools, and so on. But concentrating the population took the farmers away from their fields, using land for the agrovilles meant disturbing family burial plots, and the corruption endemic in South Vietnam did no good for the peasantry. Moreover, taking the peasants off the land meant leaving it free to the passage of the Viet Cong. No realistic amount of security could have protected the paths between the widely scattered agrovilles. That was, as Colby observed in retrospect, "the Achilles heel of the program."[5]

Maybe Colby and the CIA could do little to encourage realism from Diem and Nhu, but Bill never really made up his mind that the Vietnamese dictator and his minions were that far off. Within certain narrow confines, Colby thought, you could even see them as pragmatic practitioners of politics. For some American arguments, like those about a "fair" election or the ones raging over land reform by the Diem regime, perhaps the Vietnamese had the better answer. On land reform, Diem proposed to leave undisturbed holdings of up to about 250 acres, a large enough plot to enable the owner to rent out parcels, becoming a landlord; the Vietnamese leader insisted that this slice of people were his equivalent of the American middle class. He could not eliminate them.

Eventually Diem and Nhu convinced Colby, rather than the other way around, and the CIA man went to his grave claiming the Vietnam war could have been won with Diem in command. But while Diem succeeded with the CIA station chief, for Colby would be promoted to lead the whole CIA operation in June 1960, he could not bring along his own people. More and more, Saigon became a hothouse of political plotting, with some new rumor of a power play almost every week. On November 11, 1960, came a real coup d'état. Three battalions of tough South Vietnamese paratroopers trucked into Saigon under cover of darkness.

William E. Colby spent the evening at a formal ball, at the U.S. embassy, where the Marine Corps security detachment was hosting a celebration of the Corps' birthday. Bill in black tie and Barbara in a gown then went with Ambassador Elbridge Durbrow and his wife to the Saigon River for drinks at a popular waterfront restaurant on a boat. Late to sleep, Colby awakened about 3 A.M. as gunfire shattered the night. His home, at 16 Rue Alexandre de Rhodes, was rented from the father of a Vietnamese general, Tran Van Don, but any thought that that connection made it safe vanished as bullets began to hit the house. Out the window the CIA station chief could see tracer shells, then paratroopers running down the block toward the presidential palace, not far away. Upstairs Colby pulled together some bookcases into a crude bunker, then got the family inside. He then went to power up the two-way radio kept at home for emergencies, called in to the embassy, and readied his weapons. But little happened at Bill's house until after he left for the CIA station, and then it was simply the next-door neighbors who came to seek refuge because the Colby home seemed more solid than theirs. The paratroopers' target was Diem and by dawn they had the palace surrounded. There were tanks in the Rue de Rhodes, but Diem's palace guard, trained in the Philippines under earlier arrangements made by Ed Lansdale, held the rebels at bay.

After first light Bill was startled to see an American drop over the wall into his yard. This young diplomat, John Helble, had been sent to the palace to report on the situation but found every place suitable for cover already taken by troops. Colby enlisted Helble to watch out for Barbara and the kids and left for his post at the embassy. Helble would be one of several to win decorations for their work that day. As for the family, Barbara later telephoned embassy friends who lived five blocks away and learned things were quiet in their neighborhood. She took the kids, including infant daughter Christine, went outside and exchanged pleasantries with some troops near the house, then walked to the friends' house.

Meanwhile Bill had got down to the business of monitoring the coup d'état. The station chief soon had CIA personnel in touch with all sides in the action. Russell F. Miller, himself a former U.S. paratrooper, had also gone into the street to report. With an agency translator Miller settled in next to a Vietnamese squad, listening to their radio calls long enough to discover the location of the rebel command post. Then Miller jumped into his Ford sedan and drove there. Along the way he picked up one of the station's analysts, but that CIA officer had no stomach for the shooting—he got stuck trying to crouch under the dashboard—and begged to be let off. Before long Miller had hooked up with the paratroopers and became their conduit to the CIA.

The link to the coup's political brains would be George A. Carver, a thirty-two-year-old friend of Colby's. Both shared a bent for philosophy and a China past; though born in Kentucky, Carver had grown up in Shanghai, where his father headed the English department at the university. Both men were unusually intellectual—Phi Beta Kappas—for CIA clandestine operatives. Carver had cover as an economist with the Agency for International Development, though the Diem government had discovered his CIA connection and pseudonym, "Funaro," used in cables. Carver's assignment had been to be in touch with opposition political circles, and his was the evidence—though George personally argued against it—that Colby had relied on for warning of the coup a couple of days before the event. Based on another of the constant rumors picked out of the air by Carver who felt this had more substance than most, the warning established Carver as a seer.

Early in the morning Carver began phoning his contacts and before long was invited to the home of a lawyer related to a coup officer killed early in the fighting; at this home a political committee was meeting. Contact with the government side was maintained by Colby, who spoke several times with Ngo Dinh Nhu and went to the gate of the presidential palace at a key moment. South Vietnamese general Nguyen Khanh meanwhile climbed over the back fence of the palace to help Diem organize reinforcements, and then he opened negotiations with the plotters. At the U.S. embassy, Ambassador Durbrow ordered the CIA station to use its contacts to persuade the plotters to talk.

Talking proved to be fine with Russ Miller, but George Carver objected. Carver had already soured on Diem and believed the Viet Cong were making gains precisely because of Diem's autocratic manner. So Carver now argued with Colby; his orders were not in the interest of either the rebels or the United States. He recalled, "I bitched and moaned and explained why I thought my orders were stupid."

"George, I know your position," Bill Colby shot back. "I don't agree with you, and we haven't got time to discuss it right now."[6]

Colby's efforts succeeded in convincing the rebels to talk with the palace. Diem used the time gained to canvass military leaders and finally got troops from the Mekong Delta to intervene against the plotters. By the next morning the paratroopers surrounding Diem's palace were themselves surrounded. A number of the plotters fled to Tan Son Nhut, theoretically under rebel control. Air commander Nguyen Cao Ky learned of the coup when leaders asked him for a plane to escape the country. Ky found out that one had been an air force officer qualified on the C-47, and fifteen persons escaped on one of those planes to exile in Cambodia. But many who got away were front men, their subordinates having actually organized the plot. Diem's security services arrested nineteen officers and thirty-four civilians, including an uncle of Ngo

Dinh Nhu's wife, a former prime minister, and others. Carver's contact, the lawyer Hoang Co Thuy, never made it to the airport. Instead he hid for a night, then asked the CIA for help. The station managed to sequester Thuy, for a few days, in the house left vacant by a CIA family that had left the country. After that he was smuggled aboard an American courier flight and moved by CIA channels to Europe.

Ngo Dinh Nhu uncovered this subterfuge and also learned of other CIA men in contact with the rebels, including one with the political committee who had been heard to call up "Bill." That was Carver. Colby had cooperated with Diem, so the Vietnamese owed him something. Nevertheless, Nhu insisted Carver had intervened in Vietnamese internal affairs and wanted his head. Colby stood his ground: Carver had simply reported things going on around him and had had no role in the coup. The station chief refused to send Carver away. Then George discovered a threatening note in his mailbox, ostensibly from angry plotters but written on a typewriter known to be in the office of Saigon intelligence chief Dr. Tran Kim Tuyen. Bill Colby saw the ploy but decided the game was up: if Nhu could not expel Carver, he would likely kill the CIA man and make it look like an opposition murder, which he could then use to excuse a repression campaign. Bill decided to order Carver to leave after all. Colby took the note to Nhu, who gladly arranged for police to guard Carver's home until the CIA man had packed, as well as for armed escort on the way to Tan Son Nhut. George Carver became the sacrificial lamb.

For the most part, relations within the embassy remained congenial. The diplomats knew all about Colby's weekly meetings with Ngo Dinh Nhu. As Diem became more and more distant, impossible to see, the Colby channel actually gained in importance. In addition, Bill's first ambassador, Elbridge Durbrow, had been a top assistant in Rome when Colby served there. They were and remained friends. His successor, Frederick C. Nolting, appointed by President John F. Kennedy, saw Bill as an old Vietnam hand and among the ablest on his team, someone Diem both admired and depended on: "Colby became not only a friend but one of my most trusted advisers."[7] The CIA officer reciprocated that esteem; years afterward, when Nolting's reputation had been tarnished in the Vietnam morass, Bill cheerfully supplied a foreword to the former ambassador's memoir of those days in Saigon.

Greater dangers lurked in the hallways of CIA headquarters. Again the focus flowed from political action. Colby frankly felt the Diem regime to be the best government the United States could find in South Vietnam and reported that view to Washington, though he also sent cables that detailed the different opinions of others, such as George Carver, who held to his conclusion that Diem's style was the best thing the Viet Cong had going for it. In 1961 South Vietnam held a presidential election for the first time, and during the campaign Colby used CIA money and expertise for political actions to benefit Diem. In fact, there is a story in CIA lore of deliveries of cash to Diem's brother Nhu, cash inflated so much by black market conversion of

U.S. dollars that movers' dollies were necessary to stack the banknotes. The CIA had the Vietnamese sign a receipt for the dollie, not the cash.

In Washington, under Southeast Asia boss Charles Whitehurst, the Vietnam desk's chief of covert activity, Paul Sakwa, had been seconded from Cord Meyer's International Organizations Division, where political action made up most of the business. William A. K. Jones, Vietnam desk chief, had served in Saigon under Colby, but he had been a police and security adviser and did not care much about elections. Colby and Sakwa began to spar in cables, then the exchange reached a point that Sakwa would send something to Colby only to be answered back at headquarters by someone else entirely. Sakwa concluded that Colby had gone outside channels to others of the old OSS clique, that he was freewheeling—an "uncontrollable agent." Paul Sakwa began to write papers he sent up to the DDP, Dick Bissell. There were five Sakwa protests before the Saigon elections mooted the issue.

In the elections held on April 9, 1961, Diem received some 5,997,927 votes. His two opponents split fewer than 11 percent of the vote. Colby cabled home: "IT WAS CLEAR THAT THE PRESIDENT WANTED A SOLID MAJORITY EVERYWHERE ON HIS OWN MERITS."

At headquarters, Richard Bissell called Sakwa into his office and they had a short conversation. "I understand you've been working on Vietnam," Bissell began. "How are things there?"

"Sir," Sakwa replied, "Things there are a disaster."

"What?"

Sakwa insisted, "Yes, they are a disaster."

"Well golly," Bissell came back, "If you feel that way we'll have to take you out of the Far East Division."[8]

Sakwa became a special assistant to the DDP, where Bissell could keep a close eye on him; but Sakwa began suspecting that Colby, along with his friend Desmond FitzGerald and Charlie Whitehurst, had a private agenda of making the Vietnam situation worse in order to trigger increased U.S. intervention followed by a confrontation between the United States and the People's Republic of China.

There was one Saigon station activity that actually did have the potential to lead to an incident with the Chinese, though in 1961 it would have been only a minor one. A plane or ship could have blundered into Chinese territory in the course of the CIA's efforts to implant agents in North Vietnam. Known as Project Tiger, this activity began on Bill Colby's watch and would remain a headache through most of the Vietnam war. In 1961, a plane was lost; fortunately, it was nowhere near China. Nevertheless, it might have been better if Project Tiger had never gone forward. Bill Colby, with his experience in emplacing stay-behind networks of dubious survivability in Scandinavia and his firsthand observation of the same activity in Italy, should have been the first to question the effectiveness of Project Tiger. Here, without even the limited opportunities to submerge themselves in the North Vietnamese population available to Ed Lansdale's teams in 1954 and 1955, Vietnamese commandos were being asked to do just this. Moreover, if anything, North Vietnamese security had to be better than either the Swedish or Italian security had been.

In any case, pressures grew throughout 1960 to subject Hanoi to the same kinds of pressures besetting Saigon. A start was made with the infiltration of a single agent named Nghia. He would never be heard from again. Then Colby and the station put the project on a much firmer base. The CIA procured safe houses to train Vietnamese commandos in Saigon, Vung Tau, and Da Nang. There were momentary delays—Russ Miller and Ed Regan of the station had had an initial meeting with Ngo Dinh Can, one of Diem's brothers, in 1960, but then had come the coup. Like Carver, Regan had been pulled back to Washington while Diem cooled off, but then he returned to Saigon with new instructions to energize the program. Colby's station personnel were supplemented by Navy weapons and ship experts, who helped construct boats, configured like the Chinese junks familiar to the area but specially adapted to carry commando teams and supplies. There were also frogmen to train the Vietnamese at infiltration by sea, and Army Special Forces (Green Berets) for combat and communications training. By late 1960 Colby had nine CIA officers on the program, plus several acting as liaisons with South Vietnamese police and intelligence. A staff under Russell Miller ran the project for Colby.

Within days of assuming office, President John F. Kennedy sought briefings from Allen Dulles on the effort to infiltrate the North. On March 9, 1961, Kennedy made this project the subject of a National Security Action Memorandum (NSAM), the highest form of presidential directive employed in the Kennedy White House. Later McGeorge Bundy, Kennedy's national security adviser, pressed Dulles on what had happened to the briefing papers the CIA had supposedly assembled in response to the president's request. There could be no doubt that Project Tiger enjoyed support at the highest level of the United States government.

The CIA director's response was to recall Bill Colby from Saigon. Dulles knew that the White House had ordered a Vietnam policy review by a group under Deputy Secretary of Defense Roswell Gilpatric, and he wanted the Saigon station chief involved. The Vietnam task force presented its proposals to Kennedy's National Security Council on April 29 and shortly thereafter the president approved a revised version of them in a further NSAM. Bill Colby's stamp was on the Gilpatric group's intelligence recommendations, which included expanding the offensive (called "positive intelligence" in the jargon) and counterespionage efforts in both South and North Vietnam. Specifically the measures "include penetration of the Vietnamese Communist mechanism, dispatch of agents to North Vietnam and strengthening Vietnamese internal security services." Kennedy authorized the use of Americans if necessary in flights over North Vietnam, but pinned hopes on South Vietnamese and third country nationals—the CIA had anticommunist Chinese in mind.[9] The tone of the Gilpatric program, which emphasized immediate actions and not appeals to Saigon for Diem to make political reforms, also gratified Colby, who found it refreshingly free of the State Department's favorite rhetoric.[10]

In Saigon the CIA moved with alacrity to make good on agency promises to rachet up the infiltration program. During February another singleton agent, one Pham Chuyen, went to the North by sea. Code-named Ares, Chuyen opened radio communications with CIA case officers but he made a false move, or the operation had been known to Hanoi all along. (After the war a Saigon officer who went by the sobriquet "Francois" and had had a key role preparing commandos would claim to have been Hanoi's agent.) In any case the northerners discovered Ares's landing boat on a beach in Ha Long Bay, and at the beginning of March strengthened measures to uncover infiltration. The North Vietnamese captured Chuyen, forcing him to work his radio for their benefit, a tactic known as "doubling" an agent, which became characteristic of Hanoi's methods against Project Tiger. The North Vietnamese forced Ares to demand more supplies, which led to the January 1962 capture of the first CIA junk with its entire crew.

Meanwhile, infiltration by air gradually emerged as the preferred method. Nguyen Cao Ky, the Vietnamese air force officer commanding Tan Son Nhut airbase, found himself summoned one day to the chief of staff, the service's top leader.

"We've been working on new plans with the American CIA," said Colonel Nguyen Xuan Vinh, "to drop specially trained agents into key positions in North Vietnam. . . . What we need now from you is a highly trained group of flyers to drop the right men at the right spot."[11]

Two days later Major Ky began a program of intensive training. The CIA brought in a pilot and a navigator from Air America, both of whom had worked in the long distance penetration flights into Tibet, to drill the Vietnamese on low-altitude flying. Twenty pilots volunteered; the best of them could sustain an altitude just ten to fifteen feet above the ground. Ky innovated a technique of using two navigators for the long distance flights. One concentrated on the calculations, the other on reading the flight path by observing the ground. In the darkness there would not be much ground to see; all course changes had to be made by the clock, with the navigator counting down to the next waypoint. All the cockpit crew had to memorize the flight plan.

Major Ky came up with the basic mission profile of heading north over the sea, flying at very low altitudes to evade Hanoi's radar, then crossing the coast where a river entered the South China Sea. Ky felt confident the spy flights would not be detected during the initial penetration of North Vietnamese airspace, but returning by the same route was foolhardy, so he planned to exit North Vietnam into Laos. Ky and the other crews began their night flying by training over the mountains surrounding Dalat, where in French colonial days the elite had gone for the cooler air. Flights followed the rivers in that area through tight mountain passes in almost total darkness. It became evident the South Vietnamese had no need for their Air America trainers, and the trainers quickly disappeared. The Vietnamese were soon making their training flights in bad weather as well as good.

One night, still several weeks before the first real mission, Ky returned from his practice flight to find an American awaiting him, a slight man who wore glasses and spoke softly. It was Colby. "I remember thinking he looked like a student of philosophy," wrote Ky.[12] Colby worried about secrecy and proposed that everyone connected with Project Tiger live in a separately guarded villa inside the Tan Son Nhut complex. Nguyen Cao Ky agreed, but the regimen proved hard on his ebullient airmen, and Ky later went back to get CIA permission for at least occasional forays to the officers' club. Colby acquiesced.

Nguyen Cao Ky also insisted on flying the first mission himself.[13] A senior officer ought never to have made such a flight, and his own superiors in the South Vietnamese air force had said as much. However, Ky argued he could not ask others to do what he would not and also that he should do the mission to develop the techniques others could use afterward. For days beforehand Ky's crew practiced over twelve hours at a time, either flying or sitting in the cockpit rehearsing. The CIA built an intricate terrain model of the whole portion of North Vietnam the flight was to traverse. Ky and his crew moved to the more out of the way airbase at Bien Hoa for their final training. On May 26, 1961, hours before the scheduled spy flight, Ky flew his C-47 to Da Nang, where the mission would originate.

There was a last minute glitch departing Tan Son Nhut for the forward operating base. Major Ky sat on the runway in his plane awaiting permission to take off. Colby and CIA communications officer Sam Halpern were in Tan Son Nhut's radio hut expecting a clearance from Allen Dulles in Washington. No message came. As the minutes ticked by Colby just stood there, patient but doing nothing. Halpern, convinced CIA headquarters should be needled, offered, "Bill, I'll write the message for you myself, just send it."[14]

Colby finally agreed. He refused to use the highest priority rating, "Flash," but sent the cable with the next level of precedence, "Operational-Immediate." In about twenty minutes they had the reply, a green light. Later it transpired that Allen Dulles *had* sent his go-ahead, but the message had gotten lost at the communications relay station at Subic Bay, the Philippines.

The initial air drop involved four CIA-trained Vietnamese of Team Castor. They met Ky's air crew at Da Nang and all went out to dinner at a Chinese restaurant in the early evening before the flight. Some men worried it could be their last meal. Ky's co-pilot noticed there were thirteen men at the table and proposed to eliminate that unlucky portent by staying behind. Major Ky would not have it. Crew and passengers alike wore the cotton black pajama-like clothes common among Vietnamese peasants, and each carried about $100 worth of North Vietnamese cash, a fund to buy their way out of trouble if the plane went down or the spies were confronted by locals in their operating area. The men carried North Vietnamese cigarettes, even matches, as well.

Major Ky's plane was airborne at about 9:30 P.M. Colby and Halpern had a further moment of panic at Tan Son Nhut when Ky failed to radio confirmation of his third navigational waypoint, but it turned out the airmen had simply been too busy to send the message. Major Ky reported in when passing the next checkpoint and reached the drop zone at 1:30 A.M., May 27. As they had crossed the Red River delta, Ky imagined he could be right over the area where his battalion had fought during the French war, and others of the crew also talked of their nearby homes—all were originally from the North. The crew saw the city lights of Hanoi off their right wingtip as they headed for the mountain drop zone northwest of the northern Vietnamese capital. The return flight through Laos proved uneventful. Ky's wheels touched ground at Saigon about six in the morning. Colby met them in the hangar with a couple of cases of cold champagne for a celebration that Major Ky, at least, much enjoyed.

The Vietnamese commandos were not heard from for a long time. In actuality Team Castor, dropped into Son La province, were apprehended within three days of setting foot in North Vietnam. About a month later they came on the radio to ask for supplies. Again the North Vietnamese had "doubled" the communications man.

In Saigon the CIA loaded a South Vietnamese C-47 for a resupply mission on July 1. Major Ky intended to fly this plane for his third incursion into the North and left the office early to prepare—he needed to call a girlfriend and cancel the date they had set for that evening. On his way through Tan Son Nhut's housing area Ky was stopped by one of his best pilots, Lieutenant Phan Thanh Van, who invited Ky in for a drink. The commander declined because of his mission, whereupon Van volunteered to take over Ky's date or fly the plane instead. Ky saw Van as popular with the ladies and much preferred to have him on an airplane. Thus Lieutenant Van was the aircraft commander that night when the C-47 was hit by anti-aircraft fire as it crossed the North Vietnamese coast. Van was thrown through the cockpit window, his face lacerated. He and several others survived to be put on trial in Hanoi that November. The North Vietnamese staged a three-day trial but carefully avoided connecting the air mission with Team Castor, preserving the fiction that the CIA's Vietnamese commandos were active and productive.

Several missions into the commando program it underwent review within the agency. Colby showed up at Tan Son Nhut one day with a delegation of Americans and asked Major Ky to fly them to Hue. Ky assumed the men were CIA people come to review Project Tiger, though it is more likely this was a general inspection of CIA efforts in Vietnam. In any case, while the trip to Hue went smoothly, on the return flight Ky engaged in some acrobatics of the same sort required on the Project Tiger missions. Ky flew the C-47 so low its prop wash blew foam off waves in the South China Sea.

"Ky," Colby joked once they stood on the ground again, "The next time you fly me like that so close to the water, let me know beforehand and I'll bring my fishing rod."[15]

Major Ky became a friend of Bill Colby's and recalls many times they got together for dinner in Saigon. That day on the asphalt at Tan Son Nhut was the only time Ky ever saw the CIA man smile.

In the meantime, during the weeks after the original launch of Team Castor, the CIA and Saigon's special services had sent up two more agent teams, both of which disappeared without a trace, and both of which, according to American records, then attempted to reconnect, playing a double game through 1962. One message contained a secret sign that the radio operator was working under duress. The fiction that these teams remained in action was the sole mitigating factor in the loss of commandos that had become the norm for Project Tiger. The station chief believed nothing much had been accomplished but Washington kept pressing for action. As Colby wound up his tour in Saigon a major disaster punctuated the experience, for on May 16, 1962, another seven-man team was lost in the North. Of the eight commando teams sent to North Vietnam during Bill Colby's tenure as station chief, none survived to complete its mission and return. The teams appearing in U.S. records as operating successfully in 1964 were in actuality under enemy control.

These efforts can only be seen as tragic. Initially, Colby's task, as he later described it to Sedgwick Tourison, a military intelligence expert in Vietnam, had been to get some kind of framework up and going. The teams were targeted at places they were familiar with or where they might know someone, and most were sent to the hinterlands where Hanoi's security forces could be expected to be weaker. Colby hoped to establish bases from which the lowlands could eventually be penetrated, but the dismal record of the teams made that impossible.[16]

Another aspect of the framework, the air effort the CIA code-named Haylift, absorbed a good deal of Colby's attention. To provide cover he had the CIA create a phony corporation registered in Delaware, just like Air America. Vietnam Air Transport (VIAT) had just one plane; when that C-47 crashed, the CIA got another plane, a better one, the longer range C-54. Again Air America personnel helped the Vietnamese air force and Chinese Nationalists, who were by now active in the North Vietnam air drops, learn the new plane. The CIA also went to the U.S. Air Force for help with better flight paths. Officers at Takhli, Thailand, who had assisted the agency with its air operation into Tibet—Lieutenant Colonel Harry Aderholt and Major Larry Ropka—pitched in. When the VIAT C-54 also went down (it crashed into a mountain during a 1962 rainstorm), any doubts about the need for a fresh look evaporated. A new routine emerged: aircraft first flew to Nha Trang, shortening the operational missions. Eventually the Americans built a special barracks for crews there. Nguyen Cao Ky, who thought VIAT a very successful security measure, formed an independent unit in 1962 for his pilots working on the project. It became the Vietnamese 83rd Special Operations Group and continued on covert missions throughout the war. No more airplanes were lost in the North.

Ky and Colby continued to worry about security, but they saw little improvement. Some twenty-six Vietnamese commandos were lost during 1961. For 1962 the number increased to sixty-eight, and in 1963 losses rose to no fewer than 123. That became the CIA's final year on Project Tiger, which was then handed over to the U.S. military. By then Colby stood at the head of CIA's Far East Division and had his doubts about Tiger. Herbert Weisshart, a CIA man who went to Saigon to do psychological warfare and served as deputy of the military unit engaged in the continuing commando program, decided that Colby was holding back Project Tiger because it represented a diversion of resources from South Vietnam. In the end, the military's success rate was no better than Colby's: 450 more Vietnamese were lost from then through 1968 when infiltration by air ended. Hanoi had been enormously successful in maintaining its security. Decades later, in September 1995, Captain Do Van Tien, who had been the South Vietnamese deputy chief of the unit cooperating with the CIA on Project Tiger (and the man known as "Francois"), went on Hanoi television to tell that all along he had been a spy betraying details of the Tiger program. There were other places where leaks may have occurred as well, including the Saigon high command and the offices of President Diem.

Well might Colby brood about the security. The whole question of preserving secrecy of activities remained intractable throughout the U.S.–Vietnam involvement. Some Vietnamese nationalists were willing to work with Hanoi or the Viet Cong; many of the revolutionaries had brothers, fathers, uncles, or cousins in Saigon's government or its armed forces; always there would be people willing to inform whoever made the price right. Bill Colby took the position that the United States *had* to work *with* Saigon and that therefore there could be no alternative. To the extent that Diem's regime had been infiltrated by Viet Cong informants, Americans simply had to understand and work around that problem. As it applied to the commando operation specifically, Ed Regan, an aide to project chief Russ Miller put it succinctly: "It is a fair statement that none of us had any great hopes for the operation."[17] Other officers, CIA men or military attached to the agency, men like Sam Halpern and William R. Corson, uniformly agree that Bill Colby's attitude toward counterintelligence posed a problem in the Vietnam context. This became a headache, a migraine even, and returned later.

Symptomatic of the attitude that eventually became a problem would be Colby's relationship with a French doctor in Saigon. They met a few times and Bill apparently thought the connection entirely social, for he ignored the CIA regulation that an officer report all contacts with individuals who might possibly be intelligence sources. It turned out later that the CIA intercepted radio transmissions from the Frenchman to Russians. In France, security services apprehended the doctor in 1972 passing documents to Russian intelligence. All this cast the early 1960s association between the doctor and Colby in a different light. James Angleton set his counterintelligence inquisitors to work on the matter, embarrassing Colby and giving Angleton ammunition to use when differences developed later between the two men.*

Bill Colby's characteristic faith showed in his handling of recruitments and his refusal to believe the French doctor an enemy agent. That faith also displayed itself in his deepening attachment to Ngo Dinh Diem and his determination, during these early years, to succeed with the Project Tiger commando missions. From one point of view Colby's stance could be considered one of steadfast determination. From another it could be seen as ignorant and naive. It is suggestive that there is no evidence that Colby made any effort to close down the useless Project Tiger commando missions until late 1963, when the program changed into something even bigger, as will be seen presently. Only two of the nine teams infiltrated during his tenure as station chief survived to be handed over to U.S. military control. Contact with two others was lost in June 1963 and January 1964 respectively.

Meanwhile, impatient for progress in all areas in Vietnam, in October 1961 Kennedy sent an investigating team to Saigon under General Maxwell D. Taylor and Walt W. Rostow. At just this moment Colby was drawn away from his post to a meeting of CIA chiefs of station in the Far East that took place at a U.S. resort compound at Baguio in the Philippines. There the CIA men were to brief John McCone, whom JFK had appointed to replace Allen Dulles and would soon take over as director of central intelligence. Bringing McCone up to speed on Vietnam meant Colby got back to Saigon just as Taylor and Rostow were wrapping up their work and barely had time to shake his hand. Amazingly, when the Taylor-Rostow group left Saigon they proceeded to Baguio to draft their report. Colby might have had more in-depth contact if he had stayed right where he was with McCone.

Things went better with the intelligence representatives on the Taylor-Rostow group, who were Ed Lansdale for the Pentagon and David Smith for the CIA. Smith was supposed to look into Saigon's covert capabilities, what covert offensive actions should be considered, and the possibilities for reducing direct U.S. participation (and increasing that of third country nationals). All of these considerations added up to taking a look at Project Tiger, but the conclusion was simply to push it harder. Smith also had instructions to examine the extent of dissatisfaction toward the Diem government. That he found to be significant, though possible to reduce given the right political strategy.

* A French security dragnet in the Bois de Boulogne in July 1971 following Russians picked up an exchange of information with the doctor, given the pseudonym Vincent Gregoire. When the agent attempted another handover of information to the Russians at the same place a year later he was arrested. French interrogations established that Gregoire had been recruited in Saigon by the National Liberation Front (NLF) in 1967, however, and since his spying had focused on the South Vietnamese and the United States, the French never sent him to prison. The Russians had handled this spy as a favor to the NLF (Thierry Wolton, *Le KGB en France*. Paris: Bernard Grasset, 1986, pp. 138–141).

Lansdale's instructions were to inquire into unconventional warfare techniques, how these could be carried to the enemy, and whether preparations were adequate. He met with Bill Colby on October 21, with the CIA station chief providing a *tour d' horizon* on activities in progress. Colby explained that South Vietnam had around 3,000 people in all areas of unconventional warfare, that these were carrying out covert operations into North Vietnam and Laos (there were 41 patrols into Laos during 1961–62), and that they were conducting irregular warfare in South Vietnam. Saigon relied on fourteen-man action teams that could be reinforced by six-man heavy weapons sections, with backup intervention units of rangers (133 men to a company). There was also an elementary clandestine radio section and a few psychological warfare specialists. Colby detailed the basic training in small unit tactics, describing how the most promising candidates were singled out for advanced clandestine instruction for the commando program. Most of the other units were deployed in counterguerrilla roles in three South Vietnamese provinces. In the covert annex to the final Taylor-Rostow report, Lansdale's conclusions from what he heard from Colby and saw elsewhere were that the effort was generally well conceived, adequately implemented, but much too small in scale.[18]

On the intelligence side, David Smith found that the numerous South Vietnamese intelligence and security services suffered from a lack of coordination with each other, poor communications, not enough trained people, and inadequate ability to evaluate intelligence at both regional and national levels. Two reasons for hope were offered, first, CIA training programs that Bill Colby managed were beginning to show results; second, Saigon's creation of a Central Intelligence Organization (CIO) modeled on the CIA was expected to improve capabilities in all areas. An initial group of forty-five CIO specialists were to complete training in February 1962 and would become the nucleus for expansion.[19]

Despite the policy review, operations continued to follow typical patterns. Reporting the status of his projects on January 4, 1962, station chief Colby noted that the junk sent to resupply the agent Ares had been turned back by bad weather (the next time the maritime unit tried this mission the junk and all its crew would be captured), the commando team near Dien Bien Phu had sent the danger signal that they were under enemy control, and another agent team had been out of contact for more than a month; a patrol had been sent into Laos but results had yet to become available. Training and recruiting were bright spots: some Laotians had been enlisted to enter North Vietnam in the area of Vinh; district intelligence officers had finished training and had been sent into highland areas with radiomen; and the Diem government had approved the use of Chinese Nationalists—twenty aircrews plus fifty commando trainers. Perhaps the most positive note was that the Indian newspaper *Hindustan Times* had published a favorable article on South Vietnam after its reporter had been briefed and "guided" by the CIA during his visit to Saigon.[20]

As for the intelligence organization, a reasonable benchmark is the assessment Bill Colby sent Langley when CIA director John McCone asked for an analysis he could give to the National Security Council's Special Group (Counterinsurgency). Completed at the very end of Colby's tour in Saigon, embodied in a CIA report of June 26, 1962, the analysis featured commentary on each of the South Vietnamese intelligence organizations. Colby saw the new Central Intelligence Organization as a "fledgling national intelligence service [which] . . . appears to present some hope for a professional, coordinated, evaluated approach." Realistically, however, Colby noted, "We cannot expect professional results from it for a considerable period of time." On existing units like the National Police and Security Service, station chief Colby concurred with the conclusions of the Taylor-Rostow mission and others that these were wanting; the Military Intelligence Service was improving but slowly; military counterintelligence "could, but does not, make a real contribution"; Vietnamese radio intelligence was improving and had provided some useful information; and Diem's personal intelligence service, SEPES by its French initials, "is not considered an effective tool for collection of intelligence on the [National Liberation Front]." As to the Saigon station itself, most of its recent expansion, Bill Colby noted, "has been directed toward action projects in paramilitary and psychological warfare fields."[21] The best example was right up in South Vietnam's Central Highlands.

BY FAR THE MOST significant CIA project Bill Colby began while chief of station in Saigon concerned Vietnam's uplands tribal minorities, called "montagnards" (or colloquially, "yards") after the French word for a mountain man. The idea would be to arm and train the tribesmen to fight in light infantry units in the Central Highlands, their home territories, which, by square mileage, actually comprised over half the land mass of South Vietnam. Viet Cong encroachment in the Central Highlands, greatly feared by Diem and his generals, had already begun. Over six thousand tribesmen and several thousand other minorities regrouped to North Vietnam after the 1954 Geneva agreements. In 1960, when the revolutionaries formed their National Liberation Front, a montagnard became one of its vice presidents. Some American advisers wanted to secure the highlands by forcibly relocating the montagnards, creating depopulated zones the army could then shell and sweep with impunity. Certain CIA paramilitary advisers wished to set up special commando units to patrol the mountains. Other military men, like Colby's opposite number, General Lionel McGarr, head of the military advisory group, favored technological solutions such as mining the mountains or blocking the borders with defense lines in hopes of keeping out the Viet Cong.

The idea for the montagnard project came from outside official circles altogether. David A. Nuttle worked the Central Highlands for a private church-funded humanitarian relief organization called the International Voluntary Services (IVS), which had been active in Vietnam since 1957. Nuttle traveled the highlands on a motorbike, knew the tribes, and had become expert on one, the Rhadé, whose language he had picked up and among whom he had lived and hunted. Through IVS, Nuttle published, in Ban Me Thuot, the provincial capital at the southern end of the highlands, a detailed ethnography of the Rhadé. The tribe thought enough of Nuttle that they gave him a name, "Y-Deo," for his masterful hunting. Dave, as he called himself, was convinced the Rhadé and other montagnards would fight for themselves if given the opportunity.

In Saigon, Nuttle ran into an Army colonel, a CIA man in mufti, one Gilbert Layton, first sent to Saigon to supervise the military instruction of Vietnamese recruited for Project Tiger. Layton heard about the highlands situation but told Nuttle the Vietnamese army's rangers, a newly formed elite force, could handle it. Nuttle thought otherwise. There were deep cultural differences between the montagnards and the lowland Vietnamese, who hated them. Diem had specifically been preparing the highlands to accommodate large numbers of Vietnamese, altering the previous population balance. Dave convinced "Chink" Layton that although the Vietnamese might operate in the mountains, they would not do much to prevent Viet Cong inroads among montagnards. Layton agreed to take the opinion to Bill Colby.

Gil Layton earned the sobriquet "Chink" in the CIA, where he had worked at the secret Pacific training base on Saipan, imparting military knowledge to Koreans, Tibetans, Nationalist Chinese, and others. Before that, Chink had never had anything to do with China. In fact, he was a native Iowan, an enlistee in the Iowa National Guard's cavalry outfit, and had fought with George S. Patton's Third Army in World War II. Like Colby, Layton had earned both the Bronze and Silver Stars. In 1944, age thirty-three, Layton had been with one of Patton's units that first broke through German lines to break the siege of Bastogne during the Battle of the Bulge. For the CIA, which he joined in 1950, a contemporary of Colby, Layton had done tours in Germany and Turkey. Like Colby again, Layton helped plan stay-behind networks. When Dave Nuttle suggested a montagnard project, Chink readily recognized its necessary features.

Colby himself was uneasy about the highlands. The Vietnamese invited him to one meeting where they laid out development plans for a new village, complete with maps and charts, accounts of how roads would be built to connect with existing highways, all brand new—the village did not then exist and no Vietnamese lived there. Diem's obvious constituency was the refugees from the North who had fled after the 1954 Geneva agreements, and his clear purpose was to place a core of Vietnamese in the highlands. But Diem did not follow up with a political program. The plans instantly reminded Bill of Italy, where Christian Democratic governments had curried popular favor by similar programs. Italians who had fled to caves during the war were brought to a whole new standard of living, but the Christian Democrats had made no effort to enlist their support. Before long, in each new Italian village, the communists came and rented a storefront, talked to people, harped on their problems, and soon garnered support that might have gone to the governing party. In the same way, Colby remembered his summer trying to unionize gas station employees in Washington, D.C. His organizers had kept pushing on only one thing—grievances. Such successes as were obtained came that way, by harnessing people's anger. As far as the Central Highlands were concerned, David Nuttle's proposals for the montagnards had a social-political component because they aimed at an existing people and started by recognizing their sentiments. Colby arranged for Nuttle to attend a meeting of the U.S. embassy council to discuss policy for the Central Highlands.

At the meeting, the exposition of General McGarr's plan for forced resettlement of the montagnards, followed by unrestricted military operations, left Nuttle cold. He argued that the McGarr plan had to fail because there was no way to block the hundreds, if not thousands, of mountain trails. The rugged hills would also make it impossible for the Vietnamese army to maneuver with its big, cumbersome units. Ambassador Nolting asked for alternatives. Nuttle then presented his concept of organizing the montagnards to defend themselves. A pilot program would show whether the idea could work, and such an experiment could be conducted with the Rhadé montagnards. Ambassador Nolting told Nuttle he would be informed what decision had been made.

Meanwhile, station chief Colby pulled out the stops to create a CIA action program both political and paramilitary in nature, not some repetition of the Italian failure. Agency personnel would coordinate, true, but Colby wished to avoid the perception that the CIA had created its own private army, so he got the U.S. Army to provide some of its Green Berets to do the training. Economic and social programs were a primary ingredient and would be administered by the U.S. Agency for International Development. Equipment and supplies could come from CIA stocks. The whole would be called the Village Defense Program. Colby got Nolting to agree to the initiative as a separate embassy line item and convinced Des FitzGerald at CIA to approve it as an official CIA project. The hardest to convince would be Diem, and Bill Colby did that through Ngo Dinh Nhu. Vietnamese special forces responsible to Nhu were made the official leaders of the experiment, and, Colby found, Nhu seemed receptive to the philosophy behind the concept, in part because the Vietnamese leader had already begun casting about for some new formula to energize his own political war effort.

Next the CIA interceded with International Voluntary Services to release Dave Nuttle from his contract and the Village Defense Program innovator became a CIA contract officer. Bill Colby, Nuttle recalls, tapped him on the shoulder and said, "The CIA needs you to conduct a village defense experiment with the Montagnard."[22] On October 4, 1961, Nuttle signed his CIA contract.

By late October the CIA station chief had secured all necessary high-level clearances. At that point Nuttle, an Army Special Forces medical sergeant, and Captain Pho, of Diem's CIA, called the Presidential Survey Office, established themselves at Ban Me Thuot to begin the experiment. Joined by one of Colby's senior operations officers, Nuttle briefed the top American corps adviser and the Vietnamese province chief. The American's conventional thinking remained unswayed, but he did not oppose the CIA's experiment. The province chief already had written instructions from Ngo Dinh Nhu that were quite cautious—to permit this in just one village.

Nuttle knew the headman of the village Buon Enao, about ten kilometers from Ban Me Thuot; he was fluent in the Rhadé tribal language, and also had a bilingual Rhadé interpreter who proved very useful. When they arrived, they found that the headman's daughter was ill; the interpreter worked with the Green Beret medic and the Rhadé shaman to restore her health, further cementing good relations with the tribe, Nuttle and the CIA man, joined later by Chink Layton, began two weeks of intense discussions with the Rhadé. The tribe feared Saigon's power, but the Viet Cong had begun extorting food and money in the area and posed an immediate threat. The chief agreed to cooperate. The Village Defense Program was off the ground.

A measure of the antipathy the Vietnamese had for the CIA initiative was that Nhu forced Colby to agree that the agency would not arm the montagnards with any modern weapons without Vietnamese approval. In mid-November, the day following completion of a village clinic, Colonel Le Quang Tung, head of Diem's Presidential Survey Office, visited Buon Enao along with Layton of the CIA. It was clear the Rhadé were doing what they had promised, so Tung agreed they might have weapons beyond the spears and bows that had served them up to that point. Gil Layton had thoughtfully packed CIA weapons on their helicopter and these were immediately distributed.

Meanwhile, Rhadé tribespeople who had been forced to join the Viet Cong returned and helped identify others who could be turned, as plans were made for more extensive intelligence gathering. Aside from the clinic, a village store would be set up, which cut down on price gouging by Vietnamese traders, who were also often Viet Cong spies. Numerous South Vietnamese flags were flown over Buon Enao. The village defense team showed their confidence in the Rhadé by moving to live in the village. Additional social programs included water purification and other sanitation efforts.

A month after Colonel Tung's visit, Ngo Dinh Nhu himself came to Buon Enao, accompanied by Colby and Layton. The CIA station chief, who had talked over the tactics of hunting tigers with Nhu, persuaded him to stop by while on a hunting trip. Nuttle and the others made a point of emphasizing their support for Vietnamese authority. Captain Pho had only good things to say about his American colleagues. Impressed, Nhu approved expansion of the village defense effort and instructed his province chief to supervise the extension beyond the single village. Radio posts were to be installed in the newly adherent villages to inform the Vietnamese army if they were attacked, and a special montagnard strike force would be created to protect a village while its volunteers were away being trained as the defense force as well as to act as a reserve for the entire area. Expansion brought greater demands for expert help, so in February 1962 American Green Berets began supporting village defense in a big way.

The first Green Berets were Captain Ron Shackleton and a half dozen men from Special Forces Team A-113 on Okinawa. They stayed in Saigon at a CIA safe house to be briefed, flew to Ban Me Thuot on February 14, 1962, then quickly moved to Buon Enao. They were carried on a CIA plane—an unmarked C-46 transport with a Nationalist Chinese crew. With Buon Enao as a center, a security zone expanded steadily outward, and soon there were other zones too. By the end of 1962 the project had mobilized 6,000 montagnard strike force troops plus 19,000 village defense militia. Needing a new name for the forces, Bill Colby christened them "Civilian Irregular Defense Groups" (CIDGs).

Colby credits the success of the village defense program with convincing Ngo Dinh Nhu to proceed with a nationwide effort that would be quite similar, the "strategic hamlet" program. Sir Robert Thompson, a British expert with experience in Malaya, proposed the strategic hamlets in November 1961. In Malaya local populations had been regrouped into "new villages" for improved security and to cut them off from the guerrilla organization. Thompson proposed this for South Vietnam, but what he advised and what the Vietnamese carried out were two very different things. The CIA station chief saw Thompson's concept as impractical for Vietnam due to its origin in the distinct ethnic and physical context of Malaya. Colby and Nhu held extensive discussions on this point. Strategic hamlets in Vietnam could not be merely an administrative arrangement combined with military security cordons.

Unfortunately the social components Bill Colby saw as crucial to the strategic hamlet program, a view Colby believed was shared by Nhu, were in fact absent from the program implemented. Forcible relocation of peasants, corruption, poor security, and a lack of efforts to reach out to the people were hallmarks of strategic hamlets. Hanoi and northern Vietnamese observers complained after the war about the 12,000 strategic hamlets and the American "special warfare," an argument Colby claimed as evidence that the program was working and the enemy was being defeated.[23] Much more likely was that the hamlets inconvenienced the Viet Cong in the short term, by erecting obstacles to their contact with the peasantry, but lost their effectiveness over time as the Viet Cong evolved new tactics, and the peasants' grievances against the Saigon regime accumulated.

What happened at Buon Enao and with the CIDG program is a case in point. Saigon waited until the Americans had done the heavy lifting and created what looked like successful machinery, then demanded that the cleared zone revert to their entire control, with strike force montagnards subject to drafting into the South Vietnamese army. The villages would be turned over between September 1962 and June of the following year. The Vietnamese dismantled the medical clinic and stopped paying the Rhadé women the Americans had trained as medics. Saigon demanded that the weapons be taken back from the CIDG and set a target of 4,000 to be collected. The strike force was turned over to Saigon control in April 1963 and the Vietnamese were to be responsible for paying them, beginning April 30. At the end of July, they remained unpaid. Ron Shackleton considered what happened a travesty, and later quoted a 5th Special Forces Group study of the CIDG program: "By the end of 1963, the Buon Enao complex was disorganized and most of its effectiveness had been lost."[24]

David Nuttle, scandalized with what the Vietnamese were doing and the lack of interest in opposing them among the conventionally minded U.S. military, left Vietnam in October 1962. He took his case to President Kennedy's National Security Council, whose Special Group (Counterinsurgency) held responsibility for all CIA covert projects in Vietnam. By then Colby had returned to Washington as well; but preoccupied with other matters, he could do little to help.

The realities of South Vietnamese attitudes and actions stand in sharp contrast to William E. Colby's reflections. It was understandable that CIA subordinates left Vietnam in disgust, that South Vietnamese paratroopers launched their coup against Diem, that air force pilots tried to bomb him in 1962, and that there would be more army coups d'état later. Saigon's leaders were more than out of touch. Ngo Dinh Diem surrounded himself with an impenetrable cloud of political-philosophical gibberish, reinforced by a circle of relatives willing to shill for him, not least of them Ngo Dinh Nhu. Hanoi's bosses, focused on nationalist credibility, in fact believed that their most serious competition as a nationalist figure was Diem, but if so, that demonstrates how limited were the leadership resources in South Vietnam. There is little to substantiate William E. Colby's retrospective assertions that the United States could have won the war with Diem.

The most important consequence of Colby's weekly sessions with Ngo Dinh Nhu, meanwhile, would be Nhu's impact on Colby. The faith Bill began to develop in the Saigon leaders became so strong he would hold his course despite discrepant evidence. Then and later Colby would see things that happened in Vietnam as robbing Diem of victory, rather than events that flowed from Diem's refusal to grasp opportunities for effective action. It would be personally tragic for Bill that his view carried less and less weight in a Washington increasingly frustrated at South Vietnamese *immobilisme*. Even more poignant, Bill Colby would be witnessing Washington's new doubts at firsthand.

7

A Bigger Stage to Play On

BILL COLBY MAY OR MAY NOT have had a private channel to Des Fitz-Gerald, but the two were unquestionably close, both personally and professionally. FitzGerald gave advice on private schools in the United States—Colby sent son Jonathan home to boarding school while he was in Vietnam—and got suggestions from Colby on places to visit in Europe. As Bill drew near the end of his tour in Saigon, Des offered the station chief the job of chief of Far East operations.* Super-competent, quiet Colby, working directly in FitzGerald's office, could be a perfect counterpoint to the swashbuckling division chief. Des could stake out broad vistas and make claims for what the Far East Division could do; Colby would organize the division's resources and manage the execution of the CIA's schemes.

Not that this happened right away. Colby returned to Washington only after extensive leave-taking and a world tour. He took the family to a farewell audience with Diem, saw Nhu numerous times, and toured the country. Colby checked up on the CIA's numerous special projects, such as the montagnard mobilization and the similar "Sea Swallows" militia set up in Ben Tre province by the Catholic priest Father Hoa. The South Vietnamese commander in the Central Highlands presented him with a stuffed tiger pelt. Above Da Nang a subordinate took Barbara and Catherine Colby for a ride across the beautiful Hai Van Pass, while Bill flew with the Vietnamese corps commander and the army chief of staff, then General Nguyen Khanh, to survey the A Shau valley and then meet his family at the old imperial capital of Hue.

After Vietnam, the family made a gradual progression westward. The

---

* The clandestine service component of the CIA continued to be known as the Directorate of Plans (DDP), though it carried out operations that were called "projects." In a 1973 reorganization the DDP would in fact be renamed the Directorate of Operations. To avoid confusion in this narrative, except where DDP is being referred to by its formal title, its function, as well as that of such personnel as Bill Colby here, will be recorded as "operations."

Colbys visited the Taj Mahal in India; Jerusalem in Palestine; the Greek Islands; Italy, including Rome and the Vatican; France, including the grotto at Lourdes. The prevalence of destinations with religious themes was an indication of Colby's Catholic dedication. Indeed, he would eventually be connected in CIA gossip with a circle of Roman Catholic operations officers at the agency; the gossip would make him a leader of this circle. This would become an unusual time from a religious point of view for Catholics at the Central Intelligence Agency, for the new director of central intelligence, John McCone, was a staunch Roman Catholic himself.

What is more usually noted about McCone is that he happened to be Republican, appointed in November 1961 by the Democratic president John F. Kennedy. The selection of a figure from a different political party, apart from McCone's other attributes, represented an effort to help President Kennedy counter criticism of the CIA in the wake of the spectacular failure of the agency's attempt to invade Cuba at the Bay of Pigs in April 1961. Everything that could have gone wrong with that operation did, starting with the assumption that the Cuban people would rise up against Castro if only they were given a chance. At the technical level there had been mistakes about such factors as whether the reefs at the Bay of Pigs had enough water over them to permit the passage of landing craft. When Colby thought about it, the Bay of Pigs fiasco looked a lot like his abortive scheme to dynamite German railroad tunnels in Norway during the big war—consultation with experts would have saved a lot of energy.

For months following the Bay of Pigs the CIA remained in disarray. There was a six-week-long investigation of what went wrong by a presidential board chaired by General Maxwell D. Taylor, and a six-month-long look by CIA inspector general Lyman D. Kirkpatrick. The president's Foreign Intelligence Advisory Board held its own inquiry that lasted through December 1961. There were also closed hearings before the Senate Foreign Relations Committee. The failure put an end to the tenure of Allen Dulles as head of the agency and resulted in the resignation of Dick Bissell as head of the DDP. Richard Helms, Bissell's replacement as director of operations, came from the espionage, not the covert action, side of the clandestine service.

President Kennedy reinvigorated the intelligence advisory board, which he had briefly abolished, as well as the National Security Council (NSC) subcommittee responsible for approving covert actions. Kennedy put regulations in place requiring any proposed covert action costing more than $25,000 to have the explicit approval of the NSC subcommittee, called the Special Group (Augmented). In addition, he issued an NSC directive requiring the CIA to hand over its role in military-style activities to the United States military. The latter directive, NSAM-57, directly impacted CIA actions in Vietnam, forcing the agency to give over its montagnard program and others to the Green Berets. As if these fresh restrictions were not enough, sheer chaos ensued beginning in November 1961, when the agency moved from its buildings in downtown Washington, D.C., to a spanking new headquarters complex across the Potomac River in Langley, Virginia.

With the CIA, for the first time in its history, in the news as an object of public criticism, the shakedown of the Langley complex, and the jaundiced Kennedy administration attitude after the Bay of Pigs, not to mention sudden domination of the DDP by the spy clique, it must have seemed to Colby like a good time to let the dust settle before reaching Washington. Bill Colby had more than tourism in mind when bringing his family home from Vietnam on the slow track.

SOME YEARS LATER congressional investigators collected statistics on covert action approvals during different epochs of CIA history. The data were enlightening but, in truth, during the Kennedy years a key transition occurred. Sparked in the beginning by the Bay of Pigs mess, change meant simultaneously more and different procedures to be followed in setting up CIA projects. Change *did not* mean less covert action—John F. Kennedy remained committed to the overthrow of Castro in Cuba even after the Bay of Pigs, and globally he proved no less enamored of covert operations than Dwight D. Eisenhower, who had been an enthusiast.

President Eisenhower had continued and strengthened the National Security Council's Special Group, a unit that had overall authority for covert action. Kennedy altered the name from 5412 Group to Special Group (Augmented), but in early 1962 he subdivided functions and established a second unit, the Special Group (Counterinsurgency). Despite this multiplication of formal structures, however, much as was the case within the Kennedy White House, casual relationships became as important as bureaucratic channels in the business of intelligence. For example, a procedure evolved whereby covert action proposals were first approved by CIA station chiefs, then DDP division chiefs and the deputy director, then were forwarded by the director of central intelligence to the Special Group (CI).

But apart from the policy papers there was an informal circuit in Kennedy's "Camelot." The evening receptions and dinner parties featured many of the key individuals who figured in the formal channels. For the Special Group (CI), the president's brother, Robert F. Kennedy, who had become attorney general, was a prime mover in the secret war against Castro as well as with covert actions more generally. Desmond FitzGerald moved in the same circles, giving DDP's Far East Division extra access beyond the policy councils.

This access enabled the CIA to make its best pitch, officers felt at the time. Certainly the Far East Division had a full plate, as Bill Colby found when he reached Langley to join FitzGerald. In Japan, which had joined the United States in a defense treaty during Eisenhower's final year, the CIA engaged in classical political action, shoring up the ruling liberal Democratic Party using methods Colby had helped pioneer. In Taiwan, where the United States found itself allied with Chinese Nationalists, the CIA needed local help to implement aerial reconnaissance programs using U-2 spy planes, whereas the Chinese Nationalists wanted CIA support to mount new paramilitary efforts on the Chinese mainland. We have seen something already of the activities the Far East Division had under way in Vietnam, and shortly we shall survey similar CIA operations in adjoining Laos. In Thailand the agency had an extensive program of assistance to Thai police and paramilitary forces, including enlisting Thai aid to operations in Laos. In Singapore there was political action backing the prime minister, Lee Kuan Yew. The Philippines, which had been a prime theater for similar CIA action in the previous decade, was now mainly quiescent, but nearby Indonesia, where the agency had mounted another paramilitary operation, had become an espionage and political action target. In all these countries, and others too, there were constant clandestine efforts under way to expose Russian spies or recruit them to CIA service, just as Hanoi had been doing with the commandos Bill Colby had been sending to North Vietnam.

One operation Bill Colby had missed in the 1950s, known to the CIA by the digraph* ST/CIRCUS, involved Tibet, where rebels were actively fighting the Chinese communists. The CIA trained partisan leaders, weapons experts, and communications men for the Tibetan tribes; the agency also supplied weapons and equipment. Recruits crossed the mountains into Nepal or India, were spirited away to CIA bases, and returned via long-distance flights staged through Thailand and planned by the same American airmen who helped Colby with his North Vietnam missions. In any case, Project Circus turned golden for the Far East Division in 1961, when Khamba Tribesmen overran the headquarters of a Chinese division, capturing 1,600 pages of People's Liberation Army secret documents, the single biggest intelligence breakthrough in the secret war against China.

Colby reentered CIA Far Eastern activities at a high level just as the Tibetan operation had to be recast. Air supply missions had had to be canceled after the shootdown of Francis Gary Powers, when President Eisenhower ended all overflights of communist territory. Overland treks were still made from India, but when Jack Kennedy entered office his ambassador to India, John Kenneth Galbraith, scuttled plans to support Tibet from there. Des Fitz-Gerald and Colby scrambled to create a new supply system through the mountain kingdom of Nepal, which suddenly sprouted a CIA station headed by Howard ("Rocky") Stone. Once manager of an ice cream bar, Stone had worked on the project for a CIA coup in Iran in 1953, then later in the decade failed in an attempt to engineer a similar action in Syria.

---

* Historically the CIA used what it called a "digraph" to identify operations, equipment, agents, and other important items. The "di" in the graph meant the identification had two parts, the first being a two-letter combination. That combination typically specified the region, country, or function that the codename concerned. The second portion of the digraph consisted of a word, the code name proper. In general it is quite common to refer to a CIA project solely by its codename (the word portion of the digraph). Except as necessary for quotations or for continuity of the narrative, that will be the practice here.

Colby presided over a Far East Division review of China area operations that he forwarded to the Special Group in September 1963, concluding that the paramilitary effort had not been very productive, proposing instead to emphasize intelligence collection while increasing political support for the Dalai Lama so as to build a strong movement among expatriate Tibetans. Program approval came in early 1964, with a budget of $1,735,000, including a $15,000 per month subsidy (in place since 1959) for the Dalai Lama. Another aspect Colby supported, a project to train Tibetans in modern communications skills and teach them English, resulted in the purchase of a house in Ithaca, New York, and some cooperation with Cornell University. Tibetans studied there to become civil servants for the Dalai Lama.

Meanwhile surviving guerrilla forces built camps in Mustang, a mountain fastness even more remote than Nepal, with $500,000 per year in CIA support. Striving to fashion some way to utilize this force. Tibet increased its cooperation with the Indian army following the border war India fought against China in late 1962. The Indians progressively increased their control, incorporating certain Tibetan specialists in their own military. The Tibetans themselves, insisting on conducting raids out of Mustang, incensed the CIA in 1964 and later, resulting in a withdrawal of American assistance. Khamba mutinies, disillusion, and tighter foreign surveillance finally brought an end to the entire operation.

Throughout this period Vietnam continued to grow in terms of its demands on Washington officials. In May 1962 the Special Group (CI) were told that the United States would do its best to make South Vietnam a counterinsurgency laboratory. As Bill Colby returned to Langley and swung into action there, Vietnam matters figured in the agenda of virtually every Special Group meeting. In the fall of nineteen sixty-two Vietnam would be designated a "Gold" program area, which afforded extra budget priority to all CIA projects there. There were constant updates plus comprehensive issue-by-issue reviews that July and again in March nineteen sixty-three.

Among other Special Group initiatives were approval of an official U.S. doctrine for counterinsurgency, start-up of an academy to train foreign police officials, extensive programs of assistance to foreign police services, extra instruction in counterinsurgency for American government personnel (963 from the CIA participated in the months prior to the spring of 1963), and drafting and approval of counterinsurgency plans specific to countries designated by the Special Group. The CIA's Far East Division worked directly on almost half those country plans.

One country, Laos, featured a political environment so complex that a national plan seemed impractical. During this period a political arrangement to neutralize Laos under a coalition government that included anticommunists, communists, and middle-of-the-roaders in a single cabinet became the order of the day. An international agreement at Geneva to recognize the neutralization would be a key U.S. achievement. Assistant Secretary of State Averell W. Harriman negotiated the agreement and went on to become the diplomat responsible for all Far Eastern affairs. This led to friction between Harriman and the CIA's Far East officials, though the arena involved the *other* Special Group, the one that monitored covert operations rather than counterinsurgency matters. Issues before the Special Group (Augmented) in late 1962 included the CIA commando missions into North Vietnam, the Tibet project, Chinese nationalist demands for CIA help to return to the mainland, and proposals to conduct certain aerial missions in Laos. When these were not checked with Harriman he became furious. As the responsible National Security Council staff member reported to McGeorge Bundy, Kennedy's national security adviser, "In some of these activities there has not been adequate checking with FE that is, State's Far East Bureau with the result that either nothing gets done or consternation arises if something is done."[1]

In fact, the burden of consternation began falling exclusively on Colby's shoulders within weeks of the moment those words were penned. The author, NSC staffer Michael Forrestal, handled Far Eastern affairs; no one told him that a CIA U-2 spy plane had just returned pictures that showed the Russians trying to set up bases in Cuba for nuclear-armed missiles. That discovery triggered the Cuban Missile Crisis, in the middle of which U.S. officials learned that a unit of the CIA's Cuban exiles was about to stage an armed attack on Cuba. This covert action could have triggered a shooting war and proved embarrassing even to Bobby Kennedy, a major proponent of CIA raids against Castro. The Cuban exiles were recalled and the CIA project, Mongoose, immediately reorganized. Des FitzGerald would be called in to shut down the existing Cuban operation and spark-plug a new one. At the CIA's Far East Division, Bill Colby became the acting chief, and he was soon confirmed in command.

At the State Department, Averell Harriman would be Colby's opposite number. The crusty Harriman had already had his fill of the CIA during new Geneva negotiations on Laos. On a familiarization visit to Laos during the talks, Harriman had walked out on CIA officers when he felt he'd heard enough, and had ostentatiously turned off his hearing aid at meetings with others. One agency case officer, John Hasey, who had been too enthusiastic in supporting a Lao military strongman, would be transferred at Harriman's behest and over the objections of both Colby and FitzGerald. John Kennedy saw Harriman as a "separate sovereignty":[2] in Washington he was nicknamed "the Crocodile," some said, because he could be basking in the sun on the riverbank one minute and biting your head off the next.

"Harriman was not nicknamed 'The Crocodile' for nothing," Bill Colby recounts.[3] In the wake of the 1962 Geneva agreement it would be Colby's job to visit Harriman every week and brief him on conditions in Laos. The Far East Division chief became one of those subjected to Harriman's hearing aid trick: at other times "The Crocodile" provoked the CIA man until both were shouting at each other; or he would bait Colby to test him. But without doubt, Harriman enjoyed the full confidence of both President Kennedy and secretary of state Dean Rusk, so Colby handled the sallies as well as he could. Harriman, and Laos, quickly took center stage as Bill Colby's biggest headache.

THE LAOTIAN OPERATION began in Eisenhower's years, before Bill Colby ever came to Southeast Asia. Under the 1954 Geneva Accords Laos was supposed to be a neutral land with power shared between pro-Western and pro-communist political parties (the 1962 Geneva agreements were ostensibly an attempt to restore this previous status). The CIA's role came about because of the United States' distaste for the 1954 agreement along with the fierce partisanship of Secretary of State John Foster Dulles, for whom "neutralism" was a red flag. Dulles enlisted his brother Allen, then director of the CIA, in yet another political action campaign, designed to influence Laotian elections in 1958.

Political action in Laos would be carried on in the Ed Lansdale tradition rather than that of Colby. Lansdale used to talk about having a banjo on your shoulder but a carbine at your hip. All measure of propaganda, black and gray psychological warfare, and open political manipulation, rather than subtle tinkering with the odds, were keynotes in the Lansdale method. While Ed Lansdale did not himself participate in the Laos action, it was carried out by many of his former subordinates from Vietnam, men such as Rufus Phillips, who masterminded some of the village assistance programs. Using up some 10 percent of all U.S. aid to Laos for 1958, Americans suddenly helped in a big way on almost a hundred Laotian initiatives in what was openly called Operation Booster Shot. The project brought new visibility to Air America, formerly the Civil Air Transport (CAT), which made seventy-two flights into Laos for Booster Shot. The high point would be the airlift of two parachute-rigged bulldozers from Ashiya, Japan, to places where they were airdropped over northern Laos.

One indication of the utility of these U.S. aid programs would be the fate of the bulldozers: their function in the trackless Lao wilderness became clearing a road a few hundred feet long so that a tribal leader could pretend to drive the car he had been given by the Americans.

In the May elections, the Laotian communists, called the Pathet Lao, actually went on to win the majority of the twenty-one national assembly seats that were up for grabs, polling about a third of all votes cast. Political leader Souvanna Phouma of the centrist-neutralist party then went on to form a coalition government that included Pathet Lao ministers, along with some from the pro-American group known as the Committee for the Defense of National Interests (CDNI). But the United States, ostensibly in a dispute over devaluation of the Laotian currency, then denied all foreign aid. Souvanna was forced to resign, to be followed by a cabinet with links to the CDNI, whose efforts to disarm the Pathet Lao and incorporate them into the Royal Laotian Army in early 1959 led to an outbreak of fighting. When another election took place in April 1960 the rules were laid down in such a way that the Pathet Lao could not even run candidates in fifty of fifty-nine assembly districts. The resulting body of delegates were close to the CDNI and to rightist military strongman General Phoumi Nosavan. Complicit in all these maneuvers, the United States, not some communist conspiracy, bore significant responsibility for the Laotian war that began in earnest after the failed elections.

Hanoi, at that time, had not bothered much about Laos since 1954. There was a border clash between Laotian and North Vietnamese troops in December 1958, but the considered opinion of the CIA regarding the Pathet Lao troubles would be that they were an internal matter. The experts put it this way in a 1959 special national intelligence estimate:

> the communist resumption of guerrilla warfare in Laos was primarily a reaction to a stronger anticommunist posture by the Laotian government and to recent U.S. initiatives in Laos. We consider that it was undertaken mainly to protect the communist apparatus in Laos and to improve communist prospects.[4]

As late as the end of 1960, just prior to the transition from the Eisenhower administration to that of John F. Kennedy, Allen Dulles and his CIA were unable to cite evidence of intervention by Hanoi in Laos. North Vietnam's creation of the "Ho Chi Minh Trail" supply artery to South Vietnam, or more properly the expansion of that network into southern Laos, only began in the spring of 1961. By that time the CIA, and the United States, were already deeply embroiled in the land of a million elephants, as Laotians liked to call their country.

Following its predilections, the CIA played to every side in Lao politics except the Pathet Lao. Des FitzGerald's favorite would be the strongman Phoumi, to whom he assigned a full-time CIA case officer, John Hasey, who lived in the house next door and had his own back channel to communicate with headquarters without going through the local CIA station. Challenged about being out of step with the station in Vientiane, Hasey retorted, "I don't give a damn what they say!"[5] The reaction of station chief Henry Hecksher when he learned of Hasey's attitude has gone unrecorded but it cannot have been favorable. Then there was Souvanna Phouma. He too got his own CIA man, Campbell James, a distant relation of Teddy Roosevelt, heir to an oil fortune, who wowed Vientiane when his mother—a stalwart of New York society—came to visit. Veteran of CIA operations from Taiwan against the Chinese mainland, in which personal relations with Chinese nationalists had been vital, "Zup" James supplied Souvanna with fine cigars, went hunting with the Lao elite, and had them to his home for dinner. Souvanna remained out of a job—and Jack Hasey remained the top CIA man—until August 1960, when a Laotian paratroop battalion under Captain Kong Le mounted a military coup in favor of neutralism.

The resulting battle of Vientiane forced General Phoumi to flee. Other politicians also left the capital in droves, including Souvanna, who stopped only long enough to tell Campbell James that in spite of politics they would always be friends. But Kong Le brought Souvanna back to Vientiane to form a new cabinet; Souvanna, looking for a government of national unity, invited Phoumi to participate. The Laotian general refused and marched on the capital with his own army, eventually forcing out Kong Le's neutralist forces. Phoumi's coup, which had U.S. support, became the move that finally plunged Laos into open civil war. It took over a year of diplomacy and millions in U.S. aid to restore the political accommodation Washington could have had for free if it had not encouraged the breakup of the neutralist tripartite coalition.

Part of the struggle would be waged by a CIA-organized third force, a Laotian secret army composed of Hmong tribesmen, created in much the same way Bill Colby set up the montagnard program in South Vietnam. This time the mover would be a thirty-two-year-old paramilitary officer named Stewart Methven. Son of an Army officer but too young for World War II, Methven replaced Rufus Phillips in August 1959. A member of the first class to graduate from the CIA's full program at Camp Peary, Methven had previously been a trainer at the agency base on Okinawa. Laos brought him more into politics, and it was while searching for Hmong who were to be incorporated into the Lao government that he met Vang Pao, a Hmong officer of the Royal Laotian Army. Vang Pao jockeyed for power among the tribal elders of his group, and happened to be meeting with some Filipinos who worked in Laos—in another of Ed Lansdale's civic action programs—when Methven showed up. Vang Pao asked for an anvil to forge metal, a request so different from the usual demands for money and weapons that it impressed Methven. Henceforward Methven saw Vang Pao and the Hmong as reaching for a new future, one the CIA could help them attain.

Over the course of a few months Methven won approval from the station chief in Vientiane to pursue a program, and he convinced CIA officials in Thailand to help. "Red" Jantzen, the agency's head in Bangkok, had emphasized support to the Thai police. The Police Aerial Recovery Unit (PARU) agreed to supply the CIA with interpreters and radio men to assist the Americans with the Hmong, who inhabited the part of Laos where the Pathet Lao had their provisional capital and base of operations. In late 1960 Methven, Bill Lair, the CIA case officer with PARU, and a Laotian army officer from the Phoumi forces visited the Hmong and worked out an agreement mobilizing Vang Pao's Hmong for the Laotian war. By January 1961 Vang Pao had 4,300 in his *"armée clandestine,"* or secret army, as the Hmong forces would be known.

The Hmong fought well in the mountains of Laos, the alliance with them the bright star of the CIA's program in the land of a million elephants. But the rest—as well as U.S. policy writ large—melted into a gooey mess. Station chief Gordon L. Jorgensen had difficulty keeping his haughty proconsuls in line but that proved the least of his problems. After the American machinations, Souvanna Phouma refused to speak to anyone from the United States, yet *only* Souvanna had the prestige and central position to captain a unified government. The strongman now in power, General Phoumi, despite the enthusiasm of his CIA minder, would be as ineffective as he was bombastic. And the Pathet Lao saw their chance to ally with Kong Le's forces and move against the Vientiane regime. Russia started an airlift of supplies and equipment to benefit the Pathet Lao and Kong Le. With sudden access to heavy equipment and plentiful supplies, the Pathet Lao pressured the Hmong and soon came to blows with Kong Le as well.

Washington concluded the only way out of this morass would be the redimposition of a neutralist-government in Laos. The Geneva conference reconvened to negotiate an agreement for that solution, but here the anger of Souvanna came home to roost. Des FitzGerald summoned Campbell James, sending him to Souvanna in exile to beg the Lao politician's cooperation. Averell Harriman became the top U.S. negotiator at Geneva. Achieving agreement required reining in the CIA. Jack Hasey fell victim to Harriman, who engineered his recall, along with withdrawal of primary U.S. support for Phoumi. Gordon Jorgensen and Stewart Methven, not to mention FitzGerald himself, all experienced the Crocodile's hearing aid trick. Methven argued without success for more aid to the Hmong. Jorgensen had to cut back Thai cooperation and that of Air America, already flying over a thousand tons a month of assorted supplies within Laos.

Once a cease-fire had been obtained and the coalition government ordained by tripartite agreement among Lao political factions in the summer of 1962, a new Geneva agreement provided for renewed neutralization. The United States pulled out the military mission it had had masquerading as an office to evaluate aid programs. The North Vietnamese were supposed to withdraw their troops from Laos, but only a handful departed, and signs of the Vietnamese presence persisted. This state of play existed when Bill Colby arrived to work at CIA's new headquarters in Langley, Virginia. Colby attended and later was the primary CIA representative at weekly meetings in Harriman's office at the State Department, where Laos was a constant subject. The CIA did not end its involvement after the Geneva accord any more than did Hanoi. Air America continued to deliver supplies all over Laos, including to the Hmong. The tribesmen asked for guns, which led Colby to beg Harriman to approve arms shipments. Some of their conversations became quite heated.

Finally, as Colby described to an audience years later, Harriman agreed, "Okay, one hundred guns, but no attacks, only for defense."[6]

Between the fall of 1962 and the spring of 1963 there were a dozen arms shipments, each requiring Harriman's grudging consent. Colby worked on his growing unease that the Vietnamese had also remained in Laos, arguing that the United States had assumed certain responsibilities for the Hmong, who would have no chance against the Pathet Lao without CIA help.

Desmond FitzGerald's last hurrah on Laos came in December 1962. In the search for some way to communicate with the Pathet Lao, Michael Forrestal of the NSC staff suggested inviting Prince Souphanouvong to Washington. The Prince, cousin of Souvanna Phouma and a top leader of the Pathet Lao, had a hearing problem that might respond to American medical expertise and could furnish humanitarian grounds for the invitation. Desmond FitzGerald supported the idea, as did Harriman and the U.S. ambassador to Laos, Leonard Unger. But the plan was scuttled by several aides to McGeorge Bundy, President Kennedy's national security adviser, as well as Chester Cooper, the CIA's man in the White House.

Bill Colby's first big flap centered around Air America. With officers at Langley preparing a party to welcome Bill as chief of the Far East Division in his own right, soon after the new year, the Pathet Lao shot down an Air America plane on a supply flight to the Hmong. Souvanna Phouma had been told of the Air America system the previous summer and had voiced no objections at that time; now, however, he asked that flights be halted. A government minister insisted the air traffic was unauthorized, and the Pathet Lao charged Air America with ferrying arms to the Hmong secret army. Poland, one of the three countries who were members of the International Control Commission (the others being India and Canada), demanded an ICC investigation of Air America.

Damage control efforts preoccupied Colby at Langley and Harriman at Foggy Bottom (fond colloquial name for the State Department). The CIA agreed that a State Department lawyer would review the history and corporate structure of Air America and its personnel and operations, both inside and outside Laos, in the manner of a trial lawyer advising a client on litigation. The lawyer would provide an opinion as to whether the United States should submit to an ICC investigation. That review went ahead while Mike Forrestal and Roger Hilsman visited Laos to see the situation on the ground for President Kennedy. Forrestal's mid-January report posed problems for Bill Colby:

> This arrangement simply will not stand up under intense political pressure. Despite the fact that our official position is to the contrary, we do not have a firm agreement with Souvanna on supply flights to the Meo [i.e., Hmong]; and under increasing Pathet Lao pressure, he is rapidly backing away from the tacit acceptance he has given them. Add to this the problem with Air America itself. Morale among its pilots has dropped to a point where they cannot be expected to continue flights over enemy territory where they are subject to being shot down. While it is true that the danger has not increased significantly over what it was during the time of the fighting, it is a human fact that these pilots no longer feel that they are engaged in a war and consequently are no longer willing to accept the risks. . . . In addition to this, Air America has become politically about the most unpopular institution in Laos. . . . Souphanouvong has said that . . . almost any other form of American air activity would be an improvement. Souvanna Phouma and [General] Phoumi both dislike it because its personnel have grown so accustomed to behaving as if Laos were not a sovereign country, that they have behaved on occasion in an arrogant way even toward right-wing officials in Vientiane.[7]

Washington's self-examination made clear that security had been good on the Air America weapons flights to the Hmong. On food shipments, the

United States would offer to turn over this function to the Laotian government and argue that Air America had been used only because the Lao lacked major air transport capacity on their own. Later in 1963 the United States gave the Lao two C-46 aircraft acquired from Air America for the very purpose of transporting food. There could be no immediate solution to the problem of pilot morale. An invitation to the ICC to proceed with its investigation of air shipments to Kong Le and the Hmong would be acceptable. The International Control Commission itself gave up the idea when, in repeated incidents, ICC helicopters and aircraft were shot down or damaged by Pathet Lao or Kong Le Forces over the Laotian Plain of Jars, named for the ancient burial urns of a vanished civilization that dot its expanse.

The object of the Air America flights, and of Bill Colby's efforts to preserve secrecy, was the Hmong secret army, known to the CIA as Project Momentum. Colby's chain of command ran to Laos, then to Thailand, then back to Laos, due to the vital intermediary function of the Thai PARUs. At Udorn in Thailand, under the Vientiane station, would be a CIA base innocuously called the 4802 Joint Liaison Detachment, really a cover for Bill Lair who, with deputy Pat Landry, masterminded all paramilitary activities in Laos. In addition to Momentum, these included projects Hardnose, a similar effort in southern Laos, and Millpond, a covert air wing with Thai pilots who flew fighter-bombers identical to those in the Lao air force. Collectively the CIA efforts were known as Project Sky. Behind them all stood Air America, now delivering something on the order of 1,500 tons per month inside Laos.

These arrangements were working smoothly when the Lao foreign minister, a pro-Pathet Lao man, died in a hail of gunfire believed to be from his own bodyguards, who were Kong Le neutralists. Soon after, a senior Kong Le lieutenant was killed by Pathet Lao, and Pathet Lao troops attacked their erstwhile neutralist allies on the Plain of Jars. With the fat in the fire, Hmong secret army units began moving to positions that would enable them to support Kong Le. In Washington, Colby pressed for new Air America arms drops to the Hmong. Declassified cables between Vientiane and Langley demonstrate the U.S. hand in planning and analysis of Hmong strategy in this confrontation, which finally destroyed the cease-fire that had prevailed in Laos. The renewed war that began in April 1963, with all sides still pretending to observe the Geneva agreement, would continue throughout the Indochina conflict.

Almost immediately Colonel Vang Pao showed that the Hmong could have aims of their own apart from those of the CIA. A secret army unit in the Pathet Lao home province made attacks that exceeded CIA authority and escalated the war. This posed a new headache for Colby, just as President Kennedy began a fresh review of Laos policy. Cables from the station in Vientiane reported planned Hmong movements, but also warned of difficulties, as in this message of April 9: "THE PROBLEM OF HAVING THE [HMONG] SUPPORT KONG LE BUT AT THE SAME TIME TRYING TO KEEP THEM FROM GOING TOO FAR HAS BEEN IN OUR MINDS CONSTANTLY SINCE FIGHTING BROKE OUT IN EARNEST LAST WEEK."[8]

The next day President Kennedy held an NSC meeting to consider the Laotian crisis. John McCone opened with the CIA's view of the situation. Averell Harriman, asked to comment in behalf of the State Department, openly agreed with McCone's analysis and advised that Air America continue its flights in support of Vang Pao's secret army and the Kong Le forces. On the eve of a trip to Moscow, where he would meet with Russian leaders on arms control issues as well as on Laos, Harriman gave free rein to the Hmong operation. The CIA never looked back.

Langley, the Pentagon, and the State Department, temporarily in accord over Laos, began hatching plans to beef up the war effort against the Pathet Lao. Ambassador Unger began working quietly with Souvanna Phouma, keeping CIA's Gordon Jorgensen informed, to increase the amount of contact between Vang Pao and Kong Le. President Kennedy ordered U.S. naval forces to nearby positions in the South China Sea. The CIA recommended ending efforts to prevent Vang Pao's taking full offensive action—in fact, that the Hmong be encouraged to cooperate fully with Kong Le's neutralists and General Phoumi's government forces, who were being sent to the Plain of Jars in the guise of "volunteers." In several NSC meetings and private discussions from April 19 to 22, JFK approved all those measures. Bill Colby, who attended the sessions on the 19th and 20th, took notes in addition to those of the official NSC notetaker. Deputy Director Marshall S. Carter spoke for the agency the first day, McCone the second. Both pushed for stocks of arms and ammunition held in Thailand to be released to the Hmong. Kennedy approved. The president referred several times to problems in Cuba in these Laos discussions—the last Bay of Pigs prisoners were then in the course of being released by the Castro government. McCone advocated low altitude photo reconnaissance missions over Cuba regardless of Laos, but at another point warned, Colby notes, "that he did not feel the American people would accept the commitment of military forces in Laos when we were unwilling to make such . . . similar . . . activity in the case of Cuba."[9]

Preparing for the April 22 presidential meeting, the State Department studied the impact of the Geneva Agreements upon various U.S. activities in Laos. There were questions about some types of spy-plane flights, about an August 1962 series of ten Air America missions that had brought back to Vang Pao some 500 of his Hmong tribesmen, taken to Thailand for special training, and about the ammunition supply flights. The U.S. internal inquiry on Air America indicated that any ICC investigation could be faced with confidence, but if a clandestine supply flight were to be uncovered in the future, that would be a problem. The diplomats were also uncomfortable about the presence of Thai PARU scouts, as well as two CIA officers, directly with the Hmong secret army. Meanwhile, that same day Bill Colby reported for the CIA that so far there were no reports of casualties among the Vang Pao forces.

On the ground 4,500 Hmong troops helped defend the Plain of Jars. Under an April 12 agreement directly between Vang Pao and Kong Le, the Hmong were passing to Kong Le some of their CIA-supplied food and weapons.

There were further contributions by Souvanna, Phoumi, and by the CIA directly, for it had stockpiled 8,000 pallets of arms and ammunition in Thailand for immediate airdrop into Laos if needed. All questionable Air America activities had to be suspended at the end of April because ICC monitors visited the Plain of Jars together with Prime Minister Souvanna Phouma. The hiatus was extended when Pathet Lao gunfire damaged the ICC helicopters bearing the visitors. Then Kong Le's forces asked the Americans for 105mm howitzers—pretty heavy artillery—that finally was carried by Air America Caribou aircraft. Use of the CIA proprietary to move artillery pieces marked a new departure for the agency's role in the secret war.

Frustrated Washington officials, Bill Colby among them, concerned at the way the Pathet Lao seemed to have the initiative in Laos, devised a three-phase plan for U.S. action. Langley's input would be key because the CIA had become the main American action agency in Laos. Colby pressed for unleashing the Hmong, creating bigger units with more hitting power, backing them up with covert air power. There were also questions of sending regular U.S. military forces to Thailand to backstop Laos. Many proposed measures contravened the Geneva accords. In the planning meetings that went through June 1963, the category of first phase activities would be used to group together those things officials felt could be done without breaking (or at least, appearing to break) the agreements. This plan accepted direct CIA contact with "pro-West tribal groups," thus recognizing the continuing CIA presence among the Hmong; provided for greater Air America activity in support of the secret army as well as the neutralists; mandated an expansion of the CIA's Hardnose project in southern Laos, including increasing use of South Vietnamese-led cross-border patrols (that were being sponsored by the CIA in Saigon); and expanded Hmong clandestine operations both in as yet unengaged parts of the country and in Pathet Lao-dominated territory. Those activities would intensify, and much else too, if the CIA were ordered to go to Phase 2. Langley anticipated major expansion of the Hmong secret army under this option, with third-country nationals recruited to cadre special units, commando raids against Hanoi's bases in both Laos and North Vietnam, plus untraceable aircraft with either American contract pilots or third-country crews for combat action. The more minor moves could be made without violating Geneva or were plausibly deniable. At the higher level, the U.S. government itself recognized that these were "actions that involve or lead to overt violation of the Geneva Agreements and the introduction of U.S. forces within the Laos-North Vietnam conflict area."[10]

Bill Colby was in the room on June 19 when President Kennedy considered the phased plans for Laos. He heard Kennedy ask, for the first time among such a large group, about the effectiveness of bombing North Vietnam, an action that JFK apparently saw as an alternative to sending U.S. forces to Laos or Thailand. Colby felt that the president discouraged that option. John McCone commented that "the word covert is relevant" since many CIA measures included "would immediately be [come] known and suspicions exist of our involvement." McCone specifically acknowledged to President Kennedy that some of the CIA actions in Phase 1 "would be outside the Agreements."[11] Roger Hilsman of State responded that those actions might be "disavowable" if not better, and Harriman came up with the best rejoinder—that Washington would operate with the approval of Laotian premier Souvanna Phouma, effectively obviating any question of compliance with the Geneva Agreements.

On June 25, in National Security Action Memorandum No. 249, President Kennedy approved Phase 1 for execution, while ordering detailed planning for the contemplated Phase 2. The decision in NSAM 249 amounted to escalation of the war, an escalation Bill Colby supported and advocated. This decision in the summer of 1963 sheds important light on claims made in some histories that John Kennedy was about to withdraw from the Vietnam War when he died. It would have been virtually impossible to withdraw from Vietnam while simultaneously escalating the Laotian war.

At the point of the spear, CIA "control" over the Hmong in the Lao hills came down to two men and what they could achieve. By moderating Vang Pao's requests for arms and equipment, and Hmong demands for air support, and by clearly gaining Vang Pao's trust, the CIA officers stood at the very center of Project Momentum. One man, Anthony Poshepny, better known as Tony Po, spent a good deal of time hiking the backwoods of Laos. Previously involved in operations in Indonesia and Tibet, Po had become a CIA cowboy, albeit one who concerned himself with stock quotations in the *Wall Street Journal*. The junior officer, who lived in Vang Pao's village and gradually came to be the man to see for anything that was important, was a CIA man named Vincent ("Vint") Lawrence.

In the Good War, Vint's father, Captain James Lawrence, had been stationed in Algiers and had helped plan OSS operational group missions to Italy and the Mediterranean islands. A stock broker after the war, Lawrence sent his son to exclusive schools like Exeter and Princeton. Uninspired by the prep school, Vint broke loose at Princeton, where he did so well that by his senior year he had become a credible applicant for a Rhodes Scholarship. Vint managed what Bill Colby never could—to become a member of one of the eating clubs—and it would be a faculty member with the club who scouted Lawrence for the CIA. Along with a couple of dozen others, Vint was discreetly asked to a recruiting seminar. He took the invitation as an honor, like being invited to join one of the exclusive senior clubs, and ended up at CIA's Camp Peary with forty more trainees. That would be followed by the agency's paramilitary course, then the Army's Jungle Warfare Training School in Panama.

Lawrence had gone through Princeton with a commitment to the Army's Reserve Officers Training Corps (ROTC), and so he served out his military obligation while on duty with the agency. He had first been slated to work on the Tibetan project, but Vint had some French from high school and so found himself reassigned to Laos, where he arrived in February 1962. His introduction to Vang Pao came through the Hmong's dedicated IVS helper, an Iowa farmer named Edgar ("Pop") Buell, who in the summer of 1962 flew all over northern Laos with Vang Pao to select a new home base. Lawrence participated in some of these flights, returned to the United States to process out of the Army, then promptly volunteered to return to Laos and work with the Hmong. He lived at Long Tieng, the new settlement, which ultimately grew to 40,000 inhabitants, the second largest city in the country. Vint went about the business of keeping the flow of CIA support to the Hmong quiet but effective. Initially, at least, Tony Po concentrated on strategic advice to Vang Pao. But Po acquired a macabre reputation for things like offering bounties to the Hmong for severed ears of enemies they brought him, and Lawrence plowed steadily ahead. By the end of 1963, when the King of Laos visited the Hmong at Long Tieng for the first time, Lawrence was considered the head CIA man.

Bill Colby paid attention. Lawrence wrote good cables to Langley, infused not merely with the details of operations but also observations on tribal life and culture. Vint began to argue that the Hmong tactical organization, with a militia plus battalion-size special guerrilla units, had about played itself out. Vang Pao needed larger units to face the Pathet Lao, now increasingly being backed by North Vietnamese regular infantry. Colby bought the argument, advocating the change in the Washington policy councils. Laos was set for a new stage of war, but before that could happen, upheaval occurred in Saigon.

8

DEATH IN NOVEMBER

THE CENTRAL INTELLIGENCE AGENCY, more than a monolithic force of secret warriors, often seemed an uneasy alliance of principalities. Among the deepest divisions was that between the warriors and the analysts of intelligence, laborers in the vineyards of information, secret and otherwise, who distilled the predictions, observations, and careful reports the CIA furnished the president and the U.S. government. Langley's analytical component, the Directorate of Intelligence (DDI), along with the analysts in McCone's own office who assembled the fabled national intelligence estimates, are responsible for the widespread opinion among historians and other observers that Vietnam was one thing the CIA got right.

But behind the dry language of the intelligence estimates and reports lay a private, fierce struggle within the agency, a fight, to put it in human terms, for the heart of the director of central intelligence, who both headed the CIA and signed off on the estimates. By no means did analysts win all the battles, and one that occurred early in 1963 set the stage for decisions in Washington that paved America's way to a wider Indochina war. This episode also showed how close the relationship had become between Bill Colby and his director of central intelligence (DCI), John McCone. Even in retrospect observers have largely missed the importance of that deepening tie.

The issue at Langley in the spring of 1963 would be the preparation of a fresh national intelligence estimate (NIE) on Vietnam. An NIE represents the considered judgment of the intelligence community—not only the CIA but all U.S. government agencies that deal in intelligence matters—on some issue of national import. Some NIEs are requested by the president, others appear at regular intervals, yet others result from initiatives within intelligence, not least demands by the director of central intelligence. The NIE was called "Prospects in Vietnam," NIE 53–63, updating an estimate from two years before, and was initiated by Harold P. Ford, of the Far East estimates staff.

John McCone visited Vietnam for the first time in late 1962, with one of the periodic survey groups led by Secretary of Defense Robert McNamara. Though McNamara returned with glowing accounts of improvement in South Vietnam, McCone, who actually favored a much greater scale of U.S. activity, viewed the scene apprehensively. Dick Helms had accompanied McCone to McNamara's office one day in June and recorded the DCI's view that "we are merely chipping away at the toe of the glacier from the North."[1] McCone did not think American programs under way at that time, which included the strategic hamlet program, had much potential in the long term.

Given these opinions, McCone ought to have been impressed with NIE 53–63. Having taken the Office of National Estimates (ONE), which wrote the NIEs, out of the Directorate of Intelligence and put it in his own stable, McCone was not being blindsided by this paper. The initial draft of the estimate would be crafted beginning in September 1962 by Harold Ford and George Carver, who had transferred into the intelligence analysis business after his cover was blown in the 1960 coup attempt. Carver had every reason to dislike the Diem regime, and indeed he was known to believe the war could not be won with Diem at the helm, but ONE's manager for the estimate, Willard Matthias, found Carver's paper balanced. The draft had some good analysis, new data, and so on. Matthias felt the paper had organizational problems—nothing major—but most important, it only implied a possibility for swifter progress under a post-Diem Vietnamese government. There was no claim that Diem had to go. There *was* solid buttressing for the view that the Vietnam war had stalled. The January 1963 battle at Ap Bac, where Viet Cong soldiers stood their ground and defeated South Vietnamese troops backed by helicopters and armored personnel carriers, added further substance to that view.

Instead of aligning himself with the draft estimate, when it went before the United States Intelligence Board on February 27, John McCone savaged the NIE. Sherman Kent, director of ONE's parent Board of National Estimates, found himself upbraided for permitting a presentation whose conclusions were so much more somber than those of "the people who know Vietnam best."[2] McCone ordered revision based on the opinions of senior operators, vitiating the firewall that in theory protects intelligence estimates from simply telling policy makers what they want to hear. According to Director McCone, the people who knew best were Bill Colby; his chief of station, John Richardson; the Army's chief of staff and its South Vietnam commander, Ambassador Frederick Nolting, the naval commander in the Pacific, State's Roger Hilsman, and the NSC staffer for Southeast Asia, Michael Forrestal. George Carver prepared a memorandum defending the NIE, but his boss, Sherman Kent, supervised as ONE sought the opinions of those McCone had enumerated. Analysts met personally with Colby one morning at Langley to revise the paper.

The resulting NIE 53–63, which McCone approved and the CIA published on April 17, flatly concluded, "We believe that Communist progress has been blunted and that the situation is improving." The estimate credited a strengthened South Vietnamese military plus U.S. involvement for the trend. Analysts managed to preserve a warning that no persuasive data existed proving the Viet Cong had been grievously hurt and a statement that "the situation remains fragile," but the estimate exuded optimism. In what could have been a genuflection to Colby's view, the NIE concluded that "developments in the last year or two also show some promise of resolving the political weaknesses" of the Diem government, and embedded in the body of the estimate was a statement that the same developments had "gone some distance in establishing a basis for winning over the peasantry."[3] John McCone felt pleased at that moment but ultimately would be embarrassed, later apologizing to Sherman Kent for forcing the estimates staff into this kind of corrupted procedure.

Willard Matthias and Harold P. Ford, both former CIA officers with ONE or its parent board, have written about the episode of the Vietnam estimate. In explaining McCone's actions, Ford in his monograph *CIA and the Vietnam Policymakers* notes two factors of influence. Undoubtedly the more important would be Cuba—in yet another intrusion into Vietnam history—for the Board of National Estimates had erred dramatically in some special estimates on Cuba, predicting that Russia would never station nuclear weapons there and promptly proved spectacularly wrong by the Cuban Missile Crisis. The other factor would be McCone's network of friends. Ford mentions former president Dwight Eisenhower, in whose cabinet the CIA director had served, and to whom McCone was now President Kennedy's designated envoy. There was also Marine general Victor H. Krulak, the Pentagon's point man on counterinsurgency and a favorite of Jack Kennedy. Krulak and McCone were golf partners and frequent companions.

It is Bill Colby who goes unmentioned, yet it is Colby who arguably had the greatest impact on the CIA director's thinking about Vietnam. In the clandestine service of the CIA, it was Colby who was the expert, and he was also the recent station chief back from Saigon. Richard Helms deferred to Colby on matters of Far East operations; why should not McCone? In fact, McCone began taking positions and making statements very close to Bill Colby's views. McCone switched on Vietnam between summer 1962 and early 1963, and the obvious change on the seventh floor at Langley insofar as Vietnam was concerned was the arrival of Bill Colby as chief of the Far East Division. The key evidence is what John McCone himself called Colby in a 1970 interview: "The man who was most important in CIA's affairs in South Vietnam for the last ten years."[4]

In Washington in early 1963, Vietnam had momentarily ceased to be a presidential issue. The leading edge of policy would be the NSC's Special Group (Counterinsurgency). John McCone, who represented the CIA on that group, went to just one of its Vietnam deliberations during the interval before August, when political heat in Saigon attained a critical level. Richard Helms filled in at one other meeting. Colby represented the CIA twice as often as either of them. Those sessions reviewed such issues as the strategic hamlet program and the CIDG project, now slated for turnover to the U.S. military. The Special Group, without much success, also ruminated about the Vietnamese Buddhist problem.

Actually the situation in Vietnam began sharpening rapidly within just a couple of weeks of McCone's publication of his ill-starred national estimate on Vietnam. In South Vietnam, religion became a political issue dividing the Diem regime from the populace. An incident at Hue became the catalyst. It directly involved Diem's family—his brother, Ngo Dinh Thuc, happened to be the Catholic archbishop of Hue and celebrated his 25th anniversary jubilee in early May. Catholics paraded through Hue's streets bearing religious flags in violation of laws Diem had approved in 1958 prohibiting display of anything other than the national flag. A few days later, on May 8, Vietnamese Buddhists paraded to celebrate the 2,527th birthday of Buddha and, like the Catholics, they attempted to carry their flag.

The province chief was Ngo Dinh Can, another of Diem's brothers, and he ordered out the army in response to the Buddhists. When a monk (called a "bonze"), Thich Tri Quang, was denied the opportunity to broadcast an anniversary message for the occasion, ten thousand Vietnamese marched on the radio station. Can then ordered the army to suppress the Buddhists. Accounts conflict on whether the troop commander, Major Dang Sy, made any preliminary effort to disperse the crowd, but the army then fired on the civilians, and an armored car crushed some of the demonstrators. Eight people died, twenty were injured. The Diem government put out the story that the Buddhists had been killed by a hand grenade rolled into the crowd, ostensibly by a Viet Cong operative. West German doctors, however, had witnessed the entire event, confirming the Buddhist version of the incident. Tri Quang controlled the crowds, which several times threatened to get out of hand, but in Saigon on May 28 Buddhist bonzes began the first sustained protests against the Diem regime. On June 11 in a harrowing demonstration, bonze Thich Quang Duc immolated himself at the intersection of two busy Saigon streets.

"I believe that the Buddhist revolt," Colby would say in 1981, "had its major impact not in Vietnam but in the United States. When that picture of the burning bonze appeared in *Life* magazine, the party was almost over in terms of the imagery that was affecting . . . American opinion."[5] The secret warrior argued that this shift in opinion put enormous pressure on President Kennedy, on the grounds that the United States had no business supporting a regime like that of Diem, and that this led to JFK's vacillating in August, when the die would be cast for fateful moves.

Nothing if not consistent, Colby's recollection in 1981 mirrored his position inside government in 1963, and indeed his historical judgment in books and speeches until his death. It is important to recognize, however, that these arguments represent loyalties constructed during the years in Saigon. As a historical matter Colby's position is just not tenable. As the Far East spy chief saw it, the government had been winning the war, the Buddhist protests amounted to a tangential matter, and really the issue was to get on with it. In August, as we shall see shortly, when Ngo Dinh Nhu sent troops to smash the Buddhist temples, Colby would maintain that Diem had thereby eliminated the Buddhists as a political factor the same way he had done with the politico-religious sects in 1955. According to this view since Buddhist demonstrations died down in the months immediately succeeding, and because Buddhist activism had not become an issue except in the main cities, the way had been cleared to move forward. Only *American* opinion, in Colby's view, remained an obstacle. As he put this in a talk in 1996, "it was a turning point in the American psyche."[6]

Through Saigon station chief John Richardson, Colby continued to have a direct line of communication to Ngo Dinh Nhu. As far as he knew, Diem remained privy to that channel, but the CIA had no independent knowledge that that was the case. The question of what "Jocko" Richardson learned and how he interpreted it is a significant one. Born in Rangoon, later from Whittier, California, and a college classmate of Richard Nixon, Richardson's bluff manner and husky, tall body, complete with a birthmark on his neck, befitted his nickname. His knowledge of Asia remained sketchy, however. Jocko arrived at the CIA by way of the U.S. Army's Counterintelligence Corps, which had sent him to Italy in World War II. He had captained units of the CIA's predecessor organization in Trieste and Vienna after the war, in which he gained some fame in the capture of a notorious German agent, Carla Rossi. At the CIA, Richardson headed the Southeast Europe branch of DDP and served as chief of station in Athens. Not until 1958 would Jocko discover the East, and then it would be Manila, where Des FitzGerald wanted a man of action in charge. Replacing Colby in Saigon was Richardson's first exposure to Vietnam.

With French among his four or five languages, Richardson could get around in "the Paris of the Orient," but he knew very little. A good illustration would be the difficulty Jocko and his wife, Ethyl, had hiring any servants for the big, attractive home he had rented on a shady street. It seems that lot had been the site of an interrogation center used by French military intelligence, then Japanese intelligence, then the Viet Minh security forces in 1945, and finally again the French Sûreté. Thousands of captives must have passed through the house, and the Vietnamese were convinced the place had become haunted. The CIA chief ended up hiring a team of Buddhist monks who spent a week exorcising the spirits, then hung up ghost-repellent mirrors. Only then would Vietnamese consent to work at the house. Now Richardson busily fed Bill Colby's thirst for facts to argue Buddhism had no importance in Saigon.

Unfortunately for Richardson and Colby, the facts were otherwise. Eighty percent of South Vietnam's population were considered Buddhists (Saigon's embassy in Washington actually put out literature during the 1960s estimating the figure as high as 90 percent). Although a substantial portion were really only nominally Buddhist, practicing forms of animism, the remaining fraction of religious Buddhists certainly outnumbered South Vietnam's Catholics by a considerable margin.

Spearheaded by monks who were sophisticated politically but inexperienced socially, Vietnamese Buddhists continued steady protests against the Diem regime. The bonzes took care to keep American reporters like David Halberstam and Malcolm Browne appraised of their actions, contributing to Saigon government crackdowns on the journalists, which then led to negative reporting with consequent adverse shifts in opinion in the United States. This vicious circle only played against Diem. On June 16 Diem promised reforms and opened talks with the Buddhists, but talks dragged and Madame Nhu spoke sarcastically about bonze "barbeques," while Nhu himself demanded a hard line, resisting concessions. There was little evident progress.

On August 21 Nhu took advantage of recently declared martial law to use troops he controlled for destructive raids on the Buddhist pagodas, their places of worship, including one of the most important, Saigon's An Quang temple. Four companies of Nhu's Special Forces, the troops used, had been funded by the CIA at a price of $250,000 per month. Nhu's reliance on military units paid by the Americans made it look like the Buddhist repression had been carried out by the Vietnamese army and the CIA.

Throughout these vital days the Far East Division chief stayed in daily touch with Jocko Richardson. As Colby wrote, "I have to say that I didn't then—nor, in fact, do I in retrospect now—regard the Buddhist situation itself as quite the serious crisis that it was considered in Washington. Indeed, I agreed with Diem and Nhu."[7] Colby insisted that if the United States gave Diem the support he needed, Washington would be able to influence Diem to conciliate the Buddhists while continuing to fight the Viet Cong.

By his own account, Colby acknowledges that John McCone depended on his, Colby's, knowledge of the Vietnamese scene and leadership. The CIA director made a key error here because the Far East division chief's understanding of the Buddhist factor in Vietnamese politics remained far off the mark. What made the issue explosive was not where the protests occurred but the renaissance of this religion in Vietnam, a move that had been in progress for over four decades. It was on a collision course with the apparent favoritism toward Catholics of Ngo Dinh Diem, himself a staunch Catholic who had spent time in a monastery before his return to Vietnam. Diem's hodge-podge philosophy of "personalism," it is true, remained secular, in no way religious. But 700,000 of the more than 900,000 who came south after the 1954 ceasefire were Catholics, and Diem made open concessions to Catholics while Buddhists were killed for flying a flag. Of those generals in the South Vietnamese army whose religion is known, *70 percent* were raised as Catholics, in a population that was only between 10 and 20 percent Catholic overall. Revealingly, an *additional* 16 percent of Vietnamese generals *converted* to Catholicism after Diem's rise to power. Nguyen Van Thieu stood among them. Most telling of all, only four Vietnamese generals would admit to being Buddhists, out of a cohort of almost a hundred. Civilian ministers in the Diem government were of similar persuasion. One can argue that this disparity existed not just because of Diem but because of a French colonial policy that had created an indigenous elite using Catholicism as a means of ascription. But one cannot maintain, particularly as Buddhist protests were happening almost daily, that the rise of Buddhism activism lacked any importance.

The truth was that Buddhism had grown powerful over a long period. Regional religious associations dated from the 1930s, the same decade that brought the emergence of the Indochinese Communist Party, and the national association had begun by 1951. The An Quang pagoda in Saigon, built in 1950, symbolized the growth of the religion. Between 1956 and 1962 the number of higher schools for monks more than doubled; the number of pagodas rose from 3,491 to 4,766, and 1,295 of the older ones were renovated. The General Association of Buddhists, headquartered at Saigon's Xa Loi Pagoda and representing only six of the sixteen sects of Mahayana Buddhism in South Vietnam, claimed a membership of three million, with 70,000 to 90,000 in its youth groups, 3,000 monks, and 600 nuns. Beyond these numbers the reality would be that Vietnamese Buddhism wanted to flex its political muscles and, far from Diem being the issue of concern, it would take three years for the Buddhist issue to play out in South Vietnam. "I've talked to some of the leaders," Colby would say in retrospect, asserting that their ideas about how to organize a society were about as realistic as those of Ayatollah Khomeini in Iran.[8] McGeorge Bundy, who met Thich Tri Quang on a later visit to Vietnam, would have agreed. But that did not mean the bonzes had no political power; the ayatollahs, after all, took over Iran, ruling for decades. Ngo Dinh Nhu's pagoda raids represented a bid for power, a declaration of war. Just days earlier the August 16, 1963, issue of *Life* magazine had carried an interview with Madame Nhu in which she again talked of "barbeques" of Buddhist monks.

General Tran Van Don, commanding the South Vietnamese army, at headquarters when he learned on the radio of the pagoda occupation, rushed to the scene. Thirty-three persons, mostly monks, were injured as police and troops stormed the buildings; 1,420 bonzes were taken into custody, with the regime planning to send those from outside Saigon back to their monasteries. The damage included looting and destruction of priceless statuary in the pagodas. General Don had been in the room when President Diem ordered the raids to be carried out without harming anyone.

New York Times reporter David Halberstam found himself summoned to the side of the CIA's John Richardson. Halberstam had lunched with Jocko when the CIA man first took over as station chief and saw him as preoccupied with counterinsurgency, pleasant enough, and dedicated, but clearly a conservative. Halberstam was never sure he understood the things Richardson would say, but the day of the raids the CIA station chief would be crystal clear. Richardson was trying to counter the rumor current in Saigon that the CIA knew all about Nhu's raids.

"It's not true," declared Richardson, looking haggard and shaken. "We just didn't know. We just didn't *know*, I can assure you."[9]

The scrambling to avoid responsibility became widespread in Saigon. In fact, General Don's encounter with Diem took place precisely because Ngo Dinh Nhu wanted to spread the blame beyond his own door. Nhu also spoke with various groups of generals, according to CIA field reports, in ways that were rather unsettling to Washington. One conversation involved his plan to exert greater control over the land. Another, on August 15, had Nhu declaring that the United States had changed *its* policies in ways detrimental to Saigon—by concluding a treaty banning atmospheric nuclear testing with Russia—which Nhu viewed as appeasement. Nhu told the generals it was of "utmost importance" that the South Vietnamese army work more closely with his Republican Youth organization as well as Madame Nhu's Women's Solidarity Movement.[10]

The dimensions of the challenge were apparent in other quarters at Langley even as the Far East Division continued to deny its implications. By the summer of 1963 the national estimate on South Vietnam seemed so glaringly off reality that John McCone asked his estimators to revise the paper. The result appeared in mid-July in the guise of a "scope note" to NIE 53-63. This baldly concluded that "the Buddhist crisis in South Vietnam has highlighted and intensified a widespread and longstanding dissatisfaction with the Diem regime and its style of government." The CIA analysts judged it "likely" that Diem would fail to carry out his pledges to the Buddhists, with further disorder to follow, along with "better than even" chances of a coup or assassination attempt against Ngo Dinh Diem.[11]

The discussion section of the paper contained the observation that "The chances of a non-Communist coup—and of its success—would become greater in the event renewed [government]/Buddhist confrontation should lead to large-scale demonstrations in Saigon." The pagoda raids came exactly six weeks later. Only two days after Nhu's crackdown, General Don talked to his CIA contact in an effort to distance the generals from the regime's actions, hinting also at plans he could not divulge. The implication a coup was in the offing became obvious. Washington scrambled to cope with unfolding events.

One measure designed to show U.S. concern would be the replacement of Frederick Nolting as ambassador by Henry Cabot Lodge. Jack Kennedy wanted a badge of bipartisan cooperation on policy for Vietnam while Lodge, Boston Brahmin and Republican presidential contender, wished to serve in some international troublespot; Saigon fit both their agendas. Before arrival in Vietnam on August 22, Lodge stopped at Honolulu for a powwow at the seat of the United States Pacific Command. The CIA sent Bill Colby to this conference, and Nolting stopped on his way home to brief the incoming ambassador. Nolting remained a Diem supporter at this late date, as was Colby, who concerned himself with making sure Lodge was informed about CIA projects in progress in Vietnam. Senior State Department delegate would be Roger Hilsman, recent successor to Harriman as assistant secretary for the Far East, and one who had held extensive conversations with Colby about the possibility of a Saigon coup just before leaving Washington. Colby got John Richardson to supply the Saigon station's latest evaluations of the potential, which boiled down to a maybe. The view of Nhu's chances of succeeding Diem was, at best, fair in the case of an orderly transfer of power and virtually impossible otherwise. The station saw no civilian figure of stature acceptable to all factions. It would be in this setting that Colby and the others first heard the news of the pagoda raids.

Cabot Lodge arrived in Saigon the next day. No doubt Nhu's orchestration of the raids appeared to him an effort to preempt changes in U.S. policy. Nhu's American contact man, of course, remained Jocko Richardson, and Lodge also discovered soon enough, that Jocko had a house bigger than the ambassador's residence. For reasons not clear in the sources, but in which these personal factors may have figured, Lodge decided the Saigon station was less well informed than he had expected. In that climate Lodge confronted a sudden request from Vietnamese generals for a statement of what the U.S. response might be in a coup against Ngo Dinh Diem. What followed set America irrevocably on course toward a shooting war in Southeast Asia.

THERE CAN BE NO DOUBT the South Vietnamese generals, no less than the United States government, wished to disassociate themselves from Nhu's strikes against the Buddhists. Indeed, not only the generals were appalled. Tran Van Chuong, Vietnamese ambassador in Washington and the father of Madame Nhu, resigned his post with a blast at the Diem regime. All but two of the embassy staff followed him. On the American side a public statement appeared that deplored the pagoda attacks, followed by a Voice of America broadcast attributing them to Ngo Dinh Nhu, hinting at a cutoff of aid to Diem if he did not rid himself of certain associates. Nhu expected a negative response and had done his best to delay one, as indicated by the way he arranged for all telephone service (except for a single line into military headquarters) to be cut off to the U.S. embassy and residences the moment the crackdown started.

The Vietnamese political crisis quickly got personal. A Joint General Staff spokesman revealed, to refute claims of Nhu's role in the Buddhist strikes, that the action had been collectively proposed to Diem by his generals. At that point General Tran Van Don, just made chief of the Joint General Staff at Nhu's instigation, approached CIA officer Lucien Conein. The latter, a Colby colleague from Jedburgh days, was on his third tour in Vietnam, working with Vietnamese security agencies, and had known Tran Van Don for almost a decade. They crossed paths at the Saigon nightclub of the Caravelle hotel, which was hosting a party; Don brought Conein to his office at the JGS compound at Tan Son Nhut for a three-hour conversation. General Don related a full account of the South Vietnamese military's small role in Nhu's planning, described their meeting with Diem, related their doubts about Nhu, and hinted at the existence of plots against him. Conein, who was apprehensive about this meeting and who had arrived armed, was reassured. Don, who had begun scheming for a coup d'état in June, saw the CIA as the Americans and his talk with Conein as "some missionary work for the army with them."[12]

Conein's news reached an embassy electrified by the raids and the nearly simultaneous arrival of Henry Cabot Lodge. The ambassador's picture from Honolulu, and his audience with President Kennedy just before departure, had assured him of two things: that JFK worried about Saigon and wanted action there, and that coup talk had been in the wind. Colby's detailed CIA papers on potential coup forces in South Vietnam and the loyalties of prospective players made it clear that Langley was already aware that the unstable conditions in Saigon could lead to conflagration. Almost simultaneously with Conein, another channel reported similar information to Lodge. That was Don's brother-in-law, General Le Van Kim, through Agency for International Development head Rufus Phillips. A former CIA man and fellow member, with Conein, of Ed Lansdale's 1954–55 Saigon mission, Phillips had no compunction about reporting Kim's message that if the United States took a clear stand against Nhu, the South Vietnamese army would unite to oust him. Ambassador Lodge stood at the precipice not yet ready to jump. He cabled Washington: "SUGGESTION HAS BEEN MADE THAT U.S. HAS ONLY TO INDICATE TO 'GENERALS' THAT IT WOULD BE HAPPY TO SEE DIEM AND/OR NHUS GO, AND DEED WOULD BE DONE." As Lodge saw it, "SITUATION IS NOT SO SIMPLE, IN OUR VIEW."[13]

Sent shortly before midnight, this cable burst upon a surprised Washington on a Saturday morning. It demanded a response, urgently, in what seemed a fast-moving Saigon political maneuver. But President Kennedy had left for Hyannis on Cape Cod, and secreteries of state and defense Dean Rusk and Robert S. McNamara were also out of town. So was John McCone of CIA, on vacation at his sprawling home in San Marino, California. It would be left to subordinates to deal with the cable, Embassy Telegram 314 of August 24, 1963. It is important to note this, because what happened then has often been presented as a cabal in Washington to stimulate a coup in Saigon. The culprits are seen to be Averell Harriman and Roger Hilsman at the State Department, Michael Forrestal at the NSC, and Ambassador Lodge.

The first thing to understand is that some reply had to be made. Vietnamese generals talking about a coup d'etat did not make some minor issue that could be left for next week's business. Harriman had moved up to undersecretary of state, with Hilsman assistant secretary for the Far East, but he had been thinking about the problem of Ngo Dinh Nhu since at least the first months of 1962, when Averell advocated sending Nhu to Paris as Vietnamese ambassador. Hilsman and Forrestal had made a recent visit to Saigon and were well aware of the loss of confidence in Nhu. They drafted a cable, but something of this import needed top-level attention. Undersecretary of state George W. Ball, senior man in Washington that day, had gone off to Burning

Tree for a round of golf with diplomat U. Alexis Johnson. His only good approach shot of the day came on the ninth hole, and that is when Ball found Harriman and Hilsman waiting for him, with news of Lodge's cable and the text of their proposed reply. It was, Ball thought, "obviously explosive." He refused to send it without direct approval from President Kennedy, but he did not object to the cable other than to improve it: "I had thought for some time that we could not retain our self-respect as a nation so long as we supinely accepted the Nhus' noxious activities."[14]

From Foggy Bottom, Ball telephoned Hyannis Port and spoke to JFK, who seemed favorable but wanted more top-level approvals. Secretary Rusk in New York added a codicil about arms assistance to the South Vietnamese army, then approved. Roswell Gilpatric, sitting in for McNamara, approved for the secretary of defense. The chairman of the Joint Chiefs of Staff, General Maxwell Taylor, eating at a restaurant, could not be found, but Victor Krulak approved in his place. At Langley Richard Helms was duty officer that day. He too approved. Hilsman reports Helms added a remark that "the time had clearly come to take a stand."[15]

Washington's cable 243 contained this ominous language:

> US GOVERNMENT CANNOT TOLERATE SITUATION IN WHICH POWER LIES IN NHU'S HANDS. DIEM MUST BE GIVEN CHANCE TO RID HIMSELF OF NHU AND HIS COTERIE AND REPLACE THEM WITH BEST POLITICAL AND MILITARY PERSONALITIES AVAILABLE.
>
> IF, IN SPITE OF ALL YOUR EFFORTS, DIEM REMAINS OBDURATE AND REFUSES, THEN WE MUST FACE THE POSSIBILITY THAT DIEM HIMSELF CANNOT BE PRESERVED.[16]

Lodge was asked to tell the key military leaders that *unless* steps were taken to improve the Saigon situation, the United States would find it impossible to continue support for the regime. This amounted to a green light for a coup.

Trying to catch up on work of a Saturday, Bill Colby learned of the cable from Dick Helms, who eventually also reached CIA deputy director Marshall S. Carter. They decided to await Cabot Lodge's response before taking action. Cable 243 went to Washington dispatchers at 9:36 P.M. By his own account, Colby heard that evening that an important telegram had been sent and he returned to Langley, to the CIA operations center, to read it. Analyst Hal Ford writes Colby had not seen the cable, but he must have, since Bill phoned John McCone and, again by his own account, read the text. McCone wanted to see hard copy.

Soon there was a Saigon message from Jocko Richardson: at an embassy meeting the consensus had been Diem would never remove Nhu voluntarily, so the time had come for the CIA to survey the generals more seriously as to who favored a coup. Some of that came almost instantly from CIA's Alphonse G. Spera, at home for the siesta hour on the 25th when General Nguyen Khanh, a known Buddhist, stopped by. Khanh commanded the

Central Highlands, having saved Diem in the 1960 coup, and now he felt ready enough to do the opposite that he wanted to know, specifically and soon, whether U.S. aid extended beyond bland disapproval of the Nhus to concrete help for the army if it took over the government. Khanh and Spera had worked closely enough for long enough that the South Vietnamese general evidently believed he was not sticking his neck out in broaching this subject. Spera naturally went straight to Richardson.

Almost right away a cable arrived from Colby over McCone's signature (Director 63855). Langley here told Richardson it had not seen the notorious State Department cable, or been consulted on it, but that "IN CIRCUMSTANCE BELIEVE CIA MUST FULLY ACCEPT DIRECTIVES OF POLICY MAKERS." Moreover, Colby went on, this should be done despite his belief the action contemplated "APPEARS TO BE THROWING AWAY BIRD IN HAND BEFORE WE HAVE ADEQUATELY IDENTIFIED BIRDS IN BUSH, OR SONGS THEY MAY SING."[17] This put Richardson on notice that the channel Khanh had opened to the CIA represented approved agency activity.

In Bill Colby's view there were two things wrong with what happened. First, he believed a move against Ngo Dinh Nhu to be wrong, counterproductive to American interests in Vietnam. John McCone accepted that view, backed Colby up, and argued this position in the councils of government. Second, while standard procedures had been followed in securing approvals, Colby felt, the substance of the cable amounted to a policy end run around working level staffs at CIA and the Pentagon. With McCone's demand to see more, Bill Colby now mounted an end run of his own, phoning Mike Forrestal at the White House. A key actor in this episode, Forrestal knew how important the cable was, and he could not deny the CIA its say. Forrestal put Colby in touch with National Security Adviser McGeorge Bundy. The latter arranged for an Air Force executive plane, one that normally served the White House, to fly Colby to California.

So Bill spent his Sunday on a flash trip where he told the director of central intelligence how Harriman and Hilsman had engineered this move without consulting the various departments. Of course, Hilsman *was* the working level at State, as was Forrestal for the NSC staff; at the Pentagon the working member would be William P. Bundy, McGeorge's brother, and he was also away—in France on vacation. The Joint Chiefs had no authority in this situation, but Roswell Gilpatric had read the cable to General Maxwell Taylor, though only after it was sent, while Harriman also took steps to bring him in. Taylor did consider the maneuver an end run, but his boss Robert McNamara writes, "I do not share Max's view that the cable represented an egregious end run."[18]

That leaves Colby himself. The cabal on policy for dealing with Diem and Nhu was not one of Hilsman and Harriman but of the CIA.

Bill Colby and John McCone began with senior officials. One of those who get quiet and cold when they get mad, McCone was angry now. Aborting his vacation, he returned to Washington in Colby's White House jet. In a furious round of telephoning, the CIA director enlisted allies. Max Taylor proved an easy recruit. Secretary of Defense McNamara, in spite of his comment quoted above, raised questions regarding the notion of supporting a coup, beginning at a meeting JFK held on August 26 while Colby and McCone were on their way back from California.

The key White House meeting occurred late in the afternoon on August 27. McCone could not make it, nor could his deputy, General Marshall S. Carter, who had represented the agency the previous day, seconded by Richard Helms. Now Dick Helms led, with Colby as the CIA back bencher. It would be the Far East division chief who actually opened, however, with a brief account of conditions in Saigon. Colby described the situation as quiet, emphasized unrest had not spread to the countryside, and talked of the South Vietnamese generals as being divided. Helms said nothing. Secretary of state Rusk, whom Bobby Kennedy remembered as having been all over the map, actually backed up the policy in his cable, at both these meetings. John Kennedy, whom Bobby defended in a 1964 interview, expressed agreement with the policy of a coup *if* it worked. Of course no one could guarantee that.

Dean Rusk, therefore, made the key point, as early as August 26: "Unless a major change . . . can be engineered, we must actually decide whether to move our resources out or to move our troops in."[19]

The instructions would be a confirmation of the policy set on August 24 but with orders to proceed cautiously. In Saigon Ambassador Lodge came to this independently, meeting with his embassy team the same day to decide that in all actions the hand of the United States must remain hidden. John Richardson reported this approvingly to the CIA but soon incurred the ambassador's wrath. Max Taylor communicated by back channel with General Paul Harkins in Saigon, complaining about the coup policy, and Harkins handed a copy of Taylor's message to Lucien Conein, who brought it to Richardson. Lodge walked into the office to catch the CIA man red-handed and demanded he be given the document. The ambassador believed the CIA had communicated his private views without approval. From that day, Lodge denied State's cable traffic to the CIA station.

Over the short term, Colby's fears of a coup were relieved by the Vietnamese themselves, courtesy of CIA bungling. Approached by two generals, the agency went back to two. One, at the Joint General Staff, a subordinate of Tran Van Don, turned out to be poorly regarded by Nguyen Khanh. Meanwhile the Khanh approach turned into a huge fiasco when Al Spera, having gone to Pleiku for renewed contact, got arrested upon entering the army compound. The blustery Italian American demanded he be put in touch with the general, and Khanh duly got a call from his senior U.S. adviser, who reported Spera was being held at the bachelor officers' quarters. General Khanh insisted he had business with the American and Spera was released. But the agency man's purpose was to lay down a line Khanh didn't want to hear: that America would support the generals but they had to succeed on their own. And when he learned the CIA had been in touch with the Joint

General Staff Khanh exploded over the breach in security. In fact, no coup d'état took place that August.

Ngo Dinh Nhu almost certainly knew or suspected the plot. Spera's detention had been a subtle sign of displeasure and Nhu controlled Saigon's security services. The newspaper *Times of Vietnam,* a Nhu mouthpiece, printed an exposé of CIA political meddling accusing the agency of being behind coup talk in the capital. Nhu could have been speculating, he might have learned what he knew from General Harkins, or, alternatively, from his regular CIA interlocutor, John H. Richardson. Further enraged, Henry Cabot Lodge decided the CIA station chief had been the culprit. Thereafter the embassy became a cold place indeed.

But back in Washington, Richardson's evaluations of the Saigon atmosphere were the ones reported at White House meetings, which persisted through several more days. Bill Colby emphasized two things in his briefings: that troop movements were insignificant, the hidden meaning being that the generals were not doing anything; and that the United States had reached a point of no return, meaning this was the time and place to change course. Ambassador Lodge saw the same thing but felt the Rubicon had already been crossed, remarking in one cable, "There is no respectable turning back."[20]

Nor did all at Langley believe as did Bill Colby. One of his Saigon friends, George Carver, is the paradigm case. Upon seeing the State cable, Marshall Carter asked Carver for an analysis, and the latter had maintained that a coup d'état in fact represented the best hope for preserving U.S. interests, providing it happened soon and with sufficient force to avoid degenerating into civil war. In a revised memorandum on August 28, Carver raised the stark possibility that the risks of *not* attempting the coup "are even greater than those involved in trying it," since so long as Nhu remained there would be virtually no chance of achieving American goals.[21]

The generals did not move at that moment, but any chance of Colby's winning his point disappeared when Langley learned that Ngo Dinh Nhu had made contact with the North Vietnamese. During the last days of August more evidence on this point became available, while the CIA also heard about Nhu's plans to stymie any coup, which Richard Helms described to a top level meeting on August 30. Dean Rusk continued to frame the issue in the starkest—but most realistic—light. "Our present position . . . [is] stage one," Rusk told a different meeting a week later. "There may be no stage two if we decide to pull out . . . we might tell Diem that we wish him well. Diem may be able to win the war without us, but this is unlikely. Prior to actually pulling out, we might want to consider promoting a coup."[22]

As Bill Colby saw the situation, the activists in the administration had a plan and pushed hard. He grouped Dean Rusk squarely among them. One might add that their policy, courtesy of the notorious August cable, had already gone into force. But was the policy well thought through? "I do not remember one serious discussion in all that summer as to *who* would succeed Ngo Dinh Diem," Colby would say in 1996. The declassified record bears him out.[23]

On the other hand, the dissenters, principally McNamara, Taylor, and John McCone, were crippled in having no positive policy to promote. Colby acknowledges that too. McNamara, in his memoir *In Retrospect*, laments that the rush to a coup deflected the Kennedy administration from seriously considering neutralization of Vietnam, along the lines of the 1962 Laos agreement, a proposal encouraged by France at that time. Senior Hanoi officials, including politburo member and deputy foreign minister Nguyen Co Thach, acknowledged at a June 1997 conference with McNamara and other former American officials and historians, that perhaps a 1963 neutralization was a "missed opportunity" of the Vietnam war. But the unanswered question is how that end could have been achieved, and the point of departure in 1963 would have been Ngo Dinh Nhu's contacts with Hanoi. Since Nhu's purpose seems to have been primarily to remind Washington that the United States was not the only show in town, the Nhu channel could not form a serious basis for a grand negotiation on neutralization. More likely than not, Nhu would have dropped the channel as soon as either Washington or Hanoi evinced serious interest.

For a long time Colby too wrestled with the quandary of what could have been the alternative in 1963. Thirty-two years later he offered two possible outcomes, both of which he saw as preferable to what actually happened. One would have been that Diem continued in power and failed, which Colby believed would have happened in another year or two. This course required a U.S. withdrawal, and that alternative had been posed by the activist Rusk, not by any of Colby's dissenters. The other possibility Colby saw was for Diem to have left Vietnam, then returned later, resuming the strategic hamlet program. The former CIA man estimated that Diem could have had the security situation in hand by 1965, though he would have taken a few additional years to win the war. This is a false alternative. Ngo Dinh Diem had no reason to give up leadership in Saigon—unless pushed by the generals—and no mechanism by which he could give away power only to resume it later. No deal Diem could offer would have been acceptable to South Vietnamese generals ready to oust the man in a coup d'état. And such a deal could only have been imposed by the United States, which would have assumed a responsibility just as great as that acquired by promoting the generals' coup.

President Kennedy, uneasy though he was, continued to back the approved policy, angry at the dissension in his top ranks. But dissension not only existed around the table at the National Security Council. At Langley there would be dissent as well, both between the intelligence directorate and clandestine service, and within Colby's own Far East Division. The most important dissenter within the directorate of plans would be Colby, who continued to dispute the need to oust Nhu or overthrow Diem. And there were others who believed that to be the correct course. Despite his disagreement, Colby ordered John Richardson to follow instructions from Ambassador Lodge, which meant that CIA officers in the field implemented a policy their superiors opposed. Colby has argued that this is an example showing that the CIA is not a policy organization, but here the declassified record contradicts him, for it is replete with instances in which his boss, John McCone, advocated a wide variety of policies. The true question is whether the intelligence Bill Colby reported to the NSC remained objective in the face of his policy preferences.

Throughout this period unrest continued in Saigon. Nhu began slowly releasing detainees from the raids, prodded by repeated student demonstrations. Buddhists continued to march. After the flurry of activity in late August, CIA contact with the generals diminished but did not disappear. Schools were occupied by police on September 9, and protests surged outside Saigon at places that included Hue, the hill resort Dalat, the American airbase Bien Hoa, and Nha Trang and Vinh Long, where hundreds of students were arrested. The CIA reporting on this unrest, which Colby carried to the White House on September 12, was found so valuable by officials that Langley would be asked to keep its summary current. A week later General Khiem spoke to Lucien Conein, reminding the CIA that although they had not acted, the military still had a plan, and also expressing concern about Nhu's contacts with Hanoi.

John McCone had not had a plan in August, but on September 12 the CIA director personally presented a memorandum and what passed for a plan. It bore marks of Bill Colby's craftsmanship, was titled "A Program for Vietnam," and dated September 4. To pass muster with JFK the entire proposal would be cast as supplementary and simultaneous to the approved policy of graduated pressures on Diem. There were eleven points, but the main items were two: first, an emissary to be sent to Diem and Nhu, to persuade the latter to leave the country, and for certain other purposes; and second, a meeting between the Roman Catholic personality Francis Cardinal Spellman, known to Diem from earlier travels, and Archbishop Thuc, the Vietnamese leader's brother, as a second channel for persuasion.[24] The single American figure with the required close ties to Diem and Nhu, and presumptive ability to convince Nhu, was William Egan Colby.

The CIA proposal did not fly. Instead, President Kennedy decided to send Robert McNamara and General Maxwell Taylor to Saigon for another survey trip. The moment came September 16, when, at yet another State Department session, U.S. knowledge of the Saigon scene was revealed to be still abysmal. McCone had brought back from Saigon David R. Smith, the deputy station chief, for this meeting, and in addition to Colby, he also took along Huntington Sheldon, CIA's chief of current intelligence. The alternative to the CIA proposal, a pressure plan, became the consensus choice. The CIA officers were reduced to answering questions such as how Nhu was able to get away with creating the impression he had U.S. support, or whether it was true Nhu smoked opium. One true connection that Nhu could use to claim U.S. support was the fact the Special Forces unit he controlled got much of its funding (and all its equipment) from the CIA. Whatever else happened, the Vietnamese Special Forces were going to be placed squarely under regular military control. As for the rest, Kennedy wanted a new look.

David Smith, who had arrived exhausted from Saigon just that morning, barely had time to sleep off the jet lag before hitching a ride back with the survey group. Bill Bundy went along because he remained untainted by the August cable incident. John McCone could not have his emissary, but he did the next best thing and sent along Bill Colby to represent the CIA.

On the long flight out, Colby harbored notions of imitating Ed Lansdale. Colby had first met Lansdale during the Taylor-Rostow mission of 1961 when, as station chief, he had entertained the political operative. On that mission Lansdale had evaded Taylor's efforts to keep him away from Diem by presuming on his former relationship with the Vietnamese leader and simply leaving the survey group behind. Even if Lansdale had not told Colby this story, Dave Smith, it happened, had been the CIA member of the Taylor-Rostow team and had worked with Colby on Project Tiger, on introducing third-country nationals, and on an earlier investigation of real Vietnamese attitudes toward Diem. Smith was perfectly able to recount Lansdale's maneuver. Nevertheless Colby's chances as emissary would be nil—the instant the McNamara-Taylor group landed at Tan Son Nhut, Ambassador Lodge forbade Colby from seeing either Diem or Nhu.

In fact, days earlier Lodge had written a formal letter to Secretary Rusk, asking him to show it to President Kennedy; the letter requested that John Richardson be relieved in Saigon and that Ed Lansdale, specifically, be sent to replace him. On the telephone the day Colby and the others left Washington, McCone told Rusk the CIA had no confidence in Lansdale and officers would not accept him as station chief. McCone attributed the scheme to Rufus Phillips's brainwashing of Lodge. In any case Lodge, at war with Richardson, had no intention of permitting Bill Colby a free hand.

On the new mission, Colby's tasks were to discover whether and which elements of the Saigon power structure had deserted Diem, how serious a factor the student movement had become, and what the attitudes of Vietnamese officials were. Obstructed by Lodge, Colby confined his contacts to officers of the Saigon station. The division chief, who had argued to McCone before leaving that the most important thing of all would be to get Americans and Vietnamese talking about the war again, had been intensely disappointed. He wrote, "Privately I was outraged at this prohibition, coming after a trip halfway around the world, but I knew I had no option but to comply."[25]

Perhaps Colby had been away from Saigon too long or maybe he talked with the wrong people, but the Far East division chief came away with the impression that Diem and Nhu had *succeeded*, that they had pulled off a repeat of the 1955 suppression of the sects, that the Buddhist challenge had been defeated. Yet Diem's problems by September 1963 extended beyond

Buddhists; they had metastasized through the military, the students, throughout society. And indeed, on the long flight back in a windowless KC-135
transport, during which the McNamara-Taylor group crafted their report,
Colby proved unable to persuade his colleagues. The report baldly remarks:
"Discontent with the Diem/Nhu regime, which had been widespread just below the surface in recent years, has now become a seething problem." Despite
this, the report also asserted that the near-term chances the generals would
move against Diem were low, and in keeping with the predilections of Mc-
Namara and Taylor, that the United States ought not to support a coup
d'état.[26] Bill Bundy, the lead author on the report, got just two hours of sleep
during the twenty-seven-hour flight. Bundy acknowledges the contradictions
between the report's military optimism and political pessimism, and has remarked, "Neither draftsmanship nor judgment is likely to be at its best under
such working conditions."[27]

Meanwhile, the end of the line had come for Jocko Richardson. The station
chief's name appeared, first in the *Times of Vietnam*, then in articles in the
United States detailing cleavages within Cabot Lodge's embassy. The ambassador himself, frustrated in his attempt to have the CIA man relieved
through channels, is a likely source for the stories. Jocko left Saigon on
October 5. Henry Cabot Lodge moved into the house he left behind.

The Far East Division, anticipating that Richardson's relief would become
a subject at the president's next news conference, helped prepare guidance
for John Kennedy. The paper, which McCone sent over on October 8, defended the agency from charges that it was making policy, that its estimates
on South Vietnam had been wrong, that it had acted beyond its areas of
competence, and that it was in disagreement with the embassy and the military in Saigon. The guidance explicitly asserted that Richardson had been
"consistently right in his observations." President Kennedy did in fact defend
Richardson to the press on October 9.[28]

Reality quickly caught up with the impression McNamara and Taylor had
given that there was no possibility the Vietnamese generals were near action.
Even before they went to Saigon, one of the generals met Conein to say the
Vietnamese did have a plan. Colby's old friend loved to talk and recounted
these latest contacts when the division chief visited. On October 1, a day
after Colby and the rest left Vietnam, Conein accidentally encountered General Tran Van Don at Tan Son Nhut, and the Vietnamese asked the CIA man
to follow him to Nha Trang for a private chat. With Lodge unavailable, deputy
William Trueheart authorized the contact and instructed Conein to listen but
neither encourage nor discourage coup talk. The actual visit proved anticlimactic, with Don merely arranging for Conein to meet with another senior
general, Duong Van Minh, at JGS headquarters several days later.

At a height of six feet, the general was inescapably "Big" Minh, for a
Vietnamese, and the plans he laid out for Conein on October 5 proved equally
big. General Minh summarized three different options for a coup, named the
generals at the heart of the conspiracy, and demanded to know Washington's

position. He also wanted copies of the site plans and weapons inventory of the Vietnamese Special Forces camp at Long Thanh, which the CIA had previously handed over to another of the Vietnamese conspirators. Lou Conein refused to answer one way or the other, but promptly reported the exchange (CAS cable 1448, October 5, 1963).

One of General Duong Van Minh's options had explicitly provided for the assassination of Ngo Dinh Nhu. It was, Minh had even said, the easiest course. As acting chief of station with Richardson's relief, it fell to David Smith to comment on the possibility. On that day he cabled Langley that he had advised Lodge: "WE DO NOT SET OURSELVES IRREVOCABLY AGAINST THE ASSASSINATION PLOT, SINCE THE OTHER TWO ALTERNATIVES MEAN EITHER A BLOODBATH IN SAIGON OR A PROTRACTED STRUGGLE."[29]

The Smith cable set alarm bells ringing for Bill Colby. Even worse, possibly after reading this same cable, two officials on the NSC Special Group (Counterinsurgency) wondered, "in a tone somewhere between sarcastic and cynical," why Nhu had not already been disposed of.[30] Colby learned then of Cuban activities in a similar vein but resisted applying that method to Vietnam and wrote the reply that went out the next day:

WE CERTAINLY CANNOT BE IN THE POSITION OF STIMULATING, APPROVING, OR SUPPORTING ASSASSINATION, BUT ON THE OTHER HAND, WE ARE IN NO WAY RESPONSIBLE FOR STOPPING EVERY SUCH THREAT OF WHICH WE MIGHT RECEIVE EVEN PARTIAL KNOWLEDGE. WE CERTAINLY WOULD NOT FAVOR ASSASSINATION OF DIEM. WE BELIEVE ENGAGING OURSELVES BY TAKING POSITION ON THIS MATTER OPENS DOOR TOO EASILY FOR PROBES OF OUR POSITION RE OTHERS, RE SUPPORT OF REGIME, ET CETERA. CONSEQUENTLY BELIEVE BEST APPROACH IS HANDS OFF.[31]

Since Dave Smith had made remarks in the earshot of Ambassador Lodge, Langley instructed him to talk to Lodge and specifically withdraw the recommendation. Smith did so, and spoke to Trueheart also because the deputy chief of mission had been present at the original conversation. Saigon station reported on October 7 that "LODGE COMMENTED THAT HE SHARES MCCONE'S OPINION."[32]

Henry Cabot Lodge went ballistic with anger when the CIA brought him a report from another Vietnamese source a few days later, that Ngo Dinh Nhu had plans to assassinate *him* during the confusion of a protest Nhu would mount at the embassy. Lodge instructed David Smith to have his case officer pass the word back to Nhu that if such an event occurred, American retaliation would be swift and awful beyond description. A week later, at the office of Saigon's defense minister, the CIA station chief informed the Vietnamese of a fresh sanction—the CIA money to Nhu's Special Forces would be terminated until they were put under South Vietnamese army control. On October 19 the *Times of Vietnam* ran an interview with Nhu in which he accused the CIA of instigating the Buddhist troubles. Regardless of Bill Colby's loyalties, his friend Ngo Dinh Nhu had made it impossible for the United States to continue its relationship with the Diem regime.

In Washington, John McCone met privately with President Kennedy and brother Bobby on October 5, urging JFK to put all the pressure he liked on Diem but to shy away from any coup.

"If I was manager of a baseball team," McCone told Kennedy, "and I had one pitcher, I'd keep him in the box whether he was a good pitcher or not."[33]

The director of central intelligence had a point that JFK, a Boston Red Sox fan, could understand. Yet the president did not go back on his decision of August; JFK had Rusk instruct Saigon not to encourage a coup, but not to discourage one either. A few days later the CIA director testified in closed session, with Bill Colby in tow, before the Senate Foreign Relations Committee, about agency differences in Vietnam. Insisting his agency remained fully responsive to presidential control, and denying any policy role, McCone repeated his view. The United States must proceed cautiously in Vietnam, asserted the CIA chief: "We have not seen a successor government in the wings that we could say positively would be an improvement." Hanoi and the Viet Cong could gain, warned McCone, merely by sitting on the sidelines.[34]

Another meeting of the Special Group (Counterinsurgency) occurred on October 17. Here the CIA director foresaw an explosion in Saigon and proposed sending Colby to replace David Smith as acting chief of station. That, of course, would enable Bill to ride herd on Lucien Conein, Rufe Phillips, and the other Americans in touch with the plotters. McGeorge Bundy torpedoed this proposal—Colby's ties to Nhu and Diem would send the wrong signal. Besides, Bundy ruled, McCone had exceeded his authority as CIA director. A better signal would be the one sent the previous day (October 17, East Zone date), when General Richard Stilwell of Military Assistance Command Vietnam (MACV) and Dave Smith of the CIA informed Saigon's defense minister the United States would halt aid to Vietnamese Special Forces. Both men repeated this directly to the Special Forces commander on October 23.

Moving ahead in spite of Colby or McCone, the Vietnamese generals sent word to Lodge that he would be approached by either Minh or Don at a MACV reception hosted by General Paul Harkins. This channel advised that the ambassador would be asked to confirm that Conein really spoke with his authority and that of the United States. The party took place on the 18th and both South Vietnamese generals attended, but neither raised the issue with Lodge. Instead, a couple of days later a subordinate of Don's discussed coup plans and the identities of leaders with a MACV officer who carried that information to the military attaché.

On October 22 there was another party, one hosted by the British military attaché. There Paul Harkins, a protégé of Maxwell Taylor, and a man who opposed any coup from the beginning, went (without instructions) to Tran Van Don with that message, adding he would give no support (Harkins did say that if a coup occurred and failed, Don and his family could come to Harkins's house and would be given sanctuary). Confronted by Ambassador

Lodge, General Harkins replied that he interpreted President Kennedy's October 5 guidance to mean the United States opposed any move against Diem just as he did. Lodge set Harkins straight and got him to tell Don that his own view did not represent that of the United States.

Meanwhile General Tran Van Don and CIA officer Conein had discovered they shared the same Saigon dentist and had taken to having their meetings at his office for cover. "Whatever else happened," Conein would later tell journalist Stanley Karnow, "I certainly had a lot of work done on my teeth."[35] One such encounter, around the 20th, according to testimony Conein gave in the 1970s (no records exist for that day, though declassified documents confirm a meeting on the 23rd), included the case officer's passing along McCone's prohibition covering talk of assassination.

"All right, you don't like it," Don replied. "We won't talk about it anymore."[36]

The South Vietnamese were going to do what they were going to do. By his own account, Don opposed assassination, and Bill Colby later spoke to several generals who told him they had signed on to the coup plot understanding there would be no assassination of Diem or Nhu, *but* the possibility their course might lead to that act dissuaded no one.

Instead, on the evening of the 23rd General Don mentioned to Conein what Paul Harkins had told him, remarking it seemed very different from Conein's repeatedly pressing him for details of his coup plot. Don asked Conein to stay at home, on call around the clock, for the next ten days. Conein insisted that what Harkins had said was not U.S. policy, and in fact stood contrary to Washington's policy. John McCone confirmed this for himself in that city during the last ten days of October. To Jack Kennedy on the 21st the CIA director repeated his contention that Saigon was set to explode, and on the 24th he declared at another session of the Special Group (Counterinsurgency) that the United States had gotten itself too heavily involved in the contacts between Conein and the generals. For his efforts McCone earned a rebuke from Kennedy, who asked him the next day why he was so out of step with U.S. policy.

Bill Colby could have wished for no better front man than his director in this instance. When JFK pressed him, McCone shot back that the United States was handling a delicate situation in an unprofessional manner, that the generals could not provide strong leadership, and a coup would be only the first of many. At another meeting with President Kennedy on October 29, McCone insisted that a successful coup would hurt the war effort while a failed one would be a disaster. He also held out for CIA control, rejecting Robert McNamara's suggestion that the embassy set up a senior group to monitor the coup—a group that would include diplomats, military officers, and CIA men. McCone preferred to keep the reins solidly in David Smith's hands.

By this time the CIA had developed considerable data on the dispositions and loyalties of South Vietnamese military units. At the White House on

October 29 it would be Colby who led off the discussion, briefing the assembled group using a map that showed the locations of Vietnamese units of varied political hue. Colby estimated the forces on each side as roughly equal, with about twice as many troops not committed to either side. Meanwhile Lucien Conein, who had reported some talk about the conspirators needing money for their operation, held about $40,000 in CIA funds in a safe at his home. When the coup began he would carry it in a briefcase, along with a radio and a pistol, to the Joint General Staff compound.

Contrary to Colby's prediction, once the Vietnamese military went into action the morning of November 1, no forces outside Saigon sided with the Diem regime. His presidential guard remained loyal, as did the Special Forces, but Ngo Dinh Nhu outsmarted himself this time, staging a fake coup designed to get the generals to reveal themselves, for the purpose of which many of the Special Forces were sent away from Saigon. Some navy troops also remained loyal. Colby led off again at the White House that morning. The Americans had been promised two days' warning of when the plot would be put in motion, but they got only hours. Paul Harkins reported his warning as just four minutes. Pro-Diem commanders were arrested and their troops immobilized. The largest pro-Diem unit, the 9th Division, recently redeployed to the Mekong Delta area at Nhu's instigation, could not react because all the boats that might have enabled it to cross the river had been collected and moved to the opposite bank. Information remained fragmentary at this 8:00 A.M. session, but throughout the day "Critic" and "Priority" messages flowed into the capital.

Lucien Conein drove to Tan Son Nhut with his briefcase of money and a pistol. He filed several "Critic" messages through the day, including one contradicting radio broadcasts from the presidential palace, which the CIA also intercepted, to the effect that the rebellious generals had all been arrested. Ngo Dinh Diem telephoned Henry Cabot Lodge that afternoon trying to ascertain the position of the United States; Lodge lied that he did not feel able to comment. But the ambassador also offered a safe conduct for Diem and Nhu if they agreed to surrender, something Lodge had no real ability to deliver. That evening Diem and Nhu escaped the presidential palace and hid in Cholon, Saigon's twin city, at the home of a crony.

Early the next morning Diem telephoned General Duong Van Minh and said he would resign if he could choose his successor. Twenty minutes later he called back and spoke to Tran Van Don; now Diem simply wished to surrender honorably, with that safe conduct. Willing to grant such a benefit, Don asked Conein if the CIA could provide a plane to carry Diem and Nhu into exile. Conein phoned David Smith, who replied a few moments later that it would take twenty-four hours to get an aircraft. The Americans wanted to fly Diem non-stop to a place of exile where he would have the least chance to mount a counter coup; the closest plane that could do that was on Guam. Told of the delay, Duong Van Minh did not think the Ngos could be held that long.

Minh proved right. The Ngo brothers gave up at a Catholic church in Cholon. Bundled into an M-113 armored personnel carrier, their hands tied behind them, the Ngos did not even make it to Joint General Staff head-quarters. At a crossroads along the way the vehicle halted. The brothers were cut down by a hail of bullets. The perpetrators were Major Duong Huu Nghia, an armor officer; and Captain Nguyen Van Nhung, General Minh's body-guard. Minh lied about the circumstances of these events, and the Vietnamese put out several versions of what had happened. Bill Colby always believed the murderer to be Captain Nhung. It was in fact Nhung, also, who the previous evening had murdered Colonel Le Quang Tung, Nhu's Special Forces commander, along with his brother.

Colby missed the meeting when Kennedy's advisers gathered again, at 9:15 A.M. on November 2. Intelligence analysis chief Ray Cline went instead. The president came late. All the talk stayed on general policy issues until JFK walked into the room, but the president's first comment was to wonder how serious an impact the deaths would have. At this point cables to Wash-ington contained several versions of Diem's demise, and when the group reconvened that afternoon John McCone reported there was still no direct evidence that Diem and Nhu were dead, but messages already written or about to be drafted contained more concrete information.

Getting on with the war instantly became the major concern. Even with the coup in progress on November 1, McCone had spoken of the importance of the generals maintaining a semblance of constitutionality. John Kennedy, in the opinion of the historian who worked for him, Arthur M. Schlesinger, Jr., was more distraught than at any time since the Bay of Pigs. Bill Colby agreed. Director McCone pulled Colby into the Oval Office right after one of the White House meetings to say he wanted to send the Far East Division chief to Saigon right away. It was time to get ready.

In view of Lodge's machinations during Colby's previous visit, McCone wanted President Kennedy's personal approval for a Colby trip this time around. Colby himself wanted no misunderstandings either. Exhausted though he was—Bill had been spending nights at the CIA operations center and plenty of time in White House meetings—he wanted to lay his main concerns before the president. This day the CIA man barely had time to drive home and fetch a fresh shirt. Going back downtown he stopped at church to say a prayer for Diem and Nhu. Bill asked Barbara to pray for the Saigon leaders too. At the White House, Colby reminded Kennedy his friendship with the Ngo family was known in Saigon; the generals might refuse to see him. Kennedy approved anyway. Colby wondered at how drawn and disturbed the president looked.

That night at home, Bill Colby hosted a dinner for the families of former station chief Jocko Richardson and former ambassador Frederick Nolting. He had no doubt theirs would be the only wake for the Diem regime and the Ngo brothers. Next morning he flew out of National Airport en route to Saigon.

THE FAR EAST DIVISION chief's trip of South Vietnam had its pluses and minuses. It turned out that Colby's effectiveness had hardly been impaired. If anything the generals wanted to see the spy chief even more—disappearance from the scene of Diem and brother Nhu had made Saigon leaders desperate to sound out their American allies. Cabot Lodge also proved receptive to Colby's presence and had great praise for the performance of David Smith's CIA station. There would also be a happy round of storytelling with field officer Lou Conein, while some of the agency's case officers introduced the spy chief to their Vietnamese contacts, uniformly putting their best feet forward.

General Ton That Dinh, Saigon's new minister of security and a coup maker, told Bill Colby on November 7 about plans for regaining control of Saigon's Special Forces and informed the CIA man of demands from Madame Nhu, on the telephone from California, to produce the murdered Diem or photos of the bodies. Dinh's subordinates explained their reorganization of the Saigon intelligence and police services. In other sessions Colby would discuss arrangements for mounting commando raids against North Vietnam as well as projects to place agents there. In this case it would be the American telling the South Vietnamese of plans for the CIA to hand over this function to the U.S. military.

In later years Colby would work especially closely with Tran Thien Khiem, and some idea of General Khiem's interest in secret matters can be gleaned from the fact that upon learning of Bill's meeting with a certain Saigon spy official, Khiem demanded a meeting of his own. That session took place on November 8. Khiem had become powerful—a member of the triumvirate of generals now ruling in Saigon—and warned there would be "a rather thorough review" of intelligence organization. Diem and Nhu, Colby was told, had compartmented these functions and kept them private; now the generals wanted to know all about them. The official heading the Central Intelligence Organization, said Khiem, would serve only temporarily. Once his own review had been completed, Khiem wanted Bill Colby to brief the South Vietnamese on what he had found. Colby agreed.[37]

Other generals described to Colby the new alignments of the Vietnamese military factions, maneuvers over which service would control the national center that had been created for interrogating prisoners and various operations in the different corps areas of South Vietnam. Colby met twice with Colonel Pham Ngoc Thao, later to be revealed as a National Liberation Front agent, but in 1963 regarded as a leading pacification expert and political maverick. Certain sessions that involved joint operations between Americans and South Vietnamese were of current interest to the CIA station, and Colby included paramilitary chief Gilbert Layton. Prominent South Vietnamese politicians were also on the itinerary. In all these encounters the accent would be on potential, on the possibilities that lay ahead for a reformed Saigon military.

But there remained a negative side to Colby's ledger as well. Field reports from all over South Vietnam indicated a stalled military effort. Places like

Long An province in the Mekong Delta, considered a model, had become hotbeds of Viet Cong activity. The strategic hamlet program, Colby later acknowledged, "had fallen to pieces."[38] This would be reported to Langley, as well as the message Colby carried to the Pacific Command conference, shortly to be held at Honolulu. Saigon bureaucrats had sought to placate Ngo Dinh Nhu, Diem's czar for strategic hamlets, with favorable statistics that masked the true state of affairs. Nhu himself had consistently oversold the program. The Viet Cong focused on strategic hamlets early and steadily as a major challenge to them, had occupied some of the first ones, and moved into many others at the same time as the villagers. All these trends existed wholly apart from the Buddhist crisis, which had absorbed Saigon's attention for half a year.

Problems had been noted in the national intelligence estimate that George Carver drafted and with which Colby had differed in early 1963. The problems had then been reported extensively in the American press, while Colby, his operations officers, the Pentagon, and the State Department concentrated on attacking the credibility of the reports rather than dealing with their substance. After the November coup the Viet Cong opened a sustained offensive against the strategic hamlets, with the number of incidents up by as much as 300 to 400 percent, and weaknesses in the program could no longer be disguised.

At the same time, with the whole concept of strategic hamlets closely identified with Diem, and especially Nhu, it became impolitic for the successor regime, the military junta led by General Duong Van Minh, to continue this effort. The junta had problems of its own, not least the lack of any real dynamism on the part of Minh. Colby reported as much in his trip cable to Langley, which McCone shared with McGeorge Bundy just before the Honolulu meeting.

Despite Colby's view of General Minh as wishy-washy, he always believed it had been "Big" Minh who ordered the murder of Diem and Nhu. George Carver differed there; though his assessment of Minh was the same, Carver argued that the unsure Minh would have preferred a collective decision in order to share responsibility and hedge against future blame. And Bill Colby forever rejected charges that there had been a CIA role in the assassinations, basing his view on the narrow facts of the murders and not the broader context of U.S. encouragement of the generals. Years later, pressed about CIA murders in general by an interviewer, Bill Colby exhibited his sensitivity with an angry retort, "CIA has never assassinated anybody. Including Diem."[39]

Colby would also maintain to the end of his life that the Diem assassination constituted a major U.S. policy error, that with proper backing Diem would have broadened his regime and actually won the war within the next couple of years. That is speculation supported by not a shred of evidence. Moreover, the United States *had already taken* the path Colby advocated: in 1955 Washington rejected advice to get rid of Diem from its plenipotentiary General J. Lawton Collins in favor of the importunings of the CIA's Edward Lansdale.

In 1955 Diem stood near the apogee of his popularity, still had political allies, and faced a very much weaker communist threat. If Diem had not initiated government reforms then, and still avoided them when confronted with the Buddhist crisis, there is no reason to suppose he would have done so in the wake of a (failed) coup in November 1963. Here Colby indulged in a certain self-deception. Colby's loyalty born of friendship for Diem and Ngo Dinh Nhu, commendable on a personal basis, contributed to America's deepening wounds from the Vietnam war. And Colby's influence on John McCone, greater than has ever been understood, helped trigger a distortion of the CIA's national intelligence estimates. That, in turn, countered proponents of reforms in Vietnam before the Buddhist troubles monopolized attention in both Saigon and Washington.

The Buddhist crisis itself Colby viewed through the prism of his friendships. Despite years in Saigon and status as an old Vietnam hand, Colby saw the troubles as a false issue when they began, then argued they had been surpassed. Diem was the ticket, the Buddhist crisis little more than the result of unfortunately timed photos of burning bonzes, as Colby maintained in oral histories and two volumes of memoirs. Only once—in 1969, back in Vietnam in a new role—would the spy chief express a more nuanced opinion. Then he told a *New York Times* correspondant that the Buddhist crisis of 1963 had been "a genuine popular revolt" widely supported by the Vietnamese people.[40] Perhaps, active again in a context where his political acumen came under constant scrutiny, Colby's eyes were not so much on history. But later he reverted to the contention that Diem had overcome the Buddhists, not that a nerve had been touched in the Vietnamese social fabric that would take years to calm.

Colby's steadfast opposition to a coup influenced John McCone too. But their stand took place amid CIA escalation of the war in Laos; a Laotian escalation with a vulnerable Diem still in power would have led Hanoi to actions against a weakening and daily less effective Diem regime. The recipe for defeat here is evident. Meanwhile, McCone and Colby's taking off their gloves and mixing in the policy debate put the Central Intelligence Agency beyond its mandate for speaking truth to power. This excess could perhaps have been judged helpful if there had been more serious thought to Dean Rusk's stark alternative—withdrawal from Vietnam—but the CIA also opposed that. That Colby, years after the war, believed the United States could still have won with Diem in charge is testament to loyalty greater than his wisdom.

Meanwhile, Colby's later suggestions that the CIA ought to be excused in the episode of Diem's assassination rest on the secret record of its (excessive) policy role rather than the discoverable record of its agents on the street in Saigon. Yet, as a practical matter, public and world opinion of the Diem business would inevitably be formed on the basis of the discoverable record, not the secret one. Claims such as Colby's were destined to be seen as shrill and self-serving.

For all the sound and fury it entailed, Diem's would only be the first crucial death that November. The next, and in the warp of time these have become inextricably intertwined, would be that of John F. Kennedy himself. The murder of President Kennedy came just as William E. Colby returned from Honolulu; indeed, he arrived in Washington that very afternoon. Colby and fellow officials had just arranged for the next phase in the secret war as an arc of crisis began to engulf more and more of Asia.

9

ARC OF CRISIS

FRUSTRATION DROVE BILL COLBY after the Diem assassination. He, McCone, and the CIA might have lost the policy battle in Washington, but Colby emerged determined to effect change directly, on the ground in Vietnam. This became the quiet subtext of his post-coup swing through Southeast Asia. That trip turned into the point of departure for new CIA initiatives, greatly increasing the agency's role in the Vietnam war, as well as Southeast Asia more broadly. William E. Colby created some of these projects while energizing or becoming instrumental in others. In a way he seemed to submerge his loss of friends in the Ngo family with frantic activity that might avenge them by winning the Vietnam war.

Top on Colby's list would be revamping the CIA's Saigon station. Ambassador Lodge had effectively sabotaged John Richardson, and McCone had been prevented from sending out Colby in his stead, but the Far East (FE) Division chief became determined to have his man, not Lodge's. It was a strike against acting chief of station Dave Smith that Lodge liked him, and Smith's chances were not helped by his authorship of the cable advising Langley not to dismiss assassination, an analysis Colby considered to have undercut his efforts in Washington. Smith's days in Saigon were numbered.

In Hong Kong the CIA station chief shared a Columbia connection with Colby. Peer De Silva had overlapped at the university with the FE chief for part of a year, though Colby had been in law school and De Silva studying Russian. That background naturally led to work on Russian operations, where De Silva had been on the CIA's front lines while Colby held supporting posts in Stockholm and Rome. Not only had De Silva been an Army courier into Russia; he had joined the CIA before Colby, served in Germany and Vienna—by the end as station chief—and had been a counterintelligence officer on the wartime atomic bomb development program, the Manhattan Project. In addition, Peer De Silva had been station chief in Seoul during a

Korean military coup, and so he had some experience of what that could be like. It seemed like good preparation for Saigon.

But Colby had never met Peer De Silva and knew nothing about him other than what was in the file. It was important to look him over. One quiet morning the Hong Kong station chief's phone woke him at 5 A.M. with word of an important cable for his eyes only. De Silva went to the communications room to learn that division chief Colby demanded his immediate presence in Saigon as a companion on his inspection trip. Once De Silva arrived Bill quickly divulged the truth: he was thinking of the Hong Kong spy as successor in Saigon. The division chief let out that the appointment would come in June 1964, which would have been the end of Jocko Richardson's original tour. Together, the two visited the Saigon station, the CIA's parachute rigging shed at Tan Son Nhut, the air section for the Project Tiger commando operation, its forward echelon at Nha Trang, and bases at Hue, Dalat, Kontum, Pleiku, and Dak To—the last three all in the Central Highlands. In a helicopter Colby and De Silva flew along the Laotian border to survey the mountain fastness, and overflew the montagnard striker camp of Ben Het. At Pleiku, Army Colonel Charles Wilson described the Ho Chi Minh Trail as the "Averell Harriman Memorial Highway,"[1] which must have tickled Colby, who had had to deal with Harriman during the Laotian negotiations at Geneva. At Kontum Vietnamese security officials showed them an interrogation center.

By the end of the circuit, Bill had been impressed with Peer De Silva. When Colby moved on to Thailand for a brief visit, he cabled McCone recommending De Silva's appointment to Saigon. The CIA director approved the recommendation around the time of John F. Kennedy's assassination. The CIA succession in Saigon became the subject of private conversation between McCone and new president Lyndon Baines Johnson (LBJ).

John McCone told LBJ that he had a recommendation for a great fellow to head the CIA station, but that it would be a good move only if the president were, on his part, to replace Henry Cabot Lodge. Otherwise it would be better to keep David Smith. This clearly represented payback for Lodge's sabotage of John Richardson. President Johnson replied that ordering Lodge home would be a slap in the face for the military junta, a throwback to the lost Diem. Lodge could bring himself home—as a candidate in the 1964 presidential election, for example—but LBJ was not going to replace him. McCone shot back that Johnson wanted things too easy: "Lodge would destroy [De Silva] if he opposed his assignment or did not like him, or wished to get rid of him. . . . Lodge was absolutely unconscionable in matters of this kind and he had resorted to trickery time and time again during the Eisenhower administration and that he never failed to use the newspapers in order to expose an individual or block an action."

De Silva was the dangle, Smith the unfortunate victim, whom McCone described as "a most competent officer but young and not fully experienced." While President Johnson would not budge on recalling Ambassador Lodge, he insisted, as McCone reminded him, on the best man who could be found for the Saigon station. LBJ here reiterated he wanted a "four-star man" to head the station and promised to use the power of the Oval Office to restrain the imperious ambassador—McGeorge Bundy was told to write a suitable instruction for Lodge.[2]

FROM A QUICK STOP in Laos and on to Bangkok, William E. Colby returned to Honolulu. There, at Pacific Command headquarters, the best and brightest gathered for a strategy conference that set the course of the Vietnam war for more than a year. Amid talk of the quality of the Vietnamese junta, economic and military aid levels, and increases in the Vietnamese military, Colby mostly sat silent. He intervened to clarify a question as to the relative status of South Vietnamese military men who were division commanders versus province chiefs (equal). But the CIA officer's main contributions came in smaller meetings held apart from the plenary sessions. There were two issues at Honolulu central to the CIA's interest. One of them completed discussions the Pentagon and CIA had initiated as far back as the summer of 1963. The other would be new.

As chief of the Far East Division, Colby had been the CIA's point man for months on a negotiation with the Pentagon regarding the agency's CIDG program in the Central Highlands and elsewhere. Directives approved after the Bay of Pigs held that the military ought hence forth to have responsibility for all programs primarily involving armed forces, even paramilitary ones. It had been Colby in his earlier guise as Saigon station chief who had gotten the montagnard project up and running, and as division chief in 1963 he had to turn it over to the military. The CIA could argue, and some did, that the success of the Hmong tribal project showed the agency could direct para-military actions effectively. But the montagnard effort required more Amer-ican manpower and was much more visible. In conjunction with the Pentagon, the CIA planned operation "Switchback" to turn the CIDGs completely over to the Army's Green Berets. Those arrangements were confirmed at Honolulu.

Looking out for the montagnards, however, the CIA felt uncomfortable with Army supply channels. Not only did the Army simply not have access to some items the CIA used, but agency methods of moving materials to the front were far different. Colby worried that the Army, having handed its supplies over to the Vietnamese at a port of entry, would find itself without them at the place they were to be used. The agency therefore insisted on retaining control of the supply system right through Switchback, a control it would relinquish only in 1965.

A second matter came fresh to the officials at Honolulu. Many wanted to exert more muscle against Hanoi. Robert McNamara was one, but Ambas-sador Lodge had also gone on record favoring such activities. "They just won't work, Mr. Secretary," Colby quotes himself saying.[3]

Of course, the Central Intelligence Agency had had its Project Tiger in place for a couple of years. Indeed one of Colby's goals on his just-completed inspection visit had been to check up on Tiger. The project had little to show. Agents had been exposed, whole boatloads of commandos were captured with their equipment and the boat crews, airborne teams disappeared without a trace. Indeed, one of the boat losses, involving fourteen crewmen and commandos in all, occurred at the very end of Bill Colby's time as station chief in Saigon. More than seventy Vietnamese agents, airmen, and sailors had gone missing during Colby's tour in Saigon and another 129 between then and the Honolulu meeting that now reevaluated these operations.

Once a supporter of the northern operations, Colby now opposed them, backed up by his deputy, Robert J. Myers. Having worked with the OSS in China and in the CIA paramilitary effort against the Chinese communists, Myers had direct knowledge of the vagaries of using commando teams. He also had a feel for the area, having served in many places in the Far East over more than a dozen years. His experience in Cambodia gave him reason to suspect leaks from the unit of South Vietnamese intelligence responsible for their side of the infiltration to North Vietnam. In addition, repeated visits to Laos gave Myers a window on a paramilitary operation done right, to which Project Tiger provided poor contrast. Myers maintained that communist organization of the population was such that this type of operation simply could not work, and that CIA failures in China, Korea, and Eastern Europe put that conclusion beyond a doubt.

The record is silent on whether Averell Harriman employed his hearing aid during these particular discussions, but Robert McNamara certainly turned a deaf ear. Colby finished up advocating psychological warfare as a main focus instead of military pressure, but the decision makers were not interested. McNamara responded to the claim by saying that a program of pressures run by the U.S. military would be more effective than a program run by the CIA. Colby acquiesced, finally agreeing to help the Pentagon plan this program. It would include patrol craft forays to shell coastal targets in North Vietnam, commando raids, covert bombing by unmarked planes, more intelligence missions, and so on. Psychological warfare, with Vietnamese fishermen to be captured and propagandized, and aerial leaflet drops would be included in the whole but were not an end in themselves. The project would eventually be called Operations Plan (OPLAN) 34-A, an important milestone on America's road to a shooting war in Vietnam.

Officials who met in Honolulu had barely returned to Washington when tragedy struck in Dallas. Colby sat in his office at Langley and listened with Bob Myers as the radio said that President Kennedy had been shot. The two men speculated on what changes the event might bring. The advent of Lyndon Johnson changed much, accelerating America's slide into the Vietnam quagmire.

Over the next weeks came a series of exchanges among the CIA, the Pentagon's experts, and the Military Assistance Command Vietnam (MACV) over the shape of the program to exert graduated pressure against Hanoi.

President Johnson, who promised no changes in John Kennedy's policies, interpreted JFK's stance as giving the military every resource it needed to accomplish what it held possible. President Johnson would nevertheless be warned by NSC staff aide Michael Forrestal. "Despite considerable effort," Forrestal noted of the infiltration program on December 11, "very little has come of these operations, partly because of the tight police control in the North and partly because of their small size." An expanded effort might be worthwhile, but only *"provided* we carried them out in connection with a political program designed to get a practical reaction out of Hanoi."[4]

Meanwhile Colby went ahead with military planners. He was back in Saigon in mid-December when MACV officers briefed the draft OPLAN 34-A to Secretary McNamara. The defense secretary thought the plans a good job and so told LBJ. McNamara, John McCone, and Dean Rusk jointly recommended adoption of the program in a memo to President Johnson on January 3, 1964, accompanied by an annotated target list. McGeorge Bundy concurred a few days later. The president approved OPLAN 34-A for execution beginning on January 16. Bill Colby still had his doubts and made sure the CIA did not nominate anyone for deputy commander of the 34-A force, as had been provided in the original scheme.

Colby's December 1963 visit to Saigon actually formed part of a larger tapestry. The move involved Peer De Silva in Hong Kong, whose phone rang again on a Sunday morning, December 10. This time the cable awaiting him ordered De Silva home for consultations, appointing him Saigon station chief with immediate effect. Upon reaching Washington, De Silva's first contact would be Colby, who explained the assignment had been accelerated. Next, Bill took De Silva to McCone, whom he had met only once, when all the Far East station chiefs had gathered in the Philippines to greet a then-brand new CIA director in late 1961. McCone took De Silva to the White House to meet President Johnson. It was highly unusual for a station chief to be taken to the Oval Office, but McCone saw Vietnam as important and it was LBJ himself who had spoken of a four-star CIA man for the post. De Silva passed muster.

A few days of briefings passed in a blur, and suddenly Peer De Silva found himself at Andrews Air Force Base, waiting with William E. Colby, former NSC staff deputy Karl Kaysen, and several more men to leave for Saigon with McCone. The CIA director would hook up with McNamara in Vietnam, and incidentally beard the lion Cabot Lodge in his den, for the purpose of installing De Silva in the U.S. embassy. De Silva, who had been told John McCone's trip was secret, found dozens of reporters at Tan Son Nhut upon their arrival. The CIA party had to fight their way through the crowd. It was an omen of much that would happen in Vietnam. Peer De Silva, not to mention Bill Colby, would have done well to take it to heart.

Naturally, both Colby and his CIA director saw the Lodge facet of this visit as the most challenging. John McCone had already warned De Silva not to get on the wrong side of Ambassador Lodge, and told the station chief he wanted no trouble between that officer and the ambassador. Lodge invited the McCone party to lunch at the embassy residence a day later. Without ever looking directly at De Silva, the ambassador told John McCone he neither wanted nor needed a new station chief, that he was comfortable with David Smith. The CIA director, with a tight little smile, answered that unless Lodge had a real reason for rejecting De Silva, the CIA would go on with the appointment. Both De Silva and Smith were at the lunch and felt like prize hounds at a dog show. Bill Colby, also at the lunch, joined the others in "repeatedly gazing at the ceiling as the meal finally came to an end."[5]

This whole byplay went unmentioned in the trip report McCone sent to President Johnson. Instead, the CIA director stuck to substantive issues, remarking most tellingly. "There is no organized government in South Vietnam at this time." In a conclusion he stated, "The future of the war remains in doubt," and warned that "harassing sabotage against [North Vietnam]," in other words, OPLAN 34-A, would not appreciably change the situation.[6] (Mac Bundy would repeat to LBJ in early 1964 that "McCone thinks you should understand that no great results are likely from this kind of effort.")[7] McCone's only direct reference to the CIA would be in his covering note, in which he reported the agency was about to send back to Vietnam on temporary duty a number of officers with previous Saigon experience. He especially wanted to develop sources within the Saigon government and polity. These measures bore the mark of Bill Colby's interests.

FOR MANY YEARS, in speeches, articles, interviews, and two books, William E. Colby never tired of declaring his amazement and disgust that the United States government had never considered, in the months before the death of Diem, who might replace the Saigon leader. But in fact there did exist, at CIA headquarters, a list of potential successors. The list had been created in 1962; its author, Bill Colby. The top name on that list was General Nguyen Khanh. In any event, just a few months passed before Khanh, frustrated with the sluggish military junta in Saigon, mounted another coup and emerged as South Vietnamese military strongman. Governing behind a so-called Military Revolutionary Council and then a civilian cabinet, Khanh retained power through a turbulent year of coup and countercoup, a half dozen in all, with Saigon intrigues more intense than ever.

Volatility in Vietnamese politics thus framed the operational problem for the Central Intelligence Agency, its difficulties only accentuated by the prickly ambassador at the head of the U.S. mission. Before Peer De Silva left for Hong Kong to retrieve his family, Cabot Lodge took him aside and told him that although the CIA could not be forced into selecting Lodge's preferred station chief, there were things, by God, that De Silva had better do for the ambassador. The station chief's black sedan was longer and sleeker than the ambassador's car; De Silva was to get rid of it. He also had to dispense with the shiny brass plate on his office door that proclaimed the station chief's cover job—special assistant to the ambassador. Over time Peer

De Silva overcame the delicacy of his appointment. Though McNamara would tell a Washington meeting months later, toward the end of Lodge's tenure, that relations between the ambassador and CIA station chief remained horrible, Peer De Silva stood on quite solid ground with the ambassador by the time Lodge left Saigon.

America's top spies saw this evolution at first hand during 1964, for a steady stream of them flowed through Saigon. First there were the old hands whom John McCone had promised LBJ he would be sending out on temporary duty. The idea was McCone's; he thought that these CIA officers, who already had a feel for Vietnam, could do a quiet check on the accuracy of the reports the South Vietnamese were giving Americans, thus calming Washington's doubts about the data it was getting. The officers found the embassy cooperative; if there was any obstacle it would be Paul Harkins and the U.S. military, not Lodge and the diplomats.

In four separate cables filed in mid-February the old hands agreed Vietnamese reporting had been dishonest under Diem but seemed accurate since the military coup. They also agreed the strategic hamlet program had ground to a virtual halt, and that the tide of the war was running against Saigon in all parts of the country. General Harkins promptly claimed these observations were skewed; with his prodding, the Pentagon began insisting that the CIA study mission be converted into a joint CIA-military-State Department effort. Colby managed to moot the issue by getting his people out of South Vietnam as quickly as he could.

Almost simultaneously the Saigon station hosted the visit of Langley's executive director, Lyman Kirkpatrick. Still under the cloud of his (perfectly appropriate) criticisms of the Bay of Pigs, "Kirk," as he was called, handled some hot potatoes in an effort to gain McCone's esteem. Vietnam was one. After making the rounds in the South Vietnamese capital, Kirk mentioned his desire to see the CIA maritime base at Da Nang before Switchback handed it over to the U.S. Navy. For De Silva the trip proved less of a problem than it could have been, given that the wheelchair-bound Kirkpatrick could not fit through the doors of most conventional aircraft. But the CIA had recently taken delivery of some new C-7 Caribou transports that had rear loading ramps and bay doors in the style of the big C-130 Hercules. Wheeling Kirk up the ramp was easy. There was even no problem tying him down when Kirkpatrick wanted the doors kept open on takeoff so he could see the panoramic view of Tan Son Nhut as the plane lifted away from the ground.

At Da Nang the maritime base chief, Tucker Gougelman, took the traveling party to the facility, at nearby Hoa Cam, then held a lobster cookout on the beach. Gougelmann had been running small boat operations for Project Tiger for about eighteen months, during which time a junk and its crew had been lost, and he was outspoken. Also present was Gilbert Strickler, Army reserve colonel and deputy chief of paramilitary operations at Saigon station. "Strick," who had the reputation of being able to get *anything* that existed in either the Army or CIA systems, had charge of the process of handing over CIA facilities under Switchback. Kirkpatrick and De Silva flew back to Saigon before the end of the day. In a joint cable they sent on February 10 the two officers noted the South Vietnamese population seemed completely apathetic, without enthusiasm for either side. Lyman Kirkpatrick added a personal comment: "I HAVE BEEN SHOCKED BY THE NUMBER OF OUR (CIA) PEOPLE AND OF THE MILITARY, EVEN THOSE WHOSE JOB IS ALWAYS TO SAY WE ARE WINNING, WHO FEEL THAT THE TIDE IS AGAINST US."[8]

In Washington, a White House meeting on February 20 issued orders to accelerate planning of 34-A attacks on the North. Colby gave the CIA briefing and he began this way: "The Viet Cong have taken advantage of the power vacuum . . . to score both military and psychological gains in the countryside." The tide seemed to be flowing against the Saigon regime.[9] Colby saw this for himself a couple of weeks later, when he accompanied McCone on another of the CIA director's inspections. The DCI's subsequent report agreed the strategic hamlet program had fizzled, noted suppression of bad news and overstatement of good, reported spotty intelligence and stalling of essential projects. "We conclude that prospects for a strong government are not bright," Director McCone wrote, his bottom line that the situation was worse even than when he had drawn pessimistic conclusions from his December 1963 visit.[10]

Peer De Silva, a solid product of the espionage side of the CIA's clandestine service, had no experience with political action or paramilitary initiatives when he arrived. Early word at the station had it the agency would be getting back to its "traditional" functions. But under the pressure of the deteriorating situation, De Silva needed some concrete project, and he soon encountered one. In Quang Ngai province on the Central Vietnamese coast, frustrated local villagers had lashed out against the Viet Cong. South Vietnamese officers and American officials and military men, principally Frank Scotton and Major Robert Kelly, harnessed the local sentiments to form an armed unit of villagers. De Silva sent Tom Donohue to experiment with the units on a larger scale and several more formed. Within months the local units were credited with killing 150 Viet Cong, and capturing another 200, all with their weapons, which was unheard of, and with minimal losses.

Soon De Silva saw the local units as *the* solution to the Vietnam problem. His deputy chief of station, Gordon Jorgensen, contributed a name, "People's Action Teams" (PATs). It mattered little that in spite of PAT prowess, the security situation in Quang Ngai seemed so poor that that spring the South Vietnamese considered abandoning the provincial capital. De Silva's enthusiasm also annoyed CIA officers who had been working on similar initiatives for months. In the Mekong delta, for example, Stewart Methven, who had previously worked on Project Momentum in Laos and on the montagnard mountain scout program, had created what were called "Counter-Terror Teams" (CTTs). In conjunction with a dynamic Vietnamese officer, Tran Ngoc Chau, Methven used the CTTs in precisely the same fashion as the PATs. Others created what were called "census grievance" teams, designed to draw out Vietnamese peasants, and "agitation-propaganda" teams that directly copied a Viet Cong technique. In all instances the formula involved small armed teams directly working with villagers.

Bill Colby learned of the PAT concept early and put it on his agenda to check during the next Vietnam visit. In the meantime Colby inevitably became aware of presidential frustration. Around this time, the U.S. government approved the use of high altitude U-2 reconnaissance planes to photograph Vietnam's borders with Laos and Cambodia as well as portions of North Vietnam. Director McCone took some of the pictures to the National Security Council in late April. With the CIA director doing the talking, Colby handled huge blowups of the photos and pointed out to President Johnson the features McCone mentioned. Colby found Johnson irritated as the CIA man hovered near him, growling about his coffee cup. In several episodes in which McCone displayed photographs, including the first pictures of the Chinese nuclear weapons test site at Lop Nor, the CIA declared it needed more time to analyse the intelligence. This was not a good way to gain LBJ's confidence, which only diminished as the agency proved unable to point to real progress in Vietnam.

The Far East division chief traveled to Vietnam again in May 1964. There was another big strategy conference coming up at Honolulu. Colby wanted to see the PAT initiative for himself, while John McCone had asked him, once more, to verify the accuracy of reporting out of Saigon. Cautious regarding Southeast Asian panaceas, on May 13 Colby nevertheless cabled: "I AM CONCERNED PRIMARILY AT THE TENDENCY TOWARD CHASING WILLS-OF-THE-WISP RATHER THAN CLEAVING FIRMLY TO A FUNDAMENTAL STRATEGY FOR THIS WAR."[11] Nevertheless, in Washington a week later, Bill put his name to a joint paper with the CIA's Chester Cooper, on assignment to the NSC staff, advocating massive counterinsurgency for Vietnam and Laos.

Langley continued to see Southeast Asia in a poor light, not just McCone, the FE Division, and DDP, but the intelligence analysts as well. During the run up to Honolulu in June, analysts claimed that negative trends in Vietnam had not yet even bottomed out, while John McCone told Dean Rusk on the telephone that everything in Southeast Asia hung on just two weak reeds—Nguyen Khanh in South Vietnam and Phoumi Nosavan in Laos. At the National Security Council on May 24 came extensive discussion of 34-A operations where McCone objected that "if we go into North Vietnam we should go in hard and not limit ourselves to pinpricks."[12] Colby saw Robert McNamara at one of these meetings—not this one—excitedly tell LBJ about how 34-A commandos had landed on the North Vietnamese coast and successfully blown up a couple of trucks. It took Colby back to his OSS days in Norway, when he had mindlessly exaggerated the impact on the German war machine of his blowing up a bridge on a Norwegian railroad.

When matters came to a head at Honolulu it proved more of the same. Talk of 34-A operations, previously planned shifts in numbers of military advisers and support troops like helicopter units, and economic or military aid levels predominated. Henry Cabot Lodge spoke of boosting South Vietnamese spirits by bombing the Laotian town of Tchepone on the Ho Chi Minh Trail. General William Westmoreland, newly promoted military commander, emphasized progress in the war. Director McCone took exception, insisting the downward spiral continued. Peer De Silva attended from the Saigon station and harped on the PAT project with its advantages of local knowledge and direct combating of the Viet Cong infrastructure. Other CIA staff revealed that the agency had begun supporting a Vietnam information ministry program that intended to activate as many as 200 "agitation-propaganda" teams.

One initiative had to be of special interest to the Far East Division chief. This would feature CIA political action in Saigon. With the demise of Diem's political front, the historic parties in the South were only small groupings of elite figures. In fact the only big public organization was the Vietnamese Confederation of Labor (CVT by its French-language acronym) led by Tran Quoc Buu. With his background of union organizing, and special attention to these areas for the CIA in Italy, Bill Colby had a special interest in the labor leader. Tran Quoc Buu had been in Washington less than two weeks before, with the State Department and CIA as his points of contact. Now, in Honolulu, Buu would specifically be mentioned as a possible Saigon ally who if he came out in support of the South Vietnamese government, could really build its strength.

On June 6, roughly his first opportunity following the strategy meeting in Hawaii, McGeorge Bundy took John McCone aside after a White House meeting. Bundy asked about "the question of CIA reentering Vietnam in an active role such as that which had existed prior to Operation Switchback."[13] The CIA director said he would make a maximum effort, but only if he got clear orders, and the Pentagon and the embassy agreed. The true meaning of this exchange was that the White House thought it needed all the help it could get in Vietnam.

In the end, the formal prohibition against Langley's participating in paramilitary activities in Vietnam lasted barely six months. Of course, with PATs and CTTs and agitation-propaganda teams, the Saigon station had already gotten involved. But the Bundy statement became a green light for Colby and the far East Division. The net effect would be to disconnect the CIA from the embarrassment that occurred in August, when 34-A operations contributed Washington's first overt act of force in the war.

Garnering assistance from Tran Quoc Buu soon became easier than anyone expected. Buu had headed the national labor union for a decade and built a business supplying Saigon with shrimp and cinnamon. Diem had also used Buu, by some reports, to move political slush funds through his union's foreign bank accounts. Profits from business and currency speculation enabled Buu to buy much land, including an estate at Cat Lo, near the Vietnamese seaside resort of Vung Tau. Buu became known as a warlord because he recruited a private army to protect his seafood shipments into Saigon and used Cat Lo to train the soldiers. The scheme turned sour with the fall of Diem, after which Tran Quoc Buu was in trouble. When Buu went with the wrong side in one of the 1964 coup attempts, the trouble became truly major.

Cat Lo had to be sold to raise money, and the CIA proved only too happy to buy it, while supplying other funds to the labor movement. In two months time Tom Donohue turned the Vung Tau site into a training camp for PATs, and Vietnamese recruits soon flooded in for a thirteen-week course of political and military training before returning to their homes as PAT units. Meanwhile, courtesy of his new influx of money, Tran Quoc Buu beat the latest charges, while being released at the intercession of the U.S. embassy. Some accounts claim the AFL-CIO, an American equivalent of Buu's CVT, some entities of which had strong links to the CIA, pressured the State Department to intercede for the Vietnamese labor leader. But years later, a scholar researching a project on unions in the former South Vietnam would be astonished to discover that Tran Quoc Buu and William E. Colby were on close personal terms.

Vietnamese leader Nguyen Khanh earned few points with Americans for political skills, or lack thereof. Secretary McNamara publicly lauded Khanh on one visit but later rued those remarks. Khanh, who now lives in exile in the United States, insists he got on perfectly well with Henry Cabot Lodge, but that when Maxwell Taylor took over as ambassador in the summer of 1964 his rapport with the United States vanished. Khanh's arrest of some of the South Vietnamese generals, whom he put under house arrest in Dalat, the frequency with which he shuffled the governing cabinet, and the constant coup plotting sapped American sympathy. Student and Buddhist unrest continued, and Khanh was known to consult with Buddhist figures such as Thich Tri Quang.

In the spring of 1964 John McCone objected to the tone of one of McNamara's trip reports, saying the defense secretary put too much emphasis on the possibility of a coup. By early September the CIA had completely switched views: a special national intelligence estimate (SNIE) concluded, "At present odds are against the emergence of a stable government."[14] Another SNIE followed on October 1, which baldly declared: "A coup by disgruntled South Vietnam military figures may occur at any time."[15]

The CIA estimates harped on the Buddhist factor in Vietnamese politics. When Bill Colby argued in retrospect that the Buddhists had been eliminated as a factor, he forgot this whole history. On August 25, 1964, almost exactly one year after the fateful raids on the pagodas, Colby's own station chief, Peer De Silva cabled Washington that Khanh "HAS IN EFFECT PUT HIS GOVERNMENT ENTIRELY IN THE HANDS OF TRI QUANG."[16]

It is significant that American military and diplomatic message traffic, as well as accounts of the Vietnam war, to include Colby's, almost never mention that General Khanh was himself a Buddhist.

Another simplistic element of Colby's version of the Vietnam imbroglio is his statement that "in the Washington policy discussions I gradually dropped to a minor role as the focus of intelligence support shifted from whether to support the Vietnamese government to how to employ our military forces."[17] The change did not happen merely as the result of a shifting focus in Washington. In fact, the Far East Division that Colby headed showed itself to be significantly out of step with the U.S. government as a whole. The construction Bill Colby put on this evolution in his writing obscures the real role of his operatives in Vietnam.

One case in point is that of Bob Myers, deputy chief of the FE Division. During that spring and summer Washington held two hypothetical exercises, political-military war games with the participation of senior officials as well as working level bureaucrats. Representing CIA, Myers played, as did analyst Harold Ford, in the first of these simulations. After this iteration, Myers and Ford collaborated on a paper to John McCone completely rejecting the assumptions and some outcomes of the exercise. McCone, who despised war games, then attended a session of the second exercise himself. Following the game, Myers again penned a major critique of the Vietnam exercise, which had included the kind of large-scale bombing campaign against North Vietnam that the U.S. government then had under consideration. McCone did not waver in his support of massive military action, including bombing.

Frustrated as Washington marched into this quagmire, Robert Myers left the CIA to go into publishing. He eventually became publisher of *The New Republic* magazine.

Then there was David Smith, once acting chief of station in Saigon. With the advent of Peer De Silva, Smith had been kept on as deputy for a time, but Colby then brought him back to Langley as chief of FE-4, the South Vietnam desk. Smith had opposed major military commitment in Vietnam since at least 1961. Now he responded to Washington's deliberations with a memorandum characterizing bombing as a "bankrupt" policy.[18]

As for William E. Colby, in a May 1964 paper circulated widely to the NSC, McNamara, Maxwell Taylor, and others, the old Vietnam hand warned that the Saigon government was progressing, but not quickly enough, that at the grass roots it was not working at all well, and that the enemy continued to hold the initiative and develop strength among the population. To reverse those trends Colby advocated an array of measures across the spectrum of action. On the pacification side he proposed making the province chief the key official, and his U.S. counterpart true commander of every American activity within the province, with reduced paperwork, and directly responsible to the ambassador. On the security side there should be effective implementation of the "oilspot" tactic of closely holding the terrain with numerous garrisons, with required numbers of troops to come from an expansion of militias and "combat youth." A couple of thousand American soldiers and marines should be sent to advise the militias. In the Mekong delta area, a Chinese nationalist division could be brought into Vietnam to supplement the local forces. Throughout the country, offensive tactics with artillery and general reserves should only be permitted into zones clearly dominated by the

National Liberation Front. Politically, the Saigon side should offer induce-
ments to "less extremist elements" of the Lao Dong (North Vietnamese) party
to dangle before them the prospect of "escape from the dilemma of escalating
war and increased Chinese presence."

Colby also advocated training the South Vietnamese air force for pinpoint
bombing and preparation of a scenario to justify their activation against North
Vietnam. Aggressive reconnaissance patrols across the Laotian and Cambodian borders should be ordered immediately, according to Colby's proposal,
but the main thing would be the application of the oilspot technique.[19]

In early November Colby addressed a private paper to William P. Bundy,
at that time the assistant secretary for Southeast Asia at the State Department.
Here Colby pointed to Laos as an example of apparent success at neutralization resulting from international agreement. He broached the possibility of
a fresh conference to be hosted by Souvanna Phouma and Cambodian Prince
Norodom Sihanouk to broker agreement between General Khanh and Ho Chi
Minh to terminate hostilities in Vietnam.[20]

Though Colby's suggestion for a negotiation makes no account for the
efforts the United States was making to *avoid* another Geneva-style conference, it is intriguing and represents a response to French initiatives toward
neutralizing Southeast Asia at this time. Robert McNamara now agrees the
possibility of such neutralization to have been a key missed opportunity of
the Vietnam war, but at the time the option was given short shrift. In fact
Colby here proved out of step even within the CIA, where John McCone
went on record with President Johnson that neutralization would be a victory
for Hanoi, lead to communist domination of Vietnam, and, invoking the notorious Domino Theory (which McCone's own analysts had debunked in a
June paper), further losses throughout the region.[21]

Director McCone had previously been in close concord with his Far East
Division chief on Vietnam. On neutralization the unity faltered. Possibly
Colby, the Vietnam expert, had learned that Saigon strong man Nguyen
Khanh saw possibilities for negotiation, and Colby decided on a trial balloon.
General Khanh frequently changed tack, however, and spoke also of carrying
the war North, reunifying Vietnam under Saigon's control. Americans came
to perceive Khanh's leadership as erratic, and officials like McNamara and
McGeorge Bundy actually argued that U.S. bombing of North Vietnam could
bring stability to Saigon politics. Colby did not enter the bombing debate but
he also dropped his advocacy for neutralization.

Both Colby and McCone have passed from the scene and neither left any
record how between themselves they thrashed out this disagreement, but
Colby returned to more familiar ground in another November 1964 paper he
sent to the State Department's Michael Forrestal. Renewing his advocacy of
pacification, the CIA man argued for emphasizing the civilian side of the
war: "the target would be the population, not the Viet Cong." The main
weapons would be population engagement, local auxiliaries, irregulars and
police forces; the military would be called upon only as reinforcements when

needed. Colby reiterated his oilspot scheme and concept of primacy for the province chief. Equally significant, he advocated an American chief of operations on the civilian side, who would have ambassadorial rank and be co-equal to the U.S. military commander in Vietnam, to have authority over all American civil activities.[22] Here Bill Colby had reverted to his classical role as secret warrior.

In January 1965 the Far East Division chief prepared a further "think piece" paper, one he sent to McGeorge Bundy at the White House. Commentary on negotiations had disappeared. In its place stood an invocation of "hostile, revolutionary and expanding communism" facing only weak resistance along the periphery from traditional social structures. Colby argued that the U.S. drive to counter these expanding forces had been hampered by the fragmented efforts of individual agencies. American embassies, in a fresh exposition of Colby's Vietnam formula, should have a "chief of operations" with stature equal to any military commander and responsibility for all U.S. economic, social, and political activities including those of the CIA. Titled "The Political Weapon for Political War," Colby in effect proposed a czar for political action. In many ways this proposal prefigured later Washington decisions on pacification in Vietnam.[23]

The latest Bill Colby think piece reached McGeorge Bundy just prior to the national security adviser's departure for Saigon on yet one more inspection visit for President Johnson. This trip is most remembered for the incident at Pleiku, where Viet Cong and North Vietnamese troops shelled a base and laid demolition charges that killed many Americans in their barracks. The Pleiku incident triggered U.S. retaliatory bombing of North Vietnam, which became the start of a sustained air campaign. Mac Bundy's recommendations from the scene helped LBJ make up his mind on the bombing. Ironically, both Bill Colby and Chet Cooper—CIA proponents of massive counterinsurgency, a different strategy in the war—were among Bundy's travel party.

Another feature of Mac's Vietnam trip would be his meeting with the Buddhist Tri Quang. He emerged bewildered. Bill Colby had had an identical experience, having tea with a top bonze, discovering a huge gap between his own pragmatism and the ethereal spiritualism of the Buddhist. Colby's insight, from an earlier visit, failed at forearming Bundy in this instance.

Though the reality of a unified pacification organization still lay in the future, by early 1965 the CIA was moving rapidly toward the program that defined its operational role through the remainder of the Vietnam war. When Ambassador Taylor returned to Washington for consultations that March, the CIA program, complementing proposals from the State Department, the Defense Department, and even the United States Information Service, was ready. Leading the list of a dozen items was "extension of covert support to key Buddhist leaders," one of six political actions in the classic CIA mode and hardly necessary if in fact Buddhism had been destroyed as a political force by Diem. Also to be given CIA subsidies were student groups, farmers' cooperatives, and free labor unions.[24] Agency support for Tran Quoc Buu was about to become a regular budget item. In fact, a secret study in 1966 found CIA subsidies to groups in South Vietnam running at a level of $30 million per year. That was more than Bill Colby had spent in Italy in the huge political action program of the 1950s.

Also on the list for the agency to do in Vietnam were fresh paramilitary programs. These included "flexible assistance" to "local partisan groups" where they could be found or mobilized, a typical example being Tran Quoc Buu's so-called Shrimp Soldiers. Another project would be "expansion of guerrilla and harassment teams working in Viet Cong controlled areas." Along with this was "expansion of current political action and similar teams working in disputed areas," clearly a reference to the PATs, CTTs, and "agitation-propaganda" teams. Here the CIA reported it already provided support for 3,300 indigenous fighters.[25]

Maxwell Taylor gracefully accepted the dozen CIA projects for examination within his embassy; they were staffed, discussed at length, and batted back and forth. A few, like payoffs to Buddhists and support for montagnard "development communities," did not make it; most were approved. By the summer of 1965 the CIA had a role again, far beyond espionage or intelligence analysis. Bill Colby averaged at least two visits per year to Saigon, trips necessary due to the CIA role.

These months also saw the departure of John McCone as director of central intelligence (DCI). If William Colby had been out of step with the administration for a moment, McCone had consistently marched to a tune of his own. His opposition to the Diem coup had actually earned him credit with LBJ, who also had had a high opinion of the Vietnamese leaders, but that had been surpassed by events by December 1964. When McCone traveled to Texas in that year to meet LBJ after Christmas in Johnson City, by his own account, "I said again and again that we were wrong in knocking over Diem."[26] The CIA director had constantly expressed views on policy, pressing for attacks on North Vietnam before LBJ adopted the 34-A program, then doubting such pinpricks would suffice, then pushing for a much stronger initiative. When LBJ asked McCone "if this would not mean engagement with the Chinese Communists, I responded that this was not necessarily true."[27] It remained the considered opinion of the CIA and the intelligence community, as expressed in the national estimates, that in fact Chinese intervention (and possibly Russian as well) *would* follow strong U.S. attacks on Hanoi. When President Johnson came around to considering sustained bombing of North Vietnam, McCone suddenly stepped back to warn against making that move before the installation of a stronger Saigon government. And when the bombing finally began, McCone objected that it did not go far enough. At length McCone decided Lyndon Johnson was not giving him enough time and attention, despite the DCI's practice of personally carrying to LBJ many of the CIA's daily intelligence reports. John McCone resigned in April 1965. Lyndon Johnson had a record compiled showing that McCone had had eighty-nine meetings and fourteen telephone conversations with the president. McCone's departure would be a grave loss for Bill Colby, who never again had such close rapport with a director of central intelligence.

THE MOST VISIBLE, tragic events to occur in 1965 in Far East Division's area happened in Indonesia. There, an abortive coup d'état attempted by allegedly pro-communist military figures would be followed by massive repression of the Indonesian Communist party (PKI by its Indonesian initials). The end result would be military dictatorship, on better terms with Washington, at an enormous price. The Central Intelligence Agency's perception of, and possible role in, these events demands some attention here. On the operational side at Langley it was Bill Colby who had primary responsibility.

Any examination of the Indonesian events of 1965 has to be colored by the CIA's earlier actions in that country. During Eisenhower's administration, the agency had carried out a full scale paramilitary project in Indonesia in support of a rebel movement that ultimately failed. Like the Bay of Pigs, the U.S. hand became known, the intervention revealed when a bomber crashed and its American pilot was captured. President Sukarno, against whom the CIA had aimed its intervention, not only survived the rebellion and some bungled assassination attempts but went on to enshrine a vision of "Guided Democracy" that Washington viewed as totalitarian. Combined with that, Sukarno governed from the Left, so that Washington saw him as aligned with the PKI if not actually a communist.

When John Kennedy reached the White House he made overtures to Sukarno, who was invited to visit Washington—the first time since the CIA had tried to overthrow him. The two met the week after the Bay of Pigs debacle. Early in 1962 Bobby Kennedy returned the visit. The emissary was even more important than appeared on the surface since RFK's secret function was as Kennedy's point man on covert operations. Indeed, while in Jakarta Robert Kennedy appealed to Sukarno to release Allen L. Pope, a CIA-contract pilot then languishing in an Indonesian prison. Activists demonstrated against RFK's visit, but in July 1962 Sukarno freed the pilot. The Indonesians also permitted American mediation of their territorial dispute with Holland over what became Irian Jaya, the former Dutch colony on western New Guinea.

Sukarno continued to balance between the superpowers. In the 1950s he had become a stalwart of the movement of nonaligned nations, which had irritated Washington. He relied on Russia for military and some economic aid, but in the 1960s Sukarno permitted U.S. military training for the Indonesian army. Washington was reviewing this policy in the context of the quiet war Indonesia fought with Malaysia when Lyndon Johnson succeeded John Kennedy as president. Bill Colby sat against the wall in the Cabinet Room of the White House and took notes as Johnson had the issues talked through in the National Security Council on January 7, 1964. Colby listened as Dean Rusk called Sukarno "unsavory" and "the least responsible leader of any modern State." Bobby Kennedy expressed the consensus against continuing

U.S. military aid. John McCone warned that suspending aid would hurt U.S. interests while not inducing Sukarno to give up his war against Malaysia. President Johnson did not make a decision at that moment, but $70 million in the pipeline would be delayed.[28]

In September 1964 Colby circulated a proposal for covert action from CIA officers in Indonesia. The previous month in a speech, Sukarno had denounced the United States as an enemy of Asia. There were now numerous public indications, including passage of legislation in Washington, that U.S. aid programs were being terminated. The CIA station pointed to Sukarno's tacit approval of PKI activities but held out the possibility that "there are good men in government, the armed services, and the private sector, who are willing to work for the things they believe in." The CIA advocated measures to build up strength of noncommunist and anticommunist groups, which could flex their muscles as the CIA was "encouraging direct action against the PKI as a party." Anti-PKI harrassment activities would develop the momentum of the project. "It would have to be understood at the outset," in the words of the CIA proposal, "that the purpose of the entire exercise is agitation and the instigation of internal strife between communist and noncommunist elements." Though the CIA wanted to begin with a modest program, its measure of success would be the momentum acquired, and "this would mean a widening of [the project's] scope and an intensification of its pace."[29]

The 303 Committee, President Johnson's intelligence management group, duly considered the CIA covert action proposal. This project represented exactly the sort of political action the CIA had carried out in Italy, albeit with the harder edge of fomenting direct confrontation between the PKI and anticommunist groups. However, it had taken four months for the CIA to put together the program proposal and attain the necessary approvals from other government agencies. The final paper, completed on February 23, 1965, acknowledged a danger that were Sukarno to learn of the CIA covert operation there would be further deterioration of U.S. relations with Jakarta, but it mentioned that "some funds" had already been given ("through secure mechanisms") to key persons to bolster their ability and resolve. The project would make this more systematic and move the effort to a new level. At the 303 Committee the CIA argued that the United States had to have a master plan to keep Indonesia from moving into the Chinese camp and that this justified a major effort. Otherwise even victory in Vietnam would have little meaning. McGeorge Bundy conceded that Indonesia had not received the attention it needed in U.S. government councils but that the interagency group on covert action was not the place to make such decisions. The 303 Committee nevertheless approved the CIA's Indonesia project on March 4.[30]

Meanwhile, State Department official and former NSC staffer Michael Forrestal passed through Jakarta in February, saw Sukarno, and dangled before him the possibility of a meeting with President Johnson. Sukarno complained that the CIA had a plan to assassinate him. On February 24, just as the CIA was forwarding its Indonesia plan, ambassador Howard Jones assured Sukarno that there were no such assassination plans. A month later, on March 16, Jones reported that he had given Sukarno assurances from the CIA chief for the Far East—Colby—that there were no anti-Sukarno or anti-Indonesia subversive operations. By then, of course, the CIA project had been approved and was getting into gear.[31]

In April Desmond FitzGerald came back into the picture, now as Deputy Director for Plans, CIA's top boss for covert action. Having given a face-lift to the agency's anti-Castro activities, FitzGerald succeeded Richard Helms as DDP and brought back his old Asia Hand enthusiasm. It had been Des, holding Bill Colby's Far East Division slot in the 1950s, who had presided over Washington's end of the CIA's earlier stab at getting rid of Sukarno. As for assassinations, there had been plenty of attempts on Castro in Fitz-Gerald's previous bailiwick; he cannot have been ignorant of the concept. Ambassador Jones stated in a 1971 memoir that there were as many as seven CIA murder plots against Sukarno. No independent evidence for these exists in the public record, but it is possible Sukarno's fears were not misplaced. It is now certain there was a CIA operation, though one directed at Indonesian communists rather than Sukarno himself.

President Johnson had sent diplomat Ellsworth Bunker on a survey mission to Indonesia early in 1965, much like all the ones that went to Saigon. Bunker, who had been the mediator in the Irian Jaya dispute, had the best contacts. His recommendations from this trip became the blueprint for U.S. policy at this time: Washington should play for the long term and keep the door open to friendly relations; maintain courteous communications with Sukarno while he lived (apart from alleged murder plots, Sukarno had serious kidney problems); and the United States ought to "do all we can do to prevent a communist takeover.[32]

How those policies were carried out becomes the issue. Ambassador Jones told a regional gathering of American diplomats that spring, "From our viewpoint . . . an unsuccessful coup attempt by the PKI might be the most effective development to start a reversal of political trends in Indonesia.[33] A year earlier, Jones had dropped hints to Indonesian defense minister Abdul Haris Nasution that the United States would support the Indonesian military in the event of any confrontation with the PKI, hints that Nasution carefully avoided acknowledging.

One rumor current in Jakarta circles was that the CIA funded and backed a Council of Generals led by chief of staff Vice Air Marshal Achmad Yani. The question came into the open between Sukarno and Yani during a talk that summer.

"Is it true," Sukarno asked, "that there is a Council of Generals which is assigned to evaluate my policy?"

"There is indeed such a council," Marshal Yani replied. "I myself am the head. But the council is not aimed at making an evaluation of the policy of the president."[34]

Elsewhere Yani's council has been described as a brain trust primarily concerned with personnel decisions. One may or may not credit that description, but the rumor about the CIA and the generals' council is said to have originated with the PKI. Conversely there were many rumors that the military intended to crack down on the communists. There were others that the communists were infiltrating the armed forces. As was Saigon, Jakarta in the summer of 1965 would be a hothouse of ferment. A favorite subject of speculation remained whether the PKI or the military would strike first.

One of Ellsworth Bunker's recommendations had been that the U.S. reduce the number of advisers to the Indonesian military. This served not only to show Washington's displeasure but to get Americans out of the way in a confrontation between the military and PKI. Without doubt President Johnson focused on Vietnam, where he just now struggled over the decision to commit large numbers of ground troops to a deepening war. There was not much energy left for the Sukarno question. The United States followed Bunker's suggestion, and the embassy staff and U.S. mission in Indonesia, not merely the military advisers, were pared back from several hundred in all to a few dozen Americans.

Among the Americans who remained in Jakarta was Bernardo Hugh Tovar, the CIA station chief. Hugh—Colby's forty-three-year-old subordinate did not like using his given name—was Colombian by birth; of an old military family, he became an American citizen as a young boy and eventually graduated from Harvard. His first exposure to Southeast Asia came with the Office of Strategic Services in 1945, when Tovar parachuted into Laos with the OSS "Raven" Mission. A friend of Lou Conein from that time, Tovar had worked with Ed Lansdale in the Philippines in the 1950s. He became known to Des FitzGerald, who appreciated Tovar's smoothness and sophistication and was happy to send him to Indonesia.

Nevertheless, Tovar's was a tough job. Indonesia had the third largest communist party in the world, formed as early as 1920 by Dutch radicals in the colonies. A tradition of leftist government also figured in Sukarno's "Guided Democracy." Like Bill Colby, Tovar was Catholic, in a country even more Muslim than Vietnam was Buddhist. Americans were as obvious on the streets of Jakarta as in Saigon, and unlike Saigon, here the Russians had quite a strong contingent and were very active. The concept of mobilizing anti-communist forces in Indonesia remained far easier to advocate than execute.

In August 1965, as State Department officials wrestled with the issue of withdrawals from the embassy, undersecretary George Ball asked about the CIA covert action. Langley's representative at the meeting replied that its contacts in Indonesia were so frigid that exerting any influence, "let alone any substantial covert operation," would not be possible. Similarly, on the afternoon of September 29 in Washington, William P. Bundy held a regular monthly meeting with Colby in which the Far East Division chief presented his operating plans for Indonesia for the following month. The list seemed paltry.

"We just don't have the assets," Colby explained.[35]

Within hours of that exchange a coup began in Jakarta. Hampered by great hostility in the wake of the CIA's 1958 intervention, in addition to all the CIA's other disadvantages in Indonesia, Hugh Tovar had no inkling. He spent the previous evening at a village on the outskirts of Jakarta watching a shadow play, a *wayang kulit*, a national art form. Whether that had been for enjoyment or for a clandestine rendezvous goes unrecorded. Tovar drove home on a road that passed in front of Marshal Yani's home, where all appeared normal. The coup began in the early hours of the morning with a takeover of the radio station, post office, and certain government buildings. Before 4 A.M. the plotters had secured their major objectives.

The principal leader of coup units was a colonel of Sukarno's presidential guard, with some of his men plus two paratroop battalions from outside the capital. Small units of rebels captured six key generals, breaking into their homes at gunpoint. Chief of staff Yani was among the victims, taken to an air force base and murdered later. Defense minister Nasution escaped by climbing over the garden wall behind his house.

By morning Jakarta seemed quiet. Nothing seemed amiss to Tovar during his commute to the embassy. The presence of combat troops in the streets, rather than police, though unusual, was no tip-off. Station chief Tovar only learned what was afoot in the embassy lobby, where others told him of radio broadcasts from a "September 30 Movement" revolutionary council. Then the air attaché arrived and told that he had heard shots; one of the kidnapped generals lived nearby. Taking a second drive around embattled Jakarta, Tovar realized the long-anticipated coup had begun. An embassy cable reporting the emergency went to President Johnson at 7:20 A.M.[36]

The question was, whose coup? The coup d'état of October 1 (East Zone date) would instantly be identified with the Indonesian communists, the PKI. But while there was some evidence of Chinese arms shipments to the PKI, there was none that the party had cleared the decks for the kind of fighting with the army that must follow a coup attempt. Similarly, the kidnapped generals had been taken to a field utilized by PKI women's groups, but that field was also used by military recruits and belonged to the air force. The PKI party chief fled Jakarta in an air force plane from that same field. Sukarno has also been suspected as instigator of the coup on the basis of his known antipathy for the anticommunist Indonesian armed forces. There was also the matter of participation of elements of the presidential guard in the coup action. But under interrogation after his capture, the guard colonel who had led the coup forces proved to have had *no* leftist political sympathies and to be motivated by a desire to rid the military of corruption. Sukarno *did* hold leftist views; indeed many accused him of running the country to benefit the PKI. While the PKI's newspaper briefly endorsed the September 30 Movement, it quickly went silent and party policy was to disavow the movement and regard as misguided those members who supported the rebellion. The CIA's own analysis, presented on October 6, was that the

Indonesian situation, both foreign and domestic, highly favored the PKI and showed every sign of becoming progressively more so, and there was thus little reason the PKI should approve the murder of generals or even a change of government.[37] (The U.S. ambassador differed, claiming PKI leaders had almost certainly been in on the coup planning and that the party had begun taking vigorous security measures in mid-September.)[38] These questions cannot be resolved in the present record.

On the other hand there is an entirely different dimension to the question of the origins of the coup. This starts from the fact that, within the day, coup forces that had clearly seized Jakarta gave way to, indeed were overwhelmed by, a right-wing countercoup led by Major General Suharto, chief of the army's strategic reserve command. Remarkably, when the original coup began, its forces made no attempt to take control of strategic reserve headquarters, which would obviously have paralyzed the most important opposition. More remarkably, the kidnappers of generals did not go after Suharto, who conveniently managed to be away when they struck. Meanwhile, in his official capacity, General Suharto had personally inspected both the paratroop units forming the backbone of the rebel forces just the previous day, casting doubt as to the degree of their disloyalty. It is demonstrably true that one effect of the deaths of senior generals in these events was to wipe away the entire layer of officers who might have prevented the advancement of Suharto.

General Suharto, like Sukarno whom he eventually supplanted, had but one name and was largely a cipher to Americans. Neither the ambassador nor his embassy counselor knew Suharto, nor did Hugh Tovar or his CIA deputy, the cigar-chomping Joe Lazarsky. The military attaché apparently knew a Suharto aide but not the general himself. Langley needed a full day to come up with a CIA biographic summary on the general. The agency's coup analysis paper of October 6 used this to observe that Suharto had been "long regarded as apolitical and possibly an opportunist."[39]

The question of how well the Americans knew Suharto is material to charges the CIA stood behind the 1965 coup in Indonesia. The rebels who began the coup put out the story themselves, as justification for their actions, charging in radio broadcasts that the United States was pushing the Indonesian military to overthrow the government. The September 30 Movement claimed they were preempting that maneuver. However, Indonesian military ties with the United States were limited, aid groups had been reduced, and there remained a paucity of American knowledge of the Indonesian military. On the other hand, researchers later established that the leader of coup units in one part of Java had returned from training in the United States just a month before the coup. Moreover, the plotters were seen as military professionals, not at all communist politicos. It also strains credulity that American authorities permitted themselves to be ignorant about the leader of perhaps the single most vital Indonesian military command, particularly in a climate in which it was the Indonesian military to whom the CIA had easiest access. The Suharto point is even sharper because the United States had involved itself directly in mediation of the Irian Jaya dispute and Suharto had been the Indonesian commander there. Incidentally, the paratroop battalions in the initial coup had been under Suharto's command in Irian.[40]

There is a school of thought that the coup d'etat amounted to a CIA-staged sham, a Ngo Dinh Nhu-style fake maneuver designed to permit an overwhelming counterattack. This seems to credit Langley with undue influence among the Indonesians. President Lyndon Johnson writes, "The United States played no role in the countercoup."[41] Tovar, who insists that CIA surprise at the October 1 coup does not constitute an "intelligence failure,"[42] would agree, as would Colby, that the agency had no role in the Suharto coup. So do some outside observers. George McTurnin Kahin, until his death probably America's foremost scholar of Indonesian affairs, initially agreed. "The CIA was not involved in the attempted coup of last October," Kahin told a congressional panel in early 1966.[43] Over time, however, Kahin became less rather than more certain, writing in 1995 that "the possibility of involvement of the CIA and Britain's MI-6 are still unclear and matters of ongoing dispute."[44]

One probable CIA link would be a connection to Lieutenant Colonel Ali Martopo, who headed a shadowy Suharto intelligence unit called Special Operations, formed at the time of Indonesia's confrontation with Malaysia. Martopo was and remained close to Suharto; in the space of a few years he would rise to become a senior general. Suharto repeatedly used him on delicate and sensitive matters, or on committees or investigations that had to be handled a certain way. Given Hugh Tovar's Catholic militance, it is very suggestive that in early 1966 Colonel Martopo suddenly developed a close alliance with a Catholic student group called the PMKRI.

There were other forms of assistance to the Indonesian military as well, perhaps sparked by Colby, who made a quiet visit to Jakarta immediately following the coup, flying into the same military airfield where Suharto adherents found the bodies of the senior generals kidnapped and murdered in the initial coup. Sorting through the mess, Bill reportedly stayed several days, sleeping on a couch in the office of the ambassador, now Marshall Green. He left as silently as he had come.

Photographs of the dead generals and accounts of their murders, as well as some of the kidnappings that failed, became one centerpiece of the propaganda barrage the Indonesian military used to justify their anti-PKI violence. Propaganda is a mainstay of political action. It is highly likely that Tovar's CIA station furnished advice on these matters.

It is also a matter of record in declassified documents that the CIA helped the Indonesian military with secure communications. This began as early as October 13 with quiet provision of radio sets to General Nasution and others for their personal security and communications. Before the end of October Washington formed an interagency policy group that decided the United States might provide small quantities of specific items to the Indonesian military. This would be done not through a military assistance program but rather by a covert plan in which the Pentagon would work with the CIA to ensure minimum risk of exposure. The CIA sent a radio expert to Jakarta to survey tactical communications needs and reported back in early November that Indonesian communications needs could probably be met covertly. The CIA then assembled a formal proposal, which the 303 Committee discussed on November 19. This group asked Colby to try to find items other than the latest U.S. equipment—the KW-7, KW-11, and KW-26 encryption devices were standard in U.S. forces at that time—that could be given to the Indonesians. The CIA found a stock of older KW-11s at Clark Field, but later some nonobjectionable equipment in Japan. Colby told the 303 Committee in December that the problem had been solved.[45]

Aside from communications gear the 303 Committee approved medical supplies for the Indonesian military. Colby had his station in Thailand arrange the supplies to further disguise their origin, and the station chief there met with a top Indonesian general on November 5. The Indonesians were to make a sham purchase of the supplies that would be refunded by the CIA. The general also pressed for weapons and other covert aid for Moslem groups and nationalist youths who would fight the PKI in Central Java.[46] The CIA station chief made no promises but passed the requests on to Washington.

At Langley the CIA completed a paper on November 9 that reviewed possibilities for covert assistance to the Indonesian military. The Far East Division acknowledged that the military demands "create a definite risk for us of deliberate assistance to a group which cannot be considered a legal government." The CIA also saw the Indonesian military as determined to break the back of the PKI and eliminate it as an effective political force. Given the roots and mass support of the PKI, this meant that the military in many areas would be faced with an insurgency situation. Clearly the agency was well aware of what it might get into. Its advice was not to avoid involvement but to assess carefully the political direction and longevity of the military leadership, its legal authority, and its de facto control before any overt or readily visible assistance was provided. As for covert aid, in the words of the CIA paper, "we should avoid being too cynical about [the Indonesian military's] motives and its self-interest, or too hesitant about the propriety of extending such assistance *provided* we can do so covertly, in a manner which will not embarrass them or embarrass our government." As with the medical supplies, the CIA envisioned using covert channels to deliver what was needed, or money to buy those things. The CIA felt it could steer the Indonesians to discreet dealers and transfer agents for small arms, medicines, and other items, and by these means exercise some degree of control. The agency acknowledged it had the capability to instantly ship pallets of stockpiled older foreign equipment, that modern material would take longer and be more expensive, but argued that setting up a supply line and having "equipment . . . handed by Indonesian officers to selected civilian auxiliaries" would be much more "appropriate." The CIA bottom line was that the inherent risks had to be weighed against "what may be a unique opportunity to ensure a better future for U.S. interests in Indonesia."[47]

The full panoply of CIA assistance to the Indonesian military remains shrouded in secrecy. There is the reported $40,000 worth of communications equipment in November and December 1965. There are also reports of certain types of ammunition being given, as well as four-wheel drive vehicles like jeeps. In early December, ambassador Green consulted Washington on possible cash payoffs to certain Indonesian contacts. In any case, with legal impediments to assistance in place in the United States, for a time the CIA would be the *only* conduit for U.S. aid to the Indonesian military.

Some officials in the State Department felt the agency had been "conned" into the role of military support by misinformation from Indonesian generals. At a December 4 meeting of the interagency policy group Bill Colby strove to defend the program "but was hampered somewhat by [the] necessity of arguing on policy rather than on intelligence grounds." Several times Bill repeated his point that the United States needed to show the Indonesian military that it supported their anti-PKI campaign. He received unexpected backup from White House staffers Chester L. Cooper and James C. Thomson, who interjected that the cost of the operation was a pittance compared with the advantages that could accrue to the United States from "getting in on the ground floor" with Suharto.[48] The group decided to persist in the program if only because it had gone beyond recall.

The most controversial aspect of U.S. involvement has remained the matter of lists of names given to the military. Over the next months tens of thousands died—estimates range from a Suharto government report of 78,000 to an Amnesty International estimate of more than a million deaths. A CIA report in 1968 on "The Coup That Backfired" baldly termed these events—which crushed the PKI—one of the worst episodes of mass murder of the twentieth century, ranking with Germany's Holocaust against the Jews.[49] An agency officer who had custody of the CIA's classified history of Indonesia for a time has stated that simultaneously with it the agency prepared a second, more secret, review that admitted much broader engagement in the bloodbath. At a 1984 forum on CIA covert operations this officer was virtually shouted down by Hugh Tovar and others. Controversy surged further in 1990 when journalist Kathy Kadane published an account of how the U.S. embassy provided the Indonesian military with lists of the names of PKI militants used by troops and armed youths who were the tools of the bloodbath.[50]

The U.S. embassy in Jakarta *did* maintain a card index file of noteworthy PKI members. Diplomat Robert J. Mertens, a political officer, publicly admitted at the time of the Kadane revelations that he had passed names to the Indonesians during the six-month interregnum between the countercoup and the final fall of Sukarno. Martens based his lists on the Indonesian communist press and other publicly available information and compiled them more than two years before the bloodbath. Documents declassified for publication in the official series *Foreign Relations of the United States* now provide authoritative evidence that at least three such lists, totaling hundreds of names of senior officials, embodied in messages called "airgrams," were sent to Washington. The first (and key) list was in Airgram A-398 of December 17, 1965. The State Department officially acknowledges this list was given to the Indonesian military. Later, in 1966, a cable from Jakarta states that the Indonesians seemed to have little information on their communist opposition, meaning that provision of those lists assumes great importance.[51]

According to CIA deputy chief of station Joseph Lazarsky and State Department personnel as well, the CIA contributed substantially to the PKI card files. Sets of the file, it seems, were kept in the embassy safe and within the CIA station. In the media blaze that welled up when the lists issue surfaced in 1990, attention focused primarily on Martens and his card file. But the embassy link, which provided the information to an aide of Indonesian diplomat Adam Malik, would hardly be the only U.S. channel to the Indonesians.

Langley had always been enamored of lists as an intelligence tool, and lists of communists could be used in many ways. Kathy Kadane interviewed Bill Colby on the subject of Indonesia and reports that he spoke of lists and compared the exercise to his work in Stockholm, where he had compiled similar lists of communists in Sweden in the early 1950s. Colby also talked of the need to go after the adversary's political organization in order to really cripple him; he showed a sophisticated understanding of the organizational similarities and distinctions between the PKI and the Russian and Chinese communist parties, all of which knowledge had to have flowed from the kind of research that produced lists. The question of whether the Indonesians used CIA—or any U.S.—lists of PKI members is irrelevant to the matter of whether *handing over* such lists constituted a moral offense. Moreover, on the specific issue of CIA responsibility, the agency had gone to great lengths in a *real* covert action, Guatemala, which had been considered a model in the CIA and with which Hugh Tovar was familiar, to compile lists of communists for the explicit purpose of having them killed (the "A" list) or imprisoned (the "B" list). In the Indonesian affair the surprise would be if there were *no* CIA lists.

When Kathy Kadane's charges of U.S. involvement in the coup aftermath appeared in print, another reporter queried Bill Colby on what he had said in Kadane's interview. Colby replied his remarks had been "misappropriated."[52] But Colby's context had been as a comparison between what happened in Indonesia and the Phoenix program in South Vietnam. As shall be seen presently, there was a real comparison to be made. It is likely the former CIA chieftain had been quoted accurately. At a 1988 conference at Tufts University, Bill Colby answered a question posed by Indonesia scholar Audrey Kahin by saying he had never been aware of any United States or CIA objection to or criticism of the Indonesians' 1965–66 killings of citizens for their political beliefs.[53] That does square with the record detailed here.

One more aspect of the Indonesia affair that requires comment is the assertion, made by administration defenders at the time and by some scholars since, that the United States intervention in Vietnam motivated the Indonesians and made possible their military crackdown against communism. The considered opinion of the Central Intelligence Agency, rendered in a secret May 1966 report, is this: "We have searched in vain for evidence that the U.S. display of determination in Vietnam directly influenced the outcome of the Indonesian crisis in any significant way."[54]

Officially the CIA continues to deny having anything to do with the events in Indonesia during 1965–66. The recently declassified record, however, makes it crystal clear that this was not for want of trying, and that Bill Colby's Far East Division favored the active intervention that occurred. The countercoup took the form most desired by American officials and triggered a confrontation between Indonesian communist and anticommunist groups, the achievement of which had been the goal of a CIA project. If these things happened coincidentally, the conclusion must be that they took place in spite of failure of the CIA's covert action, not that no such operation occurred. The agency then helped fuel a tragedy that continued to divide Indonesia long afterward.

In the after years, Bill Colby said little about Indonesia. By contrast to Vietnam, where he wrote much, even on the most controversial aspects, his memoirs contain but a single sentence on Indonesia, 1965. The spy chieftain describes the episode as the PKI killing the army leadership (with Sukarno's unstated approval) and then being decimated in reprisal. Colby wrote that apart from the reports it furnished, the CIA "did not have any role in the course of events themselves."[55] Elsewhere, in recounting his passion for travel, Colby describes as a high point late night conversations he had regarding Indonesian revolutionary theory. Why such talk mattered, other than as necessary to plot a course for the CIA in Jakarta, is left unsaid. Implicit is the full spectrum defense of the CIA—that the agency had nothing to do with either the coup or the bloodbath. Secret warriors who loved to hate Colby have not given him sufficient credit for holding the line in defense of the CIA on Indonesia.

Meanwhile, service in Jakarta during this year of living dangerously proved no setback at all for Hugh Tovar. What Colby did can only be interpreted to show that he thought highly of the Indonesian affair: Colby dispatched the CIA's man on the scene of the bloodbath to Laos to run the agency's secret war there, probably the Far East Division's most sensitive covert operation. The CIA remained at war; that war was a crusade, and Bill Colby had committed his life to it.

OFFICIAL INVESTIGATIONS later established that the number of covert operations carried out by the United States reached its all-time high in 1964, while CIA funds expended for political action and propaganda projects mushroomed 60 percent during the years between then and 1967. Although such projects declined in number, roughly a third were for the purpose of influencing foreign elections, about 30 percent were media or propaganda projects, and 23 percent were to create or run secret armies or carry out covert weapons transfers. The Far East Division undertook more of these projects than any of DDP's five other area divisions. In personnel terms as well, the Directorate of Plans employed approximately 6,000 officers and a quarter of them worked directly for William E. Colby. The Far East Division during his watch became the largest component of the clandestine service.

Seven of ten clandestine services officers worked on classical intelligence functions of espionage or counterespionage. Only about 1,800 were paramilitary specialists, many of them former or current military officers detached to the CIA or working for it under contract. Again the preponderance of these "knuckle-draggers," as spooks called the paramilitary officers, were in the Far East Division. Fighting a war—the Far East Division ran one in Laos and participated in another in Vietnam—tended to dictate priorities. Paramilitary experts might be in the minority, but they spent sixty cents of every DDP dollar, while the clandestine service as a whole spent 58 percent of the CIA's annual budget. Bill Colby presided over major wars in Laos and Vietnam, a minor war in Tibet, skirmishes in Korea, something (whatever that be) in Indonesia, and political actions or espionage activities throughout the Far Eastern arc of crisis.

Even this accounting does not convey a full picture of the scope of Far East Division's work. In Laos, for example, the FE Division functioned as executive agent, not just for the Central Intelligence Agency but for the entire U.S. effort. It has been estimated that the CIA's expenses in Laos funded only a tenth of the annual cost of that war. The Pentagon supplied—and paid for—weapons aid, muscular airpower, and key technical advisers and trainers. The Agency for International Development not only carried conventional foreign aid roles but also supplied food for the CIA's secret army and even certain military aid in the guise of assistance to Laotian police forces. The aggregate costs of the Laotian war stood at $300 million per year, rising to $500 million as the war stretched into the 1970s. Even with its success getting other agencies to pay portions of the bill, the CIA's paramilitary budget grew constantly, to reach an all-time high (as a percentage of budget expenditure) in 1970, not long after the agency sent Colby back to Vietnam.

Managing this far-flung empire posed challenges every day. The agency's budget hovered at the same level—about $750 million—for more than a decade. With Southeast Asia costs rapidly increasing, there was no way Colby could find the cash required without appeals for more funds. In 1964 Director McCone made the decision to give Southeast Asia priority and the CIA began to reprogram money from other accounts to support the war.

With personnel, the situation evolved similarly. The CIA station in Saigon had had about forty people when Colby arrived there. When Bill left the number had shot up to 200. By Peer De Silva's time CIA personnel had doubled again. Even within the Far East Division, Southeast Asia had not been the hot ticket during the 1950s—China and Tibet qualified there—and there were only a certain number of Vietnam specialists. When Colby reached his chief of division job, the CIA had pretty much run through its cadre of experts. Moreover, now Vietnam had begun transforming into a real war, with increased demands to match. Project Switchback resulted in a temporary diminution of demand, but Lyndon Johnson's orders for new Vietnam initiatives put the edge back on the problem. There was also the fact that, with Southeast Asia becoming what China had been, more officers wanted assignments there. Colby responded by innovating a system of rotation and opening up service selections to anyone who would volunteer. John McCone nixed that scheme. The CIA director respected the president's demands for only the best to go to Vietnam. That directive lasted only as long as McCone's tenure as DCI. Vietnam service would soon be open to anyone, even those outside the FE Division.

Meanwhile the true Vietnam experts became more disillusioned at the thought of a real war. Officers like Robert J. Myers and David Smith saw their cautions ignored and an increasing flow of demands for missions they considered impossible. The war had begun to arouse political controversy in the United States and would shortly become much more contentious. Ennui caused a trickle of resignations, early retirements, or requests for posts as far away from Vietnam as possible. Some officers left for places as remote as southern cone countries watched by the Western Hemisphere Division. Others simply left the CIA. When Colby's second, Bob Myers departed, Bill replaced him with a stalwart from Rome, who happened to be a political action expert.

Another personnel decision gave the division chief more pleasure. The agency's deputy field officer with the Hmong secret army, Vint Lawrence, proved a model of dedication. Coming home to muster out of the Army, Lawrence got a regular CIA job and immediately returned to Laos, where he worked his heart out, became intimate with Vang Pao, and gradually got into trouble with boss Tony Po, who was increasingly being bypassed by American officials who wanted to get anything done with the Hmong. When Lawrence contracted hepatitis it seemed like the end. Instead, Bill Colby, who had enjoyed his cables and thought him a bright young man (it did not hurt Lawrence to have graduated from Princeton), brought Vint to Langley as his special assistant. Colby saw this as Lawrence's chance to learn about the mysterious ways of Washington. Lawrence made a movie on Laos for CIA training classes, and he witnessed some headquarters skulduggery, but Langley was not for him. In the mid-1960s Lawrence joined the stream of officers leaving the CIA. He left with thoughts of going back to school for a doctorate in anthropology, but gave that up for the joys of political cartooning. Vint Lawrence eventually worked for Bob Myers at *The New Republic*.

More difficult management problems surrounded issues of the size and pecking order of CIA stations. Agency installations in Korea and on Taiwan had lost much of their importance since the 1950s but remained bloated with case officers spinning their wheels. Colby found his "in" tray crammed with cables reporting marginal or useless information gleaned from cocktail party gossip on the diplomatic circuit. The division chief resorted to grading the cable traffic like a school teacher ranking essays, then dividing the averages by the number of station personnel. Colby could then produce a chart showing that some small stations produced valuable information and some large ones did not. With these performance ratings in hand it became easier to force reductions in size. The demands of the Vietnam war also generated pressures that were useful in this campaign.

The biggest flap during the first part of Colby's time as Far East Division chief started, once again, in Vietnam. That morning in Saigon began the same as any other for Peer De Silva. The station chief took a break and went out on Tu Do street to buy some ceramic elephants for his wife in the Philippines. Back in the office, De Silva phoned a subordinate in a nearby embassy annex. He stood in the window talking. Absently looking into the street, he noticed an old gray Peugeot being pushed up the narrow road, unusual since that street had been closed off following the earlier bombing of a U.S. barracks in Saigon. The car appeared to have broken down; one Vietnamese who had been pushing it disappeared up a side street and the driver began arguing with the guard who came out to challenge these men. The Peugeot was a car bomb. One horrified instant before it exploded, De Silva saw the detonator, a time pencil wedged into the front seat, a scene graven on the CIA man's mind forevermore. It was March 30, 1965.

Peer De Silva was rushed to the U.S. Navy dispensary, critically injured by glass shards. One of his secretaries, twenty-one-year-old Barbara Robbins, died in the blast, as did another American, a Filipino, and nineteen Vietnamese. Almost two hundred more persons were injured. The American victims were given triage, then moved to Tan Son Nhut, where Air Force transports picked them up for immediate movement to the Philippines. From there John McCone arranged another flight, stopping only for fuel, to Washington and treatment at Bethesda Naval Medical Center. The CIA victims included several more from the typing pool and at least two case officers. Bill Colby accompanied McCone to Andrews Air Force Base to meet the medical evacuation flight, and he and Barbara later visited De Silva in the hospital.

Barely a week after the embassy bombing President Johnson ordered the landing of the first contingent of American combat troops to enter the Vietnam war, and before the summer was out LBJ made the decision to commit major forces. With Johnson having begun sustained bombing of North Vietnam a month earlier, the United States had plunged into a big war.

The bombing also crystallized renewed debate over an old issue: counterintelligence in Vietnam. Bill had fought this out with the CIA's chief counterspy Jim Angleton in his days as station chief; now the issue resurfaced. Had the agency known about Viet Cong terror plans, some response might have been possible. Angleton, whose brief included all CIA counterespionage activities, demanded a complete revamp, strengthening counterintelligence capabilities in the Saigon station and using every technique down to background investigations and lie detector tests of all Vietnamese in contact with agency people. Colby believed in standing behind the Saigon government to support it; too much counterintelligence would seem as though the Americans did not trust their Vietnamese allies and could be interpreted as trampling on Vietnamese sovereignty.

Angleton recast his concept as a vest-pocket operation of his own, like the one he had run in Italy. He summoned John Mertz, veteran of a dozen years with the agency, and sent him to Saigon to set up an activity outside the CIA station. Officers would have U.S. military cover and report on a direct channel to Angleton, completely bypassing the station and FE Division as well. Mertz had been a lawyer for the Securities and Exchange Commission, and before that an FBI special agent, and he had finely honed bureaucratic sensibilities. He went to Gordon Jorgensen to clear the counterintelligence project. The CIA station chief in turn checked it out with Army intelligence Major General Joseph C. McChristian. The latter would be happy to provide cover but made it clear the CIA men would have to come under his command. Jorgensen naturally objected to the separate communications channel. That was two strikes already. Angleton's proposal came down to a meeting at Langley among the Directorate of Plans potentates. Division chief Colby objected that adding yet one more intelligence service in Vietnam would be counterproductive. No one supported Angleton. The plan died on the vine.

Some former CIA men, or military types detached to the agency, criticize Colby for resisting counterintelligence initiatives in Vietnam. It certainly was true that Viet Cong agents were everywhere—an analyst concluded later there might be as many as 30,000. But Colby's points about trust and sovereignty were valid, and it remained true that the CIA itself infiltrated the South Vietnamese regime as extensively as possible. A major push on counterintelligence could only be done in conjunction with the South Vietnamese and it could turn up as many CIA spies as Hanoi agents.

Meanwhile John McCone had come to the end of his days at the agency. He would be replaced by Admiral William F. Raborn. A Navy technocrat, Raborn had made his name in the effort to develop missile-launching submarines and knew nothing about the CIA. Having an intelligence professional to second him seemed especially important, so Richard Helms moved up to become deputy director of central intelligence. That opened up the DDP job. The main contenders were Colby and his good friend, now masterminding the anti-Castro operation, Desmond FitzGerald. The dark horse candidate would be former Rome station chief Thomas Karamessines, reputed to be the ultimate spy, whom Helms had made his chief of operations, the number three man in DDP. Helms consulted all his division chiefs before making a recommendation, a choice with which Raborn essentially could only agree.

"Your time will come later," Dick told Bill when Colby sat down for their talk.

Colby himself advised calling on Des FitzGerald but keeping an eye out for his extravagances. Helms had already made that choice.

Only a few months later FitzGerald's extravagance would be highlighted by an FE Division snafu over Singapore. In 1960, while Des had headed FE Division, a CIA lie detector operator had gone there to "flutter" an agent. This routine inquiry soured when the CIA expert blew out the fuses in the hotel trying to work his equipment, and the episode ended with the operator, the agent, and another CIA officer from the Singapore station all in jail. Allen Dulles, according to local authorities, offered $3.3 million in ransom for the CIA officers. Prime Minister Le Kuan Yew let them go for free, but mentioned the incident in a 1965 speech, remarking on the apology Singapore had gotten from Secretary of State Dean Rusk. The State Department asked the CIA about this incident, and Colby's division denied the particulars, on the strength of which State made a public denial. Le Kuan Yew countered by showing Rusk's letter to the press. Colby's embarrassment only increased when Senator Bourke B. Hickenlooper, one of the all-powerful congressional overseers of the CIA, wanted a briefing on the affair. Langley officials told Hickenlooper what he wanted to know on September 13, 1965.

That flap would be followed by another six months later, one for which Colby could not even claim the original events had not happened on his watch. In this case an officer of the KGB, Russia's intelligence service, had been targeted for recruitment by the Tokyo station. Russian operations had a priority within DDP such that every station anywhere tried to work against agents of that country. In the Tokyo affair, David E. Murphy, chief of DDP's Soviet Division, went to Tokyo to attempt the recruitment. He arranged a meeting at an apartment building and showed up with support from officers of the FE Division's Tokyo station. The Russian prospect, however, had been setting up the CIA, and a bunch of KGB security men awaited Murphy at the meeting place.

This encounter turned into a regular brawl, with a CIA division chief punching people in the nose and getting his name in the papers. Murphy would be declared *persona non grata* by the government of Japan and expelled from the country. Again the agency's overseers wanted to hear about the incident. Senator Leverett Saltonstall would be briefed on April 15, 1966, followed by Senator John C. Stennis four days later. Bill Colby had few excuses; his inspection trips to Japan had centered on political action projects that now seemed superfluous, such as terminating support for a Japanese intellectual journal.

Senators Stennis, Saltonstall, and Hickenlooper could affect the CIA's entire budget because of their participation in the informal system of intelligence oversight existing at that time. The entire CIA had thus been affected by mistakes made in Colby's Far East Division. The division chief had a few difficult moments with his bosses. The Singapore incident, in particular, also contained a larger lesson, one that would be a precursor to what happened to Colby much later: in agency work, actions buried deep in the past could return to create tough problems in the present.

In the meantime, throughout the arc of crisis the Central Intelligence Agency kept up its barrage of projects, programs, and plain everyday spying—supervised by Bill Colby. A man whose passion for travel remained to be slaked, Colby could be seen everywhere the Far East Division worked. But the heart of the struggle, more and more, centered on Southeast Asia. Conflict in Vietnam and Laos had escalated to a new level of intensity.

10

EXHILARATION OF WAR

WHEN COLBY LEFT JAKARTA following his quiet trip to Indonesia in October 1965, he went to Thailand, and then Laos, starting the regular routine of one of his Southeast Asian inspection swings. The irony in the Laos leg of the journey is that it reversed the tour, made a few months before, by the neutralist military figure Kong Le. In its last months the Sukarno government, in keeping with its image as a paragon of the nonaligned movement, had dispatched a survey team to the Kong Le forces, invited them to send officers to Indonesia for training, and talked of providing military aid. Americans, who did not much like Kong Le to start with—in fact, the CIA had forced the replacement of U.S. military advisers with the neutralists a year earlier, when it had seemed Kong Le had expanded his holdings too much—can only have regarded it as a bonus that the Indonesian coup put a halt to possibilities of further Indonesian aid to Kong Le.

The situation in Laos in late 1965 was both the same as and different from what it had been. Kong Le's power had waned, though his neutralist army still held ground and had constituted itself as an autonomous force (only in 1968 would it be formally reintegrated into the royalist army). The national police, another key faction, had been purged after a succession of two coup attempts. The second of these, in February 1965, featured U.S. ambassador William H. Sullivan's putting his embassy (and CIA) communications system into service to keep pro-government forces abreast of fast-breaking developments. The dry season still brought with it Pathet Lao–North Vietnamese military offensives, with government troops and CIA-supported irregulars striking back during the rains. Often the same places were fought over, again and again. In 1964 the government launched a massive attack, called Operation Triangle, to recapture the Plain of Jars. A year later another campaign took place there.

Central Intelligence Agency programs remained in place throughout the country. Back in Washington for a visit, Ambassador Sullivan participated in a full-scale presentation of these in July 1965, indeed during the same week when President Johnson made the fateful decision to dispatch massive reinforcements to South Vietnam. Director Raborn told Sullivan that the CIA, moving ahead with an action program in Vietnam, really intended to take a regional approach to the entire matter. Peer De Silva—now the DCI's special assistant for Vietnam affairs, his eye injuries from the Saigon bombing stabilized if not healed—Desmond FitzGerald, and Bill Colby made up the rest of the group who met at Langley, in the director's wood-paneled conference room. Sullivan was a strong ambassador and intended to ride herd on the CIA. Agency officials tried to convince him to give them a free hand. Colby, in particular, argued that unless the CIA was able to build a base of popular support defended by some armament, it would have a hard time meeting Sullivan's demands for intelligence.

The ambassador's response went unrecorded, but in fact the CIA moved ahead in Laos on every front. Station chief Douglas Blaufarb, who had had to be convinced of the efficacy of the Hmong special guerrilla units (SGUs), had ended up a dedicated supporter. In 1964 the Hmong secret army stood at 19,000 troops, building toward a strength of 23,000. Under Project Momentum, the Hmong not only increased in number, but they also benefited from a constant stream of SGUs sent to Thailand for advanced training in a safe environment. The SGUs were also given heavier U.S. weapons, right up to 105 mm howitzers. Project Pincushion, recruiting Lao Theung in middle Laos, had 1,200 tribesmen under arms out of 2,000 authorized. The basis for the road watch teams on the Ho Chi Minh Trail, Project Hardnose, which recruited among Kha or Bru tribesmen, had 400 soldiers and aimed at 1,000. There were another 1,700 tribal soldiers in CIA secret armies in the far north of Laos. In addition the agency was starting a large-scale pacification program along the Mekong in southern Laos, it expanded Air America with additional C-7 and C-123 transports, and it continued massive political action among Lao elites in Vientiane and elsewhere.

All these things and more were checked when Colby visited that October. Unbending, distant, and reserved, Bill's idea of casual would be to take off his suit jacket. He could step out of an Air America light plane, at the most remote of airstrips, wearing a tie, often a bow tie, in ninety degree heat. On this trip Colby and Blaufarb visited Long Tieng, where he looked over Vint Lawrence exactly the way he had done with De Silva before the Saigon assignment. That is when Bill decided to bring in Lawrence as his aide. The station chief also was nearing the end of a two-year tour, so Colby faced the need to come up with a new man for Vientiane. Des FitzGerald relieved him of that headache, offering to cut short an assignment and send his man in Berlin, Theodore G. Shackley. The latter had impressed FitzGerald in Miami during the Cuban affair. As DDP, Des could have his way, and Colby had to swallow Shackley, but that turned out to be no problem. Cautious but energetic, nervous but crafty, skinny and pale as Bill himself, Shackley soon convinced the Far East Division chief that he was among the unit's finest officers.

Meanwhile Hanoi took the Laotian war to a whole new level during the 1965–66 dry season, when major reinforcements enabled the Pathet Lao and Vietnam People's Army to push back government forces on many fronts. One Hmong stronghold, Na Khang, which had held out against an earlier attack, barely survived thanks to massive aerial intervention. In fact it would be the Air Force that made the difference in the Laotian campaign as a whole that year, in three ways. First, spotters—either Laotians or Hmong, or CIA contract airmen, flying light planes—picked up targets on the ground and instantly relayed them to planes that could strike. Second, there would be a new level of intensity in air operations, not merely the Laotian air force with some covert CIA-Thai contributions, but regular missions by U.S. planes. The Air Force flew 6,219 fighter-bomber sorties over northern Laos in 1965 and 6,746 more during 1966. Third were the so-called gunships, converted transport aircraft so large they could carry numerous machine guns and even automatic cannon. Backed by this aerial armada, once the rainy season came, Vang Pao regained 90 percent of the ground lost to the Pathet Lao offensive.

Nevertheless the threat really *was* bigger, though perhaps not as looming as some of the spooks feared. Colby would recall for Lyndon Johnson's oral historian how Hanoi suddenly surged its troops from 7,000 to 70,000 implying that Vang Pao's secret army resisted this huge accretion of force. In truth the great preponderance of the North Vietnamese increase went into southern Laos, to protect and improve the Ho Chi Minh Trail. The Vietnam People's Army buildup in the north went from a few battalions to the equivalent of more than a division, but in terms of numbers of combat troops there were still fewer than 10,000. Pathet Lao made up by far the greater proportion of enemy strength in Laos.

Ted Shackley thought he was going to transform the secret war in Laos. The way it then worked, Project Momentum remained the baby of the CIA base at Udorn, Thailand, where Bill Lair carefully parceled out responsibility and stepped in to break bottlenecks. The deputy chief of base, Pat Landry, functioned as Lair's twin; indeed the two worked at desks backed against each other. They handled Vang Pao through the CIA base at Long Tieng. The air staff, under Robert Blake, later Richard Secord, either former or detached Air Force officers, took requests from Lair or direct from Hmong SGUs and passed them along to the Seventh Air Force, to Air America, or its twin, Continental Air Services. The Hmong special guerrilla units could ask for supplies, Hmong reinforcements to be shuttled by Air America, or fighter-bombers. The latter would be coordinated by spotter planes whose pilots were soon called "Ravens," for their radio call signs. Ravens and "air," meaning more air support, quickly became the most frequent demand.

A man who appreciated his perquisites, Shackley traveled once down to Udorn, but there he told Lair that henceforth the base chief would be required to fly up to Vientiane for meetings of Shackley's lieutenants at the embassy.

Shackley saw Lair's rubber band and baling wire operation as a village market, but he wanted to run a supermarket, a high-intensity covert war. Tony Po, recently wounded, would not return to Long Tieng. Instead Shackley brought in Thomas G. Clines, who had worked with him briefly in Berlin in the late 1950s and again in Miami on the anti-Castro operation. Clines, who had begun at the CIA in the mailroom, would never attain the intimacy with Vang Pao that Vint Lawrence had had, or even the easy familiarity of Tony Po, but he had something more important—the ear of Theodore Shackley.

With Shackley in place less than a month, Bill Colby came out for another inspection. The Far East chieftain visited the Hmong, to be sure, but his favorite locale would be down the Lao panhandle, around Savannakhet. There, beginning in 1964, the CIA funded extensive pacification programs along the lines Colby had been advocating at the time. Pacification consisted of an array of complementary efforts to bring security to villages, improve their economic status, and convince villagers of the effectiveness of local political administration, with all attributed to the national government in such fashion as to command loyalty.

The pacification area in the panhandle, which Colby had also seen as a reason for satisfaction on his most recent previous visit, illustrates how the reality in Laos was always so much more complex than was evident from a quick glance. The International Voluntary Services (IVS), whose workers had helped Colby mobilize the montagnards when he was station chief in Saigon, were also in Laos, and shouldered much of the village and refugee work in this part of the country. For years—right through 1970, which is our latest data point—IVS volunteers found their lives subject to uneasy accommodations between the Pathet Lao and Laotian government. Near Savannakhet, for example, at the big army garrison and air base of Seno, the largest in this part of Laos, the local commander ordered his troops not to shoot unless the Pathet Lao were obviously attacking rather than merely coming in for a night on the town. The reason, according to IVS member George Dalley, was that Laotian officers would frighten themselves if they opened fire each time Pathet Lao appeared.

Farther north there was little question of pacification. There the Hmong secret army fought a war. Visiting Bill Lair at the end of July, Colby was impressed enough to report that a "marriage" of "excellent intelligence" from CIA (courtesy of the Hmong) had "enabled outnumbered friendly units to not only contain the enemy offensive but to mount a counteroffensive."[1] Colby expressed pleasure that the situation seemed so much better than on his last visit, eight months before: "Our side in Laos has the initiative and is looking around for additional work to do." In sum, wrote the Far East division chief, "I found the situation in Laos exhilarating."[2]

Below the surface, however, Shackley's supermarket secret war marked a less effective CIA program, not a more successful one. Historians of Laos commonly date the peak Hmong war effort in 1965 or early 1966, just before the arrival of the new station chief. At Shackley's behest, Colby told Washington of a need for more personnel for CIA in Laos, and the agency fought through the 303 Committee another force increase for CIA irregulars. Shackley also presided over a new initiative with larger Hmong units, groupings of several SGUs with supporting heavy weapons or artillery, necessary because the typical Special Guerrilla Unit could no longer hold its own in the field. Meanwhile the pattern of operations in Laos remained the same. Dry season defeats followed monsoon offensives.

Essentially, the logistical advantage changed with the weather, and whichever side had the momentary advantage could add to the territory it controlled. "Air" gave the CIA the advantage in rain; raw strength reversed the tide in favor of Hanoi during dry seasons. The one inexorable trend would be that every day more Hmong fighters died. Younger and younger tribesmen went to war. The day would soon dawn when the CIA had to enlist Thais to fight in place of the Hmong rather than simply being the liaison between Americans and tribesmen. *That* would be the change Ted Shackley ushered in, not the one he expected, hardly what FE chief Colby anticipated.

In the mid-1960s, when Vint Lawrence still lived at Long Tieng, Langley's emphasis had been on nation building among the Hmong, who were encouraged to become a unified people. Intermediate and high schools were started. Lawrence's prize achievement would be the foundation of a Hmong shortwave radio station. But a tribal nation ultimately represented a challenge to the Lao monarchy. The king visited Long Tieng twice but never again after the inauguration of the Hmong radio broadcasts. Washington's basic alliance remained with the Lao state, not the tribe; there was only one way this could end.

Another aspect of Hmong culture that would prove difficult for the CIA was opium: the tribe grew poppies and used opium as a recreational and ceremonial drug. The sap of these flowers could also be turned into heroin, and indeed the northern Laos-Thailand-Burma region of Southeast Asia is known as the "Golden Triangle" for the heroin produced there. Lao military figures involved themselves in the trade, using runners to buy opium in the hills, refining the stuff themselves or passing it along in a stream that swelled the world drug trade. "Air," the same glue that held together the Laotian war effort, made the drug trade possible. Back in 1963 one of the U.S. counters to negate claims that Air America was breaching the Geneva agreement had been to give some transport planes directly to the Laotians. With pilots from the Laotian air force, the planes now belonged to senior generals and ran opium for them. Couriers could also board Air America flights with drugs in their baggage. In 1966 the Lao were doing enough flying to move 400 tons per month in official cargo; Air America flew 6,000 tons per month plus 16,000 passengers. The second of the Laotian military coups to occur on Bill Colby's watch at FE Division came in the fall of that year: an attempt by the Laotian air force's senior field commander to overthrow the corrupt generals. The coup failed.

The Vietiane CIA station, well aware of the opium trade, could do nothing. Or more properly, it did a few things, but not always with expected results. In 1967, for example, Burmese Shan tribesmen in a caravan bearing opium were attacked inside Laos by nationalist Chinese. The latter, who also came from Burma and were in the trade, were CIA allies on intelligence missions into China. But here the object seemed to be possession of the opium. The Laotian air force mobilized to bomb the contending sides, driving off the factions. But when Laotian troops took control of the drugs, these promptly disappeared into the coffers of the Lao generals. A few years afterward a team from the CIA inspector general's office conducted a formal investigation of allegations of drug trafficking by the agency. Their report exonerated the CIA, finding no evidence of direct involvement other than individual cases of "bad apples." Scott D. Breckinridge, a senior investigator on this team, writes of seeing some of the Laotian planes as he flew around the country and notes: "It also developed that high command in the Laotian Air Force had been involved, and that some air force planes had carried drugs."[3] Ted Shackley would tell his biographer in a later interview: "We found no evidence of organized trafficking by the Hmong who were involved in our paramilitary program."[4] There were nevertheless recurrent allegations of involvement by Vang Pao himself. Former national security council staffer Michael Forrestal, who visited the Hmong leader in 1963, believed he saw sacks of raw opium in the headquarters building and felt that Vang Pao kept the stuff as a sort of reserve asset.[5]

This particular controversy boiled along past Bill Colby's watch. The division chief preferred to focus on the nuts and bolts of the CIA's Laotian projects. When he visited once more in the summer of 1967, Colby reported the Hmong were accounting for over 400 dead Pathet Lao per month while contributing key intelligence for air strikes with results twice that high. By contrast, the royal Laotian army accounted for a mere seventy battle deaths per month. Is it any wonder the CIA did not wish to look too closely at drug allegations? Colby also emphasized social progress, but the major implications of his observations were programmatic. Back at Langley, the division chief would lash subordinates in the branch that covered Laos to prepare congressional briefing materials Colby could use to buttress a request for a major funding increase. The CIA had experimented with some platoon-size tribal strike units. It had had about a dozen but Shackley pushed for, and Colby went along with, a force of more than a hundred of these platoons. Starting with a pep rally in his office, Colby watched carefully for three weeks while the briefing took shape. To give the impression that the CIA already had the units and was simply talking about getting more recruits, the existing force would be divided, on paper, into "platoons" of just three men. To convey the proper sense of potential, the platoons were termed "mobile strike forces," a label used in South Vietnam for battalion-size montagnard units. Colby went ahead with the briefing and Congress gave the CIA the money for the project.

Meanwhile, Bill continued to emphasize social, political, and economic aspects—in a word, pacification. Colby's summer 1967 trip report carefully notes that there were now seventy tribal persons in the top Lao *lycée,* a high school equivalent, compared to ten in 1962. And as for pacification overall, as the FE Division chief put it, "There are small 'islands' in Vietnam proving the feasibility of this technique . . . but in Laos the program indicates how much more can be done if the process is started before the enemy grows to be a major military threat."[6]

Manifestly Bill Colby remained wedded to his preference for a formula that soon brought him to a whole new departure. In the meantime he saw Ted Shackley as a water walker. The Laotian chickens had yet to come home to roost, and Colby would no longer be with FE when that happened. In persona, Shackley and Colby bore several similarities—though Pat Landry and Bill Lair, at least, thought Shackley rather overweight when he arrived in the land of a million elephants, and Bill had no use for the motorcycle escorts Ted favored. But there was plenty to draw them together: Shackley had been in the good fight against the Russians, heading the Polish branch of the CIA's Berlin base. Ted had also been accepted at Princeton (although he had attended the University of Maryland instead), and as a youth Shackley had been an altar boy and had wanted to become a priest.

Bill Colby liked that. In 1968, with his own time at the Far East Division evaporating, Colby gave Shackley a hand up. Saigon station could use fresh blood—the chief there had been deputy previously and had been in place a long time. Bill nominated Shackley for the job. Little did he know, then, that the move would come back to bedevil him later.

Peer De Silva lasted barely a year as the Central Intelligence Agency's Special Assistant for Vietnam Affairs. In spite of his eye problems he did not feel ready for a Langley headquarters job. De Silva wanted to be in the field, needed, somewhere on the front line. Colby had another slot that needed to be filled. It was on the front, Thailand, where chief of station "Red" Jantzen had had enough. The change became part of a sweep at the top level of the CIA, when Admiral Raborn, who had never meshed well with President Johnson, chose to retire after just a year in the director's job. Richard Helms stepped in to replace him, completing a meteoric rise for this gray man of secrets. Comfortable with Colby at FE Division and FitzGerald at DDP, Helms briefly brought in a general but then turned to their former associate George Carver for the Special Assistant post that De Silva vacated to leave for Bangkok.

A legend within the agency, Robert Jantzen had become a CIA proconsul in this corner of Southeast Asia. Nicknamed for the flaming hue of his hair, Jantzen headed the CIA station in Singapore in the late 1950s. There he oversaw agency paramilitary officers, like Tony Po, in the 1958 attempt to overthrow Sukarno in Indonesia, Project Haik, as well as varied CIA initiatives in Malaysia and Singapore itself. He moved over to Thailand then—a renewed involvement on the mainland, for some of his projects had been carried out in French Indochina. Jantzen earned the esteem of U.S. ambassador U. Alexis Johnson, who took him regularly to meetings with senior Thai officials. Before long Red had become a drinking buddy of the Thai prime minister, and he got a specially miniaturized tape recorder he could wear during their sessions to capture the exact words of the Thai.

Bill Colby first knew Jantzen from Baguio, in the Philippines, during his own duty in Saigon. The practice had been for the chiefs in the Far Eastern region to gather there at least once a year to chew over the latest trends, review operations, and commune with CIA's big fish. These sessions were sometimes attended by the DCI, or the deputy director for plans, or they might be held in the presence of the FE division chief. On occasion all three came to Baguio. Colby discovered Jantzen's antics with taped drinking sessions later, as division chief in his own right. He found this tough to get used to, but accepted the fine intelligence Jantzen produced with it.

A typical demonstration of Jantzen's place in the Bangkok pecking order would be witnessed by another CIA officer in the mid-1960s. Prime Minister Sarit Thanarat came to northeast Thailand with an entourage of members of the royal family, senior officials, Buddhist priests, and foreign diplomats, including the U.S. ambassador. Sarit wanted to inspect progress on counterinsurgency, and the CIA man, Ralph McGehee, had been assigned to these programs. A ceremony was to be held. Jantzen came up for the occasion, traveling separately, and kept company with McGehee once he arrived. The two CIA officers sat in an open air bleacher far from the official one, but Sarit saw him and stopped the procession to summon Jantzen and speak to him. While the official party, including Ambassador Graham Martin, baked in the Thai sun, Sarit invited the station chief to a party that evening, then asked if he could somehow prevent Martin from attending as well.

The deteriorating relationship between Red Jantzen and Graham Martin made it progressively more difficult for the CIA to do its business in Bangkok, adding to Jantzen's frustration. The agency briefly went into eclipse with Sarit's death in 1963, but Jantzen then developed a similarly close relationship with the power behind the Thai cabinet, deputy premier Praphat Charusathien. Others complained they could not see Praphat because he was perennially closeted with the CIA man. Jantzen liked to tell a story of how he once wrestled Praphat and let the Thai win in order to keep him from anger with the American spooks. That level of diplomacy proved less successful with Martin, prickly at the best of times, and Jantzen reached the end of his rope.

From 1951 the CIA's business in Thailand revolved around help to the national police. Starting with a Miami-based CIA proprietary called the Overseas Southeast Asia Supply Company, set up by Paul Helliwell, a former OSS colonel and lawyer who had been one of that agency's leaders for its mission to Indochina at the end of World War II, the CIA funneled $35 million to start up the Thai police. Many agency officers—Bill Lair is one example—went to Thailand with Overseas Supply cover. Thomas Lobe, a scholar who systematically studied these programs, calculates that as many as 200 CIA people entered the country under Sea Supply cover during the first two years of the initiative, while seventy-six more police advisers went to Thailand with overtly acknowledged purpose.

The Thai police steadily gathered power. Aside from the Bangkok force and a large provincial force, there were several elite units. Bill Lair's assignment to the Police Aerial Recovery Unit (PARU) occurred early in the life of that entity, which by 1954 already numbered more than 300 men. In 1960, by which time the CIA-Thai alliance had put ninety-nine PARU troopers with the Hmong secret army in Laos, the PARU was building toward a strength of 550. The Border Patrol Police (BPP) formed in 1955 and, with a size of 4,500, had responsibility for security along all Thai frontiers to a depth of twenty-five miles. Then there was the Central Investigative Division, or Special Branch, a Thai security service. The police steadily gathered power until 1956 when they challenged the military for control and were suppressed, with Sarit triumphing instead the following year. The CIA's clients never regained their former political power, but they became stronger in sheer numbers, while the agency, led by Red Jantzen, built links directly to the Thai potentates.

By the mid-1960s, when Jantzen's relations with the American ambassador were deteriorating, he had been two decades in the Far East with only one short break for stateside service. That seemed enough; it was time to go home. In replacing the station chief Colby heeded the request of Ambassador Martin, who apparently had been impressed with Peer De Silva when the latter headed the CIA's outfit in Saigon. Colby understood Thailand's special role in the Southeast Asian war, providing extraterritorial bases for U.S. operations in Laos and North Vietnam, as well as manpower for the CIA secret army and as a contributor of regular military forces to South Vietnam. De Silva, Colby knew, was familiar with these issues. Bill recommended the appointment and Des FitzGerald, who remembered De Silva's coolness at the helm in the midst of a military coup in South Korea, happily approved.

The change of command would be a little hurried. De Silva got no time to assemble a team of his own for Bangkok, instead taking only a couple of key people. One, an agency sidekick named Les Greer, had worked often with De Silva and remained in the Far East after the Saigon embassy bombing. Scuttlebut attributed to him an unusual part in the Indonesian counter-coup—there were claims that Greer and a CIA team had prepared a bomb to be set off in a U.S. Information Agency library to furnish the pretext for an Indonesian anticommunist crackdown in case the PKI had managed to avoid giving offense on their own. De Silva also brought Richard Mample, a Marine colonel detached to the CIA, to be his military assistant. The station chief later described Mample as an imaginative deputy, but some CIA officers in Bangkok never did figure out just what work he did.

De Silva's main job in Bangkok would be to prevent the United States military from taking over the whole show. Thailand had insurgency problems, a couple of them, with remnants of Malay Chinese guerrillas active along the southern border, plus, in what Americans considered relevant to Laos and Vietnam, a communist guerrilla movement in the northeast. This had never amounted to more than a few thousand, and until 1963 the guerrillas had attempted nothing more than occasional assassinations of officials. Sarit, several years before his death, had blamed expatriate Lao and Vietnamese who lived in the northeast for the existence of the movement, but the CIA was not so sure. True, the agency did implicate Hanoi in a 1962 special national intelligence estimate, but in full-scale NIEs in 1966 and 1968, the main supporter of the Thai insurgency was seen to be China. Both the key political groups behind the guerrilla movement had headquarters in Beijing. Remote from the scene, however the Chinese had very limited capabilities in Thailand. The guerrillas, meanwhile, had rather limited success in mobilizing the peasantry.

Nevertheless, the United States created a military assistance command for Thailand along the same lines as MACV and constantly encouraged the Thai in a military response to the insurgency. Those kinds of activity often alienated peasants and led to results the opposite of what was intended. Still the American military had a natural advantage since a military junta ruled in Bangkok. The CIA favored programs with twin political and military aspects. De Silva felt he succeeded in staving off the U.S. military during his tour, and that meant General Richard G. Stilwell, who headed the assistance command. An element of personal conflict existed as well, since De Silva had been a West Point cadet and a member of Stilwell's class, and the two had disliked one another ever since. De Silva's physical disability complicated his work—some days he could barely get in a couple of good hours. The station chief's mood did not improve when De Silva learned that his wife and Stilwell's played in the same bridge circle. In terms of dealing with Stilwell, aide Richard Mample's knowledge of the military and his ability to act as go-between may have been his best assets.

Shortly before De Silva's arrival the Thais made both the CIA and the U.S. military happy when they established a Counter Subversion Operations Command, supposed to combine both civilian and military ministries, including the police and the army, in a single integrated effort. The command would carry out pacification programs throughout the land, with the civil administrators in charge. At the time there were 6,800 BPP, 30,000 provincial police, and 85,000 in the Thai army. The latter never ceased agitating. Though Peer De Silva insisted afterward that he convinced the Thai military to permit civilian ascendancy in pacification, when he left in early 1968 the Thais had already (October 1967) reorganized the Counter Subversion command to give the military charge of all counterinsurgency efforts, civil as well as military, in particular in the northeast. The CIA's own reports noted the civilians were relegated to the status of a policy planning board.

Division chief Colby remained satisfied with De Silva's performance, but he would be most pleased with the agency's low-level pacification efforts in the countryside. One project, the Village Defense Corps, along the same lines as the montagnard program in Vietnam, enlisted about 9,000 militia under police command. But all was not as rosy as it appeared. In the northeast Ralph McGehee created a survey system based on the census grievance and people's action team techniques used in Vietnam. Developing detailed intelligence on the communist cadre, in one province alone he found 500 enemies where the official estimates of communist numbers listed none.

At first the Thai survey would be considered a big plus and McGehee was asked to sign on for another tour beginning in the fall of 1967. That August Colby swung through Thailand on his latest inspection and McGehee's post was one of his stops. The CIA field man met the division chief at the airfield and took him to the office, where he proudly showed off file cabinets full of survey material demonstrating higher numbers of communist cadre. Bill listened and said nothing and McGehee described in detail the process by which cadre took over one sample village. "Colby seemed puzzled by my presentation," McGehee relates. "I had never seen him at a loss for words before. He looked at the ground, he looked everywhere. Finally he looked at me and said, 'We always seem to be losing.' "[7]

Division chief Colby returned to the airport in a convoy of jeeps and Land Rovers. He never went any further in the discussion with McGehee. But the incident is disturbing as evidence that the desire for progress in Southeast Asia was driving Bill Colby in the same direction as some of his myopic Washington colleagues: to deny or ignore evidence when it suited their preconceived notions. Colby's tendentiousness with respect to Ngo Dinh Diem's chances for victory has already been shown, but he did not make those arguments until the Vietnam war had actually ended. Colby's views on pacification would have operational implications during the war itself.

In October 1967, when Ralph McGehee's Thailand tour drew toward its close, station chief De Silva called him to the head office and read a cable from Colby reassigning McGehee to Taiwan. The CIA officer got only three weeks to wind up his business in Udorn; Langley disregarded several appeals from local Thai officials to keep McGehee on the job. The communist survey project MeGehee had headed was terminated.

Ralph McGehee managed to avoid genteel exile in Taiwan by returning to Langley and the Thai-Laotian desk there. At headquarters he discovered the CIA to be engaged in a furious dispute with the Military Assistance Command Vietnam over the estimates of the number of enemy forces. At Director Helms's bidding, the CIA went along with Viet Cong strength figures it knew to be low. The process was identical to what had happened with McGehee in northeast Thailand. Several implications followed. The Far East Division would be out of step pushing estimates beyond what the agency was willing to concede for Vietnam. On the operational side, claims of success made by Colby in behalf of FE stood to be tarnished by any admission the adversary was stronger, not weaker, than before. McGehee eventually returned to the field, in Vietnam. What he saw there was Bill Colby's war effort at full stride.

WHILE LANGLEY'S PLATE remained full of paramilitary and pacification projects, there were also old style affairs of espionage, deception, and betrayal. One of the most disturbing took place in a kaleidoscope of venues from Saigon to New York, Paris and Algiers, and involved General Nguyen Khanh. With its goal nothing short of a reconciliation between South Vietnam and the Viet Cong, the war seemingly hung in the balance in this affair because of the potential results it offered. Bill Colby would be the CIA's point man as events unfolded, and the importance of the potential outcome, along with America's ultimate frustration gives, reason to pause and recount this never-before-told story.[8]

As military strongman in South Vietnam, General Khanh had lurched on for a year, surviving coups, staging others, repeatedly reorganizing the Saigon government or armed forces council of top generals. Khanh boasted of a good relationship with U.S. ambassador Henry Cabot Lodge, but in the summer of 1964, when Maxwell Taylor took Lodge's place, things went downhill. The odd blindness of American ambassadors might not be entirely the fault of events, for Lodge had evicted the CIA station chief from his haunted house and turned that into the embassy residence; Maxwell Taylor continued to reside there. Taylor developed great antipathy for Nguyen Khanh. The relationship went from Taylor and Robert McNamara, each holding up one of the Vietnamese general's arms like a boxing champion, to the American ambassador dressing Khanh down like an errant cadet.

General Taylor saw his Vietnamese counterpart as astute and enterprising, but too clever for his own good, and increasingly lonely and isolated. Khanh, Taylor believed, even came to fear for his own life. All kinds of machinations occurred, such as in October 1964, when Khanh engineered the appointment as ambassador to Washington of General Tran Thien Khiem, one of his erstwhile backers and a key participant in the coup that brought Khanh to power. The Saigon strongman weathered another coup in January 1965. This time, as with the Diem coup, the CIA had such advance knowledge of coup troop movements and the like as to put in question its relationship with the plotters. In February came another coup attempted by Colonel Pham Ngoc Thao, that romantic and notorious South Vietnamese officer variously described as CIA source or Viet Cong agent, but who happened to be a close friend of Khiem's. Some observers credit Khiem with organizing this coup at long distance from Washington, D.C. Khanh survived but just days later the armed forces council stripped him of his post as commander-in-chief and sent him, in turn, off as a roving ambassador. Nguyen Khanh left South Vietnam on February 25, 1965, and reached New York on March 3.

On his side Nguyen Khanh interprets these events as definitely American-sponsored—motivated by Maxwell Taylor, carried out by Bill Colby's Far East Division of the CIA. Playing on Taylor's writings, Khanh later said the man himself was an "uncertain trumpet," and speaks of certain cables passing between Taylor and Secretary of State Dean Rusk as proof of U.S. involvement. The cables spoke of countering a Vietnamese tendency to become neutralist, that is, fearing General Khanh could become another Norodom Sihanouk. In fact, Khanh felt, peace might be at hand at that moment. He claims to have received a letter from senior leaders of the National Liberation Front (NLF) that declared a willingness to rally to the Saigon side. The South could end its civil war and reunite Vietnam in a "March North." This, Khanh maintains, is what lay behind his public statements about a "March North" in the 1964–65 period.

In the meantime, as part of its widening diplomatic circle, the NLF established relations with Algeria and posted representatives there, among the first Liberation Front officials stationed where Western countries could contact them. Later in 1965 the NLF officials were indeed in contact with Sweden, and that nation began efforts to broker a negotiation between the United States and North Vietnam. The initiative remained active from 1966 to 1968, and Washington secretly called the channel "Aspen." While it is not clear whether the CIA learned of Sweden's contact with the NLF in Algiers, in fact the agency soon had a channel of its own to the Liberation Front in Algiers, opened by a journalist acting informally for the U.S. government and then maintained by the CIA. Bill Colby attended weekly meetings of an interagency group on negotiations in Washington, chaired by W. Averell Harriman, now a Colby nemesis in a fresh incarnation.

Preoccupied with its massive military intervention in 1965, the United States did not listen very hard to talk of negotiations with the Viet Cong (as they usually called the NLF), but a year later it would be a different story. Coincidentally or not, by that time Max Taylor had left Saigon and Henry Cabot Lodge was back as ambassador. Lodge, whom Nguyen Khanh believed understood him, posed no obstacle to what now happened. Toward mid-1966—the records of this conversation apparently have not been found—General Khanh had a talk with Jasper Wilson, the U.S. colonel who had been his senior adviser, instrumental in convincing Khanh to accede peaceably to his ouster the previous year. Khanh mentioned the NLF letter, which he connected with Nguyen Huu Tho, president of the Liberation Front, and referred to the possibility of inducing mass defections from the (reconciled) Viet Cong. The possibility quickly came to the attention of the CIA.

Americans were electrified. Nguyen Khanh's remarks were taken to Dean Rusk, Robert McNamara, and President Lyndon Johnson. The State Department assigned the code name "Elm Tree" to this matter. At Langley, Bill Colby's office drew up a paper summarizing what it knew of Khanh's offer on July 7, 1966, and followed with a second memorandum about two weeks later. On July 17 Rusk sent Deputy Undersecretary of State U. Alexis Johnson to New York for a conversation with Khanh at the Waldorf-Astoria Hotel. Elm Tree acquired more substance.

Ulysses Alexis Johnson had been Max Taylor's deputy ambassador in Saigon. In fact, he had taken a demotion for that job since he had already—in the Kennedy administration—been deputy undersecretary. Johnson happened to be an old friend of Taylor's from the time when both men were language students in Japan in the 1920s. Despite affinities and his knowledge of Taylor's attitude toward Khanh, Johnson handled Elm Tree straightforwardly. He thought Khanh flamboyant and a beguiling speaker in both French and English. Their talk at the Waldorf was in a mixture of those languages, with Khanh speaking primarily in French and Johnson asking questions to clarify points.

Nguyen Khanh laid out the background by describing the origins of the Viet Minh movement in southern Vietnam during the anti-French war of resistance. In the heady days of the August Revolution of 1945, before he became a French officer, Nguyen Khanh had himself been a Viet Minh. It became the first time he understood his ancestors had not been blondes smoking Gauloise cigarettes. The southerners who made up the Viet Minh, Khanh explained, were intellectuals rather than communists and had tried to work with Diem until forced to give up all hope. Several key Viet Cong leaders went back to these roots and Khanh personally knew them. One, a Liberation Front representative in Europe, had come to Khanh apparently and explained the background to the letter Khanh had received while still strongman in Saigon. The essence was that southerners in the Front worried that Hanoi would shunt them aside, take over the movement, and govern Vietnam only for the benefit of the north. These leaders might bring over their forces to the Saigon side but they wanted to deal solely with the United States. They would form a government of national unity with the Saigon regime, ask for continued U.S. assistance, and contrive to create a true southern government. For this "conciliation" to occur, Saigon needed a different constellation of power; the current military strongman, Air Marshal Nguyen Cao Ky, was a northerner and would never cooperate. In effect Khanh had asked Washington to overthrow the Saigon regime. When Alex Johnson objected that the United States did not have that kind of control in Saigon, Khanh countered that Washington had been very successful with its intervention in the Dominican Republic in 1965.

American diplomats had a very interesting lunch ten days later in the Paris district of St. Cloud. A four-hour meal and walk in the park enabled Paul Sturm to meet Le Van Truong, the NLF European representative, "Mr. Out" by General Khanh's description. Le Van discussed unilateral ceasefires and releases of South Vietnamese prisoners the Liberation Front could make to show its bona fides. Nguyen Khanh, here going by his French name, "Raymond," witnessed the exchange. Nothing happened in the end, despite the fact that Mr. Out delivered the U.S. messages in August, as ambassador to France Chester Bohlen reported on September 30. Two weeks later Nguyen Khanh surfaced to say he had seen Mr. Out again, and the Viet Cong representative declared himself disturbed; the lack of response might signal the end of his influence with the National Liberation Front.

In the meantime the Central Intelligence Agency turned this knowledge into a project to induce mass defections. Case officers in Saigon found a go-between in touch with NLF president Nguyen Huu Tho. That person happened to be his uncle, Nguyen Huu An, who had remained in Saigon and took care of the NLF leader's family as he stayed in the bush. The CIA's choice of a code name showed extremely poor security consciousness—on American television there was a show, "The Man from U.N.C.L.E.," in which the arch enemies were an organization called "THRUSH." The CIA defection project would be called "Thrush."

Bill Colby met on September 16 with Chet Cooper, now aide to Averell Harriman, who had cooked up a program of his own for Vietnamese reconciliation and reconstruction. With him Colby had Howard Stone, chief of the Intelligence Division at the Saigon station, home for the moment to coordinate projects. The CIA wanted to make sure there would be no conflict between State Department initiatives and its Thrush operation. "Rocky" Stone confidently predicted the CIA would have some important defections soon, so confidently he talked as if the Americans could themselves determine the timing of those defections. Rocky might have known better—he had presided over a failed coup attempt in Syria and worked with the Tibetan partisans in the twilight of the Khamba revolt—but he was truly confident. This was going to be like Stone's first assignment, which had been in the CIA's successful operation in Iran in 1953.

Two days later in Saigon, Vietnamese security services arrested the uncle. There were no defections at all, by CIA timing or otherwise. Director Helms received at least fourteen memoranda on Project Thrush from his Special Assistant on Vietnam Affairs alone. Langley put on pressure, and American diplomats intervened to convince Saigon to release the uncle, Nguyen Huu An. Saigon finally did so. On November 3 a CIA case officer confronted An who, under pressure, now admitted that claims of his activities that summer and fall had all been lies. There was no channel to Nguyen Huu Tho. The next day ambassador Lodge cabled home that Project Thrush had been "LARGELY BASED ON WISHFUL THINKING."[9] In forwarding this cable to Walt Rostow at the White House, his assistant Art McCafferty commented, "In short, the Uncle is one of the best 'fiction' writers of our time."[10]

Washington went ahead and pressed the South Vietnamese to inaugurate a program for "reconciliation," along the lines of the Harriman proposal. But the Ky government was not sincere. Saigon promised a program, but General Nguyen Van Thieu insisted the Liberation Front would be dealt with as an internal security problem, not a sovereign entity. A proclamation inaugurating reconciliation, supposed to be issued on November 1, did not appear. In December Ky and Thieu, meeting with Dean Rusk, seemed to agree again, and again nothing happened. In March 1967, when President Johnson met with the South Vietnamese leaders at Guam, the U.S. side prepared extensive position papers on reconciliation and raised the issue; once more there were promises and no actions. About official Saigon's reluctance to act, at least, Nguyen Khanh appears to have been entirely correct.

There would be more Khanh soundings in 1967 under the code name "Elm Tree," and throughout the year the United States continued to press Saigon on reconciliation. The Vietnamese treated the entire issue as an adjunct of their "chieu hoi" defection program aimed at inducing individuals to leave the Viet Cong. Meanwhile, Bill Colby periodically had to report to the Harriman group on his lack of progress on mass defections, as well as the absence of any communication from the Liberation Front through the CIA channel in Algiers. Nothing seemed to work. The CIA would be drawn in repeatedly, however, meeting with Liberation Front officials in Vietnam itself in late 1967. When a further CIA channel, "Aztec," opened in Vietnam in early 1968 with discreet approaches to Ed Lansdale, officers would rush to answer frantic White House and State Department demands to produce the Project Thrush file, which by then had been forgotten.

Had a successful reconciliation taken place in 1966, the Viet Cong would have been separated from North Vietnam and a negotiated peace must have soon followed. However, there is no present evidence that the Liberation Front was actually willing to make such a deal. After almost three years of delay the South Vietnamese government finally made a reconciliation offer in July 1969. By then Nguyen Van Thieu was president in Saigon, and he made Viet Cong participation in an election the centerpiece of his first peace proposal. By then the program was a nonstarter and Washington and Hanoi were negotiating a U.S. withdrawal from Vietnam. By then too, Bill Colby would be back in South Vietnam himself, implementing the kinds of initiatives he had long advocated.

DURING THESE MIDDLE YEARS of the Vietnam war, planning the United States military buildup and organizing the air campaign against Hanoi occupied much of the attention of official Washington. That is the reason someone from the CIA could say the involvement of the agency climaxed in the Diem years and then faded into shadow. But this is a simplistic version and conceals far more than it tells about the reality of Washington waging war in Southeast Asia. The truth is the American capital was full of advocates—generals, diplomats, politicians, even spies—each with their preferred pathway out of the tunnel that was Vietnam.

William E. Colby would be such an advocate. Far from living in shadow, Colby worked hard to give his preferred solution as much visibility as it could get. Conditioned by his experience and knowledge, from World War II, from the Central Intelligence Agency, from his reading of history and politics, Colby would never have argued for a strategy of brute force. This was a man of sophistication, for whom affecting people's ideas had been the path to success in Italy, and organizing against a potential enemy's attack had been the substance of his labor in Sweden. "I was a guerrilla once myself against the Nazis," Colby writes. "I know what a guerrilla does."[11] From the beginning in Vietnam Bill had rejected force indiscriminately applied in favor of political or combined political-military approaches.

As station chief in Saigon Colby had put his weight behind early pacification programs, both the *agrovilles* and the later strategic hamlet effort. The montagnard project had added a military dimension to the political one. Initiatives like Project Tiger, the commando operation against North Vietnam, got Colby's support but rarely aroused his enthusiasm. He had been ready to jettison the commando operation in 1963 and expressed doubts when the military wanted to expand it instead into OPLAN 34-A. Colby had helped draft that plan to ensure it had some modicum of realism. By November 1964 Colby had weighed in with a proposal for a unified pacification program with a single U.S. director who would carry ambassadorial rank and be co-equal to the MACV commander—exactly the formula Washington would adopt two years later. Reporting on his inspections as Far East Division chief, Colby constantly harped on the need for, success of, or potential and opportunity for pacification and political action. The CIA twelve-point program of 1965 showed Colby's hand in its marked predilection for these types of projects. Such themes featured constantly in Colby's actions and recommendations.

Bill began 1965 accompanying national security adviser McGeorge Bundy on a visit to South Vietnam, returning on more intimate terms with this key Lyndon Johnson aide. Bundy, of course, was one of the architects of the Rolling Thunder bombing, as well as a major player in all the decisions on commitment of ground troops that President Johnson was about to make. After one of the White House meetings in which LBJ talked of the air war, Colby stayed behind to speak with Mac. The CIA division chief objected to the incessant military focus of strategy. Rather than fine-tuning the target list for Rolling Thunder, Colby observed, it would be far more useful to pay attention to the struggle for allegiance of peasants in Vietnam's villages.

"You may be right," Mac had answered, "but the structure of the American government probably won't permit it."[12]

Bundy meant that the U.S. military did not understand pacification and was going to do what it knew how to do, but this still did not mean that no one was paying attention to Colby's issue. It had been Bundy himself who gave John McCone marching orders that led to the CIA's twelve-point program in 1965. Similarly, simultaneously with approval of Rolling Thunder, Mac argued directly to the president that as soon as bombing stabilized the South Vietnamese political situation a little bit, "the most urgent order of business will then be the improvement and broadening of the pacification program."[13] As already seen, Langley engaged busily in a range of activities with this very goal throughout the year. Then came 1966, when pacification and political action became the two major pillars of U.S. strategy—and CIA operations—in Vietnam.

Far more accurate than claiming Colby's Vietnam role faded is to say that Colby's advocacy stood steady as U.S. attention to pacification waned and waxed. And it is also wrong to say Washington lacked any interest in Colby's concerns. Lyndon Johnson worried about the political, economic, and social issues—what he called the "other war"—far more than his successors. It would be LBJ, in 1966, who set in motion the activities and began creating the organization that would conduct the pacification war. Bill Colby, not at all eclipsed, held center stage.

In his final months as national security adviser to LBJ, Mac Bundy pushed for more effort on pacification. This was bread and butter for the CIA, whose entire 1965 action program aimed at winning the allegiance of Vietnamese for the Saigon regime. When Washington began talking about a high-level conference of the top people concerned with various facets of pacification, Langley jumped at the chance to showcase its progress with People's Action Teams, Counter-Terror Teams, census grievance units, and the like. The CIA volunteered its Mt. Airey retreat, near Warrenton, Virginia, as the locale for the big powwow. The conference took place from January 8 to 11, 1966.

Twin heads of the group at Mt. Airey were Leonard Unger, now heading Washington's interagency task force that dealt with Southeast Asia, and William J. Porter. Bill Colby headed the CIA's delegation. If he took to the shadows it would only be because Colby deemed it tactically desirable to have the initiative seem to be elsewhere. Behind Colby were the CIA's Special Assistant for Vietnam Affairs and its Saigon station chief, Gordon Jorgensen. The White House was represented by another Colby associate and former CIA man, now close to Mac Bundy, Chester L. Cooper. Also among the crowd would be pacification guru Edward Lansdale. If there was anyone in eclipse among this crew it was Ed Lansdale, who had returned to Saigon the previous August to run a sort of pacification clearinghouse observing the Saigon political scene and was being studiously ignored by Americans all over. Station chief Jorgensen, worried that the Vietnamese would think Lansdale the *real* CIA chief in Vietnam, kept reminding Ed to tell people he was not with the agency. Bill Colby considered Lansdale a friend, and would one day rank him as one of the ten greatest spies in history, but at Mt. Airey he was perfectly willing to ride roughshod over Lansdale's pronouncements in order to move Langley's agenda ahead.

The Saigon-based officials largely expressed themselves as satisfied with existing arrangements. The two major proposals that flowed from the Warrenton meetings—both of which would eventually be adopted—came from Washington people. Chet Cooper proposed that the status and importance attributed to pacification should be raised by making a deputy ambassador responsible for it, a man who would have actual control over the field agencies. The Pentagon's lead man suggested that MACV handle pacification by means of a separate command responsible for all such activity. After several false starts and reorganizations, a year and a half later there would be a separate pacification organization that constituted a division of MACV, headed by a civilian who ranked as deputy ambassador.

It is not surprising that the analysts who wrote the now-famous *Pentagon Papers* only a couple of years later, and while the war still raged, remarked: "Efforts to reorganize the Saigon Mission [for pacification purposes] are a recurring theme in recent history. The impetus for reorganization has consistently come from Washington."[14] William E. Colby numbered among those in Washington doing the pushing.

Barely a month later President Johnson joined the fray. LBJ took the opportunity of one of the recurrent Honolulu conferences to make clear his seriousness on the war by attending, and turning the meeting specifically into a forum on the "other war." Johnson invited South Vietnamese leaders Nguyen Van Thieu and Nguyen Cao Ky and made this a summit meeting. Then he ordered the Saigon Mission reorganization that had been discussed at Mt. Airey, making deputy ambassador William J. Porter the head of the nonmilitary effort in Vietnam. On March 28 President Johnson followed up by taking Robert W. Komer, a member of his National Security Council (NSC) staff, elevating Komer to special assistant to the president, and designating him responsible for the "other war" in Washington. To provide Komer authority, President Johnson approved National Security Action Memorandum (NSAM) 343 that same day, referring to the Honolulu conference declaration as affirming a U.S. commitment to rural construction and pacification in South Vietnam.

A second matter that Vietnamese and Americans talked over at Honolulu had been developing political support. Thieu and Ky promised elections in 1967, preceded by the elaboration of a new constitution. The convention that would draft this document would, as the Saigon government's plans matured, be elected that fall. Washington had obvious interest in the outcome, and Colby's Far East Division became executive agent for this political action. On April 26, before the South Vietnamese even set the rules for the election, a "Political Development Working Group" met in Washington to figure out how to influence it. Bill Colby spoke in favor of CIA support for individual candidates. Don Ropa, a CIA officer on detail to the NSC staff, objected that this would not help forge a broad-based political front. Afterward Des FitzGerald asked the Far East Division for a paper commenting on the alternatives. Three days later Colby's answering memo argued that there was no time to establish a regular political party; that a covert CIA influence campaign on that scale would be blown, with adverse effects; and that the best thing to do would be to select five or six candidates and back them in a limited way. The FE Division also favored sending out an expert on electoral laws to advise the embassy and the CIA station.

Ambassador Lodge complained that the CIA suggestion was too limited. Since just then Vietnam was going through yet another Buddhist crisis, with massive disruptions in the cities of Da Nang and Hue, that seemed a reasonable argument. By the same token, however, the visibility of U.S. political action was higher even than before; Colby's point about the dangers of exposure also seemed well taken. There would be no effort to build a broad movement. The Buddhist troubles continued, with slogans in some demonstrations denouncing the Thieu-Ky government as a CIA tool. As it turned out, the Buddhists fractured over the summer, with one big faction boycotting the election, though thirty-four Buddhists (as against thirty-five Catholics) were elected to a 117-seat assembly.

Reporters like Robert Shaplen, who enjoyed excellent South Vietnamese contacts, could look at the election and say it seemed about as fair as an election in Vietnam at this time could be. At Langley when the press reactions began to come in, even poker-faced Bill Colby wore a smile.

Meanwhile Bob Komer had geared up his "other war" shop at the National Security Council. Like so many other characters in this story, Komer had been with the CIA before moving over to the White House. His practice now would be to ride atop the cable traffic, monitoring the economic and pacification issues, while, much as did Colby, making periodic survey trips to South Vietnam. Komer's acerbic wit and incisive style earned him the moniker "Blowtorch Bob," and more than once he caused heartburn. There were two Komer visits that year. At the CIA his reports went first to the Special Assistant for Vietnam Affairs (SAVA), where officers decided if Komer was on target and whether Langley should contest his edicts. If so the chief of SAVA, now George A. Carver, went to Director Helms with the particulars. Carver would have something to say about *every* Komer report.

Before long Blowtorch Bob concluded that the Saigon organization for pacification had sand in its gears. William J. Porter was a good man, but the deputy ambassador had no real authority over the parts of his dinosaur; agencies could ignore Porter's orders with impunity. As for the ambassador, it was Lodge who saddled Komer with his nickname. The CIA got into the line of fire when Komer's preferred solution, to unify pacification management and operations under the military (he believed that only the military had the manpower and money to give pacification the boost it needed) became an official Pentagon proposal. The September 1966 scheme was to nominate a pacification "czar" who would control all programs in this area. In the Pentagon scheme that individual would be a deputy commander of the Military Assistance Command Vietnam, so the chain of command would stretch directly to General Westmoreland. At SAVA, George Carver objected strenuously. Not only was it a problem whether the czar was to be a civilian or a military person, but Carver also took up Colby's cause. That is, SAVA argued that assigning CIA functions, programs, or personnel to a military chain of command would create support and even legal problems. In particular, the CIA wished to avoid any assignment of the intelligence liaison with Vietnamese police and security services, or any handover to the pacification entity of its agent networks, all of which were handled by Howard Stone's Intelligence Division at Saigon station.

Langley's objections cut no mustard with President Johnson, who made it clear in October 1966 that he wished to proceed with the new unit. LBJ kept it out of military hands, however, setting up an Office of Civil Operations (OCO) under Porter. President Johnson christened the new unit at another summit conference, at Manila, a few weeks later. It would be given authority to hire 1,468 persons. Over $56 million (of $128 million) and 1.7 billion in Vietnamese piasters (of P4.0 billion) in the OCO budget came from the CIA.

Nevertheless, ambassador Porter remained challenged. Henry Cabot Lodge insisted that Porter continue his normal embassy routine even while managing OCO, and Lodge took some trips around this time, leaving Porter the full job to do. There was little time for OCO. The organization had a difficult time filling its posts, with almost 500 job slots still vacant months later. And agencies that gave OCO lip service were quick to snipe behind its back.

The Central Intelligence Agency would be one example. Bill Colby had been a champion of pacification proposals for years, and George Carver, his former Saigon case officer, agreed. Now both tried to protect the agency from OCO inroads. Colby supervised while John Hart, who took over the Saigon station in early 1966, negotiated an understanding delineating the functions each would fulfill. Hart reserved to himself and the chief of his Revolutionary Development Cadre Division wide authority, along with a veto over planning, programming, funding, and operations. This became enshrined in a formal memorandum on February 10, 1967. In practice this meant that CIA officers often refused to take direction from pacification officials in the field. The agency also supplied few officers for OCO jobs, though one of OCO's four regional directors, Vince Heymann, who controlled the Mekong Delta area, was one of Colby's clandestine service officers.

The contribution from CIA that would be of absolutely crucial importance was the subtraction of half the Saigon station, the part called the Revolutionary Development Cadre (RDC) Division, and its incorporation into OCO. This would not be so painful as it sounds because Langley had already been reconfiguring the unit in such a way that this section could be detached without disrupting CIA activities in South Vietnam. Indeed, in a way the Revolutionary Development Cadre Division became a victim of its own success. Back in 1965 the CIA had put a training center at Vung Tau for its People's Action Teams, under Tom Donohue and the Vietnamese officer Le Mai Xuan. Soon more shows got into the act, and the Counter-Terror Teams, census grievance, armed propaganda, and other kinds of teams were training Vung Tau. Before the end of the year the South Vietnamese government noticed—literally thousands of Vietnamese at a time were passing through Vung Tau—and began demanding a larger role. As CIA director Helms described it to a Senate committee a few months later, the agency then agreed to give over the Vung Tau camp, called the National Training Center, to the Vietnamese.

Rather more prosaic, in truth Tom Donohue continued a very active role at Vung Tau. The South Vietnamese *did* bring in their own camp commander, Colonel Tran Ngoc Chau, former province chief in Kien Hoa in the Mekong Delta, where he had done well on pacification and incidentally cooperated with the CIA on the inception of the Counter-Terror Team (CTT) program. An unusual character, Chau had fought with the Viet Minh from 1945 to

1952, then come over to the other side to join the Vietnamese national army. Having been a Viet Minh spy, later a battalion commander, he now marched with the first class of graduates of the South Vietnamese military academy at Dalat, where he worked as director of studies and chief of staff before the Kien Hoa assignment. Twice the province chief there, he was sent to Da Nang by the Thieu-Ky government at the time of the Buddhist troubles. A Buddhist himself, Chau could be a sympathetic overseer. He and police official Colonel Nguyen Ngoc Loan were instrumental in quelling the disturbances, at least in Quang Nam province.

Bill Colby knew of Tran Ngoc Chau from the CTT project and met him later on. Colonel Chau believed that once the South Vietnamese got up to speed, the CIA should drop into the background. The programs taught at Vung Tau, other than people's action and Counter-Terror, were identified with the rubric "revolutionary development," and Chau felt these should not be seen as CIA, which ought to provide only money and equipment. Chau went to Tom Donohue, who rejected the argument perhaps unhappy at the way Chau had eclipsed the CIA's fair-haired boy, Le Mai Xuan; he was certainly unwilling to take the agency's hand off the National Training Center. Chau looked on equably as South Vietnam's defense ministry drafted the sixteen Vietnamese instructors at Vung Tau.

In the middle of this contest, the deepening anger would be plain to see when Deputy Secretary of Defense Cyrus R. Vance visited Vung Tau in April 1966. Vance "sensed a feeling of resentment as our party walked among the trainees," and Le Mai Xuan told him that the most frequently asked question in classes was whether the United States had come to occupy Vietnam the way the French had.[15] Chau seems to have been right about the need to avoid any CIA identification with the revolutionary development program. Nevertheless the Americans did not back off. Chau went to George Jacobsen, a military expert and friend of CIA, again with no result. Saigon station chief John Hart and Bill Colby insisted on the CIA role.

Still Colby could see the handwriting on the wall. With Vietnamese demands for sole proprietorship at Vung Tau (though Tran Ngoc Chau, frustrated, would himself resign), and the White House gearing up for a civilian pacification organization (OCO), it became clear that the RDC Division of Saigon station would be requisitioned anew. As a pacification enthusiast, in the long run Colby would not be able to resist handing over such CIA elements as the RDC Division to an entity that specialized in the "other war," and so it was necessary to prepare for that event. Saigon station began to reassign agent handlers, such networks as had grown inside the division, and certain intelligence liaison relationships with Saigon government units to other components of the station.

One of the more difficult aspects of Bill Colby's job, he felt, was getting used to the idiosyncracies of his station chiefs. John L. Hart, who took over in Saigon early in 1966 would be no exception. Hart had a clipped British accent but identified with the Norman side of the Anglo-Saxon world; he spoke fluent French. In Saigon he often tried to get those around him to talk in that language—which was not difficult for the Vietnamese. A tennis player, tall and slim, Hart proved active and smart. Tennis would be his undoing, in fact, for one day on the court in late 1967 he detached the retinas of his eyes. Hart had an operation but a couple of months later it happened again and he would be invalided out of Saigon.

In any case, where Colby favored smooth political operators, John Hart had a predilection for paramilitary types. He had headed the CIA operation in Korea toward the end of the war in that country, and at the Western Hemisphere Division had been chief of the Cuban task force under Des FitzGerald, whose man he was. Like Ted Shackley, however, Hart eventually won over Colby through his actions in Vietnam.

The station chief would not be quite so successful with his own subordinates, a number of whom decided Hart was an egomaniac. Momentary impressions could lead to arbitrary decisions. One CIA man saw his career flash in front of his eyes in a Chinese restaurant one day, as he and Hart compared the relative merits of different ethnic food. Hart remarked that the CIA man seemed to him more like the kind of guy who would go down to the MACV mess for his meals. Others saw Hart as drugged out on his medications.

John Hart arrived in Vietnam at the height of the Buddhist crisis and did not shy away from visiting the hottest spots. Though he never gave up his weakness for paramilitary activity, he made some changes in programs. Uncomfortable with the connotation of "terror" and the reputation of the Counter-Terror Teams, in November 1966 Hart converted them into "Provincial Reconnaissance Units" (PRUs). He also had the PRUs give greater attention to intelligence gathering as opposed to terrorism. It was under Hart, though not at his hand, that the CIA station began giving orientations to incoming officers, as opposed to simply pointing them at their desks and beds, and taking them out for a beer. This was the onset of another major buildup of CIA strength in Vietnam—the station would soon peak at more than 700—and orientations were sorely needed. Hart regularized the wide array of different projects by setting up six regions and designating regional officers in charge with provincial ones under them. Before that the CIA had not had any formal control system in the countryside. American aid to Vietnam and much more besides (not least, measures of pacification progress) depended on population, but until John Hart came the United States did not have an accepted figure for the number of people in South Vietnam or even those who lived in Saigon. Hart knocked heads together and came up with an estimate—only a guess but as good as any other—of 14 million people. Based on such figures the CIA allocated money to influence the Vietnamese constituent assembly election of 1966 as well as the legislative and presidential elections the following year. The American candidates for the 1967 presidential election were Nguyen Van Thieu and Nguyen Cao Ky and they won with 35 percent of the vote.

Consonant with the plans to split the CIA's Revolutionary Development Cadre Division from the remainder of the station, in the fall of 1966 that unit moved to a different building in Saigon, one that until then housed the Agency for International Development. This building became the seat of the Office of Civil Operations into which the cadre division would be incorporated. From Washington Bob Komer agitated to expand the revolutionary development training program beyond Vung Tau and to build a second center at Pleiku in the Central Highlands, so fresh cadres could be turned out even faster. Komer wanted to train 35,000 South Vietnamese a year. With ongoing recruitment for the South Vietnamese army, its regional and popular forces, its police, and other institutions, the CIA felt cadre couldn't be enlisted at the rate Komer wanted. When the cadre division went to OCO, Bob Komer thought he had won that fight, but the agency turned out to be right. The pool of Vietnamese youths available was just too small—John Hart's guesstimates had been close to the mark.

Meanwhile pressure built constantly to put increased effort into pacification. Nelson Brickham had directed field operations for the CIA station and led the cadre division when it went into OCO. Tucker Gougelman had initiated in 1965 a move to establish interrogation centers in South Vietnamese provinces, and seven or eight had been completed when Brickham began working with him. Before Brickham left Saigon there would be forty-four provincial interrogation centers. Exactly that number of PRU units were available to act on any intelligence developed by the centers, ultimately a force of perhaps 5,000 troops, created and funded by the CIA and led by Americans.

What was missing was a system and Brickham supplied that too. Bob Komer, Bill Colby, everybody, wanted to get at the Viet Cong parallel hierarchy that maintained its hidden presence in Vietnamese villages. That "infrastructure," increasingly indicated using the acronym VCI, had to be identified and counteracted. Brickham was working with Vietnamese Special Branch police at the time he began seeking ways for a systematic attack on the VCI. By late 1966 he suggested that data could be developed through employing informants, interrogating prisoners, and putting spies in the VCI itself. Tools in an attack on the VCI could be arrests, precisely targeted raids or ambushes, military sweep operations, or conventional assault. Some months later, close to the end of Brickham's Saigon tour, John Hart called him into the office and asked him to build the concept for an attack on the VCI into a formal proposal.

This scheme for a fresh approach to neutralizing the VCI would be elaborated coincidentally with further changes in the U.S. organization for pacification. The OCO structure never rose to its potential; all the while Bob Komer kept arguing that until the unit for pacification formed part of the military, it would not benefit from the great resources the military enjoyed. Much the same as with the CIA in Laos, the vast majority of the real spending in South Vietnam, for pacification as for everything else, came from the

U.S. military. Komer wanted to tap that source in a more coherent fashion. General William Westmoreland, commanding the Military Assistance Command Vietnam (MACV), finally agreed to a subordinate unit for pacification; Washington agreed if MACV's unit were headed by a civilian. Lyndon Johnson appointed Robert Komer to the post. In May 1967, Komer arrived in Saigon for good—the newly minted pacification czar.

With the equivalent rank (as a civilian) of general, Komer headed a new entity called Civil Operations and Revolutionary Development Support (CORDS). The idea for an attack on the Viet Cong infrastructure got a name too—Intelligence Coordination and Exploitation (ICEX) program—courtesy of John Hart. Brickham's ICEX idea provided for a kind of central clearing house for intelligence under CORDS, which would help identify Viet Cong who could then be dealt with by any of the tools available to pacifiers. A management staff, to be headed by Komer and the ICEX chief and including Americans attached to various Vietnamese police and security services, would supervise the whole thing.

General Westmoreland acquiesced gracefully as Robert Komer, who liked the idea of targeting the VCI, constructed a major proposal around ICEX. Called "Project Take-off," Komer's proposal went right up to the White House during the summer of 1967. Komer continued to use his connections at the White House, with ambassador William K. Leonhart, to get the most favorable hearing from President Johnson. LBJ instructed U.S. government departments to cooperate with Project Take-off. The idea would be briefed to Vietnamese police director General Nguyen Ngoc Loan, who rejected it, but U.S. diplomats then went to South Vietnamese President Nguyen Van Thieu, who approved a decree in December 1967 mandating Saigon's participation. The ICEX idea became known as the Phoenix program, a name dreamed up by American advisers in the I Corps area of Vietnam when they were thinking up ways to broaden the operation.

William E. Colby thus had very little to do with the inception of the Phoenix program. That would be ironic, since Colby's name has been linked to Phoenix ever since. How Colby came to Phoenix, and the climax of the Southeast Asian war, took the crusader from Langley to Saigon and back again. It would be the most intense phase of Bill Colby's Vietnam war.

11

RISING FROM ASHES

PERHAPS BILL COLBY did not pay all that much attention to the inception of this latest scheme to destroy the Viet Cong. He was solidly in place as chief of the Far East Division of the CIA as the plan percolated up to the Washington level. The Far East Division had been a spy chief's dream— Colby captained the CIA team on the main field through some of its most important years. Colby had frustrated some agency folk, such as those gone native in the course of the Tibetan program. But modernist proponents of political action could only be inspired by a division chief whose idea of a South Vietnam visit included prodding people into action by insisting on spending a night in a remote village seen before in daylight. Colby held credit for Vietnam projects considered highly valuable. The peasant insurgency in northeast Thailand seemed to be in check, while the tribal irregular program in Laos remained vibrant and strong.

But 1967 brought problems for the Central Intelligence Agency, and some of them affected the Far East Division. Certainly the Vietnam war had an important blowback effect since that controversial conflict energized many of the leakers who fueled a series of (then) astonishing revelations about the CIA. The March issue of the magazine *Ramparts* contained an exposé telling that the intelligence agency had secretly funded a private voluntary organization, the National Student Association. Advertised by full page ads in major newspapers, including both the *Washington Post* and *New York Times*, the National Student Association story opened a pandora's box of deeper secrets. Both those papers followed with additional tales of the CIA. Columnist Jack Anderson, in pieces syndicated throughout the land, wrote of CIA plots to assassinate Cuban leader Fidel Castro. Drew Pearson, another prominent columnist, wrote of CIA payoffs to international and U.S. labor organizations of as much as $100 million per year. *Ramparts* followed up, printing interviews with former CIA trainees and disaffected case officers. Other media exposed the CIA's technique of funneling money through channels from the Ford Foundation to the Committee for a Free Europe to aid activities as diverse as those of Radio Free Europe and the Asia Society.

President Lyndon Johnson—who had some knowledge of CIA covert actions on Cuba—growled about nefarious, even criminal activity, a kind of "Murder Incorporated" on the Caribbean island. In response the inspector general of the CIA opened an internal investigation of the assassination charges. On the student association issue, even before the *Ramparts* story hit the newsstands, President Johnson ordered a policy review. Erstwhile Justice Department official and undersecretary of state Nicolas deB. Katzenbach chaired the commission. Public debate on issues of appropriate intelligence activities seemed so necessary that the Council on Foreign Relations formed its own study group. In Congress legislative proposals for congressional oversight of the CIA, which had languished for more than a decade, were headed off only by inviting extra senators, members of the Foreign Relations Committee, to participate in the tightly restricted deliberations of the small unit of the Armed Services Committee that covered intelligence work.

Langley would be forced into high gear in its efforts to cope. Director Helms became a member of the Katzenbach commission, where he could help limit the damage. Deputy Director for Plans Desmond FitzGerald kept running to put out the latest fire. There proved to be lots of work for William E. Colby too. When President Johnson asked for information on links between the CIA and the Asia Society, it was Colby's FE Division that responded. Colby had a personal interest in the assassination inquiry and whether it included the Diem case. Colby helped the inspector general conclude that the CIA had had no role in those unfortunate Saigon events. Central Intelligence Agency connections with labor movements also held meaning for Colby, who had done much in this area during his Italian tour. Labor support formed part of the classic political action recipe, one Colby had championed in Vietnam as well. In 1966 Colby had been one of the main promoters for South Vietnamese labor leader Tran Quoc Buu and a key interlocutor during Buu's Washington visit. Revelations now about the CIA and labor could only draw attention, in particular since Buu's sponsor, the American Federation of Labor (AFL-CIO) official Jay Lovestone, was now being labeled a CIA contact.

Even more embattled at CIA than Colby was his good friend Des Fitz-Gerald, responsible for the whole panoply of covert action. Worse, Des had had a direct hand in the Cuban plots against Castro. In fact, at the moment John Kennedy was assassinated in 1963, FitzGerald had been in Paris meeting one of the assassins, to hand over instructions and murder weapons. He was a direct target in the inspector general's investigation. In 1967 the shine had come off the bird-watching, poetry-loving spy, who appeared puffy and run-down to friends and spent time merely sitting in front of the television during his off hours. FitzGerald evidently had a blood circulation problem no one knew about, but the controversies of 1967 cannot have helped his health.

Trying nonetheless to keep up his usual furious pace, FitzGerald would play tennis on weekends. In the middle of a mixed doubles match with the British ambassador and his wife in 97 degree heat on a July day, FitzGerald collapsed in mid-serve. He suffered a massive coronary and never regained consciousness. On September 13, 1967, President Johnson posthumously awarded Fitz-Gerald the National Security Medal, America's highest decoration for intelligence work, for "exceptional competence and stimulating leadership," plus "unchallenged integrity matched only by his passion for anonimity."[1]

Desmond FitzGerald's death affected Bill Colby quite directly, not only personally but professionally. Of course the funeral was hard; this was a man who had commiserated with Colby on the occasion of Ngo Dinh Diem's death; a man who understood. Colby knew all the FitzGerald family. And the funeral brought Robert F. Kennedy, whom Colby had not seen since the days of President Kennedy's covert action unit, the Special Group (Counterinsurgency). Also there were Vice-President Hubert Humphrey; Averell Harriman, once Colby's nemesis at the State Department; *Washington Post* publisher's wife Kay Graham; financier Paul Mellon; and many more. Surrounding them were a host of gray-faced CIA men. Altogether a painful occasion.

Professionally, FitzGerald's demise opened up the job of Deputy Director for Plans. Colby had been in the running the last time around; obviously he was again. Among the other division chiefs in CIA's clandestine service, Colby had the biggest stake and budgets. Vietnam was the CIA's hottest war and it made sense to have an Asia man in charge of the clandestine service. The agency had also had secret wars going on in Africa—a paramilitary effort in the Congo, a coup in Ghana—but that continent was not taken very seriously on the seventh floor at Langley. The African division chief, Archie Roosevelt, had only come lately back to operations after four years in the CIA's plum diplomatic job: station chief in London. In addition, Roosevelt was primarily a Middle East specialist. As the grandson of President Theodore Roosevelt, Archie was also, perhaps, just too visible to head the clandestine service.

As for the Middle East itself, that region had just come through a third Arab-Israeli war. It was a moment for Director Helms to retain and build on expertise in the Near East and South Asian Division, not make changes at the helm. Also, James H. Critchfield, the chief of division, had recently angered White House officials through attempts to broker negotiations between the warring Arabs and Israelis; this was not the time to promote Critchfield into a position that would give him greater White House involvement. The Soviet Bloc Division, dear to Richard Helms's heart as the center of the agency's classic espionage role, remained in complete disarray due to counterintelligence problems. Far from offering candidates to head the clandestine service, the director of central intelligence felt the Soviet Bloc Division more properly needed someone from outside to take it in hand.

The other principalities of the clandestine service did not have many stellar candidates either, but it made no difference because in actuality Colby could hardly hope to compete with FitzGerald's former chief of operations, Thomas H. Karamessines. Unlike the FE Division chief, "Tom K" as he was known, had been a Helms loyalist for over a decade. Karamessines had opened the CIA's station in Athens, at the dawn of a guerrilla war America had won, and he had run the Vienna station at the height of the Cold War. Tom K bore the imprimaturs of service with the OSS and OSO, just as did Colby, but there was about him a whiff of mist-cloaked streets, the dark alleyways that shadowed spies. Karamessines had the reputation of being a master of espionage tradecraft, for Richard Helms an irresistible attraction.

Bill Colby never even heard about the DDP job. Instead, when Director Helms called Colby into his office it was to offer the Soviet and East European Division. Colby accepted. The calculation was not difficult. Twice Colby had been passed over for the top job in the clandestine service. This was not because he was some yokel in a service still dominated by Ivy Leaguers—Colby was from Princeton, Karamessines from Columbia, FitzGerald from Harvard. It was Richard Helms who came from a (slightly) lesser school, Williams. But Karamessines was a spy and FitzGerald had been a knuckle-dragger—a paramilitary devotee—and Colby was neither. Political action, though arguably one of the CIA's most successful activities, was frowned on as an offshoot of that slightly wired specialty, psychological warfare. If it came down to social differences, probably more important was Colby's staunch Roman Catholicism among the white Anglo-Saxon Protestants. Other Catholic CIA officers looked up to Colby, but there seemed to be a glass ceiling above him. The way to break through had to be to acquire the same credentials as Karamessines, as Helms, frontline espionage experience. And if Colby thus renewed his experience on Soviet matters, fallow since his Stockholm years, so much the better. Though the action might be in the Far East Division, no branch had the prestige of the Soviet one.

Thus for several months at the end of 1967, exactly those months during which the proposal to attack the Viet Cong infrastructure wound its way up through Saigon and the Washington bureaucracy, Bill Colby thought he was moving on to fresh pastures. The plan would be looked at cursorily as Colby focused on reading into the situation of the Soviet Bloc Division. It would not be long before Bill's interest became much more direct.

Meanwhile the Soviet Division—which handled all operations against Russia and its Eastern European allies, plus efforts to counter the Russians wherever they acted around the world—was in complete disarray. Essentially the division had been paralyzed by accusations that various top officers were in reality Russian spies inside the CIA, "moles" in a term of art that came into use somewhat later. At the heart of this affair stood CIA counterintelligence expert James J. Angleton and a succession of defectors from the Russian and Polish intelligence apparatus. One of these Russian agent/defectors, Anatoli Golitsin, whose CIA digraph would be AE/LADLE, gained Angleton's confidence, then began warning of a mole at a high level within CIA. Golitsin provided just enough information to make his charges seem credible and sufficient detail that his descriptions could cover many CIA officers and contract agents. He also questioned the bona fides of Yuri Nosenko, a further KGB defector who followed Golitsin into exile.

Golitsin had defected in Finland late in 1961, Nosenko in Geneva in February 1964. From the beginning the Nosenko defection tore the CIA to pieces, some siding with Angleton in a belief that Nosenko, called AE/FOX-TROT, was a false defector; some thinking Nosenko to be on the level; others wavering both ways. Foxtrot would be sequestered for years, subjected to friendly interrogation, hostile questioning, every form of truth elicitation imaginable. But there was no final answer because, as is so typical in these kinds of situations, fresh facts often change the meaning of what experts think they know. James Angleton, a poet who had written pieces for Des FitzGerald in the boss's early days, by 1967 had become as morose as FitzGerald himself.

Meanwhile chiefs and deputies in the Russia house of the CIA were sitting in a hot seat—suspicions were cast on most of them in the course of Angleton's mole hunt. This is what Bill Colby discovered when he prepared to take over the division. It was clear why Dick Helms needed an outsider for the job; only someone from outside could run the Russian division without being prejudiced against one or another of the alleged moles. The Angleton mole hunt had thoroughly compromised the CIA's operations against Russia.

Part of Bill Colby's preparation to head the Soviet Bloc Division was naturally a full briefing by CIA Counterintelligence. In a quiet office at Langley, Jim Angleton used slides and charts to superimpose details of various career paths of CIA officers to explain how each of them could secretly be a Russian agent. Angleton described a number of cases—the CIA's first chief of station in Moscow, a couple of top case officers, the current division chief, his deputy, even an officer who had been one of Angleton's main supporters in the inside politics of this affair. The division chief, David Murphy, told Bill his own theories about the "mole" burrowing within CIA. Colby wondered where it would all lead; being a lawyer by training he wanted to see evidence, but of course there was virtually none. Angleton, Murphy, and the members of all the factions arguing different sides of the case had nothing beyond conjecture. The affair increased Colby's doubts about the efficacy of CIA counterintelligence. Once he took over the division, Colby knew, he could not avoid crossing swords with Jim Angleton.

But Bill Colby would never have to deal with the morass in the Soviet Bloc Division. Instead, one of his preparatory briefings in November 1967 was interrupted by another summons to the seventh floor. As Colby entered Director Helms's office he found the CIA chief quite agitated. Helms had just returned from the White House, where President Johnson held private sessions called "Tuesday Lunches" (even when they occurred at mid-afternoon on a Friday). The President told Helms he had just met with Robert Komer, the former White House aide who now ran all pacification efforts in

Vietnam. Komer had a tale of troubles but promised progress, and he especially wanted William E. Colby for his deputy. LBJ told Helms to make it happen. Abashed at having to yank away Colby's Russian assignment, Dick Helms asked him to think overnight about a return to Vietnam. Stunned, Colby could nevertheless see that whereas his qualifications to lead the CIA's Russia house were strictly limited, he was an obvious choice for a pacification post in Vietnam. Besides, it is hard to turn down the president of the United States. Suddenly life had been transformed. Helms would instead give the Russia job to a Latin Americanist, Rolfe Kingsley. Colby's confrontation with Angleton would be postponed, though when it came it would be even worse. Most important, Bill Colby would be going back to Saigon.

SOME PARTICIPANTS and many observers argue that Vietnam became the most overanalyzed war in American history. The many trips by Robert McNamara and his successors, by John McCone, Maxwell Taylor and other generals; the frequent policy reviews; the repeated conferences at Honolulu— all bear testimony to this belief. The Central Intelligence Agency would not be left behind. Richard Helms sponsored a CIA-wide meeting on Vietnam on August 9, 1967. There was plenty of talk about the progress of the war; about bombing strategy, just then a hot topic in public debate and about to be the subject of congressional hearings; and of possible CIA initiatives. George Carver, the Special Assistant for Vietnam Affairs (SAVA), spoke up to say that whatever the United States did, it had better be done right.

Although there was a good deal of talk about pacification, and here Carver had advised Director Helms numerous times, he knew little about the latest project proposal. The SAVA chief had helped McNamara create a statistical system (called the "Hamlet Evaluation Survey" or HES, in an acronym familiar to a generation of Americans, as in "The HES data show . . .") to measure pacification progress. Carver's office also maintained and updated a Vietnam statistical handbook and attempted to convince all CIA components to use its agreed figures whenever generating reports of their own. But the newest practical pacification proposal—plans for a coordinated attack on the Viet Cong infrastructure—was something Carver knew little about. To get SAVA up to speed and give himself the best briefer on the subject, Carver got Director Helms to assign him Nelson A. Brickham.

Working with Saigon police authorities in late 1966, Brickham had composed papers advocating an operation specifically aimed at the Viet Cong infrastructure (VCI). Komer's support made the VCI project an official proposal of Military Assistance Command Vietnam, and Komer also adopted the CIA nomenclature, ICEX (for "Intelligence Coordination and Exploitation"), for its name. At the MACV level the attack on the Viet Cong infrastructure became part of an even larger scheme called Project Take-off. The MACVCORDS Directive (no. 381-41) controlling ICEX, issued July 9, provided for a small committee in Saigon that would feed instructions to officers in charge of each region. Corresponding to the South Vietnamese corps tactical zones and Saigon's capital military district, the five regions would direct South Vietnam's forty-four provinces and they the districts. At each level an ICEX committee brought together responsible officials. With ICEX designating Viet Cong targets, the CIA's Provincial Reconnaissance Units (PRUs) and the South Vietnamese National Police would be "especially focussed" and "redirected against infrastructure." The concept differed very little from what Nelson Brickham had put in his May 1967 project proposal.[2]

Attacking the Viet Cong infrastructure meant trying to uproot the whole network of National Liberation Front cadres who worked at all the levels at which ICEX would be active. The Liberation Front maintained a hierarchy of government at the hamlet, village, district, and province levels matching Saigon's. Its regions did not correspond to those of the Saigonese but had the same function. The Viet Cong also had an array of tax collectors, intelligence staffs, local guerrillas, and support groups like farmers' associations. The ICEX idea was to eliminate the infrastructure by getting rid of the members of all these parts of the parallel hierarchy. To "neutralize" became the term of art, and a Viet Cong cadre could be killed, captured, arrested, induced to desert, or compromised to his or her own side in order to be neutralized. These techniques were not in the first MACV directive but most had been in the original Brickham concept paper of November 1966.

To make space for the expected waves of new prisoners Project Take-off included an extensive program of jail construction, providing capacity for 8,000 additional detainees (to add to Saigon's existing prisons that, excluding army prison camps, could hold 25,000 persons). Even that capacity, the CORDS estimates showed, would be a couple of thousand short of the need anticipated for mid-1968. Another element of Project Take-off was to add large numbers of interrogation centers for prisoners at the district level. Additions to manpower for the South Vietnamese police were also contemplated.

No one in Washington knew these issues as well as Nelson Brickham, and when Project Take-off documents began to land on Washington desks late in July, Brickham became George Carver's point man on pacification, Take-off, and especially ICEX. The CIA had certain very specific problems with the project. Most important, the effectiveness of any attack on the VCI hinged on the quality of intelligence, and here the intent was to aim at particular individuals. Some might well be persons recruited by the CIA itself or the South Vietnamese to spy against the rest of the Viet Cong. Safeguarding CIA unilateral activities, along with those of the Saigon security forces advised by the CIA, became a continuing concern of the CIA Saigon station and Langley headquarters.

Agency officers working out of Saigon estimated there were several hundred penetrations, mostly at very low levels, into the Liberation Front apparat. There were at least some in higher ranks too, as demonstrated by a late 1967 contact between the U.S. embassy and the adversary—another of President Johnson's attempts to open peace negotiations—through an agent (the CIA and U.S. embassy had to intercede with the South Vietnamese to prevent the spy's arrest when Saigon security services uncovered his identity). Similarly there were South Vietnamese penetration operations that had CIA advice and assistance. In early 1967 the Special Branch of Saigon's National Police ran about 200 agents within the Viet Cong, and the Central Intelligence Organization, Saigon's version of the CIA, had another hundred spies among the enemy. The vast majority were district-level cadres—fewer than 10 percent of agents at that time were as high as province level within Viet Cong ranks. The CIA view would always be that all such intelligence operations should be protected from attacks on the Viet Cong infrastructure.

Another issue involved agency missions and control. One part of the Saigon station—there were almost twenty elements at various times—conducted the unilateral operations. Another gave advice to South Vietnamese intelligence; another was the liaison with the CORDS organization, another with the Agency for International Development which, through its Public Safety Office, advised Saigon police services. The PRUs were a separate CIA activity also. Other CIA elements were involved as well. Getting them all to work together would be as much a headache as deciding who would control them all. Beginning in 1966 the CIA had transferred many of its pacification elements to what became CORDS, but at the province level there remained separate CIA lines of authority for agent activity and for paramilitary operations such as the PRUs. The project for an attack on the Viet Cong infrastructure would require consolidation of the CIA command nets at both the province and the regional levels.

Then came the matter of personnel. Detecting and countering the Liberation Front's parallel hierarchy, above all, required good, solid intelligence. That meant CIA people. The agency had already given up to CORDS the officers in its Revolutionary Development Cadre organization. Now, with few exceptions, the CIA would have to furnish the regional officers-in-charge, the provincial officers-in-charge, and many of their staff people. Thus CORDS became a major destination for CIA officers being sent to Vietnam.

Meetings at Langley considered the key aspects of Project Take-off and the ICEX program. Nelson Brickham attended with Carver when Helms made the final decision in the director's office. Edward Proctor was there for the analytical side of the CIA; Colby represented the clandestine service. Reflecting his commitment to pacification as the preferred strategy in Vietnam, Colby made few objections. In fact the Far East Division chief is said never to have commented in writing. But there were others more zealously guarding the CIA's prerogatives. Project Take-off and ICEX were a done deal—President Johnson was Bob Komer's biggest fan, had sent him to Vietnam precisely to jump-start the pacification program, and Take-off had become its primary initiative. But the CIA would retain control of its agent nets, continue its monopoly of liaison with the Vietnamese security services, and maintain its role with the Provincial Reconnaissance Units. Thus the Vietnamese police and the PRUs, to become the mainstays of the war against the Viet Cong infrastructure, were not responsible to CORDS, the high command of the pacification effort.

Equally crucial meetings took place in Saigon. South Vietnamese participation in the anti-VCI program would be a sine qua non. The National Police, not the Americans, had power to arrest. Under them the Police Field Force had the largest single body of security troops that could be used against the Viet Cong infrastructure. The Special Branch had its own agent activities, as did Saigon's intelligence service, and also controlled the interrogation centers that would be a key source of information on the VCI. The Interior Ministry ran the prisons where captured VCI would be sent, and last, the Revolutionary Development Ministry, Saigon's counterpart to CORDS, held sway over the South Vietnamese side of pacification.

When Robert Komer met with Saigon officials, however, they were initially unimpressed. Not even Komer's CIA deputy for the revolutionary development cadres, Lewis J. Lapham, could move them. Lapham, standing in for CIA station chief John Hart, who had contracted eye problems, promised aid and autonomy but the South Vietnamese remained wedded to their prerogatives. Casting about for support, CORDS found some from authorities in the I Corps zone, the northern part of South Vietnam. The I Corps people even suggested a new name, "Phoenix," the bird that rises from its ashes. With regional enthusiasm behind him, Bob Komer appealed directly to South Vietnamese President Nguyen Van Thieu. The Saigon leader accepted the concept and relished the possibility of hitting the Viet Cong hierarchy directly. A Saigon directive establishing the program appeared at the end of 1967.

That was when, in Washington, President Johnson demanded that the CIA give him William E. Colby for Vietnam. By the second week of January Dick Helms had cabled Ambassador Ellsworth Bunker both about Colby and the necessity for replacing the incapacitated John Hart. Helms also consulted General Westmoreland and checked with Bob Komer about one idea, sending Colby in some supernumerary role to both work on pacification *and* run the CIA station. Komer nixed that option. With Walt Rostow at the White House, Helms considered whether Colby should be given a new gloss—the CIA called it "sheepdipping"—with brief assignment to the National Security Council staff before leaving for Saigon. By January 23 Helms and Rostow had agreed no patina was necessary. Two days later Colby sent a message to be passed along to Komer. "NEEDLESS TO SAY," the cable read, "WOULD ALSO APPRECIATE ANY SPECIFIC MATTERS YOU WOULD LIKE TO HAVE ME PREPARE OR LOOK INTO BEFORE JOINING YOU. . . . MANY THANKS FOR THE WORKBENCH ON WHICH WE CAN CONTINUE TO BUILD A STRONGER VIETNAM."[3]

The initial idea, for Colby to remain technically on CIA rolls but his salaries be reimbursed, did not fly. Instead Bill took leave from the agency for this CORDS civilian job. Soon Colby would find himself plagued by the very controls the CIA had insisted on retaining and would rue the day he had sat silent in Langley. In Saigon Bill Colby found himself again in the middle of war.

BEFORE LEAVING WASHINGTON Colby had a host of new things to take care of. One would be the Far East Division, for which Director Helms permitted Colby to select his successor. This would be William E. Nelson. At forty-seven years of age, Nelson had come a long way from Buffalo— the Army during the Big War, Columbia College, then Harvard for a master's degree in China studies at the Yenching Institute. Nelson became an Asia specialist at CIA. He had met Colby at Columbia and resumed the friendship at the agency. Both were slight, of medium height, wearing horn-rimmed eyeglasses. Colby enjoyed his inspection visits to Taiwan while Nelson headed the station there. Now Colby thought Bill Nelson an excellent choice to follow him at the Far East Division.

Naturally the other unfinished business was the Soviet Division. Colby had to hand over the job he'd not quite taken up. True to the original intention, Director Helms next chose another outsider, Rolfe Kingsley. Kingsley had had at least a watching brief on Russia, for he had worked for the CIA in Turkey and headed the station in Copenhagen. With transfers and reassignments, Kingsley would realign Russian operations; going much farther than Colby probably would have, Kingsley's reward would later be the plum CIA station in London.

Time with the family assumed great importance given Colby's imminent departure for Saigon. An outing to ice skate on the lower portion of the Chesapeake and Ohio Canal, in Georgetown, led to a bad turn and a fall for Bill; he broke his ankle. Through his final weeks at home Colby's foot stayed in a cast, which came off only the day before his departure. Bill hobbled onto his flight resting his weight on a cane.

All the family had been in Vietnam during the early days when everything seemed so much simpler, and the Colbys talked about Bill's goals for his new assignment. In one version, Colby writes that the conversation was with his wife Barbara; in another his children were favored. It was a snowy day, much warmer to be inside; and facing a job remote from the agency, not quite so secret as all the CIA work, Bill undoubtedly felt this was an opportunity to talk in greater depth than usual about what he did at the office. The theme would be self-defense for South Vietnamese villagers; Colby wanted to get guns into the hands of the people so they could protect themselves from Viet Cong depredations. This concept went far back for Colby, who had organized militias and the CIA montagnard force during his time as Saigon station chief. The latter initiative he had even called the "village defense program." But in 1968 self-defense acquired a somewhat different content.

In the interval before Colby left Washington, Hanoi and the Liberation Front struck in South Vietnam with their Tet Offensive. There was pitched battle in Saigon for almost a week and at Hue for closer to a month, though military gains were soon rolled back. For a brief moment the U.S. embassy in Saigon seemed in danger of falling to Viet Cong sappers, elite combat troops, unnerving Americans who had been fed a steady stream of official pronouncements that we were nearing victory in Vietnam. Tet attacks occurred throughout South Vietnam, except at Khe Sanh, the place MACV actually expected an assault. Nationwide combat meant a significant setback for pacification, since revolutionary development teams, the U.S. advisers helping them, and the Saigon army units protecting them were driven from the hamlets or drawn into battle.

In later years William E. Colby's view of Tet wavered even more than his view of Diem's assassination. In a memoir of the 1970s the former CIA man agreed Tet had been a military defeat for Hanoi and, in more muted voice, their political victory. That position Colby obscured further in his 1989 reprise of Vietnam as the lost victory. Then he argued that Tet had been so dramatic that dispassionate analysis of the attacks could hardly be heard against the din of the media drumroll. Although the American public suffered a shock—akin to being awakened from sleep by drenching with a bucket of cold water—Colby recalled that he and many Americans on the ground in Vietnam saw Tet as a defeat for the enemy pure and simple.

This, Colby recounted, had been the appreciation one got from the reality of the situation in Vietnam, not just its appearance on television. But on February 2, 1968, in a CIA paper they called "Operation Shock," Colby teamed up with George Carver and former station chief John Hart to present a think piece maintaining that Tet "forcefully demonstrated" the Saigon government lacked key attributes of nationhood. It could not "defend its frontiers without a half million U.S. troops," there remained a lack of popular resolution to fight, and Saigon continued to resist necessary reforms. In an action program, Colby and the others recommended that if President Nguyen Van Thieu could not show results in a hundred days, Saigon should be told the United States would "reserve its position" with regard to continued support for South Vietnam.[4] Colby was also one of a dozen senior CIA people whom Richard Helms convened in mid-February; their consensus had been that South Vietnamese troops had performed poorly during Tet, that the United States lacked a strategic concept in Vietnam, and that the outlook was for five or six more years of war. Bill Colby's arguments in the 1970s and 1980s about what Tet represented contained significant retrospective 20/20 vision and probably an aspect of atoning for guilt.

Just weeks before his death in 1996, Colby's view had again become more nuanced, although he continued to use the image of water:

> [Tet] hit the American public like a pail of cold water. It was *the* principal turning point in American public opinion towards the war. It crystallized the attitude this place was too far away, too complicated, we don't understand it, we're getting a lot of people killed, and we don't seem to be able to do anything good about it. And that was the start of the real American rejection of the experience.[5]

In this formulation, the military importance of Tet receded and the question of whether the political result had been an outcome intended by Hanoi or an accident "is kind of irrelevant."[6]

Possibly the key man to waver in the wake of Tet would be the president himself. Lyndon Johnson ordered a policy review, which concluded that the time had come to buckle down, not send more troops, to find openings to negotiate. Dean Rusk, whose role had often been to stiffen LBJ's determination, now reversed his opposition to a bombing halt.

Johnson called a panel of "wise men" from outside government to review the reviewers. At Langley the day George Carver was to brief the group, deputy George A. Allen literally took Carver by the lapels and shook him, imploring his boss to level with the advisers, warning that open rebellion at CIA would follow if Carver delivered some glossed-over version of the situation. The briefing would indeed be pessimistic, as would that from State, and the wise men startled President Johnson when they agreed with the Clifford policy review. LBJ had Carver and other briefers repeat their presentations for him personally; the result added to his doubts. Then Johnson found himself upstaged in the New Hampshire presidential primary, where antiwar candidate Eugene McCarthy received an astonishing 42 percent of the vote.

Meanwhile Bob Komer returned to Washington at the end of February. Ostensibly Komer would consult about the post-Tet status of pacification, but privately, by a CIA back channel, Ambassador Bunker told Walt Rostow that Komer was exhausted, had health problems in the family, and was temporarily discouraged. Bunker prescribed rest and begged Rostow not to permit Komer to be caught up in Washington's endless rounds of planning meetings. The effect was that Bill Colby, about to leave for Saigon, had little opportunity to exchange notes with Komer. The newly minted pacification deputy left within hours. Colby arrived at Tan Son Nhut airport aboard Pan American Airways Flight 2 on March 2, 1968.

Limping with his cane, Colby settled in at CORDS, making visits to villages in the countryside to familiarize himself with the new mission and to renew his impressions from the past. Once Robert Komer returned from his rest trip they began dividing up the work to be done. Colby was at CORDS offices in Saigon when he heard, on Armed Forces Radio, Lyndon Johnson's March 31 speech. There Johnson renounced politics and his candidacy for president in 1968 and ordered a partial bombing halt in Vietnam. The war had already changed.

SAIGON: TEEMING, RAUCOUS, a swirl of color but a jungle of private agendas, the Paris of the Orient had swollen since William E. Colby first set foot in it, almost a decade past. The war had wrought huge destruction in the countryside, making some 2 million people refugees just since Johnson's dispatch of ground troops. Many had come to the capital city, grown in size by perhaps 40 percent. Americans came too, one after another. Some came to punch their ticket and rise to a higher level; others felt Vietnam service the patriotic thing to do. Some brought hopes for progress or recipes for victory; Colby figured among that group. The CIA spy chieftain, on leave to work at CORDS, did not invent the techniques he was about to pursue; but he was a stalwart for pacification, and offered the opportunity for a command role implementing that strategy, Colby could hardly have refused.

But as it had been a decade before, Saigon remained a place of frustration. American strategies clashed with South Vietnamese politics, soldiers with spooks, diplomats talked of principle while men with stars on their shoulders plotted for power, or for revenge. Threatening someone's ricebowl, their essential stake and interests, remained the fast road to trouble. Robert Komer, "Blowtorch Bob," the boss at CORDS, always aggressive, abrasive, smart, and endlessly persuasive, threatened many ricebowls. Komer had won a key bureaucratic battle when General William Westmoreland agreed to throw MACV's military weight behind the "other war" of pacification. That had meant overriding his own intelligence chiefs, among other things, who would take a back seat and let CORDS direct the attack on the Viet Cong infrastructure.

Cooperation from the CIA itself would be another matter. Conditions for establishing that cooperation would never be as good as at the moment Colby returned to Saigon. At that point the CIA was providing most of the people working for the Phoenix central directorate in Saigon, along with a significant share of those who formed the office of the special assistant to the U.S. ambassador, which had a supervisory role over CORDS. The CIA also funded and led the PRUs and still had a big piece of the revolutionary development cadre support network, by far the largest CORDS program. Agency officers also advised, and the agency funded, Saigon's intelligence service and its Police Special Branch. Further, the CIA formed the mainstay of the chain of officers in charge of regions and provinces and their staffs. Finally, the new Saigon station chief, Lewis J. Lapham, had actually come out of CORDS, having been director of the revolutionary development cadre program when John Hart's illness forced the agency to replace him.

If anyone at CIA would be sympathetic to CORDS it would be Lapham. Eighteen years with the CIA, Lapham specialized in psychological warfare, had a Ph.D. from Harvard, and had worked for a congressional committee. He understood political purpose, had been sent to Vietnam specially to work the pacification issues, and had had Colby's blessing when he came out to Saigon in 1966. He kept his hand in Langley business by functioning as Hart's deputy, reading the cable traffic and filling in for the station chief when necessary. As a result, Lapham would be aware of the Saigon government's misgivings about the American-sponsored pacification initiatives. The National Police, whose director's loyalty went to Vice-President Nguyen Cao Ky, saw programs like Phoenix as mechanisms to eliminate opposition to Ky's competitor, President Nguyen Van Thieu. The Special Branch viewed

Phoenix as a U.S. effort to usurp its role. To others the program promised to divert attention from more important missions. Lapham's attitude was to support the Vietnamese fully, which worked out to tepid enthusiasm for CORDS.

Colby always believed in seeing things for himself. In the aftermath of Tet, that seemed more important than ever. One of his first forays would be to visit American pacification guru John Paul Vann, a controversial former Army officer employed by the U.S. Agency for International Development (USAID) to administer programs for the Mekong River delta. Colby had met Vann only once, when the man burst into his Langley office to denounce the revolutionary development cadre program as ineffective. It was true the teams expended much of their effort on security—fully half their manpower had been trained for that. Two years after Tet, CORDS still spent *80 percent* of its money on security programs, not counting funds laid out for related efforts like Phoenix, leaving just thimblefulls for the potential social programs that were supposed to be the crux of pacification. Though Colby disagreed with Vann, and now Vann had passed his prime, he would become a key ally for Colby.

In the villages it became evident that pacification really had ground to a halt with Tet. In Vinh Long province, in the heart of Vann's delta, the Hamlet Evaluation Survey data showed the number of villages under Saigon's control had fallen by almost half, from 59 to 35 percent. In Long An province, just next to Saigon, from which many Viet Cong had marched to the battles for that city, *no* hamlets were considered completely secure, and intelligence estimates of Viet Cong strength increased 50 percent from 1967 to 1968. In Hau Nghia, next to Long An, there were setbacks from Tet as well. In all three provinces a recovery phase followed Tet and by summer 1968 hamlet surveys looked as good as or better than those from before the enemy offensive, but this apparent improvement had as much to do with errors by the Liberation Front and Hanoi, who kept wasting strength in futile second and third wave attacks after no general uprising eventuated, as it did with any action by Americans or Saigon.

Americans of CORDS were well aware of the situation. In April, while Ambassador Bunker visited Washington, Bob Komer cabled him to say that although Tet had unquestionably been a setback, it seemed smaller than previously thought, whereas the attack against the VCI "is running well ahead of tough, arbitrary goals we established."[7] The hamlet evaluation survey, which showed secure villages at 67.2 percent of the total in January, had them back at 63.3 percent again by June 1968, though the lowest rated of these (the "C" category) were judged susceptible to regression. Some Liberation Front gains endured, however: Viet Cong control had dropped from a momentary high of 22 percent in February, but at 19.4 percent in June remained higher than the level (16.3 percent) in January 1968. Moreover, the contested list of hamlets had risen to 17.3 percent (from 16.4 in January).

Soon Colby got up to speed and on April 2 a MACV general order designated Bill the assistant chief of staff of MACV for CORDS, effective the next day. He continued roaming the countryside. Colby would be amused by John Paul Vann's efforts to explain to Vietnamese the very concept that water freezes so hard outside the tropics that one can skate on it, accounting for Bill's leg and cane in the early days, but the CORDS deputy's observations on Phoenix progress were less sanguine. The Vietnamese were not taking the thing seriously. They were far behind in creating district-level Phoenix committees and barely had the provincial ones up and running. In June Colby told Komer that data from the province of Dalat, the former imperial summer resort, showed the vast majority of detainees were being released. Only a few were remanded to the military courts or the provincial security committees, and those sentenced had been handled very unevenly. Colby felt it of little deterrent value if the worst sentence for an enemy cadre was just two years.

About the same time, meanwhile, Komer was turning around to journalist Robert Shaplen to brag about the anti–Viet Cong infrastructure effort, using its Vietnamese name, "Phung Hoang." Those who thought of Phoenix as a super secret operation might have been surprised to learn that Shaplen wrote of it in one of his pieces in *The New Yorker* magazine on January 20, 1968, barely three weeks after approval by South Vietnamese authorities.

Much of the improvement in the pacification situation after Tet resulted from Operation Recovery, a CORDS priority effort in the wake of the offensive. But as Colby and Komer reviewed progress that summer they determined to infuse new dynamism into all aspects of the work. Part of this would be to convince the Saigon government to commit itself fully to Phoenix; that was achieved when President Thieu, on July 1, issued a decree on the subject. Three weeks later followed a set of standing operating procedures to guide local authorities. Another piece would be to get MACV on board again— General Westmoreland had left Vietnam, his place taken by General Creighton W. Abrams. The latter supported initiatives like pacification, but CORDS's position would be stronger if Abrams could be induced to endorse the program openly. Bob Komer devised a new initiative.

Looking ahead to the 1969 plan, Bill Colby had innovations of his own, which, in the prevalent style of sloganeering, he termed the "Three Selfs." During a home visit late in August Colby presented his ideas for the campaign to Washington officials, talking so much about "People's War," the Liberation Front's name for guerrilla warfare, that one White House aide wrote, "it seems to be the catchword for next year's pacification program." Military operations and pacification were not necessarily the same, Colby argued to an audience heavily weighted with generals. His prescription amounted to Self-Help, Self-Defense, and Self-Government. The first would be the provision of small amounts of cash and commodities that village councils could allocate themselves to worthy projects, without the intrusion of the Saigon government. The last would be local elections for those village councils.

By far the longest portion of Colby's briefing he devoted to Self-Defense. Saigon's militia, composed of Regional Forces and Popular Forces, especially the latter, would be committed directly to the villages, which were to become the new basic unit for pacification. The revolutionary development cadre units would be doubled through removing their security elements, transformed into new teams and replaced by militia. A new People's Self-Defense Force would supplement these, reporting directly to village authorities. Then there was Phoenix. "Colby seemed to feel that it was moving forward through the efforts of the American advisers after some initial difficulties," reported National Security Council staffer Earl Young. "The Vietnamese are now said to comprehend its purpose and are implementing it." But, Colby emphasized, Phoenix was being held back by a slow judicial system and lack of prison facilities. The CORDS Public Safety Division, peopled by advisers from USAID, was responsible for prisons, and Young also went to a separate AID Public Safety brief on Phoenix. "Men just in from Vietnam are not so optimistic as Colby," he reported.[8]

The CORDS deputy director went on so much about People's War because he was convinced the Liberation Front and Hanoi had to be fought on their own political ground. Radio broadcasts Colby heard that spring reminded him so much of communist appeals for united front politics in the 1940s and 1950s that he felt the need to give warning. At Dalat in late May, during the same trip on which Colby had learned of the peripathetic Phoenix performance in that province, he had lectured on communist tactics at the South Vietnamese National Defense College. That summer, when Komer and Colby cooked up the idea of an Accelerated Pacification Campaign, Blowtorch Bob agreed that Colby should give a similar presentation for General Abrams. *That* could be the way to get his endorsement.

Military Assistance Command Vietnam had the custom of holding a commander's conference monthly, following a meeting on the latest intelligence information, at which strategic and policy issues could be debated by the three-star operational leaders and MACV's most senior staff officers. The MACV headquarters complex at Tan Son Nhut would be the setting on September 20 when Colby gave his talk, all of which he aired ahead of time with Komer. Colby described the structure of Hanoi's government, the dominance of the communists through their Lao Dong Party, and the technique of using interlocking structures of political plus interest groups to mask the true coloration of their leadership. There were detailed analyses of the Liberation Front, its fledgling People's Revolutionary Government, and the assorted united front groups that were surrogates. There was also coverage of the chain of political committees from the hamlet level right up to the Central Office for South Vietnam, the Liberation Front's main headquarters, that formed the real nervous system for the enemy movement. Using hamlet evaluation survey data plotted on maps, Colby showed how Viet Cong efforts expanded outward from base areas where the political committees sheltered.

The Saigon government needed to fight on every level, and fighting for the villages had to be by local security forces and institutions. The U.S. military should protect areas in dispute by screening them while threatening

Viet Cong bases by mounting incursions. Colby advocated pacification to "harden" the population centers and encouraged local elections—his "Self-Government"—to add a veneer of democratic politics. The new effort, which became the Accelerated Pacification Campaign, would be timed to culminate at Tet, 1969. Thus MACV would demonstrate great progress on the anniversary of the big enemy offensive the year before.

General Abrams followed the presentation with evident interest. "At the end," writes Colby, "he tapped his cigar thoughtfully, thanked me warmly, and gave Komer his full approval and support to go ahead."[9]

One wing of MACV headquarters housed the top CORDS people. For the next several weeks the place buzzed with activity as the Accelerated Pacification Campaign took shape. The staff used hamlet evaluation surveys (HES) to identify provinces with significant numbers of villages where extra intervention might change the HES ranking. Some provinces badly off in pacification terms were also included in hopes of keeping them from deteriorating further. Komer chose to focus on 1,000 villages and created a list of the requisite provinces, telling Washington that probably 350 villages would have increased their HES rating anyway, if progress continued at a steady pace, so that his number was not too much of a stretch. He also objected to Washington "civilian agencies," essentially a reference to the CIA, which worried too much about whether there would be "undue emphasis on numerical goals."[10] A MACV feasibility study declared the goal to be attainable, Ambassador Bunker reported a few days later, and a South Vietnamese Joint General Staff report confirmed that conclusion.

Frantic staff work culminated on October 11 in a meeting with President Nguyen Van Thieu. All the brass were there, including Bunker, Abrams, Komer, and Colby. Thieu was seconded by his interior minister and political ally General Tran Thien Khiem. The thousand village plan went over swimmingly. "The President's enthusiasm for the pacification effort was never more evident," Bunker reported to Washington. Colby and Komer went further and pushed in regard to Phoenix. Minister Khiem reported that he had recently called together responsible officials and instructed them to triple the monthly goal of 1,000 VCI neutralized. He promised a written directive on the subject. "President Thieu said that greatly increased emphasis on the importance of the program and much additional effort by the local administration, police and army will be needed." Robert Komer then pushed home the distinction between accelerated pacification and the Phoenix program: "Obviously," Komer declared, "the attack on the VC infrastructure must not focus on only 1,000 hamlets."[11]

So accelerated pacification went into effect. Within weeks, on October 23, Colby felt it necessary to insist in a memo to MACV that the effort would not be a numbers game. Similarly, in mid-November, when Saigon's top pacification official ordered provincial officials to investigate the true situation in villages, Colby refused to permit American advisers to participate for fear of damaging the integrity of the data. But in fact accelerated pacification *did* have a numbers side to it—CORDS itself changed the HES criteria used to compile the data. The ninety-seven questions that advisers answered on their monthly HES reports were modified to eliminate most of those dealing with social well-being, leaving mainly security indicators.

Meanwhile, all of this became William E. Colby's direct concern. President Johnson appointed Robert Komer his next ambassador to Turkey, promoting Colby to the top position at CORDS. Komer insisted to the White House that to do the job right, Colby, like Komer himself, would need to have the personal rank of ambassador. Johnson acceded. William E. Colby became the first officer of the Central Intelligence Agency, albeit on unpaid leave, to attain the rank of ambassador in the U.S. foreign service reserve. On November 6, 1968, Colby drove Bob Komer out to Tan Son Nhut for a flight to Hong Kong to make a connection home. On November 27 President Johnson sent Colby a letter conferring his exalted rank. The "other war" was Bill Colby's baby now.

12

THE FALL OF PHOENIX

B ILL COLBY AND BOB KOMER would both be effective as heads of Civil Operations and Revolutionary Development Support, though personally they were as different, perhaps, as it is possible to be. Bristling as the bushy mustache he sported from time to time, Blowtorch Bob trumpeted the CORDS mission in the fullest voice he could muster. The Minnesotan Colby contrasted sharply—self-effacing, quiet, and efficient where Komer would be loud and heavy-handed. Robert Komer got results by grinding away—he knew the best people, asked penetrating questions, forced responsible officials to confront the problems to which he proposed solutions. William E. Colby used determination too, but his would be steady and nonprovocative, enlisting others in a joint approach to a solution.

A couple of vignettes serve to illustrate the differences between these two captains of the pacification war. Ambassadorial rank in U.S. service equated to the rank of a four-star general. Soon after his arrival in Vietnam, Komer would be held up at the gate to MACV headquarters by a military policeman who gave precedence to the car bearing a brigadier (one-star) general. Bob Komer promptly demanded four-star license plates for his vehicle plus clear recognition by the minions. Blowtorch Bob settled for a special windshield tag and saw it as a way of bringing the military around to recognize the importance of the pacification mission.

For Colby a typical experience would be what happened in Pleiku about eighteen months into his Vietnam tour. By then the CORDS chief was well known and an object of constant attention. The occasion, an inspection of progress in handing over former Green Beret montagnard programs to the South Vietnamese, involved the traditional montagnard ceremony of drinking potent rice wine. It was something Colby had done in his time as CIA station chief, and he carried it off perfectly whereas some Americans could barely stand up after one of these bouts. Numerous official and other photographers recorded the events fully, but Colby never thought to ask for copies of the pictures.

At the office, the boss proved quite considerate of those who worked for him. Dennis G. Harter, a foreign service officer on assignment to CORDS, found himself called into the czar's office only a day or two after reaching Saigon. Bill explained that CORDS belonged to MACV, which was military, and this meant they all went home at five o'clock. Colby and Harter, however, were CORDS *civilians*. Colby made it clear *he* worked late. *But*, Harter should understand, that did not mean Harter also had to stay into the night, unless he had some special project that needed to be finished.

The CORDS director assembled a good team and got performance by inspiring loyalty. Colby kept the chief of his Phoenix central staff, Evan J. Parker, Jr., fellow CIA, who had been with Colby in the OSS, when they had both part of the Jedburgh operation. Parker had gone to Burma with OSS Detachment 101, and in turn several of his 101 comrades were now with CORDS or in Vietnam with the CIA. Indeed, many of the top echelon of Phoenix, plus most of the regional and provincial officers, Colby knew from the CIA. The chief of the *chieu hoi* program, the part of CORDS that helped the Vietnamese to induce Viet Cong to defect, was a Princeton College contemporary, Ogden Williams. Colby maintained a good relationship with General Creighton Abrams, while he and Ambassador Bunker shared a love of boating. More than once Colby helped Bunker work on the trimaran he kept docked in Saigon harbor. They were kindred spirits. Bunker had a reputation in the Foreign Service as "The Refrigerator,"[1] while Colby too would be known for his deadpan demeanor.

The new pacification czar also inherited a number of people from Komer, several of whom he relied on. Colonel Robert Montague would be one, a member of the Vietnam brain trust, a circle including such men as Vann, George Jacobsen, and, now becoming a prominent dissenter, Daniel Ellsberg. Montague had been Robert Komer's military assistant in the White House, and Bob had brought him out to help at CORDS. Colby liked Montague, and years later the two remained friends. For his expert on South Vietnamese corruption Colby retained Everett Bumgardner, one of the oldest hands not only at CORDS but someone the boss had known in Vietnam before. Bumgardner had arrived in Saigon during French days, working for the U.S. Information Agency, became an Ed Lansdale sidekick, and sort of went native, acquiring a wife from the Chinese diaspora, strongly entrenched in Saigon's sister city, Cholon.

Still, for all his trusted staff Colby knew the real story lay in the field. To overcome the language barrier, at least somewhat, Colby began his CORDS day with a 7:15 A.M. class in Vietnamese. In the field he pursued facts tirelessly. The people Colby questioned had better know the answers. The CORDS chief tried to get out of Saigon every other day; as he said to journalist David Hoffman, "You can't really learn much just sitting in that building." Often Colby would turn to Ev Parker, or Montague, or one of his other senior people and say, "Let's go."[2] They would take a helicopter or a jeep, or would board an Air America plane depending on the destination. Those to be inspected usually found out Colby was coming only as he was about to reach them. Sometimes he brought along reporters to see the fun.

One such sally came a month or so after Bill took over from Bob Komer. This was a visit to Chau Doc, capital of the province of that name, which lay out toward the Cambodian border. With a substantial fraction of its population from the Hoa Hao religious sect, long estranged from the Viet Cong, Chau Doc had been in relatively good shape. It was late afternoon when Colby alighted from his chopper and shook hands with the province officer in charge, an old CIA friend, Jim Tull. They dined together. The pacification czar went on to a talk with the Vietnamese province chief, a colonel named Hue.

"I understand, Colonel, that you have one company that only operates at night?" Colby asked over brandy.

Colonel Hue, pleased, joked he could do that because he took away the soldiers' beds at night.

"Where had that company been operating?" Hue indicated a point on the map with his index finger. Using a pencil, Colby then traced a road in that area, wondering if it was safe to use at night. Hue said that it was, claiming his brother often drove it after midnight to return to his family in Chau Doc city.

Then Bill Colby changed subjects: "And how many rifles do the People's Self-Defense Forces [PSDF] have in Chau Doc?"

The South Vietnamese province chief reported roughly 2,000 weapons in the hands of the PSDF. Colby held a list that showed 4,000. Colonel Hue replied that was a year-end target, not a current number.

Leaving the town Colby had to break his promise to CIA officer Tull, who needed dental work and whom he had offered a seat in the helicopter to military region headquarters, where Tull could get treatment. The Air America pilot, already a half hour late in Saigon, had another priority passenger waiting at Tan Son Nhut. Jim Tull nursed his toothache until morning; he did *not* use the road which Colonel Hue's troops had supposedly made safe for night travel.[3]

On another occasion, in early 1969, the CORDS chief went to Da Nang for a powwow with top officials for I Corps. With him were Bob Montague and George Jacobsen. At CORDS headquarters for the military region, downtown at 22 Bach Dang Street, Colby listened as Harry Mustakos, the CIA's regional officer in charge, defended performance on Phoenix. Mustakos argued that his PRU teams were of low quality; his intelligence limited because too many of the supposed VCI were being killed rather than captured, and thus could not be interrogated; and that Saigon had put too much emphasis on neutralizations of top-level VCI. Colby's questions were pointed and well informed, but he did nothing to excuse I Corps from its quotas for VCI neutralizations.

Pacification in I Corps had already been a subject when the CORDS chief met with President Thieu on December 9. Things in the north looked good enough that Colby wanted to add more hamlets to the list for accelerated pacification, shortening the time cadre teams would spend in each so as to cover the territory. Robert Montague prepared a set of talking points that Colby also used to argue for village councils and local initiative, and for bringing together political forces in South Vietnam. Colby followed up by meeting with General Tran Thien Khiem about a week later, and CORDS held prolonged talks with Saigon officials that culminated in South Vietnamese agreement to select hamlets for special pacification treatment solely on the basis of the HES data. In the end the Accelerated Pacification Campaign would encompass 1,200 hamlets; CORDS saw it as a great success.

Washington proved far less optimistic. The CIA, the State Department, and the international security affairs section of the Office of the Secretary of Defense all criticized claims of pacification progress. The incoming administration of Richard M. Nixon had asked for a major reassessment of Vietnam issues, which Washington agencies used to assert that pacification remained subject to backsliding, in particular if there were a repetition of something like the Tet offensive. Of course there was not, but nevertheless CORDS claims of success were weak in several places. The CIA also produced a special national intelligence estimate on pacification (SNIE 14–69), the first (and last) on this subject during the Vietnam war. This intelligence community exercise proved quite controversial. The estimate conceded current progress but argued that the time left to make up past deficiencies was uncertain: "The most common attitude among the peasants, however, continues to be one of war weariness and apathy." State Department intelligence insisted there was no evidence to support the contention that pacification was less vulnerable than it had been before Tet. The Phoenix program was acknowledged as "fairly promising," but the SNIE pointed out clearly that the Saigon government itself had given no more than lukewarm support until the summer of 1968.[4]

Altogether this was not the pretty picture that CORDS wanted to draw. Bill Colby cast about for ways to counter the doubts. The obvious one was to plant stories in the press. Within a week of the publication of the CIA's special estimate, there was a story in the *Washington Post* from a reporter friendly to Colby that used the code name "Phoenix." It noted that 8,104 Liberation Front cadres had been neutralized in 1968, and revealed the Saigon interior minister's goals for 1969 in noting that the United States hoped for 33,000 neutralizations through the rest of the year.

Meanwhile, Colby also came up with a more creative way to stymie the pacification naysayers. This stunt, a vintage one Colby would repeat, was to drive around the Mekong Delta himself. If Colby could do that, maybe CORDS had been right all along. He drove a hundred miles along Route 4, the road south from Saigon that led through the heart of the Mekong delta. There were skeletons of blown bridges and mine craters filled with dirt, but no one shot at Colby, and his feat garnered good attention from the press, Saigon to New York, and indeed as far afield as Wheeling, West Virginia. Reporter Robert Kaiser of the *Washington Post*, after listening to a few of Bill's talks, coined the term "the new optimists" for Colby's brand of American adviser.[5]*

However, building the credibility of pacification became a multifront struggle, including not only Washington and the American public but also the American advisers themselves. Komer's placing of CORDS within the U.S. military had been a brilliant maneuver, gaining resources not to be dreamed of otherwise; but by the same token the military, addicted to numerical measures of merit, had begun to play the HES numbers the same way body counts had been so important under Westmoreland. This was true on both the U.S. and South Vietnamese sides, as officers discovered that Creighton Abrams and Nguyen Van Thieu paid attention to HES data and made decisions based on them. Bill Colby had to intervene repeatedly with assorted military commands, arguing that Vietnam was *not* a numbers game, advising that they should take the numbers less seriously than the actual status of villages. Certainly officers' promotions ought not to be based on fulfillment of some norm rooted in HES.

Yet, at the same time, Colby and CORDS were obliged to push for progress that could only be monitored by numbers. This applied to the Accelerated Pacification Campaign and its successors as well as to Phoenix. The process involved an inherent and essential contradiction, one with which Bill Colby would wrestle for his entire time in Vietnam and from which there was no escape. Washington expected results. Goals existed and there was constant need to strive to achieve them, but excessive zeal in meeting the goals more often than not resulted in lowering of standards of conduct and, consequently, false assessments of progress.

Another problem that faced Colby, one that sharpened after December 1968, was the relationship between CORDS and the CIA. That month Ted Shackley came to Saigon, promoted from his stewardship of the secret war in Laos. In his own CIA incarnation, of course, Colby had accepted Des FitzGerald's sponsorship of Shackley, then come to admire the latter's

---

* One of these grandstand plays was a motorcycle tour with John Paul Vann, at Tet 1971, ending at Chau Doc in the delta. Left unsaid was that the trip at the high holiday was equivalent to an American driving around on Christmas morning, or perhaps the afternoon of the Super Bowl football game—the choice of timing automatically minimized any risk inherent in the situation. Another Colby road trip, also early in 1971, was with the British ambassador to Hue, where they drove around at night, meeting only friendly militia and patrols. Here the underlying feature of the situation was that all sides' attention was focused on Laos, where the South Vietnamese had embarked on a major invasion, and Liberation Front efforts were thus concentrated in Quang Tri and the sectors behind the invasion front, not on Hue to the south. Pacification certainly improved the security situation but the "new optimists" painted such rosy pictures they inspired skepticism.

efficiency, but in Saigon certain differences between Colby and Shackley became inevitable.

For starters, Bill Colby believed strongly that the effort in Vietnam—the politics, the security initiatives, the thinking and doing—had to at least appear to be coming from the Saigon government. That notion created several sources of tension with the CIA. For example, CORDS furnished money, both dollars and South Vietnamese currency (piastres) to Saigon, but the currency trading that filled American agencies' accounts with piastres was conducted by the Central Intelligence Agency. For its part, the CIA had an interest in CORDS positions to provide cover for agency personnel in Vietnam, while CORDS knew the CIA had expertise in the very things in which it engaged and preferred to have the CIA people really working the jobs that were supposed to be cover. And of course the CIA actually was providing key personnel to CORDS, including most of Evan Parker's central Phoenix staff in Saigon, many of the individuals in the Phoenix chain of command from the province level on up, a number of those who managed the revolutionary development cadres, and so on. In addition, the one striking force most directly useful to Phoenix, the Provincial Reconnaissance Units, were entirely a CIA entity. All this amounted to a good deal of CIA visibility, more than Colby saw as desirable in this quintessentially political war.

In some respects Bill Colby would be in direct competition with his CIA brethren. Political action had been a Colby specialty at the agency, and the whole point of CORDS was to mobilize the South Vietnamese Public in support of the Saigon government. Colby had made that very point in meetings with Thieu. But political action also remained on the CIA station's agenda. One case in point was the Vietnamese labor leader Tran Quoc Buu. Colby met with Buu a few times in 1968 and after as Buu's CVT union began getting USAID funding. Yet Shackley's station still had a case officer assigned to Buu, one who reportedly helped with letters soliciting money from American labor organizations. Money and Japanese tractors actually came from the AFL-CIO, among whose officials Jay Lovestone had been a virtual CIA contract officer. According to Lovestone's biographer Ted Morgan, in October 1969, Buu announced his creation of a political party on direct orders from the CIA.

Competition also resulted from differing interests of Saigon agencies working with the Americans. The Special Branch of the National Police and Saigon's Central Intelligence Organization were both advised and funded by Shackley's CIA station. Yet both were major contributors to the Phoenix mission that Colby ran. Special Branch, in particular, had the job of interrogating suspected VCI in province centers whose construction the CIA had paid for. Indeed Shackley actually had officers assigned to the vast majority—perhaps 90 percent—of the provincial interrogation centers. When, in 1969, the torture and mistreatment of prisoners led Colby to issue a CORDS directive for Americans to refuse to participate in and advise against such measures, the order did not apply to CIA officers at Special Branch's inter-rogation centers.

On one occasion in 1969 Colby attended a briefing in Gia Dinh province, just to the north of Saigon, where the Special Branch adviser was Ralph McGehee, who had run afoul of Colby in Thailand and had volunteered for Vietnam to escape a dead-end job. McGehee was now on a Special Branch operation called Projectile that had uncovered a Liberation Front spy network with lines right into President Thieu's office. Not waiting for the briefers to describe what an exceptional catch they had, Colby simply called for statis-tics. McGehee found the CORDS chief harried and distracted. When the Special Branch went ahead and arrested members of the spy ring, they in-cluded a close friend of Thieu's, who headed Saigon's own school for spies, and his adviser on Catholic affairs.

Colonel Nguyen Mau headed the Special Branch. He busied himself with operations like the spy ring affair, which in Mau's view was a proper role. Providing intelligence to CORDS for Phoenix activities was not a priority—Mau saw that program as a miasma of arbitrary detention, false accusation, and unjustified arrest. Mau knew something about unjustified arrests—he had been mayor of Hue in 1963, at the time Diem's brother's breakup of a Bud-dhist celebration triggered the chain of events that led to the assassination Colby still rued. The one time the CORDS chief came to visit Special Branch headquarters in Saigon, Mau waited outside to greet him. Bill Colby swept into the building after the most perfunctory of handshakes and left soon after. Colby's shortness may have had to do with Nguyen Mau's connection to Diem's downfall, but more likely it flowed from Special Branch's lack of enthusiasm for Phoenix and Colby's inability, due to its CIA counterpart relationship, to do anything about the problem. Had Colby, while still at Langley in 1967, thought through the problem of differing agency interests when ICEX was first initiated, two years later he would have been able to work with Nguyen Mau much more effectively.

The most troublesome aspect of the CORDS–CIA relationship as it per-tained to the Phoenix program centered precisely on intelligence. Ted Shack-ley actually agreed with Colby that the CIA had too high a profile, and he wanted the station to focus more on traditional intelligence functions. But that meant recruiting spies inside the same Liberation Front hierarchy that it was Bill Colby's job to destroy. Because the CIA's primacy had been rec-ognized in 1967, it could take over any valuable agent Phoenix operators developed, or stop any Phoenix operation the CIA deemed a threat to one of its own penetrations. The agency's writ ran very broadly, as recounted by then-Lieutenant Colonel Phillip Bolté, scion of an Army family, who in 1968 was province senior adviser in Quang Tin. Bolté had been told he had charge of *all* activities in his province, so he "started pushing the CIA around." That did not last long: "The next thing I knew, the CIA representative from [I Corps] and my immediate superior came down to meet with me. The . . .

representative accused me of trying to run the CIA. I said yes, because Komer told me I was to run everything. With the obvious acquiescence of my boss, he told me in no uncertain terms, 'You're not to run the CIA.' It was then I realized that I had been playing baseball using football rules. We were never able to solve the CIA problem."[6]

Bolté would be fortunate in that the agency team in his province proved cooperative, but this degree of comity often did not exist. Coordinating between CIA and CORDS became the subject of many conversations between Colby and Shackley at meetings of the embassy council, on which they both sat. It also dominated monthly gatherings of the CIA's regional officers in charge—like the I Corps man who had put Bolté in his place—who had both agency and Phoenix missions. Coordination also was discussed in the thrice-weekly sessions Shackley held at the station, to which Colby sent top Phoenix staff people. Shackley retained his veto. The tail-wagging-the-dog element to all this left Colby frustrated throughout his time in Vietnam.

FRUSTRATION WOULD ACTUALLY be a good word for 1969, a keynote for a year during which Bill Colby struggled to make the Phoenix program run smoothly and to confine it within some kind of regularized structure. The withdrawal of the CIA from its most visible roles became one issue. Others revolved around the Phoenix program. After pushing for results, Colby had to try to restrain the Phoenix apparatus, prevent it from merely generating numbers, target it better, and bring in the American advisers he needed to ride herd for CORDS. The South Vietnamese continued apathetic and that would be another issue Colby worked at arduously. Then also, Phoenix had become known and increasingly controversial in the United States, a problem that would never cease for William Egan Colby.

Project Witness had been the CIA's moniker for the Provincial Reconnaissance Units. These were the revamped Counter-Terror Teams that had existed in 1966 and before, with an official mission changed to reflect their intelligence function slightly more, the terror one somewhat less. Each province had a unit, normally of 100 to 150; some members were locals, some former Viet Cong, some criminals, some who enlisted to avoid the South Vietnamese draft, some Nung tribesmen, indigenous fighters of legendary fierceness. The teams had been commanded by Americans ranging from CIA contract officers to detached Green Berets to Navy special warfare experts known as SEALs (Sea Air Land Soldiers). Heading Project Witness for the CIA was Tucker Gougelmann, who had worked for Colby on the latter's first Vietnam assignment as station chief. Gougelman had between fifteen and thirty CIA paramilitary officers occupied full time on the PRUs, supplying them with equipment, funds, and intelligence. Gougelman's deputy, William Buckley, a former Green Beret and Korean war hero, impressed the SEALs as being a cut above the average agency type, and served as liaison with PRUs in all the military regions. The CIA's direct costs for the PRUs, roughly $7 million a year, did not include its salaries or those it reimbursed from other U.S. government agencies or paid on contract to American PRU leaders, of whom there were between 104 and 110 at different times. In addition, a significant PRU expense that would be kept off the books was counterpart funds—South Vietnamese piastres acquired by CIA currency traders and used to pay bounties for information, captured weapons, prisoners, and in some places dead bodies.

The biggest accumulated body of open material on the PRUs comes from recollections of Navy SEALs who formed a composite unit that ran the PRUs in twelve of the Mekong Delta's sixteen provinces. The assorted memoirs show why PRUs were so effective but also sound cautionary notes. Unit leaders led by example, were out with their men, often had cooperation from heavily armed U.S. SEAL teams, and developed intimate knowledge of their areas of operation. They could also call on heavy support from aircraft or river gunboats. Local PRU fighters knew something about who might be Viet Cong. Direct contact with the CIA could be quite limited—SEAL Frank F. Thornton, Jr., saw agency people just three times during his entire tour with Nha Be's PRU. Frank Bomar never saw them at all and recalls it as simple "scuttlebutt" that PRUs worked for the CIA, though he also remembers the PRU nickname as "plumbers," a word associated with the agency.[7] Colleague Frank Flynn warned his successor about the CIA overseers: "They'll shake your hand and pee in your boots at the same time," and the SEAL who heard this warning reminisced, "As usual Frank was right."[8] Michael J. Walsh, whose Chau Doc PRU would be rated the finest in southernmost Vietnam (IV Corps) in 1970, met and got a briefing from Bill Buckley, after which other SEALs told him, "If we need anything, Bill's the guy we call."[9] It was then, Walsh remembers, "I really began to understand that Phoenix was a CIA operation, with all that this entailed."[10]

Some Mekong military advisers had different nicknames for the PRUs. Ed Miles, an Army captain and pacification adviser in Hau Nghia province, one of those in which CORDS is considered to have been most successful, recalls his people openly and commonly referring to the PRUs as "assassination squads," and not relishing the memory of entering a Vietnamese village the morning after a PRU had been there.[11] In the earlier CIA scheme of counterterror, assassination had been a major technique, but by 1969–70, at least in the kingdom of the SEALs, the more common tactic had become the "snatch," an attempt to apprehend the targeted individual. More often than not the try at a kidnap or arrest turned into a firefight, in particular when the target really was VCI who had his own bodyguard. Other SEALs remember that the CIA structured incentives in various ways—by offering higher bounties for bodies than captives; by putting the bounties out for captured weapons; and so on. Procedures were not regularized until 1969.

The heavy strike teams and backup for the PRUs were the SEALs' own units, and these undertook thousands of patrol missions for the Phoenix program. Just how ambiguous the neutralization game was is well illustrated by the February 25, 1969, snatch mission of Delta Platoon SEAL Team One into the Mekong village of Thanh Phong. The seven-man unit under Navy Lieutenant Robert Kerrey had orders to capture the NLF district committee secretary whom intelligence believed to be in the village that night. The team killed villagers as they entered to preserve the secrecy of their approach, then killed more when they thought they had come under fire within the village itself. "Kerrey's Raiders," as the unit called itself, ended up with no Viet Cong captives but a body count of twenty-one civilians. That the victims were numbered among the enemy up the chain of command is attested by the award to Lieutenant Kerrey of a Silver Star for the mission.

Bob Kerrey went on to a distinguished career as a United States senator from Nebraska, then a university president. The incident at Thanh Phong remained a source of private grief for Kerrey and his raiders until 2001, when magazine and television reconstructions of the mission raised the question of whether a war crime had been perpetrated there. Unremarked amid the flurry of public debate over whether Bob Kerrey ought to be investigated on war crimes charges was the fact that this mission to Thanh Phong was merely another day in the country under the Phoenix program, a routine mission for the PRU and SEAL strike teams.

Details like Thanh Phong did not reach to Bill Colby's exalted level, but the things that happened at that village were not isolated or unique. As he would repeatedly, Colby took action to ensure greater uniformity and respect for process in Phoenix operations. In August 1969 the CORDS director asked that all American PRU advisers be required to attend lectures on South Vietnamese police procedures at the Vung Tau school.

Meanwhile the ground was shifting underneath the Provincial Reconnaissance Units. On March 31 the Saigon government issued a decree providing that the PRU teams be absorbed into the National Police. Until that time, PRUs had had no legal basis in South Vietnam, existing entirely under a cover arrangement between the CIA and the South Vietnamese Joint General Staff. The CIA would pull out of Project Witness as of June 30. Under the new arrangement the Vietnamese chief in each province had authority over the PRU and could appoint its leader, usually someone loyal to him. William Buckley, the American deputy chief for Witness, confided to associates that he had doubts about Colonel Long, the Saigon-appointed overall commander for PRUs within the National Police. The PRUs continued to enjoy CIA funding, budgeted at $5.5 million for 1969 and $6.2 million in 1970, and their U.S. advisers, regardless of the formal legal status, retained effective control of most PRU teams. While various Americans, among them General Abrams, expected Saigon to take over full responsibility for the PRUs, in fact their CIA funding continued through the end of the Vietnam war.

Among those Americans who had doubts about the handover to Saigon of the Provincial Reconnaissance Units was Director Colby. The pacification czar worried that without their American commanders the PRUs would lose effectiveness. In their final ten months under the CIA the PRUs ran 50,770 missions and tallied 7,408 VCI captured and 4,406 killed. Their own losses were 179 killed in action. The PRUs also had the lowest desertion rate among South Vietnamese forces, which was partly attributable to the fact they were paid more than army regulars—three times as much by some counts.

To enforce the changes and Saigon government control, after September 30 Americans were not supposed to go into the field with the PRUs and they were restyled advisers instead of leaders. As with the Green Berets and montagnards in the Central Highlands, however, the strictures were rather elastic. The SEALs in the delta controlled counterpart funds, as did American advisers everywhere, that could be used to reward people for information, pay bounties, buy extra equipment, food, or anything else. Those funds gave the advisers a certain actual control. In many places Vietnamese PRU leaders *were* ineffective, as Colby feared, but often Americans stepped into their places; the PRUs were hardly going to complain. In 1970 and through the spring of 1971 the PRUs accounted for a little over half of all VCI killed who were credited to the Phoenix program, including three times as many specifically targeted individuals as the next highest performing force (the National Police Field Force). However, the same data continued to show that the vast majority (87.6 percent) of dead Liberation Front cadres perished in conventional military operations. Most effective by far were the militias, the Regional Forces and Popular Forces, who accounted for two thirds (67.1 percent) of the dead cadres. Unfortunately those counted as dead from conventional operations were identified only after the fact. The truth was that although many were probably actual VCI, no one had any idea of the reality.

Meanwhile Ted Shackley's CIA station continued its proclivity for taking over any promising agent operation. When SEAL Mike Walsh did a repeat PRU tour at Dong Tam in 1971, his intelligence people had to hide their spy lists and particulars from CIA overseers who came up from Saigon for periodic surveys. Walsh later wrote: "One of the first things you learn about intelligence gathering is that the CIA can absorb any agent it wants. My tour with Phoenix confirmed this."[12]

The nature of the Provincial Reconnaissance Units raised questions of who was the enemy and what would be done to them. The notion of an attack on the Viet Cong infrastructure presupposed a level of knowledge sufficient to identify individuals, their movements and habits, even their culpability. From the CORDS perspective this intelligence problem, greatly worsened by the language barrier—which precluded most Americans from knowing much about what their counterparts were about—proved almost insurmountable.

On the South Vietnamese side there were laws on the books dating from Diem's reign, even provisions in the constitution of 1967, which defined mere membership in a communist party or front organization as a crime. From 1968 on the Vietnamese Phoenix authorities established three categories for detainees: class "A" offenders, who were VCI cadres from district level up; class "B" offenders, active with the Liberation Front in any way; and class "C" offenders, persons who had done anything to benefit the Viet Cong in any way. The categories were set under criteria developed by Colby's legal officer, Gage McAfee, but the very nomenclature evoked the prisoners hauled before war crimes trials in the wake of World War II. A detaineee by definition was an "offender," something very alien to American notions of innocence until proven guilty. To cap the system, the Saigonese had provisions for a form of preventive detainment they called "an tri" under which an "offender" could be held for two years without any charges at all.

When the time came, Bill Colby defended the system. Vietnam was not America, he argued, and the same standards of due process could not apply. South Vietnam, a nation at war, had to be able to combat its enemy, in this case a hidden parallel hierarchy. But Colby's arguments were unpersuasive. Examinations of CORDS and Phoenix, like peeling an onion, revealed more arbitrariness at every level. One could be a class "C" offender for doing nothing more than paying taxes to the Viet Cong, leaving the peasantry in quite a predicament. Many offenders in this category were people against whom there was no evidence at all. Opinion at CORDS held that "C" offenders were very low value VCI, so much so that in his drive to increase Phoenix effectiveness Colby prohibited even counting the "C" prisoners as Phoenix neutralizations from the beginning of 1969. Despite this fact, two years later data that Colby furnished to a congressional committee showed that only about a quarter of the Vietnamese prisoners in that category were being released when their sentences came up for review. Worse, the proportion of sentence extensions for category "B" prisoners ("A" offenders were almost never released) stood at about 50 percent. Thus while Americans defended Phoenix with claims that most of those arrested received short sentences (three months to a year), the system worked to ensure that lesser presumed complicity with the VCI was no guarantee of shortness of incarceration.

The system also lent itself to corruption and abuse. Suspects went on trial before a Province Security Committee, but the proceeding was not considered a legal one and there was no appeal. The suspect had no right to counsel, no right to see his dossier, testify, confront accusers, or question the prosecution. The security services could hold a detainee at several levels—for immediate tactical intelligence, for extended interrogation, for questioning at the provincial level, for purposes of building a file—for a total of forty-six days prior to submitting a case to a province committee. At the trial, three pieces of evidence were sufficient for conviction, but evidence ranged from allegation to confessions under duress to real material like captured documents. Not all province committees applied the rule equally. Moreover, in a typical meeting of several hours held once per week, the Province Security Committee handled *dozens* of cases.

The incentive structure in Phoenix was also skewed. John Paul Vann, on whom Colby increasingly relied, estimated in 1970 that the monthly expenses of a South Vietnamese province chief were roughly double his pay and allowances. For a district chief, who had no entertainment fund, the disparity was worse. But the Vietnamese jails built by CORDS, with the exception of a few national facilities like the one on Con Son island, were run by the provinces. The province chief (an appointed official, generally a military man, with greater powers than a U.S. state governor) received money for food for each prisoner on his rolls, and in 1970 CORDS increased those allowances. The opportunity for malfeasance in the jail situation is clear; the province chiefs had the incentive to fill their jails, and they had the obvious example of the South Vietnamese army's "ghost battalions," whose rolls were padded for precisely the same reason.

The jail situation puts an interesting light on an episode that occurred in the spring of 1969. Public safety officers at CORDS sought to change the direction of the incarceration effort in a direction more suited to winning hearts and minds, that old pacification saw. Led by Randolph C. Berkeley, III, director of the prison program, they wanted to recast "offenders" as citizens gone astray. To make that a national program, Berkeley, who wrote up a detailed proposal he sent to the CORDS director, wanted to create a new Saigon government ministry and convert all the provincial jails to national prisons. At the counterpart level, Berkeley would have formed a fresh CORDS directorate and also ended such CIA funding as still flowed in this channel.

Ambassador Colby called "Berk" into his office on May 3, 1969. According to a Public Safety officer who awaited Berkeley and his associates in Colby's outer office, they emerged flushed and blushed. One of the participants reported that Colby had taken his copy of Berkeley's proposal, tossed it in the trash, and demanded all copies in CORDS be destroyed.

"Colby'll run his office and ours," the participant recounted, "We'll do as we're told. If we can't live within his established organization, pack our stuff and leave."[13]

Frank Walton, another public safety expert at CORDS who sat on the unit's council, seems to have appeared as the culprit to Colby, who marked Walton for termination at the earliest opportunity.

Beyond the jail situation itself—by 1969 the capacity was there for all the people swept into the Phoenix dragnet—the system permitted protection rackets to flourish at the district and provincial levels. The story may be apocryphal that one agent rid his family of generations of debt by denouncing all his creditors as VCI, but undoubtedly there were a thousand variations on that theme. District chiefs, who needed to triple their pay to break even, could make money by keeping those who paid them *off* the suspect lists. The real Viet Cong, who had an apparatus to ransom them out, could evade Phoenix. Again the system worked against ordinary citizens. In the opinion of PRU adviser Mike Walsh: "The VCI blacklist eventually became corrupted. It became a place to put the names of these corrupt senior officers' enemies, to avoid repayment of debt or even to settle a score." Walsh believes that CORDS Americans were wrongly blamed for this, but he made sure to keep and safely store the paperwork on his VCI cases to prove at some later date that his operations had been legitimate.[14]

Michael Walsh's concern, and that of Phoenix advisers and PRU people in general, had to have been magnified by the events of June 1969 and after, culminating June 20. That night at Nha Trang, several Green Berets, convinced that one of their agents, Thai Khac Chuyen, might be a spy for Hanoi, killed the man after a long, suggestive, but inconclusive interrogation. The chain of command had been aware of the counterintelligence problem, as far up as Colonel Robert B. Rheault, leader of the 5th Special Forces Group in Vietnam; CIA regional officer in charge Dean Almy; and Ted Shackley. When investigators for the Army's Counter-Intelligence Corps examined the circumstances here, they concluded that Chuyen's execution had been murder. When General Abrams learned of the case he questioned Rheault, who seemed to be covering up for his men, and Abrams ordered a full investigation. This led to a legal inquiry and preparations for a court-martial, but only of the men directly involved, up to the level of Colonel Rheault.

Lawyers for the defendants crafted their case around the nature of the Vietnam war and the orders that had and had not been issued regarding Chuyen. The CIA had had its watching brief over espionage activity but did nothing to prevent the execution. Liberation Front intelligence and security cadres, regarded as a prime Phoenix target, were being neutralized all the time. Defense lawyers planned to call Shackley, Almy, and Bill Colby, plus several other CIA personnel as witnesses in the case, and to introduce all the war crimes and procedural issues raised. The CIA refused to permit its officers to testify and stopped cooperating with prosecutors; as a result, the charges were dropped in September 1970. However, the murder had been covered extensively in the press since the summer of 1969. Apart from any of its other consequences, this Green Beret affair heightened concerns among the American public that execution and assassination were standard procedures in Vietnam.

Another matter that had a similar impact had been simmering all along but burst into the open soon after the Chuyen murder. This had to do with Phoenix advisers. District intelligence operations coordinating centers were the basic building blocks of CORDS involvement in Phoenix, and each needed one or two Americans. During the ICEX period, when the CIA furnished all the advisers, the counterpart framework had not yet gotten down to the district level, but moral qualms against participation in a neutralization program were already recognized. The district centers were a big CORDS initiative in 1968 and brought even bigger manpower staffing needs. One of Colby's Washington trips, in the summer of 1968, centered around a CORDS request for an increment of another 120 Phoenix district advisers from the U.S. Army. By 1969, with more district centers functioning and the CIA reducing its participation to about 100, needs increased again. The Army had over 440 Phoenix advisers then, usually lieutenants or captains, and the number would eventually rise to over 700, with another twenty or more from the State Department. It was only a matter of time until moral qualms surfaced somewhere.

The time came in early 1969. A young field artillery officer, Second Lieutenant Francis T. Reitmeyer, reassigned for training as a Phoenix adviser, asked to be transferred. Rejected, he filed suit to be recognized as a conscientious objector instead. Reitmeyer had never been to Vietnam, but his instructors had told him about PRUs and Phoenix goals and his legal documents objected to being required to maintain a monthly "kill quota." Although, by his own statement, Reitmeyer had not received "assassination" training, the moral balance was at least ambiguous, especially after another trainee, Lieutenant Michael J. Cohn, joined in the petition. The court found in their favor in July. The Army prepared an appeal of the decision but dropped it several months later. Again press coverage put before the American people an issue of the ethics of neutralization.

On October 15, within days of the Army's vacating its appeal, William E. Colby issued a CORDS directive through MACV that specifically prohibited Phoenix advisers engaging in assassinations. They were enjoined to follow the laws of war just as in regular military operations, to refuse further cooperation, and to make their objections known if they encountered activities not meeting those standards. Advisers were supposed to report questionable activities to higher command. The directive, which Colby noted elsewhere was prompted when he learned that a Phoenix adviser applied for transfer due to moral qualms, added that advisers could be reassigned without prejudice to their careers.

On the other hand, Colby's directive provided also for "reasonable military force as . . . necessary."[15] Thus CORDS gave Phoenix advisers operational authority to use PRUs, Regional and Popular Forces, and the regular military against the VCI, legitimating the relationship that already existed. As for torture of prisoners and other atrocities, complaints to South Vietnamese counterparts and reports up the chain of command were not the same thing as taking action—indeed, were often not conducive to action at all. Vietnamese could tell an adviser that after he went home, *they* would still be fighting the war. Higher command, in pursuit of those elusive Pheonix neutralization goals, often overlooked transgressions or refused to intercede with South Vietnamese commanders.

Looking back on the Reitmeyer affair, historians sometimes focus on the credibility of this American, searching for inconsistencies in his claims. But Bill Colby's quick response here, issuing a CORDS directive on assassination, makes crystal clear that the pacification czar himself perceived this as a live issue that needed to be defused. Barely a month later, on November 13, journalist Seymour Hersh broke the news that U.S. Army troops at a village called My Lai had massacred hundreds of Vietnamese civilians eighteen months earlier. The Reitmeyer affair, coupled with the Chuyen murder and My Lai, went far toward convincing Americans of the veracity of assassination charges. One may argue that Reitmeyer lacked credibility, that the Green Beret affair was tangential to Phoenix, and that My Lai had nothing to do with it, but it was the perceptions of 1969 that drove public opinion.

Moreover, suspicions about Phoenix as an assassination program only gathered force, as would soon become evident.

ON A DIFFERENT LEVEL Bill Colby's tireless labor on behalf of Phoenix actually contributed to his perception problem. That is, enlisting the cooperation of Saigon government authorities had been difficult from the very inception of Phoenix. This started with Nguyen Van Thieu but extended everywhere. Toward the end of 1968, more or less, President Thieu had been convinced to come on board. Colby had then had difficulties with Thieu that really flowed from the beginning of peace talks in Paris—South Vietnamese attempts to manipulate the hamlet evaluation survey data were motivated by a desire to demonstrate maximum dominance of the population and deny similar claims by the Liberation Front. Colby convinced Thieu to give up, arguing that "there [is] no room for optimists or pessimists, only realists."[16] Thieu subsided for the moment.

Below Thieu the South Vietnamese generals commanding the different corps areas also showed lukewarm support for Phoenix. Energizing them proved a problem. In the I Corps zone the commander spoke enthusiastically but did little planning or coordination between his regular forces and the CORDS pacification activity. The II Corps commander did not even bother to talk a good line. In III Corps, the zone nearest to Saigon, there was more sustained support for both pacification in general and Phoenix in particular. In IV Corps, where the commander did not talk much one way or the other, pacification was big business, but business is what it was, and the business was money, not Phoenix.

Bill Colby worked to get both Americans and Vietnamese to make public commitments and to take CORDS and Phoenix seriously. Part of this would be his trips to different commands. Colby rarely went to villages now though earlier he had made a point of revisiting some he had first seen as CIA station chief in the early 1960s. As Bill told one reporter, "I don't even bother inspecting hamlets anymore. By the time you get out to one, they have laid on everything and it's pure bull."[17] Colby engaged himself at the province, military region (corps), and national levels; Vietnamese at those levels, after all, were the ones he needed to motivate.

Another concern was Americans at home. For this audience Colby became the apostle of pacification. Giving interviews to journalists, taking them on trips, and creating bigger affairs for visiting groups were the main action. When a church group visited South Vietnam to study the condition of political prisoners, Colby invited them to his home on a Sunday afternoon. In this case the CORDS chief could not convince his interlocutors. Father Robert F. Drinan, a Massachusetts congressman who was a prominent member of the study group, came away convinced that "Mr. Colby did his best to prevent us from acquiring any hard information." Colby also refused to concede that the South Vietnamese might use the anti-VCI effort to jail political opponents of Nguyen Van Thieu, and he professed ignorance of the poor conditions that existed for prisoners on Con Son island. Colby did acknowledge, Drinan noted, that the number of political prisoners had risen and that many had gone to prison without trial. Three weeks later, on June 21, 1969, Drinan published an article in the *Washington Post* that was quite critical of these aspects of the Vietnam imbroglio.[18]

A few months later came a case in point on this issue. It concerned Tran Ngoc Chau, by 1970 a parliamentary leader in opposition to Thieu. Bill Colby had known Chau for a decade—the South Vietnamese had been a province chief in the Mekong when the American led the CIA station. Later Chau had been mayor of Da Nang, and when Colby headed the Far East Division, Chau was the South Vietnamese chief of the revolutionary development training school at Vung Tau. Chau considered Colby a friend, but they were on opposite sides of many questions—for example, whether Diem could have triumphed against the Viet Cong. Another difference arose over revolutionary development—Chau believed it could not succeed if identified as a CIA, or even an American, program. Of course, Vung Tau was entirely funded by CIA; once it was going, Chau went to the CIA's Tom Donohue and recommended that the agency should let it go, except for providing equipment. Chau kept up his complaints, only to be reprimanded, so he resigned to become a politician. Tran Ngoc Chau kept up his American contacts, including those with the CIA; Washington derived important information from him. With a brother who was a Viet Cong officer, Chau provided a window to the other side as well; he held a series of eight meetings with his brother during 1968–69, of which he kept the CIA informed. Among the first to understand that the impact of Tet would be to move the United States to search for a way out of the war, Chau wanted reasonable negotiations and a settlement while Saigon still retained bargaining power. Of course, Nguyen Van Thieu's policy aimed to prevent any such settlement.

Chau's brother was caught up in a Police Special Branch dragnet in the spring of 1969, and his meetings with the Viet Cong eventually became known to Saigon authorities. By the end of the year there were plans to move against him. John Paul Vann, another friend of Chau's, who had encouraged his earlier protests about Vung Tau, now felt the Americans should show responsibility and get Chau out of South Vietnam. He proposed this to Colby in a memo in early January 1970. Colby refused. Later Colby and Ted Shackley, denying connections to Chau, cast him as vaguely subversive. Police seized Chau on the floor of the National Assembly a month later and he spent five years in jail or under house arrest. Bill Colby would be CIA director himself during the last days of the Saigon regime, when there was another proposal to get Chau out of the country. He did nothing to respond.

In 1970 Colby commented on Chau to Jean Sauvageot, his liaison in President Thieu's office as well as housemate and frequent interpreter on trips outside Saigon. Sauvageot recalled what the pacification czar had said: "It was very unfortunate but . . . we had our relations with the Vietnamese government to consider and had to be careful."[19]

Indeed, in the evening of January 20, 1970, Colby held a reception at his home for 156 guests, headed by Prime Minister Tran Thien Khiem.

The reception represented a victory celebration of sorts for it marked a CORDS success. Among the guests were Colonel Tran Van Hai, director general of the National Police; Ted Shackley; his deputy Joseph Lazarsky; CIA officers Philip H. Potter and Rodney Landreth; Lou Conein, now separated from the agency; John Mason, the CIA officer who had recently replaced Ev Parker at the head of the central Phoenix staff; CORDS aide Everet Bumgardner; Stephen Young; Jean Sauvageot; and John Paul Vann. A gathering of the clan, indeed, for which Barbara Colby would be present, on her only Saigon visit during Bill's tour with CORDS.

Months of hard work reached fruition in these weeks around the turn of the year. Colby had begun building for this in August 1969, when he had spoken before Saigon's American Chamber of Commerce; visited the sailors of Task Force 77 on Yankee Station, trying to get the Navy to be more sensitive to the impact of their bombing on civilians; and dined with another visiting group, which included former U.S. Saigon chargé Edmund A. Gullion, now a college dean, who had good contacts in South Vietnam. The main purpose remained getting Saigon government officials to put more weight behind pacification and Phoenix.

By the fall there had been real progress on that front. Tran Thien Khiem agreed to preside over a rally and parade, held in Saigon on October 1 under the slogan "Protection of the People from Terrorism."[20] Colby's propaganda people helped the Vietnamese with press releases and television announcements for the occasion, inaugurating a big public information campaign that reached into every province of South Vietnam by the end of the year. On November 28 President Thieu declared in a speech that "the VCI must be eliminated . . . the Communists in the end will be defeated by the *Phung Hoang* [Phoenix] program. Without *Phung Hoang* the Communist could remain indefinitely within the fabric of society, later to begin their struggle anew at some future time."[21]

With the Thieu speech, Colby had the public endorsement he sought, though there remained conflicting interests on the South Vietnamese side that added up to uneven support. For example, on December 1 the Vietnamese ended draft deferments for the interpreters on whom the Phoenix advisers were very largely dependent (only about a third of Americans at the province level and very few in the districts were fluent in Vietnamese). The assignment of South Vietnamese army personnel, originally intended to make up for about 150 unfilled positions (of 779 authorized) in the Phoenix structure, suddenly became the major source of language services. Meanwhile, by putting the Phoenix interpreters under army authority, the South Vietnamese secured a new way to keep an eye on American activity in the program.

Having public relations flacks spread the word about Phoenix made it impossible to continue claiming that this remained a secret program. In fact, it is instructive that virtually all documentation on Phoenix bears the secrecy rating of "confidential," one of the lowest categories of secret information. In any case, the United States Congress became involved when Senator J. William Fulbright's Senate Foreign Relations Committee held four days of hearings on pacification in Vietnam in February 1970. Bill Colby came home for the occasion and brought John Paul Vann and other CORDS officials with him to present a broad spectrum of information, preventing the hearings from focusing solely on Phoenix. Nevertheless the excitement ran highest on February 17, 1970, when Bill Colby appeared under oath and testified for four hours before the Foreign Relations Committee. It was unusual at that time for committee witnesses to be sworn in, which is an index of the sensitivity of this proceeding.

Colby handled the affair with lawyerly adroitness. He kept his testimony general, on the broad picture, passing over Phoenix lightly. "I am neither optimistic nor pessimistic," Colby said, evoking his exhortations of a year earlier to Nguyen Van Thieu, "about the future of this program and of Vietnam." That was for pacification. For Phoenix, Colby chose his words carefully. He was lucky because Senator Fulbright, in questioning the pacification czar, used the word "execution," not assassination.

"There has been no one legally executed," Colby said, quite accurately. "They have been detained . . . I would not want to say that no one was ever actually executed. You have not had convictions of members of the enemy apparatus in which executions followed."

In another effort to pin down the CORDS chief, New Jersey Senator Clifford Case asked if Colby was willing to "swear by all that is holy" that Phoenix was not a counterterror program.

Here a trace of annoyance crept into Colby's voice.

"I have already taken an oath," Bill Colby snapped. "There was a counterterror program, but it has been discarded as a concept." As for Provincial Reconnaissance Units, they had "once" engaged in counterterror activities but "now operate under the same kinds of rules that are normal for police services."[22]

Colby did *not* say that South Vietnamese command authority for the PRUs was barely four months old or their incorporation into the National Police had existed for less than a year, or that he himself had *opposed* PRUs' being taken over by the police. Phoenix, of course, was more than two years old at this time.

As the CORDS first team testified in Washington, at MACV headquarters John Mason's staff put the finishing touches on the Phoenix end-of-year report for 1969. It would circulate just as Colby returned to Saigon for the next round in the war. Phoenix data showed a total of 19,534 neutralizations for 1969. Part-way through the year Colby had convinced the Vietnamese to reduce their inflated goal, which had been cut back to a total of 21, 600, but even so Phoenix had fallen short. However, Phoenix had met its goals beginning in the third quarter of the year, and indications were it could continue to do so.

Neutralization data continued to show what had been seen as a problem already in 1968: few neutralizations were of senior Liberation Front cadres. Fewer than 150 of the cadres neutralized in 1969 were regional or national command (Central Office for South Vietnam, or COSVN) level people. Of these only eighty-one of the neutralizations were of designated priority targets; of them, just *one*, a regional cadre, had come from the policy-making inner sanctums of Liberation Front current affairs or revolutionary committees. That cadre had been killed, never to be interviewed. Counting both priority targets and serendipitous neutralizations, only twenty-three COSVN cadres were tabulated. Out of 19,534, these were meager results.

Questions about assassination rankled Bill Colby because he had done more than anyone to inject order and legality into Phoenix. From day one Colby had been at the forefront of efforts to get the Saigon government to set standards and stick to them. By 1970 there was already a stack of decrees, orders, and regulations, starting with November 1968 instructions that suspects be turned over to proper military or police authorities. In March 1969 had come definitions for the categories of "offenders"; in August, a circular that was more specific on handling of prisoners and evidence required to prosecute; in September, orders that village officials be told of Phoenix operations in their areas; in November, a "guarantee" for Viet Cong defendents. More such strictures were to come.

"It was documentation that I had some influence in producing," said Colby later.[23] But Colby's interest was not necessarily to create due process; it was the intelligence officer's desire to increase effectiveness, and in his view decentralization was what would make Phoenix work. As he put it in his book *Lost Victory*:

> There was also a delay before the ministries, under continued persuasion from the Central [*Phung Hoang*] Council, abandoned the finely crafted directives they were accustomed to issue from their air-conditioned offices in Saigon. But finally, accepting the transfer of direction and control of their programs to the province chiefs, they turned to their true function of supporting them.[24]

Bill Colby's view of the primacy of the province chiefs, incidentally, is a clue to his hostile reaction when CORDS public safety officials tried to propose a national prison program.

In addition to the South Vietnamese decrees and dictates, Colby put out orders for CORDS on the American side. A standard operating procedure, implemented in late 1968, laid down basic formats and concerns. After December, when Ted Shackley officially informed Colby that the CIA had completed the handover of its Phoenix assets to CORDS, there were more. Maneuvering delicately between the CIA and the military, Colby assured MACV in March 1969 that everyone was on the same side, that he did not feel CORDS owned the forces and resources he was using. In May came a CORDS directive on functions and responsibilities in the attack on the VCI.

That October Colby sponsored a CORDS seminar of advisers from every province to clarify how Americans would work with the Vietnamese, whose latest strictures were for mandatory sentencing of senior VCI captives and immediate movement of those prisoners to Con Son island or a similar national prison. There was also the Colby directive on assassinations already referred to.

But the story of Phoenix would be that legality continually bumped into goals. Pressure by CORDS staff to neutralize high-level VCI remained intense, and the 1969 neutralization figures illustrate why. Less than half the neutralizations in 1969 (9,934) were of priority targets, and the figures on really senior VCI were minuscule. But those priority targets were designated on quite minimal intelligence; repeated accounts by district advisers and by officials who visited district centers to review dossiers on alleged VCI show that most were empty. Only in early 1970 did CORDS revise its green book (named for the color of its cover) listing VCI by name and alias based on Saigon-level intelligence and what local sources could be incorporated. In an effort to focus the VCI attack more tightly, a computer-based Viet Cong Infrastructure Information System, which until the beginning of 1970 had merely generated statistics, was modified to try to maintain more current intelligence on the VCI. Colby also had CORDS develop a standard form to note information on alleged VCI and fill out the intelligence dossiers. These forms were not in fact ready until mid-1970, however.

A major feature of the Phoenix plans for 1970 would be to spend the first part of the year identifying at least 30 percent of the VCI estimated to exist but not known to authorities, then neutralize them in the third quarter. The "objective" (the word used for goal in this document) was to neutralize 1,800 "A" and "B" category VCI every month.[25] In February, to refine these plans, Colby ordered that captured VCI could no longer be counted as neutralized unless they were sentenced to prison. He also circulated a third set of standard operating procedures for Phoenix advisers. Of the 22,341 neutralizations Phoenix credited in its eventual report for 1970, there would be fewer priority target neutralizations (7,814) than in 1969; seventeen would be from COSVN and 357 from the region or subregion levels. Phoenix did do significantly better: many senior VCI defected (203 in 1970), while neutralizations of revolutionary or current affairs committee members came to 812 of the priority figure. Captured documents and interrogations indicated that the Liberation Front was worried about Phoenix. In addition, the goal for the year was met.

Phoenix results continued to be uneven, however. An analysis by central staff, using the Central Highlands (II Corps) as an example, showed that for the first half of 1970 more priority VCI were killed than sentenced. For the entire year there were 2,949 neutralizations out of a goal of 4,200, the shortfall adding up almost exactly to the goal for one quarter. Of the neutralizations, despite the big push for Phoenix identifications of the VCI, only 19 percent of cadre neutralized had been specifically targeted, and just 22 percent of the total were district level or higher cadre. The Saigon area, not the Highlands, showed the best results against VCI.

Meanwhile it remained impossible to escape from the arbitrary methods that helped make Phoenix politically counterproductive regardless of military impact. A number of 1970 directives, both South Vietnamese and American, were repeats of orders already on the books. These included the rules on informing local officials of Phoenix operations and on the length of time a detainee could be held by each level of the system. On May 18, over the signature of General Welborn Dolvin, Colby's military counterpart, CORDS reissued its directive prohibiting Americans from participating in questionable actions such as assassination or torture. The document proved identical to the 1969 version. Clearly Phoenix goals and human rights standards continued to conflict.

In August 1970 Colby encouraged the South Vietnamese to form a Justice Committee to keep a continuing watch on legal problems with the post-apprehension processing of "offenders." On November 12 he would send Prime Minister Khiem a letter recommending the "an tri" detention laws be revised to guarantee basic rights, including the right to confront an accuser, specified in Article 7 of the South Vietnamese constitution. The National Police had had an Inspectorate to deal with problems of abuse since October 1968. In its first year the unit claimed to have resolved all of the 2,000 cases referred to it, but just twenty police officers were demoted and ten dismissed. Only a dozen policemen, including some of the same people, were prose-cuted. Recourses against abuse were limited.

Emphasizing these weaknesses even more was the scandal that began in July 1970 with the visit of a U.S. congressional delegation to the prison on Con Son island. Divided into "camps," Con Son's Camp 4, the disciplinary unit, had what were called "Tiger Cages," open to the elements with bars instead of a ceiling; in them, prisoners were shackled at night to prevent their breaking through the wooden slat doors. Prisoners were given buckets for toilets and were burned by lye tossed into the cages to disinfect them. Offi-cials like Donald Bordenkircher of public safety at CORDS insist that con-ditions at Con Son were good and getting better. Even so, an observer as sympathetic as Michael Walsh, the SEAL and PRU adviser, would report that he had visited Con Son and, were he a captured VCI, he would rather make a deal with interrogators than be sent to Con Son any day. Prisoners could be sent to Camp 4 for things as simple as refusing to salute the South Vietnamese flag.

Both CORDS and the CIA station could have prevented the congressional visit and neither did so. Guided by Don Luce, an antiwar activist, journalist, and longtime relief worker in Vietnam with International Voluntary Services, the group saw some pretty horrifying things. Depending on whose account is credited, they did or did not make up others. The international press re-ported all the worst about Con Son, and the prison issue began to reverberate in American politics along with so much else about Phoenix. Public safety officer Bordenkircher eventually suspected Don Luce of being a CIA agent, rather farfetched. In any case, Bill Colby and Ellsworth Bunker prevented public safety from mounting as effective a defense as they might have. Bordenkircher charges Colby with having set up CORDS public safety to divert attention from more sensitive aspects of Phoenix. More likely is that poor coordination permitted the problem to arise, and Colby then tried to get the Con Son mess off the table as quickly as possible. In any case, in December 1970 the International Red Cross filed an official complaint about prison conditions in South Vietnam.

Also of concern would be continued halfheartedness on the part of the Saigon government. Until late 1970 Saigon never spent a dollar on Phoenix other than money funneled to it by the United States. That summer, also, the central Phoenix committee was moved out of the office of Prime Minister Khiem and put under the National Police, which meant both less visibility and less high-level South Vietnamese involvement. Bill Colby defended the move as the best way to strengthen the National Police. Robert Komer, by now out of government and an analyst at the Rand Corporation, became highly critical. Komer returned to Vietnam early that summer and spent a couple of weeks surveying CORDS. The two articles on pacification that he wrote for *Army* magazine were optimistic, but that stance would be for public consumption. Privately Komer was scathing. The consolidation of Phoenix within the police was putting one of the most crucial of the priority missions within the weakest and least effective agency. With sixty-five generals in the South Vietnamese armed forces, the senior officer working full time on Phoenix was a lieutenant colonel (until the fall of 1970 the overall head of the National Police was himself only a colonel). The Special Branch, with its CIA advice, remained a distinct entity. Perhaps not coincidentally, most provinces and districts still had incredibly poor VCI files.

Robert Komer also reported John Paul Vann's belief that half those listed as killed were being included just to meet Phoenix goals; the others, Vann told Komer, were post facto identifications. Like most problems in Vietnam, this was not new: CIA officer Orrin DeForest, who also comments on the poor files and lack of VCI organizational charts at provincial intelligence centers, writes this of the claimed losses:

> The more I learned about Phoenix, the clearer it was that the statistics were phony. Although I never could tell with any certainty what percentage of the reported VC dead were actually the result of Phoenix operations . . . most of the capturing and killing was done not by Phoenix but by the Regional and Popular forces. . . . The local PRU team might set an ambush, or get involved in a firefight, or would come across the casualties of another engagement, and all of it went into the Phoenix hopper: the guilty, the innocent, the enemy killed in action, the casual bodies along the roadside. They'd carry them in and count them up. And that was Phoenix, at least in Military Region Three. . . . I found it hard to believe it might be any different in Regions One, Two, and Four.[26]

De Forest's impression dated from early 1969, but Komer now reported the same thing in mid-1970. Moreover, Colby's strategy had been to deliberately focus on the Saigon area and the Mekong Delta—Regions 3 and 4. De Forest went on to develop one of the most effective intelligence targeting systems in Phoenix. Perhaps not coincidentally, Komer also observed in 1970 that the shift from CIA to military advisers for Phoenix robbed the program of the only field hands who were good at the game. Orrin de Forest, who based his method on conventional police techniques, furnished living proof of that point.

Meeting with Bob Komer during his trip, Bill Colby argued that the United States had made greater inroads against the VCI than here apparent from CORDS's own data. The dispute spilled over onto paper—Komer had written a RAND Corporation analytical study on the pacification mess, to which Colby crafted a point-by-point rebuttal in an October 17 letter. Komer fired back a letter of his own a month later, and forwarded both to Henry Kissinger at the White House.

One dispute involved the Hamlet Evaluation Survey (HES) statistics that the National Security Council used to back its own evaluations. The NSC's Vietnam Special Studies Group extracted an indicator for control from HES based on items related to village security, but discounted Saigon claims to control in the presence of any of five factors. Colby protested; he argued that this stacked the deck against Saigon, ignoring the dynamics of a rapidly improving situation. In a reprise of his VCI argument, Bill maintained that pacification progress was greater than evident from HES. But it had been Colby and Komer together who, at the time of the Accelerated Pacification Campaign, discarded the socioeconomic indices in HES, the very ones Bill now felt gave a better picture. Colby initiated changes in the logic of aggregation in HES, with help from RAND, that would go into effect at the end of 1970.

Meanwhile in August, Secretary of Defense Melvin R. Laird told Admiral Thomas H. Moorer that Phoenix lacked resources, emphasis, and leadership on the Vietnamese side. There were also fears that Liberation Front spies had infiltrated the program. An early draft of a CIA paper by Samuel A. Adams estimated about 20,000 enemy agents in the Saigon government and armed forces; the study was leaked to the press that fall (the final version *raised* the estimate to 30,000). Some of those spies had to be in Phoenix, given captured documents that set a priority for Liberation Front actions to counter Phoenix. Secretary Laird demanded a policy review to be completed within six weeks. Bill Colby chaired the review.

The Colby-led 1970 Phoenix review concluded that Vietnamese participation should be upgraded by having the National Police headed by a major or lieutenant general personally selected by Thieu or Khiem. Colby also recommended other measures, including computer data files and a strengthened national identity card system, to improve intelligence on the VCI. Officials of the Federal Bureau of Investigation (FBI) should be brought out to advise on rooting out Viet Cong spies. The HES scoring system must improve, and the People's Self-Defense Force, Colby's own innovation, be induced to participate in Phoenix as a primary responsibility. Colby also insisted on legal procedures to protect Vietnamese detainees as they were being handled by the Phoenix system.

For all the sound and fury, the issues toward the end of William E. Colby's tenure at CORDS were about the same as those he had found on arrival. Like frustrated grunts who slogged through muddy paddy day after day, or battled again to capture the same damned hill; like many Americans who went to Saigon hoping to change the war, Bill Colby found instead it was the war that changed him.

WINDING UP ANOTHER YEAR in command of CORDS, Ambassador Colby had a gospel of progress in South Vietnam to preach. The CORDS director could show improved HES statistics plus the results of his just-completed policy review. Taking along his deputy, Colby left for Honolulu, where he arrived early in the morning of December 14, meeting right away with Pacific theater boss Admiral John S. McCain. The next morning Colby was off for Washington, where he stayed at home from December 16 to 19. Seeing the family at night, Colby's days were filled with a seemingly endless series of briefings and exhortation sessions. But Colby's message of victory in pacification would not be universally accepted, nor would it be interpreted everywhere in the way he preferred.

Secretary Laird had asked for the policy review and had read the papers, but Colby brought him the results in person at a mid-morning encounter at the Pentagon on December 17. Much of the CORDS Phoenix review had concerned security matters, and CIA's Richard Helms sat in on Colby's presentation. That afternoon Colby saw Joint Chiefs of Staff chairman Moorer. A lunch with Henry Kissinger at the White House had to be put off, but Ambassador Colby saw the national security adviser late in the afternoon of December 18. Kissinger had just come from a private talk with the president. He and Nixon were full of plans for an invasion of Laos; indeed Kissinger's deputy, General Alexander M. Haig, had returned that same day from Saigon with the results of a canvass of U.S. senior officers and officials that had elicited preliminary plans for the Laos operation. Colby's views of pacification success were treated as peripheral, an indication that the rear area might remain quiescent during the Laotian invasion, not an opportunity to redouble efforts and push through to real victory.

Disappointment for Colby at the official level would be matched by personal difficulties. Like many government families, Colby's had been challenged by the controversies that suffused the Vietnam war. A microcosm of America in the watershed year, 1968, Colby's family began to waver after Tet. The eldest son, Jonathan, continued to support the war. He had followed his father to Princeton and had ties with people close to Richard Nixon. Jonathan would eventually serve on Henry Kissinger's National Security

Council staff. The younger ones had more doubts. Some marched in the great antiwar demonstrations of 1969. Daughter Christine, who had gone to school in Saigon when Bill had been CIA station chief, and who had defended U.S. policy in Vietnam in letters to the editor of the *Washington Post* in the mid-1960s, was especially troubled. Barbara Colby had kept much of this from Bill as he labored away at CORDS, but on this latest home visit from Vietnam the problems were more visible. Colby could not do much on a short trip, but he went back to Saigon determined at least to visit home more often.

In some respects pacification progress resulting from Phoenix was illusory or had been purchased at a political cost growing by the minute. The CIA's intelligence estimate of cadres working in the Viet Cong infrastructure had fallen, but by only around five thousand, where Phoenix claimed over twenty-two thousand neutralizations for 1970. Of course, the VCI remained in the shadows and one could dispute the statistics, but what was concrete and disturbing was that in December 1970 the International Red Cross had begun making official inquiries with respect to the handling of defendants by the South Vietnamese legal system and the treatment of detainees in the prisons. The reforms that Bill Colby had resisted in prisons, and those for which he had pressed in the legal system, remained absent or honored in the breach. The political cost would be paid in dwindling support for the Vietnam war.

As Colby had done earlier, one answer could be public moves designed to show success on the ground. With the largest fraction of the South Vietnamese population concentrated in the Mekong delta and Saigon areas, Colby had long kept the weight of CORDS efforts in those military regions. By the end of 1970 the pacification statistics seemed to confirm Colby's strategy. In addition, courtesy of CIA officer Orrin DeForest, the Americans had unprecedented insight into Liberation Front activity because the Saigon-area officer had succeeded in recruiting an agent at a middle level in one of the Front's regional commands. Bill Colby took advantage by arranging with John Paul Vann for a series of overnight stays in areas of the countryside previously contested. To cap his show of confidence, for Tet 1971 Colby and Vann rode motorcycle down National Road 2 for a hundred kilometers or so through the heart of the Mekong delta.

Colby also defended pacification on the paper front. The systems analysts in Secretary Laird's office had completed a statistical study critical of CORDS and Phoenix. General Abrams, looking for manpower spaces to cut out of the Military Assistance Command Vietnam (MACV), now eyed CORDS, buttressing his views with the Washington critique. In early January Bill Colby countered with a paper insisting that the progress was real. Again he pointed to the Mekong delta. There, where MACV had already withdrawn, the U.S. 9th Infantry Division, leaving security entirely in the hands of the South Vietnamese (and the PRUs), the number of guerrilla incidents was nevertheless down. Abrams appreciated the argument but went ahead with a decision to stop allocating American military personnel to Phoenix as of mid-year.

Ambassador Colby's organization thus achieved its peak strength, some

7,650, toward the end of 1970. By the following spring staffing had fallen to about 4,500, though Phoenix retained its full complement of 637 U.S. military advisers through the summer of 1971. Under General Abrams's orders MACV stopped filling advisory posts as the Americans reached the ends of their tours of duty, so that before the end of the year the number of military advisers in Phoenix had fallen to less than 400.

Meanwhile, Nixon administration officials asked Colby to testify again before Congress, this time about refugees, before a panel of the Senate Judiciary Committee chaired by Senator Edward M. Kennedy (D-MA). This brought Ambassador Colby home again at the end of March. Before leaving Saigon, knowing Kennedy's subcommittee had investigated certain refugee centers in South Vietnam, Colby inspected them himself. At the early April hearing, Colby got the trouble he expected. Antiwar veterans protested in the back of the committee chamber as the session went on, and Colby found his inquisitors, especially Senator Kennedy, hard to satisfy.

In his testimony the CORDS director emphasized the positive, that millions of war-related refugees had been helped to resettle, and objected to derogatory references, such as Kennedy's attempt to portray particular incidents as relating to the notorious massacre at My Lai in 1968, or to American troops who by this time were very thin on the ground in South Vietnam. While Colby insisted that war victims were being helped, however, in truth the record remained problematical. For example, on their own authority the PRU advisers and Phoenix district people could hand out bounties and pay rewards of almost three times as much as a Vietnamese was entitled to for a case of wrongful death of a family member resulting from U.S. or Saigon military operations. In 1970 almost a third of the refugees living in 646 camps—518,000 of them—still had to bear with temporary shelter. And the camps had *no* doctors at all (CORDS had one third-country national who was a doctor attached to the northernmost military region; his job was to monitor medical and sanitation conditions) and only thirty-nine health workers in all.

Bill Colby had wanted to put the focus back on the Viet Cong and had brought along a Chinese mortar to exhibit, but decided that would just have added fuel to the fire. Instead he engaged in a debate he found theological, and he impressed Senator Kennedy enough that the politician backed off a bit toward the end. Later Kennedy sent Colby a letter expressing appreciation for his comments on the refugee problem.

Back in Saigon almost the first thing Colby would do was to have CORDS sponsor a conference on the handling of displaced persons. He also took fresh initiatives to inject impetus into intelligence gathering for pacification. Advisers and PRU leaders had long been able to use rewards of almost $100 and larger amounts if these were approved by region or MACV intelligence officials. The new wrinkle for 1971 would be gearing rewards specifically to information about high-level Viet Cong. The larger amounts would be awarded for data on more senior VCI.

This high value rewards program proposal, finalized while Colby had been in Washington for his confrontation with Senator Kennedy, came to him for approval about the time of the CORDS conference. By late May the proposal had been fleshed out to the extent that projected rewards budgets were set for each of the Vietnamese military regions. Colby's favored Mekong delta would be slated for as much money as the rest of South Vietnam put together. Perhaps that was to hedge against evaporation of Saigon's claimed progress in pacification. Adding the budget for the region around that city brought the proposed fund to almost three times as much as that for the rest of South Vietnam.

Bill Colby rejected one feature of the high-value rewards program. That was a scheme for false payment vouchers to hide the sources and amounts of rewards. The CORDS director argued that with the long-standing use of bounties in many facets of Phoenix there was nothing covert or even secret about the rewards. The program went forward to be tested in four provinces before implementation throughout South Vietnam. During the summer of 1971, however, with Phoenix more controversial than ever, fear rose of adverse political consequences in the United States. That October Ambassador Ellsworth Bunker ordered cancellation of the whole high-value rewards program.

By then Bill Colby had gone, his departure from Vietnam resulting not from matters of high policy but family concerns. Over time Colby had seen both physical and mental deterioration in his epileptic daughter Catherine but had not realized how far it had gone. Barbara Colby had shielded her husband from the worst, aware of his preoccupation with the pacification war in Vietnam. Son Paul finally convinced his mother to bare the truth for Bill. After several trips home at short intervals through early 1971, Colby decided he belonged in Washington and arranged to return at the end of June, bringing to a close his second Vietnam tour of duty.

Years after the war it became fashionable in some quarters to assert that the Vietnam war had been won but the victory somehow thrown away. Colby himself took that line in the second of his two books. But that was not the perception in June 1971. Then, the outgoing CORDS director told the *New York Times*, "The war cannot be won unless the people participate." An unnamed American official who may or may not have been Colby said to the same reporter, "We are holding our own against the VC infrastructure. But the other side is still better at improving and expanding it than our side is at whittling it down."[27]

One example is Hue and its surrounding province. After the battle for that city during Tet 1968, the South Vietnamese had installed a mayor and province chief who represented an improvement of light years over his predecessor. Colby's attention to Hue was second only to his preoccupation with the Mekong delta. Americans repeatedly pointed to Hue's progress as an illustration of winning the pacification war. For one of his periodic jaunts around the countryside, Colby had selected this northern province and taken with him the British ambassador to witness the improvement. But John A. Graham, the CORDS adviser assigned to Hue city in 1971–72, recorded a multiplicity of political and security problems that collectively added up to continued instability, right through the end of Colby's reign and on to the Easter Offensive of 1972. And the northern military region recorded 328 incidents of Viet Cong terror the month before that offensive began, the highest number for any February on record. If the pacification war was to be considered won, that moment before conventional operations began to dominate the war had to be the time. In other words, "victory" failed to be convincing.

Least convinced, by 1971, was the American public. Frustrated by promises to get out of Vietnam that had turned into new escalations of the war into Cambodia and Laos, troubled by pacification that seemed to trap the Vietnamese people in misery, Americans had become disaffected. Congress reflected that attitude. Coming home to Washington, D.C., in July 1971, almost immediately Bill Colby found himself embroiled in controversy. The issue would be the Phoenix program he had directed at CORDS, which was under investigation by the House Committee on Government Operations. Accolades showered on Colby by the Saigon defense minister, General Nguyen Van Vy, CORDS officials, even reporters such as *Los Angeles Times* bureau chief George McArthur were very nice. Most laudatory had been Ellsworth Bunker's statement: "There was no one whose presence was more vital to the policy of trying to assist the Vietnamese to pick up the load for themselves."[28] But the praise faded in the face of fresh controversy.

In mid-July the committee opened hearings on Phoenix. It read into the record data declassified by the Nixon administration that covered Phoenix neutralizations since 1968, noted a study by the General Accounting Office (GAO), a congressional auditing agency that tabulated U.S. expenditures for Phoenix at $80 million, and heard testimony from the Agency for International Development. William E. Colby appeared before the panel on July 19. Unlike their questions in his previous appearances, when the CORDS director had been able to comment on overall pacification programs or on refugees, the House focused specifically on Phoenix. Colby therefore retreated to generalities—how the program had been organized, U.S. desire to protect the Vietnamese people from terrorism, Viet Cong terror statistics to compare with those for Phoenix neutralizations.

"The Phoenix program is not a program of assassination," declared Colby.[29]

The pacification czar emphasized detention and legal proceedings, and put deaths down to combat action and resisting arrest. Under questioning, of course, that was precisely what the committee wished to explore. For example, Colby faced questions about the CIA's counterterror teams; he conceded that these were predecessors of the PRUs but denied that they had had assassination as a function. Alluding to the summary execution of prisoners and the kinds of abuses he had tried to root out, Colby called that technique "an unjustifiable offense which we have been trying to work against. If you want to get bad intelligence you use bad interrogation methods. If you want to get good intelligence you had better use good interrogation methods."[30]

The former chief agreed that blacklists had been inaccurate, to put it delicately, when originally developed, but insisted the Phoenix program had been brought to "standards we can accept."[31]

In a later exchange with New York Democrat Ogden Reid, Colby admitted he could not say that Phoenix had never perpetrated the premeditated killing of a civilian in a noncombat situation, but he insisted this did not happen often. "Phoenix as a program," the CORDS director asserted, "has not done that. Individual members of it, subordinate people in it, may have done that. But as a program it is not designed to do that." As for the blacklists, Colby went on to say, "I have never been highly satisfied with the accuracies [sic] of our intelligence on the VCI."[32]

Reid, who like Colby had graduated from Columbia Law School, pushed Colby on the point of whether Phoenix met American legal standards for due process. Colby parried that line of attack by agreeing the standards were not met, pointing to his efforts to improve them, and insisting the war necessitated an operation of this sort. A worse adversary, in Colby's view, was California Republican Pete McCloskey, who had visited Vietnam and had been escorted by Frank Scotton, one of Colby's best operatives. While claiming McCloskey had not had an open mind, Colby made little apparent effort to understand what the California congressman had experienced. In fact, on his visit to South Vietnam a pistol-packing CIA officer tried to physically bar McCloskey's entry into one of the Provincial Interrogation Centers (PICs). A World War II Marine, McCloskey fearlessly barged ahead, daring the CIA man. The conditions for prisoners at the PIC had scandalized McCloskey, who now spent much of his time at the Colby hearing on this point.

The congressional hearing was tense for Bill Colby, who ultimately never escaped from the charges about Phoenix.

"My refusal to say under oath that no one had been wrongly killed in Vietnam," Colby wrote later, "was headlined as an admission of assassinations."[33]

Vietnam had become *that* contentious.

Indeed controversy crossed the doorstep and entered Bill's own home. Elder daughter Catherine had been troubled about the war before, but in 1971 an incident occurred that must have underlined some of the problems of Phoenix for Bill Colby if not all the family. Catherine's sister Christine, herself born in Saigon in 1960, had been assigned to do a report for school. She chose to write about a Vietnamese farm family, and for information Colby gave Christine a pamphlet on agriculture and other achievements in An Giang province, up against the Cambodian border. Even before the Tet offensive, An Giang had been considered 100 percent pacified, and afterward it was judged only slightly affected. Its Hoa Hao religious population disliked communists, leaving the VCI relatively weak there. The province's People's Self-Defense Force unit was considered a model of outstanding performance by such top South Vietnamese generals as Ngo Quang Truong. Christine knew little of this, but she could identify with the Buddhist farmers and their homes built of sheet metal, woodscraps, and cardboard.

Then, in November 1971, as Colby went about the process of reentry into the Central Intelligence Agency, Special Branch police and Vietnamese Phoenix province officers in An Giang arrested a suspected VCI whom they tortured to death. There had been allegations the man ran guns to the Viet Cong, but his detention and death were handled in such an arbitrary fashion as to expose as farcical Colby's long campaign for legality in Phoenix. Catherine Colby had been accustomed to talking with her father about Vietnam progress during his visits home; Colby's drawing of family attention to An Giang, followed by the Phoenix murder there, can only have upset his daughter more.

Catherine Colby's despair burgeoned with the continuing controversy over Vietnam and a growing one over the CIA. Bouts of anorexia and depression magnified the severity of her epilepsy. Treatments at a Johns Hopkins University hospital showed little result. Her health began steadily declining. Defending Phoenix in public and returning to the CIA, Bill could not set Catherine's mind at rest.

William Egan Colby never lived down that second Vietnam tour and his Phoenix stewardship. It dogged him at every turn. During the Senate hearing on his nomination to be director of central intelligence, Phoenix again featured as a most contentious issue. Once more assassination charges were aired, and Phoenix overshadowed many other aspects of the pacification effort in Vietnam. Colby defended himself by reiterating his efforts to regulate the program through CORDS directives plus those he had convinced the Saigon government to issue. On the streets of Washington appeared "Wanted" posters, in the style of the Old West, with Colby's name and his picture superimposed on an Ace of Spades. Wanted posters had been revived by the psychological warfare experts in Vietnam, and the Ace of Spades was an icon for killing in Phoenix and elsewhere. The posters were an eerie reversal of the techniques Colby himself had encouraged at CORDS.

Ultimately the record should show that Phoenix was not an assassination program per se. To that extent Colby was right and his critics mistaken. But what Phoenix *did* do, which its former czar consistently refused to acknowledge, was to elicit, indeed demand, lawlessness on the part of the Saigon regime and its American advisers. Given the elaboration of numerical goals and their use as measures of merit, it could be no other way. The push for progress institutionalized a climate in which arbitrary actions and borderline legality became the norm. And there *was* plenty of killing in Phoenix, enough to give critics pause, or operators to be tempted to play with numbers in the old Vietnam game of body counts, to chalk up results. There was also detention without charges, trial without effective legal defense, and a system in which getting into prison was easy while release remained elusive. Honor and efficiency conflicted, moderated by hate and prejudice, greed and ambition, in an environment in which success was defined by locking people up or killing them.

Ever after sensitive on the Phoenix issue, just two weeks prior to his death Bill Colby sat in the audience as a scholar explained that one of the key authors of a CIA report, among the few to have predicted the Tet Offensive of 1968, had gotten to that work as a way of avoiding service with the Phoenix predecessor called ICEX. Following the discussion, Colby approached the presenter to insist that ICEX had not been Phoenix, it had been merely another "pacification program." In this case Bill Colby had reached too far.

13

Back to Langley

Unlike the prestigious seventh floor at State Department head-quarters—inhabited by the secretary of state and a coterie of undersec-retaries, regional assistant secretaries, and the deputy secretary—the sixth floor is a warren whose denizens work foreign policy issues covering the gamut of American international interests. At Foggy Bottom, the East Asian Bureau assigned William E. Colby a temporary office on the hodge-podge sixth floor. There was some question of whether the ambassador would take a State Department job, but in truth little chance of it, for Colby remained a man of the Central Intelligence Agency. Offered the interagency group on Indochina, which back-stopped Henry Kissinger's National Security Council unit monitoring Vietnam, Colby rejected the job as a dead-end, given the U.S. policy of Vietnamization and withdrawal from Southeast Asia. Even though the CIA had no commensurate assignment ready for Colby, he pre-ferred a return to Langley to languishing in the doldrums of diplomacy.

As for the CIA, Langley had become a place very different from the one Colby left three years before. The agency's analytical performance on Viet-nam had played well during Lyndon Johnson's administration but won it no friends in the Nixon White House. Intelligence estimates on the Russians had also come under attack. Richard Nixon had made a ceremonial visit to Lang-ley in 1969, but the platitudes he mouthed paled next to the stream of vituper-ation, amply illustrated in Nixon's White House tapes, in which the president indulged privately. Director Helms—sometimes left to cool his heels outside White House meetings, on other occasions seated at the table to hear the invective—clearly saw the CIA's fall in the Washington pecking order.

The spring prior to Colby's return from Vietnam brought completion of an evaluation of the intelligence community by James R. Schlesinger, then Nixon's assistant budget chief. Quite critical of duplication in collection and of a mismatch between the data collected and the limited ability at CIA and elsewhere to absorb and use that intelligence, the Schlesinger report impressed Richard Nixon with its argument that the director of central intelligence (DCI) should exert greater authority outside the CIA. But Nixon rejected the report's leading option, which was to make the DCI into a director of *national* intelligence, which would have required legislation. Instead Nixon chose to issue an executive order requiring the DCI to assume a stronger community role but without providing real power to do so.

On the clandestine service side there were other problems. These were noted by Ray Cline, a senior officer who worked in both analysis and operations and left the CIA about this time to head the State Department's intelligence unit. Cline believed that Richard Nixon saw the CIA not as an intelligence organization but an entity to achieve White House aims by secret methods. In one example early in 1969, the president tried to get the agency to monitor the activities of his brother, Donald Nixon. The CIA refused on the grounds that its charter prohibited domestic operations. However, the agency continued and expanded its project MH/Chaos, created in LBJ's time to detect foreign connections with the antiwar movement. This operation had distinct domestic overtones, and it also had the absolute highest priority within the CIA, being run by a senior officer within the Counterintelligence Staff. A related program carried out within the United States by Jim Angleton's staff involved tracking mail, and illegally opening some of it, sent by antiwar activists. These were things to give CIA people pause.

Even in its traditional fields of action the clandestine service was rent by the divisions of Vietnam. Some at Langley viewed the war as sapping the CIA's strength for other fights, or distorting its espionage focus in favor of political and paramilitary action. In 1970 Richard Nixon ordered a covert action in Chile—one that would come to haunt both Helms and Colby—that put the CIA into a major operation in Latin America. Apart from any of its other results, the Chile affair looked to some as confirming Langley's predilection for meddling, while others were relieved the agency seemed to be regaining an operational role outside Southeast Asia. The same could be said about the CIA's loose collaboration with British intelligence in an abortive attempt that same year to assassinate Libyan dictator Muammar Gadhafi.

Bill Colby had already run regional divisions of the clandestine service and could hardly come back at that level. The DDP as a whole remained in the capable hands of Tom Karamessines, so that job, long Colby's dream, was simply not on the table. Instead Dick Helms took Bill to lunch at the Occidental Grille and offered him the post of executive director-comptroller of the CIA. This had been a dead-end for Lyman Kirkpatrick and a sinecure for an old Allen Dulles ally, Lawrence K. White, now set to retire. But the Nixon directive on the intelligence community, which stood to make Director Helms spend more time on community affairs, could potentially increase the importance of the executive director. Helms also strengthened the post by adding the comptroller role with its budget authority. Colby had to look up the word "comptroller" in the dictionary but he took the job.

Ultimately Bill Colby would decide that Helms had done him a favor, posing a task that forced the Minnesotan to broaden his knowledge of the CIA across the board. For the first time Colby had responsibilities that included the analytical and scientific sides of the CIA. And even though the Pentagon retained its control over the bulk of the national intelligence budget, the Nixon order, by giving the DCI a larger mandate, forced the military to justify their money demands in greater detail, bringing Colby into the play also. This experience gave him an unparalleled look at the capabilities of technical intelligence collection, in particular the Key Hole 11 satellite, then coming on line. The sophisticated photographic capacity of the Key Hole, the first digital readout system, combined with electronic intercept satellites and ground stations, afforded the CIA unprecedented access to secrets, even as the agency redoubled its efforts to recruit spies and enjoyed greater success against the hard targets, closed societies like China, Russia, and North Vietnam.

In his role as comptroller Colby accomplished a major revamp of CIA program practices. The divisions and offices had always held back a proportion of their money for unanticipated needs, projects that required extra expense or opportunities that suddenly materialized. Because of budget procedures that require U.S. government agencies to return unspent money to the Treasury at the end of each fiscal year, the CIA practice led to a rush to spend the extra cash as the end of the year neared, leading to many poorly conceived projects. Colby used his writ to inspect programs and the CIA's accounting system to review expenditures on a monthly basis. He made the division chiefs give up their held-back funds while promising that he could find them the extra money when they needed it. In the first year Colby not only made good on that promise but provided $20 million more than originally budgeted through reprogramming.

As befitted his long interest in political action, Colby kept an eye on the CIA's continuing activity in this field. The capability was less than it had been in the 1950s but remained significant, as demonstrated in Chile, where all information manipulation techniques were employed in a vain effort to prevent the election of Salvador Allende as president of Chile. Colby's role in the Chile affair would come on the rebound, as the CIA responded to investigations in the United States Congress, but he quickly became involved closer to home, as the agency tried to counter or prevent disclosures in the United States of information on its own activities.

The first serious effort to head off disclosures began just as Bill Colby reentered Langley's rarified atmosphere. It concerned Victor Marchetti, a fourteen-year agency man who had done the clandestine service training course but switched to analysis, specializing in Russian studies. In the Cuban Missile Crisis he had helped innovate methods for identifying the contents of shipping crates by precise measurement of the boxes in overhead photographs plus observation of objects later seen on the ground in Cuba. Marchetti's skills as a briefer led to his assignment to the agency's top budget officer and then to the post of executive assistant to Vice-Admiral Rufus Taylor, Helms's senior deputy. Like Colby, Marchetti gained a comprehensive picture of CIA activities in every field from these posts and much that he learned seemed problematical. Langley's practices with proprietaries like Air America skirted the boundaries of legality, especially upsetting when a CIA internal study could not determine how many aircraft the agency actually owned. Intelligence analysis and the national intelligence estimates, on which Marchetti had done some work, had difficulties too. Domestic intelligence activities bothered Marchetti also, and in the late 1960s he gave up his classic Cold Warrior views in favor of a perspective that the CIA should accept greater public scrutiny in an era in which détente had begun cooling the East-West conflict.

Victor Marchetti resigned from the CIA in 1969 and wrote a novel, titled *The Rope Dancer*, which exhibited some disillusionment with the CIA. Later he encountered a similarly frustrated former State Department intelligence analyst, John D. Marks, and the two proposed a nonfiction book that would be an exposé of the Central Intelligence Agency's roles and missions. Publicizing *The Rope Dancer*, which had just appeared, in October 1971, Marchetti gave an interview to United Press International in which he complained that the intelligence business had simply gotten too big, to the degree that secret agencies could start covert wars, and that CIA analysts were then under pressure to produce reports supporting the positions of the military or the operators. These were themes Marchetti and Marks emphasized in their manuscript, which became the book *The CIA and the Cult of Intelligence*. A copy of the book proposal turned up at Langley on March 12, 1972, either openly given to the agency by the publisher, Alfred A. Knopf, purloined by a CIA contact, or handed over by a Knopf employee—several versions of the story exist. Dick Helms called a meeting to decide what to do, thus involving Bill Colby.

Both Marchetti and Marks had signed secrecy agreements with their employers, so the CIA had some leverage it could use. But such agreements had hardly been enforced in the past. The agency itself had made no objection to Marchetti's novel *The Rope Dancer*. Former CIA officers from Allen Dulles to E. Howard Hunt had written books, as had Tom Braden, William F. Buckley, and others. Their products included not just novels but commentary and even nonfiction works specifically on intelligence. James McCargar, a clandestine services officer who later co-authored a book with Colby, had participated in the early 1950s paramilitary project in Albania and gone on to write a book on spies in the Cold War. Agency efforts to counter publication had more often centered on private authors, such as David Wise and Thomas B. Ross writing on the CIA as an invisible government, or Haynes Johnson on the Bay of Pigs. At the same time, Helms, Colby, and CIA general counsel Lawrence R. Houston all agreed the agency could not prosecute Marchetti and Marks on criminal grounds for disclosures of secrets because such a trial would highlight facts that Langley thought were sensitive while revealing additional secrets and triggering an avalanche of negative publicity.

Helms ordered Marchetti placed under surveillance on March 23, 1972, while Colby asked Houston's deputy, John S. Warner, to build a legal case. Director Helms then took the matter across the Potomac, where Nixon White House aide John D. Ehrlichman, at the president's direction, became point man in enlisting the Department of Justice to seek an injunction against publication without CIA review of the manuscript. Warner later met with Ehrlichman's deputy, David R. Young, to make Langley's legal argument. Justice assigned lawyers Dan McAuliffe and Irwin Goldbloom, and the case was presented to district court judge Albert V. Bryan, Jr., in Alexandria. Tom Karamessines and CIA security officer Howard J. Osborn appeared as witnesses for the agency. Although some of their testimony did not survive cross-examination, on April 18 Judge Bryan ruled in favor of the CIA. Marchetti lost on appeal. This became an effective instance of prior restraint, remarkable in the immediate wake of the Nixon administration's failure to achieve the same in the Pentagon Papers case.

Richard Helms wrote Ehrlichman on May 23 to thank the White House for its help "in what I consider historic litigation on behalf of the Central Intelligence Agency."[1] When Marchetti and Marks completed their manuscript and submitted it for vetting, the CIA deleted 339 items ranging from innocuous facts to more serious matters, some already known to the public, such as the CIA's relationship with Air America. Faced with judicial review of the deletion of 20 percent of the book, Langley offered to compromise on 168 cuts. Knopf sued to force release of the material but went to press with the book as censored. Langley got its public relations black eye anyway when the book design for *The CIA and the Cult of Intelligence* showed graphically how much had been cut and which passages the CIA had tried to suppress. Judicial review eventually determined the agency had failed to show cause for 141 of the 168 deletions it had forced, with most of the valid secrets concerned with satellites. The book actually read like a workmanlike tour of the secret world, hardly the rabid attack Colby and the others had feared. Langley was shown in a poor light.

Meanwhile, Bill Colby reacted again when the widely circulated Sunday supplement magazine *Parade* printed an article claiming the CIA to be the sole agency in the U.S. government with a writ to assassinate. Forever sensitive on this issue, Colby wanted to respond with a categorical denial in a letter to the editor. Whatever had occurred in Phoenix, Colby would always insist, had not been assassination and was not CIA. And he steadfastly rejected allegations of CIA responsibility in Diem's assassination. But when Colby looked into the overall issue to prepare a response, he swiftly discovered no categorical denial was possible. In March 1967, following allegations by columnist Drew Pearson that the CIA had colluded with organized crime in plots against Fidel Castro, Director Helms had ordered his inspector general, John S. Earman, to conduct a formal inquiry. Earman assigned Scott D.

Breckinridge and another officer on his staff to do the report, which confirmed the Castro plot allegations. Among other things, it concluded that "we may now assume that Pearson's story is not patched together from bits and pieces picked up here and there" and that trying to hush up leaks might do more harm than good, a tactic that "offers little chance of success." The investigation asked the question, "Can we plausibly deny that we plotted with gangster elements to assassinate Castro?" The answer was no. Moreover, "If an independent investigation were to be ordered, the investigators could learn everything that we have learned. Such an investigation would uncover details unknown to us, because it would have access to the non-CIA participants."[2]

Colby had heard talk of assassinations at Langley in the 1960s, but the inspector general report gave details and named names. His own friend Des FitzGerald had been involved. Limited to Cuba, the report contained nothing about CIA plots against leaders in Latin America, Africa, and Asia, but those cases waited in the wings. The CIA's own files contained "hit lists" of enemies of the state compiled during the Guatemala covert action, and Colby had to be personally aware of intelligence assistance to the Indonesian military in 1965–66. Given the skeletons in the closest, clandestine services officers were reluctant to tell Colby about instances of this kind in their areas. He had to settle for a vague response to *Parade*, but as Colby had done with CORDS on Phoenix, he drafted a CIA directive prohibiting assassinations.

Director Helms approved Colby's draft and issued it as a communitywide directive in 1972. A later congressional investigation concluded: "Considering the number of times the subject of assassination had arisen, Administration officials were remiss in not explicitly forbidding such activity."[3]

Another 1972 instance of attempts to influence public opinion on the CIA involved Colby in splitting hairs on Laos. Again the agency managed to get word of a book project, this time Random House's *The Politics of Heroin in Southeast Asia* by a twenty-six-year-old doctoral candidate in history at Yale, Alfred W. McCoy, with co-authors Cathleen B. Read and Leonard P. Adams. McCoy had done extensive research in Laos and South Vietnam and his work demonstrated participation by Laotian government officials, the Hmong secret army that fought for the CIA, and top Saigon officers in opium traffic and the heroin sales that bedeviled the U.S. military in Vietnam. The CIA had links to many characters in this sordid tale and its Air America planes were obviously the key transport mechanism throughout the hill country whence the opium came. McCoy's evidence included even examination of the accounts books of one of the Laotian generals. McCoy went public with his charges of U.S. government and CIA complicity in testimony before the foreign assistance panel of the Senate Appropriations Committee in June 1972, and followed with an article in *Harper's Magazine* the next month.

The press promptly reported the charges. Bill Colby answered one such article with a letter to the editor of the *Washington Star* on July 5. "The public record on this subject is clear," Colby wrote. "Charges of this nature have been made previously and each time have been most carefully investigated and found to be unsubstantiated." Colby cited language in a 1970 speech Richard Helms had made, plus officials from the Bureau of Narcotics and Dangerous Drugs and others.[4] Alfred McCoy rebutted Colby's defense a couple of weeks later with specific officials in Laos quoted on the use of Air America for drug movements. McCoy received further support from Tran Van Khiem, a former Saigon security chief who had investigated corruption charges for Diem and had kept up his contacts with Saigon intelligence services: "My security agents . . . firmly confirm that a few CIA agents in Indochina are involved in opium trafficking."[5]

Executive Director Colby added the drug issue to a study of the Far East Division being made by inspector general Gordon M. Stewart. The CIA inspector general report of September 1972 validated McCoy's point that the Hmong were growing poppies (the raw material for opium), that Lao officers were active in the traffic, and that Air America controls could not prevent quantities of drugs from being smuggled aboard CIA aircraft. The U.S. embassy managed to get one egregiously compromised Laotian official fired but, aside from improving controls on Air America, the CIA could do little about the overall contours of the problem. While insisting neither the CIA nor any of its senior officers had participated, approved, or tolerated the drug traffic, Stewart's report admitted concern regarding agents and local officials: "What to do about these people is a particularly troublesome problem, in view of its implications for some of our operations, particularly in Laos."[6]

Meanwhile, on July 5, the same day Colby's letter appeared in Washington, CIA lawyer Lawrence Houston sent a letter to Al McCoy's publisher, Harper & Row, demanding to see the manuscript for prepublication review, claiming the book might endanger the lives of CIA officers. The agency had already failed to get access to the book so clandestine services deputy director Cord Meyer, Jr., went to his friend and former colleague Cass Canfield, a senior editor and Harper board member. Now Harper & Row lawyers, fearing the jeopardy argument, won over company management to the review. Elisabeth Jakab, McCoy's editor, and company lawyers worked out ground rules, to which the author agreed after sounding out other publishers and discovering the legal and temporal obstacles to moving his book. McCoy insisted on full documentation of each objection and Harper & Row gave the CIA ten days for its review. Langley took a look and sent Harper & Row a twenty-page lists of cuts it wanted. After discussion with McCoy the publisher concluded there was no merit to the CIA demands and stood by its book. In view of Knopf's experience with Marchetti, Harper advanced the publication date for *The Politics of Heroin*. The CIA apparently made plans to buy up the entire print run of the McCoy book, but then the *New York Times* printed a story revealing the CIA's attempt to suppress the book and its drug charges, and Harper merely increased the size of its printing in anticipation of wider demand, including the CIA's. Once more Langley did not look very good.

Vietnam continued to strike Bill Colby close to home, and the combination of alma mater with that subject proved too powerful to resist. Colby's Princeton classmate, Robert F. Goheen, by now outgoing president of the university and a man with a reputation for bringing change and growth to Princeton, became another to testify before Congress in favor of ending the war. The fifty-two-year-old Goheen, born to a missionary family and raised in India, was sensitive to many of the nuances of this war. In the *Los Angeles Times* of July 7, 1972, Goheen warned of Americans "thinking self-righteously about our involvement in wars." He continued, "Piling the arrogance of power on top of our ignorance of a strange and distant land, we have stumbled and forced our way . . . into the lives and affairs of another people endowed with a culture very different from our own—acting as though their interests were our own, and if not, that they should be!"[7]

Bill Colby felt unable to remain silent in the face of Goheen's advocacy of setting a date certain for an end to U.S. military action, writing the Princeton president in July that the overriding issue in Vietnam was Hanoi's attempt by any means necessary to assume control of the South. Colby extolled the local defense forces and village elections he had encouraged at CORDS, programs to elicit Viet Cong ralliers, and the resettlement of refugees. He insisted the university should be researching these matters, not washing its hands of the war. Unimpressed, Goheen replied in August that it could not be good for the country for the United States to present the picture of an aggressive, neo-colonialist power.

From his post as executive director of the CIA, Colby did his best to defend both the Central Intelligence Agency and United States policy. Contrary to the image later drawn by CIA detractors, right into 1973 Colby shared the Cold War ethos of the agency's secret warriors. He did so even as several internal and external developments challenged his pristine vision of U.S. intelligence.

INSIDE LANGLEY, invisible to all outside observers of Bill Colby's efforts to protect the CIA, the executive director himself came under fire. This affair began in late 1970 when French counterintelligence became suspicious of a doctor who did much international traveling. Following the man, the French agency, *Direction du Surveillance du Territoire* (DST), observed contacts between him and Russians. Later DST watchers caught the good doctor red-handed passing information to an officer of Russian military intelligence. Not long afterward James J. Angleton launched a CIA investigation.

Saigon happened to be one of the places the Frenchman had lived and Angleton sent his officer Newton Miler to South Vietnam to reconstruct the doctor's contacts. The Frenchman had been in Saigon during the same period when William E. Colby served there as CIA station chief. Then it developed both had been members of the club Cercle Sportif, and it soon emerged that Colby and the doctor had been friends and had seen each other socially. Despite CIA regulations, Colby had never filed reports on his encounters with the doctor. In consequence Colby became a direct subject in a counterespionage case.

Angleton assigned "Scotty" Miler and another counterintelligence stalwart, Raymond G. Rocca, to do the inquiry at Langley. They sat down with the executive director to record a formal statement. Colby remembered the Frenchman only dimly and could not say much more than that they had been friends. The relationship had seemed so innocuous that Bill had never bothered recording the contacts. Scotty Miler could not establish whether the doctor had been an active Russian agent during that time in Saigon and terminated the inquiry, but Colby nevertheless ended up with a counterintelligence file in Angleton's office. The situation could only have rankled. This became one more flashpoint for increasing antipathy between Bill Colby and Jim Angleton.

Then came Watergate and yet another matter with potential to compromise Colby. The Watergate affair was named for the Washington building that Nixon administration political operatives broke into in June 1972 to plant electronic bugs in the offices of the Democratic National Committee. The affair eventually brought down the presidency of Richard Nixon. But the term has come to be applied more generally to a whole range of operations by the Nixon White House. One of these involved Colby. Nixon wished to get the CIA to hand over certain documents on the Bay of Pigs, the Diem assassination, and the murder of Dominican dictator Rafael Trujillo, which he believed could be used in political attacks on the Democrats. John Ehrlichman first asked Helms directly for the papers, and in October 1971 Director Helms took them to a meeting with Nixon, making sure the president really wanted these documents before handing them over.

A month later Ehrlichman invited Bill Colby to lunch at the White House, ostensibly to discuss his experience in Vietnam. They spoke of CORDS and pacification at this meeting on November 16, but Ehrlichman soon turned the conversation to the Diem assassination, and then raised the question of declassifying the documents Director Helms had given Richard Nixon. Colby suggested either writing an internal history of events that could be cleansed of secrets and then released, or restricting declassification to intelligence reports and analyses rather than operational accounts. At Langley Colby recounted the gist of the lunchtime talk to Helms, who sent Ehrlichman a memorandum on December 7 making essentially the same points. The White House desisted on this initiative, but Ehrlichman later put Howard Hunt, by then a former CIA officer working for the president, and David Young to work falsifying a set of documents on the Diem affair.

The Watergate break-in itself happened on June 16, 1972, a day Colby spent preoccupied with Vietnam, for his friend John Paul Vann had been killed in a helicopter crash and was buried that day at Arlington National Cemetery. The break-in occurred during the night and the burglars were caught and arrested. Howard Hunt and another former CIA officer, James W. McCord, Jr., though not with the burglars, were quickly swept up in the net. Several of the burglars themselves had been CIA contract personnel used in operations against Cuba. The question of CIA links to the Watergate scandal occurred to many; indeed, within a week of the break-in and initial arrests, Ehrlichman and White House counsel John Dean tried to get the CIA to intervene with the FBI and head off a Watergate investigation on national security grounds. Richard Nixon's orders for that maneuver, only implied at the time, became one of the facts that forced his resignation from the presidency in 1974 when his discussion of the gambit in the Oval Office emerged on a tape recording, the so-called smoking gun tape.

Director Helms, his deputy General Vernon Walters, Colby, and other top officials mulled over Watergate's implications at the DCI's staff meeting on June 19. Participants were aware of CIA's links to Hunt, McCord, and some of the burglars but were satisfied the agency had not been involved. Helms decided that Langley should distance itself from Watergate, a key reason that General Walters rejected the White House attempt later that week to get the CIA to make the FBI back off. Helms made Colby the agency point man on Watergate.

"Stay cool, volunteer nothing, because it will only be used to involve us. Just stay away from the whole damn thing," Colby later wrote was the gist of Helm's marching orders.[8]

As executive director William E. Colby's first mission would be to handle inquiries from the FBI's Alexandria field office, which conducted the Watergate investigation. Initially this seemed simple enough—to hand over data on the backgrounds of those people with CIA associations. The biggest complication was to do so without revealing anything about operations or other agency personnel. But new issues continually cropped up. Eugenio Martinez, one of the Watergate burglars working for the White House, was a CIA contract agent paid $100 per month right through the break-in. Martinez had also participated in the November 1971 burglary of the offices of California psychiatrist Fred Fielding, whose patients included Daniel Ellsberg, the defense analyst whose act of conscience in leaking secret documents on the war in Vietnam (the government history that became known as the Pentagon Papers) earned him the number one spot on an "enemies list" that Richard Nixon created. Martinez had reported on some White House activities to the CIA's Miami chief of station as well as the two case officers he had during this period. On June 19, as Helms and Colby met on controlling the fallout from the Watergate break-in, the Miami chief of station was sent a cable instructing him to monitor his agents more closely. Angered, that officer sent Langley a report Martinez had compiled three months earlier on his activities. One of the CIA case officers who had worked with Martinez had already been reassigned to Vietnam, but the second was summoned to headquarters. The case officer was told he would be kept at Langley at least until September in the event his testimony on Martinez was needed, but he remained on Washington assignment as late as 1974. Congressional investigators of Watergate were left to ponder the extent of the CIA's foreknowledge of the illegal White House activities.

Both the break-ins just mentioned had been carried out by a White House unit called the "Plumbers" that was formed in the wake of the Ellsberg leak of the Pentagon Papers. One of the co-directors of that unit was E. Howard Hunt, who had worked on the Bay of Pigs invasion, among other projects, and had retired from the agency in 1970. Hunt had recruited the action group the Plumbers used in the break-ins as well as a May 1972 incident at the United States Capitol where Ellsberg was physically assaulted. With the exception of James W. McCord, Jr., most of the Plumbers goon squad were Miami Cubans like Martinez with past CIA connections. This again raised a specter of CIA connection with Watergate. No wonder Helms wanted to distance the agency from involvement in this affair.

Agency connections with Howard Hunt posed a particular problem that would bedevil Bill Colby for almost two years. Despite Langley's almost immediate internal investigation, aspects of the story kept changing. An assistant to Walters soon told Colby that the deputy director's predecessor, Marine General Robert Cushman, had been approached by the White House in July 1971 for help in creating a disguise and false identity for a political operative. That turned out to be Hunt, who met with Cushman on July 22, 1971. Senior CIA officers had switch-activated taping systems in their offices and a tape existed of the Cushman-Hunt conversation. On January 16, 1973, Senate Majority Leader Mike Mansfield in a letter required that all evidentiary materials related to Watergate be preserved throughout government. Approximately a week later, with Richard Helms about to leave the CIA to become ambassador to Iran, the agency destroyed all tapes, along with Helms's own transcripts of both telephone and room conversations. But then General Cushman testified before Watergate hearings in August 1973 and presented a transcript of his talk with Hunt two years before. Bill Colby, on behalf of the CIA, had to explain that two tapes made by Cushman had been preserved when his safe was cleaned out at the end of 1971 as he left the CIA. The two, of which the Hunt conversation was one, had not been found in Colby's canvass for Watergate material in June 1972 so his secretary, who had previously worked for Cushman, had created a best recollection version. Then in another search in May 1973, DDCI Walters's executive assistant had found the original tape. Perplexed senators wanted to listen to the tape and Tennessee Republican Howard Baker made arrangements to do so. By then it was February 1974. The day before Baker heard the tape, CIA deputy legislative counsel Walter Pforzheimer delivered a new, different version of the transcript. Pforzheimer also brought a transcript of John Ehrlichman's side of a July 1971 telephone talk with Cushman in which the CIA, according to the notes, was told that Howard Hunt worked for the president and was to be given "carte blanche."[9] These materials supported the CIA's contention of its noninvolvement in Watergate but their appearance was rather too convenient for the agency, as Colby had to realize. (For example, Cushman's testimony was that he normally did not have his phone calls monitored, and

CIA practice in monitoring was to record both sides of a conversation, but his secretary *had* listened in on Ehrlichman and had taken shorthand notes on *only* his side of the conversation.)

The particulars of the assistance that Howard Hunt sought from the CIA also caused some difficulties for Colby as they were revealed. Hunt had gotten disguises for himself and Plumbers cohort G. Gordon Liddy. The two had gone to California to scout the office of Ellsberg psychiatrist Dr. Fielding. The photos taken on that trip were given to the CIA to develop. Technical staff from Langley met with Hunt four times at CIA safehouses to hand over the fake identity cards, a tape recorder disguised in a typewriter case, and the camera, which was hidden inside a tobacco pouch. When CIA technicians developed the film one recognized architectural styles and foliage typical of southern California, and when the set of pictures were examined together they appeared to be materials one might gather in preparation for an operation. The CIA then terminated its help to Hunt on this matter. It was August 27, 1971. The Plumbers burglary took place a week later. After Watergate the CIA handed over copies of the pictures to the FBI but said nothing about how these had led to their terminating assistance to the White House cabal.

The White House had also used Howard Hunt in its effort to assemble documents on the Diem coup that could be used to discredit Democrats on Vietnam. Hunt met with CIA officials on this in October 1971 but, as already noted, Helms and Colby had both refused cooperation here.

Then there was the matter of a psychological profile of Daniel Ellsberg created at the behest of Hunt. Helms approved the study in late July 1971, and Hunt and Liddy both attended a meeting at the CIA on August 12, handing over FBI investigative reports that CIA psychiatrists used as raw material for their study. The agency's chief psychiatrist objected to Hunt's presence and remarks both in memos and at another meeting eight days later. The first draft of the CIA study was found unsatisfactory and it was returned for revision. Sending the final product to David Young at the White House on November 9, Director Helms emphasized that CIA involvement should not be revealed in any context, formal or informal. During the subsequent investigation the CIA refused the senators access to both the memoranda of objection by CIA psychiatrists and the responses of superiors. Here Bill Colby acted to protect the internal workings of the agency.

One more CIA issue resulted from the fact that a contract employee of the agency entered the home of Plumber and former CIA officer James McCord right after the Watergate arrests. The CIA contract employee destroyed documents that might have shown agency connections with McCord at the time of the break-in. No one outside the CIA was told of this until February 1974. In fact, the preceeding month, when agency inspector general William V. Broe was reviewing all Watergate-related files for material to turn over to the Senate, the CIA security director ordered material on the McCord break-in removed from the files. In February 1974 Walter Pforzheimer prepared for Colby's signature a letter to Senate investigators certifying that all

CIA material had been turned over to them, only to discover that subordinate officials in the Office of Security, worried that evidence in the McCord break-in would be suppressed, had kept copies and refused to concur in the CIA certification. When inspector general Broe learned of this he immediately ordered the data forwarded to Congress, to the Watergate special prosecutor, and to the intelligence oversight committees, with an explanatory memorandum from the CIA Office of Security. Colby demanded and received the resignation of the director of that office.[10]

Not surprisingly, Senate investigators were unhappy with the CIA's cooperation in the Watergate affair. In a 1974 report prepared at the request of Senator Howard Baker the agency's lapses were detailed and a long list enumerated of evidence deemed relevant that the CIA had not provided. Bill Colby defended the agency in a June 28, 1974, reply, which insisted the CIA had engaged in "almost continuous exchange of information," including handing over extremely sensitive data, permitting twenty-four agency people to testify, and giving the Senate more than 700 documents. Colby mentioned that the CIA had over 160 objections to comments in the draft Senate report, which the agency had submitted during April, that were not reflected in the final version. Colby wrote, "It had been my hope that sufficient concrete evidence would have been produced to assure you that CIA had no prior knowledge of the Watergate or Ellsberg break-ins or coverups . . . [but] I realized that you had not been so assured. . . . I recognize that you have every right to subscribe to conclusions in the staff report which are at variance with those I have drawn from the evidence presented."[11] This would be a painful moment for Bill Colby.

Other excruciating passages would follow from Nixon's Watergate coverup, especially his efforts to get the CIA to head off investigation by pleading national security and the need to protect agency sources and methods. Once again the White House demand had been conveyed by John Ehrlichman. For months after June 1972 Bill Colby, as point man in charge of CIA responses to Watergate, had avoided revealing the identity of the White House emissary. Only on November 27, 1972, at the Justice Department and under direct questioning by an assistant attorney general, did Colby reveal the name. At the time Justice was hinting that if Colby did not cooperate he might be deemed an accessory. Colby's actions held the line for the CIA amid the growing scandal but left lingering doubts among observers as the details of Watergate emerged. In particular Colby's record of his November meeting at the Justice Department raised hackles. The executive director had recorded: "I danced around the room several times for 10 minutes, and then was pinned . . . with a demand for the name."[12]

Many months afterward, when William E. Colby went up before the Senate Armed Services Committee for hearings on his nomination to head the CIA, this role in Watergate, along with the Phoenix program, would be the most contentious issues. Senators Edward M. Kennedy and Sam Nunn questioned Colby at great length on the matter. The Minnesotan would have been in dire straits had the CIA's part in Watergate been very much larger than it was. Colby satisfied the senators with his testimony and insertions for the record.

Meanwhile the Nixon White House, none too pleased with the Central Intelligence Agency, took steps of its own. Richard Nixon remarked that he had protected Richard Helms from a great many things and would be echoed by John Ehrlichman. On November 20, 1972, Nixon summoned Helms to Camp David. Colby and others believed this would be a review of the CIA budget request and prepared the DCI with intensive briefings. Instead the president asked for Helms's resignation and gave him the sop of an appointment to be ambassador to Iran. On December 15 Helms and Colby were back at the White House, where John Ehrlichman and John Dean raked Colby over the coals for his revelations to the Justice Department. Colby explained what had happened and gave Ehrlichman data he could use to construct his own version of events. Of course Ehrlichman was too deeply involved for any of this to do much good and history took its course.

Other events already in motion conspired to pit Bill Colby and Richard Helms against each other in a way that would rend asunder the CIA. These centered on Project Fu/Belt, the CIA's covert action in Chile. The background goes back to September 1970, when Nixon ordered Helms to do whatever necessary to prevent Chilean socialist Salvador Allende from becoming president of that country. "If ever I carried a marshal's baton in my knapsack out of the Oval Office, it was that day," Helms recounted in a famous quote.[13] Langley carried out this action on two tracks. One was a conventional political influence effort, which had already essentially failed (in both 1964 and 1970 the CIA spent money and planted material in the Chilean press to prevent an Allende victory, succeeding in 1964 but not the second time). The second track responded to Nixon's September 15 orders and aimed at inducing the Chilean military to move against Allende and either prevent his assumption of office or overthrow him.

Both facets of CIA activity in Chile contained elements that would lead to later problems. The political influence effort involved cooperation with like-minded private corporations, in particular International Telephone and Telegraph (ITT), which acted in concert with the agency during earlier years. For the 1970 elections, ITT encouraged the CIA's intervention, which Langley at first resisted. Prodded by the Nixon administration's 40 Committee, its top policy body for intelligence matters, the CIA later moved ahead. Although ITT then pulled out of the initiative, participation in a CIA project planted boobytraps that later blew the lid off the Chile affair. Track II, the enlistment of the Chilean military, went on without the knowledge of the U.S. ambassador. Though the blackout was on Nixon's orders, it constituted a violation of long-standing directives and CIA regulations. Worse, Chilean plotters activated by the CIA effort assassinated the commander-in-chief of the Chilean military. Langley could deny responsibility only on the narrowest of technicalities. In the larger sense, the CIA truly bore a moral burden here.

The blowback for the agency began in 1972, when journalist Jack Ander-

son in a series of columns revealed the collusion between the CIA and ITT—
agency security did nothing to inhibit leaks from a private corporation. These
reports irritated the Nixon administration, already enraged by Anderson's
columns depicting the White House's inner deliberations during the India-
Pakistan war of 1971. Nixon ordered countermeasures and Helms complied.
The CIA retaliated with surveillance code named Mudhen, covering Anderson, his assistant Les Whitten, and their families. Whitten and his wife were
followed to an art gallery, their son on a beer run. Anderson's house was
staked out until his kids, turning the tables, spied out the spies and took their
pictures. The Mudhen surveillance involved the Central Intelligence Agency
in a domestic activity prohibited by its statutory authority and put another
skeleton in Langley's closet.

Apart from anything else, the emergence of the CIA-ITT connection put
the existence of a CIA operation in Chile into the public domain. There were
many in Congress who wanted to learn more about this activity. Also, by
now Allende was president of Chile, his country suffered from the economic
impact of U.S. sanctions, and there was continuing interest in whether the
CIA had had a hand in this as well. The Senate formed a special committee
to study multinational corporations, and both the Senate and House committees concerned with foreign relations held hearings on the United States and
Chile. In the interregnum between his resignation as DCI and departure for
Iran, Richard Helms was called to testify before the Senate on February 5
and 7, 1973. At the first of these hearings he sidestepped questions about the
CIA and ITT. At the second, under oath, Helms directly denied that the CIA
had passed money to politicians opposed to Allende or had attempted to
overthrow the government of Chile.

These were not matters of which Congress stood in complete ignorance.
Between 1964 and 1973 the CIA discussed Chile with congressional staffs,
committees, or individual congressmen on forty occasions; half the briefings
included mention of covert action, and about half of those also included talk
about releasing money for these purposes. According to Helms's biographer
Thomas Powers, the evening before his February 5 testimony he had been
more forthcoming privately with Missouri Senator Stuart Symington, whose
question about ITT Helms ducked at the hearing. But Congress was never
told of Track II, and Richard Helm's direct denials constituted the public
record.

William E. Colby became involved in this morass soon afterward. The
Senate subcommittee on multinationals already had contrary information
from ITT; staff told the CIA as much a week later, asking Langley to respond
to a set of five specific questions. Langley officials, focused on the fact that
no money had changed hands between ITT and the CIA in 1970, proposed
to respond that the Helms testimony had been accurate. In terms of an overall
strategy, the CIA preferred to move the issue to the more friendly forum of
the secret CIA subcommittee of the Senate Armed Services committee. A
joint meeting of members of that group, the Appropriations Committee's

CIA panel, and agency representatives actually took place on March 13. Senator Frank Church of the multinationals committee was invited to hear what the Central Intelligence Agency had to say. Bill Colby sat next to his director when the agency group appeared.

Congress, not to be mollified, pursued various inquiries. There would be more than a dozen CIA briefings on the Chile operation between March 1973 and December of the next year. Helms faced more questions during his ambassadorial nomination hearing in May 1973. Salvador Allende, following a lengthy period of economic crisis in Chile, was overthrown by General Augusto Pinochet in a military coup that September. By then Colby himself had become the director of central intelligence, in office barely a week when the coup occurred. On October 11 it would be Colby in the front seat, denying any CIA role in the coup as he spoke to the Subcommittee on Inter-American Affairs of the House Committee on Foreign Affairs. Colby did not mention that the CIA had had more than twenty-four hours' forewarning of the coup, a potential smoking gun with respect to its assertions of no role. On previous occasions Colby had been able to avoid the line of fire, but when the Chile issue again crossed the director's desk he would be in the chair.

RICHARD NIXON'S CHOICE to succeed Helms as director of Central Intelligence proved to be a man from outside the agency, James R. Schlesinger. The president gave Schlesinger the opportunity to implement the intelligence management changes he had recommended in his 1971 review of the community. A native New Yorker ten years Colby's junior, Schlesinger's forte was management; his only knowledge of intelligence was that gleaned from work in defense analysis. He was really an economist with a Harvard Ph.D. who had gone to work at the Rand Corporation in the early 1960s and had risen to direct its strategic studies program from 1967 to 1969. Nixon had made Schlesinger assistant director of what became the Office of Management and Budget and later chairman of the Atomic Energy Commission. He came to Langley from the nuclear job, with something of a reputation as a troubleshooter and a mandate from Nixon to shake things up at the Central Intelligence Agency.

Much of Schlesinger's introduction to the agency came at briefings, some of them all-day affairs, at his Atomic Energy Commission office in Germantown, Maryland. It quickly became clear he intended to do as he had advocated in 1971 and establish the DCI's leadership of the entire intelligence bureaucracy. Schlesinger also wanted to strengthen the Directorate of Intelligence within the CIA which produced the reports and estimates that helped Washington decide on policy. The CIA's operations in Southeast Asia, and in Chile for that matter, relied on paramilitary or political action specialists. The feeling was that this force exerted disproportionate power in the agency. It was necessary to have a paramilitary capability in being, but once America's active operations in Vietnam ended with the Paris Peace Agreement of January 1973, the CIA did not need such a large capability. At the time the clandestine service numbered 6,000 to 7,000 out of a total of about 17,000 CIA personnel. Schlesinger wanted to cut it back.

Bill Colby saw his own chance in this Schlesinger reorganization. The management expert would not have much use for an executive director. The job itself remained amorphous and could never really be established since directorate chiefs would always go right to the DCI. Colby saw that Schlesinger would need the most help with the clandestine service, which the new director proposed to cut back and where he had no background at all. Tom Karamessines, with a back problem, resigned when Helms was cashiered, once again opening up the job Colby had long coveted, director for plans. Though heading the directorate would effectively be a demotion for Colby, he longed to do it and convinced Schlesinger to give him his head. To take advantage of Bill's management experience, Director Schlesinger made him chairman of a committee of all the CIA deputy directors that he set up as a management coordinating body.

A whirlwind of activity followed, and with it, the first blow to Colby's reputation among CIA's Cold Warriors. The Minnesotan cooperated with Schlesinger's program for what soon would be called a "reduction-in-force"; indeed he wanted to refocus the clandestine service on its traditional role of espionage, in accord with the DCI's view that much of the dead wood at the CIA resided in his directorate. With the falloff in covert operations entailed by the winding up of the Vietnam war, this seemed a logical way to proceed.

Colby began by rechristening his unit, getting rid of the euphemistic title Directorate of Plans, renaming the service the Directorate of Operations (DO), the name it has retained ever since. Bill Colby became the first deputy director for operations (DDO). He then set up a task force to study the DO and recommend how cuts could be made. Chairing the study was Cord Meyer, second man in the DO, who had held that post under Karamessines and been acting DDO in the interregnum between Tom and Bill. For someone with knowledge of Vietnam and what capabilities were and were no longer needed, Colby appointed Charles S. Whitehurst, who had worked for him in the Far East Division.

The reduction study could only be thankless duty. Except for the wake of the Bay of Pigs, when something over 250 CIA officers had been let go, there had never been a mass cutback at the agency. Any such thing, held the conventional wisdom, would be a security risk. Meyer tried to protect the clandestine service, arguing that conventional procedures were enough— Karamessines had had a system under which the DO tried to identify and select out the bottom 3 percent of performers. But there could be no escaping the fact that the Directorate of Operations had become top-heavy. The number of CIA staff assigned overseas on clandestine service had been 35 percent higher in 1959 than in 1973 even though the DO was now much larger. At the highest levels (equivalent to civil service grades GS-16/17/18) about 70 percent of CIA people were over forty-five years old compared to half that rate at other agencies, and no less than 85 percent of CIA officers had been on the job for more than twenty years; indeed, only 13 percent of this population had been in the CIA in an executive capacity for *fewer* than twenty years. About a third of DO personnel already met one retirement criterion—that of having served overseas for five years or more. All this translated into very limited futures for the young men and women coming into the agency.

Tom Karamessines later noted how valuable the DO's information continued to be—over 30 percent of the items in the CIA typescript publication *Central Intelligence Bulletin* were credited to the clandestine service. But Jim Schlesinger, tough and abrasive, remained determined to go ahead.

"Ruthless?" Schlesinger shot back when he heard this criticism of himself, "I'm just trying to clear the aisle so I can walk."[14]

Resistance to the purge did not abate. Charlie Whitehurst termed the reduction a "Frankenstein monster."[15] Former CIA Middle East specialist Miles Copeland, by then already in retirement and living in London, saw the purge as doing away with the very DO "fuses" who might blow the whistle on questionable operations.[16] Other senior people leaked information to the press. Schlesinger was called before the House Armed Services Committee's CIA subcommittee monthly to account for his actions. There was talk of a class action suit until one day when Director Schlesinger called a number of senior officials into his office and, in their presence, telephoned the president. Schlesinger told Nixon that the CIA cutback would result in a public fight with lawsuits, leaks, and bad publicity. The president replied he would support his DCI to the hilt. After that the denizens of Langley accepted the inevitable.

Deputy Director Colby saw one of his missions as acting as a buffer between Schlesinger's ruthlessness and the CIA folk subjected to the harsh remedies of firing, retirement, or forced resignation. At the senior level and for other agency components he acted in his capacity as chief of the CIA management committee. Within the DO he acted directly. A few top people he saved by moving them into training jobs and other administrative positions; for most there was little recourse. "It wasn't long," Colby recounted in his memoirs, "before a phone call from me cast a chill on any recipient."[17]

The agency went to its congressional overseers to ask for amendment of the Central Intelligence Retirement Act of 1949, which permitted a certain number of officers to be separated from the CIA each year. In place of the old ceiling of 800 the CIA asked for special authority to let go 2,100 people. Schlesinger's reduction in force eventually pared the agency by between 1,000 and 1,800 staff, somewhere between 7 percent and 10 percent. One who did *not* leave, but whose separation from the CIA Colby had recommended to Schlesinger, was James J. Angleton.

If Colby could not get rid of Jim Angleton he could at least cut back the large Counterintelligence unit within the DO. Colby changed the DO so that counterterrorist functions were handled by the area divisions rather than

Angleton's staff. He also took away Angleton's responsibility for liaison with the Federal Bureau of Investigation and much of his previous gadfly role in vetting almost every DO activity. Some other portfolios Angleton held had to be decided at a higher pay grade, but Colby recommended that these too be taken away from the Counterintelligence Staff. One was CIA liaison with Israeli intelligence, which Jim had handled since the inception of the state of Israel. Accounts had reached Schlesinger through the DO of arbitrary and outrageous behavior on some of Angleton's visits to Tel Aviv, including threats to the CIA's regular officers in the DO's chain of command. Schlesinger chose to lift Angleton's watching brief, strengthening the line authority of the DO's Near East and South Asia Division.

One more blow to Angleton concerned CIA domestic activities. The Counterintelligence Staff included the unit under Richard Ober carrying out project MH/Chaos, the agency's monitoring of the antiwar movement and its mail-opening operation. The latter had been going on since the 1950s, while Chaos had begun as the Special Operations Group in 1967. Not only had the antiwar movement been monitored and infiltrated—the CIA accumulated over 9,000 files and lists with more than 300,000 names—but in at least two instances the agency had abetted antiwar activities in efforts to help its agents establish their bona fides. Between 1970 and mid-1972 Chaos had issued 1,764 reports and seventy-five special studies, sent over 6,150 cables and dispatches while receiving 5,854 cables and 2,404 pouched dispatches. Ober's Special Operations Group alone accounted for about fifty officers on the Counterintelligence Staff plus a great deal of computer equipment. Despite its regular reports to the FBI and an interagency group that met at the Department of Justice but worked at the behest of the White House, when Director Schlesinger asked Angleton what real intelligence Chaos had produced the counterintelligence chief could point to very little. Not only was the domestic activity illegal, the DCI pointed out, but there was no written authority for Chaos reports to the White House interagency group.

Schlesinger decided to take the Special Operations Group out of the Counterintelligence Staff and relocate it in the Office of Security, a unit of the CIA's administrative directorate. He also deemphasized Ober's project and took away its high priority. The more than sixty agents recruited by Chaos offices (all of them before July 1972) were deactivated. But Schlesinger did not, at that time, abolish the Special Operations Group. That would be left for Bill Colby.

The CIA director proved a little less forthright with regard to Angleton's mail surveillance project, considered since the early 1960s to have had significant "flap potential." The chief postal inspector of the United States at this time, William J. Cotter, happened to be a former CIA officer who had once worked on the mail project and had been aware of it since its origin in the early 1950s. In early 1973 Cotter told the CIA he would end CIA access to the mail at its New York laboratory and clearinghouse in mid-February unless the agency supplied written authorization from the attorney general or the president. Schlesinger reviewed this situation with Colby on February 15 and decided to wash his hands and turn the whole thing over to the FBI. But Angleton protested, and at another meeting soon thereafter with Colby and Schlesinger, he got the DCI to ask Cotter for a postponement while the CIA sought higher authority for the mail opening. Cotter refused, however, and the mail cover program came to its end. In its last year the CIA copied 8,700 letters, about 60 percent of them on the basis of the Chaos watch lists, photographed the envelopes of roughly 33,000, and handled in all some 4,350,000 items of U.S. mail, whose inviolability is guaranteed by statute. Bill Colby had lost this case to Angleton on the merits but won by default when the Postal Service refused to continue CIA access.

The object of all the Chaos and mail surveillance, of course, had been the political opposition to the Vietnam war. Langley saw itself as merely tracing the foreign connections of the movement in an effort to establish whether the Russians, Chinese, or Hanoi were calling the shots in American politics (the CIA never found any evidence to support this thesis), but the agency had no control over what use the Nixon White House, FBI, or other U.S. authorities made of its reports. The Paris Peace Accord on January 27, 1973, undermined this rationale for continued CIA domestic activity, however. This quasi-end to the Vietnam war also held special meaning for Bill Colby, who had invested so much of himself in the Southeast Asian conflict. Even while working at Langley, Bill took time out to lecture at the National War College in November 1971 and again a year later on the nature of revolutionary war.

Peace accords signed in Paris on January 27, 1973, brought American prisoners back from North Vietnam and provided occasion for a direct contact with Colby by the president. The agreement envisioned an Indochina-wide ceasefire, with all forces to remain in place and strict limits on subsequent military assistance. The United State was to withdraw all its remaining military forces from Indochina within sixty days and would be permitted only civilian advisers from then on. Hanoi would return all prisoners of war. Nixon watched on television as the former prisoners stepped off a plane in the Philippines, and wrote Colby a letter on February 20, 1973:

As I saw our POWs come off the plane at Clark Field, I was never so proud to be an American.

These brave men were able to return to a nation which had achieved peace with honor rather than to one which had suffered a humiliating defeat. This would not have been possible had it not been for those—like you—who served America with such dedication, whether militarily or diplomatically, throughout this long and difficult struggle.

I just want you to know how much I personally appreciate all you have done to help achieve the honorable peace we fought for.[18]

This note suggests a closer connection than Bill admitted in his 1978 memoir. While that is not true, it is a fact that Nixon's daughter Patricia, known to all as Tricia, had long been dating Edward Finch Cox. The latter was a Princeton classmate and dormitory roommate of Bill's son Jonathan Elbridge. When Jonathan married Susan Hinks of Grosse Pointe, Michigan, in August 1970, Cox was his best man and Tricia among the guests. In June 1971, when Ed Cox and Tricia Nixon married in turn, at an opulent White House ceremony, Jonathan returned the favor. The esteem was not merely social; when Jonathan finished Yale Law School he would be hired by Henry Kissinger's National Security Council staff.

Another Colby passage, a moment of great sadness in the spring of 1973, brought further indication of Richard Nixon's esteem. Broken by her experience and continuing depression, Catherine Colby died. Some in political circles and at CIA believe this to have been a suicide, which Bill Colby always denied. The event, however, brought another note from Nixon, on April 16:

> Mrs. Nixon and I were deeply saddened to learn of your daughter's death, and we want you to know that you have our heartfelt sympathy. The loss of someone so young is an especially cruel blow, but we hope that by drawing together, you and your children will find the strength to sustain you through this very sad time. Our thoughts and prayers will be with you as well.[19]

It should be noted that Nixon, increasingly embattled by the Watergate scandal, took time out from major political maneuvers to pen this note. The same day, he demanded the resignation of White House counsel John Dean, and on the 17th the president would order a new investigation, intensified but intended to focus attention on Dean, John Ehrlichman, and White House chief of staff H. R. Haldeman. On April 15 the Justice Department announced it had just learned of White House involvement in the burglary of the office of Daniel Ellsberg's psychiatrist in California. This last development brought the CIA back into Watergate.

Central to the Ellsberg burglary, of course, had been the activities of former CIA officer Howard Hunt. In the wake of the new developments, with Bill Colby attending to family matters, Director Schlesinger called in Colby's associate Cord Meyer. Hunt, now testifying before a federal grand jury and doing his best to squirm under questioning, had spoken of the help he got from the CIA. Schlesinger had not been at Langley the previous year, when Colby and Helms first waded through Watergate, and wanted to know what it was all about. Meyer undertook a review of the "Mr. Edwards" file, the dossier for Hunt's cover identity, finding in it the photographs of Ellsberg's psychiatrist's office. A CIA technician enlarged one of the photos, one that showed the psychiatrist's name. Though Colby had already given the pictures to the FBI, their significance now stood revealed. When Meyer informed the DCI, Schlesinger vented his wrath.

"What else have you people been hiding from me?" the CIA director rasped.[20]

Schlesinger soon went to a man he trusted, Bill Colby. In Bangkok on inspection, Colby read first about the Hunt burglary in the newspaper. He saw Schlesinger on returning. The DCI now wanted information on *any* action in the CIA's past, especially domestic activities, that might have flap potential. Colby consulted his management group and prepared a directive for Schlesinger to sign. The director, ready to fire anyone to get to the bottom of this affair, approved the order on May 9. All senior officials were to report immediately on any current or past agency matters that might fall outside CIA authority; anyone at the CIA could call Schlesinger's secretary (the directive gave her extension number) to record such activities; former employees could do the same; anyone at the CIA who received a questionable order should contact the director as well.

Schlesinger meanwhile limited the damage on the Hunt burglary with a statement to the CIA subcommittee of the Senate Appropriations committee. Later, Schlesinger was enraged to learn of letters he had also not been told of from Watergate defendant and former CIA man James McCord. "His anger over this had to be experienced to be believed," Colby writes, "and I experienced it, both barrels."[21] Another directive issued forth to reinforce the order of May 9.

By late May the CIA inspector general had a summary of the dubious activities that ran to more than twenty pages, but the full collection would eventually total 693. Among items judged to have flap potential were the CIA mail-opening program, surveillance of Americans within the United States, CIA infiltrations of political groups opposed to the Vietnam war, telephone wiretaps of American journalists, drug experiments on Americans, connections with organized crime (in particular during efforts to plan for the assassination of Cuban leader Fidel Castro), break-ins in American homes and offices, participation in the Nixon administration planning for an integrated approach by police and intelligence agencies and the Internal Revenue Service to combat antiwar opposition (the "Huston" plan, named after a White House aide), and other questionable projects. A CIA wag soon referred to the document as the "Family Jewels" and the name stuck.

Executive Director Colby was horrified by the collection of materials. For some years Colby had had indirect knowledge of the assassination plots against Fidel Castro. The inspector general's report of May 1967 to which Colby had access added considerable detail, documenting agency connections with organized crime figures in these plots. As Far East Division chief amid the controversial Vietnam war, Colby was in Washington when the CIA went into high gear with its operations against the antiwar opposition, and he could have learned of the creation of an agency project in this area. There is no evidence, however, that Colby knew of the various dirty tricks mentioned in the Family Jewels until the report was compiled in 1973. Colby would express disdain for the questionable activities in congressional testimony a few months later and would issue orders in August that prohibitions against these kinds of activities be incorporated into CIA regulations.

Meanwhile, on April 30, simultaneous with the resignations of White House officials Haldeman, Ehrlichman, and Dean, Attorney General Richard Kleindienst also resigned. Elliott Richardson, the secretary of defense, was named to succeed him. Shortly after Schlesinger signed the orders that resulted in the Family Jewels. Colby got a telephone call from freshly minted White House chief of staff Alexander M. Haig, Jr. General Haig told Bill that Jim Schlesinger would be appointed to succeed Richardson at the Pentagon. Richard Nixon wanted William E. Colby to be his next Director of Central Intelligence. Official confirmation reached Colby in a cable he received in Hong Kong, where he and deputy director Vernon Walters were on another leg of their Far East inspection trip. The cable arrived during a cocktail party at the home of station chief Charles Whitehurst. Told the news, euphoric CIA officers crowded around Bill with their congratulations. For the field men the news meant the directorship was coming back to a CIA professional. For Colby it was different: Watergate, with which he had wanted nothing to do, had brought him to the top post at the Central Intelligence Agency. Unfortunately for Bill Colby, the turbulence of Watergate represented only the beginning of a most difficult period.

14

THE TOP FLOOR

O N MAY 10, 1973, when Richard Nixon went before the press to an-
nounce changes at the top of his administration, William E. Colby
reached the apex of his career. Never daring to hope he might be director of
central intelligence, suddenly the seventh floor office at Langley became
Colby's own. The atmosphere at the agency changed perceptibly. Jim Schlesinger had expanded his office, taking over the adjoining conference room
called the French Room, which had separated the suites of the DCI and
DDCI. Colby's manner was egalitarian. The day after the announcement of
his appointment, Bill made a point of driving his own car to work as usual,
and rather than using the director's exclusive underground parking space and
private elevator, he put his car in the remote reaches of the employee area
and entered through the lobby's regular turnstile system. Periodically Colby
would also lunch in the employee cafeteria, inviting CIA junior officers to
his table for conversation. He inaugurated a retiree's day for former CIA
officers to visit and see how the agency had changed, and put Langley on
the itinerary for student groups coming to Washington. Colby established
reserved parking spaces for handicapped employees and programs to encourage minorities.

Paradoxically, a number of these measures contributed to the rise of antipathy toward Colby within the CIA, where older officers viewed them as
moving the agency away from its roots. But while Bill Colby's major problems at Langley still lay in the future, his more immediate difficulties were
in Congress, where the Senate had to approve his nomination as director of
central intelligence. Congress reflected the public concern over the CIA,
which, fueled by Watergate and the early revelations about the Chile operations, continued to grow.

The chance that nomination hearings could turn into a wide-ranging attack
on the CIA had to be avoided. Colby also felt the need to limit the damage
to the agency from Watergate as that scandal continued (it would drag on for

more than a year). Personally he wished to display a responsible attitude before Congress to preserve as much as possible of the formerly cozy relationship between the agency and its legislative overseers. At the moment of Colby's appointment what was happening was the Family Jewels. Colby and Schlesinger agreed the overseers needed to know about them. As a new appointee Colby would be making the rounds of key congressmen, providing an opportunity for private briefings on the CIA's new information.

First of the quiet contacts would be the chairman of the Senate's CIA subcommittee within Armed Services, John C. Stennis, a figure of enormous power who had been in the Senate for twenty-six years. Recovering at Walter Reed Army Medical Center from a minor heart ailment, Stennis, a circuit court judge for a decade before coming to Washington, felt the CIA's domestic entanglements ought to be kept out of public view. However, he sent Colby on to his vice-chairman, Missouri's Stuart Symington. The latter had been an official in the Truman administration when the CIA was created and had long been a supporter. Symington had concerns about the CIA in Watergate, and he had forced Richard Helms to go on the record on Chile, but he sided with Stennis on the Family Jewels. On the House side the Armed Services Committee chairman, F. Edward Hebert—a reporter and editor for twenty-three years, now a congressmen for thirty-three, steeped in the old ways—agreed the Family Jewels should be kept quiet. None of the three even examined the allegations in detail; all were satisfied with Colby's assurances that the CIA would be kept out of these activities in the future.

Langley's only difficulty arose with Lucien N. Nedzi, chairman of Hebert's CIA subcommittee. Nedzi represented a liberal district of Detroit bordering on Grosse Pointe, Michigan. Like Colby, a lawyer and Catholic, CIA domestic entanglements beyond Watergate troubled him. Appointed only recently to the subcommittee, Nedzi also wanted to be the new broom, willing to sweep away established practices. The CIA subcommittee chairman not only heard Colby out, he also asked to see the Family Jewels; he then sent questions demanding answers and finally wanted more specific CIA assurances. Nedzi also confronted Colby with the question the director-designate found hardest of all: why not make public the report? Colby argued that such an action might cripple the CIA, and Nedzi accepted that argument.

Judging from the account of these events in Colby's memoir, the Minnesotan never doubted the wisdom of holding back the Family Jewels in 1973. As will be seen presently, however, the appearance of material from the collection some eighteen months later would be *so* controversial it would lead to major investigations of the CIA, inflicting grievous wounds on the agency—indeed, ending Colby's intelligence career. Lucien Nedzi would also come under fire for not revealing the problematical CIA actions sooner. Moreover, in the interval, the 1974 elections would bring to Washington a "Watergate Congress," much more inclined to dispute decisions and prerogatives of the Executive.

A release of the Family Jewels in 1973, painful though it might have been, would have occurred in a more favorable political climate and at a time when the public agenda was crowded with Watergate-related issues. At a minimum the level of noise surrounding the CIA revelations would have been much higher, improving the chance that Langley's Family Jewels would have been lost in the cacophony.

A related aspect of this situation—difficult to appreciate today, when Washington is intensely partisan and the style of engagement is vicious—is the degree of comity that then existed. In not exhibiting much interest in the CIA's Family Jewels, Stennis, Symington, and Hebert followed norms long established; Nedzi's inspection was the exception. Intelligence oversight in 1973 was exercised with a light hand, if at all. One effect of Watergate and its revelations of abuses of power was to make suspect much of the interaction between the Executive, including the CIA, and Congress, leading to an erosion in bipartisan cooperation. Though the Vietnam war also contributed to that trend, the erosion would be a gradual process and any advantage would have lain in moving sooner, not later.

What Bill Colby's private briefings on the Family Jewels did achieve would be short term—a consensus that issues of CIA domestic activity would not be aired during his confirmation hearings before the Senate Armed Services Committee. Colby recalled the hearings as rough, but it was events surrounding the confirmation, not the process itself, which met that definition. Colby was harassed at his Brilley Place home by a late-night anonymous telephone caller. In the streets of Washington there were be posters, modeled on the "Wanted" posters of the notorious Phoenix program, with Colby's picture emblazoned on the icon of the Ace of Spades. His younger daughter had to listen to another caller's threat to get her father. Bill also thought about the death of Catherine. "I remember feeling, in a curiously mixed up way, that if . . . Catherine had to die, I was relieved that it had happened before these attacks began."[1]

By comparison Bill Colby's confirmation hearings were quite tame. They opened on July 2, 1973, with a session at which Stuart Symington was the only questioner. The Missouri senator pitched Colby some slow-ball questions about Vietnam—the worst of it on Phoenix—then led the nominee in a wide-ranging discourse on the CIA and the functions of intelligence. When opponents to the nomination appeared on July 20, only four senators attended the hearings and two of them left long before its end. Symington and Georgia's Sam Nunn went out of their way to discredit former CIA officers who appeared to testify on Colby in Vietnam and the CIA's order of battle estimates there and in Cambodia. Witnesses on the Phoenix program were also cut down to size by senators' aggressive questioning. Then Colby was given the opportunity to rebut his critics in a session five days later. The toughest moment concerned Watergate, not Vietnam, and came on July 25 when Senator Edward M. Kennedy grilled Colby on aspects of the CIA's involvement, especially his delay in bringing John Ehrlichman's name to the attention of investigators.

The committee reported the nomination out favorably, and the full Senate confirmed William E. Colby by a vote of 83 to 13. Colby appeared at the White House on September 4 to be sworn in as director of central intelligence at a ceremony before Barbara and the children, his father Elbridge, Jim Schlesinger, Henry Kissinger, Admiral Thomas Moorer of the Joint Chiefs of Staff, and others.

Now the CIA's reins were in Colby's hands. But along with the seventh floor suite at Langley came a host of problems for the DCI. In the next two years the worlds of intelligence, international affairs, and American politics intersected to create a thicket of difficulties any director would have had trouble wading through.

PLENTY REMAINED TO BE DONE at the Central Intelligence Agency as Bill Colby moved into the director's suite. The biggest ticket items were the machine spies, as Helms once dubbed them—technical programs for collecting information, which included reconnaissance satellites and aircraft, ground stations, ships at sea, and other mechanisms. As executive director under Helms, Colby had had his first exposure to the exotic world of collection in familiarization visits to the scientific and aerospace corporations where much of the engineering and development occurred. The CIA's own Directorate of Science and Technology performed a great deal of the design work, while construction supervision and operation of the systems was the province of the National Reconnaissance Office (NRO) and National Security Agency (NSA), military components of the intelligence community that consumed the biggest share of annual spending.

There were three programs of particular interest at the time. Two involved the NRO and NSA. During Helms's last year as director, the Nixon administration had given the go-ahead for a new generation photo satellite innocuously called the KH-11. American spy satellites were already very advanced, with capable imaging systems, but further improvements were possible. New cameras could make overhead photographs sharper, and infrared technology could give the satellites some capability even at night. Equally important, the main limiting factor in the past had been transmission of the pictures to the ground. The NRO had long used film capsules, miniature reentry vehicles that would fall through the atmosphere to be recovered. Not only were there dangers the capsules might not be snagged by the planes sent to capture them (which happened numerous times, especially in the early days), but the de-orbiting capsules might malfunction and be lost (which occurred at least twice). A major constraint was simply the number of film capsules that could be built into a satellite's payload. The KH-11 offered whole new vistas by means of a (then) novel process: pictures would be digitized using a matrix plus light-to-dark gradient numbers, then the picture could be directly "read out" by a ground station with radio. The production costs were huge, reportedly on the order of $1.8 billion. U.S. intelligence had never fielded a satellite so expensive. However, Colby shepherded the KH-

11 through development by the TRW and Lockheed corporations. First launched in 1974, the KH-11 would become the mainstay of NRO's overhead reconnaissance effort into the 1990s; even its follow-on would be an advanced KH-11 system rather than a wholly new technology.

Another type of satellite system was the kind dedicated to intercepting electronic emissions, the main work of the NSA. Here too a new and expensive system had been proposed called Argus. Addition of Argus costs with KH-11 seemed prohibitive; several interagency studies tried to refine the choices between the two. Cost increases for operating the satellites that NRO already had complicated the matter. A twelve-month delay in Argus development ensued. The issue was fought out in 1974 within the executive committee of the NRO, which Director Colby chaired. For a time the community position favored cancellation of KH-11 in favor of Argus, but Congress, horrified at its price tag, balked. After a late 1975 discussion at the National Security Council, Argus would be canceled instead.

Another major high-tech venture that degenerated into a well-publicized misfire thrust the new DCI into the kind of effort to extinguish media controversy that became depressingly familiar in Colby's time. This arose from the third of the high-tech programs: the CIA's ambitious effort to raise a sunken Russian submarine from the floor of the Pacific Ocean. The sub had foundered in the Central Pacific around February 1968. This boat, *K-129*, was of an older type, but it was a ballistic missile sub and the United States knew where it was. Potential intelligence payoffs included data on how the Russians fused their nuclear warheads, possibly also their nuclear-tipped torpedoes; Russian codes and communications equipment; documents and secret orders; plus general metallurgy and technical information. The U.S. Navy had pioneered deep submergence vehicles that could dive to great depths and the Navy had immediate interest in the submarine's recovery; but the CIA took over the program, Project Jennifer, at an early stage.

Conceived during Helms's tenure, Jennifer required creating an apparatus that could pick up large weighty objects, not just look at them. This hydraulic claw had to have a ship designed around it capable of hovering over a precise point on the ocean floor. Also necessary was a huge barge to hold the raised submarine; the barge had to be roofed to prevent Russian spy satellites from glimpsing what was afoot. Designing and constructing all these things in secrecy, training a crew to work them, and carrying out the actual recovery became a huge task. The CIA hired the Summa Corporation—owned by the reclusive billionaire Howard Hughes—to build its salvage ship, called the *Glomar Explorer*, and Lockheed Missiles and Space to design the barge. Construction of the *Glomar Explorer* began at a Chester, Pennsylvania, shipyard in 1971, to be completed in mid-1973. The vessel was homeported in Delaware.

In addition to a project staff for a front company, a subsidiary of Summa Corporation, the CIA hired 125 persons for the mission. An "A" crew would shake down the *Glomar*, sail to the site, and raise the sub. The "B" crew would disassemble the vessel, partly in an interior compartment, partly in the barge. The cover story seemed to be a natural—Howard Hughes was portrayed as wanting to mine manganese and other rare metals that were on the ocean floor in the form of nodules. Langley put over $500 million into the project, whose code name would later be changed to Zodiac; the actual raising operation was to be known as Matador, although the public continues to know it as Jennifer.

Keeping the secret became the hardest part of the effort. The Jennifer project was being developed as the Watergate investigation was going on, and staffers of Senator Sam Ervin's investigating committee, sent in search of material on Howard Hunt, visited the law firm representing him and also Howard Hughes. In the file room the staffers encountered records on Hughes that not only linked Summa's owner to the CIA but also identified *Glomar Explorer* and suggested that Hughes had used his cooperation in the CIA scheme to pressure the Nixon administration on other issues, from nuclear testing to tax abatement. Senator Ervin demanded—and got—a full-scale CIA briefing on Jennifer. Though Ervin pointedly insisted that none of his staff had security clearances nor would be subject to their strictures, there were no leaks from the Watergate committee.

Another chink in the secrecy began in the fall of 1973, about six weeks after Bill Colby took over the CIA. Reporter Seymour Hersh of the *New York Times* learned a little about Jennifer from a senior government official. A second hint came at a Washington dinner party in January 1974, but now Hersh's interlocutor went to Director Colby. By this time *Glomar* was preparing for her shakedown cruise, and Henry Kissinger's 40 Committee, the top authority on intelligence operations, had approval of the submarine recovery on its agenda. Colby met his lawyers and science advisers to figure out what to do and decided to take the bull by the horns. On February 1 his long black limousine pulled up in front of the newspaper's Washington offices and Colby met with Hersh and his editor. Downbeat and persistent, the DCI explained that Jennifer was a project in progress. He begged Hersh not only not to write about the project but not even to mention it to anyone. Hersh, who had originally seen Jennifer as an example of government waste, agreed not to pursue the story. Nailing down this agreement at a lunch in New York with the *Times*'s editorial board, on February 20 Colby took publisher Arthur O. Sulzberger aside to reiterate that talking about Jennifer could be as damaging as publishing its details. Sulzberger, Colby told a Kissinger deputy, was delighted to be trusted.

On June 5, 1974, burglars hit the Los Angeles offices of the Summa Corporation, making off with $68,000 in cash plus four cases of documents. Summa executives told the CIA the documents included a memo from a senior official to Hughes that outlined the Jennifer project. Langley panicked and set the FBI and the Los Angeles Police Department on notice to watch for the document. From one of those sources *Los Angeles Times* investigative reporters William Farr and Jerry Cohen heard of the CIA operation and began to feel around for information. So did freelance journalist James Phelan, who specialized in Hughes affairs and had lines into the *New York Times*. Sy Hersh, concentrating on Watergate, told Phelan when asked that he knew nothing about the CIA scheme. But in Los Angeles, where the burglars apparently tried to extort half a million dollars from Summa for return of the documents, the reporters continued to collect string. The documents, including the Jennifer memo, were never recovered.

In the meantime, in July the CIA made its try for the Russian sub, located about 1,700 miles northwest of Hawaii and under 16,000 feet of water. By dint of tremendous exertion the *Glomar*'s "A" crew, supervised by a senior CIA officer who went by the pseudonym "Blackjack," managed to catch the *K-129* in their deep sea claw. But the mechanism was damaged in the grappling phase, permitting the sub to shift and break apart about two-thirds of the way up. One of the nuclear missiles aboard *K-129* fell from the ship and would have been descending at a rate of eighty miles an hour when it hit bottom. The sailors on *Glomar*, terrified they would perish in a nuclear explosion, were ecstatic when nothing happened. The CIA was dejected because the part of the sub that broke off included the conning tower and portions in which they were most interested. Agency experts wanted to make another attempt, but because of strong ocean currents in these reaches of the Pacific, there was a window of only about three weeks each summer when a recovery would be possible. The repeat effort had to await the summer of 1975.

Before that could happen, on February 7, 1975, the *Los Angeles Times* printed the first story about Jennifer. Bill Colby launched an intensive effort to clamp down, convincing the Los Angeles newspaper to deemphasize its story, even though it printed more. Carl Duckett, Colby's deputy director for science and technology, followed up. Nevertheless a syndicated version of the first story circulated, as did a United Press International dispatch. However, Colby was able to get the *Los Angeles Times* to hold back, the *New York Times* not to print more than a digest of the Los Angeles story, and others, among them the *Washington Post*, the *Washington Star*, *Time*, *Newsweek*, *Parade*, three television networks, and National Public Radio, to steer clear.

By this time Sy Hersh had much more from the CIA as a condition for holding up his story. Colby's understanding with the *Times* allowed the paper to publish if any other media revealed the story, and on March 18 Jack Anderson discussed the CIA and the *Glomar Explorer* on his national radio show. The chickens of Langley's surveillance of Anderson, Mudhen, had come home to roost. Anderson called Jennifer a government boondoggle. The next morning the *New York Times* went with Sy Hersh's extensive article on the front page. Many other media followed suit.

The CIA still hoped to go forward with a 1975 recovery attempt, and on March 19 a White House meeting approved Colby's recommendation that the government should say nothing about the story. Extensive revelation brought an end to Jennifer's possibilities, however. The United States informed Russia that remains of some of its sailors had been buried at sea (in 1991 a film recording this event would be given to Moscow). The *Glomar Explorer* would spend twenty-five years in the Navy's mothball fleet and then be sold off. No one mined manganese from the ocean floor.

THE CENTRAL INTELLIGENCE AGENCY'S traditional function of espionage continued to concern Bill Colby, a concern that had grown with him since his return from Vietnam. The clandestine service put its heart into espionage, and that culture within the CIA became ever more dominant as the Vietnam war wound down and the agency pared back its knuckle-dragging paramilitary experts. Beginning with his stint as executive director, Colby had labored steadily on these issues.

Always a major CIA focus, the hard target communist countries remained difficult to penetrate. The clandestine service compensated by increasing its commitment. This did not merely involve the Soviet Bloc Division of the DO, or as it would be recast, the Soviet and Eastern Europe Division. From the 1960s on, a portion of the resources of *every* CIA station, no matter where it was located, had been used against Russian diplomats and intelligence officers in those countries. Behind the Iron Curtain and in the world at large the idea of recruiting Russians (and Chinese or Vietnamese) as agents, or spies who could report on the Russians, remained uppermost in clandestine service minds. Translating that intention into action would always be the problem.

Much of the Directorate of Operations's effort went into observing the opposition. Identifying the Russian intelligence officers in each embassy, tracking the patterns of their movement and social activity, their interests, and their contacts became the key preoccupation. A certain amount of this effort was indispensable—the CIA *had* to know who it was up against and how good they were. But Colby began to feel that much of this was wasted motion, concentrated on methodology instead of substance. Massive effort could be put into gathering background information on some Russian when it could have gone into real spying with more profitable results. More often than not, after all the background, the actual recruitment attempt would be made out of the blue, "cold" in the jargon, with no knowledge of the subject's predisposition or intentions. As far back as when Colby headed the Far East Division, the embarrassment that ensued from an attempted recruitment in Tokyo by CIA officer David Murphy had shown graphically the dangers of the cold approach. As executive director, Colby had proselytized for substance in place of preliminaries; as DCI, he could do something about it.

Colby's own method of agent recruiting had always been simply social—to meet people, become acquainted with them, know them better, and develop a relationship over time. Then the recruitment question could be popped with some idea of the response. With this approach, the prospective agent also started off with more trust in his CIA handlers. The personal relationship approach is what Director Colby emphasized—after the war stories from France, Norway, and Vietnam—when he addressed classes of CIA trainees at Camp Peary, the clandestine service's main center for junior officer training near Williamsburg, Virginia.

Another expenditure of resources that Colby viewed as a distraction from the business of espionage was the meddling of Angleton's Counterintelligence Staff. In Angleton's zeal to protect the agency from penetration by the opposition, every proposed recruitment, before being attempted, had been reviewed by his staff for the possibility of an enemy trap. Many initiatives had been disapproved because of that danger. Not only had Angleton tied the CIA in knots with his internal witch-hunts, he had also had a negative impact on the foreign intelligence mission. Colby had been surprised when James Schlesinger refused his advice to fire Angleton in the purge of 1973 but had determined to do something about it if he ever became director himself.

Now Colby *was* the director. He invited Angleton up from the staff's second floor den of thieves and the two had several long conversations. Bill listened to Angleton's intricate theories of Russian intelligence manipulation, which held that Russian state policy, even the bitter Russian-Chinese feud, was no more than a deception designed to lull the West, and the CIA in particular, into complacency while the Kremlin placed spies everywhere. Colby found Angleton's arguments convoluted, a serpentine rendering of every event as part of a huge conspiracy. As Colby believed the primary task of counterintelligence was to place the CIA's own spies within the Russian intelligence apparatus, he asked Angleton what his staff had done to fulfill this goal. He learned that the CIA had no such agents. As Director Colby saw it, the Counterintelligence Staff had never caught a spy within the CIA and had never placed any in the enemy camp. At the same time, Angleton's staff was isolated at Langley, walled off from the Soviet Division and the others as a result of mutual suspicion.

Despite these considerations, Director Colby came down the same way as had Schlesinger on the choice of whether to fire Jim Angleton. Battered by Watergate and Chile, the CIA needed stability above all; getting rid of Angleton would only create more turmoil. Colby rued his decision soon afterward. The DCI chanced to learn that one good CIA officer had languished for years in an out-of-the-way post, though no evidence could be found against him, simply because the Counterintelligence Staff, eliminating other possibilities, had decided he must be the person referred to by a Russian defector who said his service was in contact with a CIA person abroad. Then Colby heard from an official of French intelligence that the CIA's station chief in Paris, the same David Murphy who had been involved in the Tokyo incident of 1966, was a Russian spy. This tip had reached the French from Angleton. Shocked, Bill reviewed Murphy's entire file, discovering that the Counterintelligence Staff had actually investigated Murphy and cleared him, but Angleton seemingly had not accepted that result. Director Colby personally added a memorandum to Murphy's file saying he had reviewed it and had full confidence in the man, then told the French all suspicions about the station chief had long been resolved. Colby concluded that Angleton was getting in the way of foreign intelligence operations and that he had to get counterespionage into line.

Previous orders to remove Angleton from the chain of command for CIA activities in Israel also had never been implemented. Only a month after Colby took his oath as DCI, the Middle East erupted in the fierce October War of 1973. Israeli intelligence failed to predict the Arab attacks that launched the conflict. Angleton, with his cozy contacts with the Israelis, had followed their cue. Moreover, since Angleton handled the Israeli account as a tightly compartmented operation, some of the relevant intelligence never reached the CIA's own analysts. Angleton had used every argument already to dissuade Colby from taking him off the Israeli liaison mission, but the October War made it clear that existing arrangements could not be continued. In the spring of 1974, Director Colby redrew the boundaries so that the CIA station in Israel reported through the DO's own Near East and South Asia Division. He hoped Angleton would see that as a hint and take early retirement under the provisions of the agency's modified retirement act, which afforded generous benefits to those who left the agency before the end of June. But Jim Angleton stayed on; there would be one more round to the Colby-Angleton struggle.

There remained the question of making the Directorate of Operations (DO) get out there and actually line up some spies. The Soviet Division, paralyzed so utterly for so long, needed special attention. Director Colby found himself summoning its officers for pep talks, a gathering of spies equivalent to a top-secret rally before the Super Bowl. As would a coach, Colby told the players to get out there and try. Answering the inevitable comment cautioning the DO audience that recruiters had to answer to the Counterintelligence Staff, Bill encouraged the field officers to pay no heed. This DCI far preferred harvesting a few bad apples with the crop to leaving them all on the ground for fear some were rotten.

In other words, William E. Colby was prepared to accept that the CIA might mistakenly recruit a few double agents really working for the Russians, if that meant the CIA could have high-level sources in the hard-target countries. Taking counterintelligence out of the recruiting loop would later be characterized as expecting every DO person to be her own counterintelligence officer. In the 1990s, after the depredations of CIA turncoat Aldrich Ames, who became a true Russian penetration of Langley, Colby would be derided for his attitude. Because of Ames, a dozen top CIA agents were executed in Russia and more were neutralized. Espionage without counterintelligence seemed absurd. But by then the CIA had a different environment—military jargon would have called it "target rich"—with many potential recruits among Russians who were disillusioned or on the make. In the 1970s the DCI faced the opposite problem: the CIA could hardly figure out whom to recruit, because DO officers were working with Counterintelligence breathing down their backs and had constantly in mind the examples of their colleagues brought down by shadows of suspicion. Bill Colby had been subjected to the inquisition himself and could readily appreciate how counterproductive it was.

Already, in the brief months Colby spent heading the DO before his move to the top floor at Langley, he had been pushing at the envelope constricting espionage. Reaching back to his Far East Division experience, Colby had inaugurated a grading system to evaluate output throughout the clandestine service. With a more explicit track record, the divisions could see they needed better spies. The effort began to bear fruit while Colby was director of central intelligence. The CIA successfully recruited spies among Russian diplomats in Latin America, Africa, and at the United Nations, as well as significant agents among the Russian military. There were sources in the Chinese leadership as well, though sketchy knowledge of things Chinese and the immense dislocations wrought by China's Cultural Revolution kept the CIA from understanding much of what had gone on.

In general, the United States has never been satisfied with the quality of its espionage take, now termed "human intelligence" in the jargon. Virtually every review of performance from the 1950s until today, whether internal to CIA, communitywide, carried out by congressional overseers, or presidential advisory boards, has stressed the need for better human intelligence. Bill Colby did not solve the human intelligence conundrum, but he did get the Central Intelligence Agency back on track in the espionage field. His successors would benefit from Colby's efforts.

THE ESSENTIAL AIM of all CIA work is to provide support to policy makers. For a long time this had meant the White House and executive branch of government, though by the 1970s Congress was becoming an increasingly important consumer of intelligence. For the most part the CIA's knowledge was imparted in the form of reports and estimates, analyses of the world outside, and Langley maintained a full Directorate of Intelligence (DI) to craft these papers. Colby had long watched the DI analysts from afar; as director, for the first time, he had responsibility for them. As director of central intelligence, Colby also had responsibility for the national estimates, the signature product of the intelligence community, which represented the distillation of the community's knowledge about the subject of the estimate. These draft papers went before the community's top interagency committee, the United States Intelligence Board, which Bill Colby chaired in his capacity as DCI; but the estimates were his papers and Colby could force revisions in them if he so chose. In the field of analysis and estimates, as in so much else, great changes occurred during Bill Colby's time on the top floor at Langley.

As befitted this era of the Cold War, the man in charge of the DI in Colby's time was a specialist on Russia. Appointed by Richard Helms in 1971, Edward W. Proctor had led a band of CIA economists who, in their efforts to determine how much Russia spent on its military, had constructed a building-block model of the Russian economy. Their work, beginning to come under attack in the mid-1970s, had been so highly regarded at the time that the unit became the nucleus of the Office of Strategic Research, which the DI created in 1967. Proctor himself became assistant to the deputy director for intelligence. Thin and wiry, with a penchant for broad statements that nevertheless cut to the core issues, Proctor recognized his strengths and limitations. His knowledge of Russia was a strength, of course, but Proctor knew almost nothing about Southeast Asia, and analyzing the Vietnam war remained a major DI task at the time he took over. Ed Proctor solved this problem with a practical division of labor: while he handled most DI business, he delegated Vietnam work primarily to Paul V. Walsh of the Office of Economic Research.

Proctor's choice proved an uncomfortable one when Bill Colby took over the CIA. Colby had been in Vietnam with CORDS when Langley and General Abrams's MACV command sparred over how much of their supplies the North Vietnamese and Viet Cong got through Cambodian seaports as opposed to down the Ho Chi Minh Trail. Colby had sided with MACV, disagreeing with the CIA's analysis that minimized the role of Cambodia, in a study that had been directed by Paul Walsh and supervised by Proctor's then-boss, Jack Smith. Records uncovered when the United States invaded Cambodia in 1970 demonstrated that MACV had been closer to the truth than the CIA. But Proctor had protected Walsh. When Bill Colby took over the director's suite he had no quarrel with Proctor, but some doubts about Walsh.

In actuality Bill Colby's watching brief over CIA analysis had long revolved around Vietnam. During McCone's tenure as DCI there had been the notorious case of the 1963 National Intelligence Estimate (NIE), when Colby and others were interviewed to soften a pessimistic CIA analysis of trends in the war. Colby had also differed from the CIA's analytical view of the prospects for Ngo Dinh Diem. In the middle and later stages of the war the DI had been consistently pessimistic about trends in Vietnam and the effectiveness of bombing the North, analyses which by 1973 had been shown to be correct, if not exactly palatable to activists bent on fighting the war. It is a credit to Colby that despite his discomfort with the DI's analysis, he did little to change the directorate. Colby even remained mute when Ed Proctor promoted Paul Walsh to become his own assistant director.

What Colby did do was change CIA products. The weekly *Central Intelligence Bulletin* lacked immediacy and impact, the DCI believed. Colby advocated a newspaper-like publication; indeed, he had recommended such a thing as early as 1953 to DCI Allen Dulles. Now Colby had the power and used it to create the *National Intelligence Daily*, an essential CIA publication that endured for decades. Colby joked that with the entire intelligence community for a staff and highly secret status, the *Daily* was the best-appointed but worst-advertised newspaper in the world. Both the *Daily* and its twin, the even more highly classified *President's Daily Brief*, fared poorly in the Nixon White House, with the president uninterested and Henry Kissinger disputing items and delegating the work of keeping up with the material to subordinates on his National Security Council staff. When Gerald R. Ford succeeded Nixon as president of the United States, Kissinger's attitude remained the same, while Ford preferred oral presentations as a way to absorb information.

No matter what the outside reactions, Colby fully supported his publications program, especially the *National Intelligence Daily* (*NID*), which he considered a sort of CIA flagship journal. Every day he was in Washington, no matter what his major concerns, Colby made a point of seeing the NID editors to find out what they expected to feature for the next morning. Often these sessions came at the dinner hour—seven or eight in the evening. John H. Hedley, a thirty-year agency veteran who worked on the NID, recalled that Colby always came to them, not the other way around, even though the DCI could easily have demanded that they come up to the seventh floor or consulted them by phone. Hedley saw Colby's behavior as a thoughtful gesture, much like his parking in the junior officers' lot, which he continued to do. And despite the rough handling Colby had gotten on Capitol Hill and elsewhere, he was invariably pleasant and calm.

At Langley there were some who thought this was a "new" Bill Colby, a changed man, a gentler man than he had been before. Some who had dealt with Colby at the Far East Division, like Ralph McGehee, remembered a different fellow from those times. "He was . . . a lot meaner and nastier [then], and a lot dirtier," one of the old hands told journalist John Ranelagh. "A prick. Colby changed quite a lot. . . . The Colby I knew in the agency was a real sonofabitch."[2] The years as pacification boss in South Vietnam had brought the agents of change for Colby. These were the years when Bill had had to sell a program plus the notion of progress to a skeptical public as well as endure the ordeal of defending the Phoenix program against its critics. His family traumas completed the process. Colby's perception of the CIA as embattled also sensitized him as never before to the need for leaders to rally the troops. Others believed Colby had always been genteel.

Colby and the CIA brought forth fresh initiatives. One would be at the Office for Economic Research, set up in the DI to handle a subject of increasing importance to the United States. At the end of January 1973 the assistant to the president for economic affairs, Peter G. Peterson, had penned a scathing critique of intelligence support for America's international economic policy. Collection of data remained scattered throughout government, Peterson observed, with both collection and its analysis dispersed in parochial departments and no early warning capacity. The oil crisis and huge price hikes that followed the October War, when the Arab countries embargoed petroleum exports to the West, underlined Peterson's contentions. Director Colby responded by focusing a new DI unit on the economic challenge.

An event of 1974 sparked another Colby innovation. That July Greek forces on the Mediterranean island of Cyprus, which Greeks shared with a Turkish minority, overthrew the insular government, and a few days later Turkish troops invaded as well, upsetting a delicate but long-standing balance of power. Cyprus had forever been a headache in international relations and a sore point between Greece and Turkey, thus a continuing subject for intelligence observation. There had been items in the NID regarding Greek intentions as well as other reports, which Washington did not take sufficiently seriously to dissuade the Greeks from upsetting the applecart. In CIA postmortems, because there *were* some intelligence reports, people could dispute whether the U.S. government had been warned of these developments. Colby, activated by Cyprus, spurred by the advent of the October War, revamped the CIA's warning system. Colby instituted the device of the "Alert Memorandum," a paper that would furnish specific warning of an impending event. In future crises, went the idea, one need only go to the file to see whether an Alert memo had been issued to determine whether the U.S. government had had warning. As with several other Colby innovations, this continues to be the system in the U.S. intelligence community. An Alert memorandum issued in 1990 just before Iraq's invasion of Kuwait that August, is a prominent recent example but not the only one.

Another innovation at the DI would be formation of an Office of Political Research. This office enabled the CIA to compile extensive profiles of social and political movements, foreign leaders, and so on, combining Langley's increasing computer resources with expert analysts. Ed Procter and Bill Colby pooled resources for the unit, with the deputy director giving up a special research staff he had maintained within his office, and the DCI contributing the staff previously known as the Office of National Estimates, which had compiled the National Intelligence Estimates (NIEs).

Director Colby's most enduring innovation on the analytical side of the CIA lay precisely in his abolition of the Office of National Estimates, a drafting unit, and its supervisers, the Board of National Estimates (BNE). At various times the BNE and its drafters had been located in the DCI's office; at other times they had been creatures of the Directorate of Intelligence. But since 1950, they had always been responsible for writing the National Intelligence Estimates that constituted definitive judgments by U.S. intelligence.

The NIEs had come under attack early in the Nixon administration. Estimates on Russia, especially those on Russian nuclear forces and new weapons developments, had been particular targets of the Pentagon. Kissinger had called the estimates "talmudic,"[3] often differed with them, and used the NIEs only when they suited his purposes. On Vietnam, Nixon stopped asking for overall assessments of trends altogether; the administration requested only the more limited Special National Intelligence Estimates (SNIEs) on issues of immediate interest. In general, both the NIEs and the SNIEs were represented as bland, full of watered-down judgments, and submerging the views of agencies other than the CIA.

At one time membership on the board or a post at the Office of National Estimates had been seen as the apex of an analyst's career. But the BNE had largely stopped appointing members from outside the CIA (the breadth of membership had once been a strength); by 1973 it seemed to have become a pool of senior staff positions for DI careerists. Because BNE handled all subjects, members needed broad general knowledge, but some were considered too specialized in focus. Under Abbott E. Smith from 1968 to 1971, the board was also accused of failing to consult specialists, even those in the Directorate of Intelligence, on the subjects it was working. Smith's successor, John Huizenga, had made improvements, but there was still general agreement that the BNE had no access to the senior officials it was supposed to be serving and therefore was not capable of furnishing real insight to the harried men (there were no women at the time) who sat in the Cabinet Room of the White House to hammer out U.S. policy.

Even before Colby, Jim Schlesinger wanted to do something about the NIEs. At his first meeting with the board, Schlesinger had remarked, "I understand this is like a gentlemen's club. Well, I want you to know that I am no gentleman."[4] Except for important technical subjects, the DCI ordered, national estimates were to be no more than four pages long. But before there had been too much wailing and moaning Schlesinger was gone. It fell to Bill Colby to deal with this matter.

Director Colby knew of Schlesinger's concern as well as that of Nixon and Kissinger, though he insisted later the revamp had been purely internal to CIA and he had never consulted either the president or the national security adviser. The fixed positions of these analysts would lead to trouble, Colby felt. John Huizenga fought him, arguing that abolition of the corporate BNE would compromise the independence of the NIEs. Colby, of course, chaired the United States Intelligence Board (USIB), which reviewed national estimates for the community once they had been scrubbed by the board, and believed himself perfectly capable of safeguarding the quality of the papers. Moreover the NIEs were *his* papers; he could choose how he wanted them prepared. The Board of National Estimates at this time had also become especially vulnerable in another way: retirements had reduced BNE to half its normal size. Colby would have to appoint new people or change the system; he choose the latter. Huizenga resigned.

For a fresh approach, Bill Colby turned to someone he knew well. This was George Carver, his one-time case officer in Saigon. As he had been for seven years, Carver was the DCI's special assistant for Vietnam affairs. The job involved Carver in intelligence reporting but also in advice for the director, monitoring collection on his subject, and even things like early aspects of the Phoenix program. This kind of wide-ranging role had impressed

DCI Schlesinger, who appointed another special assistant to deal with the Middle East. The arrangement suited Colby also; when the time came to do something about the Board of National Estimates, Bill asked George whether that sort of special effort could not be extended to cover the entire globe. Enthusiastic as always, Carver encouraged Colby. When the DCI abolished the Board of National Estimates in October 1973, he made Carver the head of a sort of union of special assistants.

Thus was born the system of National Intelligence Officers (NIOs). Like the old special assistant, the NIO would have broad scope and work in the office of the director of central intelligence. The NIOs had specific subject areas: Southeast Asia; Northeast Asia; China; the Middle East; Russia; strategic forces; Western Europe; Latin America; Africa. Some areas were functional ones: strategic forces, conventional forces, energy, special projects, and economics. George Carver became deputy to the DCI for national intelligence. His former second, William Christisen, would be the initial NIO for Southeast Asia. Director Colby sent another subtle signal to Jim Angleton by making much-maligned DO officer David Murphy the NIO for special projects, with a watching brief over his former directorate, including the Counterintelligence Staff. Evelyn Colbert, from the State Department's intelligence unit, as NIO for Northeast Asia became the first woman to reach this exalted level in the community. James Lilley, a DO officer whom Colby had known in Laos, was an old China hand and would take the China portfolio. James Critchfield, formerly Middle East division head and chief of station in Saudi Arabia, became NIO for energy. A professional economist, Robert Slighton, would be the NIO for economics until he left for a top job at the Chase Manhattan Bank.

Director Colby made a genuflection to the old Board of National Estimates by holding over two of its members plus two of its old drafting staff as NIOs. Prominent among these was Office of National Estimates staffer Howard Stoertz, who became the NIO for strategic forces. Conscious of the Pentagon's sensitivity about the national estimates process, George Carver made a deal with the chairman of the Joint Chiefs of Staff, Admiral Thomas H. Moorer, that the NIO posts for strategic and conventional forces would be shared between civilian and military intelligence. Thus Stoertz got an Air Force colonel as his deputy, and the NIO for conventional forces would be Rear Admiral Daniel Bergin. The task of the NIO for strategic forces was extremely complex; and additionally, Stoertz also held the job of intelligence adviser to the U.S. negotiating team on arms control, and so he was often absent in Europe. Therefore, this NIO also had a second assistant, CIA man Robert Gates, who one day would become director of central intelligence in his own right.

A major advantage of the old Board of National Estimates that the NIO system lacked was its sense of collegiality. Carver tried to inject a little of that sense into his group by having no formal deputy and instead rotating that job at six-month intervals among the NIOs. Meanwhile the NIOs, though they reported direct to Colby, usually informed Carver as a courtesy. Carver made a deliberate effort to prevent the NIOs from drafting national estimates themselves. Each was given just one assistant plus a secretary. The NIOs were supposed to identify the analyst in the community best qualified to write up an NIE for drafting; then that person would be assigned temporarily to the NIO's office for the job. Of course, agency heads often wanted to protect their best people, which meant Director Colby sometimes had to browbeat them into agreeing with the temporary reassignments. The NIOs could also go entirely outside the intelligence community if the best person was to be found there. Thus the first draft of the 1975 NIE on Russian nuclear forces was written by a military analyst, and the 1976 draft by one from the Rand Corporation.

To complete the integration of the NIO system into the intelligence community, in June 1974 Director Colby made some changes in the United States Intelligence Board (USIB), making the NIO for special projects a member of a new USIB committee for Human Intelligence. The experiment worked so well that that December Colby effected more extensive changes in the entire structure of USIB committees. Under his authority to appoint members to those committees, many of the national intelligence officers now took seats at the table. Colby also gave George Carver the right to put items on the agendas for USIB committee meetings.

In addition Director Colby used the NIOs to help him redefine the way the community set requirements for data collection. The DCI began by compiling a paper, quietly using the opinions of the national intelligence officers, which set down his impressions of the vital subjects intelligence ought to be engaged with. This went beyond the long-established system for setting priority national intelligence objectives, which Colby believed had degenerated into a paper exercise. The paper went to the USIB agencies for their suggestions and amendments. The director then set about reducing the entire exchange to a set of simple questions. When some CIA gossip labeled the things "kicks," acronym-speak for Key Intelligence Questions (KIQs), the DCI adopted that very name. But the KIQs also could become a paper exercise—whereas Colby and the USIB agreed on 69 KIQs for the fiscal year 1975, the Pentagon issued its own Defense Key Intelligence Questions and came up with more than a thousand. In any case, the KIQs served as a vehicle for the community to focus on what resources would be devoted to each subject, and Colby then had the NIOs evaluate how well the USIB agencies were doing. The National Security Agency compiled the best record—about half its operations and maintenance budget for 1975 and almost three quarters of its requirements related to the KIQs. The Defense Intelligence Agency talked about KIQs but did not orient its programs to help answer them. Data on the National Reconnaissance Office remains classified, but Colby's difficulties in the collection field are suggested by the fact that he decided to add that NIO for special programs.

With Director Colby heavily involved in managing the intelligence community as a whole, the ceremonial functions of the DCI, necessary participation at National Security Council and other White House meetings, and appearances before Congress—Colby testified on more than sixty occasions during two years as DCI—he had relatively little time for the substance of intelligence analysis. Colby acknowledged later that the NIOs had never reached their full potential as management assistants, but they had nevertheless proved invaluable as managers and interpreters of information. Colby would be told of crucial developments or disputes coming down the pike and could get ready for them.

Intelligence on Russian weapons programs remained a vital subject, and Howard Stoertz readily demonstrated the worth of the NIOs. As an expert, Stoertz knew where the knowledge lay, both within the intelligence community and the wider world of aerospace. Given the realm of what was knowable, not all disputes could be resolved, but staffers like Stoertz could at least point the way forward. A good illustration is the Russian Tupolev Tu-22M, a bomber known to Washington as the Backfire. The characteristics of this jet aircraft were debated, and the differences became important in Washington's negotiations with Moscow on limiting nuclear forces.

In the late 1950s Howard Stoertz had been secretary to the Board of National Estimates at the time of the "Missile Gap," a notorious quarrel over whether Moscow led the United States in intercontinental ballistic missiles (it never did). That fracas had immediately followed a similar argument about Russian progress in long-range bombers. Moscow had stopped building bombers at that time, and, ever since, the United States had anticipated the emergence of a new Russian strategic bomber. In actuality the Russians deployed or developed several types of medium bombers in the 1960s but never a new heavy bomber. In early 1969 the NRO's spy satellites photographed a large, unidentified airplane outside a plant in the Russian city of Kazan, and intelligence decided the craft was a supersonic medium bomber. The Backfire first flew in the spring of 1970 and entered production during 1973.

By this time U.S. intelligence had become less, not more, certain of the Backfire's capabilities. Larger than previous Russian medium bombers but much less capable than the U.S. B-52, Backfire could nevertheless carry as much as the Russian heavy bombers of the 1950s. A key question became how far it could fly; if it had a long enough range it would be the equivalent of a strategic bomber, with the United States its potential target. Air Force intelligence insisted that the Backfire could be used for intercontinental attacks and should be counted as a strategic weapon. Langley's experts thought not, and through 1973 the Defense Intelligence Agency (DIA) agreed. The CIA and DIA went along with a compromise judgment in the 1971 national estimate but the consensus soon evaporated. By the time Bill Colby became director of central intelligence a battle royal over Backfire was in progress.

National Intelligence Officer Stoertz gathered the intelligence analysts but could not iron out the differences. Stoertz then went to Colby and recommended that the CIA hire outside aeronautical engineers as consultants for

a study that would use data from the different intelligence agencies to pos-
tulate the capabilities of an aircraft with those characteristics. Colby approved. The prime contractor would be McDonnell Douglas Aircraft in St.
Louis (now part of the Lockheed Martin Corporation), employing teams both
there and in California. The British aerospace industry and Royal Air Force
were asked for parallel studies. Intelligence information, furnished without
attribution, led to quite different conclusions: engineers in St. Louis decided
the Backfire's range had to be between 3,500 and 5,000 miles; those in California, working with DIA data, estimated a 4,500 to 6,000-mile range. The
British study supported the higher estimate, a paper compiled at CIA the
lower one.

Director Colby brought the issue to the National Security Council (NSC)
on January 29, 1975, remarking that the Backfire medium bomber (Colby
used that description) could now be entering service with operational medium
bomber units and that the plane could "cover the entire United States on a
one-way mission."[5] On July 25 he told the NSC that Backfire's range seemed
comparable to that of the older existing Russian jet heavy bomber called
Bison. (Most of the detail in this discussion remains classified.) By early
August the NSC discussions of Backfire had become generalized and the
subject came up at almost every meeting concerned with Russian-American
negotiation on nuclear weapons. On August 9 Colby told the NSC that "the
intelligence community differs on this issue."[6] On September 17 he used a
chart to show the degree of confidence within the community that proposed
collateral constraints to limit the Backfire could be verified. On December
22 Colby briefed the NSC on the most recent national estimate, remarking
that intelligence believed the Backfire could be used in strategic attacks
against the United States, but with the exceptions of Army and Air Force
intelligence and the DIA, "we believe it is likely that Backfires will be used
for missions in Europe and Asia, and for naval missions over the open seas."[7]

At a summit conference in Helsinki in July 1975, the United States directly
confronted Russian leaders with the intelligence on Backfire developed at the
CIA and elsewhere. Russian leader Leonid Brezhnev responded with his own
briefing on the capabilities of the bomber; he maintained the aircraft was no
strategic bomber. It was the first time Russian leaders had openly discussed
the characteristics of any of their weapons systems. Eventually, in 1979, the
Russians made certain unilateral commitments restricting this bomber during
signing of an arms limitation treaty at another summit in Vienna. This laid
the issue to rest, though by then Bill Colby had left the CIA.

The debate over the Backfire bomber, which ranged through national intelligence estimates over several years, shows how contentious the NIEs
could be. In fact, both publicly and at the secret level, the NIEs came under
attack during this same period. Publicly, Rand Corporation defense analyst
Albert K. Wohlstetter published a series of articles that maintained the NIEs
on Russian nuclear forces had systematically underestimated the pace of Russian missile deployment through the late 1960s. Secretly, based on this and

other criticisms, the President's Foreign Intelligence Advisory Board (PFIAB) specifically criticized the 1974 NIE, later setting up a panel to evaluate the intelligence estimates. One PFIAB member compiled a much more pessimistic alternative NIE. In August 1975 the board asked the president to order an experiment in "competitive" analysis under which an independent group would be asked to write an estimate and its paper compared with the formal NIE. In September, PFIAB officials met at Langley with George Carver, Howard Stoertz, and his deputy, Air Force Colonel Raymond DeBruler, pressing their demand for the competitive estimate.

Constantly sensitive to these issues, Bill Colby had innovated his national intelligence officer system precisely to offset criticisms of an inbred, isolated Ivory Tower of CIA analysts. When the Wohlstetter critique appeared in 1974 he had thought it devastating and asked subordinates for comment. Not satisfied with the responses, Colby had gone along when NIO Stoertz asked that an analyst from outside CIA prepare the initial draft of the following year's national estimate. But in 1974 he argued to the president that the substantive areas about which the president's advisory board complained were already among his key intelligence questions. In 1975 Colby similarly defended his estimating process in lengthy memoranda to both PFIAB's chairman and to the president. Colby could not see how an ad hoc group of outsiders could create a considered estimate with the quality and depth of the intelligence community's own product.

Director Colby won that battle in 1975, but he would be gone not long after. A year later the competitive experiment went ahead, carried out by a "Team B" of former officials, defense analysts, and scientists. The report they produced would not really be an NIE at all but a blunderbuss attack on every objectionable point they could find in estimates stretching far back into the 1960s. The arguments about Russian intentions and capabilities in Team B's report have themselves been shown by history to be highly distorted, but the exercise helped bias U.S. intelligence for years, not least because of the diligence of some Team B members at publicizing their views. Bill Colby did well to resist this exercise, something for which he has been given little credit.

Meanwhile, as the fight over the Russian estimates continued, a real battle came to its climax and end in Vietnam, an engagement with which William E. Colby had been so intimately associated. Oddly enough, in a memoir replete with commentary about Vietnam, Colby could spare only two paragraphs for the inglorious end of that war. Nevertheless, as it had all along, the Central Intelligence Agency had much to do with the end of the Vietnam conflict.

IN THE AFTER YEARS, Bill Colby would look back on the Vietnam war as a victory that was lost. To sustain that view Colby pointed to the success of pacification, but he never addressed the issue of the level of warfare and the conflict the United States was prepared to fight. Early on, American capability stood ready for conventional warfare while the National Liberation Front struggled for the villages. During the period of Vietnamization, Bill Colby and Creighton Abrams retooled the U.S. war effort to conduct pacification, but the American withdrawals cued Hanoi that it could essentially wait on the sidelines for Washington's exit and then settle accounts with Saigon. Hanoi's response to pacification would be a shift to conventional warfare. Nine months after Colby left Vietnam the North Vietnamese launched a massive conventional offensive that Saigon, backed by U.S. airpower, stopped only with difficulty. Kissinger and Nixon negotiated a peace accord signed at Paris in January 1973 that brought to an end the U.S. combat role in Vietnam.

Nixon briefly used American air forces during the spring of 1973 to signal Hanoi that its continued use of the Ho Chi Minh Trail to infiltrate troops and equipment to the South was not acceptable; but that spring and summer, restrictions passed by the U.S. Congress made it impossible to repeat this maneuver. The Vietnam war sputtered on as a contest between Hanoi and Saigon. In 1973 and 1974 the northerners funneled more supplies than ever down the Trail. Saigon, meanwhile, had passed the apogee of its military capability during the 1972 campaign, and slowly lost ground against the North Vietnamese.

Langley's view of all this became increasingly somber. A March 1973 CIA intelligence memorandum pointed out that while South Vietnamese troop strength remained greater overall, without the United States the South lacked the airlift and helicopter capability to maintain mobility. Moreover, in the I Corps area, Saigon maintained equivalent force only by committing the bulk of its paratroops and marines, leaving the general reserves largely denuded. The October War and consequent Arab oil embargo had the perverse effect in Vietnam of multiplying the cost to Saigon of keeping its war effort going, soaking up a considerable portion of U.S. military aid. The North Vietnamese further complicated the situation by a successful attack on Saigon's main ammunition storage depot, destroying a huge amount of munitions expensive to replace. Documents captured in late 1973 indicated that Hanoi had resolved on a series of strategic raids for the following year.

One of the early national intelligence estimates supervised by NIO William Christisen, in October 1973, concluded that the North Vietnamese believed they should return to the battlefield and that the rate of infiltration might turn the situation to Hanoi's advantage by mid-1974. A joint study by the CIA and the State Department in April 1974 then found the Vietnam situation to be a stalemate. A month later another national estimate predicted that Hanoi would mount no major offensive that year or in the first half of 1975. The Defense Intelligence Agency objected to that judgment and put a footnote in the NIE declaring there were at least even odds for a Hanoi attack in 1975. While the NIE's prediction on the fact of an offensive proved wrong (and DIA's correct), the national estimate did observe that Saigon would find it difficult to survive such an attack without U.S. airpower, and that at a minimum, large-scale U.S. logistic support would be necessary. The national estimate also proved accurate in its statement that Hanoi would reassess the situation in the summer or fall and eventually shift to a major conventional attack.

A renewed American intervention became effectively impossible after late 1973 when Congress, over a presidential veto, passed the War Powers Act. Absent the U.S. combat role, and with the Vietnam war sickening American politics, levels of aid to South Vietnam declined radically. The military aid level of 1972–73, which had stood at $2.3 billion, was slashed to $1.2 billion for the next year. The administration asked for $1.4 billion for 1974–75, but Congress approved only $1 billion and actually appropriated just $700 million (plus $450 million in economic aid).* With the South Vietnamese economy straining under the effects of oil prices and inflation and the continued prospect of heavy fighting, morale sagged. President Nguyen Van Thieu was reported as feeling abandoned. Saigon officials, U.S. diplomats, and American military officers felt obliged to mount a major public relations effort simply to secure such aid as was accorded.

At some point Washington began to understand the decline in Saigon's morale—stories of Vietnamese exaggeration of data continued rife (the old problem of the quality of information had not disappeared). Not even Saigon could hide the fact that a government outpost in the Central Highlands, well-armed, defended by 600 troops with several months' supply of food and ammunition, had surrendered the moment it came under serious threat. But here public relations began to get in the way of policy. Graham Martin, the U.S. ambassador to Saigon who replaced Ellsworth Bunker in 1973, produced rosy reports that put even the worst developments in a good light.

The CIA station lent itself to these maneuvers. By now Bill Colby had brought home Theodore Shackley and made him chief of the DO's East Asia Division (Imelda Marcos of the Philippines had groused that *Far* East as a term implied Western colonialism and Colby took the point). Taking over the station was Thomas Polgar, a CIA man of Hungarian origin who had been active in Soviet operations in Europe at the time Colby worked the same beat from Stockholm. Polgar had spent the 1960s assigned to Vienna, then went to Buenos Aires to head the CIA station in Argentina, where he had neatly

---

* Congressional cuts reflected a desire to move America beyond Vietnam but also a more complex truth. Pentagon supply experts examined accounts and had private conversations with American advisers, determining that Saigon did not actually require the full $1.4 billion, or even the $1 billion, in military aid. Meanwhile, corruption in South Vietnam ran rampant—in 1974 the United States decided to stop even trying to find out what had happened to almost $50 million in military aid already sent. This came at a time when the Department of Defense was under pressure to generate a peace dividend in the wake of the war. Typical discussions of this issue also obscure the degree to which Congress sought to restructure rather than end aid to South Vietnam. At $450 million, the congressional appropriation of economic aid for 1974–75 ran considerably higher than the administration request for $349 million. Observers who are inclined to blame the Congress for "losing" the Vietnam war because it did not vote the full amount of military aid requested also do not show just how this amount, or any other amount, could accomplish anything other than prolonging the conflict, much less win the war.

resolved an airliner hijacking by drugging some Cokes he supplied to terrorists holed up in a narrow cabin with no air conditioning in intense heat.
Hungary had become one of the countries contributing to the International
Commission for Control and Supervision monitoring implementation of the
Paris accord. Colby no doubt felt Polgar would be able to mine the Hungar-
ians for private information from Hanoi. Polgar and Martin disliked one another but presented a unified picture to Washington.

In late 1974 National Security Adviser Kissinger ordered a fresh policy
review on Vietnam known as NSSM-213. Aid levels were the principal issue
but these also depended on North Vietnamese intentions. Supervised by William Christisen, the national intelligence officer for Southeast Asia under
Colby's new system, an interagency intelligence memorandum was filed on
November 18. The paper concluded that North Vietnamese forces would not
open "a new 1972-style offensive" at least until mid-1975, though it did
expect some escalation of military activity from which Hanoi would emerge
in a somewhat stronger position. One CIA unit, the Office of Current Intelligence (OCI), forecast that diverse factors would actually bring Hanoi to
avoid *any* full scale offensive for the entire five-year period under review in
the national security study memorandum, leading to a strategy "basically
along the lines of the present middle of the road approach attempting to
exploit Saigon's weaknesses through limited military operations." Meanwhile,
South Vietnamese military performance would be rated as "reasonably effective," with some decline in recent months that had yet to reach significant
levels. In a cover letter for the intelligence study, Colby explicitly associated
himself with the optimistic OCI prediction for the next five years.[8]

Meanwhile South Vietnamese morale remained a heated subject. About
this time Polgar ordered a subordinate to draft a cable knocking down the
notion of falling morale. When the draft failed to support Polgar's view he
wrote his own report; in the words of a leading station analyst, it "was so
extreme and ludicrous his superiors at CIA headquarters refused to pass it
on to any of our regular intelligence customers, to Kissinger, the President,
or anyone else."[9] However the station as well as the Defense Attaché Office
in Saigon both reported that the enemy high command had issued orders for
a six-month campaign to begin in December 1974 aimed at defeating pacification and eliminating a third to half of Saigon's armed forces.

The newly cautious line, more than a response to intelligence, represented part of Ambassador Martin's public relations campaign. When the
North Vietnamese opened a round of attacks northwest of Saigon, overrunning
the entire province of Phuoc Long by January 1975, Martin attributed to
Saigon leaders the view he himself held:

WE ARE IN A NEW SITUATION WHICH CALLS FOR A STRONGER, BETTER OR-
GANIZED DIPLOMATIC AND PUBLIC RELATIONS RESPONSE THAN IN THE PAST.
. . . MOST IMPORTANT OF ALL THE THING WHICH MUST BE DONE IS FOR THE
[STATE] DEPARTMENT TO MOUNT A CAMPAIGN TO BRING THE WHOLE TRUTH
TO THE AMERICAN PEOPLE ABOUT THE CURRENT REALITIES IN VIETNAM.
ONLY BY SUCH A CONCERTED EFFORT CAN WE OVERCOME THE DELIB-

ERATE ORGANIZED CAMPAIGN OF LIES AND DISTORTIONS ABOUT VIETNAM
WHICH DON LUCE, FRED BRANFMAN AND THEIR COLLEAGUES IN THE IN-
DOCHINA RESOURCE CENTER [WHOM MARTIN CONSIDERED TROUBLESOME
ANTIWAR INFORMATION SOURCES] ARE CONDUCTING TO DISCREDIT OUR
VIETNAM POLICY AND PERSUADE THE CONGRESS TO REJECT IT.[10]

Since the summer of 1974 Henry Kissinger, now also secretary of state in
addition to his White House job, had permitted Martin to lead on spin-
doctoring Vietnam. Here Martin was asking for a Washington task force
whose sole concern would be propaganda on Vietnam demanding higher
levels of aid.

With one interagency group already focused on Southeast Asia, Kissinger
did not do that, but he did have the NSC staff do things to influence information before the public. Most important, the NSC ordered the CIA to draft
a report in unclassified form on communist bloc aid to Hanoi. The paper,
released to buttress Ford administration aid requests, actually showed that
Hanoi received about the same aid in 1974 as in the previous two years, and
because the Russians had raised prices for certain equipment, the CIA paper
could be read as demonstrating *less* assistance than before. Even worse, com-
parisons with U.S. aid to South Vietnam showed that Saigon received more
than Hanoi. The NSC staff demanded changes in the CIA paper, and in an
exercise that went on through March 1975, it inserted language in the CIA
draft to make its own points while still having the CIA take responsibility
for the product. Possibly currying favor with the Ford White House, possibly
pursuing his own commitment to South Vietnam, Director Colby went along
with this manipulation of intelligence, sullying CIA objectivity.

The end object of this activity would be to induce Congress to pass a $700
million supplemental military aid appropriation for South Vietnam. If successful the move would have restored the original aid level. News that Martin,
Kissinger, and others did *not* want to have revealed was that, as of January
1975, only $158.4 million of the money *already* approved had in fact been
spent. Reading the mood in Congress as hostile to additional assistance, political counselors advised Ford to do more to prepare the ground for a request,
resulting in even more pressure for things like the White House-amended
CIA paper.

Frank Snepp, lead analyst at the Saigon CIA station, on whom both Polgar
and Martin relied, had been filing reports for months warning of declining
morale and other Saigon difficulties. Snepp wondered why his opposite numbers at Langley were so much more optimistic and wrote later of his doubts
they were even looking at the same war. A Vietnam estimate, NIE 53/14–3–
74, completed on December 23, 1974, again insisted the South Vietnamese
army remained strong and resilient. Hanoi might commit part of its strategic
reserve to exploit perceived weakening in the South, but a countrywide offensive did not seem likely before 1976.

Bill Colby, who had been a friend and Columbia Law School classmate
of the Saigon CIA analyst's father, later told Snepp, "Yes, I was responsible
for the judgment nothing significant would happen until 1976."[11]

Colby reminded colleagues of that judgment in the national estimate when Kissinger called into session his Washington Special Action Group (WSAG), the crisis management unit of the National Security Council, after the fall of Phuoc Long. Both Polgar and the Defense Attaché Office reported through their channels that the NIE had been flawed and out of focus because Hanoi had greater capabilities than predicted, even without reinforcements from the North. In the immediate moment WSAG decided to do nothing.

Some indication of the equanimity that prevailed flows from another Washington concern—the upcoming presidential election in South Vietnam. In 1971 Nguyen Van Thieu had won an election marred by the absence of any real opponent. The United States wanted to avoid a repeat performance. The CIA Saigon station favored making labor leader Tran Quoc Buu, whose dealings with the agency were discussed earlier, the opposition candidate. Though well acquainted with Buu, Bill Colby rejected this proposal.

Hanoi decided early in January to extend its offensive, beginning with an attack in the foothills of the Central Highlands. In Washington, Congress debated the relative merits of a $300 million supplemental appropriation or a $750 million one-time grant to be the final installment of U.S. military assistance to South Vietnam. Contrary to Henry Kissinger's assertion, in the third volume of his memoirs, that "the North Vietnamese offensive rolled on," there would be a lull from January to the first week of March as Hanoi arrayed its forces for the new attack.[12] Saigon military commanders themselves were in disarray, with the general in charge of the Central Highlands convinced the attack would come on the plateau, not in the foothills.

The offensive opened on March 8 with roadblocks to cut off the battle area. Two days later Hanoi forces attacked the provincial capital Ban Me Thuot, which fell surprisingly rapidly. This crystallized a sense of crisis in Saigon. President Thieu met with his area commander and ordered evacuation of the Highlands to gather troops for a counterattack at Ban Me Thuot. Aware that North Vietnamese units stood poised on the major roads, Saigon forces tried to retreat using other routes not maintained for many years. Ambushed anyway, the South Vietnamese lost whatever cohesion they had had, and the retreat became a rout. On March 18 Hanoi began another series of attacks in the region of the Demilitarized Zone and there too the South Vietnamese collapsed. Within a week Hanoi's troops were at the gates of Da Nang; the storied city of Hue fell on March 26.

Such rapid deterioration stunned Washington. The CIA and State Department at first maintained that the North Vietnamese would bypass Da Nang, and Bill Colby told a WSAG meeting that Da Nang would hold, but on the March 25 Langley was forced to report in the *President's Daily Brief* that chances for keeping the city were slim. When the full National Security Council (NSC) met on March 28, Director Colby had to report the CIA's prediction that Da Nang would fall within two weeks no matter what South Vietnamese troops tried to hold it. "The Vietnamese Government has enough to control the area around Saigon and the Delta for this dry season," Colby told the NSC, "but they are likely to be defeated in 1976."[13]

Chartered ships and U.S. naval vessels began an evacuation of Da Nang, which brought out some 135,000 South Vietnamese soldiers and refugees, with another 15,000 saved by air transport. The CIA base chief in Da Nang, whom Frank Snepp pseudonymously dubbs "Custer," ignored orders to leave until the last moment. The agency's officers in the city flew out on Air America or went by sea, like Custer, but many of their Vietnamese employees and sources were left behind. The same thing happened at Nha Trang on the central Vietnamese coast, which fell on April 2. Other towns on the coast went one by one with blinding speed. The Central Highlands were already gone.

The loss of Nha Trang energized Tom Polgar into a most unusual initiative. Polgar believed in the possibility of a negotiated handover of power in Saigon, possibly due to his contacts with the Hungarian mission. Nguyen Van Thieu would never have agreed to such a measure, nor would Graham Martin.

Polgar used his CIA channels to raise the possibility, which necessarily entailed replacement of President Thieu. Polgar and his division chief, Ted Shackley, then visiting Saigon, saw Thieu on April 2 and found him noncommittal. That afternoon, with help from Frank Snepp, Polgar worked up a message premised on the need to evacuate Americans, observing that a different Saigon government might be able to negotiate with the enemy while an evacuation proceeded.

The Saigon station cable, a bombshell for Bill Colby, instantly recalled the summer of 1963, when Washington's frustration had focused on Ngo Dinh Diem. Colby wanted no part of another CIA coup. The answer he sent from Langley was plain: "IF THERE WAS ANY REMOTE CONNECTION BETWEEN US AND SUCH AN EVENT IT WOULD BE AN INSTITUTIONAL AND A NATIONAL DISASTER." Thieu ought to be saved: "IF THINGS GET COMPLICATED AT ALL, ADVISE AND I WILL RECOMMEND STRONGEST EFFORT TO FACILITATE THIEU AND FAMILY SAFE PASSAGE AND HAVEN."[14] The station should discourage any adventures, Colby told Polgar: "PLEASE MAKE MOST CLEAR TO THOSE YOU THINK IT IMPORTANT TO ADVISE THAT THEY ARE TO FLATLY REJECT EVEN A HINT THAT WE WOULD CONDONE OR PARTICIPATE IN SUCH ACTION." Tom Polgar replied on April 5 that he had already made it clear to several potential plotters that "ANY ATTEMPT TO REMOVE THIEU ALONG THE LINES OF THE 1963 EXPERIENCE WOULD BE JUST ABOUT THE SUREST WAY TO GUARANTEE A COMPLETE AND IMMEDIATE END TO AMERICAN SUPPORT FOR SOUTH VIETNAM."[15]

As Saigon struggled, so Washington tried to understand the unfolding events. As for Thieu, Director Colby had this to say at an NSC meeting on April 9:

> So far Thieu has shown considerable skill in keeping the opposition divided. He is aided by the fact that there is no single figure who his various political and military critics believe would provide more effective leadership.[16]

Colby rendered that judgment even though President Thieu had acknowledged his political weakness by firing his cabinet. In the matter of a new

government, the CIA director conceded, "There is considerable reluctance
. . . especially among important Buddhist and Catholic groups, to be associated with a Thieu government."[17] Thieu's political vulnerability would be
underlined the day before that NSC session, when a South Vietnamese air
force plane bombed the presidential palace (though it later was alleged the
pilot had secretly been a Viet Cong agent). Thieu would eventually resign on
April 21 and leave South Vietnam a few days later.

Meanwhile, the CIA director faithfully reported the substance of Saigon
station's analysis of the military situation. Colby told the same April 9 NSC
meeting that Hanoi had decided to go for broke, had moved virtually its entire
army to the South, and planned a three-pronged attack directly on Saigon.
He went on to note just how poor were South Vietnam's hopes, "long-term
prospects are bleak, no matter how well Saigon's forces acquit themselves in
the fighting that lies ahead."[18] The purpose of that White House meeting had
actually been to consider a new assessment by General Frederick C. Weyand,
Army chief of staff, who had just returned from another inspection visit to
Vietnam. Weyand presented a plan for a further injection of U.S. aid to enable
South Vietnam to reorganize for a defense of Saigon and the Mekong delta,
but even he saw the chances for America's Vietnamese allies to be marginal
at best. The price would be $722 million. The administration made that pro-
posal but also undercut it, on April 10, when President Gerald R. Ford made
a speech in which he insisted the United States had done all it could for
South Vietnam. Some observers read Ford's words as the country's washing
its hands of Vietnam.

On April 9 the National Security Council for the first time discussed the
need for an evacuation from South Vietnam. Henry Kissinger remarked that
Ambassador Martin would resist such an evacuation but promised to make
him cooperate once a decision had been made. The numbers of people who
needed to be spirited out were massive. Some 5,400 Americans plus 600
dependents were only the tip of an iceberg. There were 164,000 employees
of the United States and their dependents; third country nationals, the diplomatic corps, and relatives raised that total to 200,000. Senior Saigon officials and military with their dependents were estimated at 600,000, with an
overall total of potential evacuees as high as 1,700,000. Such an endeavor
could consume weeks or months (where only days were left) and would
require cooperation from both South and North Vietnamese.

"If I may state my views on policy," Bill Colby interjected, "It would be
that you should put your stress on the Vietnamese people."[19]

In this departure from the usual role of a CIA chief, normally restricted
to providing intelligence, Colby advocated asking Congress for enough
money to fund an evacuation of 1 to 2 million people. President Ford decided
to seek authority for an evacuation along with his request for military aid,
but he delayed the decision to proceed with the withdrawal. Ambassador
Martin brought out small numbers of Americans, aiming to keep the embassy
open as long as a negotiated end to the fighting might be possible and wanting

to retain his Air America pilots until the last moment. Martin carped about the intelligence, complaining on April 18: "I AM NOT SURPRISED THAT 'IN THE UNANIMOUS VIEW OF THE AGENCIES REPRESENTED, THE SITUATION IN VIETNAM IS RAPIDLY AND IRRETRIEVABLY APPROACHING THE WORST CASE.' ALL OF THEM WERE SAYING NOT LONG AGO THAT THERE WOULD BE NO 'GENERAL OFFENSIVE' THIS YEAR."[20]

That day, Kissinger ordered that Americans in South Vietnam be reduced to those who could be carried out by available helicopters in a single day. On April 14 Ford had asked Congress for the new military aid package, plus evacuation authority under the War Powers Act. Congress passed the authority on the April 25 but the administration had already begun its withdrawal four days earlier with a round-the-clock airlift from Tan Son Nhut. Most Americans, along with about 80,000 Vietnamese, left this way.

Meanwhile, in Saigon Tom Polgar continued to believe Hanoi could be induced to permit an orderly evacuation through Polish mediation with the government that replaced Nguyen Van Thieu's. In Washington on April 19, Colby told Kissinger's WSAG that South Vietnam faced total defeat soon, perhaps in a matter of days. Despite this rendering, and his awareness of its implications—the CIA director told the NSC on the 24th that "high risk people" ought to be moved as soon as possible—Colby seemed reluctant to ensure that Vietnamese who had worked with CIA be gotten out immediately. A case in point would be Tran Ngoc Chau, whose evacuation was rejected by East Asia Division chief Ted Shackley—Colby could have reversed that decision but declined to do so. Chau eventually arrived in the United States by immigration, but only after years in a communist reeducation camp.

In the final hours of the withdrawal, on April 29, Colby did intervene at WSAG to ensure the rescue of a thousand high-risk people then on Phu Quoc island, but that last day was chaos. Tan Son Nhut, under fire and falling to Hanoi's troops, could no longer be used to land airplanes. Helicopters had to lift people out of the U.S. embassy and nearby buildings. Some 1,400 Americans, their U.S. Marine perimeter guards, and 5,500 Vietnamese and others were saved this way. In the Mekong delta, CIA officers organized a sealift as well, bringing out about 4,000 persons. Ships at Vung Tau and a mass escape by the South Vietnamese navy brought out, overall, about 50,000 by sea. For all this, the numbers evacuated never came close to the 1,700,000 figure that had been discussed in Washington.

The end of the Vietnam war, tragic as it was, left the CIA responsible for even more tragedy. In the chaos Tom Polgar failed to make sure all files of the Saigon station had been destroyed, leaving Hanoi's security forces plentiful data to identify and track down former CIA agents who had not escaped. A few CIA officers were captured, notably Tucker Gougelman, a Colby associate from his own days in Saigon, who had gone back to try and save friends. Gougelman died under interrogation in Hanoi eleven months later. Perhaps it is not surprising that in later years Bill Colby had little desire to recall these horrible days.

PAINFUL AS IT BECAME, the debacle in Vietnam served only to punctuate Bill Colby's larger nightmare. Vietnam represented a setback for CIA operations, its intelligence product remained under attack by conservative critics, and worst of all, the agency reeled under a full-scale political attack. The last threat, fueled by Watergate, for the first time threatened the very existence of the Central Intelligence Agency. As Colby was at Langley's helm when this challenge arose, it fell to him to navigate the treacherous waters. He did his best to avoid the shoals, but controversy inexorably engulfed the CIA.

The initial impetus for the Central Intelligence Agency's headaches flowed from continuing public concern about its role in Chile from 1970 to 1973. Barely a month after the September 11, 1973, coup in Santiago that brought about Salvador Allende's suicide and a wave of repression by the Chilean military, Director Colby appeared on Capitol Hill for testimony on the affair. Denying that the intelligence community had had any foreknowledge of the coup was relatively simple—the cables that proved otherwise surfaced only in the late 1990s when the issue revived controversy over the U.S. relationship with Chilean General Augusto Pinochet, the usurper who overthrew Chilean democracy. In 1973 the details were easy to hide and Bill Colby had little direct knowledge of them. Colby had become CIA director just days before the coup. He knew the CIA had twenty-four hours' advance warning, and as deputy director for plans he had been aware of the most recent 40 Committee decision, on August 21, which made an additional $1 million (for a total of $6.5 million) available to the anti-Allende opposition. The CIA station in Santiago asked for authority in late August to develop closer contacts with the opposition but was opposed both by U.S. ambassador Nathaniel Davis and, at Langley, by Colby, no doubt with the Diem affair in mind. Langley rejected the request. But by far the largest proportion of the CIA covert operation in Chile, Project Fu/Belt, had taken place in 1970 under Dick Helms and Tom Karamessines while Bill Colby was in Vietnam.

Chile became a legal problem for the CIA in March 1973 when Richard Helms testified before a Senate committee investigating multinational corporations. He artfully misled Congress on the degree of collaboration between the CIA and the International Telephone and Telegraph Corporation, and on CIA's own account in trying to prevent Allende's election. Helms repeated the testimony later at his own confirmation hearing to be ambassador to Iran. The former DCI acted under Nixon's orders to keep the Chilean operation a secret. But some in Congress kept up the pressure, in particular Massachusetts democratic congressman Michael Harrington. Holding to the official line gnawed at people, even within the CIA, where Director Colby had issued a directive that any questionable activity be brought to the top level.

Doubts about Chile figured in the Family Jewels collection, and discomfiture was such that word leaked beyond the walls at Langley headquarters. One of the passages suppressed in Victor Marchetti's book *The CIA and the Cult of Intelligence*—the manuscript was completed in early 1974—identified both tracks of the CIA operation, although the author was mistaken on a couple of details (Marchetti had it that the American ambassador knew of the coup-assassination plot in Track II, though at Nixon's insistence the ambassador had deliberately been kept in the dark), but Marchetti had enough that was correct to impeach Helms's congressional testimony. Since Marchetti had left the agency in 1969, before Belt ever took place, he could only have learned about Chile from inside sources. Indeed, a serving officer penned a memorandum, sent up through channels, that expressed concern about the Helms testimony and obliged Colby to initiate an inquiry. The Chilean operation could not remain secret.

With Congressman Harrington still pressing, on April 22, 1974, the CIA subcommittee of House Armed Services held a hearing on Chile. Colby appeared only in closed session and limited his comments to the political action efforts of Track I, but approached Representative Lucien N. Nedzi privately to admit that the CIA's involvement had been deeper than he had disclosed. As on the Family Jewels disclosure previously, Nedzi extracted assurances from the CIA that the 1970 plots had had nothing to do with the later coup, then let the matter drop. Harrington, not a member of the CIA subcommittee, invoked congressional prerogative to examine Colby's secret testimony and later used this knowledge in a public denunciation of the CIA. Still later Harrington incorporated details of the Chile effort in the text of a bill he presented in the House of Representatives to proscribe CIA covert action.

Disquiet on the Chile front combined with concerns that had originated with CIA activities in Vietnam and Laos to lead to legislative efforts in addition to Harrington's. The most important would be an amendment to the Foreign Assistance Act offered by Iowa Senator Harold Hughes and California Representative Leo Ryan. The Hughes-Ryan Amendment provided that no funds could be expended on a covert operation unless the president found it necessary in the interest of national security and the activity was briefed in advance to eight different congressional committees. The CIA felt Hughes-Ryan crippled covert action; Colby argued against it and filed a legal brief opposing the amendment. But the legislation passed, showing how far the scales were tipping against the secret warriors of Langley. When Colby appeared at a conference on intelligence activities hosted by the Center for National Security Studies that fall, his argument that covert action had to be one item in CIA's bag of tools fell on deaf ears.

By this time the CIA effort to keep the lid on Chile was failing. With legislators seeking publicity to blow the whistle on the agency, leads floating around in censored book manuscripts, and officers exhibiting disillusionment at Langley, revelation had become inevitable. Seymour Hersh, well connected at the agency, had enough contact with Colby to be able to bring his top editor, the *New York Times*'s Abraham Rosenthal, right into the DCI's office for a private chat. Disturbed by Colby's icy blue eyes and deadpan demeanor, Rosenthal encouraged Hersh's investigative reporting. Hersh picked up the leads and confirmed them. Most important was a July 18 letter Representative Harrington had written to his committee chairman that contained details of

Colby's April testimony, including amounts of money the CIA had distributed to various Chilean groups opposing Allende. In September and October Hersh used this and other information for a series of articles detailing a more extensive CIA role in Chile than had been publicly acknowledged. Lawrence Stern of the *Washington Post* got some of the same leads and made other charges. Extensive media coverage followed.

The Ford administration scrambled to limit the damage from these reports. At a news conference on September 16, President Ford affirmed that CIA activities in Chile had been authorized; a few days later he and Kissinger briefed top congressional leaders on the program. The administration was aware that Hersh had more information—apparently including documents from Henry Kissinger's 40 Committee—the NSC unit that approved covert activities—and senior officials were very concerned. On the morning of September 24 DCI Colby told Deputy National Security Adviser Brent Scowcroft that the most recent stories were "substantially false and . . . he is prepared to say so."[21] Kissinger aides prepared a statement denying that the CIA had participated in, supported, or lent assistance to the anti-Allende coup, strikes by Chilean workers that had preceded it, or the widely noted demonstration by Chilean women known as the "march of the pots." Colby was supposed to verify the truth of the statement then issue it. No CIA denial was ever released.

Meanwhile concern over the Helms testimony problem had percolated to the seventh floor at Langley. A middle-level CIA officer used the word "perjury" to describe testimony before the Senate subcommittee that had studied multinational corporations. His memorandum, found by an officer reviewing Latin American operations for the Inspector General, raised serious doubts. The CIA's general counsel rejected the charge. But then Richard Helms's own testimony was impeached, and the inspector general referred the matter to Colby. Now the CIA director went back to the counsel, who set up a panel of three staffers for an examination. Perjury charges turned on the question of whether Helms had described the Track II Chile project and the ITT affair in his answers under oath—he had not. The panel nevertheless decided they could not determine whether testimony and facts were truly at odds, advising that this issue be left to the Justice Department for resolution. General counsel forwarded the finding to Colby on September 5, with the addition that he did not believe perjury had been committed and that a two-decade-old understanding between the CIA and Justice Department gave the agency leeway on when to refer cases to Justice. At that point Bill Colby decided to hold the line for Helms, commenting for the record on September 25: "I have decided not to refer any of the matters . . . to the Attorney General at this time. The study . . . will continue and a final decision . . . will be made whenever clear evidence is available of any criminal conduct." The DCI simultaneously determined not to bring the testimony issue before any of the congressional bodies overseeing the CIA.[22]

Unfortunately for Colby—because the result led to lasting enmity toward him by the pro-Helms faction at CIA—the Helms matter would soon be taken from his hands. The CIA legal panel rebelled. Contradicting the general counsel, they argued that no ancient CIA-Justice ground rules could be applied; the CIA had a legal obligation to permit the Department of Justice to make the final determination. Attempting to hide the issue of Helms's misleading Chile testimony would only explode later in leaks and a worse problem.

This was a tar baby, the issue could not be escaped. Bill Colby felt himself caught between past and future, between the culture of the secret warriors and the CIA's post-Watergate rededication to legality. He squared this circle by deciding to seek an opinion as to whether the 1954 accord between CIA and the Department of Justice still held. On December 21 Colby met with the acting attorney general to clarify options. The man acting as attorney general happened to be Laurence Silberman, the same Department of Justice lawyer who had pressed Colby so hard on Watergate. Silberman saw the political ramifications even if Colby did not, and he recognized that in the superheated public atmosphere surrounding allegations of the CIA in Chile, no failure to review this matter was permissible. In an odd replay of the Colby-Silberman duel over revealing the name of John Ehrlichman at the time of Watergate, the acting attorney general forced Colby to reveal the name of Richard Helms. The Department of Justice swiftly took the Helms perjury allegation under advisement, and more than a year later brought an indictment against Helms.

Shortly after the new year, Bill Colby invited Richard Helms to Langley and had him to lunch, the last social meeting of these two men. Helms told an interviewer later that Colby ought to have gone to the courts before yielding him up to the Department of Justice.[23] Helms afficionados at CIA never forgave Colby.

Yet even the Helms affair would quickly be eclipsed as the CIA at large became embroiled in massive public controversy that brought about a sea change for William E. Colby, for the Central Intelligence Agency, for the way the United States government manages and oversees the intelligence function, and for the way Americans perceive their spy agencies. Once more the catalyst would be press reporting on the CIA, again led by Seymour Hersh in the *New York Times*. Intensely interested in the domestic aspects of spying, Hersh had been collecting material all along. Some of his items dated as far back as 1966, culled from *Times* files gathered when the newspaper did its first extensive series on U.S. intelligence. Allegations of government infiltration of the political opposition to the Vietnam war added to the pile, especially when informers were uncovered and revealed their true identities and employers.

For a long time the CIA remained a shadowy presence at the edge of this black hole, its direct involvement only vaguely perceptible. But in due time Hersh learned of the existence of the Family Jewels documents, and once having scented the quarry, got closer and closer to this trove of questionable activities. Since by definition the collection consisted of accounts by CIA officers of things they feared were illegal, the Family Jewels were automatically controversial. Colby, when first seeing the document as executive director, had been relieved that the allegations were not even more explosive, but at a minimum they contained evidence on the very domestic activities Seymour Hersh was investigating. Hersh wrote a story the *Times* published on its front page on Sunday, December 22, 1974, under the headline "HUGE CIA OPERATION REPORTED IN U.S. AGAINST ANTI-WAR FORCES, OTHER DISSIDENTS IN NIXON YEARS."[24] Under that headline came news of the Family Jewels; commentaries by academics regarding legality; and revelation that the CIA had carried out "dozens" of illegal activities; among these were wiretapping, break-ins, surreptitious inspection of mail, maintaining "at least" 10,000 files on Americans, photographing and following participants at demonstrations, and creation of a network to penetrate the antiwar movement. In all this the footprints of CIA's Project MH/Chaos were plainly visible.

Bill Colby had awaited the Hersh story with trepidation. On the previous Monday, in New York to speak at the Council on Foreign Relations, Colby, who had recently become aware of Hersh's investigation, acknowledged that there had been an internal report on domestic activities and that some improprieties had emerged. But the DCI put the development in a favorable light, lauding the junior CIA officers who had had the guts to step forward with their doubts. Hersh quoted Colby as saying. "I think family skeletons are best left where they are—in the closet."[25] On Friday morning, in the final stages of his preparation, Hersh called Colby for an interview. Colby saw Hersh at his Langley office immediately. The DCI tried to tell the reporter he was mixing together what the CIA had done to discover foreign entanglements of the antiwar movement with the agency's work protecting itself from leaks and espionage penetrations. He cautioned Hersh against running the story in the form he had it. Colby's formal response, though Hersh could not quote him by name, was that "anything that we did was in the context of foreign counterintelligence and it was focused at foreign intelligence and foreign intelligence problems."[26] Sy Hersh went with the story as he had it. Colby warned Brent Scowcroft at the White House and Representative Nedzi of the proximate appearance of the Hersh story.

Hersh's colleagues at the *Times*, and subsequent observers who have looked at media response to the CIA allegations, have marveled at the skeptical reactions. Congress also proved slow to gather its forces. Lucien Nedzi, for example, confirmed that Colby had briefed him on the Family Jewels in early 1974, and told *Newsweek*, "You might call it illegalities in terms of exceeding their charter, but it certainly wasn't of the dimension . . . of what has appeared in the newspapers."[27] Washington cocktail parties resounded with gossip of how the *New York Times* had to be overreaching with Hersh's initial account and the stories that followed it.

But within the Ford administration there was no doubt of how serious the CIA furor would become. Henry Kissinger notes that the story had the effect of "a burning match in a gasoline depot."[28] Where the media, even post-Watergate, were initially taking a more relaxed view, the executive leaped instantly. When Colby telephoned the White House to report on the story he was told to talk to President Ford, then aboard Air Force One on the way to Vail, Colorado, for a ski vacation. Colby reassured Ford, but over an open, nonsecure phone line, the president demanded an immediate report. Kissinger phoned presidential assistant (chief of staff) Donald Rumsfeld the next morning at 7:30 A.M. to discuss a report. Rumsfeld confirmed the order with Gerald Ford and so instructed Kissinger in a message sent with "FLASH" precedence at 3:15 A.M. on Christmas Eve. The sensitivity of this message is indicated by the accompanying edict to show all communications on the subject, prior to dispatch, to deputy chief of staff Richard Cheney.

In another memorandum to Rumsfeld later on December 23, Kissinger advised that the White House *not* issue any statement on the CIA story, but deal with questions only if the press asked them. "We are concerned," Kissinger wrote, "that we not act in such a way as to give credence to the allegations of the *New York Times* story and create an impression that a major problem actually exists and that the Ford Administration is confronted with a scandal of major proportions."[29]

On Christmas Eve Director Colby produced a six-page report on matters connected with the *New York Times* article, attaching copies of CIA orders, some cables, and project summaries. Kissinger repeated the gist of these items in a memorandum sent to Vail on Christmas day. Kissinger remarked, "There are other activities 'in the history of the Agency,' which though unconnected with the *New York Times* article, are also open to question. I have discussed these activities with him [Colby], and must tell you that some few of them clearly were illegal, while others—though not technically illegal—raise profound moral questions. A number, while neither illegal nor morally unsound, demonstrated very poor judgment."[30]

By Christmas day President Ford had already determined to appoint a blue ribbon panel to examine the charges of illegal activities by the CIA. Kissinger's "strong recommendation" was that the panel be told to investigate only the narrow set of items in the press and the Colby report, not the broad range of CIA actions.[31] In a flurry of frantic conversations over the last days of the year White House officials discussed possible candidates, ascertained their willingness to serve, and drafted an executive order (no. 11828) setting the narrow scope for the investigation. Chaired by Vice-President Nelson A. Rockefeller, the Commission on CIA Activities Within the United States would be appointed on January 4, 1975.

By now both media and Congress were taking the CIA allegations very seriously as well. The press flowed with news and some additional revelations. On January 27 the Senate passed Resolution 21, which set up a Select

Committee to Study Governmental Operations with Respect to Intelligence. The House of Representatives set up its own investigation, by a Select Committee on Intelligence, on February 19, 1975. So began what has come to be known as the Year of Intelligence. Over the succeeding months, Bill Colby marched into his valley of darkness.

15

THE YEAR OF INTELLIGENCE

AMID THE TURMOIL within the Ford administration, as initial allegations of domestic activities by the Central Intelligence Agency mushroomed into a widening scandal, the domestic angle with its relation to Langley's Counterintelligence Staff brought to the fore the long simmering conflict between Bill Colby and Jim Angleton. Already serving on sufferance, Angleton had very little wiggle room. Director Colby continued to be concerned about Angleton's negative impact on CIA intelligence operations, especially in the area of the Middle East. Fresh grievances had arisen from Colby's discovery that Counterintelligence Staff had employed Jay Lovestone, a labor leader, whose service not only seemed to furnish little actual intelligence but also bordered on the proscribed area of domestic involvement. The imminent surfacing of the Family Jewels, many items in which involved the Counterintelligence Staff, made it imperative for the CIA to deal with its Angleton problem.

In a piece on Angleton he published in 1978, Seymour Hersh wrote that both the counterspy and the DCI were aware of his work on the CIA domestic story by the second week of December 1974. Colby had specific notice of a forthcoming *Times* story by the following Monday. Previously Colby had left Angleton in place as a token of stability at Langley, but with revelations in store about illegal operations for which Angleton had had responsibility, and which "Mother," as he was nicknamed, had fought to preserve, the old approach no longer appeared tenable. On Thursday, December 17, Colby had Angleton up to the seventh floor for a showdown. The director announced his irrevocable decision taking Angleton out of the Middle East chain of command, and then dropped the bombshell—Colby had decided to appoint a new chief of counterintelligence. He offered Angleton the kind of post-employment sinecure that has become almost *de rigeur* at CIA—the opportunity to sign on as a consultant to write a memoir for agency files.

Angleton tried every argument he could think of to convince Colby to change the decision. Director Colby terminated the meeting by telling Angleton to take a couple of days to think over the offer.

The next morning Bill Colby fielded Hersh's phone call and discovered that the *New York Times* revelations were no longer merely imminent—they were going to press over the weekend. Indeed, the identification of Angleton and a discussion of his role had been scheduled for Monday. After giving the CIA's official reactions to the story, Colby called in Angleton once again. Angleton's resignation, no longer merely desirable, was to be on Colby's desk that very day.

"This story is going to be tough to handle," Colby told Angleton. "We've talked about your leaving before. You will now leave, period."[1]

As Angleton went downstairs he encountered a colleague from the FBI, Donald Moore, who asked what was the matter. "It's horrible, Don. It's awful. You'll soon read all about it."[2]

Another colleague, awaiting Angleton in his own office, was British counterintelligence officer Peter Wright, visiting Langley on a liaison mission. Wright recalled Angleton's face as having a gray-blue pallor. "Peter, "I've just been fired," was all Angleton would say.[3]

In a last-ditch attempt to avoid the inevitable, Angleton apparently went directly to Seymour Hersh and offered to tell the reporter of other CIA deeds if Hersh would hold off on the Family Jewels stories. Hersh refused. Afterward he called up Bill Colby to warn that the overwrought Angleton had gone off the reservation. The DCI's reply has gone unrecorded.

Tuesday morning the media, hot on the scent of this story, were camped out on Angleton's doorstep. Among the fresh hunters, Columbia Broadcasting System (CBS) correspondent Daniel Schorr would play a role in the Year of Intelligence almost equal to that of Hersh. Schorr's beat had been domestic protest in the 1960s, then Watergate, but CBS reassigned him to intelligence with the revelations about Chile in the fall of 1974. Schorr arrived at Angleton's North Arlington house and found that none of the eight camera crews outside even knew whether the CIA counterspy was at home. The reporter simply walked up to the door and rang the bell; Angleton invited him in, and Schorr ended up with a four-hour exclusive interview with "Mother." Angleton retailed his standard speech about Russian conspiracies and threw in news about the differences between himself and Colby over the Middle East operations of the CIA. What other background Schorr gained here is not known, but he soon led the pack in reporting about the growing scandal, especially charges of CIA assassination plots.

Though Bill Colby may have taken momentary satisfaction at the final disposal of his nemesis James Angleton, at that moment his troubles had barely begun. The revelations of CIA domestic activity that appeared in print set off a powderkeg that soon had Colby fighting for the agency's very existence. The first level of that fight would be with the White House and its blue ribbon commission to investigate intelligence.

ON CHRISTMAS DAY 1974, when Henry Kissinger wrote President Gerald R. Ford that there were CIA actions other than those in the Colby report that raised profound moral questions or showed very poor judgment, he was referring to the assassinations issue. Meeting Colby to discuss the charges raised by the initial *New York Times* article, Kissinger had proceeded quickly until this matter came up. Agency involvement in assassinations could take the controversy to a new high. That was the reason Kissinger recommended to the president that any inquiry be kept within narrowly defined boundaries.

"Well, Bill," Kissinger had said to Colby, "When Hersh's story first came out I thought you should have flatly denied it as totally wrong, but now I see why you couldn't."[4]

An inquiry swiftly became the favored option at the White House. The alternative, simply endorsing the Colby report, put Ford in the position of defending the CIA. Doing nothing invited congressional investigation. Presidential aide Richard Cheney summarized the advantages very well: creating a panel showed Ford exercising a leadership role, offered the best prospect of heading off congressional encroachment on the executive branch, and minimized damage to the CIA while enabling Ford to avoid defending possibly illegal activity, all the while giving the president an opportunity to convince Americans that government did have integrity and sound institutions. Before President Ford returned from skiing at Vail, Cheney, Rumsfeld, Robert Hartman, Phillip Buchen, and other Ford staffers had decided on the members for a presidential commission and drafted an executive order to govern its inquiry.

William E. Colby gave up a ski vacation of his own, with the family in Pennsylvania, awaiting a presidential call or summons to Vail that never came. He concluded that the White House would distance itself from the CIA, much as the agency had done from Watergate. Dick Cheney's notion of structuring action so as to avoid having Ford take a position on the CIA allegations became the strategy. Any meeting with Director Colby was put off until the president returned to Washington and his commission had already been structured.

That encounter actually took place on January 4, 1975. Before it, President Ford met with Kissinger, who had been making his own inquiries. The national security adviser warned the president that Richard Helms had already confirmed the gist of the situation to him.

"These stories are just the tip of the iceberg," Kissinger remarked. "If they come out, blood will flow. For example, Robert Kennedy personally managed the operation on the assassination of Castro."[5]

Little wonder that Colby's reception at the White House would be decidedly frosty. Though Helms later denied having made these remarks to Kissinger and stood by the testimony he gave that the Castro assassination plots were kept from both John and Robert Kennedy, this did not matter that day in 1975. Moreover, Director Colby had another problem all his own. The Family Jewels collection, which he had briefed to both Senate and House overseers, had never been taken to the White House until now. Whether failure to show the document had resulted from confusion during the interregnum between himself and James Schlesinger or for some other reason, Colby had no idea. Schlesinger, however, knew he had not briefed the White House and reminded Colby of this state of play. Failure to inform the president contributed to the DCI's problems there. Colby reflected in retrospect that he had made an error in not pushing for more personal contact with the presidents he served, both Nixon and Ford, unlike other DCIs who had insisted on personally carrying documents to the Oval Office and so forth. It is undoubtedly correct that the lack of more intimate links between the CIA chieftain and Gerald Ford cost Colby dearly during the Year of Intelligence.

At a January 3 meeting Colby had been informed, after a discussion of his report, that Ford would appoint a commission of inquiry. White House lawyer Phil Buchen would be Ford's point man on the intelligence issues; the National Security Council staff would retain its substantive interest in intelligence matters. Kissinger, wearing his hat as secretary of state, was spending much time on negotiations with Russia, in the Middle East, and on the Vietnam crisis, as deputy national security adviser Brent Scowcroft took the lead on the NSC side.

Colby did not want to know who Ford would appoint to his commission; the CIA had to abstain from any attempt to influence the inquiry. But Director Colby, understood better than his interlocutors that Ford's delay in responding to the CIA revelations raised the political ante; the DCI expected that Ford's presidential commission would not prevent other investigations. Colby proved right. Soon after Ford announced, on January 6, the presidential commission headed by Vice-President Nelson A. Rockefeller, both the Senate and House set hearings of their own on the affair. Colby, Schlesinger, and Helms were the witnesses when the Rockefeller Commission met for the first time on January 13. The same three led off at the Senate hearings on January 15. At the latter hearing Colby's opening statement infuriated Kissinger; he regarded it as identical to the report he had given Ford at Vail, and disliked Congress having as much knowledge as the president. Compounding the transgression, in Henry's view, was that the White House had not been consulted or even advised. Bill Colby realized that and stopped at the White House on his way back to Langley, there to tell Brent Scowcroft what to expect. The gesture did not smooth ruffled feathers.

Henry Kissinger's basic complaint remains that William E. Colby, essentially, talked out of school. But Colby's report went directly to the allegations that had already appeared in public. It would be Gerald R. Ford himself, at a luncheon with top editors of the *New York Times* on January 16, who let escape the much bigger secret that the CIA had been involved in assassinations. Ford dropped that bombshell in a comment on the Rockefeller Commission and how he had restricted it—the president did not want his inquisitors to get into the "cesspool" of foreign intelligence for fear that could "ruin the U.S. image around the world." Asked what he meant, President Ford blurted that CIA operations included every sort of thing up to assassinations of foreign leaders.[6] This luncheon comment became the source of gossip in Washington quickly picked up by reporter Daniel Schorr.

On February 27 Schorr cornered Bill Colby during a background interview at CIA headquarters. Schorr asked, "Has the CIA ever killed anybody?"

"Not in this country," Colby replied.

Schorr quickly asked who, but Colby shot back "I can't talk about it." The CIA spymaster then refused to respond to a series of questions about specific individuals, but Daniel Schorr decided he had secured confirmation for the substance of President Ford's luncheon gaffe and made assassination the subject of his broadcast on CBS news the next day.[7] One acute observer judges this "a report that was to transform the 'year of intelligence.'"[8]

The mote Kissinger saw in Bill Colby's eye should not conceal the bars in those at the White House. Suddenly the West Wing's perception was of U.S. intelligence completely out of control; more precisely, Kissinger feared the CIA moving beyond *his* control. Meanwhile the public felt dismay at the CIA's seemingly unlimited actions. Both sides held a similar fear for almost opposite reasons.

President Ford carefully selected the commission he set up under Nelson Rockefeller. The chairman himself had worked with the CIA during its halcyon days of Cold War activism, when Dwight Eisenhower spoke of rollback and Allen Dulles posed as the Great White Case Officer. In fact, "Rocky" had been Ike's special assistant on Cold War strategy in the psychological and political fields. Ford, who had been a member of the House Appropriations Committee's CIA subpanel, was aware of all this. The vice-president would be a safe choice to head the group. White House files are replete with lists of names of potential members and pros and cons for their appointment. The group eventually included Ronald Reagan, leaving office as governor of California; General Lyman L. Lemnitzer; C. Douglas Dillon and John T. Connor, both former cabinet secretaries; Erwin N. Griswold, solicitor general of the United States during the first Nixon administration; and two others.

Gerald Ford also knew something about assassinations. As a fifty-year-old Michigan congressman, Ford had been selected by Lyndon Johnson to sit alongside Allen Dulles and Supreme Court chief justice Earl Warren on the Warren Commission to investigate the assassination of President John F. Kennedy. He reached back to that experience at the time of the Rockefeller Commission to tap Warren's former assistant counsel, Iowa lawyer David W. Belin, as executive director of the commission's staff.

Belin's selection as staff director did not play out quite the way the White House hoped. Heavily involved in all manner of issues related to assassination in the earlier Warren investigation, Belin had become exceptionally sensitive to allegations of this kind. His reaction to Ford's remark about assassinations was to find out the facts. He had no doubt this matter belonged on the Rockefeller agenda and presented the facts to the commissioners. Nelson Rockefeller took umbrage; his zeal to guard the CIA was such that he drew Director

Colby aside, during a break in testimony, to ask the CIA chief to tell the commissioners *less*, not more. Rocky argued that the commission mandate included only CIA activities within the United States. Though the vice-president's arguments seemed persuasive, even to Belin, Ronald Reagan electrified the group, insisting that only a full investigation would suffice. The majority sided with the governor, not the vice-president. Once the assassination charges became public knowledge, President Ford widened the commission's assignment and extended its deadline by two months.

David Belin made it his special concern to look into the assassinations question. He quickly discovered the May 1967 internal review by CIA inspector general John S. Earman. The 133-page study covered plots to kill Cuban leader Fidel Castro, identified CIA contacts with organized crime figures, put the plots in the context of CIA covert operations against Cuba, and compared this record with garbled versions that had appeared in public, notably columns by journalist Drew Pearson. As early as 1967 the Earman report had concluded that the CIA could no longer suppress the story, that it could not plausibly deny that it had plotted with "gangster elements," and that it could not imply it had merely acted as an instrument of policy.[9]

These points fully justified the need to include assassinations in any investigation of intelligence. Using the power of the Rockefeller Commission, Belin interviewed a variety of CIA officers, especially participants in the anti-Castro operations, and conducted an extensive documents search. For example, Belin reviewed the entire set of John McCone's records to identify the numerous instances when McCone had discussed Cuban operations with President Kennedy. By mid-April Belin felt able to tell White House counsel James A. Wilderotter, an aide to Phil Buchen, that the commission would have a preliminary report about assassinations ready by the end of the month. The preliminary report eventually related extensive details of the Castro initiatives and added three more cases: the deaths of Patrice Lumumba in the Congo in 1961; Rafael Trujillo in the Dominican Republic, also in 1961; and an abortive plot in the late 1950s against President Sukarno of Indonesia. There was no discussion of Diem in South Vietnam, and Belin found the CIA role minimal in the Lumumba and Trujillo cases, and unclear in that of Sukarno. There ensued major discussion of the anti-Castro operations, however. Belin ended:

> President Ford has firmly announced that assassination is not and should never be a tool of United States policy. The Executive Director of the Commission joins in this statement. It is against the constitutional and moral principles for which this Republic stands for there to be any direct or indirect participation of any agency of the United States Government in any plans involving the assassination of any person in peacetime.[10]

Despite the extensive work on CIA assassination plots against foreign leaders and the preparation of interim reviews on this issue (Belin's report ran to 86 typescript pages), the sole statement to appear in the Rockefeller Commission's final report of June 6, 1975, read:

> The Commission's staff began the required inquiry, but time did not permit a
> full investigation before this report was due. The President therefore requested
> that the materials in the possession of the Commission which bear on these
> allegations be turned over to him. This has been done.[11]

The entire substantive discussion of assassinations that appears in the Rockefeller Commission report, some eighteen pages, deals only with questions of whether certain CIA officers or contract agents had personal roles in the *Kennedy* assassination. This formed an odd reprise and extension of the Warren Commission's work and had little to do with the issues of 1975. No public outcry ensued because until now all of this has remained secret.

Completed and given to the president on June 6, 1975, the Rockefeller Commission study, as promised, confined itself to the domestic issues. President Ford essentially followed the script prepared by his staff. Even so, members of the White House staff, John O. Marsh in particular, feared that many items contained in the document could raise more questions than they settled. Days before its official presentation, officials were already poring over a working copy of the commission's final report, holding meetings to discuss it, trading advice on what to do. A couple of months afterward *Newsweek* magazine ran a brief notice that Kissinger, for fear of offending the Russians, had had a section of the document suppressed—a part that reviewed Russian communications interception activities in the United States.[12] There was such a passage and it was excised, but this falls far short of the truth about how the Rockefeller Commission's work was handled. Reported here for the first time is the fact that the Rockefeller document was extensively rewritten in the White House, as is shown by the marked up drafts in White House Files. Sections were cut and pasted in a different order or moved to different places in the narrative; a number of the commission's recommendations were revised, all with the object of softening the overall impact. For example, where the commission found that CIA infiltration of antiwar groups in the Washington area was flatly "unlawful,"[13] White House staffers changed this to read "exceeded the CIA's authority."[14] Even this formula was softer than the amendment first suggested, "exceeded statutory authority."[15] Under the final language an agency transgression could be debated; in the original it could not.

At his June 9 press conference President Ford followed a staff script in accepting the report, thanking Rockefeller Commission members and announcing public release of the document for the following day. From the inception of the Rockefeller Commission, pundits had speculated publicly that this investigation would be an exercise in whitewashing the spooks. Partly due to the way the report was handled at the White House, the end result bore out the punditry. Even though Ford solicited agency comments on the Rockefeller recommendations and issued an executive order in the fall of 1975 reorganizing certain aspects of intelligence work based on the Rockefeller suggestions, the exercise had none of the political effect the White House had hoped for. In retrospect the Rockefeller Commission investigation is hardly remembered, even by observers who follow intelligence. Director Colby thought the Rockefeller report a sober and useful summary but that "it had, of course, failed to preempt Congressional investigations of intelligence."[16] Those investigations brought the White House, and Bill Colby, much more trouble than they ever believed possible.

ON JANUARY 13, 1975, a week after creation of the Rockefeller Commission and just two days prior to Bill Colby's initial congressional testimony on CIA abuses. White House legislative aide Max L. Friedersdorf wrote the CIA director to introduce his capable staff and detail their assorted expertise. This marked a first tentative step down a path that brought the Central Intelligence Agency to a near-death experience. Neither Friedersdorf and his political bosses nor Colby's intelligence colleagues quite understood what was at stake. At the White House, Gerald Ford's concerns centered around projecting an image of presidential leadership in advance of the 1976 elections; Henry Kissinger wanted to protect foreign policy initiatives while safeguarding his own reputation, involved in various of the episodes sure to come under scrutiny. At Langley and elsewhere, the secret warriors of intelligence reacted as if any investigation of their trade was improper and somehow unpatriotic.

His sensibilities honed by burned fingers in Watergate and adversarial proceedings over Vietnam and the Phoenix program, William E. Colby had a closer understanding of the forces at work in American society. Vietnam had broken the long predisposition of Americans to think government reflected their best interests. Aside from anything else, the Phoenix controversy had taught Colby that mere statements of intent were no longer sufficient to demonstrate credibility. And Watergate, an obvious manipulation of government for partisan political ends by the White House, engendered a climate of suspicion seldom seen before in American politics. This was the fundamental reason that the Rockefeller Commission—the executive branch investigating itself—did not work, indeed could not work, as a vehicle for defusing fears about CIA activities.

The Cold War had changed, and the world with it. Nixon's administration had brought China into the international system in a new way, creating a triangular diplomacy and a competition far different from that of the high Cold War. That also meant a new CIA, peopled by men and women impatient with the prevailing knee-jerk attitudes and cult of secrecy. Under Bill Colby's offices on the seventh floor at Langley, the building seethed, riven by the cleavages between the old guard of OSS-types and the new generation of agency modernists. The director stood poised squarely between the factions, facing the problem of moving the CIA into the future despite revelation of serious misdeeds in its past. With much of his career in controversial Vietnam, Colby perhaps came better equipped to perceive the need to change. With his education as a lawyer, Colby could also see how questions of legality could derail the entire CIA enterprise.

Some held Colby's legal background or his Roman Catholicism against him, portraying him as some kind of Boy Scout or Jesuit, ridiculing such a character in the arcane world of clandestine operations. In the third volume of his memoirs, Henry Kissinger offers two possible explanations for Colby's behavior. One—which he attributes to Colby's deputy, General Vernon Walters, a close Kissinger associate—is that Bill had seen power in Washington shift to Congress, meaning the way to preserve the CIA had to be cooperation with Capitol Hill. The other explanation Kissinger gives is that Colby might have come to think intelligence methods were weakening the moral fiber of America and sought to purify it by concerting with the protest movement.[17] This uncharitable view of Colby's motives no doubt flows from the Helms stalwarts at the CIA. Walters's construction is essentially tactical. Colby himself wrote that he had learned from Watergate that the CIA's distancing strategy in that affair had had a negative impact in the long term, and that growing suspicion and hostility toward the CIA, even earlier, had begun undermining the agency's ability to operate. The antidote, in his view, was "to lift as much as possible that thick cloak of secrecy that had traditionally veiled the Agency."[18] Since, as Colby also notes, he believed in the Constitution, in Congress's constitutional right to investigate, he had no option except to cooperate. Most important, Colby later observed, "I also believed that any other approach just wouldn't work."[19] In 1975 that was an accurate analysis.

During this period Henry Kissinger held both the job of national security adviser, supervising the National Security Council staff, and secretary of state, responsible for all U.S. foreign relations. His was the task of coordinating at the top level of government, yet Kissinger relates, "the vaunted NSC machinery proved incapable of dealing simultaneously with a runaway Congress and a runaway CIA director."[20] But Kissinger, by his own account, spent the bulk of his time on three diplomatic missions to the Middle East and on the fall of Indochina. Aside from the fact that it never formed part of the role of the NSC staff to "deal" with Congress, runaway or otherwise, it was incumbent upon Kissinger, if he could not handle all the work, to give up one post or the other. Kissinger never did, until President Ford obliged him to do so. Not all the fault here lies at the door of the CIA director.

Kissinger's main complaint regarding Bill Colby is that the director of central intelligence did not check with the White House, or even inform it, before releasing various materials to congressional investigators. With Kissinger away much of the time, the day-to-day burden of the NSC involvement in the CIA investigations fell to his deputy, former Air Force general Brent Scowcroft. Wiry and balding, Scowcroft also saw the DCI as a problem—in the fall of 1997 he would joke at a conference on intelligence held at the

Gerald R. Ford Library that Bill Colby was one of the reasons he had lost his hair.

A certain segment of CIA opinion held the same view as Kissinger. Some officers despised Colby for his actions in the Helms perjury case; others who adhered to the cult of secrecy, resented him for letting out any information about the agency. Representative of that position is the opinion of CIA legislative liaison Walter L. Pforzheimer, who considered Bill a friend but thought that the things he told Congress did great damage to the CIA. "Whatever Bill had in mind on a given day, it was going to come out," Pforzheimer told an interviewer in 1998. "It didn't matter how old it was or what the issue was, once he had it in his mind to release something it was coming out. And he didn't want to be bothered with the details."[21] If just one of the ten top officials in a meeting sided with Colby, his legislative man recalled, Bill would go with that view over the other.

But there is both less and more to the problem than meets the eye. The runaway CIA director existed only in White House and like-minded agency heads. Colby frankly admits not going to the White House with his initial testimony, but NSC staff records clearly show that key Colby testimony, including a May 1975 briefing on covert operations as well as other instances, *were* both presented *and* cleared in advance at the White House. Kissinger claims he and James Schlesinger met twice with Colby in an effort to get the CIA to clamp down on revelations, but when Colby tried to argue that assassination documents should be withheld from the Rockefeller Commission, it was the White House that forced the handover. *The White House* then gave that evidence to the Senate investigating committee. And the president himself, of course, had leaked the knowledge that put assassinations onto the investigative agenda.

Bill Colby never tried to push his way into the Oval Office, and Kissinger was happy to keep the CIA director out of it. It is somewhat disingenuous to then complain that Colby was not always coming to the White House, a White House that the records show was trying to distance itself from the "CIA problem." In fact, one of Colby's two meetings with President Ford in the Oval Office—and the only such one-on-one encounter in 1975—came on May 14 when the CIA director reviewed for the president the testimony he intended to give Congress on covert operations the next day.

The attentive public, the media, and Congress did not see any runaway CIA director; rather they saw an icy spy chieftain who remained very cagey indeed. In September, when the Senate investigating committee held its first public hearing, Colby went to Congress with a briefcase full of exotic CIA weapons. Fascinated by one of the first of them, an ingenious gun for firing poison darts, the senators never got to some of the important issues on the docket for that day. Walt Pforzheimer, who had tried to convince Colby not to show any weapons, thought the exhibit was a mistake; but in showing them, Colby had thereby avoided even more damaging areas for testimony.

Pforzheimer may or may not be right that Colby was disappointed, even angry, that he had not been able to display *all* his gadgets, but from the CIA point of view Colby's maneuver proved quite successful.

In addition, the period in which Colby was most forthcoming coincided not with the high point of the congressional investigations but with the period in which they were just getting organized, and committee staff have a very different view of just how forthcoming the CIA had been.[22] The White House had its own lines into the committees, as will be seen, and made numerous determinations on what materials to hand over or suppress. There is no evidence of Bill Colby revealing anything contrary to instructions. The White House point man, not at the NSC at all, was lawyer Phil Buchen. It was Buchen who wrote the May 13, 1975, talking points Kissinger used in one of his two conversations with Colby, prior to the DCI's Oval Office session with President Ford the next day. Colby continued to feel left out on a limb, without consistent White House direction, and appealed to Ford to put someone in charge. Finally, in September 1975, President Ford set up an Intelligence Coordinating Group under John Marsh, with Buchen as a leading member. By then Colby had been subjected to contradictory pressures and orders for months.

For all this there is no doubt William E. Colby's basic strategic choice in 1975 was to open up to the investigations to the extent necessary to preserve the CIA. Some inkling of that came one Saturday morning to Bernard Knox. Colby's old OSS Jedburgh colleague, now teaching a course on Greek tragedy at George Washington University. The subject for the day was the Sophocles play *Antigone*, in which the title character, a young woman, defies the edict of her uncle, King Creon, burying the body of her brother who had been killed leading an enemy army against the home city. For doing the right thing Antigone is condemned to death, but her action pleases the gods, who drive Creon's son and wife to curse him and kill themselves. Repenting, Creon goes to free Antigone, only to discover she too has committed suicide.

As the class discussion proceeded, two dark-jacketed security men entered the hall to survey it, then returned with Bill Colby, who sat and listened to this commentary on painful moral choice. Afterward Colby went up to greet Knox, whom he had not seen in a long time. Inevitably aware of the CIA's troubles, Knox commented, "Bill, you certainly chanced on the right lecture to come to."

"Oh, I knew what you were going to talk about," Colby replied, "And I wanted to hear what you had to say."[23]

Bill Colby clearly had thought hard about the CIA's options in that Year of Intelligence. His misfortune would be that the only viable option was not popular at either the White House or the Central Intelligence Agency. Institutional survival required personal tragedy for Colby. The Greeks had had it right. Charting a course between Scylla and Charybdis would have been easier. Now it only remained to play out the moves.

AMID THE CLAMOR over press disclosures about CIA activities, after the president had decided to create an investigatory commission, it was simply not possible to avoid congressional scrutiny. The CIA oversight panels of the Senate combined for a joint hearing January 15, 1975, at which William E. Colby was the only witness. The Director of Central Intelligence insisted he wanted to put the *New York Times* allegations in perspective, then went on to deny flatly Seymour Hersh's charges of a massive illegal domestic intelligence operation. The "perspective" Colby provided stemmed from the argument that *any* government agency in twenty-seven years of service "would be hard put to avoid some wrong steps."[24] Colby's opening statement reprised the contents of his report to President Ford at Vail, omitting mention of more sensitive issues like assassination.

After a brief round of inquiries the committee went into closed session where Colby went into more details drawn from his December report. These long time CIA overseers were as friendly an audience as the director could get, and from the beginning Colby wanted to get the facts out, on the grounds that doing so would best lance the boil of public controversy. As the two-hour session ended, Senator John L. McClellan asked if Colby's testimony could be released and the DCI assented. The next day's papers were full of his appearance, with the *New York Times* reprinting most of the transcript.

Though Colby saw himself as limiting the damage, testimony showed that allegations made in December indeed had substance. Congress could also take a cue from President Ford, whose creation of the Rockefeller Commission, at a minimum, conceded that there was something here worthy of investigation. A bipartisan group of four senators, including majority leader Mike Mansfield, quickly introduced a resolution to investigate, superceded by a further proposal that passed on January 21, establishing an investigatory group of eleven, the Senate Select Committee to Study Governmental Operations with Respect to Intelligence Activities. Things began to move quite fast indeed.

One index of how quickly events evolved would be what happened to Loch K. Johnson. An academic from Georgia, a few years earlier Johnson had been a congressional fellow of the American Political Science Association, working on Capitol Hill for Idaho Democratic Senator Frank Church. Church, after three terms in the Senate, had never held any important committee chairmanship; he begged Mansfield for the assignment to the intelligence investigation and got it. By chance Loch Johnson stopped by Church's office to say hello, only to find the senator embroiled in the details of setting up his committee. On a whim Johnson expressed an interest in serving on the staff and was promptly hired, one of the first after staff director William G. Miller. Ultimately fifty-three individuals were gathered to conduct the investigation. Church and his vice-chairman, Texas Republican John Tower, sat with their colleagues as a board of directors, constituting and reconstituting a series of subcommittees to supervise parts of the investigation.

The Church committee had an eight-month deadline—much less time than was permitted to the Watergate investigators—but a lengthy list of preor-dained areas of inquiry plus the desire to do an overall review of the intel-ligence community. Senator Church wanted to get to basics and tried to collect the views of intelligence people going back to the early days of the CIA and other agencies in the wake of World War II. Bill Miller wished to focus on a few cases in great depth. The deputy staff director, New York lawyer F.A.O. ("Fritz") Schwarz, Jr., also anticipated a need to concentrate efforts in a limited number of areas, and seeking a fact-based probe, he tried to identify all the directives that presidents and directors of central intelli-gence had used to govern the CIA and the other agencies from their incep-tion. Schwarz put staff to work on lists of these documents and chronologies of the events pertaining to individual case studies. Miller and Schwarz divided the staff into four task forces: domestic intelligence (a major congressional concern), military intelligence, foreign intelligence (especially the CIA), and command and control (concentrating on the president, the National Security Council, and the leadership of the CIA).

As soon as he learned of the creation of the committee, Director Colby phoned Senator Church to offer cooperation. He met with Church and Senator John Tower, the vice-chairman, to set ground rules. Colby wanted the com-mittee staff to sign secrecy agreements akin to those used at the CIA. Church explained his plan to first accumulate a documentary record, then call wit-nesses for hearings. Colby promised free access to unclassified information and ready access to secret material, which the committee must help protect, but not to sensitive items pertaining to technical intelligence or to the names of sources. Within these limits Colby expressed willingness for CIA officers to testify without regard to their secrecy oaths. Church, who intended to issue press releases on the issues investigated, agreed to clear these in advance with Colby's people at Langley.

But Bill Colby was not the only one observing these developments. On February 28, the day after the Colby-Church meeting, President Ford had Henry Kissinger in the Oval Office for a wide-ranging review of current affairs. Amid talk of China, Russia, arms control, Vietnam, and other matters, conversation turned to the investigations and Colby. To counter the inquisi-tors, Kissinger said, "I think we need a CIA Steering Committee and White House corroboration." Colby, he declared, was "out of control."[25] Kissinger suggested lawyer Laurence Silberman to replace Colby as director of central intelligence. Silberman had told Ford he was willing to help, but only for a month or so. That seemed no solution. Things remained as they were.

A week later, on the morning of March 5, Tower and Church were invited to the White House for a half-hour seance with President Ford and Brent Scowcroft, joined at the last moment by Kissinger and Donald Rumsfeld. Talking points the NSC staff prepared for the president advised Ford to de-clare a desire to cooperate, as had Colby, but to emphasize cautionary ele-ments. The investigations should be concerned with impressions being created around the world, intelligence officers should be assured that their heads were not on the block, and disclosures would be disastrous. Ford was told it was important that he not *commit* himself to cooperate fully or provide particular categories of information, that he should avoid giving specifics or negotiating with the senators, and that he should not agree to waive executive privilege. Specific cases would be considered on their merits. Frank Church outlined the senate resolution and tried to be agreeable, emphasizing his committee's responsible intent. Ford refused to issue a written directive for governmentwide cooperation. Kissinger, described at this encounter as being "poised like an overweight tiger," interjected, "Asking for information is one thing, but going through the files is another. The covert action files are very sensitive."[26]

The president pocketed a list of the documents the Church committee wanted to see. The committee, however, made its list the subject of a formal written request to Director Colby on March 12. On four densely packed, legal size pages, the fruit of Fritz Schwarz's inquiries took shape; the Church committee asked by name for a long series of CIA internal studies plus a wide variety of organizational, structural, and budget information. National Security Council directives, which Church had requested directly from President Ford, were not on the list but were clearly within the scope of his interests. A similar solicitation of Attorney General Edward H. Levi for FBI documents went out on March 19.

The Church committee's demands set in motion maneuvers both within the intelligence community and the White House to meet the challenge. Having set ground rules with the senators. Bill Colby created a mechanism at CIA to field their inquiries. He set up an ad hoc committee of the United States Intelligence Board in late march to serve as a clearing house, point of contact, and monitoring unit for the investigators and all documents permitted to go to Congress. To head the unit Colby selected Walter N. Elder, a twenty-four-year CIA veteran. Colby had known and trusted Elder since his days with the Far East Division, when the Elder had been executive assistant to John McCone. Elder had also played an important role in the inception of the CIA's internal history program and himself had written the agency's history of McCone's tenure. A number of those history studies, including Elder's, were soon on the Church committee's document lists. When it became necessary for the CIA to establish a liaison with the parallel intelligence investigation mounted by the House of Representatives, Colby appointed Donald P. Gregg, an Asian specialist and experienced clandestine service officer whom he had known since the 1960s, most recently as the CIA's proconsul for South Vietnam's third military region when Colby had directed CORDS.

Many at CIA, particularly the stalwarts of the Helms faction within the DO, wanted to stonewall the congressional investigators and resist every request. When it began to look like Colby's CIA was not going to do that, some took matters into their own hands. David Atlee Phillips, a prominent DO officer who had played a key role in the Chile affair as well as earlier

CIA operations in Latin America, resigned to be able to speak publicly. Phillips and others on March 20 formed the Association of Retired Intelligence Officers, with a project they called "Confound," designed to muddy the waters for the investigations.

Bill Colby understood the motivations but could not agree with the course of action. His legal experience told Colby that the defendant almost always loses in an attempt to suppress evidence. In 1975 the CIA was quite clearly in the role of defendant. The better response would be to reveal a mass of documents in order to put negative information into broader context. This stance earned Colby enmity both at CIA and at the White House. That enmity, in turn, obscures the degree to which Colby actually worked to protect CIA secrets. In fact, when Colby issued his guidelines for dealing with the investigations on March 24, 1975, he provided for four levels of security regarding information. Only "the bulk" of historical, organizational, and budget data would be permitted to reside in congressional files. More sensitive data would be "sanitized" before being shown and would be retained by the originating agencies. At the third level, only congressional committee members or selected staff would be allowed to view the documents, and only on the premises of the intelligence agencies. Colby termed these "fondling" files. The last type of material would not be shown at all and would only be used to prepare briefs or briefings. This category specifically included "sensitive matters where Executive Branch prerogatives are involved," in particular memoranda to or from the president. Colby's CIA would be far less open to inquiry than his critics claimed.[27]

The White House conformed more nearly to the predilections of those who preferred secrecy. At a news conference on March 17, President Ford refused to answer a question about whether he would give the Church committee all the material it had requested on the grounds that his top advisers were still examining the request. He did say, "We will do all we can to *indicate* maximum cooperation."[28] The day Colby issued his CIA guidelines, senior officials within the White House were lamenting their continued lack of any coherent policy for responding to the Church requests. On March 29, NSC staffer Robert C. McFarlane weighed in with a detailed analysis of the various White House documents Church had asked for—national security action memoranda, decision memoranda, national security council intelligence directives. According to this analysis, the substantial bulk of material should be conceded. Higher officials annotating the list objected to many of the recommendations. Among those McFarlane himself judged too sensitive were President Kennedy's orders creating the NSC Special Group (Counterinsurgency) and shifting basic responsibility for paramilitary operations from the CIA to the military in the wake of the Bay of Pigs. Writing to Ford on April 2, counsel Philip Buchen confirmed the bulk of recommendations, including release of the Colby report.

The documents were handed over at the White House in mid-April. Simultaneously, on April 14, McFarlane argued to White House lawyer James

Wilderotter that *no* classified information should be provided the Church committee until legal exchanges confirmed the president's exclusive right to make all decisions about opening secret information to public scrutiny. It was in the context of that position, held by Henry Kissinger and Brent Scowcroft, that CIA documents began arriving at the White House for clearance. The first batch, sent by Walt Elder in late March, contained items Colby had been asked for on March 12. Then, on April 10, Church's CIA task force leader, William B. Bader, visited Langley and requested many studies from a list of CIA histories Elder showed him. This added fifty-two more volumes to the CIA materials already up for review. Though many were dry organizational histories that have been since declassified and revealed to be scanty on serious operational details, White House reviews found problem areas in almost all of them. A study of the evolution of the *Central Intelligence Bulletin* seemed objectionable because it "describes relations with the Executive Office." Another history of the development of economic intelligence that commented on the Bomber and Missile Gaps of the 1950s "describes relations with the National Security Council and other members of the intelligence community and sets forth judgments and evaluations of these relations." The problem with an account of the CIA Inspector General's Office was that that unit had worked on the Cuban Missile crisis post mortem. A history of Allen Dulles's tenure as DCI shed too much light on CIA covert operations, and one on Walter Bedell Smith had too much "rich detail" on his personal dealings with top government officials. And so on.[29] The concerns were excessive, sometimes even silly.

President Ford eventually allowed the Church committee access to these histories, with certain restrictions, but identical issues of protecting White House reputations and secret information resurfaced at every turn during the year of congressional investigations. When the Church committee took over the investigation of assassinations (with a four-month extension of its deadline), when it began to look at episodes in the Nixon administration, and especially in regard to the House investigators, the White House bristled. The differences with Ford over secrecy led Colby to try some positive reinforcement, sending the president a personal note on April 5:

> Please let me express my appreciation for your support of our intelligence activities in several recent public statements. At a time when we are under considerable public attack and criticism, your support is enormously heartening to our professionals in the field.[30]

The hackles went up almost immediately on April 24, when Church committee chief counsel Fritz Schwarz handed a White House intelligence specialist a list of new materials that were deemed necessary to interpret the December 1974 Colby report and the director's subsequent testimony on CIA illegal activities. An index of Colby's own reticence in these matters is that he sought (but failed) to withhold the CIA's notorious "Family Jewels" compilation. Now the Church committee wanted a wide variety of related documents. Meanwhile Bill Miller reported to Senator Church that the White House continued to resort to tactical devices to delay handing over materials. On April 29 Miller and Schwarz met with White House staff at the Executive Office Building for four hours, to be told the CIA had complained about their requests for agency histories. "Why does the committee want to go through these old history books?" they were asked.[31]

Again Bill Colby imposed major restrictions on access under the formula that would finally be worked out. Only five congressional investigators could see the histories, and only at Walt Elder's CIA office. The researchers could only take notes, they were not permitted to photocopy large portions of the texts. Any documents they requested as a result of picking up references in the histories would be reviewed word for word by CIA overseers; representatives of the originating agencies would look on every minute that investigators perused their documents.

Seeking to break the ring of secrecy, Senator Church next met with Vice-President Nelson Rockefeller, then moving to the final stages of his own commission inquiry. Church asked that the assassination materials compiled by the Rockefeller commission be passed along to the Church committee. Rockefeller proved noncommittal.

Two days later, on May 9, the Church committee decided to up the ante by calling a formal hearing on CIA covert operations, requiring Director Colby's testimony. A new flurry of Executive Branch activity followed. That same day Ford's top advisers (Kissinger, Rumsfeld, Buchen, and John Marsh) drafted a recommendation that Colby be authorized to brief only, rather than testify, and only Senators Church and Tower. He would be told to discuss only the general subject, with details of specific covert actions to be avoided except for "realistic hypotheticals." Their fallback position would have permitted discussion of just nine CIA actions, limited in scope as well as time. Cuba, for example, could only be covered for 1960 and 1961; Vietnam and Laos only before 1964; the Congo only between 1963 and 1966. There could be no avoiding Chile, which could be covered from 1961 to 1971. The others were Russia, Greece, Korea (to 1952 only), and Indonesia. President Ford approved general briefing only, devoid of details, and ordered Colby to have it ready for White House review by noon on May 13.[32]

The White House gambit could not succeed, however. The Church committee had full authority to call a hearing and require Colby's testimony. Ford held a preparatory meeting the afternoon of May 14 with Colby, the drafters of the May 9 proposal, plus Brent Scowcroft and defense secretary James Schlesinger. Phil Buchen's talking points prepared for Ford suggested he quote Senator Henry ("Scoop") Jackson, who had said in 1960, "The golden word of intelligence is silence." Colby was to try to get away with the private briefing, "to induce the Chairman and Ranking Minority Member to impose limitations on the further investigation of the subjects covered."[33]

Bill Colby did speak privately with Frank Church, but he could not get away without testifying. Colby and White House lawyer Roderick Hills tried to impress the chairman with delicate issues, and told Ford later that Church might agree to restrict data more tightly within his staff. Another CIA tactic, to require all its officers testifying to be accompanied by agency minders, was roundly rejected, though Colby felt he might be able to have CIA lawyers present through most of committee interviews.

Finally Director Colby strode confidently into the Church committee's specially prepared hearing room, shielded from electronic surveillance inside the Capitol Dome. As he recounted at a National Security Council meeting late that afternoon, May 15, "It was like being a prisoner in the dock, there was a real interrogation."

Gerald Ford is supposed to have ordered all White House taping systems removed after Watergate, but the minutes of his National Security Council meetings clearly can only have been compiled by a tape recorder or court reporter. Colby's remarks that day are worth quoting at length:

> All the questions were on assassination and it was like "when did you stop beating your wife?" That was all they wanted to talk about but I insisted on covering the whole range of covert action in a larger way; otherwise it would have been a disaster. I explained to them how covert operations are conducted, what are the procedures followed, what orders are given, who does what. Then I gave them some specific cases that have already been blown for the most part, such as Guatemala. This left them groping for a way to tackle the whole problem. Then I went on to propaganda and agents of influence. . . .
>   Then I talked about Radio Free Europe. And then at the end I got to assassination. I described the delicacy of the problem and how little of this sort of thing the U.S. has really done. There were attempts against Castro in the early 1960s but our information is very scarce. . . . Then they wanted to know whether we had ever had any of our own agents assassinated, you know, the Green Beret thing. I told them we never do that. I also told them that our policy and our orders are very clear: we will have nothing to do with assassination: Church ended by saying that is not enough. That to be certain we need more than orders. We need to have a law which prohibits assassination in time of peace.[34]

President Ford asked about which senators and staff had been present at the hearing.

"It is an act of insanity and national humiliation," Henry Kissinger interjected, "to have a law prohibiting the President from ordering assassination."[35]

Meanwhile Church committee staff were poring through the supporting documents Director Colby had carried to Congress for his presentation. Several items they expected to find were missing. The next morning at a breakfast Senator Frank Church told reporters there were gaps in the records. The struggle over the intelligence investigations had reached a new level.

REMARKABLE AS IT MAY SEEM, Ford administration officials came away from the Year of Intelligence saying that their relations with the Church committee had been fairly straightforward and collegial. It hardly appeared so in May 1975, with the Senate working up to hearings. Colby would appear for more detailed testimony on covert operations over three days in late May, and Church filed several additional document requests over these weeks and into June, for material on CIA domestic activities, on national intelligence estimates, and about covert action. Over this time the parallel intelligence investigation mandated by the House of Representatives had gone nowhere, but that turned out to be deceiving. Ultimately the House investigation became even more problematical than that of the Senate.

Like the Senate, the House of Representatives produced a supermajority to create its investigating committee. The vote in the House on February 19 was 286 to 120. The chairmanship went to Lucien N. Nedzi of the existing oversight unit. Nedzi had more direct experience dealing with the intelligence community than his counterparts in the Senate plus a much stronger parliamentary edge (the political lineup on the Church committee was six Democrats to five Republicans; Nedzi had seven to three). But the chairman had already been tarnished by the Chile affair—Nedzi had had to defend himself before the House Democratic Caucus following revelations on that operation—and now colleagues looked askance at a member some viewed as in the pocket of CIA. The presence on the investigating committee of Michael J. Harrington, CIA's Chile nemesis, sharpened the problem. Nedzi tried to use the exercise of hiring a staff director to homogenize his committee, encountering rancor as one candidate after another pulled out of the running (more than twenty individuals were interviewed for this job). Finally in May the committee settled on a young Watergate investigator, lawyer A. Searle Field, who then worked behind the scenes to weaken Nedzi's leadership. In early June, press reports disclosed that Nedzi, privately briefed by Bill Colby, had had prior knowledge of the CIA's Family Jewels report that he had never made the subject of House oversight proceedings.

Generating momentum for this investigation became a problem. With the committee at loggerheads, Democrats voted to create a CIA subcommittee and called a hearing for June 12. Nedzi tried to resign, was dissuaded by House leadership, and then encouraged Republican members to boycott the hearing. Director Colby came down from Langley to be the first witness only to be left standing in the hall as the Republicans failed to show up. Nedzi went ahead with his resignation, which the full House refused to accept, but he then withdrew. On July 10 the House Rules Committee agreed to reconstitute the investigation under new leadership, accepted in the full House a week later. New York Democrat Otis G. Pike took over as chairman on July 17. The new committee proved even more lopsided, with nine Democrats and just four Republicans. Two of this group had been elected with the post-Watergate 1974 Congress and four others in the antiwar upsurge of the 1970 elections.

Bill Colby could only view these developments with trepidation. To be credible the House committee had to adopt a tough line toward the intelligence community. Meanwhile the Church committee had started its detailed investigation of charges of CIA involvement in assassinations. The intelligence inquiry had become a political struggle, a battleground in the post-Watergate realignment of power between Congress and president, and the CIA needed help. Colby hit on the idea of hiring lawyers from outside the agency to assist in responding to the investigations.

In one of his most unconventional and astute moves, Director Colby went to the Washington law firm Arnold & Porter to hire Mitchell J. Rogovin as special counsel to the CIA. A former assistant attorney general in the Johnson administration and a specialist on civil liberties, Rogovin had political sense and a sterling reputation. Rogovin also had links to liberals and the New Left, most importantly as counsel to the think tank Institute for Policy Studies. Colby's offer led Rogovin to a late night meeting at his home with Marc Raskin of the Institute, along with William Watts, who had served on the Nixon NSC staff but resigned in protest over the U.S. invasion of Cambodia. Watts argued that the job could be an opportunity to create understanding between government and the Left, but Raskin saw little chance of that and feared the CIA work could be a conflict of interest. When Rogovin decided to go ahead and aid Director Colby, the Institute for Policy Studies let him go as legal counsel. With the CIA, Rogovin's service during the Year of Intelligence would be deemed so valuable that he would one day be awarded the National Security Medal, the CIA's equivalent to the Congressional Medal of Honor, becoming the only person from outside the intelligence world (except Brent Scowcroft, who earned this medal as a military man) ever to be so honored. Rogovin began working for Colby at the end of June.

Simultaneous with strengthening his legal team, Director Colby promulgated fresh orders to limit Church committee access to information on covert action. The CIA would offer in-depth briefings, but only of "certain selected covert action programs which typify categories." A few documents extracted from project files would supplement the oral presentations, while Senate investigators could ask to see (on CIA premises) appropriately sanitized files. Presidential approvals, 40 Committee minutes, and all other White House records were to be removed from any files shown, and all briefings and documents would be cleared in advance with the White House. Should Senator Church raise questions regarding access he would be sent there. Colby hoped to restrict inquiries to CIA funding of private organizations (revealed in 1967 and reviewed by the Katzenbach Report of that year), Laos, and Indonesia. With these rules Colby complied with decisions made at a White House meeting on June 27; the strictures were acceptable to presidential advisers at the time.[36]

The picture that emerges shows Bill Colby treading a careful path between a White House intent on preserving secrecy (bolstered by a faction within the CIA) and congressional investigations determined to get to the bottom of alleged CIA wrongdoing, while perhaps scoring political points. The record of the June 27 meeting shows that White House participants understood they were approving this degree of access, limited as it was, "for the purpose of avoiding a complete impasse on this issue."[37] Church committee staff went along for the same reason. But Bill Colby remained trapped at the nexus of powerful forces buffeting the Central Intelligence Agency from every angle.

Another of those angles was pressure from the White House for covert operations in Angola, even as Kissinger and others resisted the congressional inquiries into intelligence. Six months earlier Portugal, which then controlled Angola as a colony in Africa, reached an agreement with several political factions looking toward independence to be accorded in November 1975. That began a period of jockeying for power. The most powerful political party was a communist one. Within days of the Portuguese-Angolan agreement, the 40 Committee approved large increases in the CIA subsidy already being paid to the leader of another Angolan faction. Possibilities for a coalition government in Angola soon receded, and Kissinger ordered a policy review, completed on June 13, which became the focus of a National Security Council meeting on June 27, the same day Colby received his marching orders restricting congressional access to information.

Henry Kissinger's preparatory memorandum to President Ford for the meeting made clear that U.S. interests in Angola were important but not vital. The alternatives, identified from the recent policy review, were neutrality; diplomatic measures, for which Kissinger saw a general consensus that these should at least be tried before other measures; and "active support" of the anticommunist factions, assistance which, Kissinger conceded, "would have to be covert or channeled through third parties." His own account of U.S. contacts with the dictator Mobutu Sese Seko in neighboring Zaire (now called the Congo) showed that Mobutu encouraged intervention but denied having resources to act on his own, looking toward a U.S. operation from which he could hope to take a cut. Though the Kissinger memo admitted attractions of other options, it was most eloquent on the possibility of active support:

> In addition to our substantive interest in the outcome, playing an active role would demonstrate that events in Southeast Asia have not lessened our determination to protect our interests. In sum, we face an opportunity—albeit with substantial risks—to preempt the probable loss to Communism of a key developing country at a time of great uncertainty over our will and determination.[38]

The actual NSC meeting opened with Director Colby presenting the CIA briefing. Colby described the factional infighting in Angola moving toward independence, the Portuguese stance of biding time until pulling out on independence day, and international considerations. The Russians had been helping the communist faction, the Chinese oddly enough; these were the same two noncommunist groups Washington now considered assisting. Zaire had been aiding one of those groups as well. The CIA did *not* conclude that any of the factions had the upper hand; it *did* believe that both the communist and the most powerful noncommunist faction wanted a nonaligned foreign policy that would "seek to maintain some balance between East and West, *and* that *either* of these factions if it had power would have an authoritarian regime, either centralized and socialist, or highly nationalistic and personalized" (read dictatorship).[39]

President Ford's comments at the NSC session make clear that he knew little if anything about Angola. He questioned Bill Colby after the briefing on several aspects of Angolan society. Kissinger presented his three options, professing himself not in "wild agreement" with any of them. Kissinger essentially discounted neutrality and objected that the diplomatic option could not be policed; his discussion of the CIA "active support" alternative has been deleted from the current version of the meeting record. But the diplomat who had chaired the Angola policy review, which had favored negotiation, resigned in protest at how the alternatives were handled at the White House level, and other sources make clear that Kissinger favored the CIA option. Gerald Ford asked for concrete program proposals, and Director Colby promised to have one ready by early July.[40]

Secretary Kissinger at the NSC had remarked on the importance in Africa of controlling a country's capital, evidently to counteract Colby's CIA briefing, which had noted that the communist faction was most powerful in the Angolan capital. Later he evidently found the CIA reluctant to bring forward its covert operation proposal. On July 13 Kissinger held a 40 Committee meeting and ordered Colby to present a project proposal within forty-eight hours. President Ford approved a CIA effort, Project Feature, on July 17. The CIA warned that a big covert program would leak—how could it be otherwise in the year of the investigations?—and that Feature could cost as much as $100 million. Ford gave the agency $14 million immediately and increased the amount another $10.7 million a month later. Kissinger's 40 Committee gave final approval on August 8. The CIA worked with both anticommunist factions, who were also receiving support from, and were tainted by, South Africa. The Angola effort, the biggest paramilitary operation the CIA initiated during Bill Colby's watch, would be a dismal failure.

Simultaneously pressed for action on Angola and inaction in cooperating with the congressional investigations, Colby's position was a delicate one. Congressional pressures complicated the problem even more. Echoes of this inner struggle inevitably reached the press. On June 23 presidential press secretary Ron Nessen was asked whether Gerald Ford still had confidence in his CIA chief. Nessen replied affirmatively. Colby had a note hand-delivered to President Ford thanking him and ending, "We professionals deeply appreciate this confidence and take from it renewed energy."[41] But unknown to Colby, weeks earlier the White House had begun privately considering the appointment of a new director of central intelligence. By July 10 Ford had a list of fifteen possible candidates (incidentally, George H. W. Bush, the eventual appointee, was named by just three of the eight senior presidential aides involved in this matter; Henry Kissinger was not among them). At his public appearances reporters repeatedly asked Bill Colby if he expected to be fired;

he recounts "Although, as I must admit, I steadfastly tried to deny the truth of it to myself, I knew that my days were numbered."[42]

The White House problem loomed in the distance but Bill Colby's immediate headaches were on Capitol Hill. Trouble with the Pike Committee began right away. Colby disliked Pike's staff, whom he viewed as publicity seekers, a pickup team of analysts with little expertise. Pike aggravated this nagging itch by refusing to oblige his team to sign CIA-like secrecy agreements, while opening a second front by rejecting CIA-style compartmentation for storage of the documents Langley delivered. It was Mitchell Rogovin's letter laying out a system that Pike rejected, and when Rogovin and Colby then met with the chairman the encounter turned into a confrontation. Pike saw himself as protecting the prerogatives of Congress; Rogovin believed the chairman was trying to avoid charges of having been coopted by the Central Intelligence Agency. The tone is apparent in a letter Otis Pike sent the DCI on July 28: "It's a delight to receive two letters from you not stamped 'Secret' on every page. . . . You are concerned with the concept of 'need to know' and I am concerned with the concept of 'right to know' "[43]

When the Pike committee held its first public hearing on August 4, its chairman contrasted the Ford administration's rhetoric of cooperation with its practice of delay and obfuscation. The final report that would eventually leak contained the assertion that "when legal proceedings were not in the offing, the access experience was frequently one of foot-dragging, stone-walling, and careful deception."[44] The committee struck back where it could, notably in an incident over a briefcase. In this episode the White House and Pike committee were stuck over the refusal of Ford's Office of Management and Budget to supply data on intelligence budgets (an issue Pike had already raised with Colby on July 28), and White House lawyers Philip Buchen and Roderick Hills went to the committee's offices to resolve it. Hills left his briefcase with a secret document in it when the pair departed, and when they returned to retrieve it, Pike refused to hand over the briefcase. Weeks later, when the White House complained about leaks of secret data from the committee, Pike replied that his handling of classified information was far more careful than that of White House staff, citing the briefcase episode. Roderick Hills resigned soon afterward.

Altercations over the Family Jewels report typified the Pike committee–CIA relationship. Colby showed Pike the full report early on, but the CIA sent only a sanitized version when the House investigators asked for it. On further demand, Donald Gregg told the committee its top staff could review a sanitized version at Langley. Protest brought a new version of the document, still sanitized. Finally, in November, when the committee began legal action against Henry Kissinger on other documents, the CIA delivered the Family Jewels fifteen minutes before a news conference Pike had called to lambast the agency on this matter. The device of offering briefings to the chairman and vice-chairman, then to staff members—a standard practice in CIA's over-

sight history that Colby used to advantage with the Church committee—
became a source of constant irritation with the House. Otis Pike's position
remained that if the House of Representatives had intended to create a two-
person investigating committee it would have done so.

Congress had a constitutional right to investigate, so the Ford administration was obliged to respond. Colby and Rogovin sat through many meetings
in the Situation Room in the White House basement while officials denounced
the investigators, only to have to yield up the documents in question days or
weeks later. Colby's device for handling Pike finally came to be "lending"
documents to the committee, thus clearly establishing ownership in case of
legal dispute. Eventually mountains of paper overwhelmed the thirty Pike
committee staffers—over 90,000 pages. When the dust had settled and the
investigation ended, the CIA would accuse the committee of losing some of
that material. Donald Gregg would remember his liaison work with the Pike
committee as a far more difficult assignment than many of the CIA covert
operations in which he participated. Warren Milburg, an assistant who had
gone to the CIA after working with Colby in Vietnam on CORDS, agreed.
Milburg's relations with one of the Pike staffers, of diametrically opposing
views, became so intense he fell in love and married her.

Meanwhile the Senate investigation posed its own problems. Soon after
Colby's testimony on covert action the Church committee kicked off its formal inquiry into assassinations, in which a central question had to be presidential approval and cognizance of the plans. Here the Ford administration
faced contradictory impulses. The Republicans were not entirely averse to its
becoming known that Jack and Bobby Kennedy had plotted against Castro;
but on the other hand, the assassination capability had been developed under
a Republican, Eisenhower, and the most recent plots, in Chile, involved a
Nixon-Kissinger covert operation. Protecting the presidency meant shielding
leaders of both parties. That brought even tighter restrictions on information.
Investigators were permitted to view assassination materials only in the White
House Situation Room. Other documents were handed over only after repeated requests from both staff and senators. This turned out to be for good
reason. Frederick Baron, the single Church committee staffer allowed access
to the cable traffic on the case of the death of African nationalist Patrice
Lumumba, came away with what he recalled as "the clearest evidence that a
president [Eisenhower] had ordered an assassination attempt."[45] Baron, a lawyer from the "Show Me" state of Missouri and formerly aide to the director
of the National Legal Aid and Defender Association, would not have come
to that conclusion lightly.*

---

* While the committee found strong evidence that Eisenhower had ordered action against
Lumumba, along with CIA activity clearly intended to create a capability to assassinate the
Congolese leader, the Church investigators focused almost entirely on the August 1960 plot that
involved poison. Intelligence officer David W. Doyle, then CIA chief of base in the Congolese
breakaway province Katanga (which Belgium hoped to preserve as a colony), reports that the

To get a handle on the investigations, Ford administration officials forged links with friendly members and staff on both the Church and Pike committees. On the Pike committee especially, Republican vice-chairman Robert McClory worked actively to counter his own investigation. Working plans of both committees turned up in White House files; for example, William G. Miller's July 22 memo to Frank Church outlining tasks until January and postulating target dates for various hearings was in White House hands by August 5.

Pressures of the investigations built to an explosive point in September. On September 3 Director Colby sent Otis Pike a letter detailing the conditions under which CIA officers could be interviewed or would provide testimony, with Mitchell Rogovin to serve as the point of contact for these arrangements. Colby simultaneously issued an employee bulletin containing the letter plus amplifying information. Colby also took the highly unusual step of sending a similar notice to former CIA employees. Pike moved to hold a hearing on intelligence analysis in the Middle East focused on the Arab-Israeli October War of 1973 and a crisis in Cyprus during the summer of 1974. The committee asked for documents, some of which the CIA provided on September 9; Pike issued a subpoena for more the next day. Staff director A. Searle Field also asked the agency to declassify six pages of the conclusion to its postmortem on the October War so these could be read into the record.

At the hearing the CIA postmortem was read into the record by Colby's chief of current intelligence, William K. Parmenter. The CIA tried to keep secret five passages primarily regarding signals intelligence; Pike demanded that they be released, and threatened that his committee would vote later on a motion to reveal them anyway. Langley scrambled to find Colby, whom they reached on the phone, while Rogovin begged Pike to delay his committee vote. Colby agreed to declassify all the passages save one, but insisted that a phrase mentioning the CIA's knowledge of Egyptian communications networks remain secret. This Colby considered the most sensitive of all. Pike held his vote, rejected the CIA's contentions, then held a news conference describing the byplay. The next day, over protests from Rogovin and assistant attorney general Rex Lee, A. Searle Field read all five passages

---

agency's station chief in the Congo, Lawrence Devlin, rejected assassination on moral grounds and derailed the Washington-hatched schemes of August. But on September 1 the NSC Special Group approved a fresh proposal for Project Wizard, the provision of cash payoffs to various figures to oppose Lumumba, duly fired four days later. A coup overthrew the government on the 14th, with both these actions taken by persons now on the CIA payroll. Special Group decisions on October 27 and November 20 further increased aid and provided for arms and training as well. Lumumba was held prisoner and transferred to the custody of sworn enemies, of which action the CIA appears to have had advance knowledge. It remains unclear what was the CIA role in Lumumba's death on January 17, 1961. Meanwhile a Dutch scholar has developed evidence indicating Belgian complicity in the murder. A Belgian parliamentary inquiry followed, resulting in a February 2002 acknowledgment that that country bears some portion of responsibility in the murder.[46]

into the record, including the reference to Egyptian communications security.

Ford administration officials were in an uproar following this episode. When some of Kissinger's material on the Cyprus crisis also leaked, the secretary of state hit the roof. Kissinger demanded that not only should no more documents be given to Pike but that everything the committee had be taken back. Don Rumsfeld and John Marsh, who had been congressmen themselves, blanched. Short of sending in the Marines, Marsh remarked, this could not be done. Leery of starting a war with Congress, Ford did nothing. Ironically, as demonstrated by Frank J. Smist, an acute observer of these events, Kissinger himself had leaked the key information about Egyptian communications in an even more damaging form, explicitly relating the intercepts to U.S. monitoring stations in Iran. The Kissinger leak came in interviews with journalists Marvin and Bernard Kalb who published a laudatory biography of Kissinger in 1974.[47] No one in the White House brought this up. What Ford did do on September 19 was to create an Intelligence Coordinating Group in the White House chaired by John Marsh. The group began to meet daily on September 22. Colby and Rogovin represented the CIA. Brent Scowcroft represented Kissinger and the National Security Council staff.

Another of Pike's case studies, intelligence knowledge of the Tet offensive in Vietnam, simultaneously led to a second confrontation. On September 10 Pike subpoenaed documents the CIA was reluctant to supply. Pushing for materials, the committee threatened to go to court. Rogovin failed in efforts to get Pike to modify the subpoena, then again begged for time. But Director Colby had little to stand on; the CIA's own lawyers concluded, in a legal brief on September 22, that the courts would accept justicability of a subpoena, that there was "an excellent chance" courts would uphold the subpoena, that there was little chance a court would order a congressman or committee not to report on or discuss matters under their jurisdiction, and that "there does not appear to be any realistic way in which the Agency can come out the winner."[48]

Bill Colby's recourse would be negotiating a fresh understanding with the committee on provision and handling of documents. He yielded the Tet materials and preserved an uneasy truce with both the Pike and Church committees. At the White House, Colby kept the intelligence panel constantly informed on progress, briefing them, for example, on October 8 about an inquiry into domestic wiretapping by the National Security Agency pursued by a postal affairs subcommittee under Bella Abzug; and on October 13 about Pike's interest in convert operations, plus a variety of Church committee inquiries that included the CIA's use of philanthropic institutions and its reliance on cooperating individuals and corporations.

Henry Kissinger also took the floor at the meeting of October 13. At loggerheads with the Pike committee, which insisted on looking into the 1974 Cyprus crisis, Kissinger had refused to permit testimony from a diplomat who had filed protests within a State Department "dissent" channel. Kissinger then asked Ford, on September 25, to include diplomatic exchanges within the category of material to be withheld under the compromise that the administration was working out with Congress. Kissinger simultaneously sent President Ford a memorandum advocating total denial and a consequent court confrontation, unless Pike accepted White House prerogatives and control over any public release of information. On October 13 Kissinger argued these issues before Ford and the Intelligence Coordinating Group, his situation now complicated by the fact the Pike committee had already filed subpoenas for the Cyprus documents. While the record of this critical meeting is not yet in the public domain, the next day Kissinger sent Representative Pike a letter refusing to comply with the requests for the Cyprus documents.

Though Kissinger's public posture remained cooperative, privately he encouraged intransigence and worked his contacts in the media to generate negative coverage of the congressional investigators. The contrast with Bill Colby's approach is apparent. This contrast reflected badly on an already embattled CIA director. President Ford faced an election campaign in 1976 and was being accused of having an administration in disarray. His "kitchen cabinet" of close political advisers actually told Ford on October 16 that he must be seen to project stronger leadership. That same day Ford met with defense secretary James R. Schlesinger, another senior official whom Kissinger regarded as being off the reservation, to insist that the Pentagon mute its criticisms of Henry on foreign policy issues. Ford later regaled Kissinger and Brent Scowcroft with the play by play of this session.

Driven in new directions by his need to project leadership, President Ford began to consider changes at the top level of government. On October 23 he sounded out Bryce Harlow, informal factotem to Republican presidents back to Dwight Eisenhower, on the new thinking. Toward the end of October Ford came to his decision. In his memoirs, Ford puts no time to his choice and connects it primarily with feeling something had to be done about Schlesinger. Ford says he liked and respected Bill Colby and thought the CIA director smart, with both guts and integrity. But the director had lost the confidence of senior officials, most importantly Henry Kissinger.

Langley was not so much an ivory tower that Director Colby had no inkling of all that was afoot. Indeed in early October came a resurgence of talk about town that Colby had lost the support of the president. Press secretary Ron Nessen knocked down the story, but the rumors continued to fly and acquired a more concrete character. George Schulz, then heading a huge construction firm, and William D. Ruckelshaus, a former deputy attorney general, were mentioned as possible successors to Colby. A time frame began to be attached too—Colby's job at the CIA, it would be said, would not last past the new year. In a clear indication he believed these stories, in mid-October William E. Colby filed papers with the bar association in Washington to recognize his legal credentials for the practice of law in the nation's capital. The further rumor began to fly that Colby had begun talking with the law firm Arnold & Porter, which had supplied Mitchell Rogovin to the CIA, for a partnership in that firm.

Henry Kissinger's difficulties with Otis Pike reached a new peak on Friday, October 31, Halloween. Air Force One touched down at Andrews Air Force Base at 1:01 A.M. that morning, returning Gerald Ford from a political trip to Milwaukee, but just eight hours later the president met Kissinger and Brent Scowcroft in the Oval Office. They talked of Ford's impending trip to China but at least half the conversation concerned the intelligence quagmire. Kissinger, scheduled to appear that morning before Pike's committee, previewed what he would say. A Kissinger remark about postponing a planned visit to Moscow for arms control negotiations reveals him to be already aware of Ford's decision to fire top officials. Ford thought Henry's planned testimony "a damned good statement."

"Pike will blast me at the outset," Kissinger predicted. "Then I will make my statement. Then Pike will ask what is my legal authority. I will say the lawyers say it is legal."

Henry ranged across an array of issues, spoke of which Pike committee members might bring up those matters, and returning to a favorite theme, warned the committee would vote to reveal certain information. "Their purpose is to show I am the evil genius," Kissinger said.

As ever, Ford expressed concern about the flap potential of revelations. A summary passage in the meeting record was pregnant with meaning for the CIA director: "There is discussion of Colby and giving everything away."[49]

There should be little doubt what Kissinger advocated in this conversation. In some of his many encounters with journalists during the Year of Intelligence, Bill Colby had already been asked specifically why Kissinger (and Nelson Rockefeller) wanted him out of the CIA. Later Colby recounted a scathing Kissinger jibe from one of their White House meetings: "Bill, you know what you do when you go up to the Hill? You go to confession."[50] The only thing Kissinger could have been doing in the Oval Office this day was steeling President Ford's resolve to fire Director Colby.

As for Kissinger's own road to Damascus, Ford had admonished him to keep his cool. "If I explode," Kissinger replied, "It will be calculated."[51]

Otis Pike indeed opened his hearing with a commentary, but the blast aimed at the withholding of information, with Cyprus the only issue directly referred to. There was no personal attack on Kissinger. The questioning following the witness's opening statement proved pointed, but Kissinger deflected, bobbed, and weaved, all the while deferring to the distinguished representatives. On the very delicate issue of how Kissinger could claim a right to hold information on his own, independent of a president's executive privilege, Henry did what he had told Ford: relied on his lawyers. Asserting that he had not claimed independent "secretarial privilege," Kissinger stood on the grounds that he had legal authority to direct the Foreign Service as to what testimony it might provide. Kissinger also refused to testify about covert operations in open session—in particular about approvals by the 40 Committee, which (he had acknowledged to President Ford prior to the hearing) had often been granted without formal meetings. California representative Ron Dellums quoted back to him Kissinger's celebrated remark at a meeting the 40 Committee did have, on Chile on June 27, 1970: "I don't see why we need to stand by and watch a country go Communist due to the irresponsibility of its own people."[52] Kissinger again refused to be drawn in. The secretary, who had once expressed contempt for insufficiently forceful covert operations, acerbically declaring that action should not be likened to missionary work, knew these were fertile grounds for inquiry. Here he would be saved by committee rules on how much time each member could have for questioning.

The next day reporter Daniel Schorr went on television with fresh revelations about another CIA covert operation, with the Kurds in Iraq. Colby, who thought the information had likely come from the Pike committee, spent the day in Jacksonville, Florida, meeting with Egyptian officials in connection with the visit of Egyptian President Anwar Sadat. Hoping to see Sadat, Colby spent much of the afternoon and evening sitting in a car trying to be inconspicuous while Sadat did TV interviews of his own. Finally the CIA director gave up and returned to Washington, reaching National Airport after midnight, only to find an order to call Ford counselor John Marsh, no matter what the hour. Marsh summoned him to the White House for an 8 A.M. Oval Office meeting with the president.

At the appointed hour Colby found the White House deserted. There were none of the people he expected for a dissection of the Kurdish operation, which Colby assumed to be the purpose of Ford's summons. The president entered the Oval Office promptly. It would be over quickly. As soon as Ford mentioned his desire to change government structure for national security, Colby knew his hour had come. In fifteen minutes Colby was fired, offered the ambassadorship to NATO, told George Bush would replace him at CIA,* and informed that Jim Schlesinger would also be fired and Kissinger eased out of the job of national security adviser to focus on the State Department.

---

* President Ford writes that his top choice for a new CIA director was friend and Washington lawyer Edward Bennett Williams, who had not figured on any of his advisers' short lists of possible successors in July. According to biographer Evan Thomas, Williams was offered the job on November 1 and considered it overnight, listening to the objections of his children, who did not want their dad to sell off his interest in the Washington Redskins football team, and his wife, who feared Williams might not be able to keep secrets. Edward Bennett Williams turned Ford down, pleading the press of his legal business, not the least of which was his role as defense counsel for Richard Helms in the case of the Chile perjury accusations. This story is incomplete, however, since Ford's cabled invitation to George Bush to take over the CIA went out on the evening of November 1, when Williams supposedly was still considering the offer. Moreover, Bush's acceptance is time-dated at 2:45 A.M. of November 2, just five hours after the invitation (and the same interval prior to Ford's firing of Colby), hardly sufficient time to have considered so serious a matter, one with implications for Bush's political ambitions. This suggests that Bush had to have been approached privately, probably by telephone, days before the Colby firing.

Schlesinger, entering the Oval Office ten minutes after Colby left, at least got an hour of the president's time. Ford then left for Jacksonville and a dinner to honor President Sadat.

Abandoning plans for a picnic, Bill Colby instead sat with Barbara and the couple decided against the NATO job. Colby reached Jack Marsh aboard Air Force One with his answer. Then Bill spent much of the day alerting family, visiting Elbridge and Mary at their home, and Barbara's mother as well. Colby also stopped by Jim Schlesinger's house. "You know," Schlesinger remarked ruefully, "Dick Helms outlasted us both."[53] The cult of secrecy had prevailed.

IF GERALD FORD thought himself rid of Bill Colby, that notion would turn out as wrong as the idea the Rockefeller commission would preempt congressional investigations of intelligence. Those investigations proceeded without regard to changes at the top of the administration. President Ford's prospective CIA director George Bush still had to be confirmed by the Senate before he could take over at Langley. This was no time for the agency to be without a boss. Vernon Walters, who had been very close to Kissinger since the beginning of the Nixon presidency, interceded with the White House and made the argument that Colby had to be kept on until Bush had really come on board. Bill Colby sent in his letter of resignation on November 3 and then began packing his desk, only to be told by the White House to stay on the job.

President Ford announced that Director Colby would stay in place for the time being and on November 12, a week later, accepted Colby's resignation. The vagaries of the congressional confirmation process meant that Colby remained at the head of the CIA for more than two additional months past the "Halloween Massacre," as Ford's firings were soon being called. During that time the congressional investigators pretty much finished their work.

The Halloween Massacre also did nothing to solve the basic conflict between the administration and the investigators over access to information and the whole range of secrecy issues. A batch of these came to the fore just as Ford determined to go ahead with the firings. Knowing that the Church committee had reached an advanced stage on several facets of its inquiries, the White House did what it could. Church scheduled an open hearing for the supersecret National Security Agency on the eavesdropping watch list it had kept on American citizens; the NSA chief testified on October 29 after his presentation had been reviewed by the Intelligence Coordinating Group, Colby included. The Ford administration refused to send witnesses to a hearing on November 6, whereupon Church read into the record a staff report written by his analyst L. Britt Snider. On November 1, with Colby in Florida for the day, Jack Marsh went to President Ford for guidance on the open hearing Church had scheduled regarding the CIA operation in Chile. Colby here had joined with Marsh, Scowcroft, and the others in opposing any such open hearing and were willing to go along only with one held in executive session. President Ford approved their recommendation.

A matter of great anxiety was the Church committee's report on assassinations, which Ford knew to be ready for release. Again Colby favored keeping it secret. On Halloween, Ford sent Church a letter urging the committee not to make public its study of assassinations, warning of damage to the nation and harm to individuals, responsibility for which the Church committee would bear, in Ford's view, if it went public. On November 3, hours before Ford announced Colby's firing, the Church committee approved the report unanimously; the following day Church wrote Ford to say the report would be given to the full Senate and then made public. Church in fact told Senate leaders he would resign his chairmanship if his committee sided with Ford on this issue; the compromise would be exposure to the full Senate. A court approved the committee's report as well, whereupon Colby had CIA lawyers appeal. Failing that, Colby went public, holding a press conference on November 19, actually only the second such in the history of the CIA. There Director Colby repeated Ford's charges that individuals could be exposed to retaliation by extremist groups if the report were released. The Church committee, which had already deleted two thirds of the names the CIA had asked for and saw no special sensitivity about the others, rejected this maneuver.

On November 20 the Senate met in closed session to debate the Church committee assassinations report. Debate used up the allotted time while senators could not bring any motion to a vote. After the time had run out, Senator Church released the assassinations report on his committee's authority. The study thus revealed to the public laid bare much CIA skulduggery. No U.S. administration has ever been able to show that persons suffered retaliation as a result of the Church assassination report.

If Church remained an irritant, Otis Pike had become a migraine to the Ford administration. On November 6 the Pike committee issued fresh subpoenas. Now they wanted Colby to hand over material on CIA dealings with the Internal Revenue Service plus a wide variety of documents in Kissinger's possession. These included intelligence reports on Russia, Portugal, the October War, and the Cyprus crisis; meeting records and decision memoranda of the 40 Committee, the NSC intelligence and crisis groups as well as its subunit for economic intelligence; and documents on Russian compliance with nuclear arms control agreements. Colby met his subpoena the morning of November 11.

White House advisers saw themselves as substantially complying with their subpoenas, but Kissinger insisted on keeping back whatever he deemed unsuitable for congressional eyes. These were State Department memoranda to the 40 Committee and its predecessors which, it can be reported here for the first time, were of uneven importance. Only three of the ten documents concerned the Nixon administration. One of these might have confirmed U.S.

covert involvement in anti-Allende politics in Chile; another concerned a request by Jordan's King Hussein for a secret shipment of 5,000 rifles. The earlier documents concerned CIA political actions in Italy and British Guiana (1962); management of OPLAN 34-A missions in Vietnam (1964); relations with Cuban exiles and requests for aid from the Indonesian generals during the coup there (1965); U.S. help for Indian army units that employed former CIA Tibetan partisans (1966); and, handling of the documents Bolivians seized in that country when Che Guevara was killed there with CIA help in 1967. In fact, the Bolivians themselves had publicly released the documents, including Che Guevara's diary, at the time. Claims of sensitivity in this and some other cases were laughable. The Indonesia documents would have furnished evidence of U.S. collaboration with the Suharto group, and the British Guiana material revealed the existence of a covert program there the CIA had always denied, but some of the other documents were of largely historical value and, anyway, providing the documents to the Pike committee was not the same thing as making them public. Kissinger, Attorney General Edward H. Levy, and others nevertheless united in advising Ford to claim executive privilege. The president rejected the subpoena on November 14. The Pike committee answered the same day by voting to cite Henry Kissinger for contempt of Congress.

Confrontation would be postponed by President Ford's visit to China, from which he returned on December 7. Widening the dispute, Ford then denied more covert operations documents, though offering the face-saving device of having a witness read from secret documents at a closed hearing. Before the Pike–Ford differences came to a head, however, on December 24 the CIA station chief in Greece, Richard S. Welch, was assassinated outside his home in Athens when returning from work.

The Welch assassination proved a godsend for the Ford administration and the CIA. Welch's death seemed to demonstrate the dangers of disclosure as officials had so darkly hinted. Colby's top public relations man, Angus Thuermer, also muddied the waters by implicating leftist newsmagazines, specifically one called *Counterspy*, which some months before had identified Welch as the CIA chief in Peru. Thuermer implied this was why Welch had been killed. The administration turned the Welch affair into a media circus, with Ford, Kissinger, and Scowcroft along with Colby to receive the body as it arrived at Andrews Air Force Base. President Ford also attended the funeral held at Fort Myers on January 6, 1976.

The CIA performed a postmortem on the Welch affair that was partly released two years later under the Freedom of Information Act. It disclosed that Welch had been identified as a CIA man as early as 1968 in a who's who-style book printed in East Germany, and that *Counterspy* had picked up its information from articles identifying Welch in the Peruvian press. A month before the assassination the newspaper *Athens News* had named Welch and six other CIA officers in a letter to the editor. Welch also insisted upon using the same Athens house occupied by CIA chiefs for decades, a residence so well known that it was regularly pointed out on sightseeing tours of the Greek capital. Moreover, Welch had adopted a routine and had not varied his routes to or from the embassy. Worse, CIA headquarters had warned Welch against this, yet he had neglected to tighten his precautions. When all this became known, the agency attempted to dissuade the oversight committees from making the knowledge public. The final irony would be that the Greek group responsible for the Welch assassination, called the November 17 Movement, opposed to U.S. influence in Greece and government amnesties for police in torture cases, had been energized by American actions (or the lack of them) during the 1974 crisis in Cyprus. Almost twenty-six years afterward, in July 2002, Greek authorities arrested Pavlos Serifis, the November 17 member alleged to have murdered Welch.

In the climate of horror that prevailed after the Welch killing, the Pike committee, with a January 31 deadline, moved to complete its report. Staff director Field and investigator Jack Boos put aside a draft written by a consultant and spent three weeks crafting a new version. Pike wished the members to review the document when Congress returned from a recess on the 19th, and the custom was to have five days for members to assemble their comments and the committee recommendations. That left insufficient time to publish the report by the deadline. Meanwhile Ford sent a letter, classified "secret," denying Pike authority to comment on the CIA covert actions in Italy and Angola. Having seen the draft report himself, Colby followed with a letter decrying bias in the Pike report and including eighty pages of detailed comment. The CIA leaked its refutation to reporter Daniel Schorr, who had continued to cover the investigations for CBS Television throughout the Year of Intelligence. Schorr, perplexed that the *New York Times* had already begun printing news from sections of the Pike report, searched for a scoop. Whether the latest revelations were leaked by the CIA, whose Mitchell Rogovin engaged in a marathon forty-eight-hour negotiation with the committee on deletions from the document, or from the committee itself has never been established. Pike accepted some of the CIA amendments but rejected 150 others. His committee voted to release the report on January 23; within two days Schorr had the complete document. So did the *New York Times*, which printed a major story on January 26.

Chairman Pike still needed an extension to complete his report, granted by the House Rules Committee under the very unusual stricture that the document could be released only upon approval by the White House. Otis Pike could not override that regulation and failed to carry a vote on the report by the full House of Representatives on January 29. This substantial negative vote (the margin was about two to one against the committee) empowered President Ford, who duly ruled in February that the Pike report should not be released. The document had already leaked, however, and large portions of it appeared in the New York weekly *The Village Voice* on February 16. Daniel Schorr is acknowledged to be the source for the *Voice* story.

One measure of the strength of the administration counterattack against the intelligence investigations is that the leak of the Pike report itself became the subject of investigation and hearings that went on through much of 1976. The Church committee's final report appeared only in April 1976 and proved to be anticlimactic. Recommendations from both bodies eventually resulted in little action other than the formation of oversight committees for intelligence in both the House and Senate.

The Year of Intelligence had forced Bill Colby to walk a fine line among fiercely competing interests. Steeped in Cold War tradition, concerned with protecting the prerogatives of the presidency, Gerald Ford had given in to his more conservative tendencies. Playing on those tendencies, and doubtless concerned with his image, Henry Kissinger maneuvered hard to obstruct and obfuscate. The degree of Kissinger's involvement, incidentally, gives the lie to the assertion in his book *Years of Renewal* that he had been too involved in other issues to pay much attention to the intelligence investigations. White House staff faithfully represented Ford's interests, protecting Kissinger's. The secret warriors at the CIA and elsewhere cooperated splendidly. But public doubts regarding CIA operations were real, and the prerogative of the Congress was to investigate. That left William E. Colby the man in the middle, required to respond to Congress but inevitably the focus of Ford administration and CIA resentments. The result came inevitably. Colby's career, as went a term of art coined at that time, was terminated with prejudice.

Suspended between the past and future of intelligence, William E. Colby alone among the actors of the Ford administration understood that realities had changed. In post-Watergate America the mere assertion of a national security interest no longer sufficed to justify arbitrary actions. For the Central Intelligence Agency that made it necessary to redefine roles and missions, working within a political environment in which executive and legislative branches of government shared responsibility. Such an environment made the CIA more powerful than ever. Only a few short years later Colby's successor William J. Casey proved his perception to have been an accurate one.

In the meantime, to preserve the CIA Bill Colby fell on his sword. Church committee counsel F. A. O. Schwarz, who perceived Colby as "a man of steel gray," wrote of the CIA director, "He believed his decision to cooperate with the Senate probe saved the agency."[54] The delicate choices forced on Bill Colby cost his career but ultimately, in his view, were worth it. In his memoir Colby approvingly recounted a remark Kissinger made to him late in the Year of Intelligence: "Bill, I feel required to say this to you. For the longest time I believed that what you were doing was wrong, that what you should have done was to cry havoc over the investigations in the name of national security. But I have come around to believe that your strategy was really correct."[55] Nevertheless the perturbations of the year 1975 changed Colby's life in every way, even ones yet to come to the surface.

16

INTELLIGENCE IN A FREE SOCIETY

B ELOW THE SURFACE, the real work of the CIA continued, uninterrupted by the painful investigations that went on. Among Bill Colby's last acts as director of central intelligence would be orders to open contacts with the Russian secret service, the KGB. Several of the events of 1975 shook the clandestine service, starting with investigations, which included a strong attack on the CIA's use of cover identities as journalists and religious persons. The potential dangers of weak cover were highlighted by the Welch affair, the second of these shocks. A third would be the disappearance in Vienna on December 20 of Nicolas G. Shadrin, widely believed to have been abducted by Russian agents and to have died in their hands. Shadrin, a Russian defector from the 1950s who had done contract analytical work for U.S. naval intelligence and the DIA, had been sent to Vienna on behalf of the CIA to tempt the Russians, at which he seemed to have succeeded all too well. Arguments later raged over whether Shadrin had been a Russian double agent all along. In the immediate aftermath, however, especially coming simultaneously with the Welch killing, the CIA feared the Russians had decided to jettison the unwritten but long observed rule of espionage that the officers (as opposed to spies) of opposing secret services do not kill each other. Attempting to head off an incipient spy war as well as demand the return of Shadrin—then still thought to be alive—and to determine whether the KGB had had a role in the death of Richard Welch, Director Colby quietly ordered CIA officials to meet with the KGB. The encounter took place in Vienna. The Russians pleaded ignorance and were shaken by CIA accusations, but Colby's action opened a channel of communication between the enemy superpowers used repeatedly until the demise of the Soviet Union.

Russia also figured in Colby's work of intelligence advice for the U.S. government. Secretary Kissinger still pursued arms control negotiations with Moscow against the protests of critics on the right, who argued that large

Russian missiles and the Backfire bomber were violations of agreements and showed that Chairman Leonid Brezhnev could not be trusted. With an upcoming election, President Ford wanted to achieve a nuclear weapons agreement he could present as progress to the voters, and Kissinger scheduled a trip to Moscow in January 1976 to offer a compromise. On January 13 the National Security Council (NSC) met to complete its consideration of four possible options for the offer. There Gerald Ford declared his approval of a hybrid scheme that tried to placate Pentagon fears while giving Kissinger the kind of bargaining position he wanted. The CIA supplied a warning. "Brezhnev will not be under great pressure to give in to us—if anything, it will be just the opposite," Bill Colby commented. "There is an incentive to him to be a good strong leader to his 'apparatchiks' before the Party Congress."[1]

Colby's warning proved right. In Moscow Brezhnev rejected Kissinger's compromise out of hand, while Pentagon watchdogs on the U.S. delegation, present for the first time at these private meetings, reined in the secretary of state's freedom of action. There would be no agreement in 1976, and arms control, left to the subsequent Carter administration, languished for another three years. In the meantime Bill Colby's appearance at the White House on January 13 would be his swan song as an NSC adviser.

The major political challenge remained the intelligence investigations, and here Colby pitched in on the Ford administration counterattacks. Appearing before a Senate committee on January 23 the DCI appealed for a loosening of the Hughes-Ryan strictures governing CIA covert operations. In several forums he continued to criticize the Pike committee. As Otis Pike tried to put out his report, Colby heaped censure on the House effort.

Colby's efforts climaxed on January 26, a day he again appeared at the White House* to be awarded the National Security Medal. Before Christmas, Vernon Walters proposed the award for Colby, and Brent Scowcroft joined in the recommendation, citing his work in Europe in the 1950s, service as Saigon station chief, performance with CORDs in Vietnam, and, in the words of Scowcroft's paper for President Ford, "his remarkable leadership of the intelligence community since September 1973."[2] Another factor was that every DCI since 1953, when the National Security Medal had been created, had been awarded it; to have left out William E. Colby would have sent the wrong message to the denizens of Langley. In any case, at a twelve-minute ceremony at mid-afternoon, Colby stood before his family, George Bush, Walters, Mitch Rogovin, and most of the CIA's deputy directors to receive the medal. Immediately following the ceremony the director rushed

---

* Colby's memoir is in error dating the award of the National Security Medal to him on January 27. The paperwork for the award, the White House schedule proposals, and President Ford's appointment records all clearly place this event on January 26. Moreover, Colby's immediately subsequent news conference was held to respond to the *New York Times*'s revelation of the Pike report, which appeared on January 26. Daniel Schorr's writing on this episode also dates it on the 26th.

back to headquarters to face a news conference called to denounce the Pike report.

Colby's press session, held in the bubble-like auditorium outside the CIA's main building, teemed with reporters and television cameramen, threatening to overwhelm the room's 400-odd seating capacity. This would be Colby's third news conference as DCI. One in attendance was Daniel Schorr, who got the impression the administration had afoot some move to block release of the Pike report—a major impetus in his own decision to leak the document to the *Village Voice*. Actually Schorr was quite right; that same day Attorney General Edward H. Levy sent Ford a legal opinion on the advisability of a lawsuit to block publication. The paper cautioned against such a move and the president decided against it, but Colby's public denunciations represented a different track of the same effort. The DCI termed the Pike report a disservice to the nation, completely biased, containing a distorted view of U.S. intelligence, and a "bursting of the dam protecting many of our secret operations."[3] The next morning Colby had Mitchell Rogovin send Chairman Pike a letter declaring that the CIA was "deeply disturbed by the pervasive and premature leaking of your Committee's final report."[4] Many in the Ford administration felt relief, not least among them Bill Colby, when the House of Representatives voted a few days later to give the president authority to approve any official release of the report.

That House action had just taken place when, on the morning of January 30, President Ford himself came to the Bubble at Langley for the swearing in of George Bush as director of central intelligence. Colby presided and very simply introduced the CIA to these visitors as an organization of dedicated professionals who, in the face of the controversies of the Year of Intelligence, produced the best secret information around. Supreme Court Justice Potter Stewart swore Bush in at about 11:10 A.M. William Colby's CIA career was over. Taking a last suggestion from Vernon Walters, Colby slipped away directly after the ceremony, driving home in Barbara Colby's old Buick.

WILLIAM E. COLBY let little grass grow under his feet after leaving the CIA. Within days he appeared on television for an extended interview on the news show *Panorama*. Once more he lambasted the Pike report as biased and tendentious. Though acknowledging some CIA peccadillos, as he had throughout the year of the investigation, Colby argued that missteps were inevitable through the long history of any agency and that the CIA remained an excellent organization. Better, in fact, for Colby saw the CIA as henceforth operating within a framework of law, stronger than ever. He defended the use of journalistic cover by agency officers, maintaining that the issue had been overblown since the practice was being phased out.* On the events of the

---

* On the matter of cover, interestingly enough, Colby stated in this interview that it was *not* the leftist media epitomized by the magazine *Counterspy* who were primarily responsible for the death of Athens station chief Richard Welch. Colby writes of this group in his memoir

Halloween Massacre, Colby loyally fell on his sword and claimed that President Ford had always been supportive and that he (Bill) had been saying for months that a fresh face at the head of the CIA would be quite appropriate at the proper moment. As the investigations wound down this was the time.

A few weeks later Colby published an article in the *New York Times* defending the essential enterprise. Noting that "selective exposure of some of intelligence's own self-criticism gave a totally false impression of American intelligence as a whole," Colby added that the investigations had been damaging to a degree, but that they had been necessary given Watergate, Vietnam, and allegations the CIA had become a rogue elephant. Reprising the line he had taken with Gerald Ford and others, Colby concluded, "The costs of the past year were high, but they will be exceeded by the value of this strengthening of what was already the best intelligence service in the world."[5]

About the same time Bill gave a print interview to Oriana Fallaci, a noted Italian journalist of the day. He remained cool and poured coffee as Fallaci raged about CIA political manipulations in Italy, the Chile operation, assassinations, and other matters. Colby denounced Pike's work once again: "The House Committee report is totally partial, totally biased, and done to give a false impression of CIA." Fallaci also raised Vietnam. Colby defended Diem saying, "He was not a dictator."

"We did not lose the war," Colby added, in what became an idée fixe for him. "I mean, we won the guerrilla war, we lost the military war."[6]

"Terrific interview," Gerald Ford scrawled on a copy of the piece when it appeared in the March 13, 1976, issue of *The New Republic*.[7] Ford later wrote Colby a letter commenting, "you handled [the questions] with the same competence and cool professionalism you displayed while Director of Central Intelligence."[8]

As the House of Representatives went ahead to investigate Daniel Schorr and his leak of the Pike report—a development certainly gratifying to the administration—President Ford ordered a minor reorganization of the intelligence community. Ford increased the responsibilities of his President's Foreign Intelligence Advisory Board (PFIAB) and created a separate outside watchdog group for covert operations: the Intelligence Oversight Board (IOB). The roles and missions of the CIA and other agencies were left intact. Ford's most significant actions were quite different: he proposed legislation legalizing government wiretapping of private citizens* as well as a bill providing criminal penalties for leaking secret information.

(p. 450) where he concedes having lost his temper at their effort to disclaim any role in spite of having published the identities of CIA officers including Welch. Colby believed the sensational reporting of the CIA investigations around the globe, not *Counterspy* or CIA cover arrangements, were key in the Welch assassination.

* Civil libertarians for several years had been pressing for legislation that would restrict wiretapping. Their efforts had met no success. The Year of Intelligence put real teeth into those demands, but President Ford's notable political achievement lay in harnessing that energy in support of a bill that simply created a secret court to approve wiretapping, which henceforward would be permitted. Under the Foreign Intelligence Surveillance Act of 1978, typically several

Still the good soldier, William E. Colby supported these measures. That June he attended Princeton's alumni reunion, where he appeared on a panel that considered the ethics of leaks. He agreed with Daniel Schorr, also a member of the panel, on a good many First Amendment issues. They differed where Colby supported the criminal penalties for leaking embodied in Ford's proposed law. In the fall Bill published an extensive article in the journal *International Security* that made the argument for criminal penalties in greater detail.

Colby also continued to be supportive of his beloved Central Intelligence Agency. When Ford's successor, President Jimmy Carter, appointed an outsider, Admiral Stansfield Turner, as DCI, Colby dutifully showed up to help orient Turner in his new post. Turner recalled Colby as low key and warm, inspiring confidence. When Ronald Reagan, the next president, appointed lawyer William J. Casey, Colby did the same thing. Casey, an OSS veteran and previous member of PFIAB, knew Colby in both connections, and listened closely. "I'm not going to tell you how to run your railroad," Colby had said, pointing out that the CIA was there to serve and Casey could organize it any way he wanted to. The important thing remained advice to the president and if Casey did that well all the rest would follow. Touching lightly on various facets of CIA work, the clandestine service, the analysis directorate, the need for real spies in Russia and elsewhere, Colby rehearsed themes from his own CIA experience.[9] Not long afterward Casey made a misstep, appointing a businessman as director of operations in a move that quickly disintegrated. Colby then defended Casey in television interviews. When Casey got into serious trouble during the Iran-Contra affair Colby kept silent.

On Capitol Hill Colby became a fixture at a number of hearings. He continued to press for relaxation of the Hughes-Ryan strictures on notification to Congress about covert operations. Congress eventually repealed the legislation, confining the reporting requirement to intelligence committees in the House and Senate (these committees, created after the investigations of 1975, constitute the major institutional reform that flowed from those events). Executive flouting of the reporting system would become a key problem in the Iran-Contra affair.

In 1977 and later, Bill Colby also continued to defend the CIA's relationships with the media, including its use of journalism for cover purposes. When a bill to prohibit this practice lay before the House Permanent Select Committee on Intelligence in late 1977, Colby's testimony included this:

> I ask this committee to compensate for barring our intelligence from the use of American journalist credentials by reversing the tide of prohibition with respect to official cover. This committee should insist that the agencies of the United

---

hundred warrant applications are made each year. In the whole history of the court that administers the law only a handful of applications have ever been rejected. Current favorite targets are alleged drug traffickers and terrorists.

States Government incorporate in their ranks small numbers of intelligence officers under proper administration arrangements so that they are not revealed. . . . With this change our journalists can be kept immune and intelligence can be improved.[10]

Colby went along with ending questionable habits of the past but insisted upon contriving new alternatives.

A noteworthy exercise that endured through 1980 would be a congressional effort to craft law that would govern intelligence work. Colby supported this effort. In a 1978 Senate appearance the former CIA chieftain declared:

The internal regulations issued within CIA over the years and the Executive Orders issued by . . . Presidents may have been precursors to this statutory charter, but they cannot substitute for its function as an expression of our new national consensus with respect to American intelligence operating under American law. The American public, our political leadership and the dedicated personnel of American intelligence all will benefit by a plain, open expression of the function of American intelligence and the limits we Americans insist on its exercise. A clear charter for the work of intelligence will end the ambiguities and euphemisms which have characterized this field and which are the root cause of the fascination and sensationalism which have so badly harassed and discredited the honorable men and women who have devoted their lives to their country in this 'peculiar service,' as Nathan Hale called it.[11]

The highly detailed charter that formed the subject of this 1978 legislative effort failed to gain passage, and a much watered-down bill also failed two years later. To this day the sole charter governing the CIA remains the law passed at the height of the Cold War that created the agency. This National Security Act of 1947 has arguably been the source of many of the very excesses that have bedeviled intelligence work.

Bill Colby's stand on the charter issue became the most remarkable aspect of his views as a former CIA person. In most ways he represented the Cold War crusaders of the agency. One typical expression would be Colby's speech some months later to the Chicago Council on Foreign Relations. Modern intelligence, Colby maintained, is centralized, uses the best technology, works under the law, and has moved from a posture of confrontation to one of negotiation. Despite the latter statement, Colby argued covert operations were necessary and spies a staple. Defending covert operations he pointed to successes in saving Laos through the 1960s, installing a friendly government in Zaire in that decade, and saving Western Europe from communism in the 1940s and 1950s. The validity of these examples could be debated with hindsight, and Colby went on to predict that the Shah of Iran would survive the political upheavals in his country, though a period of repression would be necessary. Almost exactly a year later the Shah was overthrown and the United States embassy in Teheran occupied by fundamentalist Muslim students in a revolution that rocked the Carter administration and changed the course of American-Iranian relations for decades, with other effects throughout the Middle East. (In the mid-1980s Colby would express support for a covert operation that might overthrow the new Muslim leaders of Iran.)

Interestingly enough, Colby's work after leaving the Central Intelligence Agency combined legal activity with risk analysis, assessing nations' political stability in behalf of potential investors. Colby did this for International Business Government Counsellors Incorporated, a Washington company; for his own firm, Colby, Bailey, Werner & Associates; and for an investment newsletter he wrote for economic consulting companies. He had interests in developments in the Philippines, Thailand, and Malaysia; and he worked as a registered lobbyist for the Japanese government. In 1982 he explained the work as learning as much as possible about a company, its products, and local venture partners, and then looking at the political and demographic characteristics plus legal systems of foreign countries with a view to making recommendations as to how a business might posture itself and act in a foreign country. "The growth of the think tanks and the academic centers, the private risk consultants and analysts . . . is the obvious development from the flood of information which is around today," Colby told an interviewer.[12] Indeed this was natural work for a former intelligence officer; Richard Helms retired to establish a risk analysis business of his own.

Colby also remained attuned to Vietnam, both postwar and veteran issues garnering his interest. His legal work included efforts in behalf of the Hmong and montagnard refugees. The latter led to a most controversial episode. Approached by former CIA colleagues, Colby agreed to represent the Australian Nugan Hand Bank, which at one point wanted to acquire land on a Caribbean island, assertedly to house refugees but perhaps for more sinister purposes. The bank collapsed in 1980 when Frank Nugan, one of its principals, was found a suicide. None of the embezzlement and stock manipulation charges that followed touched Colby, but his very involvement with Nugan Hand could only be controversial, especially given the bank's extensive ties with former CIA and U.S. military figures.

Writing would be the most prominent activity, though Colby probably did more writing and speaking about intelligence issues than Vietnam. Colby's memoir *Honorable Men*, written with Peter Forbath, had substantial coverage of Vietnam, from Colby's station chief period to his time with CORDS. Forbath had a difficult time getting Bill to recount anything in a dramatic way even though many great events were wrapped up in Colby's history. It became doubly ironic that having produced an underwhelming account of his CIA career, Colby got into trouble with CIA censors. Colby had mobilized to counter Victor Marchetti and later individuals considered CIA renegades, principally Phillip Agee, who wrote a damning account of the agency's Latin American operations that named names.

Naturally Colby had signed the same secrecy agreements as Marchetti upon joining the agency, and they required that things he wrote be reviewed for classified information. Part of Bill's problem with Peter Forbath lay precisely in the self-censorship he exercised in the effort to keep secrets out of his

book, but the CIA retained its formal authority in any case. Colby and Forbath completed the manuscript in the summer of 1977 and passed it to Simon
& Schuster, their New York publisher. Only a couple of weeks later did Bill
give a copy to Stansfield Turner's CIA. Meanwhile his agent sent the book
directly to French publishers who needed to translate text for a foreign edition
of the memoir. Despite Colby's care the agency found objectionable some
names and details of operations in *Honorable Men*, but while these could be
deleted at a late stage in Simon & Schuster's publication process, nothing
was ever done about the French edition, where the CIA's secrets went straight
to press. Colby was never prosecuted, either for the technical offense of
sending off his manuscript prior to CIA review or the real one of the secrets
in the French version.

These events assume additional importance in view of what the CIA did
to another former officer, Frank Snepp, who also went to press without prepublication review. Snepp considered that his attempts from the inside to get
the CIA to reflect on its errors and responsibilities had been shunted aside.
Bill Colby had been DCI during the first part of that series of events and
had met with Snepp when both were retired and both contemplating memoirs.
Snepp remembers Colby cautioning him to submit to the CIA review, using
an analogy Bill also relied on in a February 1976 television interview: pitch-
ers of water should leak from the top not the bottom.

Concerned the CIA would use prepublication review to suppress the truth
about the Vietnam fiasco, Snepp avoided the possibility by dealing secretly
with the New York publisher Random House, which succeeded in going to
press so that the CIA learned only at the last moment what actually appeared
in his tome *Decent Interval*. Though Snepp was acknowledged to have revealed *no* secrets in *Decent Interval*, the U.S. government decided to retaliate
by suing for damages, contending Snepp improperly profited from what he
had learned as a U.S. employee. Colby, at this time on tour promoting *Honorable Men*, expressed misgivings about the lawsuit against Frank Snepp.
The defense thereupon called him as witness for the trial. The record, which
Snepp used to write a subsequent book about how his case was handled,
shows that Colby testified his own manuscript *had* been cleared by the CIA.
Colby also argued it was not the revelation of a secret that could damage the
CIA; it was the *unauthorized* disclosure of that information.

This statement was harmful to Snepp's chances. In a nutshell, that had
been Colby's strategy during the Year of Intelligence. He had decided early
that many things secret were going to come out but the key lay in positioning
the agency to be ready in each instance. It is difficult to imagine how Colby
could have testified differently. In this the spy chieftain showed himself to
be still the loyal soldier.

In content, Colby's writings on Vietnam also have the virtue of consistency.
His central themes are that the assassination of Ngo Dinh Diem constituted
an enormous error and that the United States effectively won the war during
his later days in the pacification program. Colby not only made these points

in *Honorable Men* and in a spate of articles, but he repeated them at full length in a second book, *Lost Victory*, written with CIA colleague James MacCargar and published in 1989. Each of Colby's main arguments has been considered in the present narrative. In summary, the United States had already taken Colby's preferred course on Diem, in 1955, without success; it was not entirely up to the CIA what the South Vietnamese generals did about Diem; and there is no shred of evidence that leaving Diem in power would have led to a different outcome in Vietnam. All of these objections were in the public domain during Colby's lifetime. None of them dissuaded him from holding to his views; indeed, he occasionally put forward even more extravagant versions of his themes. Only a couple of months before his death, Colby maintained in one talk that if Diem had been left in power he would have achieved total victory within two years. As for his pacification theme, the truth is that the United States fought the wrong war in Vietnam, not only at the beginning but at the end. We fought a military war when the adversary was a people in arms, and we shifted to oppose a people's war when the enemy had transitioned to a conventional strategy. All Colby's success at pacification—which would be forever marred by the excesses of "Phoenix"—could not alter the political, economic, and international realities that forced American withdrawal from South Vietnam while leaving Hanoi's forces in place. Just weeks before his death Bill regaled another audience with his account of a long series of "turning points"—one for almost every year between 1955 and 1975—every one of which he viewed as potentially leading to U.S. victory in Vietnam. Colby sounded exactly like the advocates for one or another "perfect strategy" during the Vietnam war, people to whom a few more guns or dollars would have put the outcome in our grasp. Colby remained to the end a Lost Crusader.

Where Bill Colby's arguments on Vietnam perplexed antiwar activists, his consistency would gratify those activists in the 1980s who worked in the nuclear freeze movement. Colby had taken positions favoring arms control with the Nixon and Ford administrations' NSC deliberations, and he hewed to that stance subsequently. He attempted to put in perspective conservative charges that the Russians systematically violated those arms control agreements they had signed, and he spoke in favor of nuclear arms reductions. Colby joined Robert McNamara, McGeorge Bundy, Gerard Smith, and other former senior officials in advocating a pledge that the United States would never be the first to use nuclear weapons; he perhaps went further than the others, insisting that this be unconditional. After the Reagan administration created a Strategic Defense Initiative to innovate weapons to neutralize ballistic missiles, Colby argued the best that could be done with it was trade it away in negotiations as a bargaining chip. "What you really don't need is to build it," he said.[13] Liberals would call Colby "Arms Control's Secret Weapon."[14] Once the Soviet Union disintegrated in 1991, Colby united with Paul C. Warnke in favor of halving the U.S. military budget.

Colby's stands were not simply statements in arcane policy papers. He appeared in television ads on the budget issue, and crisscrossed the country to address local groups on his concerns. Anne Hessing Cahn, who worked with the arms control advocates' Center for National Security after service with the government's Arms Control and Disarmament Agency, reports that although she frequently had to arrange and fund speakers for their outreach programs, Colby made and paid for all his own arrangements and usually drove himself to the places he was needed. Bill also joined the Center's board of directors, immersing himself further in its work.

Colby sat on corporate boards too, but those he enjoyed most were related to his interests and experience. One that deserves mention would be the board of directors of the Center for the Study of the Vietnam War at Texas Tech University in Lubbock, Texas. A professor at the university who had been a sailor and officer with riverine forces and advising the Vietnamese navy, James Reckner, founded the center and wished to recruit a high-powered board. An associate, also a history professor at Texas Tech, had been one of those young State Department detailees to CORDS under Colby. He approached Bill, who proved only too happy to oblige, and Colby became a strong supporter of the center, speaking at several of its conferences and eventually depositing papers at its Vietnam Archive.

Another Colby venture that merits mention would be a computer game published in 1995. Scripted by British author and historian James Adams, simulation *Spycraft: The Great Game* featured American and Russian agents contesting the shadowy netherworld of Cold War espionage. To make the game authentic Adams wanted real-life American and Russian intelligence officers who would give briefings, summarize cases, and furnish appropriate comments at various points in the play. Adams recruited Bill Colby as his CIA spy chief. For the Russian he got Oleg D. Kalugin, who had been the KGB's counterintelligence director at one time as well as an adviser to the chief of the post-Soviet Russian spy service. Colby had known Kalugin for some years and had been to his home in Moscow for dinner during a trip to Russia. Both men got on very well during the process of creating this game, and when it was released, Colby and Kalugin both helped promote the product.

From CIA chieftain to game impresario was a huge transformation for Bill Colby, but hardly the biggest change in his life after Langley. That would be personal trauma—the end of his marriage to Barbara Heinzen. In September 1974, at the height of his reign at the CIA, Colby had tried to give the director a more human face, going out of his way to be photographed at home with Barbara for a feature in *Time* magazine. But the Year of Intelligence took a huge toll and there were lingering feelings from the Vietnam tragedy, with Barbara having had a different attitude on the war and carrying the hurt of how Bill had handled the troubles of their daughter Christine. Over time the relationship came apart. A religious Catholic married at a church wedding, Barbara was staggered by divorce. Then came Bill's budding romance with Sally Shelton, whom he had met on Capitol Hill when she worked as a legislative aide to a senator with offices right across the hall from those of the Church committee.

Bill Colby and Sally Shelton married in 1982 and made a new life together. They bought a house in Georgetown. Bill abandoned his old sedans for a gay red Fiat Pininfarina and later the quintessential car of the 1990s, a sport-utility vehicle. Sally Shelton Colby held a succession of top jobs in government and nongovernment organizations focused on health and humanitarian issues, a nice match for Bill's own public service interests. The former spy, at last in from the cold, created for himself a newly satisfying existence.

Until those fateful days of 1996 Bill Colby plowed ahead purposefully if not always with success. Perhaps there was a twinge when he tried to make his own return to Vietnam, as so many were doing, but the Vietnamese government denied him a visa, citing his role in the Phoenix program. Some of his investment consultant colleagues chafed at the blandness of the pieces he supplied for newsletters. But there were always the trips, speeches, articles, and boards of directors. One of Colby's boards was that of a northern Virginia defense electronics concern and it met just a day or so before Bill's last trip to the vacation house. A principal of the company encountered Colby at the coffee pot during a break and found Bill strangely out of sorts, as if something was not quite right with him. When the man learned of Colby's subsequent disappearance on the Wicomico River he quickly decided he'd seen Colby after a small stroke and that a major heart attack had followed. But Bill Colby, gray man of the shadows until his end, left this world without answering questions.

WHEN ALLEN DULLES RETIRED from the Central Intelligence Agency, notwithstanding the Bay of Pigs fiasco that had brought him down, he enjoyed an eight-year run before death as a grand old man of U.S. intelligence. Colby numbered with only three other intelligence professionals to head the CIA until now. Of them, Richard Helms, three decades since Nixon ousted him from the agency, continues to enjoy status equal to the Great White Case Officer, as Dulles was known. Robert M. Gates, somewhat more controversial before his 1993 retirement, is nevertheless regarded with professional esteem. For William E. Colby there would be little of this reverence.

Without doubt Colby lost his crusade in the months leading up to and through the Year of Intelligence. His yielding up of Helms for Justice Department inquiry cost him dearly among cold warriors at Langley; his actions, faced with the congressional investigations, hurt him both at the CIA and within the White House. Here there are two major issues to be considered: Could Colby have responded differently? What does all this mean for America today?

In terms of the Senate and House investigations, the broad conclusion has to be that William E. Colby in fact saved the Central Intelligence Agency. His cooperation proved just sufficient to dissuade Congress from more forceful action, whereas Colby's careful husbanding of CIA secrets limited the inquiries in the areas Langley found most uncomfortable. The views of Robert Gates are instructive here. Deputy to William Casey and acting DCI during the Iran-Contra affair, Gates believes that it would have been necessary "to instigate a constitutional crisis only months after Nixon's resignation to try to prevent the Congress from getting CIA's documents." Absent that, President Ford "would have been forced ultimately to give way to Congress either politically or legally." The bottom line, Bob Gates is convinced, was that "resistance to the investigations would have been useless and very costly to the CIA." With a weak president, an assertive Congress, whetted appetites among the press, and public outrage at CIA excesses, there would have been no way to protect America's intelligence service.[15]

Equally important, William E. Colby was almost the only CIA maven who understood the potentialities here: a rechartered agency with a fresh imprimatur and a new national consensus could be more effective than ever. Airing the secrets and discussing the issues could permit that consensus to emerge. Redrawing the lines of authority and oversight, adopting ground rules agreed to among all the parties, would bring U.S. intelligence into a new age.

Bill Colby deserved better than he got from the denizens of both the agency and the White House.

THIS STORY has real meaning for America today. With the end of the Cold War disappeared the raison d'être for the Central Intelligence Agency. The need for knowledge of our world continues, but the spectrum of global security problems is different. For a few years the CIA stumbled around, nibbling at the edges of drug trafficking and organized crime, each the primary responsibility of another federal agency. Through the 1990s, terrorism began to seem more and more a critical national security issue. Until the attacks of September 11, 2001, when New York City and Washington, D.C., were struck by terrorists in hijacked planes, the CIA's key issues did not pass the threshhold of the crusade in which Colby and his colleagues enlisted. After 9/11 the new crusade had already begun, and the CIA is in the midst of it now.

But the statutory underpinnings for the Central Intelligence Agency have never been perfected. Not only have they not been changed to reflect the passage of the Cold War, but the legal authorities were not complete to begin with. The effort to legislate a charter for the CIA and U.S. intelligence, which gained its greatest impetus at the time of the Church and Pike investigations and afterward, atrophied without substantial results. Whatever his detractors may say, William E. Colby had a key role in avoiding that eventuality through the way he cooperated with the investigations just enough to blunt their most serious suspicions. The CIA has additional freedom of action today because its range of permissible activity was not defined nor circumscribed during the period of reforms that began while Colby directed the agency.

National security served to justify a multitude of sins during the Cold War, and freedom of action is a double-edged sword. A prime illustration from Bill Colby's own life is what happened to him as a result of the Phoenix program: A neutralization campaign against the adversary deemed perfectly logical and ordinary by its initiators became the focus of criticism on human rights grounds, tarring for life its top manager. This result occurred inevitably despite Colby's attempts to regularize the program and put it on a legal footing. It was inevitable that excesses would occur, and the result only became more controversial as public opinion on human rights grew stronger. An almost identical situation exists today in the war against terrorism. Efforts to capture members of terror networks and then interrogate them amount to a program quite similar to Phoenix. Public opinion about this activity after 9/11 has already exhibited misgivings, and a fickle public attitude may easily change to revulsion in the future.

A CIA charter might have restricted some agency operations, but it also would have protected America's spies from arbitrary discord. Because the CIA never built bridges to the American people, relying instead on appeals to secrecy in the great global struggle, there remains no consensus on the value or proper role of the Central Intelligence Agency. It is vulnerable to the revelation of some agency excess that will bring on a tidal wave of public outcry that can demolish the agency and its capabilities, even those that are truly necessary. Controversies over CIA domestic spying, drugs and collaboration in drug running, warnings missed before September 11—many are the potential catalysts for destruction. Here is where the United States needs a figure like Colby, someone to trigger a dialogue that would establish a fresh understanding of the field and the need. Absent a new consensus, there will come a day when America's spies will wish William E. Colby were still with them.

Abbreviations Used in the References

CFVN   Country File Vietnam

CI   Counterinsurgency

CIA   Central Intelligence Agency

FOIA   Freedom of Information Act

FRUS   Foreign Relations of the United States

GRFL   Gerald R. Ford Library, NARA

GRFP   Gerald R. Ford Papers

JFKL   John F. Kennedy Library, NARA

JFKP   John F. Kennedy Papers

LBJL   Lyndon Baines Johnson Library, NARA

LBJP   Lyndon Baines Johnson Papers

KSF   Kissinger-Scowcroft File

M&M   Meetings and Memoranda File

NIE   National Intelligence Estimate

NARA   National Archives and Records Administration

NLP   Nixon Library Project, NARA

NSAvrF   National Security Adviser's Files

NSC   National Security Council

NSF   National Security File

SNIE   Special National Intelligence Estimate

REFERENCES

1. The Mystery of Bill Colby

There is no literature on the demise of William E. Colby. The following narrative is drawn primarily from press accounts and interviews. I had a lunch with Paul Colby and Barbara H. Colby, but our conversation did not touch upon the disappearance and Paul's role in the search for Colby's body. I am in agreement with the view that Mr. Colby died of natural causes.

1. Paul Hendrickson, "William Colby: CIA Mystery Man," *Washington Post*, May 7, 1996, p. D8.
2. Loch K. Johnson, *A Season of Inquiry: The Senate Intelligence Investigation* (Lexington: University Press of Kentucky, 1985), p. 57.
3. Todd Shields, "Search for Ex-CIA Chief Fruitless after Six Days," *Washington Post*, May 4, 1996, p. B3.
4. Joyce Price, "Colby's Body Discovered at River's Edge," *Washington Times*, May 7, 1996, p. A14.
5. Ibid.
6. Todd Shields, "Colby's Body Found along River Shore," *Washington Post*, May 7, 1996, p. A1.

2. Baptism of Fire

There is an extensive and growing literature on the Office of Strategic Services and on special operations in the various European campaigns. Relatively little of this deals with the Colby mission to France, but there are sources to set the context. The OSS records are now available in the National Archives as Record Group 226. On the general subject of the OSS see R. Harris Smith, *OSS—The Secret History of America's First Central Intelligence Agency* (Berkeley: University of California Press, 1972); Bradley F. Smith, *The Shadow Warriors: The O.S.S. and the Origins of the C.I.A.* (New York: Basic Books, 1983); and contemporaneously, Stewart Alsop and Thomas Braden, *Sub Rosa: The OSS and American Espionage* (New York: Reynal & Hitchcock, 1946). An official account is in Kermit Roosevelt, ed., *The War Report of the OSS: v.2: The Overseas Targets* (New York: Walker & Coy, 1976). The War Diaries of OSS/London appeared on microfilm from University Press of America in 1985, and the personal diary of David Bruce for 1944–45 has also been published.

On cooperation with the British and the British style of work, see E. H. Cookridge, *Set Europe Ablaze* (New York: Thomas Y. Crowell, 1967); and David Stafford, *Britain and the European Resistance, 1940–1945* (London: Macmillan, 1980). On the effort in France, see M. R. D. Foot, *SOE in France: An Account of the Work of the British Special Operations Executive in France, 1940–1944* (London: Her Majesty's Stationery Office, 1966); William J. Casey, *The Secret War Against Hitler* (Washington: Regnery Gateway, 1988); S. J. Lewis, *Jedburgh Team Operations in Support of the 12th Army Group* (Fort Leavenworth, Kans.: U.S. Army Command and General Staff School, Combat Studies Institute, 1991); Bernard V. Moore II, *The Secret Air War over France: USAAF Special Operations Units in the French Campaign of 1944* (Maxwell Air Force Base, Ala.: Air University Press, 1993); and Anthony Cave Brown, ed., *The Secret War Report of the OSS* (New York: Berkeley Medallion Books, 1976).

For this and all succeeding chapters of this book a key source has been the various writings of William E. Colby himself. Of principal importance here have been the Colby memoirs, written with Peter Forbath, *Honorable Men: My Life in the CIA* (New York: Simon & Schuster, 1978). Also of use is Colby's paper "The Legacy of the OSS," in George C. Chalou, ed., *Secrets War: The Office of Strategic Services in World War II* (Washington: National Archives and Records Administration, 1992).

1. Colby, *Honorable Men*, p. 35.
2. Ibid., p. 37.
3. Cave Brown, *The Secret Report of the OSS*, reprinted, p. 431.

3. Tianjin to Trondheim

In addition to the OSS and SOE sources cited in the last chapter, see also Charles Cruikshank, *SOE in Scandinavia* (Oxford: Oxford University Press, 1986); and Edward Hymoff, *The OSS in World War II* (New York: Ballantine Books, 1972). A vital contribution on the Norwegian Rype mission is Colby's article, "Skis and Daggers: OSS Operations in Norway," *Studies in Intelligence*, Winter 1999–2000, pp. 53–60. On U.S. military life in China, see Barbara H. Tuchman, *Stillwell and the American Experience in China, 1911–1944* (New York: Macmillan, 1967); General Alexander A. Vandegrift with Robert Asprey, *Once a Marine: The Memoirs of General A. A. Vandegrift* (New York: Ballantine Books, 1966) for an account of an officer who lived in Tianjin and Beijing; F. Wakeman, *Policing in Shanghai, 1927–1937* (Berkeley: University of California Press, 1995); life in Tianjin specifically is the subject in Matthew Kaufman's "The American 15th Infantry Regiment in China, 1912–1938," *Journal of Military History*, v. 58, no. 1, January 1994, pp. 57–74; for the American School in Shanghai, see Ken Ringle, "Lasting Lessons from Long-Ago China," *Washington Post*, October 27, 2000, pp. C1, C8. For events at Fort Benning, see L. Albert Scipio, *The 24th Infantry at Fort Benning* (Silver Spring, Md.: Roman Publications, 1986). On Princeton University, see Varnum L. Collins, *Princeton: Past and Present* (Princeton, N.J.: Princeton University Press, 1945); also *The Modern Princeton* (Princeton, N.J.: Princeton University Press, 1947).

1. William E. Colby with James MacCargar, *Lost Victory* (Chicago: Contemporary Books, 1989), p. 19.
2. Oriana Fallaci, "The CIA's Mr. Colby," *The New Republic*, March 13, 1976, p. 16.

3. Edward Hymoff, *The OSS in World War II*, p. 303.

4. Colby, *Honorable Men*, p. 49.

4. The Crusade Begins

In addition to William E. Colby's writings there are other sources of prime importance. On "Wild Bill" Donovan, see Thomas F. Troy, *Donovan and the CIA* (Frederick, Md.: University Press of America, 1981); Anthony Cave Brown, *Wild Bill Donovan: The Last Hero* (New York: Times Books, 1982); and as cited below. The Donovan firm's activity on the CIA proprietary Civil Air Transport (later Air America) is cited in William M. Leary and William Stueck, "The Chennault Plan to Save China: U.S. Containment in Asia and the Origins of the CIA's Aerial Empire, 1949–1950," *Diplomatic History*, v. 8, no. 4, Fall 1984, pp. 349–64; and Leary, *Perilous Missions: Civil Air Transport and CIA Covert Operations in Asia* (N.p.: University of Alabama Press, 1984). On the Greek Civil War, see Lawrence S. Wittner, *American Intervention in Greece, 1943–1949* (New York: Columbia University Press, 1982), and below. On covert operations against Russia, see Harry Rositzke, *The CIA's Secret Operations* (New York: Reader's Digest Press, 1977); Nikolai Yakovlev, *CIA Target: USSR* (Moscow: Progress Publishers, 1982); Sanche de Gramont, *The Secret War* (New York: Dell Books, 1962); E. H. Cookridge, *Gehlen: Spy of the Century* (New York: Pyramid Books, 1971) and *The Net That Covers the World* (New York: Henry Holt & Company, 1955); Alfred Bilmanis, *Latvia as an Independent State* (Washington: Latvian Delegation, 1947); L. J. Ludovici, *Tomorrow Sometimes Comes* (London: Longacre, 1957); K. V. Tauras, *Guerrilla Warfare on the Amber Coast* (New York: Lithuanian Research Institute, 1962); Thomas Remeikis, *Opposition to Soviet Rule in Lithuania, 1945–1980* (New York: Institute of Lithuanian Studies Press, 1980). The best sources on Anglo-American cooperation in these operations are Tom Bower, *The Red Web: MI-6 and the KGB Master Coup* (London: Mandarin Books, 1993); Anthony Cavendish, *Inside Intelligence* (London: privately printed, 1987); and Stephen Dorril, *MI-6: Inside the Covert World of Her Majesty's Secret Intelligence Service* (New York: Free Press, 2000). On the OSO/OPC merger at CIA, see Ludwell Lee Montague, *General Walter Bedell Smith as Director of Central Intelligence, October 1950–February 1953* (University Park: Pennsylvania State University Press, 1996); and Lyman B. Kirkpatrick, Jr., *The Real CIA* (New York: Macmillan, 1968).

1. Colby, *Honorable Men*, p. 51.

2. Ibid., p. 52.

3. Corey Ford, *Donovan of OSS* (Boston: Little, Brown, 1970), p. 212.

4. James B. Kellis, *New York Times*, Op. Ed. September 17, 1977.

5. Kati Martin, *The Polk Conspiracy* (New York: Times Books, 1992).

6. Daniele Ganser, "Gladio: NATO's Top Secret Stay-Behind Army, CIA Terrorism in Europe, and the Democratic Failure to Control Secret Services, 1945–2000" (Basel University, Switzerland, Ph.D. dissertation, 2000), pp. 497–98.

7. Bower, *The Red Web*, p. 209.

5. Political Action

Here and throughout the narrative, Bill Colby's memoirs serve as a sort of extended interview taken in conjunction with other sources. On Allen W. Dulles, see Peter

Grose, *Gentleman Spy: The Life of Allen Dulles* (Boston: Houghton Mifflin, 1994). Conditions in Italy and the challenge there can be glimpsed in Christopher Duggan and Christopher Wagstaff, eds., *Italy in the Cold War: Politics, Culture, and Society, 1948–1958* (Oxford: Berg Publishers, 1995); Elisa A. Carillo, "The Italian Catholic Church and Communism," *Catholic Historical Review*, v. 77, no. 3, October 1991, pp. 644–57; and Norman Kogan, *A Political History of Postwar Italy* (New York: Praeger, 1966). On Ambassador Luce, see Stephen Shadegg, *Clare Boothe Luce: A Biography* (New York: Simon & Schuster, 1970); and Wilfred Sheed, *Clare Boothe Luce* (New York: E. P. Dutton, 1982). On the general pattern of U.S. operations, see William Blum, *The CIA: A Forgotten History* (London: Zed Books, 1986); Philip Agee and Louis Wolf, *Dirty Work: The CIA in Western Europe* (Secaucas, N.J.: Lyle Stuart, 1978); Roy Godson, *American Labor and European Politics: The AFL as a Transformational Force* (New York: Crane Russak, 1976); Sallie Pisani, *The CIA and the Marshall Plan* (Lawrence: University Press of Kansas, 1991); and Gunther Walder, " 'Waging Peace': U.S. Propaganda Activities in Italy during the Eisenhower Administration (1953–61)" (master's thesis, University of New Orleans, 1999). On James Angleton and the development of difficulties between himself and Colby, see Robin Winks, *Cloak and Gown: Scholars in the Secret War, 1939–1961* (New York: William Morrow, 1987); and Tom Mangold, *Cold Warrior: James Jesus Angleton: The CIA's Master Spy* (New York: Simon & Schuster, 1991). On the "Gladio" networks, see Ganser, "Gladio."

1. Colin Beavan, "Memoir: A Spy in the Family," *George* Magazine, October 1997, p. 76.

2. Allen W. Dulles, *The Craft of Intelligence* (New York: The New American Library, 1965), pp. 205, 212.

3. Memorandum, James S. Lay, Jr.–Harry S. Truman, January 11, 1951 (declassified May 8, 1981). Truman Library: President's Secretary's Files: NSC Meetings Series, b. 210, f.: "NSC Meeting No. 78." Quoted from "The Position of the United States with Respect to Communism in Italy" (NSC 67/1) April 21, 1951. Ibid., b. 207, f.: "NSC Meeting No. 55."

4. David C. Martin, *A Wilderness of Mirrors* (New York: Ballantine Books, 1980), p. 182.

5. Colby, *Honorable Men*, p. 119.

6. Memorandum, V. Lansing Collins–Clare Booth Luce, November 15, 1955. United States Department of State, *Foreign Relations of the United States* (hereafter *FRUS*), *1955–1957, v. 27 Western Europe and Canada* (Washington: U.S. Government Printing Office, 1992), p. 321.

6. Journey to the East

There is a substantial literature on the Vietnam war though not necessarily on its CIA aspect. On the early years of involvement, see David L. Anderson, *Trapped by Success: The Eisenhower Administration and Vietnam, 1953–1961* (New York: Columbia University Press, 1991); and James R. Arnold, *The First Domino: Eisenhower, the Military, and America's Intervention in Vietnam* (New York: William Morrow, 1991). On the plot in Cambodia, see Sihanouk below. On the beginnings of Kennedy's policy, see William J. Rust, *Kennedy in Vietnam: American Vietnam Policy, 1960–1963* (New York: Scribner's, 1985). On the role of the Special Forces, see Charles M. Simpson,

III, *Inside the Green Berets: The First Thirty Years, A History of U.S. Army Special Forces* (San Francisco: Presidio Press, 1983). On Project Tiger, see Kenneth Conboy and Dale Andradé, *Spies and Commandos: How America Lost the Secret War in North Vietnam* (Lawrence: University Press of Kansas, 2000); Richard H. Shultz, Jr., *The Secret War against Hanoi: Kennedy's and Johnson's Use of Spies, Saboteurs, and Covert Warriors in North Vietnam* (New York: HarperCollins, 1999); John L. Plaster, *SOG: The Secret Wars of America's Commandos in Vietnam* (New York: Simon & Schuster, 1977) and *SOG: A Photo History of the Secret Wars* (Boulder, Colo.: Paladin Press, 2000); and John Prados, "Commandos of Doom: Anatomy of a CIA Failure," *The VVA Veteran* Magazine, December 1997/January 1998, pp. 19–20.

1. Norodom Sihanouk with Wilfred Burchett, *My War with the CIA* (Baltimore: Penguin Books, 1974), p. 111.
2. William E. Colby, Oral History, Lyndon Baines Johnson Library, pt. 1, p. 2.
3. Ibid., p. 11.
4. Ronald Spector, *The United States Army in Vietnam: Advice and Support: The Early Years, 1941–1960* (Washington: Center for Military History, 1983), p. 332, from CIA, *Current Intelligence Weekly*, April 9, 1959.
5. Colby, Oral History, 1, p. 25.
6. Rust, *Kennedy in Vietnam*, p. 11.
7. Frederick C. Nolting, *From Trust to Tragedy: The Political Memoirs of Frederick Nolting, Kennedy's Ambassador to Diem* (New York: Praeger, 1988), p. 25.
8. U.S. Congress (93/1) Senate Armed Services, *Hearings: Nomination of William E. Colby* (Washington: U.S. Government Printing Office, 1973), pp. 84, 94–95.
9. Memorandum, Roswell Gilpatric–John F. Kennedy, "Action Program for Vietnam," April 27, 1961 (declassified June 17, 1977). Lyndon Baines Johnson Library: Lyndon Baines Johnson Papers (hereafter LBJL:LBJP): Vice-Presidential Security File, b. 4, f.: "National Security Council, 1961."
10. Colby, *Honorable Men*, p. 172.
11. Nguyen Cao Ky, *Twenty Years and Twenty Days* (New York: Stein & Day, 1976), p. 23.
12. Ibid., p. 24.
13. In both of his books on the Studies and Observation Group, John Plaster (*SOG: The Secret Wars*, p. 22; *SOG: A Photo History*, p. 10) asserts that the first air mission attempted to insert a team called Atlas and was lost, and that Ky flew the second mission. Both the Ky and Colby memoirs and the recollections of CIA officer Samuel Halpern agree that Ky's was the first northern mission. Conboy and Andradé have a detailed account of the Atlas insertion, which they show as having been from Laos in Air America helicopters during March 1962. Casualty tabulations for the commando program also show team Atlas to have been lost on March 12, 1962.
14. Samuel Halpern Interview, Washington, D.C., September 6, 1997.
15. Ky, *Twenty Years and Twenty Days*, p. 27. Note that in this book Ky writes as if this encounter took place during the training phase of Project Tiger. In a newer, much more detailed version which we have relied upon in the foregoing account, Ky clearly times this incident to the period after the onset of the penetration operations. See Nguyen Cao Ky with Marvin J. Wolf, *Buddha's Child: My Fight to Save Vietnam* (New York: St. Martin's Press, 2002), p. 58. On Ky's third actual penetration mission his aircraft became lost and nearly crashed in the South China Sea. The full account

of Nguyen Cao Ky's participation in Project Tiger can be found in *Buddha's Child*, pp. 53–63.

16. Sedgwick Tourison, *Secret Army, Secret War: Washington's Tragic Spy Operation in Vietnam* (Annapolis, Md.: Naval Institute Press, 1995), p. 36.

17. Tourison, *Secret Army*, p. 25.

18. Edward Lansdale Trip Notebook, October–November 1961, entry for October 21, 1961. National Security Archive: Collection of Lansdale FOIA Documents, b. 1. Also, Covert Annex to Taylor-Rostow Report, no date (November 3, 1961), declassified September 12, 1978. Archive: George McT. Kahin Donation.

19. Covert Annex.

20. CIA, "Status Report on Covert Actions in Vietnam," January 4, 1961 [*sic*; this should be 1962], declassified March 27, 2000. John F. Kennedy Library: John F. Kennedy Papers (hereafter JFKL:JFKP): National Security File (hereafter NSF): Country File Vietnam (hereafter CFVN) b. 204, f.: "Status Reports 1/4/62–4/4/62."

21. CIA, "Intelligence Collection and Evaluation in South Vietnam," June 26, 1962 (declassified March 31, 1994). JFKL:JFKP:NSF: Meetings and Memoranda series, b. 319, f.: "Special Group (CI) Meetings, 1961–1963."

22. David A. Nuttle, "Buon Enao," ms., no date (c. 1983), p. 9. William E. Colby Papers, Texas Tech University; Center for the Study of the Vietnam War (hereafter cited as Colby Papers).

23. William E. Colby, "Turning Points in the Vietnam War," speech, Vietnam Center at Texas Tech University, April, 18, 1996.

24. Ron Shackleton, *Village Defense: Initial Special Forces Operations in Vietnam* (Arvada, Colo.: Phoenix Press, 1975), p. 141.

7. A Bigger Stage to Play On

For CIA operations, in addition to Colby's writings, see John Prados, *Presidents' Secret Wars: CIA and Pentagon Covert Operations from World War II through the Persian Gulf* (Chicago: Ivan R. Dee Publisher, 1996). On Laos see Roger Warner, *Backfire: The CIA's Secret War in Laos and Its Link to the War in Vietnam* (New York: Simon & Schuster, 1995); and Kenneth Conboy with James Morrison, *Shadow War: The CIA's Secret War in Laos* (Boulder, Colo.: Paladin Press, 1995). On events at CIA, see Evan Thomas, *The Very Best Men: Four Who Dared: The Early Years of the CIA* (New York: Simon & Schuster, 1995).

1. Memorandum, Michael Forrestal–McGeorge Bundy, October 18, 1962 (declassified December 30, 1994). JFKL:JFKP:NSF: Meetings and Memoranda series (hereafter M&M) b. 319, f.: "Special Group (CI), 7/3/62–5/20/63."

2. David Halberstam, *The Best and the Brightest* (New York: Random House, 1972), p. 190.

3. Colby, *Honorable Men*, p. 193.

4. CIA, "The Situation in Laos" (SNIE 68–2–59), September 18, 1959 (declassified June 9, 1993), p. 1. FOIA.

5. David Wise and Thomas B. Ross, *The Invisible Government* (New York: Vintage Books, 1974), p. 149.

6. Amoun Vang Sayaovong, "William Colby, the Hmong, and the CIA," ms., no date (c. 1996), p. 3. Document circulated on Internet.

7. National Security Council Staff (Michael Forrestal), "Report on Laos," no date

(January 15, 1963), declassified January 6, 1998, pp. 4–5. JFKL:JFKP:NSF: Country File Laos, b. 132, f.: "Laos, General, 3/63."

8. CIA, Cable from Chief of Station, Vientiane, April 9, 1963 (declassified December 27, 1976). National Security Archive: George McT. Kahin Donation.

9. William E. Colby, undated notes of April 20, 1963, White House Meeting. *FRUS 1961–1963, v. 24, Laos Crisis* (Washington: U.S. Government Printing Office, 1994), p. 987.

10. Memorandum to the President, undated (June 17, 1963). Ibid., p. 1040.

11. William E. Colby, undated notes: "Operational Planning on Laos, Presidential Meeting, June 19, 1963." Ibid., p. 1032.

8. Death in November

In addition to the Colby memoir, his book *Lost Victory* becomes very relevant in this chapter: also see Colby's article "A Participant's Commentary on Vietnam," *Prologue,* v. 23, no. 1, Spring 1991, pp. 58–67. For a general account of Vietnam, see Stanley Karnow, *Vietnam: A History* (New York: Penguin Books, 1984). For the ambassadors' views, see Frederick Nolting, *From Trust to Tragedy* (Westport, Conn.: Greenwood, 1988); Henry Cabot Lodge, *The Storm Has Many Eyes: A Personal Narrative* (New York: W. W. Norton, 1973); and Anne E. Blair, *Lodge in Vietnam: A Patriot Abroad* (New Haven, Conn.: Yale University Press, 1995). For CIA views, see the oral histories with Lucien Conein that are at the Johnson Library and in the papers of the Church Committee at the National Archives; also Harold Ford, *The CIA and the Vietnam Policymakers: Three Episodes, 1962–1968* (Washington: Central Intelligence Agency/Center for the Study of Intelligence, 1998); and B. Hugh Tovar, "Vietnam Revisited: The United States and Diem's Death," *International Journal of Intelligence and Counterintelligence,* v. 5, no. 3, Fall 1992, pp. 291–312. For a dissenting view, see Ellen J. Hammer, *A Death in November: America in Vietnam, 1963* (New York: E. P. Dutton, 1987).

1. Richard Helms, notes of meeting, June 1963, in Harold Ford, *The CIA and the Vietnam Policymakers: Three Episodes, 1962–1968,* (hereafter cited as *CIA and Policymakers*), p. 11.

2. CIA, "The Situation in South Vietnam" (NIE 53–63), April 17, 1963." LBJL: LBJP: NSF: NIE series, b. 6/7, f.: "53, South Vietnam." Also see Willard C. Matthias, *America's Strategic Blunders: Intelligence Analysis and National Security Policy, 1936–1991* (University Park: Pennsylvania State University Press, 2001), pp. 185–91.

3. Ibid., pp. 2, 12.

4. John McCone, LBJL Oral History, p. 27.

5. William E. Colby, LBJL Oral History, I, p. 30.

6. William E. Colby, "Turning Points in Vietnam," speech.

7. Colby, *Honorable Men,* p. 206.

8. William E. Colby, "Why Vietnam," speech, March 6, 1996; author's notes, at conference "Vietnam: 1954–April 1965," sponsored by the Robert R. McCormick Foundation and the United States Naval Institute, 1st Marine Division Museum, Cantigny, Chicago.

9. David Halberstam, *The Making of a Quagmire* (New York: Ballantine Books, 1989), p. 250.

10. CIA, Cable Saigon–Washington TDCS-3/5577576, August 27, 1963 (declassified March 2, 1977). Declassified Documents Reference Service, 77–93(D).

11. CIA, "The Situation in Vietnam" (SNIE 53-2-63), July 10, 1963 (declassified August 25, 1995), p. 1, LBJL.

12. Tran Van Don, *Our Endless War: Inside Vietnam* (San Rafael, Calif.: Presidio Press, 1978), p. 90.

13. State Cable, Saigon 314, August 24, 1963. FRUS *1961–1963, v. 3, January–August 1963* (Washington: U.S. Government Printing Office, 1994), p. 621.

14. George Ball, *The Past Has Another Pattern* (New York: W. W. Norton, 1982), p. 371.

15. Roger Hilsman, *To Move a Nation: The Politics of Foreign Policy in the Administration of John F. Kennedy* (New York: Delta Books, 1967), p. 488.

16. State Cable, Washington–Saigon 243, August 24, 1963. *FRUS* 1963, 3, p. 629.

17. CIA Cable, DIR 63855, Ford, *CIA and Policymakers*, p. 32.

18. Robert McNamara with Brian VanDeMark, *In Retrospect: The Tragedy and Lessons of Vietnam* (New York: Vintage Books, 1997), p. 55.

19. General Victor Krulak, Memorandum for the Record, August 26, 1963. *FRUS* 1963, 3, p. 641.

20. State Cable, Saigon 375, August 29, 1963. FRUS *1963, v. 4, Vietnam, August–December 1963* (Washington: U.S. Government Printing Office, 1994), p. 21.

21. CIA, Memorandum, George Carver–Marshall S. Carter, August 28, 1963 (declassified July 18, 1996). JFKL:JFKP:NSF:CFVN, b. 198A, f.: "Vietnam, General, Memos & Misc., 8/24/63–8/31/63."

22. State, Memorandum of Conversation, September 6, 1963, 3:30 P.M. *FRUS* 1963, 4, p. 120.

23. William E. Colby at Cantigny conference.

24. CIA Paper, September 4, 1963. *FRUS* 1963, 4, p. 201.

25. Colby, *Lost Victory*, p. 144.

26. *Senator Mike Gravell Edition, The Pentagon Papers* (Boston: Beacon Press, 1972), v. II, p. 758.

27. Kai Bird, *The Color of Truth: McGeorge Bundy and William Bundy: Brothers in Arms* (New York: Simon & Schuster, 1998), p. 258.

28. CIA Draft, October 8, 1963 (declassified March 14, 1997). JFKL: JFKP: President's Office File: Departments and Agencies series, b. 72, f.: "CIA, 1963."

29. CIA, Saigon Cable (Smith–McCone), October 5, 1963. U.S. Congress (94/2) Senate Select Committee to Study Governmental Operations with Respect to Intelligence, *Interim Report: Alleged Assassination Plots Involving Foreign Leaders* (hereafter cited as Church Committee, Alleged Assassination Plots) (Washington: U.S. Government Printing Office 1976), p. 220.

30. Colby, *Honorable Men*, p. 213.

31. CIA, Washington–Saigon Cable (Colby–Smith), October 6, 1963. Church Committee, Alleged Assassination Plots, p. 221.

32. CIA, Saigon Cable (Smith–Colby), October 7, 1963. Ibid.

33. Church Committee, Alleged Assassination Plots, p. 221.

34. Ford, *CIA and Policymakers*, p. 36.

35. Karnow, *Vietnam: A History*, p. 297.

36. Church Committee, Alleged Assassination Plots, p. 221.

37. CIA, William Colby, Memorandum for the Record, November 8, 1963 (de-

classified April 24, 1995), p. 1. LBJL:LBJP:NSF:CFVN, b. 1, f.: "Vietnam Memos, v. 1 (11/63–12/63)."

38. Colby, *Honorable Men*, p. 218.
39. Oriana Fallaci, "The CIA's Mr. Colby," p. 18.
40. "Soft Spoken Pacification Chief," *New York Times*, February 14, 1969.

9. Arc of Crisis

On the agency in Vietnam at this time, see Peer De Silva, *Sub Rosa: The CIA and the Uses of Intelligence* (New York: Times Books, 1978); and Zalin Grant, *Facing the Phoenix* (New York: W. W. Norton, 1991). On events in Vietnam, generally excellent sources are George McT. Kahin, *Intervention: How America Became Involved in Vietnam* (New York: Alfred A. Knopf, 1986); and Brian VanDeMark, *Into the Quagmire: Lyndon Johnson and the Escalation of the Vietnam War* (New York: Oxford University Press, 1991). On relationships inside the CIA, read Thomas Powers, *The Man Who Kept the Secrets: Richard Helms and the CIA* (New York: Alfred A. Knopf, 1979). On Indonesia, see Arnold C. Brackman, *The Communist Collapse in Indonesia* (New York: W. W. Norton, 1969); H. W. Brands, "The Limits of Manipulation: How the United States Didn't Topple Sukarno," *Journal of American History*, v. 76, no. 3, December 1989, pp. 785–808; Harold Crouch, *The Army and Politics in Indonesia* (Ithaca, N.Y.: Cornell University Press, 1988); John Hughes, *Indonesian Upheaval* (New York: David McKay & Company, 1967); Brian May, *The Indonesian Tragedy* (London: Routledge & Kegan Paul, 1978); C. L. M. Penders and Ulf Sundhaussen, *Abdul Haris Nasution: A Political Biography* (St. Lucia: University of Queensland Press, 1985); J. M. Van Der Kroef, *Indonesia since Sukarno* (Singapore: Asia Pacific Press, 1971); and as below.

1. De Silva, *Sub Rosa*, p. 198.
2. CIA, John McCone, Memorandum for the Record, December 6, 1963 (declassified July 21, 1995). LBJL: John McCone Papers, b. 1, f.: "Meetings with the President, 11/23–12/27/63."
3. John Prados, *The Hidden History of the Vietnam War* (Chicago: Ivan R. Dee Publishers, 1995), p. 40.
4. National Security Council Staff, Memorandum, Michael Forrestal–Lyndon Johnson, December 11, 1963. *FRUS 1963*, 4, pp. 699–700.
5. De Silva, *Sub Rosa*, p. 211.
6. CIA, John McCone Report, "Highlights of Discussions in Saigon," 18–20 December 1963, *FRUS 1963*, 4, pp. 736, 738.
7. NSC Staff, Memorandum, McGeorge Bundy–Lyndon Johnson, January 7, 1964. *FRUS 1964–1968, v. 1, Vietnam, 1964* (Washington: U.S. Government Printing Office, 1992), p. 5.
8. CIA, Memorandum, Lyman Kirkpatrick/Peer De Silva–John McCone, February 10, 1964. Ibid., p. 66.
9. Ford, *CIA and Policymakers*, p. 53.
10. CIA, John McCone Report, "Memorandum on Vietnam," March 3, 1964. *FRUS 1964*, 1, p. 121.
11. CIA, Cable, Saigon 6316, May 13, 1964. Ford, *CIA and Policymakers*, fn. p. 61.
12. CIA, John McCone, Memorandum for the Record, May 25, 1964 (declassified

July 30, 1996). LBJL: John McCone Papers, b. 1, f.: "Meetings with the President, 4/1/64–28/4/65." See also Memorandum of Conversation, NSC Executive Committee, May 24, 1964. *FRUS* 1964, 1, p. 370.

13. CIA, John McCone, Memorandum for the Record, June 6, 1964 (declassified July 30, 1996). Ibid.

14. CIA, "Chances of a Stable Government in South Vietnam" (SNIE 53–64). Declassified Documents Reference Service, Series 1978–31(A).

15. CIA, "The Situation in Vietnam" (SNIE 53-2-64), October 1, 1964. *FRUS* 1964, 1, p. 806.

16. CIA, Cable, De Silva–McCone, August 25, 1964, *FRUS* 1964, 1, p. 706.

17. Colby, *Lost Victory*, p. 181.

18. CIA, Memorandum, David Smith–William E. Colby, November 19, 1964. Ford, *CIA and Policymakers*, fn. p. 74.

19. CIA, William E. Colby Paper, "The Situation," May 11, 1964 (declassified April 27, 1976). National Security Archive: Porter/Perry/Prados Donation, b. 1, f.: "Vietnam 1964–1966, Unsorted (3)."

20. CIA, Memorandum, William E. Colby–McGeorge Bundy, "Indochina," November 5, 1964, Ford, *CIA and Policymakers*, pp. 74–75. Also see CIA, Memorandum, Board of National Estimates–John McCone, "Would the Loss of South Vietnam and Laos Precipitate a 'Domino Effect' in the Far East," June 9, 1964, *FRUS* 1964, 1, pp. 484–87.

21. CIA, John McCone, "Memorandum on Vietnam," March 3, 1964. Ibid, pp. 120–27, esp. Section 6, paragraph 1 (p. 124).

22. CIA, William E. Colby Paper, "Option A Plus," no date (but with a cover slip of November 27, 1964). LBJL: Paul Warnke Papers (John McNaughton Files), b. 8, f.: "Book IV: State Material, 1964."

23. CIA, William E. Colby Paper, "The Political Weapon for Political War," no date (January 1965), declassified February 23, 1982. LBJL:LBJP:NSF: Agency File, b. 9, f.: "CIA v. 2 (2 of 2)."

24. CIA, Memorandum, Richard Helms–John McCone, March 31, 1965 (declassified October 12, 1995). LBJL:LBJP:NSF:CFVN, b. 194, f.: "McCone's 12 Points." A complete version of this paper in *FRUS 1964–1968, v. 2, Vietnam 1965* (Washington: U.S. Government Printing Office, 1996), pp. 495–97. McCone forwarded these proposals to President Johnson the same day.

25. Ibid.

26. CIA, John McCone, Memorandum for the Record, January 4, 1965 (declassified July 30, 1996). LBJL: John McCone Papers.

27. CIA, John McCone, Addendum to Memorandum for the Record, October 26, 1964 (declassified July 30, 1996). Ibid. NSC Staff, Draft Memo, McGeorge Bundy and James C. Thomson–Lyndon Johnson, June 29, 1965 (declassified April 15, 1977). JFKL: James Thomson Papers, b. 11, f.: "NSC Staff: Chronological File, 6/65."

28. NSC, Summary Record of 521st NSC Meeting, January 7, 1964. *FRUS 1964–1968, v. 26, Indonesia; Malaysia-Singapore; Philippines* (Washington: U.S. Government Printing Office, 2001), pp. 16–20, quoted p. 17.

29. CIA Paper, "Prospects for Covert Action," September 18, 1964. Ibid., pp. 161–164, quoted, p. 163.

30. CIA Paper, "Progress Report on [deleted] Covert Action in Indonesia," February 23, 1965. Ibid., pp. 234–37, quoted p. 236. Cf. fn. p. 237.

31. State Cable, Jakarta 1662, February 24, 1965. Ibid., fn. p. 240

32. NSC Staff, Draft Memorandum, McGeorge Bundy and James C. Thomson–Lyndon Johnson, June 29, 1965 (declassified April 15, 1977). JFKL: James Thomson Papers, b. 11, f.: "NSC Staff: Chronological File 6/65."

33. George and Audrey McTurnin Kahin, *Subversion as Foreign Policy: The Secret Eisenhower–Dulles Debacle in Indonesia* (New York: The New Press, 1995), p. 225.

34. Brachman, *The Communist Collapse in Indonesia*, p. 41.

35. Kai Bird, *The Color of Truth*, p. 352.

36. NSC Staff, Memorandum to Lyndon Johnson with Text of CIA Situation Report, October 1, 1965. *FRUS* 1964, 26, p. 300.

37. CIA Report, "The Upheaval in Indonesia" (OCI No. 2330/65). October 5, 1965. Ibid., pp. 310–16.

38. State Cable, Jakarta 1184, October 26, 1965. Ibid., pp. 335–37.

39. CIA Report, "Upheaval," p. 312.

40. Benedict R. Anderson and Ruth T. McVey, *A Preliminary Analysis of the October 1, 1965 Coup in Indonesia* (Ithaca, N.Y.: Cornell University Southeast Asia Program, 1971), passim. Also, John Hughes, *Indonesian Upheaval* (New York: David McKay Company, 1967), pp. 64–76.

41. Lyndon B. Johnson, *The Vantage Point: Perspectives on the Presidency, 1963–1969* (New York: Holt, Rinehart & Winston, 1971), p. 357.

42. B. Hugh Tovar, "The Indonesian Crisis of 1965–1966: A Retrospective," *International Journal of Intelligence and Counterintelligence*, v. 7, no. 3, Fall 1994, p. 323.

43. U.S. Congress (89/2) House Foreign Affairs Committee, *Hearings: United States Policy toward Asia* (Washington: U.S. Government Printing Office, 1966), p. 91.

44. Kahin and Kahin, *Subversion as Foreign Policy*, p. 228.

45. CIA Paper, "Supply of Communications Equipment to Key Anti-Communist Indonesian Army Leaders," November 17, 1965. FRUS 1964, 26, pp. 368–71 and fn. p. 371.

46. State Cable, Bangkok 920, November 5, 1965. Ibid, pp. 358–60.

47. CIA Paper, "Covert Assistance to the Indonesian Armed Forces Leaders," November 9, 1965. Ibid., pp. 361–63, quoted throughout, italics in the original.

48. State Memorandum, "Mr. Berger's Meeting with Mr. Colby," December 4, 1965. Ibid., pp. 381–82.

49. CIA Study, "Indonesia 1965: The Coup That Backfired," December 1968. Variously cited, quoted in Kathy Kadane, "U.S. Officials' Lists Aided Indonesian Bloodbath in '60s," *Washington Post*, May 21, 1990, p. A5. Also see Richard C. Howland in *Studies in Intelligence*, v. 14, Fall 1970, pp. 13–28.

50. Kathy Kadane, "U.S. Officials' Lists." Kadane's article was followed by numerous efforts at denial but also by Robert Martens' acknowledgment of having compiled lists, although he denied other elements of the account. Kadane continues to stand by her story and has on tape interviews with all the principals, on deposit with the National Security Archive, which substantiate her charges.

51. State Department Historical Office, "Editorial Note," *FRUS* 1964, 26, pp. 386–87.

52. Michael Wines, "CIA Tie Asserted in Indonesia Purge," *New York Times*, July 12, 1990, p. A12. In a version of Kadane's Indonesia story that appeared in the *San Francisco Examiner* ("Ex-Agents Say CIA Compiled Death Lists for Indonesians," May 20, 1990), Colby is reported as comparing the Indonesia lists to the

Vietnam Phoenix program's effort to identify the enemy leadership, commenting on the Phoenix program and on his intentions in that area. Kadane then writes: "In 1962, when he took over as chief of the CIA's Far East Division, Colby said he discovered the United States did not have comprehensive lists of PKI activists. Not having the lists 'could have been criticized as a gap in the intelligence system,' he said, adding they were useful for 'operation planning' and provided a picture of how the party was organized. Without such lists, he said, 'you're fighting blind.' "

"Asked if the CIA had been responsible for sending Martens, a foreign service officer, to Jakarta in 1963 to compile the lists, Colby said, 'Maybe, I don't know. Maybe we did it. I've forgotten.' "

The passage can be read as showing Colby commenting in the abstract or as containing programmatic substance. In that sense it is ambiguous. But it is clear that Kadane had not just made up her quotations from the CIA chieftain.

53. Kahin and Kahin, *Subversion as Foreign Policy*, p. 230.

54. CIA Memorandum, Office of Current Intelligence No. 0815/66, May 13, 1966. *FRUS* 1964, 26, p. 430.

55. Colby, *Honorable Men*, p. 242.

10. Exhilaration of War

William Colby's writings are not informative on the subject of Thailand. For this, see Louis E. Lomax, *Thailand: The War That Is, The War That Will Be* (New York: Vintage Books, 1967); Thomas Lobe, *United States National Security Policy and Aid to the Thailand Police* (Denver, Colo.: University of Denver Monograph Series in World Affairs, 1977); Robert J. Muscat, *Thailand and the United States: Development, Security and Foreign Aid* (New York: Columbia University Press, 1990); George K. Tanham, *Trial in Thailand* (New York: Crane, Russak, 1974); and below. Sources on Laos have already been cited, but see also David Corn, *Blonde Ghost: Ted Shackley and the CIA's Crusades* (New York: Simon & Schuster, 1994); Timothy Castle, *At War in the Shadow of Vietnam: U.S. Military Aid to the Royal Lao Government, 1955–1975* (New York: Columbia University Press, 1993) and *One Day Too Long* (New York: Columbia University Press, 1999); and Theodore Shackley, *The Third Option: An American View of Counterinsurgency Operations* (New York: Reader's Digest Press, 1981).

1. CIA Cable, Colby–Raborn, July 28, 1966. *FRUS, 1964–1968, v. 28, Vietnam 1966* (Washington: U.S. Government Printing Office, 1998), p. 484.

2. CIA, Colby Trip Report, August 16, 1966. Ibid., pp. 484–85.

3. Scott D. Breckinridge, *CIA and the Cold War* (Westport, Conn.: Praeger, 1993), p. 141.

4. David Corn, *Blonde Ghost*, p. 149.

5. Interview, Michael Forrestal, March 11, 1988.

6. CIA, Colby Trip Report, July 31, 1966. *FRUS* 1966, 28, p. 609.

7. Ralph McGehee, *Deadly Deceits: My 25 Years in the CIA* (New York: Sheridan Square Publications, 1983), p. 114.

8. This section is developed entirely from interviews and declassified documents. As early as 1965 there are speculations in State Department documents on private contacts, which the Khanh initiative served to crystallize (reporting cables and ana-

lytical memoranda on the initial meetings appear in *FRUS* 1996, 28, pp. 497–503, 519–22, 540–42, 762–63). Averell Harriman's interagency committee on peace initiatives, on which Colby was the CIA representative, discussed this matter on August 2 and 11, though Colby was not in attendance, and Harriman prepared a private memorandum for Secretary Rusk and President Johnson on August 18 (Harriman Papers, Library of Congress). A flurry of cable traffic instructed the embassy on meetings with "uncle," a National Liberation Front intermediary, at the home of "the American," most likely Edward Lansdale, and hoped for defections of senior Liberation Front officials (in particular, see State Cable 41139, September 3, 1966, and Saigon 5245 and 5246, September 5, in LBJL:LBJP:NSF: Memos to the President, b. 10, f.: "Rostow v. 12). In December 1966 Harriman aide Chester Cooper prepared a piece titled "Direct Clandestine Contact with Hanoi" (December 7, 1966, declassified September 16, 1999; LBJL:LBJP:NSF:CFVN, b. 147, f.: "Marigold"). On March 23, 1967, the same day the White House received private information on conditions under which Prime Minister Ky would be willing to negotiate with North Vietnam and the Liberation Front, Cooper held an evening meeting at his home to discuss "Negotiations with the NLF–VC" (meeting record in Harriman papers). This followed two March 17, 1967, briefing papers on "National Reconciliation" and another on policy toward the National Liberation Front that were written for the briefing book for President Johnson's summit meeting with Saigon leaders at Guam (Paul Warnke Papers at Johnson Library). In July 1967 the U.S. government publicized the defection hopes that were attached to this initiative in the paper "National Reconciliation in South Vietnam" (Department of State: Bureau of Public Affairs, *Vietnam Briefing Notes* no. 8, July 1967).

9. State Cable, Saigon 10098, November 4, 1966, *FRUS* 1966, 28, 796.

10. NSC Staff, Memorandum, Art McCafferty–Walt W. Rostow, November 4, 1966, ibid.

11. William E. Colby, "A Participant's Commentary on Vietnam," *Prologue*, v. 23, no. 1, Spring 1991, p. 62.

12. Ibid.

13. NSC Staff, Memorandum, McGeorge Bundy–Lyndon Johnson, February 7, 1965. *FRUS 1964–1968, v. 2, Vietnam January–June 1965* (Washington: U.S. Government Printing Office, 1996), p. 179.

14. United States Congress (92/1), House Armed Services Committee Print, *United States–Vietnam Relations, 1945–1967* (Pentagon Papers) (Washington: U.S. Government Printing Office, 1971), book 6, IV.C.8, p. 20.

15. Department of Defense, Report on Trip by Deputy Secretary of Defense Cyrus R. Vance, no date (April 1966) declassified March 23, 1997. LBJL:LBJP:NSF: Aides' Files, Robert W. Komer, b. 5, f.: "McNamara/Vance/McNaughton Memos."

11. Rising from Ashes

On South Vietnam and its politics, see Tran Van Don, *Our Endless War*, and Nguyen Cao Ky, *Twenty Years and Twenty Days*; Richard Critchfield, *The Long Charade: Political Subversion in the Vietnam War* (New York: Harcourt Brace, 1968); Alfred W. McCoy et al., *The Politics of Heroin in Southeast Asia* (New York: Harper & Row, 1972); and General Nguyen Duy Hinh, *The South Vietnamese Society* (Washington: Center of Military History: Indochina Monograph, 1980). On pacification in general, see Richard A. Hunt, *Pacification: The American Struggle for Vietnam's Hearts and*

Minds (Boulder, Colo.: Westview, 1995); Robert W. Komer, *Bureaucracy at War: U.S. Performance in the Vietnam Conflict* (Boulder, Colo.: Westview, 1986); Thomas W. Scoville, *Vietnam Studies: Reorganizing for Pacification Support* (Washington: Center of Military History, 1982); General Tran Dinh Tho, *Pacification* (Washington: Center of Military History: Indochina Monograph, 1980); and General Ngo Quang Truong, *Territorial Forces* (Washington: Center of Military History, 1981). On the Green Beret affair, see John S. Berry, *Those Gallant Men: On Trial in Vietnam* (San Francisco: Presidio Press, 1984); and Jeff Stein, *A Murder in Wartime: The Untold Spy Story that Changed the Course of the Vietnam War* (New York: St. Martin's Paperbacks, 1993). On the Phoenix program, see Dale Andradé, *Ashes to Ashes: The Phoenix Program and the Vietnam War* (Lexington, Mass.: D.C. Heath, 1990); Mark Moyar, *Phoenix and the Birds of Prey: The C.I.A.'s Secret Campaign to Destroy the Viet Cong* (Annapolis, Md.: Naval Institute Press, 1997); Douglas Valentine *The Phoenix Program* (New York: William Morrow, 1990); and below.

1. Lyndon B. Johnson, Medal Citation, September 13, 1967 (Johnson Papers).
2. Military Assistance Command Vietnam (MACCORDS), Directive 381–41, "Project TAKEOFF," July 9, 1967 (declassified July 21, 1995). LBJL:LBJP:NSF: Komer-Leonhart Files, b. 11, f.: "ICEX."
3. CIA. Colby cable, January 25, 1968 (declassified December 2, 1999). National Archives and Records Administration here after NARA): Records Group 59, Records of the Department of State, Records of Robert Komer, b. 1, f.: "Turkey/Vietnam."
4. Ford, *CIA and Policymakers*, p. 130.
5. William Colby Speech, "After the Cold War: Reassessing Vietnam," Texas Tech University, Vietnam Center, April 18, 1996, author's notes.
6. Ibid.
7. State Department, Cable Saigon 24351 (Komer), April 9, 1968 (declassified May 24, 1993). LBJL:LBJP:NSF: Komer-Leonhart Files, b. 19, f.: "Pacification (7)."
8. NSC Staff, Memorandum, Earl Young–William K. Leonhart, September 3, 1968. Ibid.
9. William Colby, *Lost Victory*, p. 254.
10. State Department, Cable Saigon 39602 (Komer), October 6, 1968 (declassified May 24, 1993). LBJL:LBJP:NSF: Komer-Leonhart files, f.: "Pacification (6)."
11. State Department, Cable Saigon 2484, October 13, 1968 (declassified May 24, 1993). Ibid.

12. The Fall of Phoenix

General sources are the same as those for the preceding chapter.

1. Obituary, *New York Times*, September 28, 1984, p. A1.
2. David Hoffman, "Pacification Changes Hinted by New Chief," *Washington Post*, November 18, 1968.
3. Ibid.
4. CIA Paper, "Pacification in Vietnam" (SNIE 14–69), January 16, 1969 (declassified November 11, 1978), pp. 1 (paragraph B), 14–16. FOIA.
5. Interview, Robert G. Kaiser, April 25, 2000.
6. "Winning Hearts and Minds" (Interview), *Vietnam* Magazine, v. 6, no. 5, February 1994, p. 25.

7. Dennis J. Cummings, ed., *The Men Behind the Trident* (New York: Bantam Books, 1997), p. 129.

8. Michael J. Walsh and Greg Walker, *SEAL* (New York: Pocket Books, 1994), p. 135.

9. Ibid.

10. Ibid.

11. Edward Miles Interview, June 22, 1998.

12. Walsh and Walker, *SEAL*, p. 175.

13. Donald E. Bordenkircher as told to Shirley A. Bordenkircher, *Tiger Cage: An Untold Story* (Cameron, W.Va.: Abbey Publishing, 1998), p. 93.

14. Walsh and Walker, *SEAL*, p. 126.

15. Colby, *Honorable Men*, p. 271.

16. Richard Hunt, *Pacification*, p. 195.

17. Hoffman, "Pacification Changes," p. A14.

18. United States Congress (93/1) Senate Armed Services Committee, *Hearing: Nomination of William E. Colby* (Washington: U.S. Government Printing Office, 1973), p. 32.

19. Grant, *Facing the Phoenix*, p. 302.

20. Military Assistance Command Vietnam (MACCORDS), CORDS, "Phoenix 1969 End of Year Report," February 28, 1970. National Security Archive: Earle Wheeler FOIA Documents, b. 1, f. "Vietnam."

21. Ibid., p. 3.

22. Lawrence Stern, "Anti-VC Terror Dropped," *Washington Post*, February 18, 1970, p. A2.

23. Colby Nomination Hearings, p. 148.

24. William Colby, *Lost Victory*, p. 262.

25. Military Assistance Command Vietnam (MACCORDS), CORDS, "Phung Hoang [Phoenix] 1970 End of Year Report," May 11, 1971, Annex II, Paragraph 2(a). Document courtesy of Douglas Valentine.

26. Orrin DeForest and David Chanoff, *Slow Burn: The Rise and Bitter Fall of American Intelligence in Vietnam* (New York: Simon & Schuster, 1990), pp. 42–43.

27. Alvin Shuster, "Colby, U.S. Chief of Pacification for Vietnam, Gives Up Duties and Returns Home," *New York Times*, July 1, 1971, p. 34.

28. Ibid.

29. William E. Colby, Testimony for the House Committee on Government Operations, Prepared Statement, July 1971, p. 3. Document courtesy of Douglas Valentine.

30. United States Congress (92/1) House Committee on Government Operations, *Hearings: U.S. Assistance Programs in Vietnam* (Washington: U.S. Government Printing Office, 1971), p. 190.

31. Ibid., p. 191.

32. Ibid., p. 206–7.

33. Colby, *Honorable Men*, p. 279.

13. Back to Langley

On the CIA in general through this period, see Paul W. Blackstock, "The Intelligence Community Under the Nixon Administration," *Armed Forces and Society*, v. 1, no. 2, February 1975, pp. 231–50; Victor Marchetti and John D. Marks, *The CIA and the*

Cult of Intelligence (New York: Knopf, 1974); Cord Meyer, *Facing Reality: From World Federalism to the CIA* (New York: Harper & Row, 1980); Thomas Powers, *The Man Who Kept the Secrets: Richard Helms and the CIA* (New York: Knopf, 1979); and below. There is a vast literature on Richard Nixon, his administration, and Watergate that will not be cited here, except for the book by General Vernon Walters, *Silent Missions* (New York: Doubleday, 1978). On the counterintelligence issues, see Florence F. Garbler, *CIA Wife: One Woman's Life Inside the CIA* (Santa Barbara, Calif.: Fithian Press, 1994); Seymour M. Hersh, "The Angleton Story," *New York Times Magazine*, June 25, 1978, pp. 13–15, 61–65, 68–69, 73; Tom Mangold, *Cold Warrior: James Jesus Angleton: The CIA's Master Spy Hunter* (New York: Simon & Schuster, 1991); Mark Riebling, *Wedge: The Secret War between the FBI and CIA* (New York: Knopf, 1994); and David Wise, *Molehunt: The Secret Search for Traitors That Shattered the CIA* (New York: Random House, 1992). On the CIA in Chile, see Nathaniel Davis, *The Last Two Years of Salvador Allende* (Ithaca, N.Y.: Cornell University Press, 1985); Thomas Hauser, *The Execution of Charles Horman: An American Sacrifice* (New York: Harcourt, Brace, Jovanovich, 1978); Seymour M. Hersh, *The Price of Power: Kissinger in the Nixon White House* (New York: Summit Books, 1983); David A. Phillips, *The Night Watch: 25 Years of Peculiar Service* (New York: Atheneum, 1977); Anthony Sampson, *The Sovereign State of ITT* (New York: Stein & Day, 1973); F. Sergeyev, *Chile: CIA Big Business* (Moscow: Progress Publishers, 1981); and Armando Uribe, *The Black Book of American Intervention in Chile* (Boston: Beacon Press, 1975). Material on monitoring of the Vietnam antiwar movement comes primarily from the Church Committee report and hearings, but see Richard E. Morgan, *Domestic Intelligence: Monitoring Dissent in America* (Austin: University of Texas Press, 1980).

1. CIA Letter, Richard Helms–John D. Ehrlichman, May 23, 1972. NARA: Nixon Library Project (hereafter NLP): Presidential Handwriting File, b. 17, f.: "President's Handwriting, May 1972."

2. CIA Report, Inspector General, "Report on Plots to Assassinate Fidel Castro," May 23, 1967 (declassified 1993), pp. 126, 128, 131, 132. FOIA.

3. Church Committee, Alleged Assassination Plots, p. 276.

4. William E. Colby, Letter to the Editor, *Washington Star*, July 5, 1972.

5. Tran Van Khiem, Letter to the Editor, *Washington Star*, July 20, 1972.

6. CIA Report, Inspector General, "Investigation of the Drug Situation in Southeast Asia," September 1972, p. 3. In Church Committee, *Final Report: Book I: Foreign and Military Intelligence* (Washington: U.S. Government Printing Office, 1976), p. 228.

7. Robert F. Goheen, Letter to the Editor, *Los Angeles Times*, July 7, 1972.

8. Colby, *Honorable Men*, p. 321.

9. "Revised Select Committee Report Prepared at the Request of Senator Howard H. Baker, Jr." (hereafter Baker Report), in United States Congress (93/2) Senate Government Operations Committee: *Hearings: Legislative Proposals to Strengthen Congressional Oversight of the Nation's Intelligence Agencies* (Washington: U.S. Government Printing Office, 1974), p. 122.

10. Baker Report, pp. 119–20.

11. Ibid., p. 131.

12. Colby Nomination Hearings, p. 125.

13. Church Committee, Alleged Assassination Plots, pp. 227–28.

14. Leslie Gelb, "Schlesinger for Defense, Defense for Detente," *New York Times Magazine*, April 8, 1974, p. 10.

15. Thomas Powers, *The Man Who Kept the Secrets*, p. 365.

16. Miles Copeland, *Beyond Cloak and Dagger* (New York: Pinnacle Books, 1975), pp. 304–5.

17. Colby, *Honorable Men*, p. 333.

18. White House Letter, Richard M. Nixon–William E. Colby, February 20, 1973. Colby Papers, Vietnam Archive, Texas Tech University, b. 4, f.: "Correspondence M-Z."

19. White House Letter, Richard M. Nixon–William E. Colby, April 16, 1973. Ibid.

20. Cord Meyer, *Facing Reality*, p. 160.

21. Colby, *Honorable Men*, p. 339.

14. The Top Floor

On reconnaissance satellites and the National Reconnaissance Office, see Jeffrey T. Richelson, *America's Secret Eyes in Space: The U.S. Keyhole Spy Program* (New York: Harper & Row, 1990); and William E. Burrows, *Deep Black: The Startling Truth behind America's Top-Secret Satellites* (New York: Random House, 1986). On Project Jennifer and the *Glomar Explorer*, see Seymour Hersh in the *New York Times* (March 19, 20, 1975; May 25, 1975; December 9, 10, 1976); Roy Varner and Wayne Collier, *A Matter of Risk* (New York: Random House, 1978); Clyde Burleson, *The Jennifer Project* (College Station: Texas A & M Press, 1977); Sherry Sontag and Christopher Drew, *Blind Man's Bluff: The Untold Story of American Submarine Espionage* (New York: Public Affairs Press, 1978); and Harrison Salisbury, *Without Fear or Favor* (New York: Times Books, 1980). Sources on the counterintelligence issue have been cited previously. On the national intelligence estimates, the system for producing them, the intelligence dispute over Russian nuclear forces, and the Backfire bomber case, see John Prados, *The Soviet Estimate* (Princeton, N.J.: Princeton University Press, 1986). On the last days of Saigon see Nguyen Tien Hung and Jerrold L. Schecter, *The Palace File* (New York: Harper & Row, 1986); Larry Berman, *No Peace, No Honor: Nixon, Kissinger, and Betrayal in Vietnam* (New York: Free Press, 2001); General Cao Van Vien, *The Final Collapse* (Washington: Center of Military History: Indochina Monographs, 1985); General Van Tien Dung, *Our Great Spring Victory* (New York: Monthly Review Press, 1977); Larry Englemann, *Tears before the Rain* (New York: Oxford University Press, 1990); Olivier Todd, *Cruel April* (New York: W. W. Norton, 1987); Walter Scott Dillard, *Sixty Days to Peace* (Washington: National Defense University Press, 1982); Colonel William E. Le Gro, *Vietnam from Cease-Fire to Capitulation* (Washington: Center of Military History, 1981); Francis T. McNamara with Adrian Hill, *Escape with Honor: My Last Hours in Vietnam* (Washington: Brassey's 1997); David Butler, *The Fall of Saigon* (New York: Simon & Schuster, 1985). Specific CIA accounts include James E. Parker, Jr., *Last Man Out: A Personal Account of the Vietnam War* (New York: Ballantine Books, 2000); and Frank Snepp, *Decent Interval: An Insider's Account of Saigon's Indecent End Told by the CIA's Chief Strategy Analyst in Vietnam* (New York: Vintage Books, 1978). Snepp's account of how he was treated after publication of *Decent Interval* (unfortunately beyond our scope here) is in *Irreparable Harm: A Firsthand Account of How One Agent Took on the CIA in an Epic Battle over Free Speech* (New York: Random House, 1999). Colby's and Harrison Salisbury's accounts together with U.S. government records form the basis for the material on Chile and the Seymour Hersh articles on CIA domestic activities that end this chapter.

1. Colby, *Honorable Men*, p. 347.

2. John Ranelagh, *The Agency: The Decline and Rise of the CIA* (New York: Simon & Schuster, 1986), p. 555.

3. John Prados, *The Soviet Estimate*, p. 248.

4. Leslie Gelb, "Schlesinger for Defense, Defense for Defense," *New York Times Magazine*, August 4, 1974, p. 10.

5. NSC Minutes, Meeting of January 29, 1975 (declassified May 24, 1999). Gerald R. Ford Library (hereafter GRFL): Gerald R. Ford Papers (hereafter GRFP): Kissinger–Scowcroft Files (hereafter KSF): NSC Meetings Series, b. 1, f.: "NSC Minutes, January 29, 1975."

6. NSC Minutes, Meeting of August 9, 1975 (declassified May 25, 1999). Ibid.

7. NSC Minutes, Meeting of December 22, 1975 (declassified May 25, 1999). Ibid.

8. CIA Paper, "Response to National Security Study Memorandum 213" (Interagency Intelligence Memorandum), November 18, 1974 (declassified June 5, 1980). Document courtesy of Daniel Ellsberg.

9. Frank Snepp, *Decent Interval*, p. 120.

10. State Cable, Saigon 0267, January 8, 1975 (declassified January 30, 1995). GRFL:GRFP:KSF: Office Files series, b. A1, f.: "Camp David (VN) (2)."

11. Snepp, *Decent Interval*, p. 132.

12. Henry A. Kissinger, *Years of Renewal* (New York: Simon & Schuster, 1999), p. 494.

13. NSC Minutes, Meeting of March 28, 1975 (declassified February 6, 1995). GRFP: NSC Meetings series.

14. CIA Cable, Director 4548, April 4, 1975. National Security Archive: D. Gareth Porter Donation, b. 1, f.: "Vietnam 1975."

15. CIA Cable, Saigon 050530Z April 1975. Ibid.

16. NSC Minutes, Meeting of April 8, 1975 (declassified February 6, 1995). GRFP: NSC Minutes series.

17. Ibid.

18. Ibid.

19. Ibid.

20. State Cable, Saigon 0713, April 18, 1975 (declassified August 7, 2001) GRFL: GRFP: National Security Adviser's Files (hereafter NSAvrF): Backchannel Message series, b. 3, F.: "Martin Channel 4/75 Incoming (2)."

21. NSC Staff Memorandum, Lawrence Eagleburger–Henry Kissinger, September 24, 1974 (declassified January 27, 1997). GRFL:GRFP:KSF: Presidential Country Files, b. A5, f.: "Chile 8/9/74–3/31/75."

22. CIA Memorandum, William E. Colby for the Record, September 25, 1974 (declassified January 8, 1997). GRFL:GRFP: Richard Cheney Files, Intelligence series, b. 7, f.: "Rockefeller Commission, General."

23. Helms to David Frost, May 22–23, 1978, reprinted in Ralph E. Weber, ed., *Spymasters: Ten CIA Officers in Their Own Words* (Wilmington, Del.: Scholarly Resources, 1999), p. 285.

24. *New York Times*, December 22, 1974, p. 1.

25. Ibid.

26. Ibid.

27. "A New CIA Furor," *Newsweek*, January 6, 1975, p. 10.

28. Henry Kissinger, *Years of Renewal*, p. 320.

29. NSC Staff Memorandum, Henry Kissinger–Donald H. Rumsfeld, December 23, 1974 (declassified December 23, 1992). GRFL: GRFP: Richard Cheney Files, Intelligence series, b. 6, f.: "Intelligence—General."

30. NSC Staff Memorandum, Henry Kissinger–Gerald R. Ford, December 25, 1974 (declassified September 13, 1989). Ibid., b. 5, f.: "Colby Report."

31. Ibid.

15. The Year of Intelligence

For the viewpoint of the president, see Gerald R. Ford, *A Time to Heal: The Autobiography of Gerald R. Ford* (New York: Berkeley Books, 1980); Ron Nessen, *It Sure Looks Different from the Inside* (New York: Playboy Press, 1978); John R. Greene, *The Presidency of Gerald R. Ford* (Lawrence: University Press of Kansas, 1995); and John Osborne, *The White House Watch: The Ford Years* (Washington: New Republic Press, 1978). In addition to Kissinger's memoirs and other writings, see Marvin and Bernard Kalb, *Kissinger* (New York: Dell Books, 1975), in which a notable Kissinger leak appears. Harrison Salisbury, *Without Fear or Favor* contains much on the press coverage of the period, and that is the main focus in Daniel Schorr, *Clearing the Air* (New York: Berkeley Books, 1978). Basic sources on the intelligence investigations are the committee publications: United States Congress (94/1) House Select Committee on Intelligence (Pike Committee), which produced five volumes of hearings and two of committee internal proceedings; and United States Congress (94/2) Senate Select Committee to Study Governmental Operations with Respect to Intelligence (Church Committee), which produced five volumes of reports, an interim report on covert operations in Chile and one on alleged assassination plots, and six volumes of hearings. Key documents will be cited directly in the notes and several already have been. The Pike Committee report does not appear in an official publication but is collected in *CIA: The Pike Report* (Nottingham, Eng.: Spokesman Books, 1977). For the Rockefeller report, see *Report to the President by the Commission on CIA Activities within the United States* (Washington: U.S. Government Printing Office, 1975). For works by participants, see William R. Corson, *The Armies of Ignorance: The Rise of the American Intelligence Empire* (New York: The Dial Press, 1977); Loch K. Johnson, *A Season of Inquiry* and "The CIA and the Media," *Intelligence and National Security*, v. 1, no. 2, May 1986, pp. 143–69; Gregory F. Treverton, *Covert Action: The Limits of Intervention in the Postwar World* (New York: Basic Books, 1987); and L. Britt Snider, "Recollections from the Church Committee's Investigation of NSA," *Studies in Intelligence*, Winter 1999–2000, pp. 43–51. For an official historian's view, see Gerald K. Haines, "The Pike Committee Investigation and the CIA," *Studies in Intelligence*, Winter 1998–1999, pp. 81–92. A contemporary view is in Jerry J. Berman and Morton H. Halperin, eds., *The Abuses of the Intelligence Agencies* (Washington: Center for National Security Studies, 1975). Studies of the investigations include Kathryn S. Olmstead, *Challenging the Secret Government: The Post Watergate Investigations of the CIA and FBI* (Chapel Hill: University of North Carolina Press, 1996); John M. Oseth, *Regulating U.S. Intelligence Operations: A Study in Definition of the National Interest* (Lexington: University Press of Kentucky, 1985); and Frank J. Smist, Jr., *Congress Oversees the United States Intelligence Community*,

1947–1989 (Knoxville: University of Tennessee Press, 1990). The present account reaches much deeper into White House and CIA efforts than any of these others. On the Angola covert operation, see John Stockwell, *In Search of Enemies: A CIA Story* (New York: W. W. Norton, 1978); John Marcum, *The Angolan Revolution* (Cambridge, Mass.: MIT Press, [I] 1969, [II] 1978); Nathaniel Davis, "The Angola Decision of 1975: A Personal Memoir," *Foreign Affairs*, v. 56, no. 4, Fall 1978; and William G. Hyland, *Mortal Rivals* (New York: Random House, 1987).

1. Tom Mangold, *Cold Warrior*, p. 317.
2. Mark Riebling, *Wedge*, p. 323.
3. Mangold, *Cold Warrior*, p. 317.
4. Colby, *Honorable Men*, p. 395.
5. NSC Staff, Brent Scowcroft, Memorandum of Conversation, January 4, 1975 (declassified April 20, 2000). GRFL:GRFP:NSAvrF: Memcon series, b. 8, f.: "January 4, 1975 Ford, Kissinger."
6. Harrison Salisbury, *Without Fear or Favor*, p. 537.
7. Daniel Schorr, *Clearing the Air*, p. 145.
8. Kathryn Olmstead, *Challenging the Secret Government*, p. 59.
9. CIA Report, Inspector General, "Report on Plots to Assassinate Fidel Castro," May 23, 1967, p. 131.
10. Rockefeller Commission Staff Report, David Belin, "Summary of Facts: Investigation of CIA Involvement in Plans to Assassinate Foreign Leaders," no date (June 5, 1975) declassified May 24, 2000. GRFL:GRFP: Richard Cheney Files, Intelligence series, b. 7, f.: "Report on CIA Assassination Plots (1)."
11. Commission on CIA Activities within the United States (Rockefeller Commission), *Report to the President*, June 1975. Washington: U.S. Government Printing Office, 1975, p. xi.
12. "Kissinger's Blue Pencil," *Newsweek*, August 25, 1975, p. 13.
13. Working copy of Rockefeller Commission Report, undated, p. 27; attached to Memorandum, Roderick Hills–Henry Kissinger et al., June 4, 1975. GRFL: GRFP: Richard Cheney Files, Intelligence series, b. 8, f.: "Rockefeller Commission Report: Working Copy 6/4/75."
14. Rockefeller Commission, *Report to the President*, p. 27.
15. White House Working Copy, p. 27.
16. Colby, *Honorable Men*, p. 425.
17. Henry Kissinger, *Years of Renewal*, p. 326.
18. Colby, *Honorable Men*, p. 310.
19. Ibid., p. 444.
20. Kissinger, *Years of Renewal*, p. 324.
21. William Nolte, "Interviewing an Intelligence Icon," *Studies in Intelligence*, no. 10, Winter–Spring 2001, p. 42.
22. Loch Johnson, *A Season of Inquiry*, passim.
23. Bernard Knox, Eulogy for William Colby. Courtesy of Bernard Knox.
24. William E. Colby, Prepared Statement, January 15, 1975, p. 1. GRFL:GRFP: Max L. Friedersdorf Files, Subject series, b. 10, f.: "CIA Investigation (5)."
25. NSC Staff, Brent Scowcroft, Memorandum of Conversation, February 28, 1975 (declassified January 31, 2000). GRFL:GRFP:NSAvrF: Memcon series, b. 9, f.: "February 28, 1975 Ford, Kissinger."
26. Johnson, *A Season of Inquiry*, p. 30.

27. CIA Memorandum, March 25, 1975. GRFL:GRFP: Richard Cheney Files, Intelligence series, b. 6, f.: "Congressional Investigations (1)."

28. *Public Papers of the President: Gerald R. Ford, 1975* (Washington: U.S. Government Printing Office, 1977), p. 369. Author's italics.

29. White House Analysis, Attachment to Memorandum James A. Wilderotter–Donald H. Rumsfeld et al., April, 23, 1975 (declassified January 8, 1997). GRFL: GRFP: Richard Cheney Files, Intelligence series, b. 6, f.: "Congressional Investigations (2)."

30. CIA Letter, William E. Colby–Gerald R. Ford, April 5, 1975. GRFL:GRFP: White House Central Files: Agency File, b. 19, f.: "FG 6-2 CIA 1/1/75–6/30/75."

31. Johnson, *A Season of Inquiry*, p. 41.

32. White House Memorandum, Draft Memorandum, Philip Buchen/Henry Kissinger et al.–Gerald R. Ford, May 9, 1975. GRFL:GRFP: Robert K. Wolthius Files, Subject series, b. 2, f.: "Intelligence Investigations—Church Committee (1)." President Ford's answering orders are shown in the memorandum from Brent Scowcroft to Colby (no date, declassified April 13, 1998) in ibid.

33. White House Memorandum, Philip Buchen, "Meeting with Secretaries Kissinger, Schlesinger and Director Colby," May 13, 1975. GRFL:GRFP: Presidential Handwriting File, National Security series, b. 30, f.: "Intelligence (2)."

34. NSC Minutes, Meeting of May 15, 1975, Part 3 of 3 (declassified May 24, 1999). GRFL:GRFP:KSF:NSC Minutes series, b. 1, f.: "NSC Minutes, May 15, 1975."

35. Ibid.

36. CIA Memorandum, Directive "Ground Rules for Supplying SSC Staff with Covert Action Briefings and Documents," June 30, 1975 (declassified October 21, 1992). GRFL:GRFP: Richard Cheney Files, Intelligence series, b. 6, f.: "Congressional Investigations (3)."

37. White House Memorandum, Philip Buchen for the Record, June 30, 1975. Ibid.

38. NSC Staff Memorandum, Henry Kissinger–Gerald R. Ford, June 27, 1975 (declassified July 11, 2000). GFRL:GFRP:KSF:NSC Meetings series, b. 2, f.: "NSC Minutes, June 27, 1975."

39. CIA Memorandum, "DCI Briefing for June 27, 1975 NSC Meeting," (declassified July 11, 2000). Ibid.

40. NSC Minutes, Meeting of June 27, 1975 (declassified March 28, 2001). Ibid.

41. CIA Letter, William E. Colby–Gerald R. Ford, June 23, 1975. GRFL:GRFP: NSAvrF: Name series, b. 1, f.: "Colby, William E."

42. Colby, *Honorable Men*, p. 434.

43. Congressional Letter, Otis G. Pike–William E. Colby, July 28, 1975. GRFL: GRFP: Richard Cheney Files, Intelligence series, b. 6, f.: "Congressional Investigations (3)."

44. *CIA: The Pike Report*, p. 69.

45. Frank J. Smist, *Congress Oversees the United States Intelligence Community*, p. 70. Cf. George Lardner, "Did Ike Authorize a Murder?" *Washington Post*, August 8, 2000, p. A23.

46. Ludo De Witte, *The Assassination of Lumumba* (trans. Ann Wright and Renée Fenby) (London: Verso, 2001). For the CIA account, see David W. Doyle, *True Men and Traitors* (New York: John Wiley & Sons, 2001), pp. 129–30, 145, 147–149. Doyle has rather caustic comments from his side regarding Church committee investigators.

47. Smist, pp. 185–86.

48. CIA Memorandum, Mitchell Rogovin/Paul Reichler–William Colby, September 22, 1975. GRFL:GRFP: James E. Connor Files, Intelligence series, b. 56, f.: "House Select Committee—Legal Opinions on Subpoenas for CIA Documents (1)."

49. NSC Staff Memorandum, Brent Scowcroft Memorandum of Conversation, October 31, 1975 (declassified June 24, 1994). GRFL:GRFP:KSF: Memcon series, b. A–1, f.: "Memcon 10/31/75."

50. Seymour Hersh, "Colby Says His Dismissal as CIA Chief Arose from His Cooperation in Domestic Spying Inquiries," *New York Times*, March 14, 1978, p. 12. Colby, *Honorable Men*, p. 16.

51. NSC Staff Memorandum, Brent Scowcroft Memorandum of Conversation, October 31, 1975.

52. United States Congress (94/1) House Select Committee on Intelligence. *Hearings: U.S. Intelligence Agencies and Activities: The Performance of the Intelligence Community* (Washington: U.S. Government Printing Office), Pt. 2, p. 835.

53. Anthony Lewis, "Farewell My Lovely," *New York Times*, Op-Ed, November 6, 1975.

54. F. A. O. Schwarz, Jr., "The Spy Who Would Speak," *New York Times Magazine*, December 29, 1996, p. 40.

55. Colby, *Honorable Men*, p. 450.

Chapter 16. Intelligence in a Free Society

1. NSC Minutes, Meeting of January 13, 1976 (declassified February 7, 1994). GRFL:GRFP:NSAvrF:NSC Meetings series, b. 2, f.: "Meeting of January 13, 1976."

2. White House Memorandum, Brent Scowcroft–Gerald R. Ford, January 19, 1976 (declassified February 7, 1994). GRFL:GRFP: Presidential Handwriting File, Medals and Awards series, b. 29, f.: "National Security Medal."

3. Daniel Schorr, *Clearing the Air*, p. 195.

4. CIA Letter, Mitchell Rogovin–Otis G. Pike, January 27, 1976. GRFL: Ron Nessen Papers, Subject series accretion, b. 500, f.: "Intelligence (4)."

5. William E. Colby, "After Investigating U.S. Intelligence," *New York Times*, Op-Ed, February 26, 1976.

6. Oriana Fallaci, "The CIA's Mr. Colby," *New Republic*, March 13, 1976, pp. 19, 20.

7. White House Memorandum, James Connor–John Marsh, March 8, 1976. GRFL:GRFP: White House Central File, Agency File, b. 20, f.: "FG 6-2 CIA 4/1/76–5/30/76."

8. White House Letter, Gerald R. Ford–William E. Colby, March 24, 1976. Ibid.

9. Bob Woodward, *Veil: The Secret Wars of the CIA, 1981–1987* (New York: Pocket Books, 1988), p. 50.

10. William E. Colby Statement, Excerpts, *New York Times*, December 28, 1977, p. A12.

11. United States Congress (95/2) Senate Select Committee on Intelligence. *Hearings: National Intelligence Reorganization and Reform Act of 1978* (Washington: U.S. Government Printing Office, 1978), pp. 37–38.

12. "Colby on Think Tanks," *Defense and Foreign Affairs Magazine*, March 1982, p. 12.

13. Deborah Baldwin and Peter Montgomery, "Colby: Arms Control's Secret Weapon," *Common Cause* magazine, v. 13, no. 4, July/August 1987, p. 15.

14. Ibid.

15. Robert M. Gates, *From the Shadows: The Ultimate Insider's Story of Five Presidents and How They Won the Cold War* (New York: Simon & Schuster, 1996), p. 62.

Index

Peterson, Peter G., 274–75
Pforzheimer, Walter L., 249, 250, 306–7
Pham Chuyen (code-name Ares), 76, 82
Pham Ngoc Thao, 128, 175
Phan Thanh Van, 78
Phelan, James, 268
Philby, Haroald A. R., 46–47
Phillips, David Atlee, 310
Phillips, Rufus, 95, 97, 114, 121, 124
Phoenix program: assassination accusations, 221–
    22, 226, 235, 236, 237, 243–44; Colby's role
    in, 341; competing interests, 212;
    confirmation hearings, 264; controversy, 214,
    235, 251, 264, 304, 330, 339; CORDS–CIA
    relationship, 213; criticisms of, 229, 237;
    detainment categories, 217–18, 219; effect
    on Colby, 342–43; human rights issues, 228,
    235–36; ICEX and, 238; "kill quotas," 221;
    Liberation Front and, 227; Mustakos on,
    209; origins, 188; patrol missions, 215;
    quantifiable progress, 211; secrecy of, 224–
    25; Senate Foreign Relations Committee
    hearings, 225; staff from, 208; Thieu on, 224;
    VCI neutralization, 224, 227, 232;
    Washington Post story citing, 210
Phoumi Nosavan, 96, 97–98, 99, 101, 102
Phung Hoang (Phoenix program), 224
Pike, Otis G., 315, 319, 320, 321, 324, 327, 332–
    33
Pike Committee, 319, 320, 321, 324–25, 327–28,
    329, 332–33, 334
Pinochet, Augusto, 254, 290
Pius XII (Pope), 55
"Plumbers" of Watergate, 249, 250
Polgar, Thomas, 283–84, 285–86, 287, 289
Police Aerial Recovery Unit (PARU), 97, 172
Police Field Force, 197
Police Special Branch, 201, 223
political action in CIA, 192, 254
political affiliations of Colby, 40, 41
"Political Development Working Group," 182
"The Political Weapon for Political War"
    (Colby), 145
The Politics of Heroin in Southeast Asia (McCoy),
    244, 245
Polk, George Washington, Jr., 39, 41, 49
Pope, Allen L., 147
Porter, William J., 2, 181, 182, 183–84
Portuguese-Angolan issues, 317–18
Poshepny, Anthony ("Tony Po"), 103–4, 159,
    167, 170
Postal Service, 257–58
Potter, Philip H., 65, 224
Powell, Robert I., 17–18
Powers, Francis Gary, 92
Powers, Thomas, 253
Praphat Charusathien, 171
President's Daily Brief, 274, 286
President's Foreign Intelligence Advisory Board
    (PFIAB), 90, 281, 334
Proctor, Edward W., 196, 273, 275
"A Program for Vietnam" (memorandum), 120
Project Circus, 92
Project Feature, 318
Project Fu/Belt, 252, 290
Project Gladio, 53, 54

Project Haik, 170
Project Hardnose, 165
Project Jennifer, 266–69
Project Matador, 267
Project MH/Chaos, 257, 258, 294
Project Momentum, 100, 103, 139, 165, 166
Project Pincushion, 165
Project Sky, 100
Project Take-off, 188, 194, 195, 196
Project Thrush, 178, 179
Project Tiger, 74, 75–81, 134–35, 138, 180
Project Witness, 214, 216
Project Wizard, 321
Project Zodiac, 267
propaganda, 53, 58, 135, 153
"Prospects in Vietnam" NIE 53–63, 105–6, 112
protests and demonstrations, 120, 122, 294
Province Security Committee, 218
Provincial Interrogation Centers (PICs), 236
Provincial Reconnaissance Units (PRUs):
    attacking infrastructure of Viet Cong, 195,
    196–97; bounties and rewards, 233; Counter-
    Terror Teams converted to, 186; "kill
    quotas," 221; Project Witness, 214–15;
    Senate Foreign Relations Committee
    hearings, 225; transition to South Vietnam
    responsibility, 216–17
psychological warfare, 7, 65, 135, 192, 237
Puerifoy, John, 67

Quang Duc, 108
Quang Tin, 213

Raborn, William F., 161, 165, 170
Radio Free Europe, 190
Ramparts magazine, 189, 190
Rand Corporation, 280
Ranelagh, John, 50, 274
Raskin, Marc, 316
Read, Cathleen B., 244
Reagan, Ronald, 301, 302, 335
Reckner, James, 340
reconnaissance technology, 241, 265–66, 336
recruiting CIA agents, 217, 269–70, 271–72
refugees, 233, 246, 287, 337
Regan, Ed, 75, 80
Reid, Ogden, 235–36
Reitmeyer, Francis T., 221
relationships, Colby's reliance upon, 68
religion of Colby, 4, 22, 24, 25, 36, 55, 90, 305
religious issues. *See* Buddhist crisis
Reserve Officers Training Corps (ROTC), 8, 23,
    25, 27, 103
Resistance movements, 7–18, 28
Revolutionary Development Cadre (RDC)
    Division, 184, 187
rewards program for information, 233–34
Rheault, Robert B., 220
Richardson, Elliott, 261
Richardson, John, 106, 109–12, 115–22, 127,
    132, 133
risk analysis by Colby, 337
Robbins, Barbara, 160
Rocca, Raymond G., 247
Rockefeller, Nelson A., 295, 300, 301–2, 313, 324
Rockefeller Commission, 300–304, 306, 308, 326